A Military History of the Ottomans

A MILITARY HISTORY OF THE OTTOMANS

From Osman to Atatürk

Mesut Uyar and Edward J. Erickson

PRAEGER SECURITY INTERNATIONAL
An Imprint of ABC-CLIO, LLC

ABC ⬥ CLIO

Santa Barbara, California • Denver, Colorado • Oxford, England

Copyright 2009 by Mesut Uyar and Edward J. Erickson

All rights reserved. No part of this publication may be reproduced, stored in a retrieval system, or transmitted, in any form or by any means, electronic, mechanical, photocopying, recording, or otherwise, except for the inclusion of brief quotations in a review, without prior permission in writing from the publisher.

Library of Congress Cataloging-in-Publication Data

A military history of the Ottomans : from Osman to Atatürk / by Mesut Uyar and Edward J. Erickson.
    p. cm.
  Includes bibliographical references and index.
  ISBN 978–0–275–98876–0 (hard copy : alk. paper) — ISBN 978–0–313–05603–1 (ebook)
1. Turkey. Ordu—History. 2. Turkey—History, Military. 3. Turkey—History—Ottoman Empire, 1288–1918. I. Erickson, Edward J., 1950– II. Title.
UA812.U89   2009
355.00956—dc22   2009020872

13 12 11 10 9   1 2 3 4 5

This book is also available on the World Wide Web as an eBook.
Visit www.abc-clio.com for details.

ABC-CLIO, LLC
130 Cremona Drive, P.O. Box 1911
Santa Barbara, California 93116-1911

This book is printed on acid-free paper ∞

Manufactured in the United States of America

To my wife and my daughter
İlkay and Dilara
with profound love

Contents

Preface	ix
Acknowledgments	xiii
Note on Transliteration	xv
1 Early Middle Eastern Military Systems and the Foundation of the Ottoman Military, 1300–1453	1
2 Classical Period, 1451–1606	31
3 Transformation and Reform Efforts, 1606–1826	81
4 Fighting for Survival, 1826–1858	129
5 The Beginning of the End, 1861–1918	175
Conclusion	281
Notes	285
Selected Bibliography	355
Index	365

A photo essay follows page 174.

Preface

The history of the Ottoman military in the western world tends to be episodic and focused on particular periods, leaders, or wars. A recent comprehensive guide to the literature of military history contains no specific entry beginning with the word "Ottoman."[1] There are instead the following: Kemal Atatürk; Balkan Wars; Crimean War; Greece—War of Independence; Habsburg-Ottoman Wars; Islamic Warfare; Near East Warfare; Russo-Turkish War; Suleiman the Magnificent; Turkey—armed forces; World War I (WW1): armed forces, Turkey; WW1: Balkans; WW1: Dardanelles; WW1: Mesopotamia; and WW1: Palestine. Moreover, the existing nonspecialist western historiography was written from the European perspective and was often the derivative product of faulty or biased contemporary observations by Europeans about what the Ottomans were doing. Sometimes the literature was tainted by a lingering memory of "the terrible Turk," which presented the Ottomans as the last of a long line of racially Asian destroyers of western civilization. Even though the history of the Ottoman military is by no means wholly lacking in either scholarship or ideas, no one has yet undertaken a general survey of the Ottoman military from the very beginning until the end.

A Military History of the Ottomans: From Osman to Atatürk is intended to rectify this lacuna (or, more properly, terra incognita) in military history by telling the story of the foundation, development, and transformation of the Ottoman military. However, it is not a military history of the Ottoman state and its army—rather, it is a military history of the Ottoman army. The authors recognize that since it is not a campaign and battle-oriented study, it may disappoint some readers, but we present the idea that an understanding of an army must come before descriptions of what it did. Limitations of space have kept us from providing details, and we have been forced to summarize more often than we would have liked. We have not attempted to cover naval affairs, for example, in spite of the fact that they were closely related with some of the issues covered in the text. We also had to sacrifice most of the descriptive footnotes that would have been important to the specialists. Regrettably, no historical survey of so vast a subject as the Ottoman military can possibly provide definite coverage of every topic it includes. Therefore, this book is a modest attempt to illuminate how the Ottomans built, trained, organized, led, and sustained their army over a period of nearly 700 years.

The Ottoman army had a significant effect on the history of the modern world and particularly on that of the Middle East and Europe. As the world's dominant military machine from 1300 to the mid-1700s, the Ottoman army led the way in military institutions, organizational structures, technology, and tactics. In much reduced stature thereafter, it nevertheless remained a considerable force to be counted in the balance of power through 1918. From its nomadic origins, it underwent revolutions in military affairs as well as several "transformations" (or restructuring and reorganizations to modernity) that enabled it to compete on favorable terms with the best armies of the day. This study tracks the growth of the Ottoman military as the world's first modern professional military institution from the perspective of the Ottomans themselves. It is a unitary study that details the organizational, intellectual, and institutional changes in the Ottoman army from 1300 to 1918 that made it an effective army and created its heritage. The role of politics, which played a continual and evolutionary role in the development and application of Ottoman military power, is also examined. This theme is interwoven into the narrative and provides a historical continuum in the story of the Ottoman army. It is a general historical survey that aims to introduce the Ottoman military to a wider audience, to correct a generalized lack of understanding and ignorance in the western world, and most importantly to integrate it into the mainstream of military historical scholarship. This study is also a "standalone" survey that combines an introductory view of this subject for the general-interest reader with fresh and original reference-level information for the specialist.

Throughout much of its existence, the Ottoman army was an effective fighting force with professional military institutions and organizational structures. However, the view of this army in the western world is often negative and based largely on Euro-centric narratives and histories that tended to present the Ottomans as savage and backward enemies who were only able to succeed by their sheer numerical strength, geography, stupidity of their rivals, or pure luck. This study corrects that view by using less accessible Ottoman sources (including memoirs, military studies and discussions). A general survey, however, necessarily omits details and has to rely more on secondary materials. The vast holdings of the Ottoman archives have been used in only some chapter sections. Of particular note is the use of sources from what may be termed as a renaissance of interest in Ottoman military history that occurred between 1890 and 1940. Although almost forgotten today (even in Turkey), Ottoman and later Turkish army officers during this period carried out an active dialogue oriented on discovering an understanding of the army's recent military inferiority. The battlefield and officer's clubs were the first platforms for these types of discussions, but later the debate continued in the publication of military journals and official histories. Moreover, the field diaries of the participants were published as well as criticisms and analysis. In the 1920s and 1930s, a lively debate emerged that created a favorable atmosphere for military officers to engage a public audience. These works illuminated the ethos and thinking of the army and its commanders. Unfortunately, this period ended in the 1940s, and all but a few specialists forgot about most of this work. This study revives that body of work to provide a corrective to the western historiography that is based on European interpretations, rather than Turkish interpretations, of events.

The book is organized into five basic chapters that are broadly chronological. Chapter 1 describes how an obscure, small emirate incorporated the heritage of the Central Asian steppe-nomadic military tradition, Islamic, and Byzantine military systems into a unique military system that outperformed and outlived all of its Muslim and Christian rivals. Chapter 2 describes what is termed "the Classical period" and focuses on the development of a professional standing army while conquering large tracks of land. It also discusses the army's organization, recruitment, duties, and how it generated effective combat power. Chapter 3 describes the transformation of the Ottoman military and its institutional response to increased foreign aggression and interior opposition after 1600. It also chronicles early Ottoman reform attempts to regenerate the classical system and its eventual destruction. Chapter 4 discusses the merits and failures of the Ottoman military adaptability against post-Napoleonic European militaries and the emergence of separatist nationalism. It also gives insight into how the army became an engine of modernization for the empire. Finally, Chapter 5 details the final years of the Ottoman state and its attempts to introduce contemporary European methods, equipment, and tactics. It also includes the evolution of Ottoman regeneration and reorganization that resulted in an effective army, which fought a prolonged multifront war against sophisticated and powerful enemies during the First World War.

The authors are professional regular officers from the Turkish and American armies and have records of distinguished service in combat, peacekeeping, and peacetime assignments. Although they are well qualified academically for this work, they also bring into their research and presentation a deep understanding of the dynamics of military leadership, the mechanics of how armies operate and fight, and an understanding of how soldiers react under fire. Their belief is that this unique blend of academic qualification and active service in the field brings fresh perspectives to the study of the Ottoman military. Their wish is to act as a new lens through which a modern examination and interpretation of the foundation, development, and transformation of the Ottoman military may be revealed so as to encourage further research, academic criticism, and better understanding of it. Finally, they hope to give voice to the millions of Ottoman officers and soldiers who faithfully served their state so well from the fourteenth through the twentieth centuries.

Acknowledgments

Writing this book has proved to be both challenging and stimulating. In the course of writing this text I have received invaluable help and encouragement from friends, colleagues, and family (ranging from general suggestions to detailed comments). It is my pleasure to thank these people who have helped me.

First I would like to express my gratitude to Ed Erickson, whose patience and humor were instrumental in turning our partnership into a very successful and stimulating endeavor.

The final drafts of this book benefited enormously from two readers, Virginia H. Aksan and Sinan Kuneralp. They not only provided helpful criticism and suggestions but also sent me valuable source materials.

I have found the works of certain scholars to be highly useful. They include Avigdor Levy, Caroline Finkel, Rhoads Murphey, Stanford J. Shaw, and Virginia H. Aksan, whose works are listed in the bibliography.

I have been fortunate to discuss various aspects of the Ottoman military with the late Stanford J. Shaw, whose helpful advice and thought-provoking analyses undoubtedly improved the text.

Special thanks are due to three friends. Fatih Gürses skillfully prepared the maps, Bülent Yılmazer kindly provided valuable photographs from his private collection, and Ahmet Özcan patiently tracked down rare books and articles.

I'm most grateful to my editors for their patience and understanding.

My greatest debts, however, are owed to my wife İlkay. I find it impossible to adequately to express my thanks for her constant encouragement, understanding, and love.

Finally, I note that the help these scholars have given me does not mean that they will agree with everything I have written. Naturally any errors of fact or interpretation are entirely my own responsibility.

Note on Transliteration

As a general rule, modern Turkish spelling has been employed throughout the text for the sake of clarity and simplicity. Words that have well-known English forms, such as "Pasha" and "Sheikh," are written accordingly.

It is very difficult to be consistent and simple regarding the transliteration of place names due to the frequent nationalist campaigns of assigning new names by successor states and the western preference of using classical forms. We have preferred to call place names according to their established Ottoman forms (and generally giving its modern form in parentheses), but the ones familiar to western readers have been given in their English form.

The term Ottoman is preferred over Turk, Turkish, or Turkey since it conveys an accurate meaning of a multiethnic, multireligious and multicultural empire that once ruled over a huge geography.

CHAPTER 1

Early Middle Eastern Military Systems and the Foundation of the Ottoman Military, 1300–1453

This chapter details the evolution of the Ottoman military from its origins as a steppe-nomadic cavalry force to a standing army based on infantry. In its earliest form, Turcoman (Türkmen) tribes employed Asian nomadic command and control systems, but these changed as the nomads came in contact with the Islamic and Byzantine military systems. These encounters introduced ideas into the Seljuk military, such as slave-based armies, heavy infantry, and frontier forces based on nomadic border guards. The effects of these influences, combined with strong leadership, produced a decentralized but powerful cavalry force in the foundation period of the Ottoman military. As the Ottomans entered the 1300s, their military began a transition to an infantry-based standing army led by a caste of professional officers and centered on specialized corps characterized by standardization, of which the Janissaries were the most well known. While the Ottomans expanded into Europe during the following century, they concurrently developed a multicapable army with up-to-date tactics and weaponry. By the mid-1400s, the Ottoman military possessed a professional infantry and artillery force as well as effective, albeit largely irregular, cavalry and light infantry.

Sometimes the term Turk is used interchangeably with the word Ottoman (not to mention the term Seljuk and Turcoman), which can lead to confusion on the part of the reader. Therefore, a brief review of Ottoman history through 1453 is presented to establish a contextual framework for this chapter. The earliest Turkish political entity was known as the Göktürk Empire, which extended from China to the Caspian Sea from the sixth to eighth centuries. The Turcoman successors of the Göktürks swept into the Middle East and Persia in the seventh to the eleventh centuries and established firm control over the centers of Islamic civilization. The Turcomans were displaced by the Oğuz confederation, who founded the Seljuk dynasty in 1055. The Seljuk sultan, Alp Arslan, defeated the Byzantines at Manzikert in 1071, allowing the Seljuks and Turcomans to sweep into Anatolia. The Seljuks gradually subsumed the Turcomans into their empire but themselves were overthrown by the Mongols in 1243. The people known as the Ottomans (or Ottoman Turks) emerged sometime in the mid-1200s as a Turkic tribal group led by the legendary Ertuğrul. His son, Osman I (1280–1324), established the Osmanlı dynasty (the Europeans corrupted the word Osmanlı to Ottoman) that centered on the Anatolian peninsula. The term Ottoman Empire originated with Osman, but it was his son Orhan who took the city of Bursa and then led his soldiers in 1346 across the Dardanelles into Europe, establishing the dynasty as a force to be reckoned with. The dynasty expanded under sultans such as Murad I and Bayezid I, but in 1402 Tamerlane crushed the Ottomans. Mehmed I reestablished the leadership of the house of Osman in 1413 after an internal power struggle. Murad II ruled from 1421 to 1451, and the dynasty prospered and undertook a period of great expansion in both the Balkans and in Anatolia.

The Middle Eastern Military Legacy

The rise of Ottoman Empire from an obscure small political entity is without doubt one of the most important phenomena of the late medieval period. Unfortunately, the history of the origin and foundation period of the Ottoman Empire is very problematic because of their nomadic beginnings. The illiterate nomads produced no written records, and primary sources from contemporary neighboring countries, including Byzantine chronicles, do not provide concrete and sound information. Instead, there are only occasional entries about different aspects of the Ottoman emirate, which create more questions rather than answering the original ones. In terms of military history, the situation is far worse. The available information consists of bits and pieces that were heavily contaminated with sagas and legends, which themselves reflected a religious war mentality portraying nearly all military activities from the perspective of a struggle between good and evil. Moreover nationalist interpretations of Ottoman history by the historians of the modern successor states have also contributed to this quagmire.

It is obvious that we cannot reconstruct the foundation and early periods of the Ottoman military by depending only on chronicles and narratives, which themselves were mainly the products of fifteenth-century chroniclers who were writing well after the events in question.[1] Archeological and anthropological studies would surely contribute to our understanding of Ottoman military. Due to decades of negligence, ignorance, and even open hostility, however, these studies are still in their infant stages and do not yet provide us with much needed scientific information.[2] In order to construct an understanding of early Ottoman military history, we must use not only sources and direct information about the Ottoman emirate but at the same time incorporate the heritage of the Central Asian steppe-nomadic military tradition, Islamic and Byzantine military systems, as well as information about the fellow emirates of the Central Asian march lands (Ucat).[3]

The Central Asian Steppe-Nomadic Military Tradition

Regardless of conflicting ideas about the ethnic, social, or cultural origins of the Ottoman founding fathers, geographically they came from the inner Asian steppes and the Altai Hills, linking them firmly to the Central Asian military tradition. Indeed, the real strength and weakness of the early Ottoman military were outcomes of its obvious Central Asian steppe-nomadic roots, and in this regard it bears similarities to early Turkic-Mongol armies.

The signature identity of the Central Asian military tradition was that of mounted archer, who appeared before 700 BC. With minor modifications the general tactics and weapons of these warriors did not change substantially over the following centuries. A standard mounted archer was mounted on a sturdy steppe pony and carried a composite bow (Tirkeş Ok)—made of wood, horn, sinew, and glue—as his main weapon. He also used several other weapons, including swords (Kılıç), battle axes (Balta, Teber), maces (Topuz), and sometimes even flails (Gürz). Notably he did not use javelins (Cirit) or lances. He wore leather and woolen thick-padded garments and a metal helmet (Tulga) or leather headwear. Wearing metal armor was not common, and only wealthy or the elite forces could afford the cost of armor, which was mostly chain mail. The lack of armor was also related with the capacity of the ponies, as the small horses were not able to carry heavy burdens for long periods. For most warriors, small circular shields (Kalkan) were the only protection other than the thickness of their garments.[4]

In order to overcome their lack of armor and their heavy dependence on one weapon (the composite bow), the nomadic military became highly mobile. To enhance command and coordination in highly mobile tactical environments, such as surprise attacks, ambushes and encirclements, the nomadic armies preferred to use the same battle formation most of the time. In deploying his force, the ruler or chief commander positioned himself in the center, with his best units flanked by two wings. The second in command was responsible for the left wing, which was a privileged position. A cavalry screening force covered the front, and several independent units protected the flanks and rear. Because every unit followed the same battle routine, in most of the cases flags and whistling arrows were enough to cover communication needs. Tactics were standardized as well—ruses and arrow showers began immediately after first contact, while the main formation either waited for the enemy response to the screening force or started the attack from the wings. If the enemy could not withstand the wing attacks, the wings began to encircle the enemy and the center joined the attack as well.[5]

In most battle conditions, the nomadic military forces were able to concentrate units quickly and to disperse them quickly without losing unit cohesion and morale. The fluid and well-practiced movements made commands almost unnecessary. The most common tactic was to attack the enemy in several waves and to unleash a hail of arrows without coming inside the range of the enemy weapons. Generally every line attacked three times, and then another line would replace them. When taken into account that three lines were the standard formation and each cavalryman owned two or three horses—sometimes five—every line had the chance to rest and change horses while the tempo of attack continued unabated.

Most of the time the nomadic military tried to lure the enemy into a hasty attack, so every attempt was made to provoke the enemy to anger or to give a false sense of confidence by feigning a retreat. When the enemy attacked, the feigned retreat continued until the enemy units lost unit formation and cohesion, became tired, or were lured into an unfavorable position. Then the nomadic units in the ambush attacked violently with speedy and flanking maneuvers to encircle the enemy as a whole or in several small parts. There was no escape for the trapped enemy, and frequently they were annihilated. Because of its characteristic shape and mass hunt origins the nomadic military formation was called the crescent (Hilal) formation or the wolf (Kurt) play.[6]

The success of the nomadic battle formation not only depended upon surprise, ruse, and mobility but also on better knowledge of the terrain and the weaknesses of the enemy. The nomads were sensitive to suffering heavy casualties and tried every means to preserve their cadres. The effective use of terrain and the exploitation of the enemy were important elements of their success. Even a strong army with effective command and control could lose its battle effectiveness and formation after a long advance and suffering casualties against nomadic hit-and-run tactics. But the fatal mistake for any army facing these nomads was to retreat. Against the ruthless and aggressive pursuit by the nomads even a well-ordered retreat would turn into a disaster.

A simple but effective command-control structure based on the decimal system enhanced nomadic military superiority. This command system was the general norm for all Asian nomadic militaries from the time of Hsiung-nus. In theory the biggest military unit was 10,000 strong, which was called "Tümen," and the smallest unit was composed of 10 warriors. Between these were units of 1,000 and 100 strong. In many cases the decimal system was also applied to tribal organizations.[7]

Even though the nomads were natural warriors, the strength of the mounted archers depended not on inborn qualities but on lifetime training (including unit drills and training), exercises, and battle experience. Shooting arrows accurately when mounted was an especially difficult task (especially their telltale characteristic Parthian shot; twisting backward and shooting) and required constant practice, mandating training that began during childhood. Constant clashes and skirmishes between tribes and seasonal raids against neighboring countries provided additional opportunities to gain experience and improve talent. Interestingly, nomadic militaries tended to use hunting parties as large-scale exercises. Units would encircle the hunting ground in one or two circles. By narrowing the circles game animals would be forced into packs, and the hunt began when the ruler killed a few choice animals. Hunts of this kind required a high degree of coordination and discipline by the warriors, and different unit tactics and techniques frequently were exercised as well. It was thought that a good hunter would be a good soldier.[8]

There were several inherent weaknesses within the nomadic military system. The most obvious one was the need for constant action and for maintaining a nomadic lifestyle. Without constant action, nomads easily lost their superior individual talents and unit cohesion. Sedentary life destroyed all their military value in a short time, as they were unable to change their military system accordingly. The second weakness was the heavy dependence on horses. Maintenance of a sizable force with numerous horses needed wide steppe-like pasture lands. In effect, an authentic nomadic military system had environmental limitations, and they were able to move beyond their own borders only for short durations of time. Last but not least was the static nature of the system. Even though the nomadic military system was perfected over time, it essentially remained the same. The introduction of firearms and the lack of associated structural development ended the supremacy of the nomadic military.[9]

The Mongol experience in Syria during 1310 is useful in understanding the problem of structural development. Geographically and environmentally, Syria was not suitable for large cavalry armies and could not sustain the large invading Mongol army. Confronted by highly trained Mamluk heavy cavalry with mounted archer capacity, the Mongols were unable to sustain the numerical strength necessary to defeat them. When Mongol commanders tried to create a similar heavy cavalry force their efforts failed. Their nomadic warriors were unable to change their entire tactics and techniques drastically, and they were not trainable as adults for the highly demanding task of being a mounted archer and a heavy cavalryman at the same time. The Mongol failure against a small elite Islamic force, which was highly trained (and slave-based) then served as an ideal example that many Middle Eastern peoples tried to imitate.[10]

Not all the adversaries of the nomads were capable of using the inherent weakness of their military system against them. The Seljukid[11] successes against the Byzantine military are very important in understanding the decisive superiority of the mounted archers and the future Ottoman military. Successive Byzantine emperors and commanders were unable to produce a Byzantine military that could withstand nomadic mounted archers, who did not fit into any category of their previous enemies. Moreover, the timing of the Seljukids was perfect, appearing during a time of serious disorders, which was another characteristic of the nomadic military. Even enlisting mounted archer mercenaries did not help the Byzantines.[12] The desperate attempt of Emperor Romanus IV Diogenes to field a mighty army ended in total failure against the veteran army of Sultan Alp Arslan (1063–1072) in Manzikert (Malazgirt) on August 26, 1071.

The Manzikert battle was the first major clash between the Seljukids and the west and stands as a good example of the superiority of the steppe-nomadic military tradition. Due to the unexpected speed of the Byzantine advance, Alp Arslan was not able to gather all his troops but, with confidence, applied all the standard tactics and techniques of the nomadic military. An elusive screening force successfully deceived the Byzantines and canalized them into successive ambushes by feigned retreat. An ever-increasing tempo of cavalry attacks supported by arrow showers took their toll, and eventually the Byzantine army disintegrated. Some units escaped and some mercenary units changed sides. Alp Arslan annihilated the remaining bulk of the army (including the elite Tagmata regiments) during the disorganized retreat. With the capture of the emperor the last hope of the Byzantine Empire collapsed.[13]

Islamic Military System

There was no single Islamic military system. Depending upon the geography, history, culture, and adversaries, different Islamic military traditions evolved. During the seven centuries of its evolution, before the Ottomans, however, some common identities appeared.

All early Islamic militaries were based on duality: an infantry and/or cavalry provisional army that was tribal or feudal, and a standing army that consisted of professional slave soldiers. During the foundation period of Arab-Islamic states, nomadic Arab tribes and to a certain extent villagers and city dwellers from the Arabian Peninsula were the only source of men for the army. Obviously by defeating Byzantine and Sasanian armies repeatedly, early Islamic armies showed that they were more than simply collections of tribal contingents. However, the tribal character persisted decades to come. These tribesmen tried very hard to protect their privileged military position by forbidding the conquered nations to provide men for the army. Moreover, by building distinct cities or districts removed from native populations they tried to protect their separate identity. These tribes were the backbone of the provincial army. Depending upon their tribal specialization they provided infantry and cavalry forces armed with the necessary equipment and weapons. In return, they received regular salaries from the central finance bureaucracy, which was created for this purpose. They also provided local administrative mechanisms and security troops.[14] This emphasis on protecting a privileged military position, combined with keeping the population away from the military profession, was instrumental in creating another duality, which was a privileged, tax-free military class (Askeri) and a taxed civilian population (Reaya).

This system managed to function for only a century. The nomadic Arab tribes lost their martial fervor and military qualities soon after settling and mixing with the local population. Furthermore, with the conquest of the Persian Sasanids, for the first time they came across a highly professional and complex military system. Former Sasanid officers became naturalized and allowed in the Islamic armies.[15] Due to the financial difficulties of raising cash regularly for the military salaries and because of Sasanid and Byzantine influences, a new system was introduced called the "Iqta." This assigned the taxes of a certain land to individuals in return for providing military service. There were additional responsibilities to provide justice and order, and the Iqta gained a semi-feudal character.[16]

The spiritual Caliphs were never able to control either the provincial army or the unruly royal guard units, which were ever anxious to protect their respective interests. In fact, the Umayyadid caliphs depended heavily on the Syrian army, thereby creating a large division between Syrian and Iraqi armies, which might have been the real reason behind their military weakness. Following this, the Abbasid caliphs established their regime with the help of another military group, the Khorasan tribes. But bearing in mind the experiences of the Umayyadid period they eliminated the Khorasan army after their victory. In order to build a powerful and centralized state they depended upon freedmen (Mawali) and military slaves (Ghulams). Actually,

Mawali acted as a kind of precursor to formal military slavery. Although the Umayyadids already employed them before, it was the Abbasids who created a standing army based on slaves and freed slaves.[17]

The real value of the Ghulams was their total dependence upon their masters. Because they were foreigners in terms of ethnic origin and geography they did not have any local power base and relations with the local population. They did not have families to look after and were free to allocate all their time to the needs of the military. Their minds and bodies were molded according to the needs of their masters. Another important identity of the slave soldiers was their military expertise, which the provincial armies lacked. Enlisting different racial or ethnically compact groups to create different military branches or units was also an important element in creating both military cohesion and political checks and balances. They were mostly either sturdy infantryman from mountain regions like Dailam and Northern Africa or mounted archers from the steppes like Turcomans. Offsetting this, tension and hostility between ethnically dominated military branches was rampant, and occasional armed clashes were inescapable.[18]

The original Ghulams[19] were prisoners of war or bought from middlemen who procured them from other tribes or from border warrior groups. They were mature men with existing military skills, so they needed very little additional training. Al-Mutasim (833–842) changed this system drastically. He gathered younger slaves and trained them under capable commanders and instructors. He even built a separate city Samarra for his new army. He preferred Turkish slaves to the others because none of the ethnic groups had the same level of expertise and skill as the Turks possessed as mounted archers. They were so effective that even their image and presence were enough to keep law and order.[20]

Even though Abbasids continued to enlist Ghulams from other ethnic groups, including even Christian Greeks and Armenians, they increasingly depended upon Turkish slaves who came from Central Asia and from north of the Caucasus. Unknowingly, the Abbasid caliphs introduced Turks into the Middle East with important powers. The Turks became not only very important but indispensable. Of course this Turkish military dominance created reactions and opposition from different circles, which was largely ineffective. Until the collapse of the Ottoman Empire, one of the most dominant forces of the Middle East would be Turkish military elites.[21]

The Abbasid caliphs created the basis of the Ghulam system, which had an everlasting effect on all Islamic military systems. There were two key elements: military expertise and loyalty. The candidates were trained rigorously—including religious training—as an individual and as a part of their unit. They were isolated physically and culturally from everybody except the ruler and their unit. After this hard training and isolation, they became loyal only to the ruler and to their unit, which in a sense also became their family. Thus, isolation and training were the important parts of creating a trained and loyal army.[22]

By creating a slave-based professional army, the Abbasids were also instrumental in creating, for the first time, a professional officer corps called the Quwwad (qaid is the singular form). The officers of the Abbasids were commissioned from the ranks of Ghulams, who had achieved distinction and had showed talent and capability. Because they depended upon their salary and because they came from non-aristocratic backgrounds, their professional advancement totally depended on their success in military affairs and their loyalty to the ruler.[23]

The Iqta-based provincial armies did not disappear. In fact, they remained numerically the largest part of the military, vital in battle and in preserving law and order in the provinces. In terms of politics, power, and prestige, however, they were weak. The smaller slave-based standing army was instrumental to keep them loyal and obedient to the central government and especially the ruler himself. Even some governors, following the example of their rulers, founded slave units for themselves to preserve their position and gain more power. A product of creating private armies within the state was the bypassing of centralized command and control and the removal of the bonds of direct loyalty to the ruler. Some governors were successful in carving separate states for themselves by using their Ghulam armies, as in the examples of Tulunids and Ikhshidids of Egypt.[24]

The Mamluks of Egypt perfected the Ghulam system by establishing a unique system of training[25] and promotion and, in fact, because of this perfection Mamluk became the generic name of the whole slave military system. Actually, the foundation of the Mamluk state showed the inherent danger of this system. It was a successful system as long as the central state was financially strong, but when the state fiscal mechanisms faltered, political instability and financial crisis began. The Ghulams then became the decisive actor of the internal turmoil and, in fact, became king makers. With their solidarity and military power they assigned their favorites as rulers, and in this way they broke the code of loyalty. In the long run they also destroyed their solidarity and military effectiveness by spending most of their energy and time on politics and not on their profession.[26]

Byzantine Military System

The legacy and effect of the Byzantine military system on the Ottoman military is difficult to establish, and at the same time problematic due to controversial ideas and bitter discussions it engenders. Luckily most of the discussions focus on the administrative and socioeconomic aspects of life while ignoring the military side.[27] In order to understand the probable military exchange and effects we need to take into account of the situation of the late medieval Byzantine military.

By the 1270s, the Byzantine military was no more than a ghost of its glorious past. There was no effective standing army other than foreign mercenaries and no border defense system other than small personal armed followings of local magnates and their private castles. Whereas just two decades previously, a thinly stretched but efficient Byzantine army was able keep Turcoman warriors away from its borders.

The Byzantine military system collapsed after the defeat at Manzikert in 1071,[28] but it recovered partially and managed to withstand Turkish attacks for more than a century even after losing most of the Anatolian provinces.[29] Interestingly, after the Crusaders occupied Constantinople in 1204, the Lascarids emperors of Nicaea were able to build an effective border defense system and a small but capable standing army.

The modest recreation of land based "Pronoiai" under the new name "Stratiotikai Pronoiai" was an important development, but the real power of the system depended on the border guards, called the "Akritai." In effect, the Lascarids reorganized the old and much neglected Akritai by introducing new soldiers, including Kumans—Turkic nomadic warriors coming from the Wallachia and Russian steppes[30] and even some unemployed Latin soldiers, and by reestablishing unused rules and regulations. The logic was to give land to these loose groups of soldiers for settlement with their families along the border. While protecting the border regions from the Turkish raids by using the rebuilt small castles and mobile infantry and cavalry tactics, they earned their livelihood by farming the tax-free lands. The small standing army reinforced the Akritai in the event of big attacks.

Without the huge expenses of the city of Constantinople the Lascarids managed to funnel the state income more successfully to the military.[31] After the reconquest of Constantinople in 1261, however, the emperors left the Anatolian defenses to their fate and returned their attentions to the welfare of the capital and European lands of the empire. Making things worse, in order to get cash and financial assets, land allocated to the border units was taken and given to the local magnates or court officials. It was a fatal mistake. The effectiveness of the Anatolian troops was the key element in maintaining the empire's strength. The newly landed aristocrats provided neither taxes nor military services. Then, vicious suppressions of the Akritai, who rebelled at these inequities, put an end of the system. That also might be the basic reason why some individual Byzantine soldiers were known to have served under the Ottomans. Due to the lack of funds, the Byzantine standing army disappeared in a short time. Emperor Andronikos even disbanded the navy as a cost-cutting measure, forcing Byzantine sailors to seek employment in the Turcoman emirates.[32]

For more than 70 years the Ottomans came face to face with, and fought against, the decentralized and fragmented forces of the local magnates, whom the Ottomans called "Tekfur" and possibly against the much smaller local defense forces of the villagers. Occasionally the emperors managed to send small military units, which mainly consisted of mercenaries and some additional troops of various origins against Ottomans. They were also as ineffective as the troops of the Tekfurs (i.e. Byzantine expeditions of 1300 and 1328). So it is no surprise to see that the Byzantine emperor was also derisively called Tekfur (Tekfur of Konstantiniyye) in the Ottoman chronicles.[33]

We know that some Byzantine magnates and commanders changed sides and became members of the Ottoman military.[34] However, this was probably more common at the level of the simple soldiers. Due to their limited military experiences and know-how, however, these turncoats did not have the means to affect the Ottoman military. Taking into consideration the corruption and disuse of Byzantine military institutions, it is not surprising. There were two fields that the early Ottoman military was lacking—the infantry corps and technical branches. The Ottomans managed to establish a viable infantry corps in the 1370s only after many trials and false starts. Likewise, technical branches were established only after making direct contact with the Balkan and Central European militaries. Reciprocally, the Byzantine commanders tried to imitate Turkish cavalry tactics and techniques by enlisting Turkish mercenaries, Christianized Turks (Tourkopouli), and even settling groups of nomads in suitable areas in order to get continuous military service as early as the tenth century and even mounted archers from the north of Black Sea like the Caucasian Alan mercenaries.[35]

Some of the similarities in terms of weapons, equipment, symbols, titles, and terminology probably came indirectly as a part of the Seljukid military legacy. The Seljukids fought and faced a relatively strong Byzantine military for more than a century. A kind of "zone of interaction" was created not only at the frontier but also in the big cities of both of the states. Seljukids learned many things and occasionally enlisted individual renegade Byzantine officers and soldiers into their forces. We also know that whole Byzantine units were employed during the important campaigns as dependent state units or as mercenaries. At the same time, the Seljukids recruited entire Greek units from their subject population.[36] The technical expertise of Byzantine soldiers was needed, especially for siege warfare. The Seljukids perfected torsion/kinetic artillery, mining operations, and other engineering techniques with the help of Byzantine expertise.[37] This recruitment or employment of their adversary was not only a method used by the Seljukids. The Byzantines were also employed, or they recruited Turks. Many Turkish soldiers, as individuals and as groups, served under the Byzantines. Some even achieved high distinction and became high-ranking officers.[38] So it is reasonable to suggest that most of the similarities—like Pronoia with Timar—were the outcome of Seljuk-Byzantine mutual relationships and not simply the direct product of the Ottomans.[39]

Foundation of the Ottoman Military

Gazi Warriors of the Osman Gazi

Many scholarly works try hard to present how an obscure small Ottoman political entity managed to succeed in competition with stronger political entities and finally emerge as one of the most enduring empires of the Mediterranean region. How and why did the house of the Ottomans achieve this remarkable success while its rivals, some of which were stronger than the Ottomans, perished during the various stages of this intense competition?[40] From a military perspective the important thing is to identify the basic dynamics and systems of the foundation period of the Ottoman State, leaving the puzzling and obscure political and socioeconomic processes to others.

According to the Ottoman chronicles and legends, the founders of the emirate (proto-Ottomans) arrived to the north west of Turkish-Byzantium march lands of Bithynia with the second big wave of Turcoman migration into Anatolia (1220s) after the great Mongol assault on the Middle East. We do not know their actual arrival date in the region, but they must have established their presence not later than 1260s[41] under the leadership of a certain Ertuğrul Bey.[42] They were certainly a tribal group of nomadic pastoralist Turcomans but their tribal structure and connections were probably very loose due to the general settlement policy of the Seljukid rulers. In order to protect law and order and to establish centralized control, the Seljukids always divided big tribes or clans of former tribal federations into small groups and settled them accordingly. For a period of time they remained around the Söğüt-Domaniç region and conducted raids into the nearby Byzantine territories. Probably during this brief period they remained under the nominal control of the Çobanid beys, who were the official governors general (Beylerbeyi) of northwest march lands.[43]

Several developments and drastic changes helped this obscure tribal group to become a viable politic entity.[44] The Mongol onslaught and victory against the Middle Eastern Islamic states, including the Seljukids, uprooted the Turcoman tribes and forced them to migrate in several waves to the west while at the same time destroying the effective government control imposed on them. Between the establishment of direct Mongol Ilkhanid control on Anatolia in 1277 and the rebellion of Mongol commander Sülemiş in 1298, the march lands increasingly came under the control of independent Turcoman leaders. They constantly attacked and raided Byzantine lands and carved territories for their own separate emirates and occasionally clashed with each other. In 1300 Mongol troops finally defeated Sülemiş but at the same time lost the meager control they had on the march lands.[45]

In addition, the Byzantine military system weakened and collapsed after the recapture of Constantinople in 1261 with the migration of attention and financial assets to Constantinople and to the European holdings of the empire. The neglected Anatolian defenses further weakened after the ill-fated decision to abolish land-based border units, which was the outcome of political struggle between bureaucrats and generals. An important percentage of Byzantine soldiers—especially Akritai—began to collaborate with the Turks after several of their rebellions were suppressed.[46]

Last but not least, the bigger and powerful emirates became targets of the Ilkhanids, the Seljukids, and the Crusaders several times, while the Ottomans stayed away from these dangerous attacks and, consequently, benefited from their results. When the Seljukid commander Şemseddin Yaman Candar defeated and killed the Ottomans' overlord Çobanid Mahmud Bey in 1292, the Ottomans became virtually independent.[47] Other competitors, such as the Aydınids, one of the most successful emirates of the march lands, came under the attacks of crusaders, lost its navy and key harbors, and were forcibly pacified.[48] The Catalan Company's expedition of Byzantine mercenaries in 1303 and 1304 against the rival Turcoman emirates of Karesi, Germiyan, Saruhan, and Aydın inflicted serious setbacks on those emirates' military activities as well.[49]

The founder of Ottoman dynasty, Osman Gazi[50], was selected as the leader of the tribal group after the death of his father Ertuğrul in this volatile region in 1299. He not only inherited a loose tribal group but also a favorable geographical position against the disorganized and weak Byzantine border.[51] Interestingly, he had to fight first not against Byzantines but against Germiyanid local allies and a neighboring Tatar tribe in order to secure his position.[52] Nevertheless, Osman managed to create an independent political entity after the defeat of the Byzantine army at Bapheus (Koyun-Hisar) in 1301.

The Battle of Bapheus was the outcome of a decision to attack the Ottomans in order to relieve Nicaea (modern Iznik), which was strategically and emotionally very important for both sides,[53] from Ottoman siege. The Bapheus battle is very important in developing an understanding of the composition of the early Ottoman military, which was certainly a cavalry-dominated force with limited numbers of infantry. The cavalry was composed of nomadic horse-archers of tribal origin and volunteers. They fought according to classic steppe tradition tactics: using effective intelligence about the enemy, choosing the battlefield, fighting vanguard actions, and achieving surprise at all levels, harassing the enemy with successive cavalry charges and arrow showers, using ambushes and fainted retreats to disorganize enemy battle formation and finally destroying the disorganized and fleeing enemy by encircling them.

The Byzantine commander, Mouzolon, enlisted Alan mercenary mounted archers who learned their trade from the Nogay Tatars. He also tried to get the upper hand by using ships to transport his troops in order to surprise the Ottomans. But the Ottomans already knew about the incoming assault and achieved surprise during the disembarkation of Byzantine troops from the ships. They successfully used the cover of slopes and bushes in otherwise flat terrain. The Byzantine local militia immediately lost confidence and ran away. The Alan mercenaries successfully covered the disorganized retreat, but soon they, too, were decimated. The role of Ottoman infantry is not obvious, but probably they were used in the final encirclement of the Alans.[54]

With the Bapheus victory Osman Gazi gained an important reputation as a warrior of the faith and as a strong, charismatic leader able to arouse support from his men. (Characteristically, nomadic tribes were, in many cases, simply groupings around a charismatic leader.) He began to weld together more strongly his independent-minded subordinates and, at the same time, more Turcoman warriors began to enlist under his leadership. Osman's military success against the infidels provided more material gains for his followers, which were keys to attract more warriors, settlers, dervishes, religious scholars, and former Seljukid or other emirates' officials, while at the same time protected his leadership status. Even though Nicaea did not fall as intended, various small Byzantine forts and towns were captured, and all Bithynia except the big cities was captured.[55] So this date, 1301, may be taken as the foundation date of the independent and sovereign Ottoman emirate.

The Ottoman emirate was based on a loose group of pastoralist nomadic tribes that were in the early phases of moving from nomadic life to a sedentary one. Even though semi-nomads were the core group, there were many others coming from different backgrounds and regions, including refugee villagers, artisans, and townsmen coming from inner and eastern Anatolia as well as unemployed Seljukid officials and scholars. Of course, there were fugitives from the various rebellions, especially heterodox dervishes. All these very different people with conflicting identities came to settle the very complex and fragmented frontier of Bithynia.[56] The people called the Ottomans, a terminology largely devised by early European historians, were obviously not simply a unitary nomadic tribe.

A similar and common mistake is to see early Ottoman soldiers as simple tribal Turcoman cavalry without any tactical or technical abilities, which was not the case. Ottoman mounted archers were veterans of many campaigns under the flag of the Seljukids and perhaps other Islamic powers. At the same time, many fighting as mercenaries increasingly participated in Byzantine campaigns against foreign powers or rebels. Some of them also probably participated in Alexious Philanthropenus's unsuccessful Anatolian army rebellion of 1294 and 1295.[57] Participating in military campaigns as allies or as mercenaries with the soldiers of other Turcoman political entities helped to improve their military expertise. More importantly, this also affected the relations and solidarity among themselves, which might be the reason for the mostly peaceful character of Ottoman conquests of neighboring emirates and their ability to incorporate their cadres without major problems.

The presence of strong artisans' guilds—urban brotherhoods with sufistic religious inclination (Ahis)—was also very important. These guilds were not only socioeconomic, religious, and political organizations but were at the same time paramilitary ones. The Ahis produced weapons and military equipment and provided light infantry, but their real importance was to consolidate territorial gains by establishing their branches in the occupied towns. After conquest and settlement they immediately organized socioeconomic life, established law and order, and provided defense units against possible enemy attacks. They were also instrumental in the conversion of local Christians to Islam. With the help of the Ahis the Ottomans were able to concentrate their military efforts on enemy militaries more effectively. The Ottomans enlisted some Ahi leaders as government officials like Çandarlı Kara Halil, the eponymous father of the Yaya corps and the Janissaries. The Ahis continued to provide these services during the conquest of the Balkans.[58]

The general geography and environment of Bithynia had important effects on the Ottoman military. It was a suitable place for agricultural and semi-nomadic lifestyles but not suitable for genuine nomadic life. The available pastoral fields were unable to accommodate and feed the many horses required by a genuine nomadic army, and some of the followers of Osman Gazi were already sedentary or semi-nomadic people. Moreover, the religious scholars and former officials of the Seljukids brought sedentary traditions with them, and coexistence and cohabitation with the Byzantine villages and towns also affected the new comers. Consequently, more and more Turcoman warriors began to settle and change their lifestyle drastically, which also affected the military and political system.[59]

It is obvious that continuous warfare between the Byzantines and the Ottomans had a religious character. Both sides used religion to justify and legitimize their aims and war, but at the same time they were pragmatic enough to use the services of renegades, mercenaries and were able to develop coexistence and cohabitation mechanisms. In this respect the Ottomans were more successful. They were militarily more powerful than the Byzantines, united and able to conduct joint operations, tolerant enough to accommodate all the religious and ethnic groups, and more pragmatic in borrowing and learning useful institutions and methods from the enemy. By creating local allies and collaborators and encouraging religious conversion they managed to hold the conquered territories.[60]

Together these factors provided the Ottoman wars (Gaza) against Byzantines with imperatives beyond that of a simple holy war (Jihad).[61] Although the military expansion and raids were justified by Islam, the Ottoman warriors (Gazi) were not strictly religious fighters but raiders (Akıncı) with the unshakable belief of the superiority of Islam.[62] In fact, the terms Gaza and Gazi were the clear legacy of the warrior dynamics of the Arab-Byzantine frontier of South Anatolia and the Arab-Turk frontier of Trans-Oxania. So it is not surprising to see same type of motives, legends, and heroes like Battal Gazi and Danişmend Gazi in the story of the Ottomans and, of course, similar Byzantine patterns including heroes such as Digenis Akritas.[63] The presence of heterodox dervishes instead of Islamic orthodox religious figures was also related to this aspect of these wars. Nearly all the march lords (Uc Beyleri) had notable dervishes with them, like the Sheikh Ede Bali, Geyikli Hoca, and İleri Hoca of the Ottomans[64], thereby reducing the influence of conventional religious traditions.

All these military activities against the Byzantines were conducted without a master plan or strategy but within a general pattern. The Turcoman march lords had a tendency to allocate regions—in reality just directions—to their subordinate tribes/groups for continuous raids after establishing a strong base. This decentralized way of command and control was very effective against the weak Byzantine defenses. Numerous groups of warriors from literarily every direction were conducting continuous raids into the Byzantine domains. These constant and unpredictable raids by numerous chieftains were instrumental in the collapse of the Byzantine military and also contributed to the confused statements of the Byzantine chronicles.

Unfortunately, this decentralized way of conquest also created many problems for the Turcoman emirates. Sometimes subordinate leaders became uncontrollable after becoming strong and carving a separate territory for themselves. A good example of this problem was the weakening of the Germiyanid emirate. The Germiyanid tribal group became the strongest march lords of the south and west at the end of thirteenth century. Its commanders successfully captured all the Aegean coastlands and hinterland independent of each other. Then, instead of remaining loyal to their Germiyanid lords they proclaimed their independence and established the emirates of Karesi, Saruhan, Aydın, and Menteşe.[65] Interestingly, while the leaders of the large tribal groups tried every means to remain independent of the Seljukid overlords, they were at the same time equally unsuccessful in controlling the ambitions of their subordinate commanders and tribal leaders.

The Ottomans managed to deal with this decentralization process successfully and were able to keep commanders under strict control by starting the transformation of Gazis into a standing army earlier than the other emirates. As explained earlier, there was a relentless and sometimes vicious competition between the Turcoman emirates.

Probably the future success of the Ottomans had something to do with the lessons learned during this competition, and every opportunity was used to gain more territory, booty, and fame. At the beginning Ottomans were very slow in comparison to some others like the house of Aydınids, but their slowness turned out to be an advantage in the long run because they spent more time on state building internally while externally escaping the wrath of outside powers.[66]

Turning Gazis into a Standing Army

The early Ottoman military displayed all the shortcomings of a nomadic army. It was not a standing army but rather a number of independent military groupings depending on tribal warriors and volunteers. It managed to defeat the units of local Byzantine magnates and even the mercenaries of the emperor, but at the same time it was not able to capture fortified positions and castles by direct military means. A lack of an effective infantry corps and the absence of a technical corps were the main reasons behind this deficiency. Ruse, surprise, insider collaboration, and, sometimes, natural disasters were the only means to capture castles in a short time.[67] If these methods did not produce results, then the only remaining alternative was to blockade all the approaches to the castle by means of small fortified positions (Havale), to force villagers to seek refuge in the castle and starve the castle, which strained its sources with the sheer volume of refugees into surrender. This method was time consuming and costly especially if the respective castle was big and had enough sources and provisions. Nicaea (İznik), Prusa (Bursa), and Nikomedia (İzmit) withstood the blockades 21, 11, and 6 years, respectively,[68] and in the end the rewards of the Ottomans were destroyed and desolated cities needed years of recovery.

We know that the early Ottoman military had light infantrymen[69] who were mostly volunteers from villages without any formal organization (resembling Seljukid "Haşers"[70]) and occasionally some Ahi warriors. These forces were more of a liability than an asset. According to the Ottoman chronicles Alaeddin Paşa and Çandarlı Kara Halil proposed the foundation of standing infantry units in 1325, which would also serve as the royal guard (Hassa). After the foundation decree of the Yaya (literally on foot) corps, many young villagers eager for regular incomes applied for the job and the new unit established easily. In actuality, it was not an indigenous invention as several of the other emirates also had the same type of infantry units with the same name.[71]

The Yaya corps was not an authentic standing military unit. Its soldiers continued to work on their farms during peacetime without receiving salaries but were exempt from some taxes. They joined the army when called and brought their personal weapons and equipments with them. During mobilization and war they then received a daily salary (Ulufe). Mirroring its tribal roots, the Yaya corps was initially organized according to decimal system (10, 100, 1,000). When serving as royal guards they wore high white bonnets (Ak Börk), which was the distinctive Ahi head wear differentiating them from the tribal cavalry, which wore red bonnets (Kızıl Börk).[72]

The Yaya corps did not achieve the aims and expectations of its founders, as the soldiers possessed very limited tactical and technical abilities. This was, of course, due to their part-time employment as soldiers and, while working mainly as independent villagers, their inability to participate in regular military training. At the same time, they did not have an efficient officer corps due to the fact that the officers were not very different from the volunteers, possessing common social origins and using the same weapons (the composite bow remained the main weapon) as their men. They continued to operate under the antique command-and-control system, and their lack of heavy armor made them vulnerable for the operations they were created for. Lastly, their mobilization was very difficult, especially during the harvest season.

Due to these constraints the Yaya corps degenerated from royal guards to mere line infantry and lost the right to wear the privileged white bonnets. They continued to lapse from the primary infantry corps to the secondary one in less than 40 years.[73] Interestingly, while the Yayas were losing their position and importance in the military structure their numbers continued to rise, and some of them who were able to afford horses were organized as a cavalry corps with similar organization, which was called the "Müsellem." In order to make use of excessive manpower, a new subunit called the "Ocak" (literally hearth, but figuratively a close family-like unit) was established. Five Yaya or Müsellem soldiers were organized as one Ocak. For each campaign season one of them was tasked in serial to mobilize (Eşkinci Yaya) while the others (Yamaks) stayed behind to provide services for the family of the campaigner as well as give a certain amount of money to him.[74]

The Yaya and Müsellem corps were reorganized as auxiliary corps with fixed personnel strength—about 20,000 each—after 1360. They did not receive salaries but were compensated with a tax exemption. Their status became hereditary, physically fit elder sons replacing their old or deceased fathers. Their primary duty was to provide several types of support for the army during the campaigns, including transportation, road and bridge building, and protecting supply convoys and army baggage. In the later decades additional tasks were assigned for some of the units, such as when the Gallipoli Yaya and Müsellems provided some services to the navy arsenal. Another group, the Sultanönü Müsellems, who were renamed as "Taycı," bred horses for the royal household while others provided labor and menial services to the nearby mines. Occasionally, in emergencies, they were used as combat units, as in some of the campaigns of Murad I.[75]

Even though the Yaya corps did not fulfill the expectations of the Ottoman military as an infantry corps, it managed to become a viable model for the support and auxiliary corps. It also illustrates a valuable point about the unique blend of conservatism and elasticity of the Ottoman military. The Ottoman high command showed its conservatism by not abolishing the Yayas after its failure to fulfill its original duty. But showing its elasticity, the Ottomans reorganized the corps as a support unit to perform much needed non-combatant tasks for the army. Additional tasks were also given to the whole corps or some of its units according to the new needs. This unique blend of conservatism and elasticity remained a distinctive characteristic of the Ottoman military identity to the very end.

The other demanding task for the Ottoman leaders was to reorganize the Turcoman cavalry into an efficient provincial army. There were basically three problems. The first one was lack of cohesive command and control. The Turcoman cavalrymen were loyal only to their immediate leaders and fiercely independent. In addition, they paid more attention to material gains than to the aims of the state. This was a serious handicap for conducting large unit operations and conventional battles. The second was the Turcoman leaders' tendency to create independent personal domains in the conquered territories. The obvious outcome of this decentralized way of conquest was the establishment of separate political entities. The third one was related to the inherent weakness of nomadic military. With the settlement of more tribes their cavalry began to lose martial fervor and military qualities. In order to overcome these problems the Ottoman leaders began to introduce various measures slowly in order to control and transform the Turcoman cavalry. The principal outcome of these measures was a specially tailored Seljukid Iqta system called the "Timar." Nearly all the important Turcoman emirates tried to develop their own Iqta systems during this time period.[76]

We know that during the early period of the Ottoman emirate, conquered territories were immediately divided up among the leaders of Gazis as personal domains known as "Yurtluk," but they remained under obligation to remain loyal to the emirate and to continue providing military services.[77] This system did not work well. Most of the leaders settled in their respective domains and ceased to take part in military campaigns.[78] After the first conquests in Europe a new system began to appear. There, the newly conquered territories, which remained state property, were divided according to their tax value (Timar) and given to commanders and soldiers, who were named "Timarlı Sipahi," according to their merit and contribution to the conquest. Importantly, only certain tax revenue from the land was allocated and not the ownership of the land itself. Moreover, it was not a permanent but a temporary allocation in which the state retained the right to change it if the Sipahi was not able to provide military services. The Sipahi was under the definite obligation to participate in military campaigns with his horse, weapons, and other equipment, and according to the value of allocated taxes of the land he might have to provide some armored retainers (Cebeli) as well. According to his success in battle he might increase his Timar by gaining additional lands, but if he failed to perform his tasks properly or fled from the battle he would certainly lose all his rights and would be punished.[79] Even though the Timar system did not gain its full effectiveness until the mid-fifteenth century, its efficiency was one of the main reasons behind the Ottoman military successes.[80]

As mentioned earlier, most of the Turcoman emirates tried to found similar types of standing armies as the Ottoman emirate.[81] However, the main difference and eventual success of the Ottomans was the foundation of an indigenous slave-based standing army called the "Kapıkulu Ocakları"—literally hearths of gate slaves or court slaves. The Kapıkulu Ocakları with their famous sub unit, the Janissaries (Yeniçeriler), remained the backbone of the entire Ottoman military system until the end of the eighteenth century.

We know that from the period of Osman Gazi military slaves served as royal guards, but their numbers were limited and they did not belong to a separate unit. In fact, they were members of the sultan's private staff called the "Nöker," which was essentially a Mongol institution.[82] The Nökers consisted of distinguished individuals personally selected by the sultan from tribes, slaves, and other social groups. They were required to be independent of every social connection, especially from tribal groups, and served the sultan with loyalty and with absolute obedience. Their main duty was to act as royal guards, and they performed additional duties, including messengers, ambassadors, and hound keepers, but unlike royal pages they did not perform steward duties. Some successful Nökers were also appointed to military command duties.[83]

The Ottomans certainly inherited this institution from the Seljukids[84] with some alterations, but the transformation of this institution started after crossing into Europe. Ottoman units captured countless slaves and, for the first time, a special tax called the "Pençik" (one out of five) was introduced to take one out of every five slaves for the central treasury. These slaves were trained and organized under the structure of a new corps known as the Janissaries. According to the Ottoman chronicles the Pençik was devised jointly by Kara Rüstem of Karaman and Çandarlı Kara Halil, probably after the conquest of Adrianople (Edirne) after 1369.[85] Unfortunately the foundation period of this important military institution is not clear, and the available information is very problematic.[86] But we can reconstruct the early Janissary institution by using clues from its well-developed form of mid-fifteenth century.

Only physically fit, sturdy and young slaves were selected (Pençikoğlanı), and a special training center, the "Acemi Ocağı" (hearth of the inexperienced), was founded in Gallipoli in order to train them for at least two years according to the needs of the army. In addition to their military training, the slaves worked as naval arsenal workers and oarsmen. However, after less than a decade the training system was changed drastically. Instead of using the "Acemioğlans" (novices) in exhausting maritime duties they were sent to Turkish farmlands to work in the fields and to learn the Turkish language and culture and convert to Islam.

After this initial training period, which lasted four to eight years according to the availability of training slots, they were taken to the Acemi Ocağı. It was a demanding training regime under heavy discipline and spartan conditions. Trainees learned to fight as infantry by using different weapons—especially the ubiquitous composite bows—under challenging conditions and learned to obey absolutely the orders of their superiors. Loyalty to the sultan was the key theme of the training. The constant evaluation and harsh discipline was instrumental in the selection of the future elite soldiers of the sultan. The Acemis performed all the menial duties within the training center and additional duties, like fire fighting and transporting state-owned goods, but no duties required artisanship. According to the regulations, any Acemi who somehow learned any craft was immediately dismissed from the center and might be assigned to the auxiliary services. Under normal conditions, training would last four to eight years, and when slots became available the senior Acemis would be assigned to their respective units, but only after "Kapıya Çıkma" (literally passing out to the gate)—the final examination by high-ranking officers.[87]

But, in less than 30 years after the foundation of the Janissary corps, a totally new mode of recruitment evolved, the infamous child tribute system called the "Devşirme" (literally to collect) was introduced.[88] The main idea behind this new recruitment mode was the forced tribute of selected children from their Christian families, who were then used as military slaves after a long training period that included cultural and religious training in addition to military training. This was not unusual as it might seem today, and we know that the Seljukids previously collected limited numbers of children from Christian families for special training in court duties.[89] Additionally, some Ottoman march lords independently had already collected children for their staff use. So, in a sense, the Ottoman administration simply continued these practices after blending it with the Mamluk military slave training system.

From the military perspective, the reasons for early enlistment were obvious. Prisoners of war or slaves captured during the raids were already mature men who were not very responsive to Ottoman military training. For example, the training of the main weapon of the army, the composite bow—either mounted or foot—was very demanding and time consuming. In addition to training, loyalty was also a key issue. Most of these forcefully recruited soldiers, who already had undergone hard training and who lived in prison-like conditions, were unwilling to work for a foreign power, so a substantial percentage of them were ready to desert the army in any suitable opportunity. Field commanders had to take special measures, including assigning special police units, in order to keep the number of deserters small.

The Devşirme was a brutal but efficient solution to these problems. First, a large and stable pool of men was available for selection. Most of the parents, of course, resisted the idea of giving their children, and some tried every means to keep them, including flight from the country. However, the administration and collection of the Devşirme was not a large problem thanks to the efficiency of Ottoman administrative control. Second, children were more responsive to the training, and their bodies and minds were easily molded according to the needs of the military. Third, in the long and complex training, heavy emphasis was placed on unit cohesion and élan, and very rich rewards were granted for merit and combat achievement, which combined to create intense loyalty to the institution. In fact, loyalty to the sultan never became an important issue, as in reality blind obedience to the orders of the superiors was the generally expected norm.[90] Even though the Devşirme created a much disputed legal problem by forcing a group of citizens to give up their children as future military slaves, as an institution it continued to develop into a well-regulated system at the end of fifteenth century. The secular benefits of the system were clearly more important to the state than its shaky legal base in reference to Islamic law (Sharia).[91]

It is obvious that the Janissary corps (Yeniçeri Ocağı)—literary new soldiers or troops—was established initially and later other Kapıkulu corps were created around the nucleus of Janissaries because of newly arisen needs. The Janissary corps was not the only infantry corps created by the early Ottoman commanders, but it was the first modern regular infantry in the Ottoman army. As royal guards they had the privilege of wearing white bonnets and they became the elite of the elite and, subsequently, the most famous and powerful corps of the entire Ottoman military.[92]

Of course, the Janissaries did not gain their famous reputation immediately and were not numerous enough to fulfill the army's complete requirements for infantry units. But they quickly became an important asset to counter-weight the centrifugal tendencies of unruly march lords and other local Turcoman leaders. As in the examples of the previous Islamic slave-based standing armies, the Janissaries and other Kapıkulu corps were instrumental in protecting the centralized structure of the state and its territorial integrity and in keeping other military groups loyal to the sultan. Especially after crossing into Europe, some military commanders became march lords and played important roles in terms of conquering large expanses of territory. They used the slowness of central administration to reach rapidly advancing frontiers for their benefit. They were much attuned to preserving their freedom and keeping the territories they had captured under the control of their families. Some famous Akıncı families, like the houses of Evrenos, Mihal, Turahan, and Malkoç, were founded as an outcome of their successes against both enemies and Ottoman central administration. The Kapıkulu corps initially counter-weighted the hereditary semi-independent march lords' ambitions and later completely destroyed their power bases during the mid-fifteenth century.[93] With the establishment of the Kapıkulu corps, the Ottomans constructed an effective centralized state and maintained their territorial integrity even after several succession crises. In the end, the rival Turcoman emirates were unable to establish efficient standing armies and perished one after another.[94]

The Janissaries were, at the beginning, numerically small—probably around 1,000 strong—and as an elite unit they were very precious and expensive. But the army needed large infantry units that were expendable and easy to replace. The solution was to introduce semi-mercenary infantry corps of soldiers called Azabs—literally "bachelor"—that were already employed by the other emirates[95] and generally financed by the provinces. Even though we do not know for sure the ethnic composition of Azabs, all the contemporary sources are pointing out their origin as Turcoman villagers from Western Anatolia.[96] According to government regulations, the state decided the numbers of Azabs needed for each campaign and allocated the requirements between provinces. The governors then collected the necessary financial assets to raise the allocated numbers of Azabs from the population, which was essentially one Azab per 20- or 30-person household. Finding Azabs for a particular campaign was not difficult, as there were enough unemployed or ambitious youngsters with some military experiences. Initially Azabs were part-time soldiers called up or who volunteered for a certain campaign, but in time due to the nature of prolonged and constant campaigning, most Azabs became semi-mercenaries, who broke all bonds with their villages and migrated to the provincial cities looking for employment on a continuous basis.

Governors were the senior officers of the provincial Azab units, as in the example of Timarlı Sipahis. After recruitment and commissioning officers, the governors organized the Azabs into units, which were nearly the same in organizational structure as Janissaries. Soon, nearly all the officers were permanently commissioned and governors then only renewed their licenses. The Azabs had to provide their weapons and equipment, which were closely inspected during the recruitment process. They were essentially light infantrymen and their main weapon was the composite bow. They habitually performed dangerous duties, fought in the frontlines, and were tasked to wear down the enemy. For this reason their casualty rates were very high, but their rewards were commensurately high as well. In addition to their salary, the Azabs were exempt from taxes during the campaign. Occasionally, for heroic combat achievements and meritorious service they were awarded Timar or permanent employment in the army—and most then became guards with duties in frontier castles.[97]

Even though the Azabs were essentially mercenaries (due to the constant campaigns, strong state controls, and lack of independent condottieri-type captains) they acted more like the full-time soldiers of the age. They did not have unit loyalties and their only common bonds were finding a salaried job and looting. In any event, however, the process of urban unemployment after demobilization made them the precursors of the real Ottoman mercenary system that was born after the mid-sixteenth century with the spread of hand held firearms.

Crossing into Europe: Rapid Expansion and the Turbulent Period

The relatively peaceful annexation of the Karesi emirate in 1345 to 1346 provided all the important components needed to cross the Dardanelles (Çanakkale) strait into Europe. The Karesi emirate was a maritime emirate and achieved many successes at sea until the Catalan expedition and the beginning of the succession struggles. Moreover, the Ottomans managed to enlist more captains and sailors from the other maritime emirates and from the Greeks as well. These captains and sailors had the necessary maritime expertise and technology to accomplish a crossing, and well-known Karesi gazi warriors (after enlisting into Ottoman military) encouraged the Ottoman leadership to assault the Gallipoli peninsula.[98] Indeed, the Ottomans themselves also had numbers of well-experienced veterans of European wars or raids. Many Turcoman warriors had already participated in many military operations into the Thrace and the Balkans as pirates, raiders, and especially as mercenaries of the Byzantine Empire.

The Byzantine emperors and aristocrats increasingly depended on the services of Turcoman mercenaries against Serbians and Bulgarians and even for their own internecine fights. They initially hired private groups, but after the 1320s they began to deal directly with leaders of the Turcoman emirates, including the Ottomans who began to appear as a mercenary presence after 1345. In this process Turcoman warriors learned the weakness of the Byzantines and Balkan states and became familiar with the terrain. Moreover, whatever the outcome of the particular campaign, the mercenaries looted and destroyed everything, without regard to friend or foe, and in this way contributed greatly to the internal unrest of the Balkans.[99] Following the Byzantine example, other powers also enlisted Turcoman mercenaries, including the Catalan Company. Interestingly, a group of Turcoman mercenaries—former allies of Catalans—under the command of a certain Halil Ece, on their way back to Anatolia, captured a castle on the Gallipoli peninsula in 1311 and managed to keep it for at least one year.[100]

Clearly the Ottomans began to view the crossing into Thrace as inevitable and, perhaps, even as an easy operation. Following the example of Halil Ece, Crown Prince Süleyman Paşa captured the important castle of Tzympe (Çimpe) in Gallipoli in 1352 on his way back to Anatolia, after contributing greatly to the Byzantine victory against the Serbian army at Adrianople in 1352. It is possible that some independent gazi warriors were already in possession of the castle beforehand. While the Byzantines struggled to negotiate in order to regain Tzympe in 1354, an earthquake gave the Ottomans an excellent opportunity to capture the remaining castles on the peninsula, including the city of Gallipoli itself. The Byzantines regained the city with the help of Count Amedeus VI of Savoy in 1366, but by then it was too late to turn back the Ottomans, who had established a strong foothold in Thrace. Later, the Byzantines abandoned the city of Gallipoli in 1377 without a fight.[101]

Because the Ottoman standing army was in its infancy, some military leaders—the majority of whom were former Karesi commanders—were assigned as march lords and were given areas of operation. In order to keep them under control, the crown prince was initially assigned as the overlord. But later on a Beylerbeyi was assigned to this role in the European provinces, which were named Rumeli (Rumelia). However, the agents of central administration were unable to exercise effective control and the initial military onslaught was carried out in utter disorder. Cities and towns changed hands several times, but the march lords managed to penetrate deep into western Thrace and Bulgaria following strategic advance routes.

Even though Thrace and the eastern Balkans were dotted with numerous castles, these were of limited military value against the march lords because the castles of the Byzantine and Balkan states were not part of a coordinated defense network. All of them were individual castles without the support of centralized mobile units and, except for Salonika (Selanik) and Adrianople, the Ottomans captured them easily. It was at this point that Ottoman technical units and primitive siege trains began to show their presence.

After a decade of confusion, Beylerbeyi Lala Şahin Paşa finally established effective command and control. In order to insure security in the newly conquered territories, all castles and fortifications were torn down. At the same time, many nomadic groups were forcefully settled into the conquered territories while land-based Byzantine military groups remaining in strategic locations were relocated into Anatolia. In this way Ottoman administration managed to achieve two goals: to change the ethnic composition of its European possessions and to tame the unruly character of nomads who became loyal and law-abiding citizens in a foreign environment. The newly settled nomads continued to provide military service and they were organized as Yörük (auxiliary corps), which mainly dealt with transportation and logistics.[102]

The Byzantine and Balkan states failed to create a coalition against Ottoman onslaught because political disintegration and deep social and religious problems proved instrumental in blocking all diplomatic efforts.[103] Only two important Serbian magnates, the Vukašin and Uglješa brothers, managed to join forces and collected a relatively large army. This Serbian army easily passed through Ottoman territory and reached Černomen on the Marica (Meriç) river, as most of the Ottoman army units were in the Anatolia. Lala Şahin Paşa, however, reacted resourcefully with the available forces by immediately sending a reinforced vanguard under the command of Hacı İlbeyi to reconnoiter the enemy. Hacı İlbeyi found out that the Serbian army had established the camp without security measures and, using his own initiative, he immediately launched a hasty attack on September 26, 1371. The Ottoman vanguard's sudden attack (and loud noises created by them) caused a panic inside the Serbian camp. In the confusion many Serbian soldiers were killed or drowned in the nearby river, including many of their commanders. The battle of Černomen (Sırp Sındığı, literally rout of the Serbs) greatly weakened the only regional power capable of resisting Ottoman advances. In this sense Černomen had more long-lasting effects than the more famous Kosovo battle of 1389.[104]

After the battle of Černomen new Ottoman march lords were assigned to cover the strategic routes heading inside the Balkans.[105] At the same time, many Byzantine, Serbian, and Bulgarian magnates became officially vassals of the Ottomans. From now on the Ottomans exploited the military potential of their Balkan vassals to the limit and if any of them showed insubordination their territory was immediately ransacked by the march lords and they lost everything they had.[106] Ever farsighted Murad did not forget to take measures against Venice by renewing commercial agreements and ties with Genoa.[107]

During these early phases of the invasion of the Balkans, the Ottomans showed their inherent pragmatism and adaptability to new environments, which would prove to be a key element of Ottoman administration in the coming years.[108] After the conquest of Thrace the Ottomans understood that they did not have the military means to control the entire area effectively nor were there enough Turkish nomads for Turkification programs anymore. In turn, their initial vassalage agreements preferred to use former local military and administrators in their home territories, which created a peaceful atmosphere for transformation according to the needs of the Ottoman system.[109]

Under these favorable conditions Ottoman Sultan Murad I began two important processes. The first was the standardization and bureaucratization of the entire sultanate, which the Ottoman emirate had been gradually transforming since the 1360s. Murad I sped up this transformation[110] by organizing and standardizing the Timar holdings and provincial army units assigned to them, creating a finance bureaucracy independent from the military command system and founding slave-based standing army units.

Murad I and his advisors paid special attention to the family farm system (Çiftlik). The family farm system was the nucleus of the Timar system, and this nucleus had to be preserved and transformed to meet the needs of the Timars. At the same time, an efficient family farm system that eliminated feudal domains would create incentives for the Christian peasant population to support the Ottomans. In this way the Ottomans purposefully used the wide-ranging peasants' protests and the age-old struggle between peasants and feudal lords for its own benefit. In a sense, the Ottomans enhanced effective centralized state control without making large changes in people's lives.[111] Standardization and bureaucratization helped the state deal with the daily administration of the sultanate more efficiently while making the peasants loyal and peaceful. More importantly, however, with the help of this process, disasters, defeats, and succession crises did not create large problems affecting the survival of the state. Due to the stable manpower pool and the associated flexible financial system, no loss was irreplaceable.

The second important process was related to the emirate's expansion into Anatolia. From the very beginning the Ottomans suffered great difficulty in order to legitimize their expansion against fellow emirates. But nearly all the emirates were weakening after the successes of the Ottomans, who became the unquestionable leader of the all gazis. Even the strongest emirate of the Karamanids was unable to repeat the Ottoman successes when they tried to imitate the Ottomans by attacking small Christian castles in Cilicia without success. Nevertheless, fighting against them was very difficult, and this problem is evident in the chronicles' accounts, which spoke of who tried to produce various excuses in order to legitimize the conquests in Anatolia.[112]

From the military perspective the problem was more difficult to solve. Ottoman soldiers were hesitant to fight against emirate soldiers, who were seen as comrades. At the same time, material gains and looting opportunities were limited in the Anatolia due to strict Islamic law regulations. Murad I solved this important shortcoming by using some of his new Christian vassals' military potential and standing army units. In this manner the Ottomans captured most of the territories of the neighboring emirates easily. By defeating the most powerful contender, Karamanids at Frenkyazısı in 1387, Murad I clearly showed that the conquest of Anatolia was only a matter of time.[113]

Murad I continued to pursue his creative Balkan vassal policy in Anatolia. Former sipahis of the newly conquered emirates preserved their status but lost their original land holdings and, instead, they were assigned to Rumelian timars.[114] The Anatolian vassal emirates were obligated to provide military units for European campaigns. Generally they were placed in front of the Ottoman army to perform dangerous duties, as in the example of the Hamidid archers in the Kosovo battle of 1389.[115] This policy provided several benefits. First, by performing dangerous duties the emirates' soldiers lightened the burden of the Ottoman units. Second, service within the Ottoman army was instrumental in weakening the already shaky authority of the emirates. Constantly changing alliance structures and using the military potential of the vassals to the limit would remain a keystone of the Ottoman system in the coming years.

The Battle of Kosovo (Kosova) is very important in terms of understanding Ottoman army organization and how it functioned with vassal troops after Murad's reorganization. We do not know the exact numbers, but from the available sources the composition of the Ottoman army is clear. The total numbers of the Ottoman units were probably not higher than 40,000, including the vassal troops and baggage train. The composition of the army in percentage terms was as follows: Kapıkulu units—including the palace guards—a bit more than 5 percent, Azabs and Yayas around 30 percent and cavalry troops more than 50 percent, which consisted of Akıncıs and Timarlı Sipahis evenly. The soldiers of the vassal emirates—cavalry and infantry—comprised around 10 percent, and Christian vassals probably less than 5 percent.

We know about the presence of a small light artillery unit, which played a minor role in the battle. Interestingly, the cavalry-infantry balance changed drastically from the 90 percent cavalry domination of the emirate period to a smaller 60 percent majority, which was one outcome of the reorganization. At the same time, other problems may be identified. For example, the numerical equality of Timarlı Sipahis and Akıncıs shows clearly that the Timarlı Sipahi system was not fully established and that the march lords were still very powerful. The heavy presence of the problematic Yayas was also an important weakness because they had been reduced to a secondary position and they were very unhappy about this lost status.[116] It might be said that the results of Murad's reorganization were mixed.

The deployment of troops and logistical support functioned surprisingly well. Governors and Christian vassals prepared four large logistical concentration and distribution points and various small ones along the routes of advance. Additionally, Ottoman units passed through difficult terrain, including mountain passes, without problems thanks to the preparations and deployment of auxiliary units beforehand. At the same time, an infant organization of civilian logistical elements (Orducu), which consisted of artisans, contractors, and various types of tradesmen achieved remarkable success. Most of these civilians were tasked by their respective guilds to perform services for the army during the campaign. All of them were required to supply services by using their own assets—capital, equipment, and so forth—but, of course, with a handsome profit. The state only provided security and sometimes transportation. Every individual soldier (and units as well) had to buy logistical support for themselves from the Orducus, which had a monopoly. Moreover, local tradesmen and villagers in the campaign area could only sell their merchandise and services through Orducus.[117]

Information about the actual conduct of the Battle of Kosovo is not clear. The Serbian-dominated western Balkan coalition with Bosnians, Albanians, Bulgarians, and small units from Hungary and Bohemia, under the command of Knez Lazar Hrebeljanović, took their battle positions in Kosovo before the arrival of the Ottoman army. Ottoman units deployed one day after the army's arrival on June 15, 1389. Units took their battle position according to old established system: left wing (Anatolia units), center (Kapıkulu units), and right wing (Rumeli units). The Hamidid emirate-dominated foot archers were tasked with the forward elements.

Most probably the Ottoman left wing launched the attack following the success of vanguard action. After the initial success, however, the left wing suffered heavy casualties against heavily armored Serbian and Bosnian infantry and began to retreat.

The help of the right wing prevented a possible Ottoman collapse. It is probable that the center also suffered a serious setback at the same time, during which Murad I himself was killed and many Orducus perished. Nevertheless, Ottoman units successfully counterattacked and captured many important Christian dignitaries, including the commander in chief, Knez Lazar, who were then summarily executed. The destruction of the enemy command cadres created a chaos in which the coalition units withdrew in a disorganized fashion.[118]

Both sides immediately announced themselves victorious. Most probably the Ottoman announcement was the correct one. Even though the Ottoman army did not pursue the enemy, it remained in firm possession of the battlefield. For the Ottomans it was a Phyrrhic victory, which would be nicknamed "big bloody Kosova" (Kosova Melhame-i Kübrası). The Ottoman army suffered heavy casualties, including the loss of the sultan, and only gained the upper hand after the desperate counterattack of the center and right wing. The Serbian-dominated coalition also suffered heavy casualties and, in comparison to the Ottomans, they did not have the means to replace them. By all accounts the Battle of Kosovo reinforced the Ottoman presence in the Balkans.[119]

Why the Ottoman army suffered heavy casualties and barely gained the upper hand with a last-minute maneuver deserves explanation. The obvious answer is the shortcomings related to the transformation of the military. The Kapıkulu corps were still too small to affect the outcome. The Yaya corps with light armor and problematic combat value was no match against heavily armored Balkan infantry in defensive positions. The Akıncıs were essential raiders with limited conventional cavalry capacity, and the Timarlı Sipahi corps was still in its infancy with various shortcomings. A secondary factor must be the decision to attack first. Instead of applying the old nomadic tactic of luring the enemy into an attack and then attempting to ambush them when they lost the cohesion of unit formations, the Ottomans attacked directly the heavy infantry in defensive positions. Thus, immature organizational structures combined with faulty tactics badly hurt the Ottoman army in this battle.

The new sultan, Bayezid I, after dealing successfully with a succession crisis, continued the transformation of the military while enlarging the sultanate in Europe and Anatolia. He insured that most of the former vassals lost their territories one by one and allowed the Akıncıs to raid all corners of the Balkans—even launching occasional raids into Hungary.[120] King Sigismund of Hungary realized the imminent danger of an oncoming Ottoman invasion and was able to convince several important European monarchs of the idea of a crusade. This crusading army, which mainly consisted of Hungarians and French, was completely crashed at Nicopolis (Niğbolu) due to the reckless and uncoordinated attack of the French commander, Comte de Nevers, who was lured by a successful feigned retreat and ambush by the Ottomans on September 25, 1396. For the first time, the Janissaries showed their presence and affected the outcome of the battle by successful defensive infantry tactics that included the use of sharpened stakes and ditches to annihilate the French heavy infantry. The large number of Christian losses included many famous knights, and subsequent horrendous accounts by the participants convinced Western European monarchs to stay away from the Balkans and East Europe, leaving this region to the mercy of the Ottomans. So, in a sense, Nicopolis turned out to be the last real crusade. Importantly, the Ottoman army later captured the last remaining Bulgarian strongholds and established the Danube as the strategic border in Europe.[121]

Not only did Bayezid I expand the sultanate rapidly in both directions (east and west), he also tried to transform rapidly the military. The nucleus of Bayezid's transformation was the Kapıkulu corps and slave-originated statesmen, which led to the alienation of many constituencies that were empowered under previous sultans. Bureaucratization and land registry changed the ownership of lands drastically. This, combined with an emerging centralized sultanate and increased taxes, alienated the marcher lords and nomads[122] as well as the Yayas and Azabs, who were already very angry about the loss of status and importance. In fact, Bayezid I was very unpopular among large segments of the Anatolian population, which caused many of the former Turcoman emirs to seek the help of Timur (Tamerlane). Timur was the self-made sultan of a great Central Asian Turcoman state, who just finished the conquest of Iran and became the neighbor of the Ottomans. He was more than happy to enlist the support and cooperation of the Turcoman emirs. This was a recipe for disaster, as Bayezid's excessive arrogance and confidence in the power of his military made confrontation inescapable.

Both sides faced each other at Angora (modern Ankara) on July 28, 1402. Timur, by occupying water sources and strategic ground, put Bayezid I immediately in a difficult situation. The large nomadic army of Timur, which also included elephants in front, was nearly twice the size of the Ottoman army. Paying no attention to the advice of his commanders or to the exhaustion of his army, Bayezid I launched the attack immediately from his right wing (Anatolian units). Timur's left wing lured the unwary Anatolian units into an ambush. At this decisive moment the former emirate soldiers changed sides and Bayezid's right wing collapsed completely. Timur's simultaneous attack on the Ottoman left wing (Rumeli units) was stopped by a stiff defense, but the Rumeli units lost confidence when attacked by the enemy center. A daring counterattack by Bayezid's Serbian units established contact with the center while the remaining Rumeli units decided to withdraw.

The Kapıkulu corps at the center preserved their formation and courageously faced the increasing attacks of the Timur's cavalry. Bayezid I refused to leave the battlefield, and by a fighting withdrawal pulled some of his remaining units back to a dominant hill. Part of the Ottoman center and the Serbians managed to escape before the encirclement, but most of the Janissaries and palace guards perished in a last stand, and Bayezid himself was captured by the enemy.[123]

The collapse of Ottoman army was obviously the outcome of a clash of interests and divided loyalties due to the rapid military transformation of the military. The desertion of the former emirate soldiers to the enemy provided the necessary excuse for the traditional military classes to flee. In addition to this, Timur managed to maintain the initiative from the very beginning by choosing the battlefield, controlling the water sources, and forcing the Ottomans to attack. Interestingly, the Ottoman military suffered all the problems that conventional forces had previously faced against nomadic cavalry—and the Ottomans, as previous nomads, should have known how to deal with Timur. That they did not is clear evidence of the level of transformation from nomadic cavalry to a regular infantry and cavalry force.

Some of the former emirates were restored after Timur's decision to return their former lands. Bayezid's sons immediately engaged in a civil war, and the country unofficially divided into three parts. The interregnum (Fetret) period continued for 12 years (1402–1413) with vicious internecine fighting. Some of the Akıncı families played important roles during the civil war by supporting the factions, which gave assurances for continuation of their semi-independent presence. Despite this vulnerable situation, the European domains of the sultanate remained quiet. The Balkan principalities and foreign powers like Hungary were unable to use this ideal opportunity (due to their own internal divisions, internecine fights, and succession crises) to further their interests. Instead of uniting against Ottomans, each one of the Christian entities preferred to play one pretender against the others, which instrumentally created an ever-changing and fluid network of alliances. Even most of the sultanate's Christian subjects remained loyal and did not rebel. It is evident that the Ottomans managed to establish an enduring legitimate political and administration system that had the support of the majority of the population.[124]

In the end it was the presence of both a strong Kapıkulu corps and central government functionaries that kept the centrifugal forces under control. Mehmed I followed an appeasement policy in order to unite the country again after ascending the throne. He satisfied the uneasy and troublesome traditional military classes with financial rewards, and troublemakers were eliminated quietly. He refrained from an offensive policy against his neighbors, and the primary activity of the Ottoman military remained focused on internal confrontations. Of course, the march lords were allowed to return to raiding activities after the end of the civil war[125]

Murad II immediately changed his father's appeasement policy to that of a limited offensive after successfully dealing with a succession crisis in which nearly all the march lords supported his uncle. He reconquered most of the Anatolian lands lost after Ankara battle. His offensive policy also resulted in a long but low-level confrontation with Venice and a sporadic but high-level confrontation with Hungary. While the last strongholds of Serbia fell in 1439, the Ottoman assaults into Transylvania (Erdel) failed against the talented Hungarian General John (János) Hunyadi.[126]

Hunyadi was the first European commander who understood the inherent weakness of Ottoman military at the operational and tactical levels. He launched attacks on the European domains of the Ottomans using a window of opportunity created by the seasonal nature of the Ottoman campaigns and demobilization. But he earned his fame by employing the Hussite war wagons (wagenburgen) widely against Ottoman cavalry charges. These mobile fortresses made of war wagons and light artillery were very effective against the lightly armored Ottoman cavalry and their arrow showers. The presence of heavily armored infantry strengthened Hungarian battle formations, but even the smart Hunyadi underestimated the pragmatism and adaptability of the Ottomans. Consequently, he suffered two defeats at the hands of the Ottomans, which provide important illustrations in understanding the strength of their system.

The anti-Ottoman league at this time was under the official command of Hungarian King Vladislav (Władysław) I, but Hunyadi acted as de facto commander. Their army consisted of Hungarians, Polish, Wallachians, and some other small contingents. In the previous year their assault had fallen victim to the scorched earth policy of the Ottomans and cold weather. So this time they tried to follow rivers and the coastline in order to have secure logistical support. Murad II led his army directly towards the Christians and met them near Varna on November 10, 1444. Murad II and his commanders had learned the hard way that they somehow had to lure the enemy into an attack by abandoning their defensive superiority. Both Ottoman wings attacked but collapsed against the well-entrenched, heavily armored Christians. They then conducted a hasty retreat that provoked the enemy center to follow. Vladislav led the attack, which crashed headlong to Janissaries behind sharpened stakes and ditches. After a bitter struggle the Janissaries managed to encircle the enemy command group and kill Vladislav. The death of the king and the sudden return of the fleeing Ottoman cavalry caused panic and rout. Hunyadi managed to escape, but not many of his comrades.[127]

The second encounter took place in the famous battlefield of Kosovo. Hunyadi managed to bring together his old allies and some Western mercenaries. The Ottoman army met the Christians on their way to join forces with their Albanian ally Scanderbeg on October 17, 1448. This time the roles were changed. The Ottoman army remained on the defensive behind a long line of stakes and a ditch palisade that covered the entire front. In addition to this security measure, the Kapıkulu corps at the center employed the same kind of war wagons that Hunyadi was famous for. In fact, the Ottomans founded a special military corps to use war wagons called Top Arabacıları Ocağı (Artillery Wagoners' Corps). Ottomans called their version of wagenburgen as "Tabur Cengi," which was obviously coined after Hussites' term of "Tabor."[128] The first day was spent with low levels of skirmishes. On the second day Hunyadi attacked mainly the left wing of the Ottomans without achieving any success. Then, his inspired night attack to the center was crushed before the Kapıkulu war wagons. The Ottoman wings were pulled back as if to reorganize after the previous day's attacks, and the center was left alone on its original position as a ruse to lure the enemy. Hunyadi tried his chances and attacked. The concealed wings of the Ottoman army encircled the attackers, and the Wallachians changed sides at this crucial moment. Most of the Christians were annihilated and the remaining units took refuge in a fortified camp. The next day Ottoman units captured the camp easily and found out that their arch enemy Hunyadi had already escaped.[129]

The second battle of Kosovo convinced the Europeans of the invincibility of Ottoman military might and of the impossibility of recapturing the Balkans. From now on all their efforts would focus on checking the Ottoman advance into Central Europe. The Battle of Kosovo of 1448 was also a turning point for the Ottoman military.[130] This was the first time that the Ottomans employed up-to-date battle tactics, such as war wagons and firearms, on a large scale while ingeniously combining them with traditional cavalry tactics. They defeated not simply an ordinary commander but one of the best practitioners of tactics of the age. This victory was a critical turning point, as it set the stage for the elimination of the unruly traditional military classes and for the establishment of a centralized military command structure.

CHAPTER 2

Classical Period, 1451–1606

The classical period of the Ottoman military corresponds to what Professor Stanford J. Shaw described as the period of the apogee of Ottoman power. It began with the accession of Mehmed II to the throne in 1451 and extended through the reign of Ahmed I, ending with the Long (Habsburg) War in 1606. During this period the Ottomans conquered the residual Byzantine state, which had been reduced to the city of Constantinople, pushed north to the Danube and east into Anatolia. At the apex of the Ottoman conquests in the mid-1500s, Süleyman the Magnificent pushed deep into Hungary and Mesopotamia and made the empire the master of the eastern Mediterranean Sea. Later, sultans advanced into southern Russia, Caucasia, Persia, and North Africa. In concert with these military successes, the empire transformed itself into a sophisticated administrative entity of great strength, which encouraged diversity, culture, learning, and religious activity.

The enduring western view of the signature characteristics of Ottoman military identity originated in this time frame. That view was constructed out of a seemingly endless series of European defeats against the superior Ottomans. That identity included armies composed of vast numbers of soldiers, giant cannons, and bombards, relentless Janissary warriors, and swarms of reckless auxiliary soldiers. It was an identity that rekindled ancient European memories of limitless Persian and Mongol hordes. It became the material from which nightmares were born and generations of European children learned to pray for delivery from the "Terrible Turk."

This chapter develops the institutionalization of a professional standing army of Janissaries, household cavalry, and artillery forces in the Classical period of the Ottoman military. It also outlines the evolution of the varied corps of professional service support organizations that enabled the Ottoman military to operate effectively in distant theaters of war. Provincial forces are examined as well as frontier forces and auxiliary corps (under various names). Ottoman command and control is presented, and precombat preparations and operations are explained. The chapter concludes with an analysis of the Ottoman military's effectiveness and its structural shortcomings, which scholars tend to neglect in its Classical period of operations in diverse theaters of war.

Mehmed II and the Conquest of Constantinople

The final accession of Mehmed II to the throne was a keystone in the history of the Ottoman military. Mehmed not only changed the Ottoman Sultanate into an empire but also dramatically transformed the military into an effective centralized armed force and rid the army of traditionally unruly elements. In opposition to the commonly held opinion that the real military transformation started before the conquest of Constantinople, Mehmed actually used the conquest of Constantinople as a pretense to strengthen his position and to transform the military. During his first and brief reign after the voluntary abdication of his father Murad II (1444–1446), he faced strong opposition from some of the leading viziers, especially grand vizier Çandarlı Halil Pasha, and from aristocratic Turkish families. These opposition groups tried every method to block his reforms and ambitious plans and, in the end, incited the Janissaries to mutiny (the Buçuk Tepe incident) and dethroned him.[1]

During his forced exile, Mehmed prepared a detailed plan to deal with the politicized and unruly elements within the military. After his reinstatement to the throne he immediately sacked key military commanders, including the Ağa of Janissaries, Kazancı Doğan, and appointed trusted lieutenants to these positions. His next step was to enforce widescale disciplinary measures and harsh punishments, but even these measures did not satisfy him. In order to control the Janissary corps more completely and to insure their loyalty, he reorganized their organizational structure and introduced the largest palace guard unit, the Sekban (hound keepers), into the corps. The Sekbans became an integral part of the corps in a short time but at the same time preserved their separate identity and name.[2]

After effectively curbing the Janissaries, Mehmed turned his attention to the technical corps of the army—especially the artillery. His fascination of military technology was instrumental in the refoundation of the artillery corps, which previously was an ad hoc timariot unit with a very loose organizational structure. He first turned the artillery into a salaried standing army unit, which allowed him to deploy it quickly to distant points.[3] To modernize the artillery he employed European cannon founders and technicians like the legendary Hungarian (or Transylvanian) master Urban (or Orban)[4] and he also mobilized all available local military technicians, craftsmen, and gunsmiths. Edirne (Adrianople) became a large foundry locus where various groups of founders and technicians refined their designs under the personal supervision of Mehmed. Many cast and wrought-iron cannons were produced. His newly reorganized artillery batteries tested these new cannons as a part of their continuous training program. Unfortunately, the details of the artillery reorganization and preparation for siege operations, including the gunpowder and saltpeter industries, remain unclear. But we do know that at least four giant bombards (bigger than 40 cm diameter)[5] and about 74 medium cannons were produced and organized into 14 siege and four fortress artillery batteries. There were also an estimated 15 more field batteries equipped with light wrought-iron pieces.[6]

Transportation of cannons and the siege train from Edirne to Constantinople turned out to be as demanding as the production phase. Nearly all the population of Thrace was mobilized in addition to Turcoman camel and oxen drivers coming from Anatolia. The engineer corps constructed new roads and bridges and improved old ones. During the rainy season it took 64 days (February 1 to April 5, 1453) for the siege train to arrive at Constantinople. It is probable that a field gun foundry was also established somewhere near the city.[7]

By taking into account the experiences of four failed sieges of his ancestors and numerous blockades, Mehmed paid special attention to securing the borders and establishing naval supremacy. His diplomacy was based upon appeasement and concessions to achieve a desired level of security in his Balkan rear. Mehmed easily pacified his troublesome neighbors, the Karamanids of Anatolia and the Byzantine despots of Morea, by brief military incursions.[8] However, establishing naval supremacy needed more effort and time, and he built more than a hundred naval vessels, the bulk of which came from the Gallipoli dockyards. But interestingly most of them were small vessels, and only 20 of them were galleys—and there were no galleons or other types of large ships. As far as we can understand from the available data, the probable reasons behind not constructing large ships were a lack of know-how and limited numbers of experienced captains and trained crew. In fact, nearly all Mehmed's captains and crew were the legacy of various maritime Turcoman emirates, and their experiences were limited to piracy and raids.[9] To compensate for these limitations, Mehmed assigned one of his trusted lieutenants from his royal household, Baltaoğlu Süleyman Bey, as the admiral of the navy. However, his preference for loyalty rather than experience proved instrumental in the failure of the navy during the siege.[10]

As a careful leader Mehmed did not rely on the navy alone for the enforcement of the blockade of Constantinople. He decided to close the Bosporus by building a new fortress, which would be located on the opposite shore of the existing one in Asia (Anadolu Hisarı or Güzelce Hisar). He accelerated the construction of the four large towers by assigning one each to his favorite viziers. In four and half months (April–August 1452) the construction of the European fortress (Rumeli Hisarı or Boğazkesen) was finished thanks to the ambitious viziers and mobilization of entire western Black Sea region. Even though the design and architecture of Rumeli Hisarı with high masonry walls and four circular towers certainly belonged to the classical medieval style and was old-fashioned according to contemporary Italian examples, it still was a remarkable accomplishment. The main works were designed to protect extensions of the fortress (Hisar-ı Beççe) containing large bore cannons overlooking the sea from land and amphibious attacks. This extension with its lower walls and suitable openings was an ideal gunnery position up to 20 large cannons. Additionally, light cannons and kinetic artillery were positioned on various parts of the main fortress. Rumeli Hisarı with its older counterpart on the other side effectively blocked all sea traffic to and from the Black Sea.[11]

After two long years of preparation, Mehmed and the main part of the army arrived at Constantinople just after the siege train on April 6, 1453. He carefully positioned his troops against the famous land walls of Theodosius.[12] Anatolian army units were positioned on the right wing (in the south) in three groups covering half of the walls. The Kapıkulu corps remained in the center in two groups, and Rumelia army units covered the left wing (in the north) with two groups. The remaining Rumelia army units covered the geographically separated suburb of Galata. Most of the heavy artillery batteries were positioned in the center under the direct command of the sultan himself. Due to the highly inflated numbers given by the contemporary chronicles, the exact size of Mehmed's army is difficult to estimate, but its combat strength must been about 100,000 (including the volunteers but excluding the non-combatant units).[13]

Mehmed's army was very large compared with the standards of the time. The command, control, and logistical requirements were daunting. In addition to the sheer size of the army, only half of the men belonged to the standing army and the rest were volunteers and mercenaries. Some of the volunteers and mercenaries were well organized and properly equipped, but most of them were loosely organized groups coming from all corners of the Anatolia and the Balkans, which were not only Turk but also Bulgarian, Serb, Albanian, Greek, and even some Latin warriors.[14] Mehmed organized them into operational groups and assigned commanders from his standing units, who were officers with superior ability and authority. Any misconduct or violations were harshly punished, and some of the timariot units were tasked to establish screening lines around the army in order to deal with desertion and criminality.

The level of effective planning and organization was more evident in logistical and administrative issues. The Orducus opened large markets and workshops to meet all the needs of the soldiers. Well stocked field depots provided necessary food and fodder regularly without creating problems for the local population. Law and order was strictly established, and even the presence of thousands of camp followers did not affect the order in the well-regulated camps.

The siege of Constantinople began with artillery fire. The giant bombards damaged the walls, but confounding the estimates of Mehmed's experts did not destroy them. Actually, these giant bombards were already out of fashion in Europe because of immobility, slow reloading, long cooling, and difficulty of aiming.[15] These limitations enabled the defenders under the able leadership of Giovanni Longo di Giustinianni of Genoa to repair the walls and build up palisades during the long pauses, rendering the slow-firing cannons ineffective.[16] Classical siege engines like mobile siege towers and various types of kinetic artillery were also employed, but they only wore down some parts of the walls. Mehmed also tried various tactics and techniques, including night assaults and mining operations. The Lağımcı (miners-sappers) corps, which was reinforced with Serbian miners from Novo Brdo, managed to dig at least five tunnels under the walls, but all of them failed because of successful counter-mining operations. Surprisingly, the Byzantine army reinforced by the civilian population, foreign mercenaries, and volunteers successfully withstood these ingenious attacks by using an elaborate defensive system.[17]

In addition to these discouraging results and the ever increasing casualty figures, the Ottoman navy failed to breach the boom closing the entrance of Golden Horn and was unable to enforce the blockade effectively. Four large Christian supply ships ran the blockade after a day-long naval skirmish on April 20. The faulty command of Süleyman Bey and the ineffectiveness of medium and small Ottoman vessels against the large enemy ships were the main reasons for failure. A furious Mehmed sacked and punished the impotent admiral, but great damage was already done to the morale of the besieging army as well as strengthening the defenders.[18]

The ever resourceful Mehmed immediately sped up one of the most daring and brilliant plans of the age: the moving of ships overland across the hills into the Christian anchorage in the Golden Horn. In a short time a special causeway was built using greased logs, and about 70 small vessels were transported over the hills into the Golden Horn in a single night (April 22). Complete surprise was achieved. The Ottoman vessels under the protection of artillery were able to force the Byzantine fleet to seek refugee near the entrance away from the vulnerable parts of the sea walls. This forced Giustinianni to remove units from the land walls to face a new threat. Moreover, he had to reinforce these units with additional soldiers when Ottoman units built a new floating bridge over the Golden Horn, enabling them to move units more freely. The Christian situation in the Golden Horn became desperate when a newly designed large mortar had begun to shell the Byzantine fleet, sinking some of them. According to several witnesses Mehmed personally directed and was involved in the design of this particular mortar.[19]

Even though the Byzantine defenses and morale were increasingly weakened (particularly after seeing Ottoman vessels in the Golden Horn) the Ottoman side also suffered significant problems. The conservative governing elite under the leadership of Çandarlı Halil Pasha was increasingly unhappy and vocal with each passing day. They were certain about the impossibility of the fall of Constantinople and were uneasy with the increasing risk of a European army of relief coming to the aid of the city. However, the real reason for their opposition was an ever-increasing struggle between the aristocratic families and the Kuls of the sultan. They wanted to preserve their political power and hereditary positions within the government. They were well aware of the grand design of Mehmed and their fate at his hands when the city fell. In addition to this opposition, the failure of two massive frontal assaults and high numbers of casualties convinced an important percentage of Mehmed's soldiers of the futility of the continuation of the siege.[20]

Mehmed once again displayed his leadership abilities in the climatic conclusion of the siege. He convinced the respected religious figures and ulema to support the siege and he encouraged his soldiers by talking about divine omens and signs. He also made use of the financial expectations and greed of the soldiers by promising three days of looting and plunder. All his available units were organized into three waves and positioned mainly against three breaches, which had finally been created in the walls. The final assault started before dawn on May 29, 1453. The first wave consisted of mercenaries and volunteers who bore the brunt of the attack and were virtually annihilated, but at the same time wore out the defense further. Azabs attacked as a second wave and nearly scaled the walls. At this critical moment Mehmed ordered the final wave of Janissaries to attack. The defense collapsed after a last stand, and Ottoman soldiers poured into the city. The Ottoman navy left its position and joined the looting as well. This created an opportunity for some of the defenders to flee by sea.[21] At the end of a brief period of carnage and looting Mehmed (using his new and prestigious title Fatih or the Conqueror) enforced law and order. He immediately started rebuilding and began the development of his new capital. From this date until the collapse of the empire, Constantinople or Istanbul remained the capital of the Ottoman Empire.

The conquest of Constantinople was seen by the Christian and Muslim worlds as the realization of apocalyptic oracles and as the beginning of a new era. The first losers of this new era were aristocratic Turkish families and the old military classes. Mehmed eliminated leading members of the opposition immediately. As in the example of Çandarlı Halil Pasha they were first stripped of their positions and sent into exile. Later on, one by one, they were executed and their power bases completely destroyed by the confiscation of assets and exile of family members.[22]

The second group of losers was the unruly traditional military classes, especially the semi-independent frontier units: the Akıncıs and Turcoman tribal warriors. Of course their power bases were already weakened after the Kapıkulu corps became the most powerful Ottoman military force, but the fall of Constantinople turned out to be the final blow. This effectively and symbolically ended the frontier emirate mentality and structure of the military. From this point either they accepted their reduced status and became a kind of timariot unit under close surveillance of functionaries of the centralized government or continued their opposition and lost everything.[23] The Akıncıs passed through this process more easily than the nomadic warriors who lost most of their privileges as a military class and actually became part of the Reaya. However, not all of the nomadic tribes consented; an important percentage of them migrated to the east to reestablish their fortunes in eastern Anatolia and Iran.

Why did the city fall after withstanding dozens of sieges over hundreds of years? The common answer is because of the giant bombards. We know that one of the most important shortcomings of the unsuccessful 1422 siege was lack of heavy cannons. We also know that Mehmed's siege artillery batteries destroyed the walls and demoralized Byzantines. But it is also obvious that defenders managed to repair the breaches and damaged walls successfully and for a brief time regained their confidence. Regardless of the merits of the cannons, the real reason behind the victory was the leadership of Fatih Sultan Mehmed and the efficient Ottoman military machine that he created. While the Ottoman military previously made use of the capabilities of cannons, Mehmed led them properly and even involved himself personally in designing, manufacturing, and firing. However, it was his flexible leadership style that capitalized on innovation that turned the tide. Without the dynamic presence of Mehmed himself Constantinople likely might have stood another siege.[24]

The Military Organization

Kapıkulu Ocakları: Sultan's Standing Army

Janissaries

Being the nucleus of all the standing forces of the empire and reflecting the increasing importance of infantry in combat, the Janissaries became the most important corps in terms of combat effort and remained so until the end of the seventeenth century. Without doubt Mehmed II played an important role not only by defining and creating a new mission and organizational structure for the corps, but more importantly for providing opportunities for it to gain prestige and reputation. For example, he purposefully allocated the prestigious final victorious assault on the walls of Constantinople to the Janissaries and publicized their role in public. The unfortunate Azabs and other auxiliary troops were decimated in order to wear down the enemy and received no public acclaim.

Mehmed continued his reorganization of the Janissaries after the conquest of Constantinople. He replaced the old military scribes who were raised within the corps with civilian scribes independent of the corps hierarchy in order to prepare muster lists in which all details of individual soldiers were kept. This kept financial spending under the direct control of the government.[25] He moved the main Janissary barracks from the city of Edirne and founded a new Acemi Ocağı in addition to the one in Gallipoli. The Istanbul Acemi Ocağı became the biggest Janissary military training institution in a short time—reaching a strength of 3,000 to 4,000 men organized into 31 Odas (companies). Although the original length of the training period—eight to nine years—was preserved, in reality, due to the constant nature of campaigns and increasing number of assignments to the provinces, the average length of stay in the hearth was between five to six years.[26] In addition to military training the Acemis continued to carry out various manual labor tasks for the palace and official institutions. They were also tasked to provide security and other services during the absence of Janissary combat units.[27]

Of interest, while the Devşirme became the main source of the Janissary and other corps, the practice of selecting youth just after the conquest of large towns continued on. Mehmed II was especially very keen on carrying out the selection by himself.[28] Ideally every seven years several regiment commanders of the Janissary corps were tasked to collect/select youths, each one to a particular province. Even though youngsters from villages were preferred, occasionally sons of local notables were also chosen. Each 40 family unit had to provide one youth (preferably between the age groups of 14 to 18). There were several examples in which the Devşirme was ordered in five-year, or even three-year cycles. With the increased bureaucratization and standardization the government enforced detailed recruitment procedures and various control measures, and it became very a strict operation. However, cases of abuse and misconduct continued to be reported, such as receiving bribes, frightening locals, abstaining from one village over collecting from another. So the strict regulations and controls managed to limit these abuses but not completely stop them.[29]

The European provinces were the main source of the Devşirme but were not the only ones. The government also applied the Devşirme to Anatolian provinces from time to time. In addition to Muslim recruitment, the government targeted the Southern Slav groups more often but refrained from recruiting from some nations (i.e., Russians, Persians, Jews, and Gypsies). The administration perceived Russians and Persians as unruly and treacherous, Jews as a mercantile class, and Gypsies as unworthy and corrupt. The Bosnians remained a favorite Devşirme target group even after converting to Islam, and they were sought after especially as personnel for royal household duties and for the artillery corps.[30]

With the passage of time and with increasing numbers of senior soldiers within the corps, the government decided to relax the non-marriage rule and gave permission for marriage to limited numbers of old and meritorious soldiers during the mid-sixteenth century. This limited relaxation effectively became a major policy change after the sons of Kapıkulu soldiers (Kuloğlu) gained acceptance in the corps. The repercussions of this policy change remained minimal during this period, but as will be seen, became an important factor after the beginning of the seventeenth century.[31]

The organizational structure and command and control system of the Janissary corps changed dramatically after the addition of the Sekban units, which was the outcome of a deliberate decision to reinforce the loyalty of the corps to the sultan. However, in relatively short time the loyalty of the corps became problematic once again. Sultan Bayezid II[32] discovered that a particular commander of the Sekban units (Sekbanbaşı) was involved in a conspiracy against him. He immediately sacked him and changed the policy of assigning Sekbanbaşı to the post of Yeniçeri Ağası (commander in chief of the Janissary corps). Instead, he decided to assign Ağas from his household in order to be sure of the loyalty of the corps. This assignment policy continued without change until 1641, and thereafter Ağas were assigned from within the corps. Following his father's approach Bayezid founded the Ağa Bölükleri (commander's own regiments) as the personal retinue of the Ağa in order to give him power and leverage within the corps.[33]

After these two drastic changes the structure of the corps became stable and did not change except that the numbers of regiments continued to rise until the end of the sixteenth century. The final number of regiments were 101 Cemaat (or Yaya) Ortas, 61 Ağa Bölükleri and 34 Sekban Ortas.[34] Although the number of regiments then stabilized, the personnel strength the corps continued to rise from 8 to 10,000 during the mid-sixteenth century to 13,357 in 1560 and growing to over 35,000 at the end of the sixteenth century. This unintended rise is understakable when taking into account the increasing need for trained infantry and the successful introduction and use of firearms by the Janissaries.[35]

The Janissary Ortas were the first permanent infantry regiments in all of Europe and were founded at least 100 years before any other example.[36] Originally the entire corps was organized as a single regiment but later, with the increase in strength, each of the Ortas became a separate regiment with distinctive heraldries and traditions. Until the mid-sixteenth century additional regiments were founded in order to perform special tasks but later, because of the increasing need for musketeers, the size and numbers of specialized regiments multiplied. For example, the 82nd Zenberekçi Orta was founded to use heavy steel crossbows (Zenberek), likewise the 22nd and 92nd Tüfenkci Ortas were founded to provide training and assistance in the use of firearms. Not all the activations of new regiments were related to weapon systems. For example, the 64th Zağarcı, 68th Turnacı and 71st Seksoncu (Samsoncu) Ortas were founded to breed hounds and other animals of prey and to participate in royal hunting parties. Of course, over time, all became standard infantry regiments, and their original hunting duties became a legacy and were enshrined in regimental symbology.[37]

The élan and cohesion within each regiment was very strong. The Janissaries were very proud of their respective regiments and they generally identified themselves with the units so much that each regiment became something of a great family. Most of the men tattooed the symbols of the units on their shoulders. Interestingly, the most revered object for entire Janissary corps was the sacred cauldron "Kazan-ı Şerif." Similarly, the cauldrons of each regiment were more sacred than their respective standards or flags.[38]

Another symbol of Janissary prestige and identification was their distinctive uniforms. Initially their distinctive high white bonnets were their signature, but later on detailed uniform regulations were put into use that clearly defined all the different uniforms of the Janissaries and other Kapıkulu corps. Obviously the Ottoman government understood the importance of uniforms in order to promote élan, raise morale and discipline, and for the practical application of differentiating friend and foe. Moreover, the Ottomans were well ahead of their counterparts by standardizing uniforms for their troops at least 200 years before any European state.[39] The government regularly issued the uniform, including an overcoat and shoes (or the monetary value of it) to each soldier. The uniforms were simple but functional and sturdy. The colors of the uniforms and shoes showed the status, such as yellow shoes for high-ranking officers, black for junior officers, and red for soldiers. A variety of head gear was also instrumental in establishing rank, unit, and merit, such as awarding heroic soldiers with a distinctive turban.[40]

Clearly in the beginning, by employing varied cosmetic apparel, the government went to great lengths to create identities and élan. However, later through spending military careers together, facing dangers, and sharing the harsh life of a soldier, these shared identities became self sustaining and became strong traditions in their own right. The intimate connection with the Bektaşi religious order and its increased activities within the corps also played an important role in this sense.[41] Not surprisingly, the harshest punishment for any Janissary was not capital punishment but to be sacked from his regiment. The obvious outcome of this élan and cohesion was bitter competition between the regiments. Regiment members used every opportunity (especially combat) to outperform other regiments so as to receive more financial awards and to gain fame. However, the Janissaries always stood together against all other groups including, occasionally, the sultan. And clearly this unity deterred them from any permanent alliance to a particular military commander. The solidarity within the corps later became very dangerous for the government after the politicization of the corps, which made use of this solidarity to start uprisings or launch coups.[42]

The command and control system and the role of officers are unclear today and there is no specific study concerning these issues. We know a great deal about the protocols, the uniforms, and the administrative functions of the officers, but there is very little information about their combat duties, inner system, or the interactions between them. The officer corps of the Janissaries was not separated from the other ranks, and there was no separate officer training school or training corps. Except for the posts of Yeniçeri Ağası and Sekbanbaşı all military officers were commissioned from within the membership of the corps. Each regiment trained and selected its own officers within the regiment according to seniority, merit, and courage. So, in theory, except for the posts of "Çorbacı" or "Bölükbaşı" (regiment commander) all officer positions within the regiment were allocated only to the members of the regiment. In case of any vacancy, that position would most likely be filled by promoting the next ranking senior person. Certainly one of the most bizarre aspects of the Janissaries was the naming of titles for its officer corps. Most of the junior and middle-ranking Janissary officer titles were closely related with kitchen terminology, such as naming regiment commanders as Çorbacı (soup maker), quartermaster officers as Aşçıbaşı (chief cook), or lieutenants as Odabaşı (chief of chamber). This was due not because officers spent more time for supervising food supply than leading in war, but rather to the revered status of regimental cauldrons![43]

The promotion system for higher command posts was a bit complicated. There was a clear hierarchy above the level of regimental commander in which some posts were more prestigious and higher in rank than others. Essentially after promotion to a regimental command, an officer looked forward to an opening at the prestigious super-regimental level of posts called the "Katar Ağaları" (commanders of the convoy). In case of filling an opening at this level every Ağa below the selectee would move up. The vacancy at the bottom was then filled by a meritorious commander of a regiment. That meant that after getting assigned to the lowest Katar Ağaları post, an officer would be promoted automatically to any vacancy in the higher posts.[44]

Due to the linear promotion system, if the sultan or Yeniçeri Ağası decided to pass over a high-ranking officer for promotion to a certain position, he had no alternative but to grant him a suitable Timar and send him out of the corps with honor. There was another alternative for low ranking officers in addition to granting a Timar, which was reassignment to the household cavalry (Kapıkulu Süvarileri) regiments with better pay. So, in a sense, the linear promotion system provided job security by protecting the rights of the individual.[45] The linear promotion system would become a great problem after the end of seventeenth century, but during the classical period it eliminated such corrupt practices as favoritism, birth rights, or selling and purchasing commissions, whereas European armies continued to suffer these problems for two more centuries.[46]

The static nature of the organizational structure after Süleyman I – Kanuni (the lawgiver) Sultan Süleyman, who was also known as "the Magnificent," created various problems, the most important of which, in terms of command and control, was the lack of a military staff under the direct control of Yeniçeri Ağası. This might be understandable during the foundation period with a corps of only a 1,000 strong or perhaps even the 15,000 strong corps of the sixteenth century. But especially after the rapid increase of the corps during the Long War (1593–1606) and because of the introduction of new tactics and combat formations, the military staff became essential. However, the Ottomans failed to create military staffs and, consequently, the Yeniçeri Ağası, with only civilian assistants (Ağa Divanı) who had very limited military experience, lost effective operational command and control. An associated problem in command at lower levels was a shortage of officers. The number of officer positions within the regiments remained constant even after increases in personnel strength. As the strength of regiments rose from its original numbers of 100 to about 700 during the seventeenth century, the number of officer positions remained unchanged at five, and only the number of NCO positions increased. To compensate some NCO positions, notably the Odabaşı, they were upgraded to officer positions.[47]

In terms of social security and welfare the Janissary corps had the best system and more rights than any other corps in the empire and which certainly exceeded those in contemporary Europe as well. The Janissaries were entitled to receive a salary (Ulufe) every three months. The government always paid special attention to paying the salaries regularly, keeping them competitive and in line with market prices. The government also provided food and other expendables at fixed prices, which in turn became a sort of supplementary income during the inflationist periods. Salaries were always paid according to very detailed financial arrangements and involved a ceremony where Janissaries pledged their loyalty and dedication to the sultan and his government. This affirmation of loyalty might be the reason why the Janissaries were given a special payment at every succession of the new sovereign. Additionally, the Ottoman government made use of financial awards effectively and gave special bonuses during difficult campaigns or after its successful outcome. In truth, the competitive and regular salary was a critical factor in maintaining the élan of the corps and, ultimately, in generating combat success. At the same time, it was instrumental in both attracting recruits and for creating reasons to remain in the corps as professional soldiers. This economic incentive, therefore, was to become an important issue at the end of the classical period with the influx of personnel recruited from non-Devşirme backgrounds.[48]

In addition to promotion opportunities, Janissaries who served loyally and honestly but who demonstrated average talent and limited achievement had the right of retirement within and outside the corps and could also be granted Timars. These old Janissaries could be assigned to frontier fortresses with a good pension or remained within the main barracks (Korucu or Oturak) to perform some simple tasks—mainly during the campaigns—and were awarded a reasonable pension. Additionally, the families of fallen Janissaries were also taken good care of by the state. The male descendant was guaranteed admittance to the Acemi Ocağı, and occasionally financial aids were granted whereby regiments provided allowances from the regimental fund. Interestingly, in order to increase money in the funds, the fund-raising officer of the regiment generally invested the money into the market by giving loans with interest, which eventually became economically important to the empire.[49]

The Janissaries were light infantrymen—although there were very limited numbers of privileged mounted Janissaries involved in traditional hunting duties[50] but the corps remained foot soldiers until the very end. Initially all were equipped with composite bows and swords. They also used a special short spear, battleaxes, and other infantry weapons but only as secondary weapons or on special ceremonial occasions. Over time the Janissaries acquired some of the weapons of their adversaries as preferred weapons, the Mamluk sword, Damascene knife, and European battleaxe for example. Most probably firearms were introduced into the corps during the first half of fifteenth century. As far as we know from the available sources, only a few regiments were initially equipped with firearms, but as firearms reliability grew the remainder of the corps acquired them. Additionally, a kind of primitive hand grenade (Elkumbarası) became a well-liked and common weapon after the 1560s.[51]

The Ottoman leadership came to understand the potential and importance of firearms in a remarkably short time. However, they insisted on keeping composite bows while most European nations (a notable exception was the English insistence on keeping the longbow up until 1589) discontinued the old missile weapons that required long and continuous training because they could replace them with easily learned firearms. A rare blend of pragmatism and conservatism played an important role in this decision. The Ottomans had great faith in the capability of their traditional main weapon—the composite bow. Moreover, early firearms (arquebuses and match-lock muskets) were often faulty, unreliable, and slow. In comparison, composite bows were accurate, reliable, and had a high rate of fire (nine to 10 shots per minute against one shot per two to three minutes). A well-trained archer also had greater effective range of up to 300 meters, whereas hitting a target with a firearm farther than 70 meters was pure coincidence.[52]

To maintain proficiency in archery the Janissaries had the advantage of the Acemi Ocağı in which every soldier spent a mandatory average of six years. After this long training period, on the job training within the regiments and weekly weapons training under the control of gunnery specialists gave ample opportunities to succeed in marksmanship. This was such an institutional priority that commanders took active roles, for example the 54th Ağa Bölük commander was the master archer, and Tüfenkcibaşı was the master gunner of the whole corps. Thus, the Ottomans had unique advantages enabling them to maintain composite bows side by side with firearms, which compensated for the shortcomings of the early firearms.[53]

For these reasons archery reached its apex of development during the classical period, and most of the famous Ottoman archers, such as Tozkoparan İskender, Takyecikulu Şüca, Miralem Ahmed Ağa, came from this time. The inevitable decline of the bow as a combat weapon started after the massive influx of muskets into nearly all standing army units. However, archery as a sport remained an important part of Janissaries' daily life and commanders encouraged its continuance.[54] As a byproduct of regular and continuous weapons and marksmanship training, either as a part of combat training or as a sporting activity, the government successfully dealt with the inevitable entropy of barracks life during peacetime.

We have very limited information about Janissary combat formations and how they actually fought other than the "Tabur Cengi" formation. Generally they positioned artillery at the center, and often a screen of Azabs covered their front and household cavalry positioned behind them or on the flanks. We also know that the Janissaries preferred several rows of deep formations and achieved a continuous barrage of fire by rotating rows forward. They were able to maintain this formation even against heavy enemy fire because of their discipline, courage, and training. Occasionally, some regiments were positioned within linear trenches during defensive battles,[55] but in the open, taking cover against incoming fire or breaking from the lines were always seen as cowardly acts.[56] To keep this from happening, junior officers, NCOs, and elderly soldiers were tasked to keep the lines intact and in combat their duties were focussed on this important task.

The Janissaries mainly employed the deep formations described previously for defensive purposes. Unfortunately, we do not know many of the details of their offensive formations, which remain problematic. Although there were several instances where deep formations were employed offensively, but as far as the available sources state the Janissaries preferred to launch all out assault at the first real opportunity. This usually occurred when the enemy main body was within close proximity and had already lost coherent battle formation. The Janissaries then unleashed themselves with full speed and in loose regimental formations.[57] Loose regimental assault formations remained the norm of the classical period but soon lost in importance as the number of musketeers rose within the corps.

The Janissaries preferred fighting against European enemies with the exception of fighting in Wallachia and Moldavia, rather than in the east—even though battles against the Europeans were more deadly. The reasons were very simple. First, fighting against fellow Muslims was always difficult from the moral and motivational view. Second, as regular light infantry, the Janissaries were reluctant to fight against enemies against which they could not use their tactics, techniques, and weapons. On the eastern and the southern frontiers, most of the time the Janissaries faced light cavalry enemies who used nomadic tactics and techniques and consequently proved elusive and difficult foes. Even when nomadic enemies decided to face the Ottomans in a pitched battle, the Janissaries suffered degradation in the effective application of their combat potential. For this reason the timariot and household cavalry units were essential for the successful combat performance of the Ottomans against eastern enemies.

Even though the Ottoman government paid special attention to logistics and welfare of the Janissaries, life in military, especially during campaigns, was very difficult. With their sound training background and spartan lifestyle in the barracks, however, the Janissaries were well adapted to these hardships. The men were very sturdy and faced easily the difficulties of the long and constant campaigns. They were able to march continuously with heavy burdens through difficult terrain, often under constant enemy harassment. The Janissaries proved their value continuously during this period. They fought obediently in most instances without regard for their individual safety and rarely fled or surrendered.[58] Sometimes even their presence was enough to frighten an adversary. Mahmud Pasha made use of their reputation by ordering his engineers to wear Janissary uniforms to frighten the defenders of Smenderovo (Semendire) to surrender—a ruse that actually worked well.[59]

Because of their loyalty, combat effectiveness, and reliability, the government began to assign new tasks to the corps. Beginning with Mehmed II, the Janissaries were tasked to guard important fortresses for periods of up to three years in a row.⁶⁰ Moreover, during the final years of Süleyman I, Janissary garrisons were established in important provincial centers to control the ambitions of the governors and to provide law and order due to the unreliability or ineffectiveness of the Sipahis in carrying out these duties. Small units of Janissaries were tasked temporarily to carry out these duties. In this respect, providing law and order in Istanbul was the main peacetime duty of the Janissaries stationed there. Different tasks involving law and order duties, such as guarding important institutions and embassies, police, fire, and constabulary duties were also assigned to some regiments.⁶¹

The Household Cavalry (Kapıkulu Süvarileri)

"Kapıkulu Süvarileri Ocağı" (literally the Hearth of the Cavalrymen of Gate Slaves) was most probably founded by Murad I as a royal guard unit. Logically the first regiment, the "Silahdar," was manned initially from royal servants and pages. Its initial strength probably did not exceed 100. Subsequently, following the Islamic-Seljukid tradition of enlisting the sons of the leading aristocratic families, a second regiment, the "Sipah," was founded. In a short time both regiments became very attractive assignments due to high salaries and proximity to the sultan. Later, four other regiments (Bölükat-ı Erbaa) were founded simultaneously; two "Ulufeci" (salaried men) and two "Gureba" (poor, stranger) regiments. They were commonly called the "Altı Bölük Halkı" (literally, people of six regiments).⁶²

During the military reorganization of Mehmed II the force gained its permanent character and organization. The Sipah became the most prestigious regiment, followed in turn by the Silahtar, the Ulufecis, and the Gurebas. At the same time, the recruitment policy changed drastically and sons of the nobles were taken out of the recruitment pool. Mehmed introduced merit, valor, and loyalty as the guiding criteria for enlistment. Pages of the palace school (Enderun İçoğlanları) and youths from other royal schools were assigned, according to their talent, merit, and age, to the first two regiments. Meritorious and veteran Janissaries were assigned also to the first four regiments as an award, which amazed contemporary western observers.⁶³ The last two regiments, the Gurebas, were filled with military personnel and volunteers who routinely displayed extreme bravery and valor in combat. There was also a promotion system between the regiments. For example, if the cavalrymen in the low-ranking regiments showed merit and proved themselves in combat they would be promoted to the high-ranking regiments. During the sixteenth century the sons of the Süvaris (Veledeş) gained access to the regiments in an apprenticeship status as well.⁶⁴

The army's organizational structure was very simple. The "Bölük" (file or section) was the basic unit, which originally consisted of eight to 10 cavalrymen but later reached levels of 25 to 30. The other units below the regiment were temporary tactical formations, and there were five junior and mid-ranking officer positions as well as one scribe position within each regiment. These officers were commissioned within each regiment according to valor, merit, seniority, and the availability of vacant positions, but the regiment commanders (Bölük Ağaları) were generally assigned from the palace.[65]

The numerical strength increased continuously from a mid-fifteenth century strength of 8,000 men to 20,869 men in 1609. The increase affected the Sipah and Silahdar regiments while the strength of Ulufecis and Gurebas remained relatively unchanged at about 1,000 each. But the available combat strength doubled if the apprentices and armed servants were added in the total.[66]

With the increase in regiments and in strength, the Süvaris became more of an elite corps than a royal guard unit. Their weapons were nearly the same as the Sipahis, but their armor and mounts were of better quality.[67] Later during the last quarter of the sixteenth century about 10 percent of the Süvaris began to use firearms in addition to their traditional weapons. The Süvaris, having many former Janissaries within their ranks, were probably more adaptable to firearms than the Sipahis.[68] The cavalrymen of first four regiments brought armed servants with them according to their respective salary. They always moved with the sultan or the commander in chief and positioned themselves around him in battle. The Silahdar regiment was also tasked to monitor road building and maintenance activity of the engineers and other auxiliary units. All regiments stayed in their assigned positions during battles to protect the sultan, high-ranking officials, the treasury, and the standard. However, they often took part in combat in the final moments to reinforce successful attacks or to save the day. Some of the Süvaris were also tasked to perform courier duties.[69]

We also know that Süvari companies were attached frequently to various types of provincial expeditionary forces as reinforcements. The main reason behind these assignments was to enforce discipline on, and to control, the provincial units. Additionally, the government tried very hard to keep the military readiness of the Süvaris high by keeping them busy. For example, two Süvari companies from the Gureba regiments were tasked to reinforce a raiding mission of Akıncıs into Hungary in 1475.[70]

During peacetime only Sipah and Silahdar formations remained in and around Istanbul. All the other regiments were deployed in nearby provinces. This was a function of the limited amounts of grazing pastures around the city. However, some of their personnel were assigned away on temporary border guard duties. They also performed several administrative duties, of which tax collection was the most important. Tax collection was an important and profitable duty, which was open to corruption and was instrumental in the eventual decay of the organization.[71] In addition to these classical tasks, during the final years of Süleyman I, they were ordered to monitor the loyalty of the Sipahis and to provide security in the provinces. Even though the Janissaries also carried out similar duties due to their long history of presence and established relations, the Süvaris remained more powerful in the provinces in contrast to their weakness in İstanbul.[72]

The Süvaris and Janissaries together were used initially to keep provincial army units loyal, but later sultans and high officials began to use the Süvaris against Janissaries to counterbalance their political power. This policy created an everlasting tension and hostility between both corps. Even though Süvaris had high salaries and prestigious positions they were never able to gain more political power than the Janissaries, and their contribution to Ottoman military might remained limited.[73]

The Artillery Corps (Topçu Ocağı)

We know that the Ottomans began to use cannons during the first battle of Kosovo (1389), but we do not know how and when a standing artillery corps was founded. Most probably the first artillery units were founded during the reign of Bayezid I.[74] However, they were more or less independent units created around a particular master gunner-founder to perform services during a certain campaign or siege. This ad hoc arrangement remained until the accession of Mehmed II. In order to achieve his grand design, the conquest of Constantinople, he enlisted all the available European and native master gunners, cannon founders, and other engineers/ technicians and organized them into a single corps, the Topçu Ocağı (literally hearth of the cannoneers).[75]

With the conquest of Constantinople the newly founded artillery corps became legendary not only within the Ottoman military but also within the Old World as well. Their importance was soon proven again during the battle of Otlukbeli (Başkent) against the Akkoyunlu Sultanate. In this battle, Ottoman artillery employed in concert with war wagons created havoc within the ranks of the nomadic Akkoyunlu army. While other factors such as discipline were important, the artillery overshadowed the rest.[76] The continuous campaigns of Mehmed created a conducive atmosphere, opportunities, and the financial assets for the artillery corps to improve its organizational structure, increase personnel, and acquire new weapons.

The post-Mehmed artillery corps essentially consisted of two main branches, cannon foundries and field artillery units. After their initial experience with ad hoc artillery units, the Ottomans initially emphasized cannon production and secondly the gunners. The first cannon foundry was established in Edirne and later moved to Istanbul, where it was known as the Tophane-i Amire (the Imperial Cannon Foundry).[77] The Tophane remained the biggest and most important foundry of the military until the end of the empire. Various foundries were opened and later closed in provincial centers according to the current needs of the time. Some of these local foundries even surpassed the Tophane in terms of importance and production, but only briefly and usually during the conduct of a particular campaign. It was also a common practice for Ottoman expeditionary forces to carry the necessary materials and to cast cannons in front of besieged fortifications.[78] Field casting operations were so practical and effective that there were reported cases of casting done on mountaintops.[79] The field casting operations generally remained under the control of the Tophane (and occasionally local foundries) until the creation of an expeditionary cannon foundry company in 1667.[80]

The quality of Ottoman cannons in terms of casting and design is still a controversial topic. According to both contemporary observers of the Ottoman Empire and modern scholars, Ottoman cannons clearly lagged behind the West European designs by clinging to older huge bombards of poor-quality metal composition.[81] However, modern researchers are revising this commonly held conviction. According to recent findings, Ottoman military engineers managed to produce cannons with up-to-date designs in line with their European counterparts until the beginning of eighteenth century. The impressive series of siege victories against the modern fortresses of Hungary during the second half of sixteenth century also proved the level of Ottoman artillery technology and its field application to be on par with Europe. Additionally, most of the technologically related problems that affected the Ottoman artillery system were common problems also affecting its archenemies, the Habsburg Empire and Venice. Last, but not least, it is almost impossible to validate some of the commonly held notions concerning the Ottoman artillery, such as the alleged inferior metal composition, without conducting extensive research and scientific analysis on the cannon themselves.[82]

In reality, the empire had distinctive advantages in comparison to its rivals. Importantly, and in opposition to most of the European states, the empire had the necessary mineral ore deposits (except tin) and made use of them in more than 25 gunpowder mills and 19 cannon foundries in the various corners of its provinces (excluding smaller or temporary facilities). The Ottomans established a very effective administrative-financial bureaucracy in order to control cannon production and to meet the needs of the military conducting campaigns in various theaters.[83]

The Ottoman Empire did not suffer difficulty in enlisting European military engineers and technicians when needed during this period. In truth, its European enemies were unable to enforce restrictions on technology transfer and were unable to stop the transmission of military knowledge.[84] Likewise, Ottoman restrictions against Iran did not work either and Ottoman-trained master gunners and founders became sought-after specialists, not only in Iran, but also in Central Asia, Afghanistan, and India.[85] Constant campaigns and increasing numbers of sieges provided adequate opportunities for Ottoman military engineers to practice their profession and enabled them to follow developments taking place in the enemy camps. Thanks to its efficient military-administrative structure, the Ottomans had both the means to imitate and to improve new weapons and to change its arsenal in a relatively short time.

Even though cannon casting and gunpowder production remained the critical foundation, the real strength of the Ottoman artillery certainly lay with the soldiers of its field and fortress units. Understandably, cannons alone cannot conquer fortresses and defeat enemy armies, and only well-trained and properly organized and led artillery units can achieve success on the battlefield. Until the beginning of seventeenth century, the Ottoman artillery remained the only standing and salaried corps of its kind, and its biggest institutional advantage was the privilege of selecting the best and brightest from the Acemi Ocağı. The Şakirds (artillery novices) passed through an intensive and demanding on-the-job training program—normally four to five years—before finding empty slots. Even after becoming regular soldiers they participated in mandatory training two days a week under the immediate control of master gunners. In addition to intensive training, continuous campaigns and actual combat gave them ample opportunities to excel in their trade.[86]

The strength of field artillery corps rose from a modest figure of 250 in 1453 to 1,204 in 1567 and 2,827 in 1598 (excluding the personnel in border fortresses and provincial artillery units). These soldiers were organized into Cemaats (regiments) of approximately 100 personnel, which later rose to 250. The numbers of Cemaats were also increased following the increase of personnel from a few to 72 in 1687, all of which were stationed in Istanbul. The first Cemaat was the personal unit of the Topçubaşı (commander of artillery corps) and comprised more than 500 men, who were organized into five Bölüks (companies). Not surprisingly, the strength of the Ottoman artillery exceeded all of its enemies together and remained so until the beginning of the seventeenth century.[87]

In addition to their regular assignments cannoneers of standing artillery corps had to serve at least three consecutive years in border fortresses. Organized under the command of a Sertopi (chief artillery officer), the duty of these cannoneers of a given fortress was to be ready for action against possible attacks and also to improve the defense systems. However, in time the increased number of border fortresses and the cannons positioned within proved that the military needed to enlist increasing numbers of local men as artillery soldiers (Yerlikulu Topçu). Thus, the main duty of cannoneers changed and they began to provide leadership, technical expertise, and assistance to the more numerous local artillery soldiers. In a sense they were training and transmitting current tactics and techniques to these local soldiers, who were permanent members of that particular fortress. At the same time, artillery officers from Istanbul conducted regular inspections in these distant fortresses in order to maintain high levels of training and readiness.[88]

The importance of fortress artillery rose after the capture of the key fortress city of Buda (Budin) in 1541. In order to guard the newly conquered Hungarian provinces the Hungarian defense system was revitalized by repairing old fortresses and building new ones after the peace treaty of 1568. Fortress artillery units became so critical that more locals were recruited as cannoneers—some salaried and others as timariot—and consequently four cannon foundries and three gunpowder mills were founded in Hungary. The continuous nature of warfare even during peacetime and rapid technological changes provided a lively environment for the Ottoman cannoneers to improve their level of training and combat readiness.[89]

The expeditionary artillery units were more or less self-sufficient, carrying all key materials in addition to cannons and an ammunition load of 100 balls and gunpowder for each cannon. These units had the emergency capacity to produce repair parts and a limited amount of gunpowder without the support of field casting units. These mobile artillery units were commonly positioned in the center of the Tabur Cengi combat formation, in front of Janissaries but behind a thin screen of Azabs. They were rarely positioned on the flanks.[90]

The artillery corps remained a prestigious branch during the entire life of the Ottoman military. Even the subsequent degeneration, corruption, and decades of neglect did not change this status. In fact, most of the later reform efforts targeted this corps first and then the other corps. It outlived all the other Kapıkulu corps and transformed into a new organization after 1826.

Other Technical Branches

The most important technical branch after artillery was, without doubt, the Cebeci Ocağı (the hearth of armorers). We do not know the exact date of its foundation, but probably armorers within the Janissary corps were organized into a separate corps at the beginning of fifteenth century. Evidentially, the Cebecis gained their distinctive organizational structure during the reign of Mehmed II. Mehmed garrisoned the new corps around church of Hagia Sophia (Ayasofya) by allocating several Byzantine buildings to it and by building new barracks, which remained its home until the end of the empire.[91]

The main duty of the Cebecis was to manufacture weapons, including the firearms, armor, trenching tools, and related combat equipment of the Janissaries. At the same time they were responsible to fix or repair broken equipment and to store it during peacetime. As a general rule, all weapons and armor remained in depots under properly controlled conditions during peacetime. Janissaries were not allowed to use this equipment except on campaigns and for designated combat training. The Cebecis carefully issued weapons, armor, ammunition (300 rounds for muskets), and other equipment to each soldier before battles and collected it after the battle. The Cebecis always transported all this equipment back and forth with special wagons and, interestingly, even the Janissaries did not get their weapons and equipment until reaching the combat zone. Within this system firearms received special priority. Obviously, by issuing weapons only during actual combat or special training the government attempted to keep the arsenal in proper condition and, more importantly, to stop any loss, theft, or uncontrolled diffusion of weapons to unauthorized persons.[92]

The personnel strength of the Cebecis rose at the same rate as the Janissary corps; 451 in 1514 to 789 in 1567 and 3,000 in 1598 (excluding the personnel in border fortresses and provincial Cebeci units). According to its final organizational structure the armorer corps was organized into 38 Ortas (regiments). The first Orta was the personal unit of the Cebecibaşı (commander of the armorer corps) and was organized into 59 Bölüks (companies). Essentially all of these Ortas and Bölüks were divided into four distinctive skill-sets: weapon manufacturers, repairmen, gunpowder amelioration specialists, and combat equipment manufacturers. There were also a bombardier Orta and an engineering Orta tasked to produce equipment related with their areas of expertise.[93] Following the traditions of guilds each Cebeci unit was also an on-the-job training facility, and their officers were often more like master trainers than military officials.[94]

In order to provide standard and high-quality raw and semi-finished materials to the Cebecis the government devised an elaborate supply chain in which particular provinces were tasked to provide specific materials. This supply system was also flexible enough to increase its capacity during emergency situations. Additionally, the government made use of the capabilities of civilian manufacturers and craftsmen for bulk consignments. The Cebecibaşı was responsible for regular inventories of the stocks and for replacing missing or spoiled equipment. He also sent special inspection teams to monitor the depots and check the equipment issued to garrisons in provinces.[95]

Like the artillery corps the Cebecis also had to serve three years consecutively in border fortresses and field depots. Similarly, the increase of permanent fortress garrisons forced the formation of provincial Cebeci units over which regular Cebecis acted as trainers or master craftsmen during their temporary assignments in the border fortresses.[96]

It is apparent that towards the end of sixteenth century the quality of Cebeci services and products began to decline in comparison to its potential and previous record. In fact, most of the Janissaries began to buy personal muskets from the civilian market rather than to use government-issued types, which were seen as faulty, old-fashioned, and cumbersome. As a result a new workshop was founded in 1578, directly under the control of the Ağa of Janissary corps and independent of the Cebeci corps. Thereafter some essential services and production began to be carried out by this workshop, like the production of hand grenades as well as selected repair and maintenance services.[97]

Two of the remaining three principal technical branches were directly related to the artillery corps. The first was the Top Arabacıları Ocağı (hearth of artillery wagoners), and as previously mentioned, was a corps specially tailored to support the Tabur Cengi battle formation.[98] Clearly, its foundation originated with the battles of Varna in 1444 and Kosovo in 1448 (and not in the late fifteenth century as some scholars have suggested). Unfortunately because of misunderstanding or misinterpretation, most of the modern Ottomanist literature treats this corps only as an artillery transportation corps and pays no attention to its key combat role. In reality its transportation role was very minor[99]—a job the government preferred to task various support elements to transport cannons and their related equipment.

The Ottomans modified the Hussite wagenburgen tactics and techniques in their Tabur Cengi. In place of the protection and defensive role of western European pikemen formations for the arquebus/musket carrying infantry, the Ottomans used the wagons of the Arabacıs. Obviously in comparison to the European pikemen-musketeer formation, the Tabur Cengi was a more defensive and static battle formation. Due to its custom-built wagons, however, it had better and faster long-distance transportation capability, whereas pikemen marched carrying their own heavy equipment and often arrived tired. So it could be said that the Ottomans sacrificed tactical mobility in order to achieve strategic mobility. Against all these limitations we know that on several occasions the Tabur Cengi was used offensively, like a mobile fortress slowly but destructively attacking the enemy battle formation.[100]

The basic mechanism of the Tabur was simple but very difficult to apply. Before the start of the battle war wagons were chained together and cannons were placed within. Several Janissary units armed with heavy arquebuses/muskets were also positioned with the cannoners, and the remaining Janissaries—several rows deep—remained within the formation. The Ottoman wings, by outflanking or feigned retreat, would try to force the main body of the enemy army towards this fortress. The Azab screen would retreat immediately after showing brief resistance in order to disorganize enemy attack. Artillery and heavy arquebuses/muskets would fire first and further wear down the enemy and disorganize its assault formations. Then the Janissaries, with light weapons, began firing in volleys by rotating the ranks. Finally, a counterattack would then start when the enemy lost cohesion and heart.[101] The success of this battle formation depended upon constant practice of combined arms and strict discipline. Any disharmony or failure would certainly result in a disaster. Unfortunately, today the exact details of this tactical application and especially the role of the Arabacı corps (and design of their wagons) are missing.

The Tabur achieved a frightening reputation among the rivals of the Ottomans in the east and west. The Hungarians and Habsburgs tried to create their own version of the Tabur or to invent methods to counter it like the pike-based formations of Giorgio Basta and Raimondo Montecuccoli.[102] The Safavids of Persia learned their lesson dearly after their catastrophic defeat against the Ottoman Tabur at the Battle of Çaldıran in 1514. Surprisingly, the Safavids created their own Tabur and used it successfully against the nomadic Uzbek army in the Battle of Jam in 1527. The reputation of the Tabur reached even to India, and the founder of the Mughal dynasty, Babur Khan, gained the victory of Khanua thanks to a successful application of the Tabur.[103]

Similar to the other Kapıkulu corps, the Acemi Ocağı was the main source of personnel for the wagoners. Obviously the wagoners' corps never became a preferred choice for the men of the Acemis and, in compensation, the government gave it increased priority by tasking certain provinces to provide the best material and the finest horses. Additionally, none other than the prestigious Tophane armory was tasked to produce and repair the wagons.[104]

The personnel strength of the wagoners' corps rose for a period of time (correlating with the increase of artillery) from 372 in 1514 to 678 in 1567 and reached its peak in the classical period, 700 in 1598. They were organized into Bölüks (regiments) of approximately 100 personnel (excluding cadets). The numbers of regiments reached a peak of 63 at the end of the sixteenth century. Thereafter, due to their uniquely tailored role (and unlike the artillery corps) their personnel strength remained constant and even decreased after combat losses in battle. After the battle of Mohacs (Mohaç) in 1526, sieges and counter-sieges, with occasional small-scale battles, became the dominant pattern of combat on the European front. Coupled with the Safavid reluctance to face the Ottoman military in pitched battles, the wagoners' corps began to lose its importance and was increasingly employed simply in its transportation role. After the battle of Mezö-Keresztes (Haçova) in 1596, the transportation of cannons became their primary duty.[105]

The second artillery related corps was the Humbaracı Ocağı (the hearth of bombardiers). In fact, it was not a true independent corps during the classical period and remained so until 1731. It consisted of three separate units, the manufacturers of explosive mortar shells, who were organized under the Cebecis and the salaried bombardiers, who fell under the artillery corps. The third unit was composed of timariot bombardiers, who were enlisted in fortresses from Hungary and Bosnia. There were also individuals or small units serving on naval vessels. The bombardiers played a minor role except during several siege operations (such as the Rhodes campaign of 1522) during this period, becoming marginalized by the end of the sixteenth century. Only the timariot bombardiers, who were mainly Bosnians, managed to survive the changing times to become the core cadre of the 1731 reforms.[106]

The last technical corps was a loose group of engineering-related specialists organized under or controlled by the Lağımcı Ocağı (The Hearth of Miners). Originally the corps was founded to provide engineering support for siege operations during the reign of Mehmed II. The main task of the Lağımcıs was to dig mines under the walls of enemy fortresses, to place explosives there, and to ignite them at the proper moment.[107] They also performed counter-mining operations, and a unit of miners was always present in the forces assigned to every important fortress. Additionally, they were responsible for field duties as sappers and dug trenches, gunnery positions, and other earthen works for siege operations.[108]

Except a few salaried Lağımcıs organized under the Cebeci corps, who were tasked to produce engineering equipment, the remainder were timariots. This administrative-financial setup is understandable when taking into account the increased dominance of siege and counter-siege operations against Hungary and Habsburg domains. Due to its timariot nature, limited tactical capability, and loose organizational structure, the Lağımcı corps did not have a clearly defined organizational hierarchy and, in reality, it was more an auxiliary combat support unit than a part of the standing army. This explains why ad hoc tactical groupings of actual Lağımcıs carried out specialized assignments most of the time and why the army often depended upon mobilization of auxiliary military units and civilian elements to perform engineering tasks during campaigns. While the auxiliary units with their own command and control systems were very efficient, this was not the case with the civilian elements. Although some of the civilians came from occupations suitable for engineering tasks (like professional miners) many of them were villagers without effective organization and capable of only performing simple labor.[109]

Not surprisingly, the Lağımcıs had the support of an empire's personnel and material strength and were far more capable in siege and counter-siege operations than its contemporary counterparts. The conquest of Cyprus (Kıbrıs) was an obvious example in this respect. Both of the main fortresses—Nicosia (Lefkoşa) and Famagusta (Magosa)—were constructed or modernized in line with the latest Italian designs (trace italienne) during the 1550s and 1560s. The Christian fortresses had reinforced garrisons and plenty of firepower. The Ottoman expeditionary forces commander, Lala Mustafa Pasha, initially decided to storm Nicosia with a combination of artillery firepower and an all-out assault without listening to the advice of veterans from the Hungarian campaigns. After the costly first assault, he gave up storming the fortress and ordered the Lağımcıs, reinforced with professional miners, to begin time-consuming but efficient sapping and mining operations. Ottoman mines in close cooperation with artillery demolished the southern side of the fortress, and Nicosia fell on September 9, 1570.[110]

The siege operation against Famagusta turned out to be more costly and time consuming. Due to its unique topographical position with natural obstacles and a more elaborate defensive system, Mustafa Pasha had to depend upon more on his Lağımcı units from the very start of operations. The Ottomans dug lines of trenches entirely surrounding the land walls, constructed fortified gunnery positions, and conducted mining operations. Famagusta finally fell after withstanding a siege of 82 days to a combination of mining operations and seven general assaults. In the siege of Famagusta, Ottoman operations and tactics presaged the important identities (including parallel siege lines and zigzag approach trenches) of the French siege system that Sébastien Vauban devised 100 years later.[111]

While not directly in combat, the government began to task the Lağımcıs to provide technical expertise for road-bridge building and maintenance. Most probably, however, engineers and architects independent of the corps carried out the leadership of these projects, whereas the Lağımcıs carried out the duties of mid-level technical leadership and expertise. The Lağımcıs also took an active part in building small fortress or fortified camps, but their role in masonry fortress building is not clear. The loose organization of the Lağımcıs remained until the reforms of Selim III in the 1790s which saw, for the first time in Ottoman history, the actual separation of military field engineering and architectural construction.[112]

Provincial Army (Eyalet Askerleri)

The Timariot Cavalry (Tımarlı Sipahi)

The Timariot cavalry gained its distinctive character after the wide-scale reforms of the Mehmed II, who removed hereditary local magnates from the military and took over their private estates. He also reorganized the organizational structure of the cavalry and introduced various control mechanisms. Even though his son Bayezid II had to return some of the confiscated lands to their previous owners as a means of appeasement, most of the Mehmed's regulations remained and were reinforced further with the amendments of Süleyman I.[113]

There were three categories of Timar estates according to their tax values; Timar (between 2,000 and 19, 999 akçe [asper]), "Zeamet" (20,000–99,999 akçe) and "Has" (more than 100,000 akçe). In actuality, these fiscal groupings must be taken as general rules and not as absolute reality because there were various examples in which the government applied the rules unevenly and made exceptions.[114] The Has estates were generally allocated for the royal family, viziers, and some high-ranking commanders/governors and carried no direct military obligations—except for the Beylerbeyis (governor generals), who had to subsidize their personal retinue or household.[115] The Zeamet estates were generally given to senior military officers according to their ranks, which left the smaller Timars for common Sipahis and junior officers.[116]

The central government generally granted the Timar estates.[117] However, the Beylerbeyis could also grant Timars below 5,000–6,000 akçe. During the foundation period, nomadic warriors easily received Timars based on to their military contributions. Some members of the aristocracy in newly conquered territories (regardless of their religion) were able to acquire Timars depending on their loyalty to the empire. In later periods, the government put restrictions and detailed rules in place for the granting of Timars. According to these strict rules, only sons of Sipahis, court officials, Kapıkulu officers, and occasionally Kapıkulu soldiers could qualify for the award of Timars. The only legal way for others (Ecnebi) to get a Timar was to demonstrate exceptional and multiple acts of bravery during combat. In effect, the government was keen to keep the Sipahis a privileged class separate from ordinary citizens. Unfortunately, the corruption and nepotism of Beylerbeyis (who had a tendency to use Timar grants to subsidize their personal retinue) forced Süleyman put further restrictions in place and as well as reemphasize the importance of controls.[118]

The policy to grant Timars to the local aristocracy of newly conquered territories was deliberate. There were two reasons behind this policy. The first one was very obvious: to integrate the territory into the empire quickly without many problem. The second one was to make effective and rapid use of the military potential of the population. As already explained in the Chapter 1, the Ottomans simply did not have the manpower pool necessary to conquer both the Balkans and the Middle East by themselves. They needed the help and active collaboration of the locals to continue their military campaigns, and the Timar system turned out to be a very successful way to integrate the local aristocracy into Ottoman military-administrative system. In the meantime, many Christian Sipahis converted to Islam and were reassigned to other parts of the empire so as to cut their connections with their country of origin.[119]

The Ottoman government granted Timars to other military groups and nonmilitary individuals. Fortress guards, cannoneers, bombardiers, and regional militia officers were the main non-cavalry groups that were granted Timars. Additionally, nonmilitary individuals such as minor court functionaries, scholars, clergymen, and scribes were also included and these grants to nonmilitary individuals increased at the end of sixteenth century with the loss of military importance of Sipahis.[120]

Basically the Sipahi was a light cavalryman armed with composite bow, sword, mace, and flail (and occasionally with a spear). A metal helmet, chain mail armor, padded garments, and a circular shield provided basic protection.[121] Depending upon wealth, province, and personal choices, of course, there were slight differences in weapons and armor. In terms of weapons, armor, and military techniques, they looked like nomadic mounted archers, but essentially they were more like a conventional light cavalry due to effective and strict command and control, a capability for combined operations with infantry, and an ability to conduct various additional combat duties.

The individual Sipahi was under the obligation to participate in military campaigns with all necessary weapons, equipment, and a horse. For each extra 3,000 (in some provinces 2,000) akçe he had to provide one more armored retainer. The Zaim (Zeamet holder) was under the obligation to provide armed retainers for each extra 5,000 akçe, and after 15,000 akçe a kitchen, saddler, and tents. Moreover, both the Sipahi and the Zaim also brought various kinds of servants with them.[122]

The basic unit was the 1,000 strong Alay (regiment) under the command of Alaybeyi (colonel) and three to four Subaşıs (captains). The Alaybeyi was under the obligation to monitor training and readiness, but his main duty seems to have been warning his unit four to three months before the start of the campaign season and making sure all his Sipahis were present. The Alay then mustered in the province center with other Alays and moved to the regional assembly area under the command of Sancakbeyi (province governor). After passing through the inspection of Beylerbeyi, which was aimed to ensure that the basic standards of weapons and equipment were met, as well as the preparation of muster lists, the units marched to the concentration points.

Additional inspections and musters would also take place, generally while passing a selected point such as an important bridge. If any of the Sipahi failed to muster without an acceptable excuse, he immediately lost his estate and other rights. The loss of a Timar estate was a serious punishment, and if the Sipahi was not able secure another Timar in seven years, he would lose his Askeri class position and would return to the Reaya. The only way to regain a Timar was to show exceptional bravery in combat, and the government was more than happy to make use of the potential of ex-Sipahis by promising them assignment of Timars. If he was not able to provide the necessary weapons, equipment, and armed retainers he would be punished severely (sometimes including mutilations, as during the reign of Selim I). However, mobilization of Sipahis continued to create problems. During the Long War (1593–1606), due to nearly continuous mobilization, the campaign seasons overlapped with other requirements, such as internal security duties. The government found no permanent solution to this situation and it remained a problem.[123]

The exact dates and numbers involved in the changes of personnel strength of the Sipahis are unknown today, but at the peak of their power during last quarter of the sixteenth century they reached the strength of 83,550, and if the armed retainers are added the numbers increase to more than 100,000. The Asian provinces provided 42,855 Sipahis, while the European ones provided 40,695 Sipahis. However, the provinces were never able to provide more than 70,000 Sipahis with their armed retainers at once because of geographical distances, other demanding military, and administrative tasks, a requirement to leave one-tenth of their numbers to take care of estates, and, finally, individual excused absences. So, in any given campaign their numbers were normally about 40,000–50,000 strong. The limits on the total mobilization of Sipahis actually produced an important advantage, which was to leave a large reserve force at home that could be used in emergency situations.[124]

Traditionally, the Sipahi units were always positioned at the wings of the battle formation. Depending upon the continent of operations, either Anatolian or Rumelian Sipahis would be positioned at the right wing. If the battle took place in Asia, Anatolian Sipahis would be at the right wing and in Europe just the opposite. The remaining provincial Sipahis, usually of inferior numerical strengths, then simply reinforced either left or right wing as necessary. The Azabs or other provincial infantry units also positioned with them. Contradicting common beliefs the Sipahis generally fought together with the infantry except during flanking attacks and when in pursuit. Wing attacks were the trademark of the Sipahis. Generally one wing started the flank attack, and based on the outcome of the initial skirmishes the other wing joined the battle. The basic idea behind this maneuver was to fix and encircle the enemy and to force it towards the Janissaries within the Tabur Cengi formation. If the enemy became disorganized and lost most of their cohesion then the Janissaries left their fortified positions and attacked to deliver a final crushing blow. Most of the time one wing or sometimes both of them feigned retreat and ambushed the enemy pursuing units with Ottoman infantry. After the collapse of the enemy battle formation the Sipahis would relentlessly pursue the fleeing enemy. This old and simple battle formation worked well in most cases and was greatly admired by contemporary European observers.[125]

During defensive operations the Sipahis either remained behind the infantry supporting them with showers of arrows, or similarly to European heavy cavalry tactics they joined the infantry defensive formations in dismounted role (sometimes acting as officers or role models for the infantry). They always looked for the opportunity to make use of any weakness within the attacking enemy formation. Commonly used tactics and techniques were diversionary attacks, sudden change of wings, raids behind the enemy lines, and various kinds of lures. But obviously as in the example of Mercidabık battle of 1516, defensive operations remained difficult for both the Sipahis and for the commanders, who were challenged to handle the Sipahis properly.[126] Most of the time commanders preferred to position Sipahis behind a natural barrier or man-made obstacle in order to give them protection and confidence.

An interesting aspect of the multifunctionality of the Sipahis was their service with the navy. The Sipahis, like Janissaries, frequently took part in naval campaigns as a marine unit. Because of the similarity between galley fighting compared with fortress assaults and defense, the Ottomans never felt the need to create specific marine units and used regular land forces instead. The Sipahis were always the most numerous of troops of any naval expedition, as in the example of the Malta campaign in 1565 during which most of the Anatolian Sipahis took part.[127]

The Ottoman government tried to use Timar estates as a material incentive in order to enhance combat effectiveness and promote valor. If a Sipahi showed bravery and merit he would immediately receive financial awards, and sometimes land was added to his Timar estate. At the same time, however, mercenaries and volunteers tried very hard to win a Timar. There were many examples of Timar grants to various volunteers or mercenaries due to their valor and merit. Even the restrictions of Süleyman II did not stop this influx. For example, a volunteer named Hacı Mehmed managed to accumulate most of the important Timars of Požega province in less than 40 years after a brief but successful military career.[128] The government carefully made use of these incentives and encouraged competition, but it was not always successful in handling the tension and hatred that arose between groups attempting to gain Timars. In order to maintain this competitive environment, the government zealously curbed large Timars after the death of their holders. The sons of Sipahis were allowed to receive only a part of their fathers' original estates, and the excess land was automatically allocated toward future incentives.[129]

The Sipahis also performed other military tasks, such as providing security to baggage trains or supply convoys, participating in siege operations as dismounted archers, or establishing lines of contravallation. They also had important military and administrative duties during peacetime. While high-ranking Sipahi officers served as administrative officials, common Sipahis were also tasked to assist in various administrative duties ranging from law enforcement to tax collection. Moreover, they were occasionally employed as interior security units conducting counterinsurgency missions, pacifying volatile regions, and policing organized banditry.[130]

Even though the seasonal nature of mobilization was a serious military handicap, the Sipahis remained vital and the largest element of the Ottoman military during the classical period. Their success or failure generally decided the outcome of battles. They were especially effective against nomadic enemies like the Safavids and in internal security duties like suppressing Turcoman rebels. Obviously their combat value decreased after the wide-scale introduction of firearms, but they were still seen as a dangerous adversary by some sixteenth century observers, including the famous Habsburg General Lazarus von Schwendi.[131]

At the same time, they performed important administrative and financial services to the state. For this reason the government put much emphasis on the protection and maintenance of the Timar system. Various control mechanisms were invented and fervently introduced into the system, including periodical surveys of estates and population counts. The Timar holders were required to provide the necessary current data. Because the welfare of the system depended upon new conquests or on the ability to convert fertile lands into new Timars (so as to accommodate the interests of ever-increasing numbers of warriors), any stagnation immediately produced internal problems and conflicts. This inherent weakness became a vital issue at the end of the sixteenth century.

Frontier Units (Serhat Kulu)

The Akıncıs were the most important of the frontier units on the western frontier during the classical period. Their numbers reached 40,000 during the mid-fifteenth century and passed 50,000 at the beginning of sixteenth century. The Chapter 1 already noted that Akıncıs, as the direct successors of Gazi marcher lords, were the main group of provincial cavalry until the enlargement of the Sipahis. Moreover, the conquest of Thrace, Morae, Bulgaria, and Serbia became possible only after the continuous and destructive raids of the Akıncıs. The government paid special attention to control the activities and the personnel of the Akıncı groups (most of which were organized under the control of hereditary Akıncı families) by issuing licenses and keeping strict muster lists. Obviously the government wanted the Akıncıs to conduct raids within the parameters of overall strategy as well as to tax them effectively. However, it was nearly impossible to control the hundreds of small groups operating independently and, as often as not, in their own interests.[132]

The government had to reach a compromise with these small groups by introducing the "Harami" (bandit) category. This essentially gave a free hand to groups of less than 100 to conduct raids into enemy territory after coordinating their activity with regional Akıncı leaders and paying a tax after the successful end of the raid. This was an uneasy compromise for the government that, not surprisingly, created an occasional crisis with neighboring countries. From the perspective of the government, however, Akıncı and Harami activities were useful for wearing down the enemy, were very profitable, and, more importantly, acted as a safety valve in releasing the dangerous pressure of unemployed and volatile youth.[133]

Nearly every spring large and small raiding parties poured into enemy territories in every possible way.[134] By using methods of disguise and rapid movement these groups penetrated deep into target regions in small parties, gathered together to launch the attacks, and then withdrew with booty and slaves. The Akıncıs always enlisted Martoloses (or local collaborators) in order to acquire accurate intelligence about the enemy and terrain. The government often tasked the Akıncıs to conduct vicious raids into enemy regions, either before the start of the campaign in order to weaken the enemy and terrify the population or as a means of punishment for misdeeds. The Akıncıs managed to launch raids deep into Habsburg, Venetian, and Polish domains as early as the 1480s.[135]

In addition to the main activity of raiding, the Akıncıs provided valuable services during the campaigns. With their intimate knowledge of terrain and local connections they were priceless scouts and vanguard units that always operated three to five days in front of the main body, securing critical points and capturing prisoners for interrogation. The Akıncıs were also well-known for their daring spoiling attacks on enemy units trying to reach the battlefield in proper formation. Sometimes they were tasked to provide provisions for the army by looting the enemy territory, but it was always difficult to control and command the Akıncıs during campaigns.[136]

They also had several inherent combat vulnerabilities and problems. First, they were almost useless during in conventional battles if employed as conventional light cavalry. In most of the cases, they preferred to flee rather than to stand and face the enemy directly. Second, they saw every combat action from the perspective of personal gain. So, if the chances of looting were slim and conditions of the campaign were harsh, then it was very difficult to keep them obedient. Lastly, they had contentious relations with the standing army because the presence of the unruly and troublesome Akıncıs was potentially harmful to the discipline and order of the regular units. Often commanders tried to keep them apart from the conventional army, but there were not always successful in their efforts.

Although these institutional shortcomings created problems, they were not too large or difficult to manage. Their loyalty to the sultan (and state as a whole) was the biggest problem because they remained troublesome and tried to protect their independence at all costs. The Akıncıs actively took part in every Ottoman succession crisis and often provided sanctuary for pretenders of the throne.[137] So it is not surprising that Ottoman sultans starting with Bayezid I tried to curb the power bases of hereditary Akıncı leaders and introduce more controls. These policies were carried out, but the Akıncıs continued to produce political problems on a lesser scale.

In addition to the deliberate policy of the government, several other factors weakened the Akıncıs. The first factor was the increasing participation of Crimean Tatar units in the army's campaigns, which performed the same tasks that the Akıncıs had provided. In numerical terms the arrival of up to 50,000 Tatars was enough to insure the chance of success in any campaign. Beginning with the Moldavia campaign of 1484, the Crimean khans began to send light cavalry units to support Ottoman expeditionary armies. Initially their contribution was limited and unpredictably haphazard, but later on their contributions became an important characteristic of Ottoman effectiveness. In fact, the presence of Crimean units became so essential to the army that during the Long War (1593–1606) their late arrival postponed major operations. The Khans tried to preserve their semi-independent status even during the conduct of the military operations. Due to their increased political dependence on the Ottoman Empire, however, their militaries became increasingly an integral part of the Ottoman military.[138]

A second factor was the increased awareness and capacity of the neighboring states to counter Akıncı raids—especially after the beginning of sixteenth century. Hungary launched a massive construction campaign of building fortresses (which the Habsburg Empire continued on more successfully). They built not only large fortresses but also various types of small fortifications specially designed against the Akıncıs. Additionally, they raised village defense units and created regional mobile troops to support them. Most often these territorial defense units preferred to attack Akıncı units returning to their home bases. This tactic was a logical choice because it was very difficult to prevent the unpredictable and irregular Akıncı attacks. However, the returning Akıncıs were very vulnerable because of their long baggage trains, which consisted of booty and slaves. The Akıncı raiding parties increasingly suffered casualties against the territorial defense units' ambushes and, occasionally, large-scale disasters literally wiped out whole groups of Akıncıs.[139]

A third related factor was the operational pause of the Ottomans between the 1470s and the 1520s during which the western frontier of the empire was stabilized and, for the first time, the government had time to deal with the defense of the frontier provinces. This situation provided opportunities for some of the more ambitious and talented frontier province governors to fill these defensive requirements. At first they raised province defense units, but soon these units proved capable of cross-frontier raiding operations and developed into a sort of dual-purpose unit. They performed better than the hereditary Akıncı families because they were more loyal to the central government. The famous first governor of Bosnia, İsa Bey (İsakoğlu), was a very good example of this type of effective leader, who was able to create an effective military capability.[140]

At the same time this new generation of governors founded a totally new kind of frontier light cavalry unit, called "Deli" (Daredevil or literally "crazy"), as their personal retinues. The Bosnian and Semendire governors created the first Delis. But the leader most associated with these troops was the Bosnian governor, Gazi Hüsrev Bey (better known as Husrevbegova), who employed about 10,000 of them so effectively that other frontier and inland district governors of Rumelia began to imitate him.

The Delis were a totally different type of Ottoman soldier. Most of them were recent converts to Islam (usually from Bosnian, Serb, and Croat origins) and were fanatically dedicated to wage war against infidels. They wore exaggerated and wild costumes as uniforms, which were a mixture of furs and feathers of animals of prey. Their weapons also looked terrifying with exaggerated features and accessories. However, all these served a very important purpose, which was to terrify the enemy. With their wild and vicious outfits and their almost supernatural courage and daring the Delis became contemporary phenomena, and sometimes their presence alone intimidated enemy units.[141] Moreover, in addition to their raiding potential, they turned out to be more useful than the Akıncıs in conventional military duties due to their superior command, control, and organizational structure.

Not surprisingly as the importance and prestige of the Akıncıs decreased the government began to assign them combat service support duties, such as road clearance or menial tasks associated with siege engineering during the campaigns at the end of sixteenth century.[142] It is probable that the Akıncıs would have met the same fate of other auxiliary units had the disastrous defeat of Yergöğü (Giurgiu) not taken place. During the ill-fated campaign of 1595, an Ottoman expeditionary force with a majority of Akıncı units swept through Wallachia to locate and destroy the rebellious Voivode Michael's army. Michael stayed away from the Ottomans but launched an unexpected attack when the Ottomans concentrated around Yergöğü in order to cross the Danube River. Koca Sinan Pasha, the Ottoman commander, held the Akıncıs as the last component of his army to cross the bridge (perhaps to insure that he might properly tax them). In any case, the hapless Akıncıs bore the brunt of the Michael's attack and were literally decimated, and only a handful managed to survive. Yergöğü sealed the fate of the Akıncıs and they never regained their old status or personnel strength.

However, the new formations that had taken the place of the Akıncıs also demonstrated shortcomings in addition to their positive qualities. The Tatars had a tendency to see war as a means to acquire booty and often had little regard for friend or foe. Consequently, they had a notorious reputation for disciplinary problems, but since they did not have the potential to create political or military problems (like the Akıncıs) the Ottomans tolerated their behavior. Similarly, the problematic characteristics of the Deli units interfered with their employment. They were a part of the personal retinue of a particular governor, and at the end of that governor's assignment they were dismissed. The Delis then had to seek another patron or find another job. This was usually not a problem for the men because their numbers were limited and there was a constant need for experienced light cavalry. This shortcoming did not create large problems during the classical period in which the employment opportunities were generally high. However, it would become a part of a wider mercenary problem in the following centuries.

Because of the strategic orientation of the empire, difficult terrain, and limited opportunities for booty, Akıncıs or similar types of formations were not raised initially at the eastern and southern frontiers. Instead, the government tried to fill this vacuum by making use of semi-independent tribal political entities like the Kurds,

Turcomans, Circassians, and Arabs. In this regard the Kurdish tribes and federations especially played an important role against the Safavids. However, the government had to spend sizable amounts of money and had to negotiate with them continuously in order to keep them loyal and under control. Increasing the presence of permanent fortress garrisons did help, but did not solve, the structural problem of the ever fluid allegiances and loyalties of greedy tribal chiefs.[143]

In addition to the Delis, frontier province governors hired various mercenary-type auxiliary groups, Azabs, Martoloses, Farisans as mercenary cavalrymen very similar to Delis, as well as local cannoneers and the like for manning fortresses. Often Janissary and other Kapıkulu corps personnel serving on a rotational basis would establish a core cadre that was supported by mercenaries (even though their numbers usually exceeded the Kapıkulu soldiers).[144] In times of emergency governors also enlisted volunteers (Gönüllü) for a limited period of time from locally available men with a cash salary or the promises of a Timar estate. If the number of the volunteers was insufficient then every fifth household had to provide one soldier (Beşli), who then served without the salary and other inducements.[145]

Over time the differences in origin between Gönüllüs and Beşlis disappeared, but their names remained in use. The emergency recruitment of Gönüllüs or Beşlis for border defense created an additional attraction for youngsters who were willing to prove themselves in combat in order to win a secure income. It is likely that many of these men served voluntarily and temporarily within the fortress garrisons gaining combat experience and military know-how, which were the essentials for better military employment. After the mid-sixteenth century the frontier provinces in Europe were saturated with of all sorts of mercenaries seeking employment. At that time, the traditional mercenaries, who came from Turcoman stock, lost their importance, and Bosnian, Serbian, and Albanian mercenaries established a new majority. Obviously Christian mercenaries were an integral part of these employment seekers, and most of the Muslim mercenaries were either first- or second-generation converts. Thereafter, it is safe to say that the Gönüllü category became a generic name for all mercenaries in and around frontier provinces.[146]

Auxiliary Corps and Units

Probably the most problematic, least understood, and largely ignored parts of the classical Ottoman military were its auxiliary corps and units. Even though their numbers largely exceeded the standing corps they remained in its shadow. With their various categories and constantly changing names, even identifying the roles of each of the auxiliary units and their development is very difficult. Consequently, the focus in this section is more on their functions and their contributions to the overall combat effort than to their elusive names.

Using the same weapons and coming from the same Turcoman stock the Azabs had many similarities with the Akıncıs, and they were the backbone of the auxiliary infantry units. As already pointed out in Chapter 1, the Azabs were provincially recruited and financed light infantry soldiers with their own junior officers but under the command of state-appointed provincial officials. Initially Turcoman villagers were the backbone of the Azabs, but later on freebooters of all sorts began to make their presence felt in the ranks. It is uncertain whether Christians were recruited into the Azabs, but there were no special restrictions banning it, and most probably a certain percentage of the soldiers were Christians. Over time, the Azabs lost their village connections and became a sort of unemployed urban mercenary group waiting in provincial centers for recruitment.

The Azabs were a cheap and expandable group of soldiers that were organized into loose units. They were always first to attack and first to face an enemy attack. They provided their own weapons and equipment, which were obviously below the standards of standing army units. Composite bows and swords remained their main weapons. Interestingly, with the appearance of large numbers of arquebus/musket-carrying infantry units during the last quarter of sixteenth century, the Azabs disappeared from the Ottoman documentary record[147] and the Sekbans, Sarıcas, Tüfenkcis, and Levends appeared instead. Additionally, during this century the government began granting larger Timar lands to provincial governors in order to finance their personal retinues, which were organized and armed better than the Azabs. Most probably the Azabs increasingly adopted firearms or enlisted into a governor's personal retinue and, for these reasons, were reclassified into new categories and names.

The precursors of the Azabs, the Yayas and Müsellems were no longer identified as combat units but served as role models for all auxiliary units, and they performed various combat service support duties during the classical period. However, their loss of status and the ever-increasing burden of constant mobilization caused them leave their hereditary lands and to evade their campaign duties. The government's reform and reorganization efforts to correct this did not produce results, and almost all these units were abolished in 1582.[148]

The most important and largest of the combat service support groups were the Derbendcis. As a legacy of the Seljukid and Ilkhanid periods the Derbend was already a well-known organization under different names. The Ottoman government rehabilitated and transformed the Derbend system into a component of its own military administrative structure. By rehabilitating the Derbendcis, the Ottomans released conventional military units from routine internal duties, such as guarding and repairing roads, bridges, and passes, and performing constabulary duties in the countryside. Generally entire villages or communities were tasked to perform these duties and were compensated with an exemption from taxes and forced labor. In some cases, groups of people were relocated to formerly uninhabited but critical places to serve as Derbencis. The value of their service became very important after the increase of banditry at the end of seventeenth century.[149]

Derbendci status was hereditary and compulsory. When individuals or groups left the area to escape from duty, the government immediately sent units to find them and forcefully return them to their abandoned post—itself obviously demanding. In order to lighten this burden and maintain control the Ottomans organized them into a very simple unit structure of 30 men (Tabl), within which they performed rotational duties. Initially they were armed with light weapons, but with the later wide-scale distribution of firearms they too began to use firearms and kept crime at low levels. Unfortunately, the poorly motivated Derbendcis proved no match against the gangs composed of former soldiers that increasingly became a very large problem at the end of the seventeenth century. In the end the government was forced to hire Muslim or Christian mercenaries to insure the continued service of the problematic Derbends.[150]

Oddly, nomads were another important combat service support group. The government's policy towards nomads was conflicted, and it saw them either as unruly elements to be disciplined or as a cheap source of untapped manpower. Thousands of them were forcefully relocated from Anatolia to Rumelia[151] and organized into auxiliary military groups (more than 30,000) under different names depending upon their ethnic or regional origins, such as the Yörüks, Tatars, and Canbazs. This policy achieved several purposes simultaneously. Nomads became loyal subjects in these foreign regions and began to serve in the campaigns as light infantry (very similar to the Yayas), but in a short time they were relieved of combatant status and were tasked to provide transportation services to the military. They served with their pack animals, and chief among these were camels, which became important assets on campaign. These animals were sturdy, able to carry large burdens (especially light artillery pieces), and able to traverse difficult terrain better than wagons. But as the baggage trains of the army increased over time the nomadic elements could not meet all requirements, and the army was forced to hire civilian-owned camels and their drivers.[152]

The Ottoman government with its inherent pragmatism and adaptability made use of the military potential of its conquered nations by bringing them into the system according to specific regulations. The Ottoman government enlisted Mamluks of Egypt but kept them in low and medium level posts only. Understandably Turkish speaking Mamluks were very valuable assets as highly trained cavalry and compensated for the numerical weakness of the Ottoman garrison in Egypt. However, this policy did not work well in Syria where local Mamluks wanting higher posts decided to rebel and were completely destroyed in retaliation by the Ottomans.[153] Differing from the Mamluk experience (and at the other end of the spectrum) the Ottomans included local higher aristocrats in the Balkans, who received certain parts of their former lands as Timars in exchange of loyalty and military service. However the number of these Balkan aristocrats within the Ottoman system remained a minority and they were assimilated over time into the wider Ottoman Askeri class. In effect, Ottoman rapprochement with lower ranking local aristocracy and with other military classes brought a wider military capacity into being and became more permanent than originally planned.

The best known and, most probably, the first established Christian military group in Ottoman service was the Martolos (likely from the Greek Armatolos). Because it was the original word used for Christians in the army, the word Martolos became a kind of generic term describing all sorts of both Christian military groups and individuals. Additionally, Martolos was the given name for all Christian spies, pathfinders, messengers,[154] Danube boatmen, and fortress guards.[155] Interestingly, Christian renegades fighting within the Akıncı units were also called Martolos. It was natural then to find more Martoloses in the frontier regions than inland provinces. During the reign of Süleyman I local Christian constabularies began to be called Martoloses as well, especially the ones stationed in regions chronically infested with brigandage like Monte Negro (Karadağ) and Morae.[156]

The Voynuk (after South Slavic term Vojnik) groups were generally organized in Southern Serbia, Macedonia, and Bulgaria. There were also small numbers of them in Bosnia and the Danube-Sava region. Even though some Voynuks performed similar tasks as the Martoloses, the bulk of them were tasked initially to defend and secure Macedonia and Bulgaria. Later they acted as auxiliary transportation units for the expeditionary armies and provided fresh fodder for the royal stables.[157]

The Eflak (Vlach) groups came from a totally different background. They were Romanian-speaking nomadic groups that once lived in the mountainous regions of Serbia, Macedonia, Herzegovina, and northern Greece. The Ottoman government applied the same policy, which it had applied to nomadic Turcomans, and tasked them to provide nearly the same services; providing beasts of burden and drivers. They were also tasked to provide security especially against brigands.[158]

The Pandor (after Hungarian term Pandorak) groups were clearly atypical. At the end of the sixteenth century, the government tried to release all Christian auxiliaries from combat duties, but it decided to raise the Pandors in order to deal effectively with brigandage. This was a natural outcome of increased reliance on various types of mercenaries who were using firearms (as the Pandors then did). The basic differences between the Pandors compared to other Ottoman mercenary groups were their recruitment from mostly Christian Reaya and their often being tasked to perform static defense duties against bandits equipped with firearms, what were in a sense Derbendci duties (i.e., the securing of fortresses, critical bridges, and passes). They were mainly based in Bosnia and Serbia, but there were also small numbers of them in Bulgaria and Greece.[159]

The Cerehor or Serehor (after the Seljukid term to define mercenary) groups emerged out of an emergency policy of total mobilization of the civilian population. The Cerehors initially were a kind of mercenary mobilized from Muslim and Christian Reaya to perform combat duties for a very short term during extraordinary periods. An example of their use may be found in the eastern campaign of 1472, in which every four or five households had to provide one soldier with weapon and provisions. In a relatively short time at the end of the fifteenth century, however, they became entirely labor battalions levied from the Christian Reaya and engaged in large-scale civil or military construction efforts (especially in Hungary, Bosnia, and Serbia).[160]

These diverse Christian military groups with puzzling names (derived from their origins or regions) essentially served the same purpose and followed the same pattern from their foundations to eventual demise. The government initially made use them as combat units with minor organizational changes that maintained Christians as junior officers, who served under Ottoman senior and middle-ranking officers. These Christian fighters used their traditional weapons and fought according to traditional tactics and techniques. They also performed much needed scouting, reconnaissance, and flank protection duties by making use of their intimate knowledge of the terrain and population.[161] Importantly, they also served as agents of transmitting military technology and techniques.[162] In compensation for their combat services they often kept their hereditary small lands, were exempted from several taxes, and occasionally received financial awards for their merit and loyalty.

Obviously their defensive capacity was their most valued capability for the government. The Ottoman system needed time to set up its military-administrative organization in newly conquered territories. Often troubles began immediately as the expeditionary forces returned to winter quarters, which played into the hands of local uprisings (sometimes corresponding to an influx of foreign troops as well). The Christian auxiliary groups played a critical role during this period of establishing the Ottoman system in new provinces by guarding the important castles (like Vidin), roads, passes, and bridges, by supporting the small Ottoman garrison forces there, and by repressing local rebellions and brigandage.[163]

However, their importance as combat forces decreased eventually as the Ottomans established their military-administrative system with its normal complement of provincial troops and large numbers of fortress guards. All of the Christian auxiliary groups peaked in importance about 70 years after the conquest of the particular region in which they were based. The only exceptions were the groups on the frontier region of Hungary and in the provinces of Bosnia and Semendire. In those locations, the government preferred to transform them into combat service support roles instead of abolishing them.

Not surprisingly, the government applied the same methods and organizational structure it had employed during the transformation of the Yaya corps. Almost all these former Christian combat groups organized around the nucleus of an Ocak, which were renamed as Gönder (lance with flag). Each Gönder consisted of five to 10 soldiers, and for every campaign only one soldier was mobilized (in turn) whereas the others provided only money for his campaign needs. The mobilized soldiers then joined the campaign with the necessary mounts and equipment under the command of their own junior officers (i.e., knez, lagator, primkur) and supervision of Ottoman provincial officials. The Gönders performed mostly combat support service duties, such as repairing roads and bridges, carrying provisions, protecting baggage trains, supporting sappers (and occasionally serving as miners), providing fodder, and the like.[164]

At the end of the sixteenth century, the government began to change the entire concept and increasingly used Christian auxiliary groups simply as labor battalions performing all sorts of civil and military menial duties (with the exception of the Pandors and some Martoloses). At the same time, the government tried to curb the numbers and to limit the tax exemption status in order to increase much needed tax revenues. This policy was carried out slowly because of the conservatism of the system and so as not to alienate these groups. But even this cautious policy was destined to create large problems within the auxiliary groups, who were already unhappy with the decline of their status and increasingly menial duties, and this would become a contentious issue well into the seventeenth century.[165]

The policy of employing Christian auxiliary units did not work in all of the European provinces of the empire. It did not work well in Hungary especially, where the Hungarians refused to participate in these units and government decided not to force the issue because of security and loyalty issues.[166] Nevertheless, it worked well generally in the other parts of the empire. In short, during the foundation and classical periods the Ottoman government tapped and made use of its Christian citizens' military potential, effectively according to the demands of the particular time and situation (their overall numbers exceeded 80,000 during the sixteenth century).[167] The Ottomans demonstrated a unique form of pragmatism and elasticity by blending practicality with conservatism. Obviously the government saw the use of auxiliary Christian units as combat units in a temporary and expedient sense and tried to use only former military classes (as well as keeping ordinary villagers away as much as possible). Thereafter, with the exception of some frontier province units, the government changed their combat roles into combat service support role after traditional provincial units were established.

Interestingly, while the government managed to tap the military potential of its conquered peoples, it was also able to keep the natural leaders of the society loyal to the government. However, there were several unintended consequences of this policy, the chief among them was that by organizing effectively the local aristocracy in continued leadership roles, the government actually helped to preserve pre-Ottoman local institutions. These local institutions would become insurgent centers of gravity during the national awakenings and uprisings at the end of the eighteenth century.[168]

The Effectiveness of the Military

The Ottoman military of the classical period was neither "nearly perfect" nor was it simply a good imitator, which are the two opposite views that come from both traditional academic and popular works about this subject. The real classical Ottoman military achieved great victories but also suffered defeats; it did imitate European models and experiences but managed to produce original concepts and practices that were, in turn, imitated by the Europeans. The Ottoman military was, overall, an effective force relative to its principal opponents and proved capable of providing a viable military capability in support of the political objectives of the Ottoman state.

The army of Mehmed II's reign is instrumental in understanding how a victorious army operated with serious shortcomings. The army of the conqueror (of Constantinople—the most famous city fortress) suffered severe setbacks in all five of the large siege operations that it undertook.[169] The Belgrade siege of 1456 was literally a disaster. The besieging army did not manage to blockade the fortress effectively and the Ottoman Danube flotilla suffered a humiliating defeat as well. The staunch enemy of Ottomans, Hunyadi relieved the city in the nick of time. Mehmed and his army threw off these setbacks and continued the operation even more stubbornly. When Ottoman cannons and mining succeeded in destroying the outer walls Ottoman units poured into the city. However, they were ambushed and decimated. Effective

Hungarian counterattacks not only forced the Ottomans to give up but nearly wiped out the Ottoman headquarters. (Even the Sultan himself was wounded in this attack.) The severely beaten Ottoman army withdrew but remained in good order.[170]

The Hungarians defended Jajče successfully in 1464.[171] Two famous fortresses of Albania; Kroja (Alacahisar), and Shkoder (İşkodra) withstood three (1466, 1467 and 1477) and two (1474 and 1478) long and costly sieges, respectively, and surrendered only after long negotiations.[172] Similarly, the main fortress of Rhodes did not give up against the mighty army of Mesih Pasha in 1480.[173] Explanations of why the Ottomans failed do not satisfactorily account for their problems and sometimes hinge on the notion that they did not achieve immense numerical superiority.

The real problem was Mehmed II himself, who was over ambitious and paid scant attention to the limitations of the army that he had radically transformed. Mehmed's army desperately needed time to accommodate all these changes and to deal with the antagonism of old military classes. However, the army conducted nearly continuous campaigns on all fronts every year without any opportunity for rest and reorganization. Even though its numerical strength seemed enormous, in reality it was overstretched and often exhausted. At the same time, Mehmed often disregarded the technological shortcomings of his cannons, which were immobile, slow, faulty, and difficult to aim.

Against all these shortcomings Mehmed's army functioned better than any of its counterparts. Ottoman besiegers successfully built furnaces and cast various types of cannons in front of the fortress in most of the above sieges. In most cases the army properly constructed lines of circumvallation and contravallation and employed effective masking forces. Mehmed's miners showed remarkable talent, performance, and zeal and actually set a new standard that was followed by European countries. However, in some cases, simple shortcomings were enough to change the tide, as in the example of the failure of the Ottoman Danube flotilla or natural obstacles that were so great to overcome in a short time. Mehmed's over confidence and sometime inability to understand the limits of his army were common problems also.

Nevertheless, the same army achieved remarkable success during the campaign of Negroponte (Eğriboz) in 1470. The successful joint operation of the Ottoman army and navy (including building floating bridges out of ships and transporting ships overland) sealed the fate of the island and its main castle. Another successful joint operation was conducted in the famous campaign of Otranto, Italy, in 1481, where the Ottoman army managed to capture the fortress in 13 days. It was an extraordinary victory brought about mainly by the element of surprise. Moreover, it was carried out efficiently, showing clearly that the Ottomans learned their lessons.[174]

The reign of Bayezid II Sofu (the Pious) gave the army much needed rest, rehabilitation, and reorganization time. A succession crisis forced him to appease his European enemies and, except for raids and occasional small-scale border conflicts, the Hungarian and Venetian borders remained calm and stable. Bayezid tried to keep clear of the Safavids of Iran and the drastic sociopolitical developments taking place in eastern Anatolia.[175] Focusing on other fronts, he undertook two limited but problematic campaigns against the Moldavians and the Mamluks.

The Moldavian (Boğdan) campaign was a risky undertaking from the very beginning. The army rank and file vividly remembered the disastrous campaign of 1475 in which the expeditionary forces were decimated as well as the problematic victory of 1476. Moldavia, because of its geography and terrain features, was not a viable country for the Ottoman military to conduct its classical combat tactics, techniques, or effectively use its cannons. The enemy preferred to fight unconventionally and skillfully made use of forests and marshlands instead of facing the Ottomans in conventional battles. There was no large city, which with its capture might force the enemy to surrender. Moreover, the Ottomans went into a barren trackless country with extremely limited resources and without the support of their famous logistics networks.[176]

Bayezid decided to launch the Moldavian campaign in 1484 in order to satisfy the standing military units (especially the Janissaries), which were frustrated by a prolonged absence of military activity. Ottoman expeditionary forces easily passed through Wallachia (Eflak) but immediately began to suffer problems in the inhospitable environment of Moldavia. Although it was a limited undertaking, the Ottomans had the support of large Crimean Tatar contingent. The lessons learned in previous campaigns paid off and, in contrast to previous campaigns, they did not try to search for the Moldavian army but focused on the coastal fortifications of Chilia (Kili) and Akkirman. Both of these were captured after brief siege operations of nine and 12 days, respectively. These two fortresses would become very important for safeguarding Ottoman interests in the northern Black Sea region. In the short term, however, the undefeated Moldavians preserved their military potential and continued to create problems. Their later attacks on Ottoman units and allies provoked two limited Ottoman campaigns in 1485 and 1486.[177]

Bayezid's campaigns against the Mamluks were inescapable due to the imperial interests of the Ottoman Empire and the collapse of buffer states between them and the Mamluks. After a brief period of border conflicts Bayezid decided to force the Mamluks out of southern Anatolia, and the Ottoman expeditionary force, which mainly consisted of provincial units, that was sent there easily conquered Cilicia in 1485. However, overconfident Ottoman commanders were later caught unprepared and severely defeated in Adana on February 9, 1486. Bayezid responded by ordering another limited campaign with a small detachment of Janissaries supporting the provincial units. This campaign also ended with a humiliating defeat at the Second Adana battle on March 15, 1486.[178]

The second defeat was a major blow to the prestige of the empire. Bayezid ordered yet another campaign the following year, and the expeditionary force, this time heavily reinforced with Janissaries and other standing army units, also had the support of the navy. Once again Ottoman army captured Cilicia easily. The Ottoman navy also initially achieved remarkable success against the Mamluk army that had been caught between the coast and the mountains, but an unexpected storm destroyed the fleet. On August 16, 1488, both armies faced each other near Adana at Ağaçayırı. At first the Ottoman army succeeded in breaking down the right flank of the Mamluks, but simultaneously the Ottoman right wing also suffered casualties and disintegrated. The soldiers from Karaman province fled without fighting, forcing all Ottoman units to retreat. Interestingly, the Mamluks also retreated at the same time but to an area close by the battlefield. They hurriedly returned and claimed both the field and victory. As it retreated, Turcoman tribes attacked the disorganized Ottoman army in the mountains and it suffered more casualties.[179]

In addition to the piecemeal and escalatory Ottoman approach to the conflict, a mixture of structural, loyalty, and command-control problems were the main reasons behind the series of Ottoman defeats at the hand of a militarily weaker state. The Ottoman army was accustomed to the centralized battle command of the sultan himself (or his grand vizier), but instead Bayezid remained in the capital and handed over command to one of his junior governors without clear instructions. During the conduct of all three campaigns Bayezid's governors became involved in personal disputes and sabotaged each other. Some Ottoman units also turned out to be disloyal and not capable of standing in the line of battle. In addition to the men from Karaman, the Anatolian Sipahis, as a whole, were unhappy with the increased centralization of the state and their reduced status in accordance with standing army and were reluctant to fight hard. Additionally, some soldiers were affected by the Shiite propaganda of Iran and their loyalty to the empire became controversial. Their half-hearted participation was evident during these campaigns (especially the disloyalty and treachery of the Karaman Sipahis).[180]

These two problems were temporary issues, and Bayezid's successor, Selim I Yavuz (the Grim), overcame them in time. However, the structural problem of fighting against nomadic cavalry was more daunting and remained. The Mamluks were the finest nomadic cavalry of the day and enjoyed a conventional military capability as well. As already mentioned, the Ottoman military like other conventional armies did not like to fight against nomadic cavalry. Surprisingly, the nomadic origins of the Ottomans did not help them and, in some ways, became a liability. Obviously, any nomadic enemy naïve enough to face the Ottoman army in a pitched battle had little chance of success because the Ottoman professional infantry and firepower would pin the cavalry, allowing it no opportunity to escape. Nevertheless, against all odds the Mamluks engaged in three pitched battles and defeated the Ottoman army in every case. These results happened in the first two battles because the Ottomans were neither ready to face a nomadic-type cavalry nor were they able to apply their classical light cavalry and infantry combined operations properly due to the lack of standing infantry units. In the third battle, loyalty problems by provincial troops insured the Ottoman defeat.

This structural problem of engaging nomadic cavalry was already known to the Ottoman high command from its experiences in the Ankara battle of 1402 and more recently from the Otlukbeli battle of 1473. In the Otlukbeli campaign, Akkoyunlu nomadic cavalry literally wiped out the entire Ottoman vanguard after luring them into an ambush before the battle. However, the Ottoman army managed to defeat the Akkoyunlu troops decisively because of two factors: Mehmed II did not insist on rigidly employing a classical battle formation, and in the main battle the Akkoyunlu did not act like nomadic cavalry but as conventional cavalry. This gave the Ottomans a golden opportunity to engage, pin, and destroy their enemy.[181]

The Iranian campaign of Selim I is instrumental in understanding the increased capacity of the Ottoman military but it also gave a false sense of confidence to the government regarding the structural problem of how to overcome the army's vulnerability against nomadic enemies. Sultan Selim took the throne in the succession crisis with the help of the Janissaries, who were tired of Bayezid's passive military policies and who were agitating for increased military activity against the Safavids. It became more than obvious for Selim that the empire must fight in order to prevent a military rebellion and to cement his authority at home. He immediately began military preparations and, in the mean time, heavy-handedly pacified the troublesome Alevi Turcoman tribes.[182]

The mobilization of personnel and logistical capacity was performed efficiently and units joined the main army in two large concentration areas. After concentration, the Ottoman expeditionary army covered 2,445 km in 123 days mostly in good order. In addition to the auxiliary combat service support units, thousands of civilians and packed animals were mobilized (contemporary Ottoman sources mention the mobilization of 20,000 camels). The Ottoman navy undertook important logistical responsibilities by ferrying provisions to Trabzon harbor. As the campaign progressed, Shah İsmail of the Safavids followed a scorched-earth strategy by moving civilians and destroying everything of value on the Ottoman's avenue of advance. For this reason, the careful logistical planning, large-scale mobilization, and coordination effort barely met the needs of the army in such inhospitable and ravaged territory.[183]

Selim made use of financial awards effectively to motivate soldiers from the very beginning, and he allocated units for interior security and as strategic reserves. These measures turned out to be wise decisions because the disaffected Akıncıs and Anatolian Sipahis were already infected by Shiite propaganda and not willing to fight against them. Additionally, the harsh conditions of the campaign caused immense suffering at the level of the individual soldier. Moreover, Selim had to deal with two serious Janissary disorders. With these factors on his mind and not improving, when the Iranian army's presence was discovered at Çaldıran field Selim immediately decided to attack.[184]

Surprisingly, Shah İsmail decided to face the Ottomans in a pitched battle even though most of his Turcoman commanders preferred traditional nomadic tactics. He made the mistake of underestimating the real capacity of the Ottoman military machine due to its poor performance against the Mamluks, and he had no idea about the effects of firearms.[185] Selim employed the classical Ottoman battle formation with minor alterations by which he placed artillery in front of both flanks in addition to the cannons in the center.

The Safavid wings launched all-out assaults from both flanks. The Azab screen in front of the Ottoman right wing retreated in time and the Safavid left wing perished against artillery fire. However, the Azabs on the left wing did not retreat in a timely manner, and the Safavid right wing managed to reach the Ottoman left wing before effective artillery fire could be brought to bear and succeeded in defeating it. The Janissaries in Tabur Cengi formation, under the heavy supporting fire of artillery, then launched a series of counterattacks that restored the right wing and beat back the Safavid Turcoman cavalry, which had managed to reach almost to Selim's headquarters. The tide turned in favor of the Ottomans and, in less than 14 hours, Shah Ismail lost most of his army and barely escaped with his live.[186]

The Safavids never again challenged the Ottomans in a pitched battle and stayed away from Tabur formations except against isolated and weak Ottoman units when they were absolutely certain of their superiority. In effect, they understood both their newfound vulnerability and Ottoman logistical weaknesses, choosing to remain with their preferred scorched-earth strategy. For their part, the Ottomans understood that small expeditionary forces with limited baggage trains were easy prey for the Safavids. So in order to achieve decisive results there was no alternative than to deploy large expeditionary forces, which had to traverse barren and inhospitable regions with long logistic convoys. These also proved somewhat vulnerable while searching for an elusive enemy who preferred hit-and-run tactics. The Ottomans captured the Safavid fortresses in Azerbaijan and held them easily, but full control proved impossible because Ottomans were never able to extend their military-administrative system into Azerbaijan. Thus, the Ottoman troops there remained solely dependent upon vulnerable resupply from the Ottoman provinces in Anatolia. Making matters worse, after the return of the Ottoman expeditionary forces, the Safavids immediately counterattacked and captured some of the lost fortresses. Later, they also launched siege operations against Ottoman fortresses, which provoked another equally inconclusive Ottoman campaign. This extended stalemate of fortress wars and low-level border conflict hemorrhaged the strength of both states.[187]

Not surprisingly, the Ottoman military continued to suffer the same problems during the suppression of the nomadic tribes' rebellions. The pacification of the Taurus (Toros) mountains in southeast Anatolia took many years, with many failures and casualties. The nomads continued to rebel in every opportunity and, as in the examples of Şahkulu of 1511, Nur Ali of 1512, and Kalender Çelebi of 1527, their rebellions occasionally affected wider areas, and several large campaigns were required to suppress them. Even though the Ottoman Sipahis made use of nomadic cavalry tactics effectively against European enemies, they continued to fail against real nomadic cavalry, and the presence of reinforcing Janissary infantry was essential for the success of the Sipahis against nomads. This is understandable because as conventional light cavalry they had inherent weaknesses when operating without infantry and, additionally, as always they were reluctant to fight against Turcomans. Consequently, the Janissaries provided the required defensive means and firepower, while the same time kept the Sipahis under close scrutiny.[188]

An obvious outcome of facing enemies mainly based on nomadic cavalry was to keep the traditional cavalry corps intact.[189] This was a difficult and contentious decision for the Ottoman government. The dynamics of the western frontiers increasingly required more infantry with firearms and artillery, which were not at all suited to deal with nomadic cavalry that refrained from pitched battles. The Ottomans did not have the luxury of affording two different armies that specialized according to the capabilities of two completely different types of enemy. Instead, the Ottomans used the same army with minor organizational and tactical changes against all of their adversaries.

Selim's campaign against the Mamluks was a larger undertaking than the Iran campaign. The main grouping of the Ottoman army began marching on June 5, 1516, collecting units from various concentration areas, and it managed to reach the Mercidabık battlefield on August 24, 1516. Once again the Mamluks risked facing the Ottoman army in a pitched battle. Surprisingly, the battle raged in a very similar manner to the Çaldıran model. The Mamluks attacked with both wings and successfully disorganized the Ottoman right wing. But the battle was saved and won by Janissaries supporting the wings and launching vicious counterattacks.[190]

Not satisfied with his victory Selim pushed on toward Egypt. The army spent two and half months making logistical preparations to cross the Sinai desert. Then, in a single week, the army passed through the desert with limited casualties thanks to the efforts of logistic convoys that moved a day ahead of the army and opened water supply points. Six days later Selim attacked the Mamluk army on January 22, 1517, which this time awaited the Ottomans in a fortified defensive line (reinforced with 200 artillery pieces) at Ridaniye. Instead of launching a frontal assault, Selim fixed the Mamluks with a small force and sent his main group around the flanks to attack the Mamluk rear. The Mamluk cavalry perished under heavy Ottoman firepower, whereas their own cannons remained useless in static defensive positions.[191]

Interestingly, the victorious Ottoman army faced its greatest difficulties and suffered the most casualties not during any of the two pitched battles but during the four-day uprising in Cairo (Kahire). The Ottoman army was unable to make the best use of its technological superiority against a determined enemy dug into Cairo's highly dense and anarchic streets. After a shocking numbers of casualties, Selim ordered his artillery to clear avenues with fire, enabling the Ottoman forces to clear the city slowly but methodically. After a blood bath of house-to-house fighting, law and order was finally restored.[192]

The limitations of the well trained, well-equipped, and highly motivated Ottoman army became even more evident during the conquest of Albania (1456–1478) against primitive, but capable, warrior tribes, which made effective use of the rugged mountainous terrain. Here the Ottoman-trained warrior hero Skanderbeg (George Kastrioti) displayed outstanding unconventional combat leadership and defeated a series of Ottoman expeditions (arguably with considerable assistance from foreigners, including the Venetians and the Papacy). Indeed, some of the most vicious combat actions of the entire classical period took place in Albania. The Ottoman army managed to hold its ground and, against the odds, increased its control over Albania while simultaneously conducting other campaigns. Typically, the ever-pragmatic government managed to enlist increasing numbers of Albanian nobles and made use of their military potential. In the end a mixture of conventional large unit and mission-oriented small unit operations pacified the entire region. A second rebellion again created large problems in 1481, but Ottoman provincial units managed to suppress it (with limited help of the central government), albeit in seven years.[193]

The reign of Süleyman I is generally considered to be period of greatest accomplishment in the classical Ottoman military system. At the same time, this period is also known for the beginning of corrupt practices that led to the start of a long period of decay. However, this idealized picture makes it difficult to assess the combat performance and effectiveness of the Ottoman military without taking into consideration the effects of far-reaching military developments then taking place. A thorough understanding and evaluation of Süleyman's period must properly include a discussion of contemporary Western European military affairs.

Süleyman achieved his remarkable feats at the very beginning of his reign without altering the military that he had inherited from his father. His handling of the Hungarian campaign of 1521 was controversial to say the least. In contrast to the well-established system of careful planning, the young sultan launched the largest military operation in the Balkans in 57 years without either a clear objective or the necessary preparations. Overlaid on this was a bitter struggle between his high-ranking officials in which most of them disregarded sound military principles and requirements and paid attention instead to their own vested interests.[194]

The Hungarians were very weak and disunited, but Süleyman was not able to take advantage of this golden opportunity. The main part of his expeditionary forces wandered around the Sava River and spent time investing minor fortresses like Szabasc (Böğürdelen). Thanks only to the desperate efforts of Piri Mehmed Pasha, Süleyman sent part of his army against the only prime target within reach—Belgrade, which was the keystone of the Hungarian defensive system. The Ottoman Danube flotilla effectively sealed the city against any reinforcement or relief force. After more than 20 days, many fruitless discussions, hesitation, orders and counter-orders, the main army joined the siege with its full firepower. In seven days the outer walls of the city were breached and the defenders of the inner castle capitulated after withstanding Ottoman artillery, mines, and assaults for 21 days on August 29, 1521.[195]

Süleyman achieved his second feat in Rhodes in 1522. Once again Süleyman made use of his father's valuable inheritance by this time using the navy. The Ottoman navy transported the entire army and its siege train and isolated the island. The main fortress was a contemporary fortification system of modern design, and the defenders stocked abundant supplies well before the start of the operation. The siege continued on for five months and drew out of the campaign season. But, in the end, the proud Knights of St John gave up against the besieger's stubbornness and effective methods at the end of December 1522.[196]

In short, thanks to the legacy of Selim I, Süleyman succeeded in capturing two fortresses easily that the legendary Mehmed II had not. The Ottoman military machine, which was long accustomed to centralized command, functioned effectively despite power struggles between sectarian high officials. Surprisingly, the military passed through this period without any permanent damage. In addition to the remarkable performance of the standing army, Bosnian and Semendire provincial forces on their own managed to destroy most of the fortified bases of the Hungarian first line of defenses between 1521 and 1526.[197]

Süleyman then led his army into Hungary with surprising speed (marching 1,500 kilometers in 129 days) to exploit the weakness of the Hungarian defense system. King Louise (Lajos) II made a fatal strategic mistake by deciding to face the Ottoman army in a pitched battle at Mohacs (Mohaç) on August 29, 1526. The Ottoman army units were positioned according to the classical battle formation; provincial units on the wings and the Tabur Cengi formation (consisting of 150 wagons and 4,000 Janissaries in nine rows) in the center. The only difference was keeping the Bosnia Delis as a mobile reserve in the Ottoman rear. Hungarian commanders confidently decided to attack in two columns in order to make the best use of their heavy cavalry. It was a recipe for disaster. The Ottoman screening forces on both wings, mainly Akıncıs and Sipahis, feigned retreat and lured the enemy heavy cavalry towards the Tabur formation. The Ottoman artillery and Janissary musketeers opened fire at close quarters, decimating most of the cavalry. At the same time, Delis, Akıncıs, and some Sipahi units encircled the Hungarian army and blocked most of its escape routes. Most of the routed Hungarian soldiers perished either at the hands of encircling forces or drowned trying to escape through a swamp. In a single battle Süleyman decisively destroyed both the army and the hopes of the Hungarians.[198]

Mohacs not only decided the fate of Hungary but also drastically transformed the battle environment and face of the combat in the western theater. After Mohacs, the Habsburgs, who had replaced the Hungarians as the Ottoman's principal adversary, launched a large construction campaign of renovating old fortresses and building new ones based on the latest Italian designs. This was congruent with contemporary Western European experiences and pitched battles, and short decisive wars became very rare, whereas long wars of sieges and reliefs became the norm. Süleyman conducted seven large campaigns against Hungary between 1529 and 1566. Although the borders of the empire moved further west, none of the campaigns achieved the decisive victory that would have led to the stability and security the Ottomans required. This inconclusive state of events—in which fortresses changed hands, new ones were built, and the personnel strength of fortress garrisons ever increased—continued to dominate the Ottoman northwestern frontier until the end of the seventeenth century.[199]

Even though the continuous Ottoman military campaigns in the Hungarian theater of operations consumed much energy and military sources, the most interesting and, in a way controversial, military undertaking of the period turned out to be joint naval and land operations against Portugal in the Red Sea and Indian Ocean region during the first half of the sixteenth century. This undertaking is important in understanding not only the Ottoman military capacity and its structural limitations but also the global view, concept, aims, and strategy of the governing elite. Against the modern common misperceptions the sixteenth century Ottoman Empire was not a reactive economic entity, solely driven by the motive of territorial expansion. The control of trade routes, critical harbors, and passes and expelling a potentially dangerous naval power were the main motives behind the Ottoman campaigns in the Indian Ocean theater of operations.

Surprisingly, the first steps towards this military undertaking were taken after the urgent requests coming from an ardent opponent, the Mamluk Sultanate. The Mamluks were famed cavalrymen but they had no naval capacity whatsoever. So they showed feeble resistance against the carefully planned and launched Portuguese naval onslaught of 1503 to 1505, targeting the Muslim hegemony on the spice and other luxurious items' trade.[200] Simultaneously with the Mamluks, several Muslim emirates and trade colonies sought Ottoman help. Furthermore, frequent Portuguese naval incursions seriously undermined the security of the Islamic holy cities (Mecca and Medina). The Ottoman administration welcomed these developments and saw in them golden chances to expand its sphere of influence into Mamluk domains. Military experts (mariners, armorers, and canon founders), weapons, and equipment were dispatched in two parties in 1507 and 1510, respectively. This official military mission gave a further boost to the Ottoman mercenaries, and many more joined their comrades who already established a position or place.[201]

The Ottoman military advisors and assistance did not alter the situation. The Mamluks and their allies neither managed to beat back the Portuguese nor proved able to defend Muslim positions and interests. After each defeat and setback the Mamluks immediately asked for more help. In the end they became a literal dependency of the Ottomans, where after most of the local Muslim political entities saw the Ottomans as their sole protector. Thus, all parties (including Venetians whose monopoly on the spice trade was threatened by the Portuguese) welcomed the Ottoman conquest of Egypt and the demise of the Mamluks in 1517, and some of the entities immediately asked for vassalage as in the example of Sharifian Emirate of Hejaz.[202]

The Ottomans showed their presence at once by beating back the Portuguese naval raid targeting Jeddah in 1517. The Ottomans slowly but methodically secured their position. The Mamluk garrison of Yemen surrendered in 1520, followed by the fall of Baghdad in 1534. By securing the Red Sea and establishing a powerful presence in the Persian Gulf, the Ottomans gained a strategic advantage against the Portuguese, which they immediately capitalized on. A sizable fleet of 40 galleys and 25 other vessels were assembled under the command of Hadım Süleyman Pasha and set sail in 1538. Süleyman Pasha cunningly captured Aden but was unable to conquer Diu in India due to ill-will between local allies. His two expeditions to capture the critical Portuguese naval base of Hormuz also failed to materialize. Two other admirals had to be dispatched to bring back the fleet from Persian Gulf to Red Sea, but in vain. The Ottoman fleet perished after series of naval engagements and storms.[203]

For a period of time these reverses did not discourage the Ottoman governing elite and commanders on the ground. Grand Vizier Sokullu Mehmed Pasha and his protégés tried to overcome this impasse by drastically altering the status quo. They revived the idea of a canal to join the Red Sea with the Mediterranean (following nearly the same path of the modern Suez Canal) not only to sail the navy directly from its main base but also to revive commerce. Unfortunately for the empire the project was terminated immediately after the initial ground work.[204] They also sent small groups of military experts and weapons to the Muslim emirates of India and the East Indies (chief among them the Sultanate of Atjeh at Sumatra).[205]

The priorities of other theaters of operations, increasing competition with the Safavids of Persia and Mughals of India and ever present internecine fights between small Muslim entities were instrumental in curtailing the Ottoman military presence in the region. For example, between 1562 and 1568, the Ottomans lost control of nearly the entire Yemen province and reinstated the authority only after a year-long bloody campaign.[206] In the end both Ottomans and Portuguese unofficially had to recognize the other side's sphere of influence and tried to consolidate their bases and network of alliances. The Ottomans kept the Portuguese out of the Red Sea and secured their hold on the northern side of the Persian Gulf with the conquest of Basra in 1546 and al Hasa in 1552. However, their quest to control the Persian Gulf and Indian Ocean ultimately failed. Of course, small-scale engagements and occasional naval raids continued on. Most often governors decided to use a window of opportunity to extend their control or gain booty without the approval of the central administration. For example, an Hasa governor launched a surprise attack against Portuguese base in Bahrain in 1559, which ended with a humiliating defeat.[207] A certain corsair Mir Ali Bey with the support of the Yemen governor launched a more daring attack in order to expel Portuguese from Africa's Swahili coastline (especially Mombasa) in 1588. He achieved some success initially but was defeated by an alliance of Portuguese and local tribes.[208]

For most of the modern commentators the Ottoman military effort to expel the Portuguese from the Indian Ocean was an overly ambitious and faulty decision. They are right to point out the technological constraints such as the Mediterranean galleys' poor design for the job of continuous control of high seas or the Ottoman military's difficulty in conducting operations far away from its main support bases. However, they tend to ignore the great achievements, like establishing absolute control of the Red Sea and the northern Persian Gulf, the enormous prestige of protecting the traditional realm of Islam (including guarding the holy cities), and restoring the volume of traditional trade up until the mid-seventeenth century with relatively modest commitments. It was not Portugal, which was soundly defeated by Dutch navy at Amboyna in 1605, but the Netherlands and Britain that would overtake the Ottoman-controlled trade routes during the second half of the seventeenth century.[209]

About the same time the inconclusive, unpredictable, and expensive nature of large campaigns, low-level border conflicts and raids (kleinkrieg) gained importance and became the essential part of the battle environment and lifestyle of the Ottoman-Habsburg frontier after the long reign of Süleyman. This situation was exaggerated by frontier populations, which consisted of thousands of mercenaries who sought employment through war. Within certain limits both sides tolerated these raids and conflicts within. Occasionally, events spiraled out of control, however, provoking large campaigns. The Long War (Langekrieg) of 1593 to 1606 was a good example of this type of escalation. In 1592, the governor of Bosnia, Telli Hasan Pasha, increased the level of raids and began to conduct medium-sized attacks against specific targets by using his provincial units only, although he probably had the tacit support of some high-ranking government officials. Initially, he achieved a series of successes but suffered a decisive defeat near Sisak in which nearly all his army was wiped out and he himself was killed. The new Grand Vizier, Koca Sinan Pasha, used this incident as well as a popular mood inclined toward war to break the long peace.[210]

The ambitious Sinan Pasha began the war eagerly but did not show the same enthusiasm during the actual start of the military campaign. The army mobilization was very slow and haphazard after long decades of inaction on the western frontier and from the repercussions of the draining and tiring Iranian campaign. Consequently, the campaign season of 1593 was wasted, and real combat activity only began in 1594 when the Ottomans easily captured Raab (Yanık) and Papa. However, a joint revolt and defection of the Danubean principalities of Wallachia, Moldovia, and Transylvania negated these gains and put the army in the very difficult position of facing two fronts at the same time. Moreover, the revolt threatened the security of the Danube River communications, which was essential for the supply of the army. The Wallachian campaign of 1595 to suppress the revolt ended with a humiliating defeat and huge loss of life. In the meantime, Habsburg forces captured the strategic fortress of Gran (Estergon).[211]

The ever-resourceful Ottoman government immediately reacted to the consequences of these disasters, which had damaged especially the morale and motivation of the standing army corps. A new campaign was organized, and the reluctant sultan, Mehmed III, was persuaded to lead the expeditionary force in person. The presence of the sultan gave a big boost to army morale, and it advanced to the main objective, the modern fortress of Eger (Eğri), in good order. The Ottomans demonstrated their pragmatism and receptivity once again by applying the same effective siege artillery tactics that their Habsburg enemies had used against Estergon, and Eğri capitulated on October 12, 1596.[212]

After the successful resolution of the siege, the Ottoman army had to face the relief force. Initially the Ottoman high command underestimated the danger and sent only the vanguard to deal with them. After the defeat and retreat of the vanguard, however, it decided to advance and attack the enemy with the entire army. The Habsburg army was deployed mainly in well-fortified defensive wagenburgen formations and it controlled all the passes in the swampy region of Mezökeresztes (Haçova). Even though captured prisoners had revealed the enemy strength and intentions two days before, the Ottoman high command insisted on an offensive strategy after spending only a single day passing through the swamps and thereafter deploying immediately into combat formation. The entire Ottoman first line joined the assault on October 26. The daring Ottoman plan failed, the assaulting units were stopped by massive firepower, and were then routed by Habsburg counterattacks. Fortunately, the Habsburg units gave up pursuit to loot the Ottoman camp. The day was saved at the very last moment with the daring counterattack of auxiliary units and cavalry against the Habsburg flanks and rear. As the disorganized and looting Habsburg soldiers panicked, the retreating Ottoman units immediately turned around and joined the auxiliary units. The Habsburg army suffered huge casualties in the following mayhem, and the Tatars decimated the remainder during the pursuit.[213]

The Ottoman high command ended the campaign and returned to winter quarters instead of exploiting the advantage gained by these two victories. The reason was understandable considering the command elements of the army in this campaign. Except for a few operational level commanders, none of the military or civilian members of the high command (including the sultan) had the knowledge, experience, or courage to lead the army forward. This failure is contrasted by the strong performance of the standing army corps and provincial units, which executed their combat tasks properly and in some cases better than in previous campaigns. The Habsburg side also had the same leadership problems as well as other structural problems, such as mercenaries and the conflicting interests of regional magnates. The outcome of this mutually inarticulate strategic vision was to drag the war out into a series of seasonal campaigns launched against each others' fortresses.

The Long War continued on for 10 more years, during which both armies, the Habsburgs especially, avoided large-scale battles. Because of the unpredictability of the outcome of pitched battles, both sides focused more on smaller battles revolving around key fortresses. After the disastrous year of 1598 in which Yanık was lost and the Ottoman army suffered numerous difficulties caused by harsh weather, the balance began to tip to the advantage of the Ottomans. Repeated attempts by the Habsburgs to capture Buda (Budin), the capital of Ottoman Hungary, failed whereas the Ottomans captured the mighty fortress of Kanisza (Kanije) and managed to keep it against all odds. The rebellious Danubean principalities, likewise, could not withstand the sheer weight of the war and one by one gave up. An unexpected revolt of the Transylvanians against the Habsburgs effectively wiped out the remaining chances of Habsburg success, while the Ottomans reconquered strategic Estergon. Once again, however, the Ottomans were unable to exploit their success effectively. This time it had nothing to do with the government or the strategic direction of the war but, rather, because of the collapse of the eastern frontier defensive system against a new Safavid offensive and the immediate security threat of renewed popular revolts (Celali). The Long War concluded with the Zsitvatorok peace agreement of 1606, which itself was the outcome of mutual exhaustion and other urgent issues.[214]

Even though the Ottoman government failed to achieve a complete victory in the Long War it still gained considerable advantage by retaining such critical territorial conquests as Kanije and Eğri. This forced the Habsburgs to spend large amounts of money and time to build up a new defensive line against the Ottomans.[215] Another advantage occurred with the influx of large numbers of western mercenaries, who introduced new weapon systems, tactics, and techniques into the Ottoman military.[216] The Ottoman military benefited greatly from these new innovations, thanks to its receptivity and pragmatism. For the first time in Ottoman history, the government enlisted groups of mercenaries who had deserted from the Habsburg camp. The most well-known example involved the desertion of a French mercenary unit in the Papa fortress to the Ottoman side on August 1600. Afterwards, they served on various campaigns during the Long War, and some of them continued to serve well after the end of war.[217] Even though this was extraordinary and not representative of a generalized trend, it demonstrates that the Ottoman government of the seventeenth century was far from being the reactionary and conservative organ that is still a commonly held conviction about its identity today.

Moreover, the length and difficulty of the war forced the Ottoman military to the limits of its capabilities and drastically transformed it. In order to meet the requirements of war, the Ottoman government had to reorganize the empire's financial system and to recruit or mobilize all available manpower. The obvious outcome of the financial reorganization and enlargement of eligible population groups to the privileged Askeri class not only changed the face of the military but also had a huge impact on Ottoman society as a whole. Moreover, the increased need for musketeers further weakened the traditional military classes, especially the Sipahis and other cavalry corps.[218]

From every aspect, the Ottoman military ended the war with a completely different army. Instead of mounted archers in loose formations, the army employed infantry with firearms in deep formations of several rows of men. Instead of a regionally based provincial army, a salary-based standing army supported by provincial mercenaries became the dominant military organization. Moreover, that army was becoming highly evolved as an institution that had formalized ranks, corps of specialists, training, and battlefield flexibility. Therefore, it can be safely said that the classical period of the Ottoman military effectively ended with the signing of the Zsitvatorok agreement on November 11, 1606.

CHAPTER 3

Transformation and Reform Efforts, 1606–1826

For the Ottoman military the seventeenth century was a very turbulent and problematic period. While the sultans consolidated their hold on the northern Balkans, the empire lost its grip on western Iran and most of northern Caucasia. Nevertheless, the Ottoman military in this period demonstrated great strength in its ability to stage and support logistically large numbers of mobilized forces. However, the seasonal nature of Ottoman war making and campaigning crippled efforts to sustain combat power at the frontiers of the empire on a continuing basis.

The Ottoman high tide reached the gates of Vienna in 1683, only to fail because of faulty command decisions and internal deficiencies. This enabled the resurgent Habsburgs and their Polish allies to reclaim provinces in Hungary, Podolia, Transylvania, and, to a certain extent, Wallachia, which had long been lost to Ottoman power, while the Russians and Venetians would also carve off pieces of the empire. As the Ottomans entered the 1700s, it was apparent to the Ottoman elite that many of their problems were associated with the declining effectiveness of their military forces, both standing and provincial.

A reformist movement began as early as the mid-1600s, and it matured into a significant force in Ottoman military affairs in the 1700s. Much of the discourse regarding the direction of reform pitted traditional Ottoman ideas from the classical period against the modern tactical innovations of contemporary Europe. Many of the reformers themselves were not exclusively men with military backgrounds, and the tempo and thrust of reform efforts varied through the years. Reversals of policy took place as well, which both accelerated and retarded overall progress. Finally, reformers, identifiable by their alignment with contemporary European ideas—mainly those of Bourbon, France—effectively moved the empire's military in the late 1700s toward a regular army organized and trained according to contemporary European models. The reform period culminated in the destruction of the traditional centers of Ottoman military power. First, the Sipahis were eradicated as a class, followed by the transformation of provincial forces, and finally, the elite Janissary corps and its associated forces were destroyed in their entirety. This ended a military architecture and tradition that had characterized the Ottoman army's identity since the 1300s.

This chapter covers the transformation of the Ottoman military and its institutional response to increased foreign aggression and interior opposition. It explains the evolution of competing reform efforts in a search to restore the effectiveness of the military. The chapter concludes with the demise of an army that had existed for hundreds of years, setting the stage for the reconstruction of a reformed military.

Transformation

The end of the Long War has been generally seen by scholars as the end of Ottoman military superiority and the beginning of stagnation and eventual decline. According to these authors, an influx of American silver and an associated price revolution, demographic pressures, the rise of Western European military states, and economic hegemony were instrumental in the corruption of the classical Ottoman military-administrative system. In turn, the Ottoman Empire simply did not have the means to compete with the European militaries, which were undergoing a wide-ranging technological transformation, and consequently, its decline was a forgone conclusion.[1] This line of scholarship grew out of the inaccurate views of contemporary observers of the Ottoman Empire, combined with well-established Eurocentric tendencies to apply different standards to the Islamic and non-western Ottoman Empire.[2] It should not come as a surprise that the so-called "long and inevitable decline" became, and remains, the dominant theme of received Ottoman history in this period.

The criticism of the political, economic, cultural, and social shortcomings of this body of thought is beyond the scope of this work, but recent revisionist literature has already begun to dismantle this school.[3] From the military perspective, declinists have difficulty in explaining the Ottoman victories and military successes—other than pointing out factors such as unusual leadership, geographical difficulties, or simple luck. This difficulty is even more evident when trying to explain the relative ease with which the Ottoman government overcame serious military defeats and setbacks, including the battle of Lepanto (1571), the fall of Baghdad (1623), and the long campaign of Crete (1645–1669).[4] In this period, an ever-resourceful government continued to overcome its problems by creative or pragmatic methods, although it must be said that sometimes the solutions themselves were instrumental in the creation of even larger secondary problems.

The theory of decline is also unable to explain the rapid transformation of the Ottoman military against the threat raised by the Habsburgs or its ability to fight on the eastern and western frontiers at the same time. In truth, following contemporary European trends,[5] the Ottoman military transformed itself slowly but decisively by increasing its size, introducing new firearms *enmasse*, and increasingly making use of siege and counter-siege operations. Obviously, a totally new approach is needed to explain the Ottoman military of the seventeenth century, but the first focus must be on the increased capability of the Ottoman military's logistical and manpower systems in order to explain why this period should be labeled as a "transformation" rather than a "decline."

Logistics

The classical Ottoman military was well known for its advanced logistical system, which was much more effective than any used by European militaries during the sixteenth century.[6] The Ottoman government was well aware of the importance of regular salaries as well as the proper feeding of the army. However, in order to meet the demands of wars of attrition, which frequently dragged on for years without a clear outcome in the heavily fortified networks of fortresses on Hungarian frontier or the hostile mountainous buffer territories of the Iranian frontier, the Ottoman government had to develop even more effective and intricate systems. At the same time, the government had to solve the daunting task of funding the increased costs of manning the expeditionary armies. (Those sent against the new absolutist kingdoms of Europe, for example, were five times costlier than the previous century.)[7].

The contemporary Ottoman logistical system can be divided into three functional parts: movement, active campaigning, and winter quartering.[8] Due to the seasonal nature of Ottoman campaigns—usually between the end of March to the end of September—moving large numbers of soldiers, horses, and other pack animals from the core provinces to the frontier regions was a critical activity. To this end, the government enforced a very strict system of military corridors (Kol) in order to keep the combat strength of the expeditionary forces high, transport them rapidly, and cause minimum disruptions to the lives of citizens living in close proximity to the military corridors. The Ottoman campaign planners had about 180 days to conduct the campaign, including deployment and return. Even a delay of 15 days was potentially a serious problem, especially if winter arrived early, as in the example of the campaign of 1529, during which a two-week delay and early winter nearly wiped out the victorious army of Süleyman I.[9]

There were three military corridors in the Balkans and another three in Anatolia and the southern provinces. In most cases, the expeditionary armies marched in several packets and used multiple corridors in order to lighten the burden on particular districts. Each one of the corridors was carefully measured, and provincial authorities were charged with the upkeep of roads and bridges and were required to supply the marching army.[10]

Several auxiliary corps were founded to provide certain services related to the movement of the expeditionary forces. Chief among them was, without doubt, the Derbendcis—composed of villagers tasked with the upkeep and maintenance of roads and bridges and expected to provide security against bandits within their area of responsibility. The Yörüks, Eflaks, Voynuks, Martoloses, and the like were not only tasked to provide pack animals with drivers but also to serve as a regular transportation corps. The frequent mobilizations and the introduction of new control measures, including assigning more commanding officers from the standing army, created a more coherent, organized, and disciplined structure. Additionally, they continued to provide their classical services, such as emergency road repair and guarding logistic convoys and baggage trains.

The daily supply of the marching army and its billeting was the duty of the districts along the military corridors. The local judges (Kadı) were tasked to coordinate and make available prearranged amount of provisions at the billets (Menzil), which were positioned within their subdistricts at intervals four to eight hours of marching distance from each other.[11] Additionally, villagers were encouraged to sell their products at reasonable profit to the Orducus and other military contractors. Similarly to European soldiers, every Ottoman soldier bought his food and fodder for his animal at his own personal expense. To accommodate this, the government was under the obligation to provide enough supplies at a reasonable price to standing army units. In common practice, standing army regiments purchased enough food and fodder for the entire regiment and collected payments accordingly. The Sipahis were expected to bring necessary amounts of money and provisions for themselves and their retinue. They dealt with the contractors directly, and the government only provided additional funds late in the campaign season.[12]

Thanks to these meticulous preparations, the movement of expeditionary units most often worked quite well, especially in the European theater of operations. However, several factors were critical for the efficient functioning of this system. These were regular payment of the soldiers, good harvests, law and order and, most importantly, terminating campaigns quickly and prior to the end of the season. In this respect the Iranian campaigns were always difficult due to the lack of productive villages and farmlands along the corridors, greater marching distances, hostile nomads, and the scorched-earth tactics of the Iranians. For these campaigns the government continuously tasked adjacent provinces to supply provisions and arranged additional sea or land transportation.[13] Despite these arrangements, the Ottoman army continued to suffer privations during nearly all of the Iranian campaigns (which certainly was an important part of its poor performance there).

The active campaigning period began when the bulk of the army passed the main staging centers near the frontiers of the empire, such as Belgrade, Bender, Diyarbakır, Mosul, Erzurum, or Kars. At that point logistical difficulties became more pronounced, and precampaign preparations, magazines, and depots increased in importance. It can be safely said that Ottoman staging centers were the first permanent magazines in Europe, originating at least 50 years before the famous magazines of le Tellier and Louvois of France.[14] In addition, the large depots within the inner fortresses were instrumental in keeping provisions in proper condition by renewing the stocks regularly and selling the excess at the end of the campaign season. In this way the government effectively prevented spoil and misuse.

In the European theater of operations, the Ottoman government was able to solve the logistics of campaigning relatively easily, thanks to the presence of its strong flotillas on the Danube River[15] and the agricultural capacity of its vassal states of Transylvania and Wallachia. The government tried to protect border societies from pillaging and foraging—but not always successfully. The Crimean Tatar units especially created problems, and Ottoman control measures rarely worked on them. Often the Tatars were employed conducting foraging raids deep into enemy territory in order to keep them happy and to provide additional sources of supply. During campaigns, carrying enough necessary provisions with the army itself was the least desirable logistical choice, but it was often the only possible solution in the Iranian campaigns and occasionally in the Habsburg campaigns.[16] In this regard, camels and their camel drivers (mostly Yörüks) played a critical role.

The Orducus played an important role during all phases of the campaign, but especially during an active phase by acting as contractors, artisans (both production and repair), service personnel (medical), personnel care, including cooking and baking, and financial services (loans, slave buying, and the distribution of plunder). Their presence and markets (Ordubazar) were especially vital for the provincial units, which did not receive the same level of combat service support that the standing army corps received. Even though they generally brought some service personnel with them, these were not enough to cover the wide ranging needs of an expeditionary soldier. Not surprisingly, the standing army units also depended on the services of the Orducus to provide services that the regular combat service supports corps could not provide.[17]

The increased importance of logistics also affected the Orducu system. During most of the classical period the guilds of artisans and tradesmen of three large western cities (Istanbul, Edirne, and Bursa) had a monopoly to provide for all of the Orducus during campaigns. Beginning in the last half of sixteenth century, however, the government made a strategic decision to distribute support for the Orducus to other provincial centers' guilds according to centrally arranged lists. This drastic policy change pleased most, but not all, of the cities. Some cities preferred to pay a special exception tax rather than use their tradesmen for unspecified reasons. Most probably up until the end of the seventeenth century, the willingness of tradesmen and artisans to take part in military campaigns remained high because of high profits that clearly exceeded the risks. Even though the government increasingly had to hire artisans with cash salaries to perform services, the Orducus remained an important but diminishing part of the military until after the end of the seventeenth century.[18] So it is not surprising to see the guilds continuing to play a role as late as the military rebellion of 1730, when the government cancelled the long projected campaign in Iran.[19]

At the end of the campaign season the Ottoman army was accustomed to return to their home provinces or peacetime barracks. This was very important for the Sipahis and other provincial units, especially since they had to deal with their estates, collect taxes, and protect their interests. Increasingly, however, the government had to maintain part of the army in winter quarters near the frontiers so as to have reserves against possible out-of-season enemy attacks or to start the next campaign early. This new policy created serious tensions within the retained provincial units and created numerous disciplinary problems and occasional disorders. In addition to these problems, winter quartering required strict order and discipline as well as detailed planning beforehand so as to arrange provisions and other logistical needs.[20] The presence of gunpowder mills, cannon casting foundries and strong artisan guilds in main staging areas provided a large advantage to the Ottoman military during their winter quartering.[21]

The Ottoman campaigns of the seventeenth century were launched with three times more soldiers and five to six times more firearms and cannons than in the previous century. The obvious outcome of this remarkable growth was an increasing need for logistics in terms of more pack animals and wagons, more provisions and ammunition, better and larger billets, depots, and magazines. In contrast to their European counterparts, the Ottomans were able to reconfigure their old logistical system into a larger, but still effective, system that was relatively less corrupt and which created minimum disruptions on the provinces along the military corridors or hosting staging areas. At the same time, the vast size and varied capacity of the empire turned out to be a great advantage in subsidizing campaigns at one frontier with the resources of other regions.[22]

The Ottoman logistical transformation becomes more apparent when compared to the experiences of the Thirty Years War during, which the concentration of more than 20,000 soldiers in a given area became the exception rather than the norm.[23] By contrast, the Ottoman government was able to move and concentrate up to 80,000 combatant soldiers, thereby securing decisive numerical superiority in any given campaign.[24] Moreover, the government demonstrated an understanding of the importance of balancing local and military needs and managed to preserve regional economies while milking their capacity so as to keep the military corridors intact but never turning them into economic wastelands.[25]

However, the Hungarian frontier regions did not profit from this policy due to constant siege and counter-siege operations as well as the never-ending raids and counter-raids. Moreover, the Ottoman Hungarian provinces never managed to recover completely from the destruction of the Long War and only partly managed to support the needs of the Ottoman permanent garrisons (whereas they had managed to supply all needs during the 1570s). Surprisingly, even during the disastrous War of the Holy Alliance (1684–1699) Ottoman expeditionary forces tried to protect civilians from the effects of continuous combat conditions and, most of the time, managed to pay for the provisions provided by the villagers.[26]

The Ottoman expeditionary army had other crucial advantages as well. The average Ottoman soldier was sturdier, consumed fewer luxury goods, and contended more easily with the difficult conditions of the campaigns than his fellow European counterpart. In times of crisis when the government was unable to pay salaries or unable to feed the army, the Ottoman regular soldiers generally withstood these hard conditions rather than desert. Nevertheless, they were prone to rebellion, and it was very difficult to cool them afterwards. The Ottoman camps were free of alcohol, which not only reduced the need to allocate transportation for carrying barrels of alcoholic beverages but also reduced alcohol-related troubles as well. Additionally, the numbers of unofficial camp followers remained very limited, whereas in any given European army their numbers far exceeded the actual numbers of combat soldiers.[27]

In short, even though the personnel strength and the baggage train of the Ottoman expeditionary forces dramatically increased, the government still managed to maintain the high standards of logistics seen during the classical period and, in some respects, exceeded it. Throughout this period, Ottoman soldiers generally remained qualitatively and quantitatively superior to their contemporaries because of better rations, more reliable supply systems, and better sanitation and health services.

Financing the War

In financing the wars, the Ottoman Empire demonstrated adaptability and achieved high levels of transformational success. This success becomes remarkable when taking into account the structural limitations that the government dealt with, combined with an unwillingness to launch drastic changes. The first obstacle was the economic structure of the country. The Ottoman Empire had a medieval-type agrarian economy, which had limited surplus capacity, was short of ready cash, and possessed scant resources required to support the newly evolving gunpowder mass army. The Ottomans did not have the means to compete with countries accumulating large amounts of cash from commerce and banking, especially the Dutch Republic. The conservative governing elite had neither the understanding of economic developments occurring in Western European countries nor was it willing to make drastic changes.[28]

The second limitation was directly linked to the first. The government was well known for its dislike of making drastic changes or abolishing any traditional military corps or institutions. Understandably this conservatism resulted from the government's unwillingness to face the sociopolitical consequences of any radical change. Regarding army logistics, instead of institutional change, either new combat support tasks were assigned to old corps or they were left to perform their old tasks side by side with the new corps, which were essentially founded to deal with the shortcomings of the old corps.[29] The outcome of these two different courses of actions was the same: the slow death of the elder and obsolescent corps. As already pointed out in the previous chapters, this policy worked to a certain extant during the foundation and classical periods, as reflected in the experiences of the Yaya and Akıncı corps.

The wars of the seventeenth century were very expensive due to the increasing costs of salary payments—from 65.8 million silver aspers in 1527 to 285.9 million aspers in 1660.[30] Costly siege and counter-siege operations combined with rising inflation added to the government's fiscal woes. The Ottoman government tried to solve this problem by introducing classical methods, such as debasing the currency, short-term domestic loans, introducing new taxes, and the sale of excess administrative and military posts. These classical methods did not provide the necessary relief and, instead, created new problems, including social unrest and insubordination. For this reason the government unwillingly introduced new methods, such as in-cash taxes instead of in-kind taxes, tax-farming, and reassignment of the timariot estates, which were essentially related with each other.[31] Moreover, the government began to focus renewed attention on effective tax collection, more effective bureaucratic procedures, and better bookkeeping.[32]

Extraordinary wartime taxes (Avarız) became a part of the regular tax structure during the seventeenth century. Additionally, the government began to insist on turning the in-kind nature of these taxes into in-cash collections. It was an understandable policy change due to the fact that transporting the collected in-kind taxes became a nightmare, frequently resulting in spoilage of the provisions. The in-cash alternative was more elastic and became essential for the payment of the salaries (in addition to monies saved in transport fees). Moreover, the purchase of provisions from the provinces near the war zones helped the economy and created more incentives for agriculture. Most of the villagers and other taxpayers were not happy with the changing nature of tax collection, however, and it created large problems for which the government was unable to find satisfactory solutions.[33]

Except for direct borrowing, tax-farming was an expedient alternative for an agrarian state like the Ottoman Empire to extract surplus resources from its citizens. This evolved in order to produce regular and predictable cash flows to meet the expenses of modern warfare.[34] However, the only possible lands available for this were the timariot estates of the Sipahis, and the government was already unhappy with the combat performance of the Sipahis, who were militarily useless against the European musketeers and artillery. Additionally, they were increasingly unwilling to take part in long campaigns, preferring instead to pay exemption fees (Bedel).[35] So, the government chose to finance its new infantry units at the expense of the Sipahis. However, it began to reassign the estates slowly because of institutional conservatism, the continuing need for light cavalry against the non-European enemies, and the potentially disruptive socioeconomic problems. It was not an overt and drastic policy change, and most members of the governing elite probably did not understand the potential consequences, as it appeared to be simply a part of an already ongoing process.[36]

Furthermore, there were other victims of the new fiscal policies. The government slowly but surely reduced the personnel strength of the expensive Kapıkulu Süvaris and their salary payments from 130.6 million aspers in 1609 to 67 million aspers in 1692.[37] Various auxiliary units lost their tax-free status, and instead exemption fees began to be collected from them and some even lost the estates that had been allocated to them.[38] However, the biggest loser (after the Sipahis) was the Ottoman navy. By decreasing both naval activity and naval vessels, the government managed to divert large sums of money to land campaigns. Unfortunately, this saving created large problems and could be characterized as penny-wise but pound-foolish. During the Cretan campaigns (1645–1669) the weak Ottoman navy suffered humiliating reverses and was unable to support the expeditionary force and enforce an effective blockade.[39]

In addition to the vested interests of the traditional military corps, the government had to face the villagers and townsmen who were provoked by the new fiscal policies and heavy taxes. The change from timariot-based tax collection to the tax-farming system by itself was a very traumatic process, and the introduction of permanent war taxes soured the relations between government and subjects even more. However, the most dangerous problem turned out to be not the increased financial burden but its side effect, which was the breakdown of law and order. The citizens of the empire had to deal with various rebels, large groups of bandits, unruly nomads, unemployed religious students, and mercenaries, all of which were the product of the heavy burden of war. The government managed to deal with the opposition coming from different groups either by disciplinary measures and using one group against another or by simply introducing new control measures and agents.

With the help of the new fiscal policies the Ottoman government increased Janissary personnel strength and manned critical fortresses. Even after internal savings and the additional tax revenue, however, it was financially impossible to enlist both the necessary numbers of Janissaries and man all of the important fortresses.[40] In order to utilize the revenues economically, the government hired more musket-bearing mercenaries for its campaigns and fortresses. The mercenaries were cheap and easily demobilized after the end of campaigns. Additionally, they could be used on internal security duties as well. The government was well aware of the consequences of depending heavily on mercenaries, but it was unable to find any other feasible and satisfactory solution.

The Ottoman financial reorganization and increased professionalism achieved important results, and without these the empire would not likely have been able to face the difficulties of the seventeenth century.[41] Even with this renewed capacity, however, the Ottomans several times fell victim to the massive financial burdens of the long wars and the maintenance of the fortress zones. The government demonstrated its flexibility and pragmatism during these crises, but very often it paid a steep price for resolution. The importance of this crisis management capacity becomes clearer when taking into account the frequent bankruptcies of all the great powers of the age (with Spain being the most prominent).[42] Unfortunately, these unique and effective solutions were seen as corrupt practices by contemporary observers and became the starting point of the so-called "advise literature" that will be dealt in the next section.

Similar to European experiences, one of the most far-reaching and unpredictable outcomes of the increased importance of supplying and financing the war effort was the growth of bureaucracy in terms of size and power.[43] Until the seventeenth century the Ottoman governing elite was composed of the military-administrative (Seyfiyye) and the judiciary-religious (Ulema) classes. (The remaining class of scribes [Kalemiyye] were politically very weak.) Interestingly, instead of gaining more power from the continuous war conditions, the military-administrative class began to lose its hold on the decision-making process because the attritional nature of the wars failed to produce decisive victories. In contrast, the central bureaucracy was rightly seen as successful due to its financial and logistical performance, and its members were increasingly awarded with provincial administrative posts, thus limiting the chances of military commanders to advance within the system. The development of a larger and politically stronger bureaucracy began to challenge the traditional power holders only after the second half of the seventeenth century, however, and it established dominance afterwards.[44]

Manpower

Without doubt the obvious winners of the seventeenth century military transformation were the Janissaries and the cannoneers (Topçus). A few other technical corps also benefited from the transformation, like the armorers (Cebecis) and the miners (Lağımcıs), but not the household cavalrymen (Süvaris) and wagoners' (Arabacıs). Being a very expensive light cavalry corps, the Süvaris were unable to withstand the financial compromises of the transformation and could not protect their privileges effectively. For the Arabacıs, the situation was grimmer. Their specialized mode of combat formation, the Tabur, lost its value against the new firearms, which had longer ranges and better accuracy. So, they only managed to protect their place in the force structure because of the conservatism of the government and by becoming totally an artillery transportation corps.

The Janissaries, as musket-bearing light infantry with long established regimental structures and built-in combat support arms, were a more than ideal corps for the new battle environment. For this reason the government understandably increased their personnel strength[45] and tasked them with additional duties. More and more Janissaries were trained and sent to provinces for policing due to the increased unreliability and ineffectiveness of the Sipahis as well as to frontier regions because of the changing nature of wars from those of pitched battles to those of siege and counter-siege operations. In 1685, there were 13,793 Janissaries guarding 36 fortresses out of a total strength of 31,790. This figure would rise to 53,966 (including local Janissaries) guarding 68 fortresses by 1750.[46]

In addition to the rise in the numbers of Janissaries serving in the provinces and frontier regions, their temporary rotational service system was also changed in the meantime. At the end of the century most of them were serving in the same province permanently and had already established family and socioeconomic relations with the local society. In doing so they became part of local politics and power struggles, much like their predecessors had in Istanbul and Egypt. Whatever the merits of this policy in the short and middle term, the Janissaries who were assigned to provinces permanently lost their military value and became more or less a police force. So, any statistics that count them as combatants give a false picture of their actual strength.[47]

The rapid increase in strength transformed the corps drastically. The main mode of recruitment, the Devşirme, had already lost its dominance with the relaxation of the non-marriage rule, and sons of Janissaries (Kuloğlu) gained favored admission to the corps. Even though the Devşirme practice continued on until the middle of the eighteenth century, Kuloğlus—not to be confused with the Kuloğlus of North African provinces—became the main source of manpower for the corps. Interestingly, even the availability of the Kuloğlus did not fulfill the demand for soldiers, and the government had to recruit from other groups—mainly from the urban unemployed, excess members of guilds, and recent immigrants from the countryside—who had been seen as unreliable during the classical period. From time to time volunteers under the name of Kul Karındaşı (brother of the corps), which is sometimes used interchangeably with another term Yamak (apprentice), were recruited with the promise of enrollment in Janissary corps if they served three years with distinction. Thus, the recruitment base moved from provinces to urban centers.[48]

The first victim of the new sources of manpower was the Acemi Ocağı. There was no need to send new recruits, who already were native Turkish speakers and practicing Muslims, to Turkish families. Additionally, most of them had already spent time within the corps as apprentices with their fathers or relatives, and they already learned their trade without much need for formal Acemi training. Even though the Acemi Ocağı remained in use, its period decreased from five to six years to one to two years.[49]

The decrease in Acemi training combined with the recruitment of Kuloğlus and urban youth had far-reaching results. In the short term it was a welcome development in terms of manning and finance. In the middle and long term, however, the Janissaries lost their privileged position of a small, highly trained special corps and became more or less a corps of line infantry with basic skills. Moreover, family connections and vested interests within the socioeconomic fabric became more important than loyalty to the sultan. Of course, they lost their homogeneity and in some respect their cohesion also. Instead, the Janissaries became the leaders or opinion makers of the urban middle class and divided into factions or small interest groups. The government accepted this reality by making an important policy change and resumed assigning the Yeniçeri Ağası within the corps in 1641. Not surprisingly, in four years Ağas from the ranks gained promotion to the rank of vizierate for the first time.[50] This predictable development would have significant effects on the future of the empire (which will be dealt with in the "Reform Efforts" section).

The ever-increasing requirements of the new combat environment and fiscal limitations were instrumental in forcing the government to make use of two older practices on a wider scale. The first was reducing the real salary payments by debasing the currency. This policy, as before, caused widespread unrest and occasional rebellions, but it achieved several decades of relief for the government.[51] The reduction of the salaries, however, forced the professional soldiers to search for other ways to earn a living. Corruption and abuse were obvious outcomes, but the most important development, which was also very similar to the contemporary European examples,[52] was establishing private small businesses and becoming part of the artisans' guilds and city labor market at the end of the seventeenth century.[53] Recent research shows that Kapıkulu soldiers were already part of the empire's commercial activity[54], but participation in secondary commercial-artisan related jobs were obviously born out of the government's deliberate policy of reducing the salaries by means of debasement.

The second practice was the massive recruitment of mercenaries. The mercenaries were always a part of the Ottoman military under different names and categories. So, in essence this was not a completely new development; it was just the continuation of old practices according to the requirements of the new combat environment under new names. At the end of the sixteenth century several categories of mercenaries disappeared from the official documents and new categories appeared that understandably specialized on firearms.

The term Levend (or its plural form, Levendat) was the generic name of musket-bearing, mostly infantry but also cavalry, mercenary groups of the seventeenth and eighteenth centuries that were also labeled under different names, including Sekban,

Sarıca, Deli, Faris, Gönüllü, and the like. Originally, Levend was the name given to the marines of the Ottoman pirate flotillas during the fifteenth century. Over time it became the generic name of all mercenaries, but it was most often associated with those recruited as the personal retinue of high provincial officials.[55]

For more than a century the governing elite and high provincial officials gained control of fertile lands by assigning them to members of their personal retinue. The Ottoman high officials were well accustomed to use their personal retinue in a way that imitated the sultan's household. The personal retinue of the provincial officials played an important role as the core of the provincial forces, including the Sipahis, during the classical period. They were known as Cebeli (armed retinue) and most likely the main body of them was light cavalry. They were not seen as mercenaries by contemporary observers, but in real sense they were. These so-called Cebelis made contracts with Ottoman officials individually or as part of a small group. Therefore, being part of the personnel retinue of an official, their contract totally depended upon the term of that particular official, and they had to find another employer when their former one's term ended.[56]

The government hesitated between encouraging high officials to raise stronger and better-armed retinues and trying to promote the rights of low-ranking timariots. The government continued to enforce the constant rotation of its officials and conducted frequent inspections, but only to curb the formation of local power bases by governors and not to curtail the enlistment of retinues.[57] The government actively encouraged a vicious competition to raise a larger but cheaper army. The provincial governors acted as official military contractors or commissioners to recruit as many men as possible. Success in raising larger and well-trained musket-bearing units was always handsomely rewarded by having one's expenses reimbursed. However, any failure generally would ruin a career.[58]

The proliferation of mercenaries during the seventeenth century coincided with a change of their respective names. The Levends, in contrast to their predecessors, had more solidarity and group cohesion. This increased solidarity was understandable given the fact that they spent years in war and peace fighting together, searching for employment together, and generally trying to survive together. Employment as part of a large group gave the mercenaries a better bargaining position vis-à-vis provincial officials or other government officials. We can safely say that at this stage the Ottoman system created its own "free companies."

Sui generis mercenary company commanders, Bölükbaşı (captain), and Başbölükbaşı (head of captains), began to collect men around themselves, and after arming and giving very basic training (leaving further training to actual combat) began to look for employment. Depending on their prestige, strength, and market conditions, they would make a contract either with a provincial officer or directly with the central government's representative (these Levends generally classified as Miri Levend). At the end of their contract, company commanders tried to find another employer in order to keep their private units intact since otherwise they had little means to keep them together. In the worst-case scenario, company commanders sometimes chose banditry.[59] One interesting characteristic of the Ottoman mercenaries was their preference to seek employment distant from their original province. For example, the most famous mercenary group, the western Anatolians (to which the famous Kazdağlıs of Egypt belonged), sought employment in European and North African provinces while the Albanians tried their chance in Anatolia.[60]

How was the battle performance of these new types of large mercenary units? If the Ottoman chronicles' statements are taken at face value, they were militarily useless, financially ruinous, but most importantly a danger to the Ottoman system akin to cancer cells. Most modern scholars have nearly the same idea about them.[61] From our perspective this common opinion does not represent the reality of the seventeenth century and simply offers a superficial and deceptive view.

Before starting an analysis of the Ottoman mercenaries, one must remain impartial and avoid the modern ethical tendency to label all mercenaries as evil. First, without the presence of large units of Levends, the Ottomans could not withstand the onslaught of their increasingly powerful enemies, and these became relatively important in reversing numerically inferior odds.

The list of accomplishments is long, but the following examples are enough to refute the negative claims about the mercenaries. During the two long Iranian campaigns of 1578–1591 and 1603–1612 the government had to depend increasingly on mercenaries when its traditional military units proved incapable of fighting any longer. Later, Özdemiroğlu Osman Pasha recruited record numbers of mercenaries by promising enrollment to Janissary corps and achieved a series of victories in difficult terrain without the help of an effective logistics system.[62] More than two-thirds of the famous defenders of Kanitzsa (Kanije) of 1601 were actually mercenaries who withstood the impressive army of King Ferdinand for three months and inflicted huge losses under the able command of Tiryaki Hasan Pasha.[63] Similarly, the successful outcome of the Polish campaign of 1620 against stronger Polish forces became possible thanks to the personal retinues of several provincial governors.[64]

Second, after the rapid enlargement of the Kapıkulu corps and the disuse of Devşirme system the socioethnic difference between mercenaries and Kapıkulu soldiers literally disappeared. This development is understandable when taking into account that the aim of many Ottoman mercenaries was to secure permanent employment within the standing corps. The mercenaries were more willing to take risks in order to gain enlistment than the Kapıkulu soldiers, who felt themselves secure enough and were less willing to risk what they already had. They more or less came from the same social backgrounds; many were uprooted villagers, unemployed urban youth from big cities like Istanbul, peasants from mountainous regions like Bosnia, Albania, and Caucasus, and from the traditional breeding ground of mercenaries—western Anatolia.[65] Due to the lack of archival studies we do not know the exact religious composition of the mercenaries. We know the presence of totally Christian mercenary groups like the Pandors, which were founded during this century. If taken at face value some of the documents labeling various Albanian mercenaries as non-Muslims, then it is safe to say that Christians were still numerous within the mercenary ranks.[66] Obviously, the majority of Christian mercenaries converted to Islam at some stage of their service in order to have better chances of employment within the standing corps.

Third, the mercenaries were in every way cheaper than Kapıkulu soldiers. Their salary was relatively low, and they received it haphazardly. Most often their equipment and weapons were second rate. Surprisingly, however, they proved to be as willing and courageous as the Kapıkulu soldiers, but obviously were not as trained and talented as the standing corps men. They had no job security, and at the end of the campaign season they had to find other jobs in order to survive during the winter. It was very difficult (but not impossible) to find temporary jobs in the inelastic Ottoman economy. These winter period jobs mainly involved guarding frontier fortresses, serving in military construction work, or policing the provinces against bandits. In contrast, the Kapıkulu soldiers increasingly spent these winter periods working in their well-established civilian secondary jobs.

Last, but not least, the Levends following the tradition of their predecessors sought employment in foreign countries, including the erstwhile enemy of the Ottoman Empire, Iran.[67] Unfortunately, there exists very limited information about the real dimensions of Ottoman mercenaries serving abroad. The available sources only provide information about some spectacular incidents, like the presence of Karaman mercenaries under command of a certain Mehmed in Yemen before the Ottoman conquest[68], Ottoman musketeers that were employed by Indian emirs, and some isolated individuals like artillery experts Ali Kuli, Mustafa Rumi, Kara Hasan, and sea-captain Cihangir Han in the service of the Mughals.[69] No scholarly work has examined the Ottoman Christian mercenary groups (chief among them were the Stradiotis, which were mostly a Sipahi-type light cavalry serving under various flags)[70] and their origins, similarities, and differences from other Ottoman mercenary categories.

The most common criticism about the mercenaries is their alleged role in military rebellions, social disorder, and banditry. According to this view the unemployed mercenaries (Kapısız Levendat) "roamed the countryside" and caused great problems after the end of Long War and Iranian campaigns.[71] Even though their presence in these social upheavals is undeniable, recent research shows clearly that neither their role nor the social upheavals were as significant as originally thought. In reality, the government recruited large numbers of them for guarding fortresses, policing the provinces, and for other duties, which was instrumental in keeping the number of unemployed mercenaries lower than previously stated by scholars. Moreover, most of the mercenaries of Habsburg campaigns came from the Rumelian (European) provinces—chief among them Bosnians and Albanians—not from Anatolia, where the most of the rebellions and social upheavals took place. Not surprisingly, most of the rebels of Anatolia were actually nomads and Sipahis, who were alienated by the new policies of the government.

In addition, we must not forget similar developments affecting Europe. In terms of military rebellions and disorders especially, there was a clear and corresponding trend during the early modern period. The long and attritional wars pushed the European militaries, which were trying to accommodate transformation, to the limits. As in the famous example of the Spanish Army of Flanders, most of the expeditionary armies of the age suffered a series of rebellions and disorders. So, increased numbers of military rebellions and disorders were not something unique to the Ottoman military of the seventeenth century but characteristic of all militaries of the time. Indeed, most of the time the Ottoman government easily manipulated the rebels and accommodated their requests better than most of the European states.[72]

In short, the Ottoman mercenaries became indispensable and performed important duties as long as they were kept under control. Being cheap and affordable soldiers, they literally became the cannon fodder of long and costly campaigns. Naturally this caused the composition of the provincial troops to change drastically, and the percentage of mercenaries rose from half of the provincial troop strength in 1609 to two- thirds at the end of the century.[73] The problematic side of this development was that for the first time in the history of the empire mercenaries surpassed the numbers of the standing units. This abnormality becomes clearer when bearing in mind the change in Europe after the end of the Thirty Years War, particularly after the 1650s, in which mercenaries began to be seen as threats rather than assets.[74] In actuality, the Ottoman mercenaries became a significant problem after the end of the seventeenth century as a consequence of the devastating results of the War of the Holy Alliance.

Another important aspect of the military transformation was the appearance and increase of high-ranking officers who were recruited and trained outside the established officer training system. According to the classical system, an officer could be commissioned in three ways: on-the-job training within the Kapıkulu corps, attendance at the three palace schools (Enderun [Topkapı Palace], Galatasaray, and İbrahimpaşa), and participation in the timariot system. The officers of auxiliary units and mercenaries did not have the same rights of the privileged officers of the central government who were part of the military-administrative class (Askeri). However, with the rise of vizier families, governors, and other grandees and the vitality of their personal retinue for the conduct of campaigns, their households began to recruit and train prospective officer candidates. The grandees increasingly began to assign personnel from their household to high military posts, and patron-client relations became the most important element in this system. The share of the grandee household members rose gradually and achieved dominance at the end of the sixteenth century. In fact, proportions would rise to nearly two-thirds of all provincial high-ranking posts during the second quarter of the seventeenth century. The Kapıkulu corps managed to keep these protégés out of the regiments but not out of the high-ranking positions, and palace school graduates were actually bypassed and most of the time had to satisfy themselves with the positions within the palace.[75]

Unfortunately, there is a dearth of necessary data to compare the performance of protégés with classically trained officers, but it is known that bureaucrats from households did achieve remarkable success. Moreover, Grandee households provided new opportunities for youngsters from decent backgrounds and became a new channel of social mobility, but for obvious reasons patron-client relations factionalized the Ottoman military-administrative system. From a military perspective, however, this practice was instrumental in causing the military training institutions to fall into disuse from neglect. As a result, the classical institutions were left to a problematic fate for more than one and half centuries. Due to this long neglect and antiquated practices, the military reformers of the eighteenth and early nineteenth centuries found it difficult to use the formal institutions as a springboard to launch reforms. In fact, to the contrary these institutions became an obstacle blocking the foundation of more modern structures.

Side Effects of Transformation: Rebellions and Banditry

As already pointed out, the most deleterious side effects of the transformation were widespread popular rebellions, social unrest, and banditry. Obviously the new fiscal policies and socioeconomic transformation were instrumental in creating fertile ground for these crises. However, the role of military transformation in this, other than wartime taxes, is not clear.[76] Likewise, it remains difficult to answer questions such as the role of the diffusion of firearms into society, the factor of mercenaries, and the increasing presence of Janissaries in the provinces.

The military rebellions and unrest were nothing new to the government. They were sporadic and most of the time had limited effects, but some proved devastating as exemplified by the succession crisis of 1481. The death of Mehmed II created a power vacuum, which the governing elite suffered to fill in a timely manner. The opposition, which consisted of losers of the military reforms of Mehmed II, namely the Sipahis, Azabs, nomads, and other provincial units, launched a desperate attack but failed against the might of the Kapıkulu corps. In the example of the crisis of 1481, one group of the elite always manipulated these rebellions for their own personal or political benefit. Seeing these rebellions as a completely military-related problem is erroneous.[77]

During the classical period the government successfully balanced provincial units with the Kapıkulu corps, and even corps within the Kapıkulu were played against each other. When the military transformation of the seventeenth century effectively destroyed the power base of the Sipahis, the government lost them as a balancing weight against the Kapıkulu corps. We know that the government tried to use the military potential of the Levends against Kapıkulu corps several times, as in the notorious example of using Yeğen Osman's armed followers. But none of them brought success and instead made the situation more dangerous. The current data does not support the suggestion of wide-scale power struggles between the Kapıkulu corps and mercenaries.[78]

The second important development (previously mentioned) was the enormous increase of musket-bearing mercenaries, who began to fill the ranks of the military, which destroyed the balance of power in the provinces. However, by themselves these two developments did not create the necessary tension for the so-called "Celali" rebellions. Other factors also need to be considered. First, we need to identify who the Celalis were and then explain their connections with the Ottoman military.

The year 1595 is generally seen as the starting date of wide-scale rebellions and banditry.[79] However, the generic name for these rebels and bandits, Celali, appears to have been born earlier in 1519 after the rebellion of Sheikh Celal. Most of the original Celalis were nomadic tribesmen, unemployed Sipahis, and members of various heterodox sects. During the 1550s another group appeared as Celalis, and these were students of the rural religious schools (Suhte or Softa). According to the Ottoman chronicle accounts, however, the real start of the mass unrest only became possible after the sacking of thousands of Sipahis, who had refused to take part in campaigns or fled during the combat actions at the beginning of Long War. Even though the archival documents do not support this widely accepted claim, we know that large numbers of landless Sipahis were present in Anatolia. Some mercenaries joined these groups later on but not in large numbers and most often only for a limited period of time. Why then is there is a tendency to identify Celalis with mercenaries? The answer is simple. The social origins of most of these groups, including the students, were the same—young peasants and urban unemployed.[80]

The identification problem becomes more difficult when Ottoman counterinsurgency or stabilization operations are taken into consideration. Most of the time, in terms of social origin, there was no difference between the government forces and the Celalis. Moreover, members of both groups had a habit of changing sides. To make the issue more complex, the local people even had great difficulty differentiating who was representing legitimate authority due to the large number of rebellious governors or other officials. This gave rise to another interesting identity of the Celalis. Leaders were necessary in order to attract and incite large groups to rebellion. Without the leadership of disaffected government officials, like Abaza Mehmed Pasha, the rebellion had no chance of success.[81]

What was the role of the diffusion of firearms into Ottoman society? Obviously, musket-bearing rebels, bandits, or villagers created a significant security problem, but by themselves firearms did not create the problem. The government followed a dubious approach. On one hand, measures were enforced in order to stop diffusion (especially after 1524), but on the other hand the government showed reluctance to arm mercenaries and asked them to provide their own firearms.[82] As a consequence, after discharge from the military, mercenaries returned back to their provinces with their personally owned firearms. Thus, the accumulated knowledge of manufacturing and using firearms was instrumental in the creation of rebel armies of several thousand strong, as in the example of Canbulatoğlu of Syria who managed to collect a force of more than 30,000 musket-bearing men. However, the government still had enough power to control the diffusion by enforcing import bans (in fact, only a very few provinces like Palestine had foreign supply channels), by maintaining tight control on manufacturing and by forcefully collecting all firearms from nonmilitary classes, as in the example of Kayseri province at the beginning of the seventeenth century.[83]

In reality, it was the Ottoman government's own policies that created the volatile atmosphere of rebellion and banditry in which government-trained disaffected officials led the unemployed villagers, students, timariots, and mercenaries, who manned the rebel armies and bandit gangs. This situation was not an intentional governmental decision but rather the outcome of the application of its decisions. At this point the government also manipulated the situation for its own benefit, in terms of financing the military and war effort more effectively by increasing the tax-burden of villagers and by employing armed groups as cheaply as possible and then getting rid of them as soon as possible. Interestingly, the rebels and bandits actually acted as additional tax collectors by squeezing villagers more—but of course they did not share their collections with the state! Nevertheless, by using these financial tricks as a kind of *de facto* wage (and for equipment and weapons) the rebel armies became in a sense a cheap and ready source of manpower for the government. This is not surprising when taking into account the readiness of the rebels and bandits to join the government ranks with the promise of a good salary or position.[84]

The level of the Ottoman government's manipulation is more visible when the foundation of provincial militia (İlerleri) is taken into account. The public policy of the state was to stop the diffusion of firearms and disband all armed groups during this period, but in reality the government founded provincial militias under the pretext of protecting small towns and villages against Celalis. Village and urban youth were organized into 30 to 40 men-strong units under the command of locally selected officers (Yiğitbaşı) who were under the operational control of district judges. The state provided the weapons, but the locals provided the financial means. So the government managed to militarize Ottoman society further without any additional costs, and additional militia gave the government another means to manipulate and balance power relationships within the provinces.[85]

The large-scale rebellions and banditry affected the country as a whole but did not damage overall military strength. When the government decided to repress and eliminate all armed groups after the need for their presence ended or after some of them became a real threat, like Kalenderoğlu Mehmed Pasha, strong counterinsurgency forces were sent to the rebellious regions. Most of the time the Celalis surrendered without a fight and were forgiven. The infamous campaign of Kuyucu Murad Pasha (1607–1610) put a definite end to this era of anarchy, which had lasted approximately 15 years. By 1610, all the major rebel groups were defeated and thousands of Celalis were executed.[86]

The Second Siege of Vienna and the Turn of the Tide

The Second Siege of Vienna

The second siege of the Vienna is generally seen not only as a disastrous defeat but also an inevitable one. According to common interpretations, the Ottoman governing elite just did not comprehend the limitations of its decaying military and began an overly ambitious undertaking.[87] In reality, the transformed Ottoman military functioned properly from the beginning of the campaign to the final defeat at Parkany on October 7, 1683, and victory was lost at the very last minute because of the personal misjudgment of the commander in chief.

From available accounts we can safely say that the Ottoman government under the able control of the ambitious Grand Vizier Merzifonlu Kara Mustafa Pasha made use of Habsburg vulnerabilities and escalated a well-calculated crisis that led to war. The obvious aim was to safeguard the Ottoman interests in Hungary and to end frequent Habsburg interventions in the affairs of Transylvania and Wallachia. Even though Mustafa Pasha underestimated the military potential of Habsburg allies, foremost among them Poland, the flow of events justified his overall assessment of Habsburg vulnerabilities and military weakness.[88] The consequent disastrous outcome was largely the result of his slow and poor combat leadership.

The rebellion and relative success of Hungarian nobles under the leadership of Count Imre Thököly created a unique opportunity that the Ottoman high command had sought for many decades. In contrast to modern scholars who pay more attention to the active combat potential of Thököly, the Ottomans saw his strengths more in terms of combat intelligence, logistics, combat support services, and pacification of local populations.[89]

Mustafa Pasha, like his predecessors, decided to negate Habsburg technological advantages by the personnel strength of the Ottoman military. He skillfully mobilized the military potential of the empire. In addition to the standard provinces contributing forces, elite units from Egypt, Aleppo, and Damascus, numbering 3,000, 1,500 and 1,500, respectively, were also mobilized. The composition of the expeditionary forces is instrumental in understanding the difference of the late seventeenth century military from that of the classical age. The musket-bearing Janissary corps was still the backbone of the force with 40,000 strong, but provincial troops barely exceeded that number. Not surprisingly, most of the provincial units were actually the personal retinues of the governors (essentially very similar to the Janissaries) and interestingly the campaign accounts also show the presence of a 6,000-man Grand Vizier's retinue and 2,000 man retinue of the Ağa of Janissaries. Obviously, the timariot troops were, by now, more or less defunct, but importantly the high command had to balance the conflicting interests of various governors in order to establish an effective command and control system.[90]

The vanguard of the expeditionary army began its march forward from Edirne without much ceremony at the end of March 1683, while Habsburg envoys were still trying desperately to end the crisis peacefully. The ever-confident supreme military commander, Mustafa Pasha, paid no attention to speed, and even unexpected rain showers and bad road conditions did not worry him. The main body of the army reached Belgrade on May 3 and the last elements on May 24. After the reorganization, Mustafa Pasha reached the forward staging base at Osijek (Ösek) on June 2.

There are conflicting accounts of the march and the expeditionary forces. Even the same observers gave contradictory accounts, as in the example of the Habsburg envoy Caprara. He began his account by praising the enormous effort of the marching units under heavy rain immediately after the start of the march. However, he described the same units as disorderly and weak in the last stages. If one takes into account the sheer size of the expeditionary force; approximately 100,000 men in combat units and nearly the same amount of combat service support personnel and camp followers, which followed different but coordinated routes, then the conflicting and contradictory accounts are understandable.[91]

Mustafa Pasha displayed his ambitions during the war council of Szekesfehervar (İstolni Belgrat) on June 26. For the first time he announced the unexpected target of the campaign—the city of Vienna. Most probably he had the covert support of the Sultan, Mehmed IV, and his inner circle, but most of his immediate subordinates would have preferred to target the fortress of Raab (Yanık) rather than Vienna. Despite this dissension, Mustafa Pasha managed to silence or convince all his generals to conform to his plan. From a military perspective this choice was logical. Raab was a very strong fortress, renovated into an impregnable fortification by Montecuccoli, which would be very difficult to capture. Additionally, it was very difficult for the Ottomans to hold the fortress and its surrounding fortified zone as had happened previously in its first capture in 1594 and its eventual surrender four years later. More importantly, however, its capture would not tip the balance to the advantage of the Ottomans because the Habsburgs would immediately surround the fortress with a new fortified belt and negate its military value, as had happened previously at Ersekujvar (Uyvar).[92]

In contrast, Vienna had all the advantages that the Ottomans were looking for. Its capture would be a sensational victory and provide a strategic advantage. Some parts of its fortification were neglected and of problematic value, and having a large civilian population it was more vulnerable than Raab. Furthermore, a direct assault towards Vienna had the potential to surprise, disrupt, and dislocate the Habsburg forces. At the same time, its capture might shatter the enemy's will to fight and frighten the civilian population. The crafty Mustafa Pasha also paid special attention by enlisting neutral Hungarian nobles to assist him in achieving this spectacular victory.[93]

Ottoman and Tatar raiders and Thököly's Hungarian units began their raiding and destruction campaign at the beginning of June while the Habsburg commander in chief, Charles of Lorraine, was planning for a preemptive strike against both Uyvar or Estergom. In doing so, Charles wasted any chance of a preemptive strike against the Ottoman expeditionary forces. This was due to his wavering and to the inherent weakness of the Habsburg military in terms of a lack of effective command, control, and decision-making as well as from the conflicting interests of the nobles. Moreover, while he was receiving and giving orders and counter-orders the Ottoman raiders and their allies increased their activity and began to roam and burn down practically all parts of the countryside to the east of Linz and Opponitz. The daring and ever-increasing activities of Ottoman raiders were instrumental in frightening the civilian population and disturbed most of the Habsburg's efforts to establish defensive measures.[94]

Mustafa Pasha achieved complete surprise when his forward elements brushed aside weak defenders around Ungarisch-Altenburg and the high tempo of Ottoman units dislocated the main body of Habsburg forces, which were still expecting an attack towards Raab on July 7. After several clashes Charles had no choice other than to pull back all of his units, and the Emperor Leopold I fled to a secure location—leaving Vienna to its fate for the time being. At this critical junction Mustafa Pasha failed to either press on the demoralized and disorganized enemy forces or to march quickly towards Vienna. Instead, he suddenly slowed down and began to move his units at a leisurely pace. Charles used this breathing space to send some infantry regiments to Vienna while the Viennese spent it making last-minute defensive preparations.[95]

The main body of the Ottoman army reached the city and began siege preparations on July 13. Mustafa Pasha found out to his regret that his forward elements had mistakenly burned down several tons of timber that would have been very useful for constructing earthen siege works.[96] For a plan Mustafa Pasha and his engineers had a model to apply—that of the long and bloody Cretan campaign. During this 24-year-long campaign (1645–1669) Ottoman expeditionary forces conducted several siege operations against modern and massive Venetian fortresses. The last and most important siege operation was launched against Candia (Kandiya) and lasted three years. Because of the ineffectiveness of their artillery against modern fortification, the Ottomans depended solely on mining and engineering operations. At Candia the Ottoman engineers chose the St. Andrea bastion and directed most of their mining and engineering activity against this bastion. Even though the defenders concentrated most of their forces in and around St. Andrea, the Ottomans did capture the bastion and the fortress after 1,369 successful explosions of mines and 69 assaults, but at the heavy cost of nearly 60,000 casualties over three long years.[97]

Closely following the experiences and lessons learned from the Cretan campaign, and making use of intelligence about the fortifications and defensive system (other than recent modifications) given by renegades and spies, Ottoman engineers and miners slowly but professionally and methodically chose the next target. This time they chose the Burg bastion, prepared plans, and then dug and constructed lines of circumvallation, parallels, zig zag trenches (Sıçan Yolu), protected gunnery positions (Domuz Damı), and earthen ramparts (Tabya). Mustafa Pasha disregarded the establishment of lines of contravallation that would defend the besiegers against a possible relieving force. This lack of lines of contravallation was also one of the peculiarities of the Cretan campaign. Similarly, the masking force was also neglected by allocating only several light cavalry squadrons and observation posts to it. Above all, Mustafa Pasha did not bring the heavy artillery pieces to Vienna that were available in Budin and Belgrade. We know that several generals and staff members repeatedly pointed out the importance of these. However, without any apparent reason other than over confidence and arrogance he did not add heavy artillery into the siege train and only brought approximately 30 medium and 95 light cannons to Vienna.[98]

The siege strategy gave ample opportunities to the Viennese defenders, including the concentration of forces around the Burg bastion, moving units and workers with relative ease, and most importantly bidding time for the arrival of the relieving force. Additionally, by employing mining operations massively the Ottomans forced the Viennese to learn how to conduct counter-mining operations in the meantime.[99]

The Ottoman miners patiently and methodically dug towards the bastion. They made excellent use of the terrain and the suburban buildings. The elaborate designs of the entire siege earthen works were much appreciated later by observers and survivors of the siege. The first attack was launched on July 23 after an unsuccessful mine explosion. Two days later Ottoman volunteers (Serdengeçti), who were rewarded with cash prizes or permanent employment to the standing corps, penetrated the outer defenses but were repulsed. Inch-by-inch Ottoman miners and volunteers fought their way into the fortifications. At last on August 12, volunteers captured a part of the inner defenses of the bastion. It was one of the turning points of the siege, and suddenly victory seemed very near. However, the defenders managed to restrict Ottoman gains, and the Ottoman volunteers were unable to penetrate further without the support of powerful artillery.[100]

In the meantime, the Habsburgs and their allies slowly but surely gathered their forces, and even slow columns of Polish units reached the border. Surprisingly, Mustafa Pasha did not seem to understand the urgency of the situation and failed to pay much attention to the activities of his cavalry units and his allies. His confidence in the military potential of Thököly turned out to be faulty, and he did not stop or disrupt the concentration of the Habsburg forces. Thököly launched several attacks, essentially raids, repeatedly between August 22 and 24—all of which failed. Poor command decisions combined with the unreliability of some of his troops resulted in the loss of the 6,000-strong Ottoman screening force. Making matters worse, instead of focusing on the enemy build up, gathering intelligence, and conducting reconnaissance, the remaining Ottoman light cavalry continued burning and pillaging the countryside.[101]

The Ottoman besiegers finally increased their attacks, and bit by bit the main defensive lines began to crumble after vicious and bloody fights between September 2 and 8. Victory seemed closer than ever before, but still Mustafa Pasha seemed unable to concentrate the might of the Ottoman army and gave defenders time to reorganize the defenses. Obviously he not only underestimated the will of the Viennese defenders but also undervalued artillery and other technical means needed to capture the city. The slow and leisurely tempo of the siege gave the Habsburgs time to gather relieving forces, and Mustafa Pasha's neglect to take security measures, including lines of contravallation and masking force, left his units unprotected. Surprisingly, several captured enemy prisoners had already informed him of the enemy plans and their concentration, but the ever-optimistic Mustafa Pasha insisted on the continuation of the siege without allocating any forces for the protection of his own army.[102]

Even at the very last minute Mustafa Pasha only redirected two-thirds of the besiegers to counter the relieving force on September 12, 1683. Pressed between a strong fortress and a strong relieving force, without any effective artillery support and defensive protection, the Ottoman army in a loose formation of 28,000 men faced the 80,000 men of the Habsburgs and their allies. The so-called battle of Kahlenberg was actually an anarchic series of clashes in which none of the commanders had effective control of their respective troops. After several desperate standoffs the Ottoman units began to crumble under the attacks of superior Habsburg and Polish forces. Adding to the confusion, Tatars, Hungarians, and Wallachians left their Ottoman masters in the middle of the battle and fled. Mustafa Pasha's late order to reinforce the battle with other besieging units did not help, and his combat units fled one by one, leaving 10,000 casualties and thousands of support personnel behind. The victorious allies raced towards the Ottoman camp for looting, leaving the Ottoman units to flee the field almost unhindered.[103]

The defeat was disastrous, and although it had an especially damaging affect on morale caused by the seemingly narrow loss of a spectacular victory, the main body of the expeditionary force managed to escape and regroup. The main problem after the battle was not reviving the beaten army, but managing a crisis in command. Everybody within the Ottoman government and military began to look for scapegoats. Mustafa Pasha summarily executed several generals in order to cover his own failures, but without success. Then rival interest groups managed to convince Mehmed IV to execute Mustafa Pasha, which was duly done—leaving the beaten army without a commander. Against all odds the regrouped Ottoman force faced the victorious Polish forces at Parkany (Ciğerdelen) on October 7. Amazingly, the demoralized Ottoman force beat the Poles, but at a price, their unreliable Tatar and Hungarian allies fled away once again. Two days later the Poles, reinforced by the arrival of Habsburg units, crushed the now outnumbered and vulnerable Ottoman defenders—only 2,200 of them managed to escape, leaving 9,000 casualties and 1,200 captured.[104]

While the Ottoman military was suffering from the aftershocks of an unforeseen defeat and without effective strategic and operational leadership due to the purge and death of numerous commanders, the Habsburgs, the Polish-Lithuanian Commonwealth, Venice, and the Papacy announced the establishment of the Holy Alliance in March 1684. Suddenly the Ottoman Empire was engaged in an unexpected, multifront war (which was to last about 16 years). The administration mobilized all the available manpower and brought into force several emergency decrees, which effectively abolished all the exemptions.[105] The performance of Ottoman military during the War of the Holy Alliance is very complex and difficult to portray. On the one hand, the Ottoman military suffered from humiliating defeats—mostly against the Habsburgs, rebellions, and the loss of nearly all of Hungary. On the other hand, it was a period of heroic defenses, such as the defense of Budin (the first lasted 108 days in 1684 and the second and the final lasted 78 days in 1686), Kanisza (a four-year blockade and siege), Belgrade, Chios (Sakız), Azov, and Kamenets in Podolia. There were occasionally surprising victories like the recapture of Belgrade and Niš and the battles of Kačanik (January 2, 1690), Lugos (September 22, 1695), Bega (Ulaş) (August 20, 1696) as well as desperate efforts like the battles of Szlankamen (Salankamen) (August 19, 1691), and Zenta (September 11, 1697). Time after time, outnumbered and demoralized Ottoman units managed to defeat or stop Habsburg, Venetian, and Polish forces, which paid dearly for their underestimation of the military potential and will of the Ottoman military. But obviously the Ottoman military of 1699, after the treaty of Karlowitz (Karlofça) ended the war, was totally different from the proud besiegers of Vienna of 1683.[106]

Various factors affected the conduct of Ottoman military performance during the War of the Holy Alliance as well as the outcome. It is evident that the Ottoman failure had more to do with politics and diplomacy than with the military. Even though Ottoman military shortcomings, especially in leadership and in the artillery corps, were clear, these did not greatly affect the outcome. The Ottoman governing elite's myopia in international politics and diplomacy to forecast and understand the possibility and danger of an alliance or coalition due to the recent changes and shifting patterns was the main reason for the Ottoman collapse.[107]

The first and most important result of the War of the Holy Alliance was the abrupt end of the relatively successful military transformation.[108] The trained and battle hardened cadres of the transformed military were lost without any chance of renewal by new cadres. The situation in terms of the officer corps was more desperate. The Ottoman officer training system depended upon time-consuming and meticulous on-the-job training within the corps. The system was not capable of training large numbers of officers in times of need. Moreover, the oral tradition of passing know-how and experiences was very vulnerable to the unexpected loss of old cadres, in which centuries-old knowledge could be lost forever. Indeed, this was the case during this traumatic period. With heavy officer casualties, high rotations of personnel, and the sudden introduction of massive numbers of recruits within the standing army corps, the traditional officer training system collapsed. This development would become the largest problem for Ottoman military reformers during the eighteenth century.

The second result was actually not a new issue but rather the worsening of an old problem: military rebellions and politicization. The standing military corps, especially the Janissaries, increasingly became a tool of the competing political elites. The units rebelled frequently, even during campaigns, without consideration of the possible negative results. The worst example of this took place during the campaign season of 1687. Most of the soldiers of the standing army corps rebelled after the fateful decision of the commander in chief, Sarı Süleyman Pasha, to conduct a dangerous maneuver during a storm on August 27, 1687. The rebels chose a new commander and marched on Istanbul, leaving the frontier fortress garrisons to their fate. An appeasement policy and concessions did not stop the rebels, and they reached Istanbul while Habsburg contingents conquered the weakly defended border regions. The rebels caused havoc within the capital city, dethroned Mehmed IV, and executed many high-ranking officials. The anarchic rule of the rebels ended only after a rising by the citizens of Istanbul in April 1688, during which many ringleaders perished. This military rebellion not only ruined the campaign season of 1687 and 1688 but was instrumental in the fall of many fortresses, including Belgrade.[109]

The third result was a reversal of Ottoman military strategy from the offensive to the defensive. Even though dreams of reconquering the lost provinces continued on until the treaty of Pasarowitz, in reality the governing elite and most high-ranking officers recognized the importance of fortifications and the reorganization of the entire military based on the considerations of an overall defensive strategy. Embedded in this drastic change, the frontier regions and the provincial units guarding them gained importance while the centralized standing corps lost it.[110] The psychological impact of this change was enormous for the army (and the public as a whole), who were well accustomed to an offensive and ever victorious military tradition. Clearly this change also affected the prestige and the power of the military within the Ottoman system. The Ottoman military would not recover from this loss of power, prestige, and face until the second half of the nineteenth century.

The fourth result was actually more political than military. It was the mass exodus of Muslims living to the north of Danube to the south and the increasing unrest of Christians living around the Danube. The outcome of these developments, from a military perspective, was the increasing disloyalty of the Christian auxiliary troops, a requirement to allocate more troops for interior security missions (including the suppression of uprisings in the Banat and Čiprovci in 1688 and Karpoš in 1689), and an increasing dependence on the Muslim population for recruitment and levies. The disastrous defeat did, however, increase the solidarity and unity of the Muslim groups who became more willing to fight and pay the costs of the wars. Even if the immediate political and military impact of these developments were limited, its psychological and social effects were still very important. For the first time the disloyalty of Christian subjects began to be seen as a significant problem, and the general attitude toward Christian auxiliary units changed totally, regarding them as liabilities rather than as assets. Consequently, their role in the frontier defensive system was diminished and Muslim groups replaced them.[111]

The Rise of the Governors and the Provincial Units

The Treaty of Karlowitz effectively fixed the Ottoman-Habsburg border around the Danube River and its tributaries and the Ottoman military had to accustom itself to this strategic change.[112] As already discussed, the Ottoman military lost its strategic offensive capability against the Habsburgs (but not against other adversaries) and retained only a very limited theatre offensive capability. So, it is no great wonder that the Ottoman government was more than satisfied to rely on a defensive strategy first against the Habsburgs and later against the Russians. By this time the standing army corps was already overstretched from constant campaigns and rebellions elsewhere, and they were far from the old corps in terms of combat efficiency and discipline. The new Grand Vizier, Amcazade Hüseyin Pasha, reduced the inflated numbers of standing corps by half, but even this harsh measure did not increase the military quality of the remaining soldiers. Consequently, the Istanbul-based standing corps was not the ideal candidate to man distant border fortresses permanently.[113]

There was a military necessity to tolerate the rule of strong governors and other provincial magnates. The Ottoman government's policy basically acknowledged an already ongoing process, which gave the entire responsibility for the defense and interior security of border provinces to their governor generals and Ayans (provincial magnates). The governors already had powerful personal retinues (financed by seizing estates and assigning them to their household members). The new policy gave them rights to create or reorganize provincial units (other than timariots) according to the geography of the border. All of the soldiers, including cannoneers, were to be locally recruited from volunteers or villagers and organized into companies. One or several companies would be grouped under a company grade officer, who was responsible for a border region that included small fortresses, towers, and guard houses. (In Bosnia, for example, a Kapudan [captain] was responsible for an area called a Kapudanlık [Kaptanija].) Even though the government more or less gave free hand to the governors, it still held sanction authority and paid special attention to the commissioning and assignment of officers. Additionally, by keeping the assignment and allocation of cash funds (Ocaklık) for the wages of these units, the government had a strong lever to control them.[114]

The province of Bosnia provides the best and most important example of these new militia-like border defense units. Thanks to the efforts of a series of competent governors, chief among them Hekimoğlu Ali Pasha, Bosnian provincial defense units achieved a high standard of effectiveness and kept it for a century. Highly motivated and well-funded, trained, and led Bosnian units not only defended their respective regions properly but also conducted offensive operations against the Habsburg military border region (Militär Gränitz or Vojna Krajina)[115] and the superior Habsburg conventional forces. They played an important role in the recapture of Belgrade during the Ottoman-Habsburg War of 1737–1739.[116]

Interestingly, at the start of the hostilities, strong elite mobile forces numbering 5,000 men were called to reinforce the Russian front, which crippled the defense of Bosnia. The Habsburg forces under the command of Prince Hildburghausen entered into Bosnia using five different approaches on June 29, 1737. The reorganized Bosnian units under retired field grade Ottoman officers managed to annihilate one of the Habsburg columns in Ostravica on July 22 and focused on the main group, which had already laid siege to Banjaluka (Banaluka). They secretly approached the confident and careless besiegers and launched a daring raid, capturing their camp and most of the artillery park on July 24. The confused and panic-stricken Habsburg force suffered difficulty in withstanding the Bosnian attacks and retreating towards the Vrbas River and unknowingly fell into a well-prepared ambush. Only half of the combat troops managed to swim to the other side, leaving their comrades and support units to the mercy of Bosnians. The disaster, in terms of casualties, was larger than the Ottoman defeat at Vienna, nearly 40,000 Habsburg casualties. The Habsburgs not only lost any chance of continuing their offensive against vicious joint Ottoman-Bosnian attacks but they soon lost all the territory they had conquered in 1717 and eventually Belgrade.[117]

Not all the provinces followed the Bosnian pattern, and in most of the southern and eastern provinces and in Northern Black Sea region the Ottoman government had to depend more on tribal leaders, including Cossacks hetmans, Arab Sheikhs, and other local magnates and acknowledge their already well-established semi-autonomous rule. However, their loyalty was always problematic and their frequent underhanded deals with enemies were notorious. Of course, constant negotiations and bargaining was the norm. As a result, the massive Ottoman northern and eastern fortresses like Kili, Özü, Akkirman, Kars, and Erzurum were tasked not only to stop enemy advances until the arrival of the main army and act as forward staging bases but were also necessary to keep the locals loyal.[118]

The government had to solve difficult problems like allocating financial resources for the expanses of the increasingly expensive fortresses, providing up-to-date weapons and equipment, and procuring massive amounts of gunpowder. In terms of recruiting fortress garrisons in the east, the government had to depend more on mercenaries and tribal warriors because of the proven uselessness and unwillingness of the Janissaries. Even though both of these groups were very problematic and rebellious, in order to carry out the tedious and dangerous job of guarding the fortresses, the government had no alternative but to keep them in line using all sorts of methods and tools.[119]

The Russo-Turkish War of 1711 provides a good example of the importance of fortresses in the victorious outcome of the campaign. The Russian Czar, Peter I, began hostilities using inaccurate intelligence estimates that underestimated the military might of the Ottomans and their allies (Tatars and Cossacks) and which exaggerated unrest in Moldavia and Wallachia. Peter was right to target the Ottoman fortresses and forward mounting bases at the delta of the Danube—especially İbrail and Kalas. However, the Ottoman expeditionary forces marched faster than estimated, and by making better use of terrain they reached the staging bases before the Russians. The ever-stubborn Peter did not understand the vulnerability of his situation, and after several wrong maneuvers to counter Ottoman advance became mired in the marshlands of Pruth on July 18, 1711. The Janissary assaults (albeit unwilling) put the already tired Russians, who were worn down by heat and illness, into a desperate situation. Unfortunately, the Ottoman commander in chief, Baltacı Süleyman Pasha, instead of destroying the weakening Russians was easily satisfied with Peter's offer of peace that returned the Azov fortress and several other small concessions to the Ottomans.[120]

Whatever the limitations of Süleyman Pasha as a military leader and a diplomat, the campaign of 1711 showed clearly the virtues of an Ottoman defensive strategy against Russia, which would remain the same until 1850s. Unfortunately, we do not know the details of the military government system of either the eastern provinces or the Black Sea region. (Indeed, the field needs more monographs on technical details of this region—especially during eighteenth century).[121]

The province of Damascus (Şam) provides a totally unique example of military organization. In 1708 the government surprisingly lifted the obligation of Damascus to provide units for military campaigns while, at the same time, tried desperately to mobilize untapped manpower sources. Instead, it tasked Damascene units with the responsibility for the organization and execution of the pilgrimage (Haj) to Mecca and Medina and also for interior security duties (especially against unruly nomadic tribes). Actually, by rendering this difficult and strange decision, the government was openly recognizing its limitations and difficulties in mobilizing and transporting the military manpower of Damascus to the faraway theatres of war and, at the same, stabilize the province during the absence of its military.[122]

Damascus never provided enough manpower and always experienced difficulty in fulfilling its military obligations. Moreover, the meager Damascene units (only about 500 soldiers were available for campaigns) either showed up very late or so exhausted that they practically had no value in any campaign. So, from a military perspective the absence of these troops had little effect on the overall combat efficiency of the Ottoman military machine. In turn, they would be more useful by stabilizing the province and providing protection for the pilgrimage. The successful execution of the yearly pilgrimage was very important for the prestige and legitimacy of the empire in the eyes of the entire Muslim world. However, increasing Bedouin attacks on pilgrimage convoys and other difficulties in execution (including billeting and providing transport) caused the Ottomans to come under serious criticism. Thus, from a political perspective the allocation of Damascene units for the pilgrimage was a wise decision. Additionally, the Damascus governor came under the obligation of paying an exemption fee for not participating in campaigns, which generated revenues for the state.[123]

The complex composition of the Damascene military is important in understanding the difficulties of the Ottoman government in terms of making use of the empire's potential. There were four main military groups in Damascus. The first group was composed of local Janissaries (Yerli), who were the successors of the Janissary unit left to guard the city after its conquest in 1516. The second group was the so-called Imperial Janissaries (commonly called Kapıkulu by the locals), who were positioned in Damascus after a large military rebellion in 1659. Both of these groups had already become part of the local society and politics and had practically no military value. The third group was composed of mercenaries, in general service to the governors as a part of their retinue. This group was actually a strange mixture of Anatolian Levends, Kurdish musketeers, and North African mercenaries. The fourth group was timariot cavalry. They were the biggest group during the sixteenth century and the first half of the seventeenth century. However, their numerical and military strength reduced rapidly during the last quarter of the seventeenth century. Most of the estates were allocated or captured by the governors, Ayans, or Janissaries. As a group they ceased to exist at the beginning of the eighteenth century. All of these groups had difficulty cooperating with each other and preferred to spend their time in local politics and trade rather than on military matters. However, instead of abolishing them the Ottoman government mobilized them for pilgrimage and stabilization duties.[124]

Surprisingly, the policy worked and produced results until the 1750s. The government effectively curbed the numbers of Janissaries, sometimes violently as in the example of the local Janissary rebellion and suppression of February 1746, and used different groups to balance different interests. By limiting the Damascus governors' opportunity for promotion within the system, the government forced them to focus more on local matters and achieved effective control over the province.[125]

Both the Bosnian and Damascus models are instructive in understanding the difficulties facing the Ottoman Empire and its pragmatic solutions in meeting them. While the government managed to defend its borders by using locals more and giving them freedom of action in Bosnia, it managed to fight effectively against internal troublemakers and rebels by following different formula in Damascus. Moreover, these two divergent, but complementary, policies limited the ambitions of governors and Ayans (provincial magnates) for at least another century and helped make them dependent on the central government.[126]

The rise of the governors and their households accelerated the demise of the Kapıkulu corps, the sultan's household, and the sultan himself. Unfortunately for the empire, the successful policies and decisions of the sixteenth and seventeenth centuries eventually created the nemesis of the system—successful local families, who excelled within the Ottoman military administrative tradition and used it for their own benefit. Despite the fact that most of the Ayans did not strive for an independent rule and were mostly interested in their own welfare and prestige, their increased local autonomy caused the decentralization of the empire during the last quarter of the eighteenth century and first half of the nineteenth century. In this regard the empire was out of step with Europe, where absolutism was on the rise and strong kings were centralizing their power in nation-states.[127]

Early Reform Efforts

The first discussions about military reforms began surprisingly early during the so-called "Golden Age of Süleyman the Magnificent" which, according to the classical scholars, was the apex of Ottoman military power. Also surprisingly, it was the members of the new bureaucracy who first formulated the dialogue of reform. These ideas began to circulate within the governing elite of the empire in the form of "advice literature" (Nasihatname). The form of advice literature was a well-established literary tradition within Islamic literature. The basic idea behind this literary tradition had been to advise the kings to govern their society justly and wisely and to pass on the accumulated experiences of the previous generations. Thus, this well-recognized and respected tradition gave the early reformers the means to voice their ideas freely as long as they remained within the literary format.[128]

Lütfi Pasha, Gelibolulu Mustafa Ali, Hasan Kafi el-Akhisari, Veysi Efendi, and Katib Çelebi were some of the famous early reformers, who wrote down their ideas in the form of advice literature. However, the best known reform writer was, without doubt, Koçi Bey, who presented his work to Murad IV in 1631. Koçi Bey actually compiled all the important points of his predecessors and rewrote them in a beautiful style.[129] Most of these writers, including the anonymous ones, were conservatives who belonged to the new bureaucracy, and they recommended the reestablishment and conservation of idealized institutions from the classical period of the Golden Age.[130]

A full discussion of the reformer's political, socioeconomic, and religious ideas is outside the parameters of this study, and the focus instead is on their criticisms of the Ottoman military and their recommendations. As might be expected from their highly conservative and traditionalist approach, they identified the main reason behind the deterioration of the military as corruption and disuse of the classical military institutions, which they immediately linked to the lost virtues of a centralized, efficient, and rational classical system. They saw the growth of the Kapıkulu corps, especially the Janissaries, and introduction of foreign elements (Ecnebi or Saplama) into the corps as instrumental in increasing corruption and in causing poor performance.[131] Additionally, the Timar system was neglected and afterwards weakened by assigning estates to nonmilitary groups or individuals. In this way the government destroyed the balance between the standing corps and provincial units, which had been the backbone of the Ottoman military system.[132]

According to the writers, the only satisfactory solution to the ever-mounting number of military problems was to reintroduce the classical system—not the real one but a highly idealized one—and its regulations with renewed energy and harsh punishments. In their view dramatic action was required. For example, the sale of offices, bribes, and all other corrupt practices must be stopped at once. The personnel strength of the Kapıkulu corps must be reduced and purified of foreign elements. The Sipahis must be strengthened by reorganization and by the restoration of their estates. But, above all, military command must be united under the absolute leadership of the sultan himself. The sultan must lead the army and personally establish the example for his soldiers.[133]

Except Hasan Kafi, who actually observed the Long War,[134] none of the advice literature authors had any idea of the changing combat environment, the effects of the introduction and diffusion of new firearms, or the requirements of extended attritional wars. Their general unawareness of international developments, their rigid approach to problems, and their complete hostility to the rise of new elites, especially protégé bureaucrats, as well as their unfamiliarity with a monetary economy and firearms literally blinded them. Fortunately for the empire the elasticity and pragmatism of the Ottoman military administrative system, which the advice authors despised, turned out to be the backbone of Ottoman survival. Moreover, even though their suggestions did find some receptive ears and eager sultans, in reality these suggestions turned out to be unpractical and received only lip service from the leading members of the government.[135]

Surprisingly, the influence of the advice authors on historians of the following centuries and modern scholars was more powerful than on their contemporaries. Some modern scholars have taken the advice authors' flawed descriptions of the classical period (and their arguments about the decline of the empire, which were actually devised more according to Ibni Khaldun's cycle of governance than reality) without question and without confirming these ideas through archival documentation. In fact, the advice authors were not neutral observers of developments and trends but just the opposite; they were active participants in the struggle for power. So their views most of the time were self-serving (and were the views of the losers as well), as in the example of Gelibolulu Mustafa Ali, who longed for the idealized past. Indeed, this lack of honest objectivity was the main reason why they encountered difficulty in understanding military transformation within the country and abroad.[136]

As can be expected, the early military reformers conducted their limited reforms without any coordinated strategic plan or target. In reality these were more of a kind of disciplinary operation than real reforms. After the tragic end of the Osman II Genç (young) attempt to reorganize the Kapıkulu corps in 1622, Murad IV (1628–1640) and the viziers of Köprülü family (1656–1676) successfully carried out their respective limited military reforms and harsh disciplinary operations effectively. Hundreds of officials and thousands of Kapıkulu soldiers were sacked and some of them executed. Wide-scale inspections and harsh punishments helped to correct corrupt financial-administrative practices and limited bribes and abuses.[137] Thanks to these disciplinary operations, more effective Ottoman expeditionary forces successfully conducted a series of long-range campaigns against specific targets like Revan (1635), Baghdad (1638–1639), Varat (1660), Uyvar (1663), Kamanets (1672), and Çehrin (1678).[138]

However, these early reforms achieved only limited and short-term results because the reformers still misunderstood the actual dynamics of the military transformation in Europe. From our perspective the main difficulty of the early reformers centered on their professional occupations. None of them, either authors of the advice literature or the leaders of the reforms, came from the military classes. Most of them came from the bureaucracy and others from the judiciary-religious class. Moreover, most of these new bureaucrats were part of the new patron-client relationship that negated significantly the role of sultan and palace. The bureaucrats were recruited and trained by high officials within households, and promotion within the system depended not only on their personal success but more often on the efficiency of connections.[139] In effect this led to unqualified and inexperienced individuals, in positions of power, attempting to change complex systems.

The change of composition of the governing elite brought many advantages, including the widening of the recruitment base and further increasing social mobility. With the decline of the old palace schools and Kapıkulu training system, however, the new elite had no means to acquire military know-how other than actual field experience, which was something very rare until the third quarter of the eighteenth century. In short, they understood the need for reforms but suffered difficulty in understanding the requirements of the military profession and the new dynamics of the battlefield. Similar to contemporary European experiences, while the bureaucracy became prominent, the military profession lost its popularity and power within the government.[140]

In fact, the empire had the necessary military experience and understandings needed for the success of military reforms. Ottoman combat unit commanders and officers, especially the ones on the Habsburg frontier, were already aware of the new military developments and were actually applying them successfully against the enemy.[141] However, they had difficulty in passing these proficiencies as well as new technical developments to the central government functionaries because of an oral tradition and on-the-job training system that tended to keep information within their unit structure. Unfortunately, this traditional system was very fragile when held against sudden losses of too many cadre during disasters, such as had occurred after the second siege of Vienna, and sometimes valuable information and insights were lost in this manner. Finally, the malaise caused by long decades of military and financial neglect and hemorrhaging effectively negated hundred years of accumulated knowledge.

Without having a good understanding of new military requirements the early reformers perceived most of the problems as related to a lack of discipline and a disregard for classical rules and regulations. So the obvious solution for them was to enforce classical methods and regulations harshly without any restraint of concessions.[142]

Murad IV and the Köprülü viziers became famous for their harsh punishments and summary executions. Similarly, Kuyucu Murad Pasha suppressed the wide-scale Celali rebellions with massacres and the burning down of entire regions.

For obvious reasons the reform efforts remained totally a function of the personality of the leaders. Reforms tended not to be institutionalized and, furthermore, remained isolated from the rank and file. So, relative success depended upon the personal determination, decisiveness, and consistency of leaders themselves. Leaders often made use of the conflicting interests between different military groups against each other in order to carry out their reform measures. At the same time, they frequently gave concessions to powerful individuals or groups to keep them loyal. These shortsighted power politics brought immediate but temporary success. In the long run, relations between the institutions deteriorated further and excessive use of force pushed the system to its limits, making it more fragile than ever before. In short, ineffective reforms caused the Ottoman Empire to continue fighting extended campaign seasons and prolonged sieges and counter-sieges with ill-disciplined and poorly trained forces. A final legacy of these early failed reforms was a training system that remained firmly rooted in oral and on-the-job traditions without any formal institutions or formal written system, which encouraged a regime of secrecy as the norm against outsiders and other Ottoman groups.

Eighteenth Century Reforms until Selim III

The Treaty of Passarowitz (Pasarofça) of 1718 was instrumental in ending any hope of recovering the lost provinces and was also seen as the final blow to the image of Ottoman military invincibility. However, it also provided a much needed long period of peace after the series of devastating wars and it began a new era—the so-called Tulip Period (Lale Devri) (1718–1730). The Tulip Period was, in all ways, a turning point in the history of the Ottoman military because for the first time most members of the governing elite not only accepted European military superiority but also perceived the need to understand the reasons behind it.[143]

Ahmed III gave wide-ranging responsibilities and power to his son-in-law Grand Vizier Damad İbrahim Pasha (Nevşehirli), who was to play an important role in carrying out new reforms. Following the chief recommendation of the advice literature he tried to maintain peace at all costs while reforming the empire. His second move was to send Yirmisekiz Çelebi Mehmed Efendi as an ambassador to France in order to gain first-hand impressions about all aspects of change in contemporary Europe. Contrary to the conventional modern perception (many still believe in the presence of an early form of an "iron curtain"), the Ottoman governing elite never lost contact with Europe. The problem was that these contacts remained within small groups of the elite, which could neither influence the decision-making process nor become part of the common understanding until the second quarter of the eighteenth century.[144]

Çelebi Mehmed fulfilled his arduous duty with success during his brief plenipotentiary of 1720–1721. He visited a variety of places and carefully noted all details as well as his impressions. In a way his observations were like snapshot photos of French society and institutions. But surprisingly he paid little attention to military matters, and he wrote almost nothing about the French army, making no concrete military observations. However, Çelebi Mehmed's return and the materials he brought created an excitement within the Ottoman governing elite and intellectual classes. His major findings were highly appreciated by the government and had profound effects on Ottoman politics. Unfortunately, the real reason behind the plenipotentiary was forgotten and a kind of hysteric Francophilia set in. Instead of focusing on the basic findings of the mission, the Ottoman governing elite preferred to imitate French high society's manners and tastes by building luxurious European-style mansions and gardens (not to forget the craze for tulips) and by importing large quantities of luxurious consumer goods. Their extravaganza was destined to alienate large segments of the society.[145]

In addition to diplomatic fact-finding visits, other new windows and opportunities opened for the Ottomans. Many foreign embassies were opened, and the empire became a favorite destination for Europeans for a variety of reasons during the eighteenth century. The new government made use of these European visitors as well as a few renegades. These Europeans came from all strata of the society and many had their own agendas, like the bizarre and ambitious Huguenot project. A Huguenot officer named de Rochefort proposed establishing modern European-style regiments equipped with modern weapons and equipment in exchange for estates to be assigned to Huguenot refugees for settlement. He also promised to set up modern industrial workshops. After long discussions, the government rejected his project for understandable reasons, including the inherent danger of assigning lands to European immigrants.[146]

Several others with less ambitious proposals for employment were able to gain the confidence of the government. We know that various European officers and technicians were employed within the Ottoman military, but only after converting to Islam. The military did not ask them to be pious Muslims and only superficial conversion was enough to gain employment. But even so this requirement turned out to be a serious barrier for most of the talented European officers, who could easily find jobs in less demanding countries like Russia or the Americas.

The most prominent reform effort of this period, the establishment of the first Turkish printing house, was achieved by a modest Hungarian or Transylvanian renegade named İbrahim Müteferrika, with the support of Damad İbrahim Pasha and Said Mehmed Efendi, in 1727. Even though this reform was not a military reform, it affected the military educational system drastically in the coming decades. It also provides a case study to understand the shortcomings and structural problems of both the Ottoman reforms and reformers.

The Ottoman governing elite learned the importance of printing and printing presses approximately 300 years late (surprising some of the contemporary observers)[147] from several sources, thanks to a renegade and the plenipotentiary of Çelebi Mehmed. In fact, several minority groups already founded their presses. For example, Jewish refugees from Spain established one in 1495 and brought their accumulated experience to the empire. Similarly, the Ottoman vassal state of Transylvania became an important printing center of Eastern Europe during the sixteenth century, but this development also did not affect the Ottoman Empire.[148] However, instead of making use of locally available know-how and technical expertise, the government preferred to import it. One can see the repetitions of this pattern—an inability to use locally available know-how—again and again in the history of Ottoman reforms, in this case delaying progress by hundreds of years.

The Müteferrika Press did not fulfill the expectations of its founders. The first book, which was a dictionary, was published two years after the establishment of the press, and the press managed to publish just 17 books, of which only three were science related, during its 16 years of existence. This is a clear example of a second structural problem. The Ottoman reformers had a tendency to move very cautiously and did not have the courage to face opposition and the wider public. Because of this tendency the actual output of reform projects were mere shadows of their original projections, never meeting expectations and sporadically affecting the system in the long term.

In contrast to commonly held opinions, the religious establishment and conservatives showed only a limited reaction to the press and did not block this reform.[149] However, the new press was unable to capture the interest of government officials, intellectuals, and the public, and so demand for its products failed to materialize. The press was unable to sell even its limited titles and bankrupted in a short while, and its backers lost interest in the endeavor. This provides an example of the third structural problem. Often the capricious Ottoman reformers lost interest soon after launching a reform project and moved on to other projects, forgetting the reasons for establishing it in the first place and paying scant attention to its subsequent fate.[150]

İbrahim Müteferrika played a small but crucial role, not only founding the press but also writing an important booklet in which he tried to present the real reasons behind Europe's superiority. After describing the important aspects of the Enlightenment and the new political structure of the European states he tried to point out the Ottoman shortcomings. He suggested the largest problem for the empire was not a generalized ignorance of everything coming out of Europe but rather a casual disregard for critical new scientific and technological developments. This ignorance also affected the military, which was falling behind because it lacked a trained officer corps and an effective command-control system. Müteferrika also tried to explain some aspects of modern European militaries and introduced the first Turkish versions of several key military terms.[151]

In 1730, a localized disorder escalated and turned to a popular and violent rebellion (so-called Patrona Halil rebellion), which indirectly put an end to the reforms. It was an extraordinary rebellion in which nearly all segments and groups of Istanbul joined the rebels. (Artisans and small merchants especially played a crucial role.)[152] Even though the rebels did not specifically target the reforms but the dissolute governing elite, by losing its protectors and supporters the reforms were left to their fate and eventually faded away.[153] The spirit of reform remained within a closely knit group of officials, but it remained secretive and weak until the arrival of the French military mission in 1774.

The most important reform of this interim period (1730–1770) was the reform of the Humbaracı Ocağı (bombardier corps). The Humbaracı corps was not an independent corps and played a minor military role throughout the classical period. During the seventeenth century it even lost its minor role and became more or less extinct; an organization on paper only. According to the reformers, however, under the leadership of Grand Vizier Topal Osman Pasha it was an ideal candidate for transformation. The corps had no effective socioeconomic power base and its personnel strength was minimal. Moreover, it was a totally technical corps, and changing it would not provoke the resistance of conservatives. Osman Pasha had an additional asset in the person of a French aristocrat, who had taken refuge in the Ottoman Empire and willing employment in its military.

Claude Alexandre Comte de Bonneval was an unusual personality. He was a very talented and daring officer, but he was also well known for his quick temper and incompatible character. Because of this volatile combination he had to take refuge first with the Habsburgs in 1706 and then with the Ottomans in 1729. In order not to be handed back to the Habsburgs he converted to Islam and took a new name, Ahmed. His presence was immediately noticed and Osman Pasha took him under his protection, invested him with the rank of governor general (Beylerbeyi), and tasked him to reorganize the Humbaracıs into a modern European-style technical corps.[154]

Bonneval, or with his new name and title Humbaracı Ahmed Pasha, immediately started the reorganization with the help of three other French renegades and two French officers, who were assigned by the French government. First a new salaried corps with a strength of 300 personnel was established, followed by the construction of custom-built barracks. Due to the timariot legacy of the corps nearly all the personnel were recruited from Bosnia, but the most important part of this reform package was the establishment of a technical school within the corps, the Hendesehane (school of geometry).

The Hendesehane was a modest school with limited enrollment. However, it was the first European-style military high school in the empire and turned out to be the forefather of all Ottoman military technical schools. Historical information about the new corps and the school is very limited, but it is known that because of the secretive and timid approach of the governing elite it did not become a springboard for progress as planned. It affected only several hundred soldiers and suffered huge problems due to constant interventions, financial problems, and simple ignorance. The ambitious political maneuvers of the complex Bonneval did not help, and he was exiled in 1738 due to his political activities, which were unrelated to his role in military reforms. Like the ones before it, the Humbaracı reforms faded away in the meantime.[155]

Another Grand Vizier, Koca (also known as Mektupçu) Ragıb Pasha (1755–1773), tried to reenergize the corps and its school by collecting the old Humbaracıs while continuing its modern training and education system. He even managed to conduct field exercises. However, his efforts also failed and did not produce any meaningful or permanent results.[156]

This interim period was also instrumental for the rise of a new generation of reformist bureaucrats. Two important experiences made them distinct from their predecessors: combat experiences and direct contacts with Europe in official capacities. Ahmed Resmi Efendi (1700–1783) was an early example of this new generation. After classical scribal training Ahmed Resmi served as ambassador to Vienna (1757–1758) and Berlin (1763–1764). Additionally, he performed important administrative duties at the front during the disastrous Ottoman-Russian war of 1768–1774, and he was the chief Ottoman negotiator of the Küçük Kaynarca peace treaty. Thanks to this unique combination of experiences he witnessed the direct results of the empire's structural problems and was familiar with its military deficiencies.[157]

In contrast to previous Ottoman diplomatic reports, Ahmed Resmi gave sound military information about the countries he had visited. His descriptions of the Prussian military are especially revealing in understanding his perceptions and priorities. He noted that living conditions for Prussian soldiers were very hard. Their provisions were meager and accommodations more than Spartan, but surprisingly they continuously participated in rigorous training and maneuvers. Similarly, their command-control and discipline were very good. At this point he switched his focus from soldiers to their officers. Obviously he was impressed by the gentlemen academies (rittersakademie) of the Prussians in which boys from aristocratic families underwent a long and application-based military training. He saw no negatives and was obviously unaware of the limitations of this type of institution (or, of course, the current discussions on the establishment of academic military institutions).[158]

Ahmed Resmi's portrait of Frederick the Great is a combination of his reformist tendency and oriental training. He drew an idealized picture of Frederick for Ottoman consumption in order to voice his ideas about what a savior of the Ottoman Empire might appear as. According to Ahmed Resmi, Frederick was a good leader and governor, who spent most of his time in the act of governance but whose most important identity was his apparent military talent and military leadership.[159] Not surprisingly, Ahmed Resmi's vision of an idealized Prussian military machine would become a format for new generations of reforms, which (knowingly or unknowingly) repeated Ahmed Resmi's themes again and again. Indeed, Prussia/Germany remained a model for Ottoman military behaviors until the very end of the empire.

The disastrous Ottoman-Russian War of 1768–1774 was not only a turning point for the empire but also for many reformers, including Ahmed Resmi. The war, in contrast to common perceptions, was forced upon the Ottomans by increasingly aggressive Russian incursions against Poland and the Crimea as well as by the hostile activities of warrior Tatar refugees. However, the period of long peace and further neglect of the standing corps had already taken its toll, and the absence of trained and experienced military leadership had spawned an ill-trained, ill-disciplined, and totally unreliable force. The Ottoman military was no match for the veteran Russian army of the Seven Years' War (1756–1763), which had mastered not only the effective use of fire and maneuver combinations of infantry and artillery but the spoiling raids of light cavalry. Moreover, because of infighting between the elites and clashes of interest, the government failed to make effective use of the veterans of the last war, who were actually old and far from positions of influence. The only positive aspect of the military was its capability to achieve numerical superiority on the battlefield. Not surprisingly, mercenaries, tribal levies, and various militia-type conscript units made up the majority of the expeditionary forces in the succeeding campaign seasons.[160]

From the very beginning the government suffered many problems that included the mobilization of manpower and the stockpiling of logistical materials in the forward staging bases. The collapse of the classical logistics system further limited the capacity of the Ottoman military. The campaign season of 1768 was wasted, and the limited Ottoman assaults did not provide any relief during the season of 1769. Even though Ottoman fortress garrisons fought bravely and desperately, the Russian army under the able command of Peter Rumiantsev advanced into Ottoman territory. At the same time the Greeks of Morea rebelled with Russian support and encouragement, effectively pinning down many provincial units. More importantly, the Russian Baltic fleet unexpectedly appeared in the Mediterranean Sea and burned the Ottoman fleet while in its harbor of Çeşme (near İzmir) on July 7, 1770. The Ottoman army, because of command and control problems and demoralized with recent events, was unable to bring its numerical superiority to bear against the tired and disease-stricken Russian army. Rumiantsev relentlessly crushed Ottoman units appearing in his way. Finally at Kartal (Kagul) on August 1, 1770, the Ottoman main army faced the victorious but weak Russian army. A Russian night attack failed but further weakened the Ottoman will to fight. In the morning the numerically superior Ottoman army melted against the Russian artillery and was routed. As a consequence of the defeat the Russians conquered most parts of the northern Danube region.[161]

The twin disasters of Kartal and Çeşme compelled the Ottomans to revitalize and improve their war effort. The overall command of the campaign was at last given to veteran military commanders—but it was too little and too late. Without the availability of trained operational and tactical leadership, and with a morally collapsed and materially crippled army, neither commander, Silahdar Mehmed Pasha nor Muhsinzade Mehmed Pasha, had the means to change the outcome of the war. Making matters worse, the ever-factionalized government demonstrated its inefficiency in the diplomatic field in addition to its apparent failure to direct strategically the war effort. Unable to face Russian military might, incapable of benefiting from Russian domestic problems like the Pugachev's rebellion, and unable to mobilize support from other countries, the government wasted the meager capacity of its military.[162]

The twin disasters also forced the French government into action, as it was alarmed with possible Russian incursions into French political and economic fields of influence. Even though the Ottoman government refused French ambassador St. Priest's comprehensive plan for sending a large and robust military advisory team, it accepted the services of François Baron de Tott and several other Frenchmen. De Tott, who was a self-made military engineer, immediately began working by first improving the coastal defenses of the Bosporus (Boğaziçi) and Dardanelles (Çanakkale) straits. Then he directed the construction of a new cannon foundry and gunpowder works in Hasköy-Istanbul. But more comprehensive reforms had to wait until the end of the war.[163]

At Kozluca on June 20, 1774, inferior numbers of Russians routed an Ottoman expeditionary force, and the last available forces melted against the advancing Russian units without any effective resistance at Şumnu on June 30. The government had no alternative than to ask for peace and threw itself on the mercy of Russia. The treaty of Küçük Kaynarca in 1774 practically ended Ottoman suzerainty over the Crimean Tatars and ceded an important strip of Black Sea coastline to Russia. However, the most important outcome of the treaty was the moral collapse of the governing elite and the nation as a whole. The poor performance of the Ottoman military surprised even the most pessimistic observers and showed clearly the futility of halfhearted reform efforts.[164]

As an active participant of the campaigns and peace negotiations Ahmed Resmi examined the structural problems within the system and tried to transmit his combat and plenipotentiary experiences to the governing elite in several works, including his famous book *Hulâsatü'l İtibar*. He began his examination with a general criticism of Ottoman foreign policy and the government's faulty decision-making process. He found the Ottoman governing elite did not have the ability to develop an effective foreign policy against the Habsburgs and Russia. The decision to wage the recent war against Russia was based upon faulty and exaggerated information, without any understanding of the empire's own military capacity. The Ottoman military did not have the capability to carry out offensive campaigns against the Russians and lost much of its meager resource base during the war. So at this critical point, he cautioned the government must preserve peace and avoid any aggressive policy in order to gain time to carry out wide-ranging reforms.[165]

Ahmed Resmi was more than critical of the current status of the military. He reasoned that the classical military corps had already collapsed and were militarily useless. Moreover, the mercenaries, tribal levies, and militia units had limited capability and were very difficult to control. The logistical system existed on paper only and, in addition to the corruption of finance officials, the expeditionary units were looting and ravaging along the routes of march. More importantly, the command and control system was not functioning properly because of the lack of a trained officer corps and a capable high command. In short, the Ottoman military was more like a mob than an army. In actuality, with this analysis, he confirmed the St. Priest reports about the Ottoman military.[166]

In contrast to this brilliant and unique analysis Ahmed Resmi was unable to provide any sound remedy or formulate reforms to deal with the military problems. Similar to his predecessors, all he could do was emphasize classical values, virtues, and disciplinary measures and offer some suggestions to adapt to European tactics and techniques. In truth, the new generation of bureaucrats was more than convinced about the need for military reforms but still had difficulty in formulating effective ones.[167]

The series of defeats and later the humiliating peace treaty provided ample opportunity to the reformers for the continuation and extension of the activities of de Tott.

The first significant effort established a new artillery corps, Sürat Topçu Ocağı (the hearth of rapid-fire artillery), resulting primarily from the experiences with deadly Russian artillery fire. The Sürat corps was a modest effort with only 25 cannons and 250 cannoneers, but as the first modern European-style unit its establishment was an important milestone in the history of Ottoman military reforms. Even if the self-proclaimed achievements of de Tott[168] (that included new barracks, uniforms, modern equipment, and training) are downplayed, the Sürat corps immediately became the pride of the reformers and gave a boost to other efforts, including the foundation of a new Hendesehane in Hasköy. The new school of geometry was actually founded with the help of an English renegade Kampel Mustafa Ağa (Count Ramsay Campbell), probably in 1774, and it was basically similar to the old Hendesehane of Bonneval. It used both the intellectual legacy and the physical remnants of the old Hendesehane to restart education in the basic sciences and introductory military engineering.[169]

The opening of a rival school to Hendesehane in 1776 by Chief Admiral of the Navy Cezayirli Gazi Hasan Pasha, the only hero of Çeşme disaster, illustrates an inherent dilemma within the Ottoman reform movement. Previously the patron-client relationships and interest-based factions within the governing elite had been the most important factors in the decision-making process and in carrying out the decisions. Regardless of the merits of any reform project the members of the elite had a tendency to see them from the perspective of their interests. So if the success of a project had the potential to empower further a rival faction they did not hesitate to sabotage it or try to counter it. The case of Hasan Pasha's effort, which represented strong factions, provides an interesting example. The small and inconsequential Sürat corps' Hendesehane did not succeed and disappeared during late 1780s, but Hasan Pasha's school managed to live on and became a success story afterwards by turning into the Mühendishane-i Bahri Hümayun (the Imperial Naval Engineering School) in 1784.[170]

Regrettably, most classical and even many modern scholars found it easy to label these factions as either progressive or reactionary without paying attention to the inherent dynamics of the governing elite. The struggle within the governing elite showed itself more clearly when related to the fate of the French military advisory team. The numbers of French advisors numbered around 20 in 1775 and rose to 300 in 1780 (after the return of de Tott in 1776) amidst growing opposition. The problematic character of the new French Ambassador Choiseul Gouffier, a well-known philhellene, and the sudden discovery of French secret deals with rebellious magnates in Egypt damaged the reputation of the military advisory team. The discovery of Şehzade (prince) Selim's secret correspondence with French King Louis XVI and an alleged associated plot to dethrone the current sultan, Abdülhamid I, destroyed the balance. As a result, the most daring reformer of the era, Halil Hamid Pasha, was first dismissed and later executed because of growing anti-French feelings in 1785. Nevertheless, the French team remained in the country up until the start of hostilities between the Ottomans and the Habsburg-Russian alliance in 1787.[171]

The Nizam-ı Cedid Reforms

Selim III ascended the throne during the Ottoman-Habsburg-Russian War of 1787–1791. He gained the confidence of many high officials previously as a prince by showing great interest in military matters. He was unable to change the course of the war but used the disastrous ending of the war as a pretext to convince even the most traditional and conservative officials of the necessity for military reforms. Like previous reform efforts, the Nizam-ı Cedid reforms were born of military defeat.

Selim actually started discussions for reform during the war. He collected more than 200 high officials and other dignitaries (including two foreigners) as a kind of advisory council in May 1789. After several heated gatherings, some of the participants, totaling 24 in all, presented their ideas in pamphlets. As can be expected, most of the participants came from nonmilitary backgrounds (mainly from the bureaucracy) and only two pamphlet authors were military officers (and one of these was a French officer). Most of the pamphleteers proposed traditional types of reform similar to previous efforts, and only a couple of them proposed wide-ranging reforms including, for example, the establishment of European-style infantry corps. Most recommended that the new corps must recruit personnel from the healthy population of Anatolia and Rumelia and that it must be kept away from the disruption of Istanbul. Actually, they advocated simply making use of an already available manpower pool, namely the mercenaries, for the direct use of the state. Not surprisingly, however, even the most radical reformer, Tatarcık Abdullah Efendi (an influential member of Ulema), did not dare to propose the disbandment of the Kapıkulu corps. In some ways they were trying to find a magic formula for reforming the Kapıkulu corps, whereas subconsciously they knew the impossibility of it.[172]

Selim was partially satisfied with the outcome of his advisory council's recommendations in which he made use of his lieutenants to voice his ideas as their own. He still felt the need to get first-hand information regarding military developments in Europe and he sent one his most talented and trusted lieutenants, Ebubekir Ratib Efendi, to Vienna as an ambassador to gather accurate information about its military. Ratib managed to visit most of the important military institutions, including the military academy and engineering school, civilian high schools, and libraries during his brief embassy (November 1791–September 1792). He delivered two reports, one of which was about his military observations.[173]

Similarly to Ahmed Resmi, Ratib made use of his combat experiences and effectively identified the strength of the Habsburgs, which he felt was an academically trained officer corps. He noted that the successful integration of military technology into combat units required highly trained officers. These officers were needed, not only to lead the men in the combat but also to train them according to the demands of the new dynamics of warfare. Therefore, he reasoned, if the government would like to have a strong army it had no alternative other than establishing at least one academic military institution for the training of officers. He even coined a name for it, the Akademi Militar (military academy). Because the empire did not have the necessary technical expertise, Ratib recommended following the example of Russian

Tsar Peter I, and thought directors, teachers, and other specialists must be imported from Europe. He ended his report with a provocative sentence; "the Russians did it, why not us?"[174]

Ratib became the most influential individual involved in carrying out the military reforms of the period. He personally brought in a group of European military advisors during his brief term as the secretary of foreign affairs (June 14, 1794–August 19, 1796). But, unfortunately, he too fell victim to inner court struggles and was executed on November 22, 1799.[175] The tragic fate of Ratib is instrumental in understanding a particularly important problem of the Ottoman reforms. As already pointed out, the interest-based patron-client relations continuously poisoned the reform efforts. The Ottoman high officials always looked through the lens of their personal and group interests, and the reforms themselves became a way to gain more power, prestige, and income. Regardless of the merits of any project or individual, if success had the potential to adversely affect their interests they were quick to sabotage or discredit it by any means. The inner group's struggles and personality issues remained the most damaging and enduring problem throughout the history of the Ottoman reforms.

Selim officially began his military reforms with the publication of new regulations for the Kapıkulu corps in 1792. The officially announced aim was the reorganization of the corps according to classical regulations and ideals. As might be expected, the targets of the so-called reforms seem modest and reasonable: reestablishment of a hierarchy and the reorganization of the officer corps, a general reduction of the size of each corps, a prohibition of the sale of pay-tickets, the enforcement of regular training, construction of new barracks, and the introduction of new weapons and equipment. In order to achieve these goals and limit corruption and nepotism the government assigned new supervisors from the inner court. For a brief period of time even the assignment of trainers and experts from outside the corps was forbidden.[176]

These problematic reforms ended with very modest success. None of the targets were achieved for the Janissary and Süvari corps because of well-organized reactions. The size of the Janissaries rose against all attempts of reduction from 54,458 in 1794 to 98,539 in 1806. The timid introduction of reforms merely encouraged the ringleaders of hard-core criminal elements within the Janissaries to such a degree that their insolent behavior alarmed Ottoman society.[177]

The halfhearted attempt to reform the Sipahis also failed, not because of their reaction but because by this point the Sipahis had no organizational architecture at all. Their system and organization existed only on paper for many years And, while the government, on one hand, tried to revive the organization, on the other hand, by allocating the land estates to new reform projects it destroyed any chance of resurrecting this class.[178]

However, the government achieved encouraging results within the technical corps, which were long-time comrades of Janissaries, including the Topçu, Humbaracı, Arabacı, and Lağımcı (all except the Cebeci corps). It is obvious that past reforms made the technical corps more ready for change. All four corps underwent a swift cleaning and got rid of troublesome and useless elements. New personnel were recruited, for the Topçu and Humbaracı, from Bosnia once again. With the help of

European trainers and experts a higher standard was achieved and a number of new weapons and equipment were introduced. Similarly, the government became successful in the projects to modernize the Tophane-i Amire (imperial cannon foundry) and the gunpowder mills. Initially French, and later British and Swedish, experts and foremen opened new facilities and reorganized the old ones. In terms of gunpowder especially, the empire achieved superior quality and managed to meet its constantly growing demands for several decades.[179]

Selim and his intimate circle of lieutenants launched the radical part of the reforms secretly behind the cover of Kapıkulu reform attempts. The main idea was to establish a modern European-style infantry corps and later use this corps as a core around which a totally modern military could be created. Indeed, the name of the new infantry corps, the Nizam-ı Cedid (literally new regiment or order), became the name of the entire reform package and era. Fortunately, a quick start was possible because Koca Yusuf Pasha had already conducted trials with Russian and German deserters and prisoners during the war. He collected them into a company-size infantry unit, armed with captured weapons, and conducted several training exercises and maneuvers. This makeshift unit took the first tentative steps towards the establishment of a new infantry corps.[180]

After the end of the war this unit was secretly stationed away from public eyes in Levend near Istanbul and reinforced with recruits from the urban unemployed in April 1792. The British Embassy provided some infantry weapons and equipment and several French soldiers of fortune were hired as trainers and advisors. The new unit secretly continued its training for two more years, during which a separate treasury (İrad-ı Cedid) deriving its revenue from seized timariot estates was founded to finance it independently of the traditional corps. Soon, additional foreign experts and new weapons were introduced.[181]

The timid and fearful reformers did not dare to reveal the identity of an independent Nizam-ı Cedid corps (even after two years of existence) and tried to conceal it up by embedding it within the organizational structure of the Bostancı Ocağı (the hearth of gardeners), which was the personal regiment of the sultan. The new corps continued to grow under this camouflage, with the introduction of additional recruits coming from households of the Anatolian Ayans. The first regiment was established in Levend in 1795 and the second one in Üsküdar in 1799. With growing confidence Selim ordered the establishment of additional units, albeit under the control of the Ayans in Anatolia. At least nine provinces carried out the order, and for the first time recruitment of villagers began. After this strategic decision the size of the corps rose rapidly from 9,300 in 1801 to 24,000 in 1806.[182]

The level of confidence of the government may be seen by its efforts to announce or, in a way, propagandize the military reforms and their results to Ottoman and European officials and intellectuals. A book titled *Koca Sekbanbaşı Risalesi* was written, in very understandable language, to answer questions and to show the military merits of the reforms to wider intellectual circles.[183] Similarly, for the first time the government ordered the writing of books for European audiences. Two books were prepared and published by Mahmud Raif Efendi: (*Tableau des Nouveaux Règlement de L'Empire Ottoman*) and Küçük Seyyid Mustafa Efendi (*Diatribe de L'Ingénieur Séid Moustapha Sur L'Etat Actuel de L'Art Militaire, du Génie, et des Sciences a Constantinople*) in 1798 and 1803, respectively. In a short time, they caught the interest of European statesmen and intellectuals.[184]

Surprisingly, the most important and enduring reform of the Nizam period, the establishment of the first modern military school of the empire, was launched in 1795 without fanfare and was unknown to even some of the reformers. The Mühendishane-i Berri Hümayun (the Imperial Military Engineering School) was not only the first modern military school but also the first modern high school of the empire. Even though it was built on the remnants and legacy of various military technical schools of past reforms, it was the brainchild of two modest reformers, Ebubekir Ratib Efendi and the official interpreter of the Swedish Embassy, Mouradgea d'Ohsson (Muradcan Tosunyan). Both of them proposed nearly the same ideas, most likely unknown to each other: the establishment of a highly academic military school for all military branches with the help of foreign experts. D'Ohsson, as a former Ottoman citizen of Armenian origins, additionally asked for the inclusion of non-Muslim students.[185]

Selim accepted the proposals but limited the broad concept to a narrowly defined technical school within the structure of bombardier and miners' corps. As such, in the mainstream of the Nizam army infantry units continued to follow traditional on-the-job officer training patterns, in which seniority and loyalty to regiments took precedent over merit and loyalty to the sultan. Thus, the much debated cornerstone of the reforms, an academically trained officers corps, received only partial support from the government. A small but functional building was constructed with a modern library and press. Although several foreign experts were hired, special care was given to bring in the best and brightest Ottoman scholars also. The school remained modest, with limited enrollment up until the 1830s. But its modest size actually helped its survival during the disastrous end of the Nizam-ı Cedid reforms. Contrary to its purpose, its first graduates were actually assigned to infantry regiments to reinforce the weak command and control system instead of their original military engineering posts.[186]

Unfortunately, while the government had to struggle with domestic opposition a new war suddenly forced itself upon the empire, this time not from its traditional enemies but from a traditional friend—France. The new revolutionary French Republic decided to accomplish the grand design of crippling the British Empire by capturing Ottoman Egypt. A French expeditionary army under the command of Napoleon easily crushed Ottoman provincial troops in two pitched battles and captured Cairo in July 22, 1798. The war caught the government unaware and completely unprepared. It did not have combat-ready forces, other than the personal retinues of governors and other local magnates, in position to resist the French. Fortunately the British Royal Navy sank Napoleon's fleet, isolating the French, and the powerful governor of Syria, Cezzar Ahmed Pasha, stopped the French advance by the successful defense of Akka (Acre) (March 19 to May 21, 1799) by mainly using his own mercenary troops.[187]

The Ottoman military proved repeatedly unable to defeat the weak and isolated French forces in Egypt. Two Ottoman amphibious operations in 1799 ended with total failure. In the meantime the government spent enormous amounts of money recruiting all available manpower and bribing standing units to mobilize for war. The outcome, the so-called grand army of Yusuf Ziya Pasha, was not an army but a horde without effective command and control or a competent officer corps. Most of the members of the Kapıkulu corps remained in and around Istanbul, and only a portion of them participated (albeit with much protest). Similarly, the provincial Janissaries also tried their best to evade duty. The government had to depend on mercenaries more than ever. Interestingly, for the first time in the history of the empire Albanian and Caucasian mercenaries were more numerous than the traditional mercenaries of Anatolia and Rumelia. The only positive feature of the grand army was the presence of regular artillery and engineers units under the command of trained officers, including 70-year old Campbell Mustafa Ağa.[188]

Thanks to eyewitness accounts of a British military mission under the command of General Koehler, consisting of 75 members, there exists a clear picture of the Ottoman grand army and the reasons behind its disastrous campaign. The grand army marched slowly with much confusion and anarchy and, of course, it left a trail of destruction behind itself. The irregularity and anarchy of its camps were notorious, during which units constantly clashed with each other. Not surprisingly, Yusuf Ziya Pasha continued to recruit and forcefully levy soldiers along the way in order to compensate for a constant drain of sickness and desertion. Strangely, some of the governors tried their best to lure mercenaries from within the grand army to their provincial units.[189]

According to the British observers the Ottoman soldiers had all the basic qualities (for example, bravery, sturdiness, and the will to fight) to be excellent warriors. However, due to the lack of an efficient officer corps, basic military training, and discipline, they were more or less useless against a European enemy.[190] As can be expected, Yusuf Ziya Pasha's grand army was beaten immediately after reaching Egypt by a weak but professional French expeditionary army at Heliopolis on March 20, 1800. The French forces finally gave up only after the introduction of British units and the arrival of additional Ottoman units on June 27, 1801. For the government the only bright side of the Ottoman-French War of 1798–1802 was the outstanding performance of the Nizam soldiers from the original two Istanbul regiments. A battalion-size Nizam reinforcement turned the tide of the Akka defense, and the 3,000 well-trained Nizam soldiers fought proficiently while the remaining Ottoman units performed poorly during the last phase of the campaign.[191]

The foreign problems did not end with the final peace with France in 1802. The Russian army invaded the principalities of Moldavia and Wallachia in 1806, starting a war that would last more than five years. The Ottoman military once again performed poorly, and in spite of its numerical superiority it lost most of the pitched battles and only displayed limited and ineffective resistance in the defense of its fortresses. A series of rebellions further destabilized the empire. The government effectively lost control not only of the distant provinces like Egypt, Baghdad, and Syria, but also of most of the core provinces to the Ayans, who had official titles like Tepedelenli Ali Pasha of Yanya, Pazvantoğlu Osman Ağa of Vidin, Canikli Ali Pasha of Trabzon, Çapanoğlu Mustafa Pasha of Yozgat, and Cezzar Ahmed Pasha of Syria.[192]

As a consequence of these wars and domestic struggles the Nizam corps, while expanding in size, rapidly became weaker instead of stronger. The government was unable to increase the numbers of trained officers, and except for the original two regiments all other Nizam units became liabilities rather than assets. The provincial Nizam units were poorly trained, ill-disciplined, lacking effective command and control, and, as the retinues of Ayans, showed limited loyalty to the central government. The government encountered difficulty in mobilizing them during the campaigns as it had with the Janissaries. Furthermore, following in the footsteps of the Janissaries they created the same type of problems against civilian populations, such as looting, robbery, and devastation. The apparent failure of Nizam units to stabilize the provinces and widen the control of the central government further weakened the reformist camp. It also gave encouragement to increasing opposition against reform, as happened after the failure of the important Nizam commander Kadı Abdurrahman Pasha in Konya between 1803 and 1804 and his disastrous attempt to spread the Nizam order to Edirne in 1806.[193]

Selim was equally unsuccessful in uniting different interest groups within the reformist camp. Different factions sabotaged the activities of each other and occasionally caused the elimination of important figures like Ratib Efendi. It is no great wonder that a small disorder within the guards of the Istanbul straits defenses turned into a full-scale rebellion (the so-called Kabakçı Mustafa rebellion) in a very short time under these circumstances on May 25, 1807. Selim failed to show the determination to face the rebels by using his faithful two Nizam regiments, which had the capability to suppress the rebellion. Instead, he tried to appease the rebels by accepting their initial demands, which included the execution of reformist officials and some his intimate friends. This surprisingly soft and timid approach simply encouraged the rebels, and other dissidents joined them. The rebels attacked and massacred the Nizam soldiers who had been left to their fate by the government. Finally, Selim was forced to abdicate, and a new sultan, Mustafa IV, ascended to the throne.[194]

A final attempt of an important Ayan Alemdar, Mustafa Pasha, who was persuaded to intervene by political refugees from Istanbul (better known as Rusçuk Yaranı), from the Danubean province of Rusçuk to save Selim, did not succeed. Selim was killed while his rescuers were forcing their way into the palace on July 28, 1808. Mustafa Pasha subsequently dethroned Mustafa IV and gave the throne to a young prince, Mahmud II. The Alemdar incident clearly shows the sorry state of the empire—the provincial forces of a local magnate defeated the rebels that the government of a mighty empire had been unable to deal with.[195]

Mustafa Pasha, in the role of kingmaker, confidently tried to continue the Nizam reforms (with the help of Rusçuk Yaranı) under a new name, the Sekban-Cedid, while simultaneously hunting down the rebels. He was also instrumental in collecting important provincial magnates to make a Magna Carta-type agreement with the state, in which the state acknowledged the rights and legitimacy of magnates and in return magnates were obligated to support military reforms. The Sened-i İttifak (deed of agreement) might be important in terms of the history of constitutional law, but in reality it was one of the lowest points in the power of the Ottoman central government.

Mustafa Pasha's harsh rule alienated almost everyone, including the new sultan, and when the Janissaries rebelled against his rule on November 16, 1808, Mustafa Pasha had to fight with only a few supporters. The rebellion lasted nearly a week and caused a bloodbath throughout the city of Istanbul. In the end Mahmud II was forced to consent to all the demands of the rebels. The Sekban-ı Cedid was abolished and all the privileges of Kapıkulu corps were renewed.[196]

After the destructive Janissary rebellions of 1807 and 1808, Mahmud did not make any overt reform attempts and waited patiently until 1822. However, this period turned out to be more difficult than the preceding decades. Mahmud had to deal with additional serious crises and wars. The Ottoman-Russian War of 1806–1812 continued on amidst the rebellions within the country. Ottoman expeditionary forces (composed of mostly provincial troops of the Ayans) did show stiff defense and achieved some feats, but they were more like a horde than an army. The two-pronged Russian assault penetrated into Rumelia and Georgia. Luckily for the Ottomans the epidemics, hunger, and the incoming French offensive forced Russians to give up their desire to conquer Moldovia and Wallachia.[197] A minor conflict between Serbs and local Janissaries turned into a medium-level rebellion in 1804 and became a full-fledged insurrection with Russian support in 1807. The government managed to suppress the rebellion in 1813 only after the Russians withdrew their support because of the clauses of the Bucharest Peace Treaty of 1812 and Napoleon's ill-fated invasion.[198]

Mahmud slowly and patiently tried to strengthen and reinforce both his personal and the central government's authority. He dealt with the powerful Ayans one by one while assigning his loyal lieutenants to critical posts. Some of the magnates were easily eliminated, like Çapanoğulları of central Anatolia and Veli Pasha of eastern Anatolia. However, others seriously challenged the government like Tepedelenli Ali Pasha of Yanya (Janina), whose rebellion lasted two years and provided a suitable atmosphere for the Greek rebellion of Morea in 1821.[199]

The Ottoman expeditionary force was mainly composed of mercenary troops of the provincial grandees. There were Delis coming from eastern and southern Anatolia, Kurdish, and Turcoman tribal warriors, and all sorts of mercenaries and volunteers from Balkan provinces. Interestingly, Albanians fought on both sides. As can be expected, neither the administration nor the provincial grandees managed to enforce effective command-control and discipline. The troops fought independent of each other, and the unconventional nature of the conflict further increased the chaos and anarchy. Making matters worse, Ottoman units had to fight without logistical support, and thereby epidemics, cold, and hunger took their toll.[200] Mahmud had no alternative than to call on the help of the most important and dangerous Ayan of the empire, the governor of Egypt, Kavalalı Mehmed Ali Pasha, (better known as Mohammed Ali Pasha) in order to suppress the Greek rebellion.[201]

Previously in 1811, Mehmed Ali Pasha successfully launched new military reforms in Egypt. Initially he imitated Selim's Nizam-ı Cedid reforms and even called his new army by the same name, but later, with the arrival of foreign experts who were mainly French officers, Egyptian reforms changed course. The backbone of the Egyptian reforms, an officer training corps, was established in 1816. Instead of providing extended academic training, Mehmed Ali Pasha preferred short military courses based on practical applications. Later on, however, a more academic school, the Hendesehane, was founded in 1821. Selected students were also sent to France for further military and engineering training, totaling 115 students by 1833. Mehmed Ali Pasha's other preference provided the final identity and shape of his army: an army trained by the French, commanded by Turkish officers, and composed of Egyptian villagers. He also managed to reorganize not only the military and navy but also the socioeconomic structure of the provinces in order to establish a strong economic base for the continuation of his reforms.[202]

The Egyptian army and navy under the able command of İbrahim Pasha helped the Ottoman expeditionary forces in suppressing the Greek rebellion. İbrahim Pasha not only made effective use of his well-trained and well-equipped infantry and artillery units but also exploited intelligence, terrain, and the excessive confidence of the rebels. The assignment of the talented Mehmed Reşid Pasha, as the commander in chief of the Ottoman expeditionary force, was instrumental in further strengthening the Ottoman position. Both commanders led their troops into rugged terrain, and in a series of successful battles and sieges that was crowned with the conquest of Messolonghi on April 10, 1826, crushed the rebel army.[203] The Greek rebels achieved their aim of independence only after the active military and political incursions of Britain, France, and Russia. The combat efficiency of the provincial army of Egypt, especially its officer corps and command and control structure, impressed and in a way terrified Mahmud, who once again comprehended the importance of military reforms. The reforms of Mehmed Ali Pasha directly and indirectly affected the course of Ottoman military reforms, and Egyptian trained officers played key roles in its development after the 1830s.[204]

Mahmud's determination and his methodical approach began to produce results after 1822. He managed to eliminate key figures from conservative circles one by one and replaced them with his trusted lieutenants. Not surprisingly, his trusted men were also conservative in thinking, but they were pragmatically trying to gain more power by siding with the sultan. He then focused on creating a web of alliances with bureaucrats, military commanders, and, more critically, with the important members of the Ulema (judiciary-religious) class. He gained their confidence by granting concessions and gaining control of key posts with his lieutenants. As a third step he made sure that the technical corps of the Kapıkulu remained loyal to him. For the first time all the important groups were united and the would-be allies of the Kapıkulu corps were neutralized.[205]

Mahmud's last move was to destroy the last hopes of conservative reformers, who were still adamant on the possibility of a reorganization of the Kapıkulu corps by launching the last attempt to reform the Janissary corps. This was known as the

Eşkinci (campaigner) project. All Mahmud's high officials, dignitaries, and high-ranking Janissary officers approved the project on May 28, 1826. Actually, it was a very modest restructuring. Selected soldiers from the corps would man 51 new companies. Even though they would remain part of the corps, they were obligated to take part in all individual and collective training according to European models. Of course, neither Mahmud nor any of the reformers had faith in the success of this partial reform effort. In reality they were simply looking for a legitimate pretext to deal with the Janissaries once for all. Janissary ringleaders immediately reacted to the reforms and lost any legitimacy they had by revolting.[206]

Mahmud acted swiftly and aggressively against the rebels on June 15, 1826. All of the important officials and loyal Janissary officers immediately gathered around the sultan. The technical corps of the Kapıkulu mobilized and occupied critical locations within the city of Istanbul. The Ulema representatives easily gathered the civil population and provoked them against the Janissaries. The Janissary corps was perplexed by these events and was caught completely unprepared. Only its embedded technical corps Cebecis still remained loyal. After initial skirmishes, the hard core of the rebels dug into their barracks while others ran for their lives. Under intense artillery fire and concentric assaults by the grand alliance the last Janissary resistance melted away. During this so-called Vaka-i Hayriyye (the auspicious event) hundreds of Janissaries were killed. Mahmud officially disbanded the Janissary corps and its allied and affiliated corps, chief among them the Cebecis, two days later. The reformers hunted down the remaining important leaders of the rebellious corps, and the Janissaries in the provinces soon shared the same fate. The hysteria lasted a couple of weeks, and at the end of the month, except in Bosnia, all the branches of the Janissary corps and affiliated units were eliminated.[207]

The bloody end of the Janissary corps, which had been the pioneering regular infantry of the early modern world, marked the end of an era. The reformers not only cleared the last obstacles but also destroyed the last hopes of revitalizing the classical military system. However, the technologically oriented reformers neglected or ignored the political, social, and economic costs of such a significant structural change, which at the time seemed solely military. Surprisingly, the following generations of military reformers, who were in turn still ill informed and ill equipped to deal with these costs, began to see themselves as social engineers dealing with other aspects and problems of the empire. This would become the principal internal structural problem that the Ottoman military would have to fight against while simultaneously facing ever-increasing foreign and domestic enemies.

CHAPTER 4

Fighting for Survival, 1826–1858

After the conclusion of the Napoleonic Wars in 1815, the empires of Europe found themselves confronting the emergence of nationalism on a wide scale. Additionally the forces of the Industrial Revolution and rapidly evolving market economies added new stresses on monarchies struggling to retain their grip on subject peoples. The Ottoman Empire experienced these movements as well but, perhaps, to a much greater extent than contemporary Europe. The Ottoman Empire was finding that governing a geographically extended multinational and multiethnic empire was becoming more difficult with each passing year. A new generation of sultans and members of the governing elite evolved, who were convinced of the need for modernization and westernization (both terms have been used synonymously and interchangeably) and who were committed to change in order to keep the empire intact.

The destruction of the Janissaries removed the last serious barrier to modernity and began the process of change. Various reformers, some of whom possessed solid military credentials and others not, began to deconstruct the traditional corps of the Ottoman army. These reformers attempted, in a variety of ways, to construct a modern standing army based on European models. They also began the establishment of specialized training institutions that coalesced as the Ottoman Military Academy, the trained graduates of which were soon caught in an intragovernment competition for their services. Corresponding changes in Ottoman society resulting from the Tanzimat reforms further destabilized the traditional strengths of the military as the forces of nationalism swept through the empire.

Perennial wars in the 1800s with the ancient Ottoman adversary, Russia, damaged the empire severely and resulted in the loss of territory and prestige. However, the series of Ottoman-Russian wars compelled the reform movement to examine the structure of the army itself with a view toward correcting its weaknesses. Consequently, the Ottoman military evolved a European-style regular army backed up by a reserve system. The entire military was based on a conscription system, but there were competing pressures that created large and unwieldy masses of ill-trained irregular cavalry. This transformation of the Ottoman military was poorly thought out and poorly planned and failed to provide the empire with a sharp instrument of military power. While it enjoyed some limited successes on the battlefield, its performance in combat was largely poor.

The Crimean War brought this period to a close by exposing the profound institutional weaknesses of the Ottoman Empire's military. Moreover, most of the efforts of academy-trained Ottoman officers, as well as refugee European officers, failed to produce a combat-capable army and the commanders necessary to lead it. Despite these setbacks, the seeds of change were sown as a generation of young officers gained valuable combat experience, and the fledgling military academy began to produce graduates in greater numbers. In truth, this period of transformation was probably more valuable for the Ottoman military in the destruction of its antique institutions than for any long-lasting and effective changes that emerged from it.

Delusion and Reality
The Victorious Soldiers of the Prophet Muhammed

Sultan Mahmud II and his inner circle were more than sure that their long-cherished dream of founding a modern military was within their immediate reach after the bloody end of the Janissaries. However, even though Mahmud meticulously and patiently planned and prepared for the destruction of the Janissaries and the classical military system (for nearly 18 years), he simply had no concrete ideas or master plan and no able advisors to help him found a new military.[1] He and the administration were equally ignorant and unprepared for the drastic changes of the post-Napoleonic world order and disintegration of the empire due to the rise of nationalism and separatist movements within his Christian subjects. Additionally, they underestimated the will of Russia to sabotage any reform, which would strengthen the Ottoman military. Furthermore, the empire encountered difficulty in filling the socioeconomic and moral vacuum that was created by the abolishment of the Janissaries. The sudden disappearance of the old order, as well as the values and patterns related with it, was instrumental in the creation of a moral crisis that the administration was ill-equipped to handle. In a way, the administration "had taken the heart and soul out of the people" without replacing them with new ones.[2]

The hunt for the surviving Janissaries and their local collaborators continued on for several months more. The administration made a fatal mistake of seeing all of the provincial Janissaries in the same light as the imperial ones.[3] The vicious suppression destroyed local balances and created serious problems, especially in Bosnia within which there was already preexisting widespread resistance (beginning around 1813) against Mahmud's political and administrative centralization. The decree abolishing the Janissaries added fuel to the fire and for more than a year the Bosnians withstood the enforcement of the decree in their province. Even after finding a relatively peaceful solution, the administration remained unpopular, and well-intended but poorly and crudely carried out reforms within the province further alienated the Muslim population. This hostility would remain until the 1840s, and the administration was not able to make use of the military potential of Bosnia for decades to come.[4]

Mahmud initially tried to obtain military experts seconded to him from the governor of Egypt, Kavalalı Mehmed Ali Pasha. Not surprisingly, Mehmed Ali Pasha politely refused this wish under the pretext that his officers were not trained enough to act as expert trainers.[5] The accounts of contemporary western observers regarding the presence and significance of Egyptian experts in the army's rebirth were unfounded.[6] In fact, only one Egyptian officer, Davud Ağa, who happened to be spending his leave in Istanbul, enrolled individually into the new army. The ongoing Greek rebellion and subsequent international crisis effectively blocked any chances of getting military aid from European countries as well. The prestige and public image of the empire, by this time, was so low that even the ever-present European soldiers of fortune were missing. Consequently, Mahmud had no other choice than to follow the blueprints of the defunct Nizam-ı Cedit project of the late Selim III. Not only was the regulation of the new military, the Asakir-i Mansure-i Muhammediye (literally victorious soldiers of the prophet Muhammed), a copy of the old Nizam regulation with minor changes, but the uniforms and unit structure were also close copies. Similarly, most of the initial commanding officers (two out of three) and NCOs of the Mansure were none other than the old cadres of the Nizam.[7]

According to its establishment decree, the Mansure did not combine all the standing army corps into one but merely replaced the Janissary corps. Thus, all the existent corps kept their traditional independence and most of their vested interests in a system within which the Mansure was nothing more than *primus inter pares*. Moreover, in order to insure loyalty, the administration unwillingly stayed away from comprehensive reforms of the old technical corps of Kapıkulu, chief among them the Topçus, which had played a critical role during the final suppression of the Janissary rebellion. Obviously, this was a temporary measure—as a determined, but patient, reformer Mahmud was waiting for a suitable time frame to reform these corps also. However, he underestimated or neglected the urgency of the foreign threats to the empire. The luxury of ample time was about to run out.[8]

Even though the old technical corps enjoyed their traditional privileges a few years more, Mahmud, who was well experienced with military rebellions, knew the importance of the imperial guard unit in maintaining his own security. He soon abolished the ill-trained and ill-equipped Bostancı Ocağı (hearth of gardeners or more properly palace guard regiment), which also performed various menial tasks around the palace. In its place a completely new imperial guard regiment was formed under the disguise of the old name, Bostancıyan-ı Hassa (however, it was frequently called simply Hassa [imperial]), in August 1826. For the first time in the history of the empire, imperial guards were assigned exclusively military duties. The best and brightest members of the old corps and talented recruits were selected for the new imperial guard regiment.[9]

The strength of the regiment initially corresponded with its original task and mission, but it grew to over 11,000 by 1835, becoming an army in itself. Mahmud intentionally kept the guards out of the Mansure command structure, thereby reinforcing its separate and independent role. For his own purposes, the Hassa was a useful tool as an additional balancing and manipulating force that remained under his immediate control. But his insistence on regarding the guards as his private domain, keeping them nearby at all times, created a tradition in which the imperial guard units seldom took part in combat in faraway theaters. In doing so, he unintentionally curbed the combat efficiency of his army by keeping the elite regiments out of war, as in the example of the Ottoman-Russian War of 1828–1829.[10]

As usual, the urban unemployed of Istanbul willingly filled the empty slots of the first three regiments (Tertib). And most of the Istanbul-based grandees were more than happy to staff the officers and rank and file of the new regiments with their retinues in order to protect their vested interests. So in a span of less than two weeks, the Sultan and the public began to admire joyfully the parades of new Mansure units (albeit without proper uniforms and equipment). In the meantime, the number of the regiments, each with 12 musket companies and an authorized strength of 1,527 men, rose to eight. To the astonishment of all contemporary European military observers, Mansure officers tried to train their units according to pre-Napoleonic infantry tactics and technical norms. The lack of military expertise was so obvious that even teaching rudimentary military skills turned out to be almost impossible. And, of course, without an effective centralized command and control structure, the regiments passed through completely different and independent types of training programs that varied according to the tastes of their commanding officers. Additionally, all the regiment commanders tried their best to invent battle formations, often in ridiculously weird geometrical forms, in order to please their willing, but militarily ignorant, sultan.[11]

The recruitment and establishment of new regiments did not go well in the provinces either. In addition to the distrust and doubts about the new regime and its reforms, the public was uncomfortable with recruitment policies. Even though the administration announced the temporary nature of the military service, the public understood it as a lifelong commitment. Once again the administration collaborated with grandees—this time provincial ones. Generous offers of land and financial incentives started a race between neighboring provinces, and the western Anatolian provinces actually exceeded their allocated personnel quotas. However, the extension of the Mansure army slowed down in Syrian and eastern Anatolian provinces and in Bosnia, Serbia, and Macedonia as well. Naturally, its establishment did not penetrate into Iraq or the Arabian Peninsula where voluntary recruitment was unknown.[12]

The administration was still resourceful enough to find ingenious solutions to daunting problems. The establishment of the Silistire Cavalry Regiment was a very good example in this sense. The financial constraints and precedence given to the Mansure infantry regiments effectively curbed any chances of establishing regular cavalry units. As a result, the administration decided to raise a cavalry regiment from Silistire, where several ethnic groups already possessed suitable mounts and cavalry expertise. Showing a rare level of elasticity, not only the Muslim groups (Tatars and Turcomans), but also Christian Cossacks, were put under obligation to provide allocated numbers of cavalrymen according to their populations. The new Silistire Cavalry Regiment, which was established on November 16, 1826, consisted of two wings; a Tatar wing and a mixed Turcoman-Cossack wing, with a combined strength of 1,323 men. Even though the rebellion of Greeks and Serbs further increased the strength of ethnic- and religious-based sectarian movements in the empire, Mahmud tried his best to preserve good relations. While integrating Christians into the regiment, he worked with Muslim religious authorities to motivate the new soldiers with increased religious indoctrination. The recruitment of Christian Cossacks into the regular army showed clearly the elasticity and resourcefulness of the administration.[13]

The establishment of the regular cavalry corps began after February 1827, but it progressed slowly, and the administration was unable to accommodate old Turkish cavalry traditions with modern European practices. And the much-cherished project to revive the old, and more or less defunct, cavalry corps or groups, like timariot cavalry (Sipahi) and nomadic groups (Yörüks or Evlad-ı Fatihan corps), turned out to be a waste of valuable time, assets, and personnel. As Selim III discovered with sorrow, any attempts to reawaken these ancient institutions and groups were not congruent with the socioeconomic realities of modern Ottoman society. As a result, an empire founded by horse-archers, who played an important role in the establishment of light cavalry traditions in Europe and the Middle East, had no effective cavalry corps except for two or three excellent cavalry regiments (which were generally quartered in and around Istanbul). And sadly, for horsemen, the Ottoman military continued to depend on tribal levies or volunteers of dubious military value who were liabilities rather than assets most of the time.[14]

The problems increased hand in hand with the increase in the number of Mansure soldiers. Uniforms, equipment, and weapons remained unresolved problems through 1829. Making things worse, wide-scale anarchy and a hysteria of destruction after the abolition of the Janissary corps resulted in the burning of nearly all large military barracks, and there were no barracks available for the new Mansure units. The administration initiated a large construction campaign to build three barracks amidst much confusion and financial problems while trying to cope with the daunting task of providing salaries and daily rations to a varied assortment of military personnel. Interestingly, the administration turned out to be more talented in solving housing and logistics problems than in training the new military cadres.[15]

Against all odds and amidst much privation, the administration was still keen on the enlargement of the Mansure army. The government decided to establish new Mansure regiments in the provinces and chose neighboring Anatolian and Rumelian provinces because of the increased proximity and presence of central authority. In a relatively short time, new provincial regiments were founded one by one by competing governors between August and September 1826. Somehow, the administration decided to send officers from the already thin cadres of the Istanbul regiments to prospective regiments in the provinces in order to establish a common nucleus to promote standardization. As can be expected with this sudden enlargement, the Mansure army plunged into chaos during the first months of 1827. The trial and error approach and tendency to apply patches instead of dealing with problems as a whole were instrumental in creating this crisis. The solution to the chaos came from a controversial figure named Grand Admiral Mehmed Hüsrev Pasha.

Hüsrev Pasha was a very conservative military leader and, as the *beau ideal* of the old system, he was more than satisfied with the old corrupt practices. But he was at the same time very pragmatic and, in fact, an opportunist. He knew that in order to please Mahmud and gain more power he needed to prove himself as an ardent reformer.[16] Immediately after the announcement of the establishment of the Mansure army, he began to collect military experts, translators, and bright youngsters into his retinue. He secretly trained a naval infantry battalion according to the Napoleonic era French system by making use of a renegade ex-French NCO named Sardunyalı Hurşid (Gaillard of Sardinia), while the administration itself was desperately looking for a model and experts. His translators rapidly translated European military manuals and regulations even though he was not well versed in reading. After nearly a year-long preparation, he staged a magnificent war game with his battalion in the presence of the Sultan and other dignitaries. Mahmud was more than amazed and immediately ordered the introduction of Hüsrev's training system, known as Hüsrevi, and soon followed the reorganization of all Mansure units according to Hüsrev's model.[17]

As the new favorite of the Sultan, Hüsrev was assigned as the commander in chief of Mansure troops on May 8, 1827, which effectively put an end to the chaos. Hüsrev Pasha changed the Mansure army drastically, and the practices of the Nizam-ı Cedid were discontinued. The modern regiment (Alay), battalion (Tabur), and company (Bölük) organizational structures were introduced, albeit slowly due to the ongoing war with Russia. The first modern infantry regiment was founded in February 1829, and the transformation of the rest of the regiments continued until the end of 1831. This new unit structure effectively curbed the independence of the different military corps, and in less than two years the unification of all corps into a single army was more or less finished. Hüsrev Pasha did not neglect to place members of his retinue into critical posts, and quite literally the Mansure army became his domain.[18]

The weakest part of the Ottoman military was its officer corps, which did not benefit from the ongoing reforms and even lost much of its proficiency. Earlier, Mahmud had tried his best to resuscitate the classical officer training system, especially the palace school (Enderun), by turning it into a springboard for further reforms, well before the abolishment of the Janissary corps. He personally took part in classical military training exercises and even excelled at some military sports including archery, Cirit (a cavalry game based on javelin attack and defense), Tomak (a kind of martial art with heavy wooden clubs), and wrestling.[19] But these efforts were largely unsuccessful. After the start of the Mansure reforms, he supported and further increased military training. He picked the best and brightest men within the imperial household and palace guards and organized them into an infantry company and a cavalry squadron, which later expanded into a battalion with additional units such as artillery, waggoners, and a military band. Success in any military related subject was immediately rewarded with promotion or gifts.[20]

The training center had no real program other than the caprice of the sultan. Mahmud happily tested various ideas, including opening a special primary school for the training center, as well as weird combat formations and maneuvers. However, none of them produced meaningful results other than entertaining the sultan himself. Similarly, there were no regulations concerning examinations, scoring, and graduation. All of these depended upon the Sultan and one's connections. Most often, appearance and bearing was enough to gain favors and promotion. As the sole officer training center, the palace school graduates were promoted easily and were assigned to critical military posts. Inevitably, dignitaries demanded and succeeded in forcing the acceptance of their sons into this makeshift training center—making it even more corrupt and anarchic.[21]

Eventually, Mahmud tired of this project and was increasingly dissatisfied with it, due to the poor performance of its graduates. Essentially, the palace school cadets were no more than playmates for the Sultan, and because of the lack of military expertise and sound training programs, their skills tended to be childishly showy rather than warlike and practical. Patronage and paternalistic relationships designed to please the Sultan took precedence over real military issues. The ever-present disciplinary problems and intergroup struggles aggravated the situation. The necessary excuse for abolishing the school appeared only when a majority of the cadets repeatedly refused to attend Hüsrev Pasha's rigorous training, and it was duly abolished in May 1830.[22] The only legacy of this experiment was the court band (Mızıka-i Hümayun), which survived intact. Neither Mahmud nor any reformer paid attention to the lessons learned and consequently no benefits accrued from either successes or failures. This would remain as an inherent problem afflicting all the reform efforts of the period.

Reality and Humiliation: The Ottoman-Russian War of 1828–1829 and the Rebellion of Kavalalı Mehmed Ali Pasha

The brief peace ended with a Russian declaration of war against the Ottoman Empire on April 26, 1828. A long list of Russian demands was compounded by the further humiliation of granting more rights for Greeks and other Balkan Christians, leaving the empire with no recourse other than war.[23] It was a war that was forced upon the empire against its will. Moreover, in its entire history, the empire had never been so unprepared for war. Even though militarily useless, the destruction of the Janissaries created a vacuum within the sociopolitical structure of the empire and alienated some groups and, in the case of Bosnia, the whole province. During the war, the Bosnians refused to send any provincial troops, which were about 40,000 strong, thereby sabotaging the Balkan defenses.[24]

Except for two strong guard (Hassa) regiments of 6,000 men, the Ottoman regular army had 33 poorly trained Mansure regiments (totaling 16,500 men), four regular cavalry regiments (3,600 men), engineers (2,600 men), and 92 field artillery batteries. Mahmud's decision to keep most of the Istanbul regiments of the Mansure for the defense of the capital city and its immediate surroundings, including the Straits, further constrained Ottoman military capabilities. The administration had no other choice than to recruit as many volunteers, mercenaries, and tribal warriors as it could.

The proclamation of a holy war against much hated Russians did produce results in all of the core provinces in which provincial magnates recruited hundreds of volunteers in addition to their retinues. Traditional mercenaries like the Albanians and western Anatolians joined the army under their chieftains, whereas the Arab provinces stayed away from contributing to the war effort. Similarly, the Kurdish tribes of the east stayed neutral and followed a wait-and-see policy due to their uneasiness with the reformist administration. Even though the numbers of the irregulars fluctuated greatly during the war, it is safe to say that their numbers exceeded 80,000.[25]

Interestingly, for the first time, the administration classified all of these groups into one category called Başıbozuks (literally "broken heads" or "crazies," but the word came to define irregulars) in order to differentiate them from regular units. The Başıbozuks would remain an important part of the Ottoman expeditionary armies up until the 1880s. Their colorful and exotic clothes (in comparison to the dull uniforms of the regulars), artistically ornamented weapons, daring attacks, and anarchic camps captured the imagination of the western travelers of the nineteenth century. But in reality, only the tribal warriors had magnificent outfits, and most of the rest were poor villagers and urban unemployed who were trying desperately to earn a living. There were two types of irregulars, varying according to their contracts. The majority made contracts with a certain governor or a provincial magnate, whereas only a small minority made contracts directly with the central government.[26]

The Ottoman strategy depended totally on fortresses and static defense lines. The Danube River and the fortresses of İbrail (Brailow), Varna, Silistire, Rusçuk (Ruse), Vidin (the last four better known as Kale-i Erbaa, quadrilateral fortresses),[27] and several other smaller ones were the first and main line of defense. The provinces of Moldavia and Wallachia were left undefended other than the presence of light cavalry harassment parties. Şumnu (Shumla) and three other mountain passes were fortified and were planned to be held by the commander in chief himself. The obvious vulnerabilities of the Ottoman defense system were its static nature, old and neglected fortifications, lack of mobile reserves, and wide gaps between the fortifications.[28]

The situation on the Caucasian front was even grimmer. Only a small portion of the regular army, four regiments, was supporting a fledgling army of 30,000 irregulars. The fortresses of Batum, Kars, Ardahan, Ahıska (Akhaltzikhe), Ahılkelek (Akhalkalaki), and Bayezid were the backbone of the defense, but they were isolated fortresses without any means of mutual support or connection. Additionally, all of them were old types of fortifications and were weakened further by decades of neglect. In a way, the real defense of the Caucasus depended on the martial spirit of the people and on the weaknesses of the Russian military lines of communication and logistics.

Based on poor Ottoman performance during the Greek rebellion and on imaginary intelligence estimates, the Russian high command estimated that the Ottoman European defenses would crumble easily and that Russian forward elements would reach Edirne during the campaign season of 1828. The initial phase of the campaign reinforced this overoptimistic estimate. The Russian army began crossing the Pruth River on May 7, 1828, and without facing any major Ottoman resistance, reached Dobruca in three days. Surprisingly, the Ottoman defenders did not make use of the formidable Danube River to stop or delay the Russian invaders, and the Russians laid siege to İbrail with minimum casualties. The defenders of İbrail initially showed determination and bravery. However, the sudden collapse of the Dobruca defensive system, combined with no possibility of an immediate relieving force, affected the defenders, who lost heart. The fortress surrendered with large amounts of provisions and ammunition on June 17.[29]

The confidence and expectations of the Russian high command were further increased after the inspiring victory of Pazarcık over the Ottoman main army. This was the result of the devastating superiority of the Russian field artillery. But the Ottomans managed to stop the Russian advance in front of the Şumnu fortifications, as they had in the previous Russian invasions of 1774 and 1810, by making effective use of terrain and earthen fortifications. The confidence of the defenders increased in the meantime, and the Russians seemed stupefied by ingenious Ottoman night attacks and never-ending cavalry harassment. The Şumnu defense effectively stalled the faulty Russian campaign and any hope the Russians had of finishing the war before the start of the winter season.[30]

Similarly, the fortresses of Varna and Silistire conducted stiff defenses and further blocked any flanking maneuver that would bypass Şumnu or secure the Russian lines of communication. In both of these cases, the Ottoman defenders surprised the Russian besiegers with various active defense methods, including constant counterattacks and cavalry action, effective earthen fortifications, and countermining operations. Most importantly, the defenders kept morale high despite heavy casualty figures and much privation. Moreover, the civilian populations of both cities showed remarkable enthusiasm for the war and actively contributed to the defense. Unknowingly within the eyesight of a relieving army, the defenders of Varna gave up on October 11 after four months of enduring constant artillery fire and enemy assaults, losing most of its cadres (6,000 defenders remained alive out of the original strength of 22,000). To achieve this result, the besiegers received heavy reinforcements of soldiers, artillery, and engineers several times, and the Russian Tsar even visited his army to boost its morale.[31]

Silistire, which was a relatively weak fortress in comparison to Varna and İbrail, managed to carry on until the advent of winter, when the Russian besiegers had to abandon the siege and retreat to their winter quarters.[32] Obviously, the Russian high command did not achieve its overambitious goal, but the high casualty figures, more than 40,000, were seen as evidence of success, which caused the relief of the top ranking Russian commanders. On the other hand, Mahmud and his close circle perceived the successful defense of Şumnu and Silistire (as well as the extended fight for Varna) as victories. They stubbornly dreamed of driving away the Russian invaders during the next campaign season, while paying no attention to the structural problems within the Ottoman military, the ultimate fall of Varna, and the series of humiliating defeats on the Caucasus front.[33]

Interestingly, the Caucasus front received scant attention from both warring parties. From the very beginning, the Ottoman high command left the eastern provinces to their fate by sending limited numbers of regular units and artillery. Moreover, the

Ottomans set their hopes on the success of an Iranian general attack in 1826 into Russian Caucasia, which turned out to be a huge strategic error. After suffering horrific defeats and a Russian invasion into Azerbaijan, the Iranians signed the humiliating Treaty of Türkmençay in which they withdrew from the Caucasus altogether. Additionally, the Russian Army of the Caucasus captured huge amounts of provisions and ammunition that subsidized the Russian war effort against the Ottomans. The Ottomans also committed the obvious folly of letting Russian military contractors buy all the surplus food and fodder in the region just before the start of hostilities, further crippling Ottoman defenses.[34]

The Russians started combat operations by besieging the fortress of Anapa on May 18, 1828, while the main army under the able command of General Ivan Fedorovich Paskievitch crossed into Ottoman territory on May 26. After a brief resistance, the Anapa fortress surrendered on June 23. The equally unprepared, but militarily stronger, Kars fortress shared the same fate and fell on the same day. The Kars fortress was not only a strategic fortification, but also the pride of the Ottoman Caucasus defenses; it had played an important role previously by withstanding an Iranian siege in 1735 and a Russian siege in 1807. The fall of Kars effectively destroyed the Ottoman Caucasian defensive posture and shocked the entire region, while the fall of the seemingly unimportant fortress of Anapa demoralized and neutralized all the neighboring northern Caucasian nations.[35]

The Ottoman main army did try to save Kars but was defeated, and only the outbreak of plague temporarily stopped the Russian advance. Paskievitch successfully deceived the Ottoman high command and, instead of advancing in the direction of Erzurum and facing the Ottoman main army, he turned back to attack the Ahalkelek fortress. The bravery of the garrison merely delayed the inevitable outcome, and the fortress surrendered on August 15. The Ottoman army rushed to protect the Ahıska fortress. But once again, Ottoman troops arrived late and were defeated by the well-positioned Russian artillery. The defenders of Ahıska, including the townsmen, desperately fought back, but lacking effective command and control and modern fortifications, their bravery caused little hardship for the Russian besiegers.[36]

The victorious army of Paskievitch further strengthened its gains by easily capturing Bayezid and some other minor fortifications with the help of a wait-and-see policy of the Kurdish tribes. So in five months' time, Russians achieved nearly all their aims, except the port of Batum, by capturing four large and various smaller fortified cities with an army of only 18,000 regulars and a handful of irregulars. The Ottoman army failed to conduct any serious resistance and was defeated repeatedly thanks to the leadership of Paskievitch and the efficiency of his artillery.[37]

The defeated Ottoman Army of the Caucasus was then subjected to a structural reorganization that included changing all high-ranking commanders and raising additional units (albeit all were irregulars). For the first time, the Ottomans chose an offensive strategy for the campaign season of 1829. Their plan was to launch feint attacks against Kars and an amphibious landing near Batum in order to surprise and confuse the Russians, which would facilitate the main effort; the attack and capture of Ahıska. The plan was more than brilliant, and the Russians were unprepared for such a bold enemy undertaking. However, the Ottoman commanders and units had neither the means nor the training to carry out such an ambitious plan. Thus, the feint attacks did not divert any Russian troops, and the main effort failed in every aspect even though the Russian defenses were weak. The defeated Ottoman units again retreated in disorder on March 16, 1829.[38]

The failed Ottoman offensive provided ample opportunities for the Russians, which Paskievitch relentlessly took advantage of by launching concentric offensives. The Russian troops passed through the main Ottoman defense line on the massive Soğanlı block by using undefended mountain roads and passes, thanks to defective Ottoman preparations and slow reactions. After skillfully dislocating and dividing the Ottoman defenders into two groups, he attacked the main group and easily routed it. The second group dispersed without any resistance. Paskievitch continued his offensive, without loosing momentum, towards Erzurum, which held the geographic key to Anatolia. There were no effective military units left to defend the city, and by making use of various collaborators, especially the strong Armenian minority, Paskievitch destroyed the will to fight of the civilian population and their leadership, who gave up on July 9. A last-minute Ottoman attack by Kurdish tribes against the Bayezid fortress failed to alter the situation.[39]

The Ottoman Army of the Balkans shared the same fate as the Caucasus army, even though Sultan Mahmud and Ottoman high command dreamed of a victory at the beginning of the campaign season. Against high hopes, the Ottoman army did not receive enough reinforcements and was unready for the campaign in terms of everything—and chief among the shortages was morale. The new Ottoman commander in chief, Grand Vizier Reşid Mehmed Pasha, a protégé of Hüsrev Pasha, was the most talented general of the empire. However, he had difficulty seeing the realities on the ground, and he possessed very limited means of command and control over his units scattered around the combat zone. In contrast, the Russians made major changes in their overall strategy after the bitter lessons of the previous year and not only reinforced the expeditionary forces but also assigned better commanders, like the new commander in chief General Diebitsch.[40]

The Russians captured the critical harbor city of Süzebol with a lightning attack, once again thanks to the ever-careless Ottoman defenders and faulty defensive strategy. The Ottoman joint land and naval attack to recapture Süzebol failed and with it also any chance of keeping the coastal road secure.[41] The optimistic Reşid Pasha paid scant attention to this development and instead attacked the Russian concentration around Prevadi on May 27. Even though this attack surprised the Russians, it did not achieve any significant result other than increasing the confidence of Reşid Pasha. He repeated the attack, this time targeting the Kozluca concentration, by stripping all the units from within the Şumnu fortifications. General Diebitsch gathered timely intelligence about the Ottoman movements, became aware of the Reşid Pasha's intentions, and decided to surround him. The Russian units maneuvered swiftly and encircled the advancing Ottoman army in Gülefçe (Kulewtscha) on June 11. The cavalry-heavy Ottoman army fought back valiantly and launched desperate attacks that melted against Russian artillery. Nevertheless, these attacks saved the army from complete annihilation, and a few Ottoman units managed to escape. Reşid Pasha returned to Şumnu with two or three under-strength regiments—all the others having dissipated or having been captured.[42]

In the meantime, the Russians concentrated a sizable force to capture Silistire, the only remaining Ottoman Danubean fortress. In direct contrast to their able stand against the Russians during the previous year, the garrison of Silistire was completely unprepared for a new siege. The garrison had neither built new fortifications nor repaired the old ones. Moreover, the Ottomans did not even destroy the Russian trenches, gunnery positions, and other besieging works surrounding the city. So the Russians were able to renew easily the siege from their former positions. There was also conflict between the original garrison and Anatolian reinforcement units. The defeat of Gülefçe further weakened morale and increased the tension between defenders; one side tried to find ways for surrender while the other side launched desperate sorties. In the end, massive Russian artillery and rocket fire convinced the defenders of the futility of resistance, and they surrendered on July 30.[43]

General Diebitsch decided not to waste any time capturing the Ottoman fortifications but force-marched towards Edirne instead, bypassing all remaining defensive positions. He divided his army along two corridors, one following the coastal road, the other following the direction of Aydos-İslimiye-Edirne. Incredibly, the Ottoman commanders, instead of blocking the Russian advance with all available forces and attacking its rear, remained in their original defensive positions or retreated away from the theater of operations. Russian units drove toward Edirne, as if in a race, crushing makeshift volunteer units opposing the advance. Panic and the absence of any leadership were more than evident when the Edirne garrison of 15,000 surrendered without a fight against a Russian army of 30,000 that was very tired, without provisions, and afflicted by plague on August 20.[44]

Even though the treatment of the Ottoman Empire in the Treaty of Edirne in terms of territory lost seemed lenient; in reality the Russian Empire acquired critical locations that could act as springboards both in the Balkans and Caucasus for future campaigns.[45] The Treaty of Edirne further bruised the already tarnished self-confidence and morale of the Ottoman military and empire as a whole. The major shortcomings of the Mansure reforms (previously discussed) crippled the Ottoman war effort, but the war itself clarified and illuminated them thoroughly. The first and foremost problem was clearly the faulty decision-making process caused largely by a lack of trained military commanders at all levels. The ignorance of military art and science was so obvious that even fundamental issues were neglected or done superficially, such as poor logistical management, lack of mobilization and movement plans, complete lack of unity of command and coordination, total absence of security and, as always, ever-present corruption.[46] Most of the time nonmilitary issues took precedence and the Ottoman military remained at the bottom of the government's priority list. The best example in this respect was, without doubt, the allocation and positioning of the armies. Due to the concerns related to internal security, the fragile balance of sociopolitical power, and Mahmud's personal preferences, the elite regiments of the army remained out of the actual theater of operations throughout the war. Waiting for a fantastic victory, while paying scant attention to the old and much neglected state of the Danubean and Caucasian defenses, was more than enough to show the ineffectiveness of the high command's leadership in the war effort.[47]

A second important problem was not actually directly related to the Ottoman military but rather to the sociopolitical transformation of the empire. The rapid growth of nationalist feelings and separatist aims within the Christian communities of the Balkans broke the bonds of loyalty to the empire. And, of course, increased foreign meddling aroused their suspicions toward the Ottomans. Even though nationalism did not spread to all corners of the Balkans immediately, and in fact most of the people preferred to watch events passively, the administration had limited means to affect this process and fight against direct and indirect foreign interventions. The impact of this ongoing process on the Ottoman military was obvious; Muslim citizens became the sole group that the empire could rely on militarily.

As already pointed out in previous chapters, even though Islam was a very important element in the identity of the Ottoman Empire, Christian communities remained an important part of the military. But developments after the Greek rebellion changed this paradigm drastically and, except for the Cossack cavalry of the Silistire regiment and some Christian Albanian mercenaries, we can safely say that the combat components of the Ottoman military became a totally Muslim force at this point in history. The active collaboration of some of the Christian groups during the Russian occupation and the subsequent migration of thousands of them—about 20,000 Bulgarians and 90,000 Armenians—with the retreating Russian forces further reinforced the suspicions of the administration and the Muslim population.[48]

In addition to being unable to make use of the potential of the Christian communities, the administration proved equally incapable of mobilizing the Muslim population for the war effort. In truth, part of the reason for this was the alienation of important segments of the Muslim population, which opposed the radical and harsh nature of the Mansure reforms. In most of the empire's towns and cities, the civilian populations passively sat out the war and Russian invasions, while the Bosnians completely refused to serve the sultan at all. The last-minute call to arms also failed and the Russians passed through the country with limited opposition. This alienation turned out to be a temporary problem, and the administration managed to solve it later, but it cost dearly during the war.[49]

The third problem was the poor combination of leadership and manpower. For the first time in decades, the Ottoman military displayed absolute obedience, but obedience itself proved of small value, as the ill-trained, ill-equipped, and poorly led Mansure regiments were no match for Russian line infantry. In addition to bravery, sturdiness, and obedience, the military actually had some defensive skills. But these were not suitable for offensive operations, and any complex maneuvers were impossible. The artillery corps was the best trained element of the Mansure army, but the number of batteries was insufficient relative to the size of the army and, moreover, their cannons were inferior.[50]

Similarly, the Ottoman commanders could not make use of the potential of the Başıbozuks, the major component of the army. The Başıbozuks were mainly light cavalrymen who, by definition, were ill-suited for employment against conventional infantry-artillery combined forces. In order to achieve conventional effectiveness and to preserve an acceptable level of discipline, they required the presence of regular units alongside them, which seldom happened. The collapse of the Caucasian defenses was the apparent outcome of the massive use of Başıbozuks without the backup of the regulars.[51] However, the Başıbozuks had excellent potential to create havoc behind enemy lines, to attack isolated units, to conduct raids, reconnaissance, and other intelligence duties, to lay ambushes, and to complete other irregular tasks. And, in contrast to regular units, they were almost indestructible, because they could immediately disperse, escape, and regroup afterwards. They were also cheap, expendable, and less dependent on conventional logistics systems.

Ottoman commanders at all levels stubbornly tried to employ them as regular forces. For example, 3,000 Başıbozuk cavalry were ordered to defend the harbor city of Süzebol, which did not work for understandable reasons. Similarly the all-Başıbozuk cavalry force of Viryon Ömer Pasha was ordered to relieve Varna, which was an impossible mission from the beginning. Ömer Pasha did achieve some success against the Russian screening force at Kurttepe but was unable to proceed toward the main Russian army and watched helplessly the fall of Varna. However, the Başıbozuks achieved remarkable results when employed according to their potential as in the example of the successful raids of the Vidin and Rusçuk Başıbozuk units into Wallachia against Russian convoys and isolated units in which they spread fear and deprived the enemy of provisions (albeit temporarily).[52] Unfortunately for the Ottomans, the high command never thought through the potential of massed continuous attacks against the already thinly stretched Russian logistics lines.

Last, but not least, Mahmud's fascination with appearance and bearing, rather than with the structural and inner elements of the military reforms, gave a false sense of confidence to most of the reformers. Mahmud liked to toy with new uniforms, equipment, and buildings. Valuable resources and time were expended on these at the cost of training, organization, and leadership. The new units spent week after week on parade and marching in close order drills to satisfy their sovereign. The acceptance, or in reality the enforcement, of European-style uniforms and the equipment related with it, was without doubt also a major misstep by the reformers. Obviously, the new uniforms set the new soldiers completely apart from the defunct old corps. However, the new uniforms were received by the Muslim public with distrust and disdain and, in some cases, open hostility. Even western observers found the new uniforms simply awkward, and they longed for the magnificent outfits of the past. In the words of von Moltke, the Ottoman army "was composed of men disciplined after the European fashion, wearing Russian jackets, and Turkish trousers; with Tartar saddles and French stirrups, and English sabers."[53]

As a conclusion, even though the Ottoman military surprised the Russians greatly and inflicted heavy casualties,[54] it shattered the dreams of its sovereign and embarrassed the public as a whole. Furthermore, the war annihilated many of the new military cadres that the administration worked so hard to train. Therefore, Mahmud once again had to rebuild his army—find and train new recruits, buy weapons and equipment, and more importantly, find a solution for training the future officer corps. Unfortunately for Mahmud, the end of foreign aggression was followed by a dangerous internal aggression, the rebellion of Governor of Egypt Kavalalı Mehmed Ali Pasha.[55]

As mentioned in the previous chapter, political and administrative centralization and the elimination of powerful magnates were key elements of Mahmud's reforms. Mahmud skillfully eliminated most of the magnates by watching for the ideal opportunity, then using one against the other or assimilating them into his administration. But these methods did not always work as in the example of Tepedelenli Ali Pasha, whose insurrection facilitated the Greek rebellion and independence. And the most important and independent-minded magnate, Kavalalı Mehmed Ali Pasha, controlled the rich and distant province of Egypt.

He was well aware that Mahmud would do his best to remove him at the earliest opportunity. Moreover, he was more than frustrated and disappointed at not getting what he thought he deserved for his important services in suppressing the Wahabi rebellion in the Hejaz (1811–1816) and the Greek rebellion. The reward he sought was his long-cherished dream of controlling the governorates of all the Syrian provinces in addition to his current post. Even though he was not thinking of independence at this stage, his insistence on widening his control, along with a concession of hereditary rights in Egypt, in reality was nothing less than carving out an almost completely independent entity (in a way restoration of the old Mamluk Sultanate of Egypt and Syria) at the expense of the Ottoman Empire. Several other minor factors also contributed to his rebellion, such as his growing dislike of Mahmud and his inner circle and the increasing number of Egyptian refugees taking shelter in Akka province.[56]

Mehmed Ali Pasha's army (imitating his predecessor Ali Bey's campaign) rolled into Syria under the command of his son, İbrahim Pasha. Surprising even the most pessimistic observer of the Ottoman Empire, İbrahim Pasha easily crossed the Sinai desert and captured Yafa (Jaffa) and Hayfa (Haifa) 15 days after the start of hostilities on November 2, 1831. The mighty fortress of Akka and its stubborn defenders stopped the advance for six months (December 4, 1831–May 27, 1832), but the cities of the Syrian provinces, including Damascus, rapidly fell afterwards. The civilian population heartily welcomed the invaders and in some cases actively supported them. The Ottoman administration was not able to mobilize the might of the empire and tried in vain to end the crisis peacefully. Readily available forces, once again mostly irregular cavalry, were sent in piecemeal and were defeated completely.[57]

İbrahim Pasha, with growing confidence and boldness, was able to defeat two Ottoman armies separately in two battles, Humus (July 2) and Bilan (July 29), by maintaining momentum and achieving surprise. His army managed to pass the formidable Taurus Mountains and poured into Southern Anatolia. At this critical stage, İbrahim Pasha, instead of sticking to the original plan of conquering only the Syrian provinces, decided to advance into Anatolia. However, the need for rest, reinforcements, resupplying, and reorganization put an effective brake on his operations for more than four months, during which time the Ottoman administration managed to mobilize its available resources and established four new army groups.[58]

İbrahim Pasha foresaw trouble and decided once again to advance and crush the nearest Ottoman army before it joined forces with the others. It was a headlong dash into the unknown during the coldest time of winter, and hundreds of Egyptian soldiers froze to death. The unlucky commander in chief of the Russian war, Mehmed Reşid Pasha, was once again the Ottoman commanding officer. His army was mainly composed of Başıbozuks from Albania and Macedonia. Bearing in mind the problematic nature of depending solely on irregulars, Reşid Pasha decided to wait for incoming reinforcements and retreated away from the Egyptian provincial army. But he hesitated at the very last moment and turned back towards the enemy. The hesitation of Reşid Pasha damaged the already weak morale of the soldiers, and the poorly led and disoriented (due to misty weather) Ottoman army attacked the well-entrenched enemy on the Konya plains on December 21.

İbrahim Pasha skillfully concentrated his artillery's decisive weight of fire on the blindly attacking Ottoman units. The Ottoman artillery, although superior in numbers, did not fire back effectively due to a faulty decision to distribute cannons to the few infantry battalions that were available. An Egyptian cavalry counterattack kept the Ottomans off balance, thereby further destroying their combat formations and cohesion. To make things worse, Reşid Pasha was captured, and the disorganized Ottoman units panicked when they realized their commander was captured. The survivors fled, leaving most of their cannons and baggage behind.[59]

The unfortunate Mahmud was left with few choices other than to ask for help from his archenemy, Russia. The arrival of Russian troops in Istanbul as well as British diplomatic intervention soon stopped the advance of İbrahim Pasha. After tortuous negotiations, the Ottoman delegation had to accept the embarrassing demands of Mehmed Ali Pasha and duly signed the Treaty of Kütahya on May 5, 1833, in which all governorates of the Syrian provinces and Adana were given to Mehmed Ali Pasha.[60]

Unifying the Command, Training the Officer Corps, and Recruiting the Peasants

The Ottoman administration and public received a huge shock after a series of defeats suffered at the hands of a rebellious governor's army dramatically exposed the weakness of the military. The level of trauma was so great that it literally erased the humiliation suffered during the Greek rebellion and the recent Russian war. Actually the empire was on the point of collapse. It had not only lost two major wars, but also enemies appeared in front of its capital twice. However, Sultan Mahmud showed his determination and, with unwavering belief in the merits of military reforms, began a new package of reforms targeting the high command structure and the officer corps.[61]

As already mentioned, Mahmud did not envision a unified military under single command and control structure. He merely replaced the Janissaries with the Mansure and kept most of the remaining old corps intact. So the newly created post of Serasker (commander in chief), regardless of its seemingly important title, was nothing more than the commander of the Mansure, at most a kind of *primus inter pares*. Over the passage of time and during the introduction of new reforms, the absurdity of a decentralized military structure with independent corps became evident. However, several factors delayed the introduction of a unified command system. Chief among them was a lack of military know-how and understanding of the importance of a single command and control structure and associated general staff duties. Secondly, Mahmud, following old Ottoman traditions, liked to play one person or group against another and always remained suspicious of his immediate commanders. He saw the single command concept as a dangerous rival to his own authority, and his insistence in creating a separate imperial guard army (Hassa) was the outcome of this suspicion.[62]

Interestingly, the totally new concept of unified command was introduced thanks to the conservative, but power hungry, Hüsrev Pasha, who became Serasker in May 1827. The recent series of disasters and ever-present crisis atmosphere helped him greatly to consolidate power into his own hands. Hüsrev Pasha, by assigning his protégés from his wide household, was able to control most of the important nerve centers of the Ottoman military. At the zenith of his power, there were more than 30 generals and dozens of other ranking officers from his household in office. Thereafter, most of the independent corps, albeit unofficially, were brought under the control of the Serasker. Hüsrev Pasha also managed to diminish the power of the Nazır (superintendent) position, a civilian high official responsible for financial and administrativel issues, created to check the power of the Serasker.[63]

Hüsrev Pasha understood quite well that military knowledge was the key to power under Sultan Mahmud. To achieve a complete monopoly on military knowledge, he created a private staff of foreign experts, translators, and other useful personnel. So without knowing it, he created a makeshift but still the first-ever modern military staff in the empire. Not surprisingly, some of his staff personnel would achieve great fame and power later on, as in the example of Michael Latas, who was better known as Ömer Lütfü Pasha, the famous commander of the Crimean War. Little by little Hüsrev's private staff became the model for an official military staff for the Serasker. Consequently, the Seraskeriye (literally the office of the commander in chief) not only provided its traditional duty of scribal services but, more importantly, performed military staff duties as well. But obviously this process moved painfully slowly and, as might be expected, mirror organizations were established by rival organizations, chief among them the guards (Hassa).

This series of reorganizations and reforms destroyed the independent institutional structures of various corps such as the distribution of artillery units into divisions, and they became an organizational part of the Mansure. Experienced former commanders of the independent corps became noncommanding staff officers of the Serasker, thereby introducing the first real elements of a modern general staff system. Of course, the modern general staff system remained a novelty for the Ottoman military up until the end of the Crimean War; nevertheless, the Military Academy began to train general staff officers, modeled on the French example, after 1844. However, we must bear in mind that the Ottoman general staff was still in its infancy long after its adoption by the highly developed militaries of western Europe. Similarly, former civilian institutions of ordnance and military equipment manufacturing became subordinate organs of the Seraskeriye.[64]

Mahmud's preference of establishing military councils at all levels, the highest one, Dar-i Şura-ı Askeri (council for military affairs), affected the development of Seraskeriye adversely. As mentioned before, gathering all the grandees and high officials became an important mechanism of consensus and legitimization for the reforms starting with Selim III. But Mahmud's insistence on establishing councils at all levels and his tendency to listen to them for nearly all major issues became a problem. Day-to-day meddling in the command and control of combat actions in faraway theaters created a parallel command structure to the Seraskeriye, thereby destroying the unity of the military hierarchy. Furthermore, high-ranking commanders personally had to establish and preserve good relations with council members in Istanbul. Even though Mahmud was often able to direct the decision-making process according to his wishes, council members still had enough power to manipulate many aspects of life within the military. Clearly these councils played an important role in the formulation of military reforms by providing various interest groups with a voice for their ideas. This duality of checks and balances between councils and the Seraskeriye continued on for several decades, but by the 1880s the councils lost their influence and power and became solely posts for elderly generals.[65]

The essence of the new reform package was the establishment of an educational institution in which future officers would be trained according to current European models and standards. Mahmud and his commanders were aware of the high standards achieved by the Mehmed Ali Pasha's army, but it was the performance of its officers during the recent war that astonished them the most. It was probably the ethnic and sociocultural origins of Mehmed Ali Pasha's officers that played the most important role in this development. Although Mehmed Ali Pasha recruited Egyptian peasants for the ranks of his army, he trained and assigned Turkish-speaking officers who were well versed in Ottoman culture. Interestingly, he recruited most of them from Istanbul and other big cities of the empire with the private permission of Mahmud. And in some cases Egyptian recruiters lured the students from the newly founded schools to which Mahmud attached special importance.[66] As a result, the high level of training and expertise achieved by the fellow officers of the Egyptian provincial army impressed the Ottoman high command more than that of the Europeans. Additionally, several Egyptian-trained deserters played important roles as lecturers and administrators, notably Selim Satıh Pasha.

Out of frustration and following the example of Egypt[67] closely, the administration decided to send bright youngsters to Europe in order to set up a firm base of trained officers to launch further reforms. Not surprisingly, Hüsrev Pasha once again proactively sent four youngsters from his household to France in 1830, well before the start of discussions within the government circles. These four students achieved immediate professional success after their return to country that one of them (İbrahim Edhem Pasha) was able to achieve the rank of Grand Vizierate.[68] A few years later, the administration dispatched the first groups of students to Austria and Britain. In contrast to the success of Hüsrev's protégés, these students encountered immense difficulties in adjusting themselves to the European atmosphere and lifestyle. They were not only lacking the necessary language skills, but also the secondary-school-level educational background to continue their education. So they were obliged to study at preparatory schools or took private lessons in order to qualify for admission to military academies or other schools of higher education.

The practice of sending students to European countries continued on in spite of the founding of Military Academy and other institutions of higher education. The numbers of problems grew geometrically with the increase of students. At the end, the administration decided to establish an Ottoman-led preparatory school so as to give intensive training and to supervise the students more thoroughly.[69] The Mekteb-i Osmani (L'École Impériale Ottomane) was founded in Paris in 1857. The French government showed special interest and took the school under the control and patronage of the Ministry of Education. The Ottoman students were gathered and put under the supervision of an Ottoman officer and taught by the specially selected French lecturers. Even though the students were supposed to be selected from the Ottoman high schools according to their academic success, a sizable percentage of them were either relatives or protégés of the grandees. Thanks to the spirit of Tanzimat, Christian students from different ethnic groups were also dispatched.[70]

Unfortunately for the empire, this novel and very expensive experience failed from the very beginning. Obviously, the heavy presence of children from influential parentage did instrumentally weaken the discipline, order, and academic excellence. The insubordination and breaches of rules were rife. Students were neither very willing to fulfill the academic requirements nor did they have the proper background. Finally, the administration decided to give up keeping a school in Paris and instead accelerated the preparations for the founding of a high school (the famed Lyceé of Galatasaray, Mekteb-i Sultani) with French-sanctioned curriculum. The Mekteb-i Osmani was abolished after barely seven years in existence in 1864.[71]

It was the establishment of a new military educational institution, namely the Mekteb-i Ulum-u Harbiye (Turkish Military Academy), in 1834 that turned out to be the zenith of Mahmud's military reforms and one of the most important turning points in the history of the Ottoman modernization. As mentioned in the previous chapter, some military schools had been opened before the Military Academy. But either they disappeared in a short time, or they were purely technical schools with very limited enrollments. Therefore, except for a few engineers and artillery officers, none of the Ottoman officers were academically trained. The majority of the junior officers were rankers (Alaylı literally from the regiment) without even primary school education, and their identical social and military origins with the private soldiers caused problems in terms of respect to higher ranks and discipline. In most cases the clients of grandees and protégés of the sultan occupied high-ranking military posts. Few officers ever reached high rank without having support of the sultan or a grandee, whereas a few junior scribes managed to obtain commissions by making use of their literary talents in an army of illiterates. As can be expected, most of the generals had no military background and experience, thanks to the patron-client relationship, which promoted the according to court politics. Likewise the rankers had limited capacity to command units above company level.[72] As a consequence, the Ottoman Empire depended on connections or chance and talent, rather than on a developmental system, for manning its high command.

In this respect, following the origins and career patterns of some of the famous Ottoman military figures illustrates the inner workings of the Ottoman officer corps during this period. The unlucky but famous commander of the Russian wars and Greek and Mehmed Ali Pasha rebellions, Mehmed Reşid Pasha was one of the most successful members of Hüsrev Pasha's household (which produced more than 30 generals). The author of the Nizip disaster, Hafız Pasha, was a protégé of Mahmud and was promoted to lieutenant-general rank in three years after commissioning as a major in 1827. Mustafa Zarif Pasha received his commission at the age of 14 due to his scribal skills and became a general at the age of 27. He had no command and combat experience, but still he was assigned as the commander of the Kars army in the initial phase of the Crimean War immediately after a series of blunders and defeats. Not surprisingly, he became the author of the Gökdere (Kurudere) disaster in which the Ottoman forces lost all offensive capacity.[73]

Cast against this paternalistic and ineffective atmosphere and in contrast to earlier schools, the new Military Academy was something totally different. The main idea behind its establishment was to educate as many cadets as possible in the European style for an expanding new army. In this way, reformers thought to overcome the deficiencies of the Ottoman military system. And at the same time they wished to have officers who understood European ideas in every respect, who themselves would prove able to continue the reforms, not only in the military, but in other institutions of the empire. For this reason the reformers preferred to follow the French military educational system instead of a short-term officer corps training system like the one Kavalalı Mehmed Ali Paşa had successfully founded in Egypt.[74] It is no surprise that the founding father of the academy was a highly trained civilian bureaucrat who was commissioned as a military officer later in his career; Mehmed Namık Pasha.[75]

Namık Pasha, following the fashion of his time, advocated for the French model, the French military school L'Ecole Spéciale Militaire de Saint-Cyr, which provided purely military vocational education with specific emphasis on theoretical studies.[76] According to his vision, the school needed to be self-sufficient without need for pre-requisites from any other institution. Consequently, an old barracks (Maçka Kışlası) isolated from the civilian quarters of Istanbul was chosen and refurbished. A state-of-the-art indoor amphitheater, library, and printing-press facility was constructed. And he did not forget to build a mosque to silence criticism coming from religious circles. It is evident that Mahmud preferred not to place this critical institution under the control of Hüsrev Pasha, who was already very powerful. Moreover, Mahmud was also aware that the conservative Hüsrev Pasha would try to keep it as traditional as possible and certainly would place many of his retinue as cadets, thereby making the future officer corps part of his household. Therefore the Academy was not placed within the Mansure structure but instead under the structure of the Hassa or, more correctly, under the direct control of the sultan himself.[77]

The role of Namık Pasha and the establishment of the academy showed clear similarities to the example of the U. S. Military Academy at West Point and its founder Slyvanus Thayer Mahan. But, in contrast to America, the empire did not have a satisfactory primary and secondary educational system. Making things more difficult, the elite and even the middle class preferred not to enroll their sons in this new school, which was perceived as an un-Islamic and sinfully western institution. Consequently, the administration had few alternatives other than to enroll forcefully young soldiers and to collect orphans or the sons of the poor.[78] This development disconnected cadets from the patronage system but insured that they were almost entirely illiterate.

Therefore, the first cadets began their training by learning how to read and write, and other lessons were provided at the primary level of education. After six years, cadets began to take secondary and high school lessons. The main focus of their training concerned the application of their future military duties, and they took courses like "Military Engineering," "Military Ballistics," and "Strategy and Operational Art." Nevertheless, the founders and supporters (especially the civilian bureaucrats) of the new academy understood the western educational system as a magic medicine that could by itself transform the whole state and society and soon included lessons that would provide useful civilian skills such as "City Planning," "Art," "Politics and International Politics," and "Civil Engineering." In turn the new Military Academy began to train its cadets in a broad range of western ideas, and it became a safe haven against reactionary opposition.[79]

Without waiting for the fruits of the new officer training reforms, Mahmud broke the uneasy peace with Mehmed Ali Pasha after long military preparations and after receiving encouraging news of rebellions against the new Egyptian authority in Syria in 1839. His expeditionary army commanded by Hafız Pasha was better in many respects than previous armies, but command and control remained problematic due to the absence of a properly trained officer corps. Even the presence of a four-man Prussian military advisory team under the leadership of Captain Helmuth von Moltke, who would later become famous as Field Marshal Moltke, did not help much, and poor leadership prevailed. The expeditionary army of some 70,000 strong reached the plains of Nizip with only 28,000 men because of poor logistics, infectious diseases, and desertion (most of the soldiers were forcefully recruited and deserted at the first instance).[80] Unfortunately, Hafız Pasha paid attention to the oracles of his fortune-tellers rather than the advice of his military staff, including the Prussians, deciding to move into defensive positions, thereby giving the initiative totally to the Egyptians.[81]

The Egyptian provincial army was in much worse condition than it had been before after spending six years as an army of occupation in Syria. Frequent rebellions, a hostile population, harsh working conditions, poor logistics, and inadequate finances had destroyed the élan of the army. Only the iron will and discipline of İbrahim Pasha maintained its unity. Hundreds of Egyptian soldiers, including some officers, deserted and joined the Ottoman army after it reached Nizip. But at this critical moment, İbrahim Pasha showed once again the importance of leadership and knowledge of military art. He pinpointed the weakness of the Ottoman defensive positions and waited two days until exhaustion began to affect the Ottoman army. Then Egyptian infantry attacked the Ottoman positions as cavalry finished a flanking maneuver, and artillery weakened Ottoman morale further. The Ottoman defense collapsed, and units fled in panic. Oddly, Egyptian officers and soldiers continued to desert their then-victorious army.[82]

It is easy to understand the desertion of Egyptian soldiers who were forcefully recruited, who endured much hardship away from their hometowns, and who were fighting for a cause that had no value for them.[83] But the reasons for the desertion of officers were more complex and totally different from those of their soldiers. Nearly all of the officers were Turkish speakers and products of Ottoman culture. Most of them saw themselves as part of the Ottoman system and society, and many experienced conflicts in identity and loyalty when actual combat started. Beginning with the invasion of Anatolia, initially a few individuals but later on increasing numbers of them deserted to the Ottoman army, even after the series of victories.[84] For example, the talented artillery commander of the Konya battle, Selim Satıh Pasha, who played a decisive role, second only to İbrahim Pasha, deserted a few months after this remarkable achievement. Later on, Selim Pasha played an important role as the third superintendent of the Turkish Military Academy between 1837 and 1841.[85]

Sultan Mahmud died just before the news of disaster reached the capital. His lifelong dream of creating a modern military suffered yet another blow, and the empire was saved only by the efforts of Britain and its reluctant allies, the Habsburgs and Russians. The Egyptian army shattered into pieces after a brief campaign by a joint British and Ottoman army, starting with the amphibious landing in Lebanon on September 10, 1840, and following rapidly with the capture of Beirut, Akka, and the battle of Kaletülmeydan. Only a fraction of the once proud and victorious army escaped back to Egypt, and Mehmed Ali Pasha had to give up most of his gains in order to keep the governorship of semi-independent Egypt, agreeing to the reduction of his army (to a miniscule 18,000) and a similar concession that left only a small fraction of his once mighty navy.[86]

Amidst this continuous atmosphere of conflict and ever-increasing urgent calls from field commanders, the first cadets continued their training without interference for another eight years.[87] But when the first graduates received their diplomas in 1848, initial results were far from satisfactory. Only 10 officers were commissioned, which was dramatically insufficient for an army starved for officers. And there was another problem. This tiny number of officers amounted to the only available government officials in the empire who were trained in modern European methods, and there was a high demand for their services from all departments in the government. In the end, none of the graduates went to their posts, which were originally to have been as company grade officers in regiments. Some remained in the academy as lecturers, while others were assigned to high level posts in the civil departments.[88] This situation continued for almost a decade.

The Ottoman line infantry and cavalry units received their first academy graduates during the Crimean War—20 years after the founding of the academy. And, unfortunately, these pioneers had to struggle more with the elder generation of officers, who were anxious to protect their own vested interests, rather than fight against the Russians. The British military advisor of the Kars fortress, Colonel Fenwick Williams, wrote of the bitter experiences of 14 academy graduates and the insults and degradation they suffered at the hands of the older generation. Not surprisingly, and to the detriment of the eastern army, most of them found ways to transfer to better assignments in Istanbul.[89]

For obvious reasons, and thwarting the high expectations of its adherents, the effects of the new academic military education were not felt immediately. The effects proved long-term as development only came in a series of small and halting steps, which clearly frustrated the governing elite and high-ranking Ottoman officers. They had tended to forget the inertia of the sociocultural climate in which the new generation of cadets had been grown, and the military schools themselves absorbed a large share of the trained officers. And without setting up crash training programs in the most needed specialities, moving quickly from backwardness to modernity proved an elusive dream.

This trend continued well into the 1860s when the academy finally began to graduate more than 50 officers per year. After the establishment of civilian academies and other technical schools beginning in 1859, the demand for Military Academy graduates decreased. But already a tradition was established, and Military Academy graduates continued to serve in other governmental departments either full-time or part-time. One outcome of this tradition was, of course, that multiple pressures came from other departments to change the structure of academy academics and nonmilitary changes were made to the curriculum.[90]

After 1845, several French officers or ex-officers began to serve at the Military Academy as lecturers. But it is interesting to note that none of them served as instructors for the core academic courses such as "Mathematics" or "Engineering." They were teachers of "Cavalry," "Fencing," and, of course, "French." We do not know the exact reason, but this practice soon became a tradition. From that time on, all foreign officers assigned to the Military Academy served as instructors of military technical application lessons and foreign language education.[91]

Over time, Military Academy graduates were able to affect all aspects of Ottoman life. Not only did they change the Ottoman military system, but also the civilian governmental system and society. Many graduates were assigned to different civilian posts and many of the successful officers served as teachers in secondary and high schools, mainly as teachers of "Mathematics," "Physics," "Chemistry," and "French." Most of the pioneers of contemporary Ottoman art were officers, and many famous writers and poets of the period were, in fact, graduates of the Military Academy.[92] So 20 years after its establishment, the Military Academy became an attractive opportunity for a young man who wanted to obtain a modern education at a prestigious school, which itself had become the empire's most important agent of social mobility. Interestingly, the lower classes remained the main source of cadets, even after the rapid elevation of the prestige of the academy-trained officer corps. The absence of aristocracy within the officer corps and its egalitarian nature always surprised and sometimes shocked contemporary western observers who were not accustomed to seeing black Africans wearing officer uniforms or the lack of class differences between the rank and file.[93]

While the Ottoman administration was trying desperately to create an academically trained officer corps, unexpected developments in eastern Europe immediately before the Crimean War provided unique opportunities and a temporary relief, namely the arrival of hundreds of Hungarian and Polish refugees and other adventurers. These refugees were escaping from Habsburg and Russian armies, which viciously suppressed the Hungarian and Polish rebellions of 1848–1849. The merciless suppressions and follow-up persecutions forced not only the leaders and revolutionary cadres but also civilian sympathizers to flee into the Ottoman Empire. We know that the numbers of ex-military within the initial group of refugees in Vidin reached 6,778 in September 1849.

The Ottoman administration showed remarkable courage and withstood intense political and military pressure from the Habsburgs and Russians and did not hand back the refugees. Only two small groups of revolutionaries, men such as Lajos Kossuth, for example, were detained temporarily in two separate cities (Kütahya and Haleb) far away from the Habsburg border in order not to escalate the crisis. However, the majority of refugees freely went where they wanted. The defiance of the Ottoman Empire so affected and gave hope to the Hungarian and Polish refugees in western Europe that refugee organizations began to send volunteers to the empire to enlist in the Ottoman military.[94]

The administration immediately understood the value of these willing former revolutionaries and commissioned them according to their former ranks. For the first time, the Ottoman administration did not ask for conversion to Islam, but many of them eventually converted anyway. Jozef Bem, for instance, was commissioned as a lieutenant-general (Ferik), converted to Islam, and adopted the Turkish name of Murad Pasha, whereas Richard Debaufre Guyon and at least 20 others preserved their religion but received ranks commensurate with their previous military backgrounds and achievements. During the height of enlistment, a special military committee was established within the Military Academy, which examined each candidate and commissioned them accordingly. But, of course, several worthless adventurers and rascals were commissioned as well. From the initial groups of refugees, more than 200 officers were assigned to different units in Rumelia and Istanbul as commanders, up to and including divisional command positions and key staff officers, in March 1850. The numbers increased afterwards with more revolutionaries seeking an opportunity to fight against the Russians, given the escalation of the political crisis which led to the Crimean War. Sensing opportunity in the coming war, all sorts of adventurers and soldiers of fortune, coming from all over the world, followed the footsteps of the former revolutionaries.[95]

Many formed combat units, the most well-known revolutionary being Michal Czajkowski (Mehmed Sadık Pasha), who pioneered the formation of Cossack cavalry regiments solely from refugees and Wallachians. Another officer, a Pole named Wladyslaw Zamoyski, followed his example and founded a Cossack division under the command of a British expeditionary force. However, the real military contribution of the refugees was, without doubt, introducing and providing modern command and staff functions into the Ottoman military. Their expertise changed the Ottoman officer corps drastically, and the effects of this change became apparent very quickly during the final years of the Crimean War. Obviously, some of them were frustrated with the slowness of change and the sociocultural character of Ottoman society in general and returned to western European countries after the war, but a remarkable percentage of them became naturalized citizens. They became part of society and continued to provide not only military but also other professional services as doctors, engineers, teachers, and artists.[96]

Good information exists about the revolutionary leaders, but this is not so for the rank and file soldiers. How many refugees actually enlisted? How many of them took part in combat actions? And finally, how many of them naturalized and settled permanently? The answers are unclear today; however, we know that they played an important role in Ottoman modernization not only directly but also by influencing the Ottoman middle classes and intellectuals. For obvious reasons, their most important and lasting effect turned out to be ideological. Being the rank and file of failed nationalist revolutions, they acted as agents of ideological change by introducing revolutionary nationalism into the governing elite, intelligentsia, and wider public of a multinational empire. Not surprisingly, the first known Turkish nationalist interpretation of the Ottoman past and present was written by a Polish convert, Mustafa Celaleddin Pasha (Konstanty Borzecki).[97] Unfortunately, current levels of scholarship are not enough to understand the real dimensions or consequences of their contributions.

The years of 1833 and 1834 were important not only for the giant steps taken towards the creation of an academically trained officer corps, but also for the attempts to address the problem of manning the Mansure regiments. As already examined, Mahmud and his staff achieved remarkable success in the recruitment of soldiers for his new army. In less than one year after the abolishment of the Janissary corps, the administration managed to recruit 25,000 soldiers manning 19 infantry regiments. But unfortunately, the Ottoman-Russian War of 1828–1829 and the Mehmed Ali Pasha rebellion annihilated two armies and exhausted all readily available manpower. Moreover, poor sanitation and health services—even the founding of the Imperial Medical School (Mekteb-i Tıbbiye) in 1826 did not help much—frequent outbreaks of epidemics, privation, and harsh conditions killed or incapacitated more soldiers than did the actual combat actions (a pattern typical of early nineteenth century armies in general). In short, taking into account other factors, we can easily say that the military put the empire on the verge of complete collapse and bankruptcy.[98]

Following the traditions of his predecessor, Mahmud arranged several meetings with high officials and other grandees in May 1834, in order to find a permanent solution to the ever-increasing demand for soldiers. The arbitrary nature of current recruitment and the limited chances of being discharged from military service not only frightened the public (and in a sense dried up the personnel pool), but also damaged local economies by removing manpower from production. Moreover, founding new regiments and staffing them permanently was very expensive and already forced the fragile state treasury to the limits of solvency. Therefore, whatever solution was mandated had to be demographically and economically viable and, additionally, acceptable to the public.[99]

In reality, Mahmud found a solution well before the start of the meetings—the establishment of a hybrid reserve-militia system called the Redif-i Asakir-i Mansure or, in short, the Redif (literally the reserve). According to available documents and modern interpretations, it seems that it was inspired by the Prussian reserve system (Landwehr).[100] But its essential components and its character as a whole were so different that, at this stage, the Prussian connection must be taken with caution. The essence of the system was to establish Redif battalions with a strength of 1,426 men, nearly double the strength of regular battalions, which would be manned and financed by the provinces.[101]

The Redif soldiers continued their trades but lived under the obligation of participating in weekly, monthly, and yearly training, according to the harvest seasons and local customs. All weapons and equipment were collected after training and remained in storage in provincial depots. The soldiers wore their uniforms only during training and war, whereas officers were under the obligation to wear them all the time. But interestingly, soldiers had to wear their fezzes all the time as a visible sign of their status. In compensation, the government paid them a portion of the regular soldier salary during peacetime and full salary during mobilization and war. Moreover, they were exempted from conscription to regular units or any other extraordinary levies.[102]

Even though the administration was well aware of the merits of universal conscription after witnessing the success of Mehmed Ali Pasha's army, it did not enforce it, but merely tried to levy a portion of the population instead. This method needed the active collaboration of the grandees and required strict rules to protect the vulnerable (such as families with single male heirs). The provincial magnates were needed to carry out the project, because they were the ones who knew the region and population and who had enough leverage to convince or force the peasants to give their sons as soldiers and to manage tax collection and the allocation of tasks. As a reward for providing these services, they would have the right to appoint men to the officer posts, like Prussian Junkers, and oversee spending. Therefore, by handing over some of the administrative tasks and rights as government agents, Mahmud actually relaxed his centralization policy and provided additional socioeconomic power to the provinces. As might be expected, the grandees happily agreed upon the Redif project, and it was officially announced on July 8, 1834.

Similar to previous experiences, the project was carried out rapidly in Rumelia and western and inner Anatolia, but slowly in the outer provinces. Not surprisingly, problems began to appear with the establishment of each Redif battalion.

The administration was suddenly faced with the immense task of training and equipping the rank and file of the Redifs. The regular units already consumed the available trainers and equipment, and financial constraints limited any prospect of bulk purchases from foreign or domestic suppliers. To make matters worse, corrupt officials and greedy provincial magnates immediately diverted the tax resources allocated to the Redifs. Obviously, without the presence of a high command hierarchy, it was nearly impossible to control or monitor the myriad of issues related to independent battalions located great distances from one another.[103]

Hüsrev Pasha once again saved the day by presenting a draft proposal for a completely new Redif organization. Actually, the proposal was prepared by making use of Prussian regulations and probably used input from Captain Moltke and other foreign advisors.[104] Apparently, his private advisors and translators were more talented and better led than the more numerous imperial ones. The indebted Sultan approved the draft and implemented it during the summer of 1836. The new regulation simplified most of the complex rules and removed the nonfeasible ones. Consequently, the training program was rationalized by reducing the allocated time for training, and the role of the regular army was increased by assigning more regular officer trainers. Additionally, Redif units had to come to Istanbul or important military centers sequentially at least once in two years. The role of the provincial elite in the commission and assignment of Redif officers was decreased, and centralized approval and control was mandated.

However, the most important change was the establishment of regular army unit structures in the Redif organizational architecture. The battalions would have the same strength as regular battalions, and a structure of regiments, brigades, divisions, and field armies was also established. Initially, five field army commands were formed, and influential generals were assigned both as commander and governor-general of the respective provinces (in a way returning to the classical unification of local military and administration under a centrally assigned military commander). The role of the Redif field army commanders, who were the central government's direct functionaries, became so important that provincial magnates literally lost what power they had before. Consequently, Mahmud, with a very surprising twist, gained greater ability to control his provinces than before the Redif project.[105]

Without doubt, the bright progress reports prepared by the governor-generals about the establishment of new units and their personal strengths were often simply deceitful. The provincial magnates were very angry for obvious reasons, and they tried their best to sabotage or block the application of the new regulations. But they did not have means to unite forces, so their opposition only slowed down the expansion of Redif units. In addition to the active opposition of the magnates and of the suspicious, and sometimes hostile, peasants, the absence of reliable census figures and effective law enforcement organizations was a problem. This situation forced the inexperienced, and more often corrupt, officials to revert to old arbitrary measures in which some provinces and some groups provided more soldiers but others less.

Interestingly, the administration neglected to prepare and enforce a conscription law or regulation in the late 1830s (the first conscription law would be enacted in

1846). It was no wonder this vacuum gave ample opportunities for corrupt officials to abuse their extraordinary power, especially during wartime when the hard-pressed administration paid attention only to quantity. Thousands of reluctant peasants, without any medical or physical selection, ended up in military units, while the limited surplus of the state treasury and the allocated taxes of the provinces continued to end up in the coffers of corrupt high officials instead of going to Redif units and their personnel.[106]

Against this dismal background, the administration achieved remarkable success by trying different methods and showing unusual zeal in the establishment and manning of new regiments. Mahmud's instinct to push on, justly or unjustly, after each disastrous defeat, but at heavy price (which according to some "consumed the heart's core of the empire") was remarkable. When examined in comparison to traditional exemptions, the actual burden of conscription on Anatolian and Rumelian Muslim peasants becomes clearer. The non-Muslim groups (except Cossacks and Albanians), imams and students of religious schools, artisans and other professionals, populations of holy places (citizens of Mecca and Medina), and Istanbul were all exempted from military service. And naturally, wealthy citizens always evaded service, either by paying an exemption tax or through bribes or the sending of substitutes.

The effect of the population liable for military service was profound. The only available official estimate dates from the year 1837, which stated losses in rough numbers as around 106,000 regular soldiers, including 17,000 discharged and pensioners, but excluding the losses of irregulars and militia, in a bit more than 10 years. This means that thousands of Anatolian and Rumelian peasant soldiers perished or were maimed at their most productive ages. Understandably, in order to escape from government recruiters, thousands took refuge in the mountains or deserts, which caused further depopulation and loss of revenues. When taking into account the fact that only the Muslim population was affected by this levy, the change of demographic balances and its effect on political, social, and economic life becomes more apparent. Moreover, the Russian invasion of Rumelia and Mehmed Ali Pasha's invasion of Syria and Anatolia destroyed or damaged large tracks of land, forcing thousands to flee from their homes, thereby causing further privation and confusion in conscription.[107]

The Tanzimat and the Ottoman Military in a Proto-World War (The Crimean War)

The Tanzimat imperial edict of 1839 was a significant breaking point with the past in that it provided basic constitutional rights to Ottoman subjects. It was actually something in between realizing contemporary developments in Europe and trying to achieve a compromise with the disaffected ethnic and religious groups within the empire. For the first time, an Ottoman sultan promised to give guarantees for security of life and property, to show respect for basic civil rights, to enforce equal and fair taxes, to provide open and fair trials, and to provide an obligation to place all religious groups on an equal footing. In exchange, the Sultan asked for his subjects' loyalty to himself and the empire and encouraged unity under an obscure ideology known as Ottomanism. The obvious military outcome of this drastic constitutional document was that military service suddenly became the duty of all citizens, thereby putting all citizens, regardless of religion, under the obligation of providing soldiers. Of course, with its just and humanitarian approach, the Tanzimat reduced the term of military service and fixed the period of service for each recruit.[108]

Unfortunately, neither was the Muslim population ready to see all other religious groups on the same footing and serving together in the military nor were non-Muslim groups ready to give up their privilege of not serving in the military. Actually, both sides looked at the issue in more pragmatic terms. The Muslims saw their monopoly on the military and weapons as a safeguard against increasingly rebellious and separatist non-Muslim groups. Similarly, non-Muslims were not willing to sacrifice their sons for the never-ending wars of the empire. Their centuries-old exemption from service provided ample opportunity to focus on economic activities, either agricultural or commercial, which thereby increased their prosperity and welfare. In the end, the administration willingly found a compromise in which non-Muslims continued to be exempted from military service by paying a certain amount of money yearly. In reality, it was simply a continuation of the centuries of selective taxation.

The Tanzimat did not increase the pool of the recruits or lighten the burden of the Muslim population, especially for ethnic Turks. But it played an important role in the empire by further opening the doors of opportunity in terms of education, literature, and intellectualism, providing a suitable climate for change and the means to modernize not only military, but also civilian education. It is nearly impossible to understand the birth of the later reformist generation without examining the impact of the Tanzimat. Unfortunately, the empire did not have the opportunity of long periods of peace and tranquility to carry out the demands of such wide-ranging reforms. The ever-present foreign and internal aggression increased the tension between different groups, disrupted economic activity, and dried up the manpower pool. Just 14 years after the proclamation of the Tanzimat edict, the empire unwillingly became the focal point of the first modern war in world history—the Crimean War, which can also be categorized as a proto-world war.

The political crisis, which led to the Crimean War, was actually the outcome of continuous Russian aggression and plans to control strategic parts of the Ottoman Empire. Russian ambitions were thinly disguised as concerns for several sacred places in Jerusalem and additional protections for Orthodox Christians, which were presented as the pretexts of the current crisis. The Ottoman government was fully aware of the horror and military humiliations of the series of Ottoman-Russian wars of the last 100 years, the wars of 1768–1774, 1787–1792, 1806–1812 and 1828–1829, but against this legacy and all odds stood firm against the new Russian demands and threats. The joint intervention of Britain and France (which were concerned by the rapid expansion of Russian territory and influence towards the Mediterranean and Middle East) in the dispute and their increasing support of the Ottomans did not deter the Russians but played an important role in increasing Ottoman confidence and defiance.[109]

Interestingly, at this critical stage, while the leaders of Britain and France were trying to save the Ottoman Empire from its nemesis, Russia, the European view of the empire could only be characterized as ignominious. This was due largely to several influential authors and travelers, chief among them Charles Mac Farlane, who drew a completely pessimistic and prejudiced picture of the Ottoman reforms and the new Ottoman military in the period just before the Crimean War. According to these observers, the reforms of Mahmud and his successors destroyed the religiously based fanatical dedication of Ottoman soldiers by enforcing European rules and regulations, because "the Turk can only be formidable as a Turk; attempt to modernize, to Europeanize his habits, his mind, or even his costume and he will lose all his power." They were right in certain aspects. For example, the imitation of a European-type cavalry system disregarded the realities of a multinational and geographically dispersed empire and played an important role in the destruction of the famous Turkish light cavalry tradition, which forced the empire in turn to depend continuously on mostly tribal irregular cavalry.[110] However, in most respects, these pessimistic observers were wrong. And their accounts misrepresented the achievements of the reforms and created a stereotype in which the empire was commonly seen as a "sick man" in a state of hopeless decay.[111]

The common European perception of the empire gave courage to Tsar Nicholas I and made his military advisors overconfident. The Russian General Staff initially prepared and recommended bold plans, such as a daring naval attack and amphibious landing targeting the Bosporus and Istanbul and similar bold amphibious operations targeting other important nerve centers. But in the end, the tsar gave approval to the safest alternatives; the occupation of the Principalities (Moldavia and Wallachia) and being ready to launch attacks on the Caucasian front. This decision for war was actually a political one without a sound military basis, a political push to force the Ottomans to accept Russian demands. Even though the Russian General Staff had plans to go further into Ottoman territory in case of need, in reality the plans were on paper only and were unrealistic and totally useless in the field. Furthermore, the Russian military was unready to carry out any comprehensive war plan against the Ottomans without weakening other parts of the empire.[112]

Against this background, Nicholas ordered his commanders to begin the invasion of the Principalities on May 28, 1853, which was duly carried out after a month-long concentration with the crossing of Pruth (Prut) River on July 3. Thanks to the clauses of the Edirne Treaty of 1829 in which all the Ottoman fortresses and fortifications within the Principalities had been demolished, Russian troops easily invaded the entire region, and the undefended capital of Wallachia, Bucharest (Bükreş) was captured 12 days later. Due to the limited nature of the invasion, Russian vanguard units stayed away from the forward defense positions of the Ottomans on the northern side of the Danube. Instead of frightening the Ottoman administration and public, the Russian occupation enraged them. The French- and British-led diplomatic initiative lost its importance, and all negotiations were stopped. As could be expected, the Ottoman commander of the Danubean front, Ömer Lütfü Pasha, after receiving authorization, defiantly asked his Russian counterpart to pull all his forces out of the Principalities on October 4, which was essentially a declaration of war.[113]

The Ottoman army of the Tanzimat period was, against all pessimistic observations and analysis, obviously superior to its predecessors in all aspects (except for the cavalry corps), but it was still in the midst of rapid modernization and reorganization. Some corps and units modernized relatively well, whereas others remained more or less the same. The new military regulations in effect following the famous Tanzimat imperial edict played an important role in improving the conditions of the rank and file, remedying some of the widespread abuses and restructuring the Ottoman military. Starting with the Rıza Pasha Reforms of 1843, the chaotic mass of units organized under five field army commands, excluding the African provinces, were named after areas they were based in—Hassa, Dersaadet (Istanbul), Anadolu (Anatolia), Rumeli (Rumelia), and Arabistan (Arabia but actually Syria only)—and drew soldiers from their respective provinces. The number of field armies was increased to six with the addition of the Army of Baghdad and the Second Army was relocated and renamed as Army of Şumnu in 1848. The others renamed according to the city location of their command posts, but still their old names were used interchangeably with the new ones: Hassa, Manastır (Bitola)-Rumeli, Erzurum-Anadolu, and Şam (Damascus)-Arabistan.[114]

With the establishment of field armies and changes in the recruitment system, the regular part of the army was renamed the Asakir-i Nizamiye-i Şahane (literally imperial regular soldiers or commonly known as Nizam troops), and the reserve component was renamed as the Asakir-i Redif-i Şahane (imperial reserve soldiers), which retained the moniker Redif. To support the dual Nizam-Redif architecture, a new conscription system was formulated with the enactment of the Kura Nizamnamesi in 1846. According to this new law, the eligible male population of the provinces would assemble in front of an official council, would undergo medical and physical check-ups, and would be divided by lot. The unlucky citizens would be inducted into Nizam units, whereas the lucky ones would be classified as Redif and continue to take part in annual lots until passing the age of 26. The Nizam soldiers were obligated for a five-year duration of active service, to be followed by seven years in the reserve. So, in theory, Redif units consisted of experienced veteran Nizam soldiers and inexperienced and partially trained men.

The field army commanders had both Nizam and Redif units under their commands, thereby abolishing the previous parallel but separate command structure. According to the logic of the new regulations, the Nizam troops could be deployed to any part of the empire depending on the circumstances, whereas the Redifs were allocated for duties in and around their home provinces. However, the Crimean War would show the fallacy of this optimistic thinking, during which the available Redif units of Rumelia were sent to the Caucasus to alleviate the hemorrhage of combat losses.

The magnificent façade of newly constructed barracks barely disguised the infancy of and lack of an effective command and control structure of the field armies. At all of the army headquarters, administrative and logistics elements were missing and existed on paper only. Trained officers remained, especially at the level of senior commanders and staff officers, a rarity, even after the arrival of several hundred Hungarian and Polish refugee officers and later a small number of British military advisors. Not surprisingly, the administration and high command paid limited attention to following a standardized field army structure and both the Danubean and the Caucasian fronts during the Crimean War were organized around specific commanding generals and the geographic alignment of fortresses.[115]

The new regulations of the Tanzimat period clearly improved the conditions of the Ottoman soldiers, but at the same time, like the façades of the new barracks, camouflaged most of the major problems and shortcomings. Many peasant soldiers were absolutely alien to basics of military life like discipline, timetables, and personal hygiene. The administration had difficulty assigning officers to the Nizam units and had almost no trained officers left to man the Redif units. Similarly, the training of Redifs remained anarchic and haphazard in some provinces or, worse, amounted to nothing at all in others. The provincial nature of conscription also affected the combat value of the respective units. Thanks to constant warfare and rebellions, Rumelian and western Anatolian units, which were also lucky to have most of the trained and experienced officers, were battle-hardened. This was not so for the Syrian and Iraqi units in which most of their officers and soldiers had no military experience whatsoever. Moreover, Turkish-speaking officers there had difficulty communicating with their Arabic-speaking soldiers in addition to experiencing cultural problems.

Overall, the Ottoman army had a nominal combat strength of 480,000, including volunteers and units from African provinces of Egypt, Libya (Trablusgarb), and Tunis. The 123,000 Nizamiye (regular) soldiers were well trained, especially the artillery corps, and more or less properly equipped. They were superior to the Russians in several respects; for example, more than 12 elite battalions (Şişhaneci) were armed with Minié rifles (the Russians had none and were unready for their deadly effects). However, the effectiveness of Redif soldiers and the Başıbozuks remained problematic, and their combat value was very limited even under ideal conditions. In the confusion of war, the misidentification of these forces was the reason why western military observers encountered difficulty in describing the complicated and often conflicting combat performance of regulars and others in the Army of the Danube and the Army of the Caucasus.[116]

The Ottoman war council accepted a strategic plan in which the Danubean front would remain in an active defense, conducting only limited attacks and harassment raids, while the Caucasun front would launch attacks deep into Russian territory and try to capture dominant ground, blocking Russian approach roads while keeping the Kars, Batum, and Bayezid fortresses secure with strong garrisons. However, the optimistic Sultan Abdülmecid and his advisors paid little attention to the force composition and other operational, tactical, and technical issues.[117] They thought that assigning the best and brightest generals that the empire had as commanders of both fronts would be enough to deal with all the problems. A renegade Habsburg officer (he might have actually been an ex-NCO as some contemporary sources stated), Ömer Lütfü Pasha, was chosen to defend the Danubean region. And one of the first academically trained Turkish officers and graduate of the Vienna Military Academy (Theresianische Militarakademie), Abdülkerim Nadir Pasha (better known as Çırpanlı Abdi) was chosen to lead offensive operations into the Russian Caucasus.

Ömer Pasha was lucky in most respects. Except for a few regiments, all of the elite imperial guard divisions with their artillery regiments were under his command. His Rumelian line infantry regiments and his reserve units were superior to their eastern Anatolian and Syrian counterparts. Moreover, the veteran Egyptian regiments were also assigned to the Danubean army.[118] In terms of logistics and transportation, he had the advantage of better roads, proximity to Istanbul, and major military workshops and foundries but, above all, he was in the midst of the breadbasket of the empire. In contrast, two-thirds of Nadir Pasha's army in Caucasia consisted of Başıbozuks of all sorts and tribal levies. Not only were his soldiers second rate, but also their weapons, equipment and, more importantly, their officers, were too (except for a few academy graduates and Hungarian and Polish refugee officers). Logistics and transportation in the Caucasus and eastern Anatolia were a nightmare and remained so well into the twentieth century. To make things worse, command and control relationships were not established properly, and the Army of Batum remained independent and reported directly to Istanbul throughout the campaign. In fact, the numerical majority of forces in the Caucasus was independent and gave confidence only to Sultan Abdülmecid and his novice advisors, which included the British Ambassador, Lord Stratford Canning.[119] Thus, the most capable and well-supplied Ottoman forces were tied to a defensive strategy, while far less capable forces took the offensive in a distant theater.

After repeated orders and urgings from Istanbul and the apparent passivity of Russians, the commanders on the Caucasus front reluctantly and timidly launched attacks in three directions, targeting Şevketil (St. Nicola), Gümrü (Alexandropol), and Ahıska-Ahılkelek. The timing was more than perfect. The main Russian units were far from the border, and the border garrisons were unprepared. The fall of the lightly defended small harbor of Şevketil and the defeat of a relieving force on October 24, 1853, encouraged everyone and was seen as an early sign of easy victory. Surprisingly, this minor success frightened the Russian commander in chief, General Count Mikhail Voronzov, so much so that he ordered the evacuation of all coastal fortifications up to Anapa.[120]

Unfortunately for the Ottoman side, neither Nadir Pasha, who was leading the assault towards Gümrü, nor Ali Rıza Pasha marching against Ahılkelek, saw the exceptional opportunities that now existed. There was no master plan or coordinated strategic aim. Both commanders were simply advancing for the sake of obeying orders. Furthermore, the previous disasters and humiliations so discouraged them that they did not dare to launch an all-out offensive, using but a small portion of their units and keeping operations as limited as possible. Without motivation, morale, or good leadership, the lightly armed Ottoman assault formations still managed to reach Ahıska and Gümrü. Ali Rıza Pasha did not have enough firepower to subdue the Ahıska fortress, which should have been evident from the very beginning, and asked for heavy artillery. While Ali Rıza Pasha was waiting for the artillery for nearly a week, the Russian relieving force managed to reach and attack him near Süflis (Sadzel) on November 13. Ali Rıza Pasha was unable to make effective use of his numerically stronger force or to take advantage of terrain or employ the support of the local population. The regular Russian infantry and cavalry easily routed the largely irregular Ottoman force and captured Ali Riza's cannons and baggage.[121]

In the meantime, Nadir Pasha managed to defeat the Russian screening force but instead of pressing on toward his target of Gümrü, making use of apparently surprising the Russians, he continued to advance cautiously, thereby giving the Russians time to recover. Nadir Pasha immediately lost heart when the news of Ali Rıza Pasha's rout reached him, and he decided to retreat to the safety of Gedikler, which blocked the approaches to Kars. He then left command to his chief of staff Ahmed Pasha and returned to Kars. This sudden retrograde move provided fresh opportunities for the Russians, and they immediately capitalized on them by moving the then-available forces located near Ahıska-Ahılkelek. However, Ahmed Pasha, one of the first academically trained staff officers, decided to ignore Nadir Pasha's orders and, instead, approved a daring plan devised by renegade advisors.

The main idea was to fix the advancing Russians with a frontal assault near Gedikler and destroy their columns by means of a flanking maneuver on their right flank with regular cavalry and infantry, while conducting a subsidiary flanking maneuver to their left with irregular cavalry. The plan was inspired, but the planners paid no attention to the level of training and experience of the units involved. The attack was launched as planned on December 1, but the Russian commander Prince Bebutov took security measures against flanking attacks and immediately counterattacked toward the Ottoman artillery positions, capturing them after a bloody encounter. The irregular cavalry merely harassed the Russian left, while the main assault group launched its attack late and without artillery support. The element of surprise melted against stiff Russian defense and counterattacks. The Russians were able to capture half of the Ottoman cannons and most of the baggage, but were unable to pursue the retreating Ottomans. As might be expected, the irregular cavalry immediately disappeared and fled to their hometowns, whereas the few Nizam troops withdrew in relatively good order. Interestingly, the Ottoman high command relieved Nadir Pasha from command and assigned the author of the Gedikler disaster, Ahmed Pasha, in his place.[122]

One day before the Gedikler defeat, the Russian Black Sea Fleet attacked and destroyed an Ottoman fleet harboring in Sinop. The Sinop disaster and Gedikler defeat effectively crippled Ottoman offensive capacity, thereby securing the Russian position in the Caucasus. However, the dimensions of the Sinop disaster (actually only twelve light frigates and four transport ships were destroyed) were exaggerated immensely by the British and French media, and the apparent passivity of the Allied fleet (which seemed to give free hand to the Russians) created an uproar in Britain and France. Consequently, they declared war on Russia on January 27, 1854, and both decided to send troops to the region. In a way, these twin disasters reversed the pattern of Ottoman misfortunes.[123]

The Gedikler battle showed clearly that no matter what the merits of plans, the Ottoman army did not have the means to carry out complex offensive maneuvers. There were simply not enough officers to command and control poorly trained soldiers, and a complete lack of effective communications negated any advantage of simultaneous maneuvers. Moreover, Ahmed Pasha and his advisors neglected the vital component of morale. The rank and file of the army had little faith in their commanders and in themselves. The recent rout of Süflis, relinquishing the attack on Gümrü, and the legacy of a century-long series of defeats demoralized the soldiers and, sometimes, even the appearance of Russians was enough to scare them. Unfortunately, most of the Ottoman commanders and their foreign advisors did not understand this serious limitation. Some, like Nadir Pasha, so underestimated the capacity of the units they commanded that they invented excuses not to do anything at all. Whereas others, like Ahmed Pasha, fascinated with their ambitious plans, paid no attention to how their half-trained units without enough officers could carry them out.

While the ill-equipped and poorly led Army of the Caucasus suffered a series of blunders and defeats, the Army of the Danube under the able command of Ömer Pasha, who had elite units and better equipment, launched medium-sized surprise attacks within Wallachia with remarkable efficiency. Ömer Pasha understood the Russian reluctance to cross the Danube and anticipated the operations of local Russian commanders and their weaknesses. After good and detailed reconnaissance and what might today be called a "combat intelligence campaign," he ordered the Vidin garrison to cross the Danube and capture Kalafat, which was duly carried out on October 28, 1853. The capture of Kalafat effectively blocked the Russian connection to its ally Serbia and secured the Vidin fortress.

Immediately after this success and a series of supporting harassment raids, the Ottoman Totrakan garrison attacked and occupied Olteniça (Oltenitsa) easily on November 2, while the Silistire and Rusçuk garrisons kept the Russians occupied with harassment raids and demonstration attacks. This time the Russian commander in chief, Prince Mikhail Gorchakov, ordered his local commanders to attack decisively the recent Ottoman gains. The overconfident Russians attacked Olteniça leisurely two days later. Ottoman troops beat the Russians back and inflicted heavy casualties and, before the second wave of Russians attacked, retreated to the safety of the Danube. Ömer Pasha continued his aggressive offensive strategy by continuous active reconnaissance and learned of a Russian buildup against Kalafat. He immediately launched a surprise attack on Çitate (Cetatea), inflicted heavy casualties, and destroyed the buildup on January 6.[124]

The combat actions of Ömer Pasha between November and January clearly neutralized Russian concentration along the Danube, except for the Dobruca region at the mouth of the river. The small, but continuous, victories gave a moral boost not only to his soldiers but also to the Ottoman public and, thanks to newspapers, to the European public as well. He showed effective combat leadership by conducting aggressive reconnaissance, directing shock action against enemy weakness, avoiding unnecessary casualties, and employing clear mission-oriented orders. By taking advantage of fleeting opportunities, he kept the enemy off balance and thus served to reduce the probability of enemy counteraction. Although he was a capable commander, he also had a distinctive advantage in terms of the quality of officers and troops.

The arrival of the first group of allied soldiers at Gallipoli and Istanbul forced the Russians to change their strategic plans. The main idea was to capture Edirne before the allied troops could come into action. The Russian General Staff showed once again the same myopia and overconfidence by reviving Diebitsch's 1829 plan without paying attention to the apparent improvement of the Ottoman military. Surprisingly, they still could not grasp the drastic changes and improvement within Ottoman military. The initial part of the plan was carried out easily by occupying the lightly defended Dobruca. However, the second part of the plan, the capture of Silistire, turned out to be impossible even though the expected allied units failed to arrive on time.[125]

The Russian planners correctly saw the poor state of the Silistire fortifications, which had been left to crumble after the last siege. But, they did not anticipate the rare combination of a talented commander, Musa Pasha, and the presence of elite units (a highly trained guard divisional group and veteran Egyptian battalions). The Russian attacks started on May 16, 1854, without sealing off Silistire, so Ottoman reinforcements and provisions continued to arrive. The victorious commander of the previous war, Count Paskievitch, had little regard for the Ottoman military, and his faulty leadership negated the advantages of the Russians. The defenders of Silistire beat back three major assaults even after their beloved commanding general, Musa Pasha, was killed. The massive toll of casualties and allied concentration in Varna harbor forced the tactical commander, Prince Gorchakov, to abandon the siege and retreat on June 21. A hasty attack by Hasan Pasha against the Russian garrison in Yerköy (Giorgio) sped up the withdrawal, and the entire Danube basin, except a portion of the Dobruca, was evacuated by the Russians.[126]

A Habsburg memorandum to Russia effectively finished military operations in the Balkans, and the Russian army of occupation pulled back its last unit in mid-August. The Ottoman administration then tried in vain to convince Britain and France to send their now unoccupied troops in Varna and Istanbul to the Caucasus. However, it was unable to persuade their allies to do this. Neither Britain nor France was willing to face the Russians in the Caucasus, where neither country had important interests. Rather their strategic interests seemed to lie in the destruction of the Russian Black Sea Fleet and its naval bases, chief among them Sevastopol (Sivastopol). Interestingly, the allies not only managed to move the main theater of operations to the Crimea, but also persuaded the Ottomans to contribute a contingent of 20,000 men. In the end, the Caucasus front only received 7,000 Tunisian regular troops and a few other small units. In a flawed strategic decision, the Tunisians reinforced the Batum Army, which was already strong, instead of reinforcing the deeply shaken and demoralized Kars Army.[127]

Meanwhile, the Russians turned their attention to the troublesome Caucasian tribes, especially those under the leadership of Sheikh Shamil, as well as the Circassians and other lowland tribes. Shamil's guerrilla army had never recovered from a comprehensive Russian pacification campaign that lasted for seven years. It was apparent from the start that, without substantial foreign support, he could only harass the Russians and little more. Moreover, the Circassians were incapable of unification and were unwilling to cooperate with Shamil. In essence, the uneasy tribes and groups were waiting for Ottoman victories and direct military aid. As a result, the Ottoman administration and its local commanders were unable to make use of these tribes other than sending imperial decrees and a few military advisors. Small groups of tribesmen landed in various locations but, due to the irregular character of the forces concerned, they acted more like pirates looting the coastlines than like regular units trying to achieve military aims. Therefore, without aid and faced with a series of Ottoman defeats, their rebellious and volatile natures cooled and further divided them. The Russians did make use of the calmness of the front to move more units to deal with the Caucasian tribes. Consequently, they were able to successfully deal with several tribal groups and isolate the others between January and July 1854.[128]

The Ottoman commanders on the Caucasus front did start limited offensive actions, albeit reluctantly, after repeated urgings from Istanbul. They lost thousands of their soldiers to epidemics caused by poor sanitation, inadequate rations, and the ever-problematic medical services.[129] A surprise attack of 8,000 irregulars of the Batum Army against Russian positions in Nigoeti on June 8, 1854 was beaten back and provoked the Russians to attack the Ottoman defensive line around the Çolok River. Ahmed Selim Pasha positioned his troops properly but neglected to destroy or control a key bridge. General Andronikov captured the bridge and attacked furiously the Ottoman left wing on June 15. The stiff Ottoman defense caused heavy casualties, and it seems some Georgian and Polish soldiers took this opportunity to change sides. This was followed by Russian units infiltrating the Ottoman rear, while a frontal attack destroyed the Ottoman artillery, which was located too close to the frontline. During the following disorganized retreat, most of the cannons and baggage were lost. The defeat of Çolok completely neutralized the Batum Army until the end of 1854, thus giving the Russians the opportunity to leave a weak screening force in the area and concentrate their army on Kars.[130]

After their victory against the Ottoman left, the Russians advanced against the Ottoman right flank (Bayezid Army) to further isolate the Kars Army. The Russian forces in Erevan (Revan) marched through mountain tracks and defiles and surprised Selim Pasha's Bayezid Army in defensive positions at the Çilli and Çengel passes on June 29. The Nizam troops stopped the Russian attacks for a period of time, but the panicked flight of Kurdish irregulars compounded by the slowness of reserve forces destroyed their morale and cohesion, and they ultimately fled. The Russians captured the Bayezid fortress easily on July 19, thereby cutting Ottoman communications with Iran. Not surprisingly, the isolated Iranian government signed an agreement secretly with the Russians a few months later and stayed neutral throughout the war.[131]

The new commander of the Kars Army, Mustafa Zarif Pasha (who was originally an army scribe without combat experience)[132] moved against the Russian buildup near Gökdere (also known as Kurudere) as slowly as possible without paying attention to the defeats on his left and right flanks. He leisurely positioned his army against the Russians and began to wait. The Russian commander, Prince Bebutov, became frustrated after waiting three weeks for the Ottoman assault and decided to attack on August 5. Zarif Pasha countered the Russian move by launching a hasty attack. Actually, he was following a plan devised by Hurşid Pasha (Richard Debaufre Guyon) and İsmail Pasha to fix the Russian army with a frontal attack and destroy it with flanking attacks from both sides. Initially, a highly important hill was captured by the Ottoman irregular cavalry and jeopardized the Russian assault formation. However, the flanking forces failed to attack at the same time and were beaten back separately after bloody hand-to-hand combat. Once again, the flight of irregulars further weakened and demoralized the Ottoman regular units, which gave up and abandoned the fight. Bebutov was unable to pursue the completely disorganized Ottomans and wasted a golden opportunity to capture the Kars fortress.[133]

The Kars Army essentially was crippled, suffering 8,000 casualties, 2,500 prisoners, and the desertion of 10,000 irregulars. It was not only demoralized, humiliated, and isolated, but also afflicted with limited chances of survival due to a lack of adequate provisions and outdated fortifications. The British decision to send a technical military advisory team to Kars before the Gökdere disaster turned out to be a very wise decision.[134] The arrival of British military advisors and later their leader Colonel Fenwick Williams on September 24, combined with the assignment of the able Ahmed Vasfi Pasha as commander after a few months of foot dragging, changed dramatically the shape and destiny of the garrison. Thanks to Russian inactivity and a complete absence of military action, the defenders managed, with the help of the civilian population, to improve the fortifications and gun emplacements. Continuous training and arrival of some additional officers heightened the combat readiness and quality of the units. However, the poor living conditions, lack of effective medical support, problematic logistics, and corruption caused immense numbers of casualties and limited any chance of offensive operations or even harassment sorties. To make things worse, no reinforcements arrived in terms of units, weapons, or provisions.[135]

The main reason for the obvious neglect of Kars was the opening of the Crimean front. Both British and French decision-makers hoped to finish the war in a short time by attacking the heart of the Russian navy.[136] The allied fleet and transport vessels crossed the Black Sea leisurely and reached their destination on September 13, 1854, and in five days disembarked more than 50,000 soldiers. The commanders of the allied forces, Marshal St. Arnaud and Lord Raglan, then overconfidently continued their leisurely approach in their advance to Sevastopol without enemy resistance. The lack of pack animals and a surplus of heavy baggage slowed down the advance.[137] The Russian commander, the notorious diplomat of the crisis Prince A. S. Menshikov, was waiting for them on the far bank of the Alma River. The 7,000-man Ottoman division of Süleyman Pasha was under the command of French commander Marshal St. Arnaud. Arnaud decided to use one French division and the Ottomans on his right wing to conduct a flanking attack. His main units remained in the center, and he planned to use British units to flank the Russians from the left. The Ottoman division advanced immediately after French General Bosquet's division and when the French wheeled to the left, they continued forward and pushed the Russian light cavalry back, thereby securing the road to Sevastopol. Thanks to effective naval artillery support, the Ottomans suffered few casualties. Arnaud's plan turned out to be a success, even though the British were unable to perform the flanking movement and instead conducted a frontal attack.[138]

To the amazement of the Russians, the allies did not make use of their victory by pursuing the defeated and demoralized Russian units or conducting a hasty attack against Sevastopol. Instead, they returned to their leisurely rhythm by resting two days and starting the advance only after replenishing. They finally arrived at Sevastopol on September 25, but instead of initiating a siege or launching hasty attacks, they waited two more weeks to settle in, thereby giving the Russians ample time to make last-minute preparations and reorganize. The first allied assault was launched on October 17. The French suffered heavy casualties and were unable to capture their objectives, whereas the British were successful locally but not aggressive enough to penetrate deeply into the Russian defenses.[139]

The role of the Ottoman division during the initial stage of the siege is not clear. Most probably it also took part in the costly French attack. Additionally, thanks to the miscalculation and neglect of allied quartermasters, it suffered further casualties because of poor diet and lack of provisions. But, its role in the Balaclava (Balıklıova) battle is well known, albeit not with glory. The Russian main army group attacked the relatively weakly defended allied security perimeter around Voronzov Ridge. At least four Ottoman battalions reinforced with artillery gunners, some 2,000 men (more or less) manned five poorly fortified redoubts that established the forward defensive line.[140] What happened at these redoubts during the early morning of October 25 is still shrouded in mystery. According to the commonly accepted version, the Ottoman soldiers cowardly fled when the first Russian shells began to land, leaving their cannons behind. The day was saved thanks to the British Heavy Cavalry Brigade and the famous "thin red line" of the 93rd Highlander Regiment. The alleged cowardly behavior then became so established in the minds of the allied commanders that Lord Raglan refused to assign Ottoman troops to reinforce his weak defensive forces at Inkerman Ridge just before the battle of the same name.[141]

Recent research, however, including battlefield archeology, provides a completely different story and corresponds to the version of events contained in the modern official Turkish military history. According to these recent findings, the Ottoman battalions in the redoubts, especially the ones in Redoubt One, defended their positions and stopped the massive Russian assault for more than two hours with only their rifles; the British 12 pounder iron cannons located there could not be used without help. Their efforts gained valuable time for the British to react effectively. The battalion in Redoubt One was literally annihilated and the others, after suffering heavy casualties, were forced to retreat. They did not flee, because we know that some of them regrouped with the 93rd Highland Regiment and manned the famous "thin red line." It is evident that Ottoman soldiers were also heroes at Balaclava.[142] However, because of factors including racial xenophobia, language barriers, and lack of representation at the war council in Crimea, their valor was tarnished, and they were chosen as scapegoats and blamed for many of the blunders that occurred during the battle.[143]

Neglected by their government and despised by their allies, harsh winter, diseases, and the poor quality of rations soon took their toll, and the combat strength of the Ottoman division fell below 5,000 in mid-November 1854.[144] The Ottoman government, now under serious political pressure, urgently ordered Ömer Pasha, who was planning to capture Bessarabia, to reinforce the Crimean front. Ömer Pasha arrived in the theater with three divisions, one of them Egyptian, in January 1855 and was ordered to cover Eupatoria (Güzelova) against an expected Russian assault. The Russians launched their long-anticipated attack after infiltrating several small units during the early hours of February 16. The surprise attack achieved only limited success; the Ottoman defenders beat back the Russians with the help of naval gunfire support. From the military perspective, it was a small battle with relatively modest casualties, but it effectively destroyed the Russian threat from Eupatoria and created a crisis in St. Petersburg. In turn, Prince Menshikov was relieved of command and, suffering further deterioration of health, Tsar Nicholas himself passed away a few weeks later. Importantly, this success restored the tarnished image of Ottoman soldiers.[145]

With the arrival of Ömer Pasha, the Ottomans were represented with a seat at the war council. For the first time in the Crimean War, the Ottoman army began to affect the decision-making process at the operational level. And, at last, after spending months at menial tasks, Ottoman units began to make their presence known more prestigiously in combat operations such as the one against Kertch on May 24 and, more importantly, during the last Russian assault of Tchernaya on August 16.[146]

Ömer Pasha continued to criticize the decision to send his army to the Crimea even after Ottoman contributions resulted in the successful outcome of several operations. He rightfully saw the Caucasus and Bessarabia as more important to the strategic interests of the empire. Frustrated with the impasse in Crimea, he secretly went to Istanbul and arranged a private talk with Sultan Abdülmecid on July 17, 1855. He managed to convince the Sultan on the merits of his plan to move the Ottoman army from Crimea to the Caucasus in order to save the Kars garrison from capitulation and occupy an important portion of Georgia. But, unfortunately, allied diplomatic and military representatives blocked this move, and the Ottoman contingent remained in Crimea until well after the fall of Sevastopol.[147]

The situation in the Caucasus changed from bad to worse for the Kars Army while the government focused on Crimean operations. The new Russian commander, Count Muravyev, was obviously not a talented general, but he was sturdy, cool, and battle-hardened. He received clear orders to secure a military advantage that would be useful at the upcoming diplomatic negotiations. He managed to reorganize the Russian Army of the Caucasus according to his strategic aim of the conquest of Kars. He was so obsessed with Kars that he paid limited attention to other opportunities. He failed to anticipate the obvious improvements within Kars and similarly refused to see the structural differences in the current Ottoman army from the army of 1829.[148]

The Russian army, 30,000 strong, crossed the Arpaçay and poured into Ottoman territory on May 24, 1855. Muravyev allocated a quarter of his army for masking the Kars garrison and advanced further into Anatolia. The Russian vanguard easily captured the important Soğanlık block and destroyed the temporary logistics depots located there. The only available unit on the ground was the weak division of Eleşkirt, which withdrew without showing any resistance. Clumsy Russian maneuvers to block its escape routes failed. Interestingly, two more important dominant terrain features were abandoned, and Muravyev reached the last defensive line in front of the key fortress city of Erzurum on June 22. Instead of attacking the panic-stricken city with its ramshackle fortifications and ill-trained, poorly led garrison, he returned to his obsession with Kars, leaving only screening forces blocking the approach roads to his rear. His obsessive and short-sighted strategy without doubt saved the empire from a disastrous defeat that most probably would have negated the advantages gained by the fall of Sevastopol.[149]

Muravyev immediately understood the futility of a direct assault on the Kars fortifications without a siege train, so he decided to seal off Kars with his superior cavalry and starve the garrison into submission. The siege officially started on June 17, but the garrison managed to keep contact with the outside for at least one month longer. Interestingly, neither of the nearby Ottoman commanders, under these suitable conditions, tried to help the Kars garrison in terms of reinforcements and provisions. This was also true for the administration, which was trying desperately to convince its allies to send direct military aid to Kars or release its troops in Crimea. Likewise, it failed to order its commanders in Batum, Erzurum, or Oltu to help the heroic defenders of Kars. The apparent cowardly behavior of these commanders remained unpunished amidst the ever-increasing calls for help coming from Kars.[150]

Ahmed Vasfi Pasha managed to preserve the élan and cohesion of the Kars garrison, which suffered high casualties each day due to malnutrition and a deadly cholera outbreak. He also showed a rare talent of diplomacy by eagerly cooperating with his British military advisors and making effective use of foreign expertise. The Anatolian and Syrian Nizam battalions established the backbone of the city's defense. Their unwavering obedience and stoic approach to difficulties kept the other units, and especially the irregulars, in line. At this critical stage, the news of the fall of Sevastopol and the decision to release Ömer Pasha's army gave a strong boost to the morale of the defenders of Kars. Reciprocally, the same news disturbed Muravyev for the first time, and he decided to launch a massive frontal attack with all his troops.[151]

The Russian plan depended on three factors for success: a night advance, surprise, and a coordinated final attack. However, the Russian units were unable to achieve the high standards that the plan required. The defenders were alerted prematurely by the sudden movement of Russian units and were waiting for the incoming assault. Secrecy and darkness disoriented most of the assault formations, and some units mistakenly attacked the strongest sides of the fortifications instead of the planned vulnerable points, while others became mixed up with adjacent units.

Because of delays, the Russian infantry started the assault under broad daylight conditions on September 29. To make things worse for the Russians, their archaic close assault column formations provided excellent opportunities for Ottoman artillery and Minié rifle fire. Deadly Ottoman fire annihilated row after row of Russian soldiers. The survivors, who had managed to penetrate into the fortifications, were beaten back with well-drilled counterattacks. The Ottoman rank and file reacted to every Russian move with courage and ingenuity. When Muravyev ordered the retreat in the middle of the day, he already had lost more than half of his troops. However, he stubbornly continued the enforcement of a blockade instead of retreating to Georgia. Unfortunately, the defenders could not make use of this crushing victory due to a lack of horses and the physical limitations of disease-ridden and half-starved soldiers.[152]

The long-awaited relief operation of Ömer Pasha began with an amphibious landing at Suhumkale (Sokhumi) on October 3. Ömer Pasha hoped to divert the Russians from Kars, but he miscalculated the stubbornness of Muravyev and the distance to Kars. Instead of maintaining momentum by pressing on the surprised Russians, he leisurely spent 12 days preparing for his advance and resting. He defeated the forces of Prince Bagration in the battle of Ingur on November 6 but did not pursue the defeated enemy. Without realizing that Kars capitulated just one day after his victory, Ömer Pasha lost more valuable time by spending another 12 days in Zugdidi.[153]

The Ottoman army bogged down in the marshes when the rainy season began but, at last, the Ottoman army advanced. Bagration applied a traditional scorched earth policy and destroyed everything that might be useful for the Ottomans, including the vital bridges. Under these adverse conditions, the Ottoman soldiers obediently continued to march, but they collapsed within striking distance of the planned objective of Kutaisi on December 7. Ömer Pasha had no alternative than to retreat to the nearest harbor. The defeated expeditionary force finally reached Redutkale harbor at the beginning of February 1856, losing half of its strength on the way without fighting. The Ottoman evacuation to Batum continued well into March.[154]

The Crimean War, which can be classified as the first modern war or proto-world war, played an important role in the modernization of the Ottoman military. Even though the Ottoman military was still far below the level of its western counterparts (in terms of quality and quantity), it managed to inflict repeated defeats on its most implacable enemy, the Russian military, for the first time in 100 years. We can safely say that the dream of Mahmud II was finally validated; the Ottoman military could protect its homeland if the reforms continued unabated.

While the Ottoman units became familiar with modern tactics and techniques and brand-new weapons and equipment, the Ottoman military as an institution also benefited. Its command and control structure improved, the standards of its officer corps were raised, and, for the first time in centuries, its military medical system improved, thanks to the opening of large British and French hospitals in Istanbul.[155]

On the other hand, the Crimean War camouflaged serious institutional problems that the Ottoman military had no means to solve.

The war clearly showed the importance of an industrial power base and modern finances. Understandably, the archaic agrarian economy of the Ottomans did not have the means to support a modern war effort. Except for limited production in a few small military workshops and gunpowder mills, every bit and piece of military equipment had to be imported. Initially, thousands of percussion muskets were imported, which were soon augmented by muzzle-loading Minié rifles from Belgium and France. It followed that the Ottoman military encountered immense difficulties in terms of ordnance maintenance, once again due to the lack of an industrial base and trained personnel. The state treasury was in ruins even after receiving sizable foreign loans. Emergency war taxes, mobilization of Redif units, and forced levies to replace casualties disrupted local economies so much that even wealthy provinces encountered problems overcoming these immense burdens. Thousands of soldiers perished or were maimed during the war, thereby further crippling the local economies. In this respect, the situation in the eastern provinces was more desperate. All of this was exaggerated by the poor state of logistics, itself an outcome of poor finances and widespread corruption at all levels.[156]

Once again, the Ottoman government and units on the ground were unable to effectively use the potential of their own country and people. For example, the Kars garrison capitulated because of starvation, but the Russian besiegers were able to get an important percentage of their provisions and fodder from the very region which Ottoman quartermasters were unable to collect from. Due to faulty bureaucracy and lack of coordination and transportation, provisions collected in temporary depots were either destroyed by the Russians or simply looted by the locals.[157]

In part, the administration's obvious inability to mobilize people and resources was a product of conflicting multiethnic and religious identities in an empire during the turbulent age of nationalism. While the Christian minorities were increasingly conscious of their respective identities and sympathized with the empire's archenemy Russia, the Muslim population still respected the norms of bygone classical times, and their lack of national identity limited their contribution to the war effort. The indifference of some of the Muslim groups was so striking and baffling that western observers could not understand it.[158]

The performance of the Ottoman officer corps was mixed. The numbers of academic graduates were limited, and their superiors were unable to make effective use of their talents and expertise. Patron-client relationships and favoritism in promotion continued to worsen the already chaotic situation of the corps. The arrival and inclusion of Polish and Hungarian refugees did improve the quality of the officer corps, but most of the time they were employed as staff officers or technical experts and rarely assigned as combat unit commanders. And the sudden introduction of hundreds of foreign officers with dubious backgrounds obviously increased the suspicion and anger of Ottoman officers.[159] Furthermore, the Ottoman military continued to encounter difficulty accommodating and making use of the talents and expertise of British military advisors and other temporarily hired foreign officers. Although there was certainly improvement in terms of relations with foreigners in comparison with previous decades,[160] religious identity and traditional antagonisms still disrupted the acquisition of modern European military skills. Discussions and disputes were rampant between Ottoman and foreign officers. Most of the Ottoman officers did not understand why some foreigners with disputable reputations were assigned to superior positions. At least four commanding generals were sacked, because they could not work in harmony with British General Williams. Furthermore, language and cultural barriers remained a large obstacle and foreign officers' ignorance of the capabilities of the Ottoman military and their eagerness to prove themselves sometimes created massive fiascoes like Gedikler and Gökdere.[161]

Most of the contemporary western military observers of the Ottoman army were highly critical of the performance of its officers. Except for a few, like Adolphus Slade who spent decades within the Ottoman military, most of them easily labeled the entire Ottoman officers corps "cowards," "ignorant," "imbecilic," "corrupt," commissioned and promoted "solely and entirely on interest of the very worst description." Interestingly, they made a clear distinction between officers and soldiers, whom they admired very much. Of course, they did not place them on the same footing with European soldiers, but still they praised their obedience, sturdiness, and bravery. They perceived Ottoman soldiers as excellent fighters but only in defensive operations. In nearly all accounts, European authors differentiated the Anatolian peasant soldier from all other ethnic groups. So, in reality, they were not praising all Ottoman soldiers, but specifically Anatolian regular soldiers. According to them, the main deficiency of the soldiers was once again the officer corps; "the Turkish soldier, if properly officered, might be made equal to any in the world."[162]

The obvious outcome of a "raw materials that had been spoiled" perception was the establishment of Ottoman units officered and paid by Europeans. British Ambassador Canning and his military advisors managed to convince the British government to finance this project after getting the approval of Sultan Abdülmecid during the spring of 1854. The main idea was to establish an irregular cavalry force similar to irregular Indian cavalry. According to the original plan, eight regiments, each 600 strong, of Başıbozuks would be recruited from Macedonia, Albania, and Syria. Only the commanding general and some of his immediate staff would be Ottoman; all others would be hired from the British regular and colonial army on an individual basis. Later, due to the language barrier, shortage of time, and accommodation of tribal leaders, it was decided to man all the company grade positions with natives. Interestingly, Canning and his British generals insisted upon preserving the irregular characteristics of the Başıbozuks as much as possible. According to them, the value of these forces was their inherent savage warrior instincts and their irregular tactics and techniques.[163]

The original cadres were collected in June 1854 during the allied buildup in Varna. The French expeditionary force also tested the same idea nearly at the same time, but on a much smaller scale. At the end of 1854, British recruiters were sent to designated provinces to recruit Başıbozuks. As might be expected, they had to deal with tribal leaders or chieftains first and, only after bribing them and local officials, were they able to recruit soldiers. The recruits were transferred to Gallipoli to organize into a regimental system, receive equipment, and meet with their British officers. General Beatson took over command and more than 100 British officers, who were mostly veterans of colonial forces, were assigned. The experiment turned out to be more troublesome than expected. It was nearly impossible to introduce even basic discipline and elementary training to the irregular recruits. Even the colonial experience did not help the British officers get along with their units, and the language barrier remained unsolved. Therefore, so-called company grade native officers actually became the real commanders.[164] The British Başıbozuk regiments, informally named Beatson's Horse, were ordered to march to Şumnu in April 1855. The Ottoman high command remained suspicious of British aims and uncertain of the combat efficiency of the units. It is certain that no Ottoman field commander wanted these troops within his corps. Fortunately, the war ended before this weird unit could take part in combat actions. Canning tried every means to hand over the unit to the Ottomans without changing its British designed structure and composition. For obvious reasons, the Ottoman high command refused this offer and the unit disbanded in September 1855.[165]

While General Beatson and his staff tried very hard to create a reasonably disciplined irregular cavalry corps, increasing casualty figures and public outcry at home forced British planners to compensate for the loss of regular British soldiers from other sources. The ingenious idea of establishing a Cossack regular cavalry division from mainly Polish refugees did not progress as it had been anticipated. In the end, some British officers proposed the idea of getting raw recruits or reserve soldiers from the Ottoman military directly, without getting into the recruitment business. After much pressure, the Ottoman administration gave its approval on February 11, 1855.[166]

Similar to Beatson's Horse, the British administration would provide the necessary financial means, commanding generals, staff, and high-ranking officers, whereas the Ottomans would provide company grade officers, interpreters, and soldiers. British Lieutenant General Vivian was assigned as the commanding general of this regular unit with 10 generals and 51 officers. General Vivian and his staff managed to achieve remarkable progress in a short time, reaching a personnel strength of 10,000 (in comparison to Beatson's Horse) by making use of already available Redif regiments and semi-trained recruits. Even a regular cavalry regiment from the Dersaadet Army was given on a loan basis to General Vivian. The first group finished its organization and actually took part in the last combat actions in the Crimea while the main group continued its training and organization.[167] The disbandment of the Vivian corps was achieved easily; the on-loan units returned to their own original commands, whereas the Redifs continued their service in their provincial regiments. The British government spent remarkable amounts of money, assets, and personnel on these dubious projects. But, interestingly, they did not show the same interest in helping the regular Ottoman army in terms of financial assets and know-how, except by assigning a few individual officers.

The seemingly victorious end of the Crimean War gave much hope and a feeling of security to most members of the government. As a sudden consequence, the

Ottoman military seemed irrelevant and lost its favored priority position. The administration turned away and left the military to an uncertain future. The sudden shift of attention of the reformers from military issues to civilian ones, chiefly administrative, initially gave the war-weary Ottoman military a period in which to rest and reorganize as well as to scale down its highly inflated numbers of personnel. However, it mishandled this reduction and the transformation to peacetime organization, without a grand plan and without the necessary institutional mechanisms. For understandable reasons, a sizeable percentage of the émigrés and other foreign officers resigned after the war. But the most damaging decision of the demobilization was to permit the assignment of academy-trained officers (Mektebli) to administrative or diplomatic posts. Many highly trained officers with combat experiences were lost during this crucial reorganization and transformation period. Consequently, the army's units were left to uneducated rankers (Alaylıs) once again.

Soldiers were discharged haphazardly, and a golden opportunity to establish a real NCO corps was lost. Not surprisingly, most of the irregulars did not hand over army-issued weapons, equipment, or horses to their military owners. In a way, tribal warriors and other mercenary groups that were traditional troublemakers were armed at the expense of government. Thus, it is no great wonder that as the empire approached the twentieth century, the primary duty of its peacetime army was to suppress brigandage and tribal unrest.

As a conclusion, in this period the Ottoman military, institutionally, benefited in two areas: nearly all the junior officers, the future leaders of the Ottoman-Russian War of 1877–1878, gained combat experience in a modern war, and the military educational system progressed greatly. However, the problematic conscription and training of soldiers remained as it had always been. The battalion remained as the basic building block unit, and all the higher unit structures were destined to remain on paper only, without sound staff or administrative and logistical attachments. Obviously, the Ottoman generals did not grasp the importance of a branch-specialized regimental training and administrative system. Similarly, brigade and division structures continued as artificial constructs largely existing on paper, which seemingly were not understood as to their combat role or in the context of combined arms warfare.

Regimental Janissary officers (from left to right): Çorbacı (commander of regiment), Odabaşı (lieutenant), Kethüdabey (one of the most prestigious regiment commanders), Orta Çavuşu (officer in charge of execution of sentences), Salma Çukadar (constabulary officer), and armored Janissary.

Different Janissary uniforms (from left to right): Harbacı (halberdier), daily uniform, parade uniform, Solak (ceremonial guard), and soldier carrying the wages.

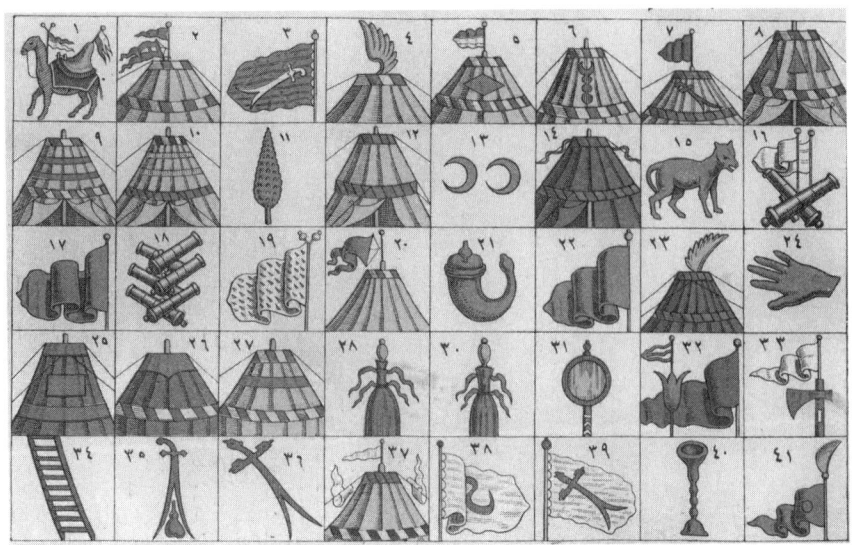

Coat of arms of Janissary Cemaat (Yaya) Ortas from the first to forty-first.

A group of soldiers and officers from different corps (from left to right): Sipahi, Lağımcı (miner), Cebeciler Kethüdası (second in charge of armorer corps), and Topçubaşı (commander of artillery corps).

Mahmud II period uniforms after 1830 (from left to right): Muzikacı (bandsman), naval officer, infantry officer, Harbiyeli (Military Academy cadet), infantryman, and marine.

Abdülmecid period uniforms (from left to right): cavalryman, infantryman, artilleryman, artillery officer, naval gunnery officer, and marine.

Abdülhamid period uniforms (from left to right): cavalry captain, artillery brigadier general, cavalry major general, infantry major general (grand uniform), medical officer, and sapper.

Old Maçka Barracks in 1836 (picture drawn for the book of Julia Pardoe), the first building of the Mekteb-i Harbiye (Military Academy). The mosque was built in order to give assurance to conservatives.

Friday parade of the 2nd Field Army in front of Edirne Barracks at the beginning of the twentieth century.

Military garrison and citizens of a Macedonian town celebrating the coronation anniversary of Abdulhamid II with mass prayers.

Arrival of first train to Medina station after the opening of Hejaz railway. Not surprisingly, the first group of passengers was no other than an infantry contingent.

A group photo of officers of an unidentified infantry regiment at the beginning of the twentieth century. Notice the presence of a black African officer.

Officers of a Macedonian garrison with some civilians, proudly showing the armlets of the 1908 Constitution Revolution.

Staff and patients of a military hospital in Syria (most probably Damascus Hospital). Notice the presence of tribal warriors and Black Sea region irregulars.

Arab Hamidiye Tribal Cavalry Regiment personnel during an inspection. They were equipped with military issue heavy lances, which was nontraditional.

Second-grade cadets of the Military Academy posing inside the Pangaltı Barracks after 1909. The cosmopolitan nature and the heavy presence of Arabs are striking.

Ottoman Şehzades (princes) wearing different military uniforms, posing with the academic and military staff of the Military Academy.

Joint Ottoman-Serbian prisoner-of-war exchange commission with representatives of the International Red Cross Committee after the end of the Balkan War.

Cadets from various military secondary schools conducting field training at the Black Sea entrance of the Bosporus immediately after the mobilization of 1914.

German officers and sailors from Göben and Breslau with Ottoman military personnel taking part in a field day.

High school students undergoing machine gun training at Infantry Officer Training Corps (Piyade Zabit Talimgâhı) in Istanbul just before the commencement of World War I.

Fahreddin (Türkkan) Pasha and his staff during the defense of Medina. [Courtesy of Bulent Yilmazer]

XV Ottoman Army Corps commander Yakup Şevki (Subaşı) Pasha with his staff (including Austro-Hungarian and German officers) at the Galicia front in 1916. [Courtesy of Bulent Yilmazer]

I (Caucasian) Army Corps commander Kazım (Karabekir) Pasha with his private staff at the Caucasus front in 1918. [Courtesy of Bulent Yilmazer]

Ottoman and German aviators in Yeşilköy-Istanbul. [Courtesy of Bulent Yilmazer]

Ottoman and Austro-Hungarian officers in a Russian prisoner of war camp in Siberia.

Kuleli Military Secondary School cadets before their escape from Istanbul to Ankara in order to join Mustafa Kemal (Atatürk) Pasha's nationalist army in 1920.

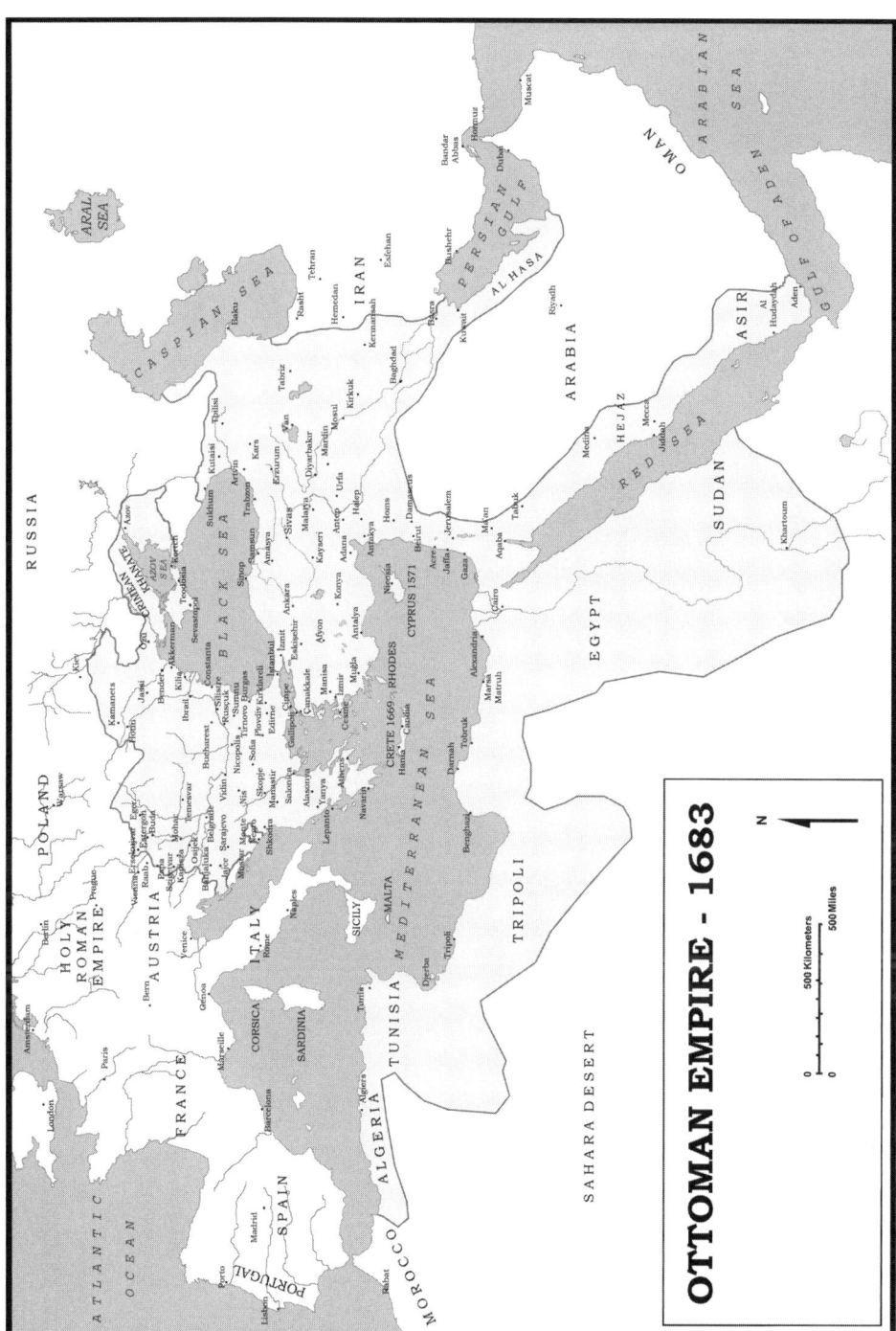
[Courtesy of Fatih Gürses]

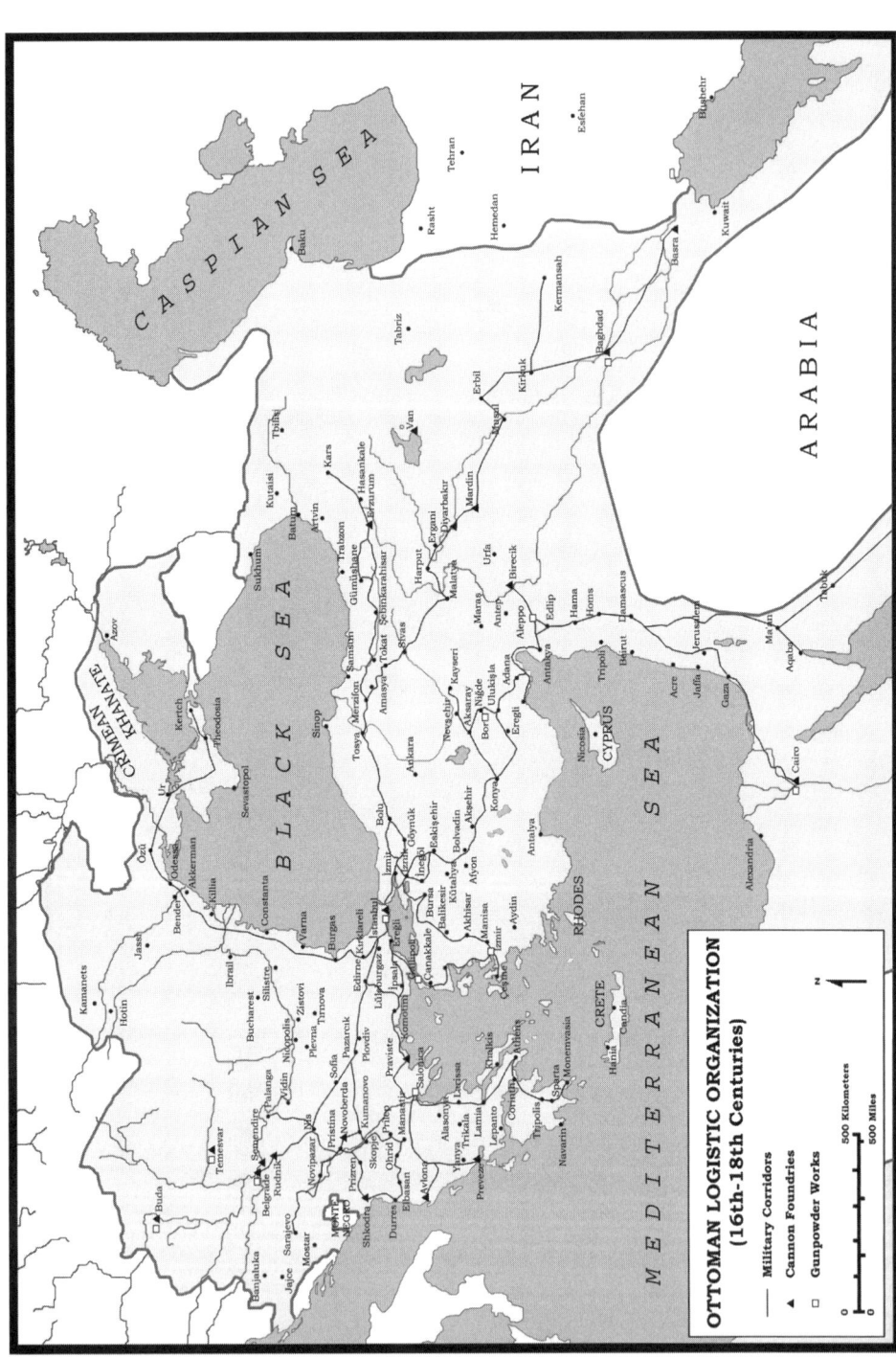

[Courtesy of Fatih Gürses]

[Courtesy of Fatih Gürses]

CHAPTER 5

The Beginning of the End, 1861–1918

In this period the Ottoman Empire was known as the "Sick Man of Europe" and was subjected to the interventions and machinations of the Great Powers that sought to benefit from the empire's collapse. The nearly penniless agrarian peasant state became a target for the forces of ethnic nationalism that fought to dismember it and a market for greedy western entrepreneurs who controlled its economy for private gain. Against this tide of enmity stood a small group of patriotic reformers dedicated to saving their country through modernity and westernization. The Ottoman military was a significant force in this movement and often broke new ground as the Ottoman Empire tried to catch up to the nation states of industrialized Europe.

Reform in the military came largely in the guise of technical schools and military academies for training new officers. There were periodic reform packages, but these tended to polarize the officer corps along the lines of academy educated officers and regimental officers. The tradition of bringing in European experts to train and organize the military was revived and the army, in particular, entered a period of profound transgenerational German influence.

Wars against Russia resulted in disastrous defeats and the loss of territory in the Caucasus. Crete was lost to Greece, and the Italians took Libya and the Dodecanese Islands in 1911. The Balkan Wars of 1912–1913 saw the Ottoman army decisively defeated and driven from its European provinces that had been held since the 1400s. The catastrophic losses of Albania, Macedonia, Salonika, and Kosovo, as well as casualties approaching a quarter million men represent the nadir of Ottoman military fortunes.

Out of the Balkan Wars, a newly energized and youthful officer corps emerged that revitalized the army. Unprepared for a multifront war against the heavily industrialized Entente powers, the Ottoman military struggled to deploy its forces in a coherent manner in the First World War. Early campaigns, Sarıkamış in particular, were a disaster, but by 1916 the army had won the Gallipoli Campaign and captured a small British army at Kut al Amara. The keys to these successes were the corps of highly trained Ottoman officers produced by the Ottoman military's educational institutions. For the first time since the 1680s, the Ottoman army consistently defeated its European enemies. In many ways, its performance represented a renaissance of Ottoman military capacity. In the end, the empire, bankrupt and blockaded, could not match the resources of its enemies and after two further years of drawn out combat signed an armistice. Unlike the Russian army and the Bulgarian army, which collapsed, or the French army, which mutinied, the Ottoman army fought loyally until the end.

Triumph of the Autocracy and Technical Reformism

The death of Sultan Abdülmecid on June 25, 1861 and the ascent of Abdülaziz to the throne were generally perceived as a victory for the reactionaries. Abdülaziz certainly did not have the elegance and refined manners of his predecessor; he was just the opposite. He was a professional wrestler, who had a wide-framed muscular body without any trace of refinement. He was not only rude, vulgar, and hot-tempered, but also hateful of all polished manners and the rules of European diplomatic protocol. And he was deeply suspicious of all sociocultural reforms. Without doubt Abdülaziz was a traditional autocrat, who merely used modern technology and methods to further increase and widen his control.[1]

Both contemporary observers and modern commentators seem to have missed his fascination with all aspects of the military, while labeling him as a reactionary and antireformist, who had little understanding of modern life. In fact, Abdülaziz had the same curiosity and fondness for the military displayed by his father Mahmud II. Like Mahmud, he liked to watch military parades and weapons firing exercises, to inspect units and barracks, to design uniforms and headgear, and even enjoyed wrestling with his soldiers. Thanks to his enthusiasm and emphasis on military matters, the Ottoman military managed to rid itself of the apathy and general lethargy that it had fallen into after the Crimean War.[2] His fascination with the technical aspects of his army enabled Ottoman military purchasing agents to acquire and import thousands of new weapons and a variety of new equipment (albeit with ruinous financial consequences).[3]

During the Crimean War, except for ineffectual naval bombardments and the transportation of troops, the Ottoman navy remained a self-made prisoner in its own bases. This now changed, and the navy benefited greatly from the sultan's fascination with new technology. A completely new fleet of up-to-date ironclad cruisers and monitors were purchased from Britain and France. The imperial shipyard in Hasköy was entirely refurbished according to modern British designs under the supervision of British and American engineers and foremen. But, unfortunately, neither Abdülaziz nor his naval advisors paid serious attention to the officers and other ranks that would man this fleet. The old Imperial Naval Engineering School (the Mühendishane-i Bahri Hümayun) provided only limited numbers of officers, and there was no training center for the equally important mechanics and petty officers. So, although it became the third largest navy in Europe, the Ottoman navy did not fulfill the expectations of its sovereign.[4]

Interestingly, Abdülaziz's suspicions of European intellectual and cultural movements did not block reforms within the military educational system. He assigned the founding father of the Ottoman Military Academy, Namık Pasha, as the new commander in chief on July 1, 1861, thereby giving additional stimulus to military educational reforms.[5] New military high schools were opened in nearly all the core provinces and in cities hosting field army headquarters.[6] These schools were specially tailored to support the requirements of the semi-engineering curricula of the Military Academy (Harbiye) and Military Engineering School (Mühendishane). In doing this, Abdülaziz started a process which his successor Abdülhamid II would follow with increased zeal. By increasing the number of military secondary schools and allowing cost-free admission for all citizens, the administration deliberately created social mobility channels for the poor and shaped the identity of the future officer corps. In effect, the Ottomans created an elite corps of men with common backgrounds, who underwent highly technical training and dedicated their lives to the military.[7]

The elitist approach to military education continued on during the term of Abdülaziz. The administration still insisted on a very comprehensive education that, under the circumstances, could only accommodate a limited number of cadets. Thanks to the high academic levels of the semi-engineering curriculum, graduates (the Mekteblis) achieved remarkable success in various technical duties such as fortification, road and bridge construction, and even building barracks and drinking water facilities. However, several contemporary observers were highly critical of deficiencies in practical application lessons and of a general ignorance in military theory and strategy caused by the allocation of more time for engineering subjects.[8] But the most significant shortfall of the Military Academy educational system remained its limited capacity to satisfy the ever-increasing demand for academically trained officers (the Mektebli or literally "from the school").

The shortage of Mekteblis caused problems for the army high command, which had to find enough qualified officers to man its ever-increasing number of command and staff positions. The only available source outside the Military Academy was the army itself. The Ottoman military was long-accustomed to commissioning able soldiers, who were called Alaylı (literally from the regiment), and certain regiments and battalions performed the task of an unofficial officer training corps in every field army. Unfortunately, even though the Alaylı officers were experienced small unit leaders and had good relations with their soldiers, most of them were illiterate and had a very limited understanding of modern combat tactics and techniques. At the same time, they were politically very conservative and, in fact, often openly rebellious against academy-trained officers (the Mektebli), as well as hostile toward European-style training and administration.[9]

To provide an understanding of the seriousness of the situation, out of 20,000 regular officers in the Ottoman army of 1877, only 1,600 of them were from the academy. Furthermore, there were just 132 school-trained general staff officers for seven field armies. The artillery corps was more fortunate in this respect because Mektebli officers constituted 20 percent of its entire total of artillery officers. As a result of this higher Mektebli representation, the relative combat efficiency and success of the Ottoman artillery corps, compared to the rest of the army, was much greater. Slowly, but surely, the Mekteblis permanently changed the face of the army. Even the appearance and bearing of the military changed drastically as the heavily caricatured older generation of officers with dozens of orderlies and long baggage trains disappeared and was replaced by a young and scholarly-looking new generation.[10]

Additionally, the Ottoman army, which suffered huge difficulties in training and accommodating officers, did not have a professional noncommissioned officer corps and often, experienced senior soldiers were dragooned to perform NCO duties. At the root of the administration's neglect of NCO training was its complete lack of understanding of the important role of NCOs.[11] In turn, as a result of the combination of the lack of an NCO corps, Alaylı officers of limited capacity, and semi-trained soldiers, Mektebli officers were often overstretched to cover many of the duties of all these groups. Thus, it was a common sight to see high-ranking officers doing the artillery gunner's job of aiming the cannon or general staff officers conducting reconnaissance (instead of cavalry troopers). As could be expected, the fatality rate of the Mekteblis jumped to record levels during actual battles.[12]

Surprisingly, the general structure of the Ottoman military remained the same after the Crimean War. The administration and high-ranking generals did very little to improve the institutional architecture of the military. The reasons for the defeats—the inefficiency of the logistical system, the major shortcomings of the Redif system, and the like—were largely ignored. The army even failed to benefit from the revolutionary experiments of Florence Nightingale, who founded the modern system of nursing in the Ottoman army barracks at Selimiye in Uskadar (Scutari) during her stay in Istanbul. Just before the outbreak of the Ottoman-Russian War of 1877–1878, instead of building its own medical corps, the administration tried to hire as many foreign doctors (even using newspaper ads) as it could to man military hospitals.[13] Consequently, the absence of an effective field medical service caused thousands to perish in epidemics without ever having the chance to fight the Russians. Moreover, there was no mechanism to institutionalize lessons learned by units and individuals for the benefit of the entire system. The apparent lack of a coherent punishment and reward system also illustrates apathy toward the importance of combat experiences. The combat performance of many effective high-ranking officers was often ignored, and many of the court-martialed authors of military disasters soon returned to their former positions, thanks to their connections and patron-client relationships.[14]

After wasting valuable time, the first concrete step toward modernization was taken in 1869 by Hüseyin Avni Pasha, the most famous Mektebli officer of the time. Once again, the decision to reorganize was made not because of lessons learned by Ottoman soldiers but because of the effects of international military dynamics. The unexpected Prussian victory against Austria in 1866 was due in part to their comprehensive conscription system, which soon became greatly admired by European generals, causing waves of transformation. Inevitably these waves also affected the

Ottoman military. The Ottoman conscription regulation of 1869 was inspired by the recent Prussian success but, by preserving the basic identity of the 1843 regulation, fell well short of making effective changes.[15]

The general structure of the army was preserved as it had been, with only one important change: the reduction of the independent status of the Hassa corps into a prestigious but normal field army. Several regiments continued to serve as imperial guards, and the Hassa, under its new name the First (Dersaadet) Army, continued to receive the best and brightest men of the Ottoman rmy. Importantly, the artificial and cumbersome dual command and control structure at last came to an end. The number of field armies increased to seven with the founding of the Seventh (Yemen) Army in Sana, which was needed to deal with both continuous rebellions and with the increasingly important Red Sea Straits (in order to control navigation by the British and French into the region). The other field armies preserved their structures and bases with minor changes—the Second (Tuna) Army in Şumnu, the Third (Rumeli) Army in Manastır, the Fourth (Anadolu) Army in Erzurum, the Fifth (Suriye) Army in Damascus, and the Sixth (Arabistan) Army in Baghdad. Likewise, the fortress commands, composed of two fortress regions and 42 fortresses, preserved their independent status with their local troops. The independent border guard battalions in the Bosnian, Greek, and Montenegrin border regions were organized into three independent regiments.[16]

The Redif or reserve system, which preserved its main identity even through the Crimean War, clearly showed its structural shortcomings and the fallacy of its foundational principles. Obviously, without functional unit architecture, fair and sustainable recruitment policies, properly trained officers, regular training, proper weapons and equipment, and, most importantly, without establishing coordination and interoperability with the regular army, the Redif was destined to remain a defunct organization. Hüseyin Avni Pasha optimistically thought to overcome these problems in the middle term. He paid more attention to increasing the number of Redifs than to improving the quality of them. With a stroke of the pen, the period of obligatory military service increased from 12 years to 20 years; however, the selection of recruits by the drawing of lots remained in force. The unlucky lot drawers would serve four years as regular soldiers and two years as İhtiyat (active reserve), and the cavalry and artillery corps would serve five and one years, respectively. Then, after discharge, the unfortunate soldier had to spend six years in the Redif, which was divided into two classes (the first three years as Mukaddem and the second three years as Sani). Finally, following the Prussian categories closely, an additional service category of eight years, the Müstahfız (literally old guard, a kind of territorial defense soldier modeled after the Prussian Heimwehr), was added after the end of Redif service. The lucky lot drawers, and the men who managed to evade regular service, would spend 12 years (in Redif service and after-service—the same obligation as held by regulars). In practice, though, most of the unit commanders applied the regular service period as six years of continuous service, paying no attention to the new İhtiyat category. Similarly, the Müstafhız category was stillborn. The Ottoman military did not have the means to accommodate such a category, nor was it demographically feasible. So, during the mobilization for the Ottoman-Russian War of 1877–1878, for all intents and purposes, Müstahfız units merged into the Redif system.[17]

The new regulation did not change the recruitment regions but doubled the number of regiments each region had to provide. Theoretically, each recruitment region provided two Redif Mukaddem, two Redif Sani, and two Müstahfız battalions in addition to its regular soldier quota. Defying all logic, the administration decided to assign discharged regular soldiers to entirely separate Redif battalions (Kısm-ı Evvel) instead of mixing them together with raw Redif soldiers. Indeed, the spirit of this decision clearly showed how little faith the administration had in its Redif soldiers, who had no regular service experience. In short, the administration achieved its recruitment goals by applying the clauses of the 1869 Regulation as closely as possible, albeit, without consideration for quality. A grand total of 343,000 Redif soldiers were mobilized for the Ottoman-Russian War of 1877–1878, but the level of training and élan was so different between units that contemporary western observers had difficulty making general evaluations.[18]

Not surprisingly, there were no clauses in the new regulation about the conscription of non-Muslim citizens. Previously, the new imperial rescript of 1856 (Islahat Fermanı) reinforced the rules of the Tanzimat Rescript regarding the equality of all citizens regardless of faith. This meant, theoretically, all citizens had the right and obligation to serve in the military but, in reality, neither did the administration force the issue, nor did the non-Muslims ask for it. Both sides agreed upon the continuation of a payment of poll-tax in exchange for military service, but under a new name. Moreover, with the disappearance of the Cossack Cavalry Regiment, Christian Albanian mercenaries, and Greek sailors from the ranks of the army and navy, by the 1870s the Ottoman military consisted of only Muslim rank and file. The only exception was the medical corps, which was traditionally a non-Muslim profession in the empire.

The 1869 regulation was obviously a half-hearted attempt to create a larger mass army that could fight the archenemy Russia on two fronts. Unfortunately, between 1869 and 1877, the Ottoman military was employed almost exclusively in counterinsurgency operations or other interior security duties. So, while the administration deliberately tried to train, equip, and organize an army to defend the empire against Russia, for most of this period a sizable percentage of the Ottoman military was deployed on low-level, but bloody, internal security duties. We can generically group the internal security problems into three categories: separatist nationalist rebellions, traditional banditry and tribal unrest, and outbreaks of social violence. The empire had the necessary power and traditions to deal with the two latter problems but not with the nationalist movements.

The Christian peoples of the Balkans began to demand separate national states after the success of the Greek independence movement and were encouraged by increasing levels of Russian help and propaganda (especially after Pan-Slavism became the official ideology of the Russian state). The already autonomous provinces of Romania, Serbia, and Montenegro asked for more territory and full independence. Additionally, the island of Crete, the Bulgarians, Serbs in Bosnia, and

Herzegovina either asked for a separate homeland or unification with their brothers. Even though the administration understood the grave dangers that these independence movements posed, it was unable to mobilize its civil departments and, knowingly or unknowingly, left these problems to military commanders. But as the most efficient branch of the government, the Ottoman military was more capable and resourceful than the civil administration or the Foreign Service; this was probably the only real option for the empire. While the army might not have been able to stop a Russian onslaught, it was more than capable of suppressing rebellions and social unrest or fighting against banditry. However, the military did not have the means to solve completely the issues regarding captive populations, and its victories only achieved temporary peace and stability, not durable solutions. The conflicts dragged on, and the increasingly desperate measures of the Ottoman army increased the misery of the empire's Christian subjects, which provided excellent opportunities for Russia to intervene.

The administration's zeal to implement the new field army structure and the demands of counterinsurgency operations collided and, in the end, a dangerous tradition was created, namely, the Müfreze (literally independent detachment). Essentially, each Müfreze was a mission-oriented temporary grouping of available units around a certain commander, which in most cases was named after the commander. Sometimes, however, the mission itself became the name of the Müfreze, like the famous Fırka-i İslahiyye (literally the division of forced reform) of 1865. It consisted of 15 infantry battalions, two cavalry regiments, several artillery batteries, and various Başıbozuk cavalry. The nucleus of this unit was established around seven veteran Albanian battalions of the Montenegrin Campaign of 1863–1864. And its commanding general was none other than the victorious commander of the same campaign, Lofçalı Derviş Pasha. Derviş Pasha collected the other units on the way to his mission area, the province of Kozan (northeast Cilicia), and this temporary grouping fought there until it was disbanded one year later. Then, however, instead of returning to their mother units, most of the former battalions of the Fırka-i İslahiyye became part of a new Müfreze assigned to suppress rebels in Lebanon.[19]

The problem was that the constantly increasing counterinsurgency operations required more and more Müfrezes each year, and often the supposedly temporary organizations became permanent due to the chronic nature of most of the problems. Thus, many Ottoman army battalions spent more time under these temporary groupings than under their mother regiments and brigades. The administration's preference for pulling battalions and creating temporary groupings instead of employing established regiments and brigades reinforced the paper-only character of units higher than battalions. This Müfreze tradition also destroyed the careers of officers who spent more time in Müfrezes than in their original assigned posts.[20] For example, the famous commander of Plevne defense, Osman Nuri Pasha, spent more time conducting counterinsurgency operations than conventional warfare. After a brief service as staff officer during the Crimean War, he fought against rebels, bandits, or tribal warriors in nearly every corner of the empire from Lebanon to

Crete, and from Yemen to the various parts of the Balkans.[21] The same career pattern appears in the service records of most high-ranking Ottoman officers of this time.

Moreover, the administration made use of its military for all kinds of law enforcement duties including tax collection. Except for some of the elite units, all regular units had to allocate a remarkable percentage of their time for these kinds of non-military tasks. The situation was far worse for some of the field armies like the Fourth, Fifth, and Sixth Armies, where their areas of responsibility were infested with banditry and tribal unrest. These kinds of law enforcement duties not only adversely affected the military qualities of the units involved, but also corrupted officers by providing lucrative opportunities for personal gain.[22]

Unfortunately for Abdülaziz, his one-sided support for military education and his dislike of political opposition and intellectual movements created the nemesis that led to the downfall of the sultanate. Several intellectuals, who were sent into exile or had escaped from prosecution, gathered in Paris and other important European capitals and formed an opposition group. The new group, which called itself the Yeni Osmanlılar (literally "new Ottomans") but was better known in Europe as Jeune Turcs or Young Turks, was totally different from the interest-based opposition of the past. They soon began to broadcast their support for constitutional governance and reforms. Although they, themselves, had no power, they managed to affect the rising elite, notably the Mektebli officers, with their new ideology, which was called Osmanlılık (Ottomanism). Ottomanism resembled Habsburg official ideology and was a kind of patriotism that asked for loyalty to the empire from all of its citizens in exchange for more political and economic freedom and equality. It was the natural response of Ottoman intellectuals to the increasing nationalist and separatist revolutionary movements of the Christian communities in the empire. And they naively believed that the proclamation of a constitution based on this idea would immediately stop the nationalist movements and integrate all groups regardless of faith and ethnicity.[23]

As these events transpired, Abdülaziz began to feel suspicious of everything, including his beloved military. There was, in fact, some truth behind this, as most of the Mekteblis questioned his autocratic way of governing and his huge expenditures of money on projects of personal interest. Moreover, their long counterinsurgency experiences showed them clearly the failure of the administration, and some were even infected with the political ideals of the rebels. By sacking several influential generals without any apparent reason, Abdülaziz strengthened the opposition. After much discussion and several failures, the most famous Mektebli, Hüseyin Avni Pasha, created a powerful conspiracy ring that included the Grand Vizier Mehmed Rüştü Pasha and famous civil reformer Mithat Pasha. He also convinced the charismatic young superintendent of the Military Academy, Süleyman Hüsnü Pasha, to carry out a coup d'état with cadets. Abdülaziz fell victim to his own arrogance by disregarding early warnings and by failing to create a strong and loyal imperial guard. For several days in late May 1876, theology students (Softa) rioted in front of the Grand Vizier's offices (Bab-ı Âli or better known as the Sublime Porte), and the crowds increased with every passing day. The cadet battalion and several other military units then intervened and easily conquered the palace. The conspirators dethroned the sultan on May 30, 1876. After a brief reign by the mentally ill Murad V, Abdülhamid II ascended the throne on August 31, 1876, by promising constitutional governance.[24]

Abdülhamid involuntarily proclaimed the constitution on December 23, just before the oncoming war, as he had promised the conspirators. But the wily sultan made use of several incidents, including the murder of chief conspirator Hüseyin Avni Pasha, to play the conspirators against each other. He also sent the civil head of the coup d'état, Mithat Pasha, into exile. Thus, in a relatively short time, he secured his position and replaced powerful figures with loyal ones, and the war soon provided him with a reason to dissolve the parliament.[25]

Mixed Results: The Ottoman-Russian War of 1877–1878

The Ottoman government did not fully understand the level of isolation into which it had fallen during the previous decade, especially after the so-called "Bulgarian horrors" (a term widely used in Europe to describe the excesses of the counterinsurgency campaign waged there by the Ottomans). The heavy-handed tactics and techniques of the Ottoman army, coupled with exaggerated stories in western newspapers, worsened the already tarnished image of the empire. The friendship and solidarity of the Crimean War period was quickly forgotten, and any negative news about the Ottoman Empire and Turks fueled European public hostility, thereby increasing Ottoman isolation. The fate of the empire or so-called "Eastern Question" became a topic of everyday talk in parliaments and newspaper columns, thanks to efforts of several influential leaders, of which British politician and Prime Minister William Gladstone was the most famous.[26]

This bad publicity gave Russian diplomats additional reasons to ask for further rights and reforms for the Orthodox Christian communities of the empire. Unaware of the empire's isolation and very confident of its military after much exaggerated victories against Serbia and Montenegro in 1876, neither the new sultan nor any of his advisors were willing to grant more concessions to either their own Christians or to Russia. Moreover, they simply did not comprehend the drastic changes in the balance of European politics caused by the rise of Prussia and the humiliation of the Habsburgs and France at the hands of Bismarck, which jeopardized the position of Russia. Rigid Ottoman diplomacy frustrated Britain and France, because both saw extended reforms as a solution and both were equally anxious not to destroy their respective relations with Russia. The new administration not only ignored last-minute chances for peace, but also further strengthened Russia's position by paying no attention to Romanian requests for autonomy. Frustrated Romania would become a valuable ally of the Russians. War became inevitable and bad crisis management and publicity isolated the Ottoman Empire further.[27]

The new sultan's eagerness to command and control every aspect of the war effort destroyed the already problematic Ottoman decision-making process and command hierarchy. Abdülhamid assigned Redif Pasha, who was an Alaylı general with a dubious career but well known for his loyalty to the throne, as the new Serasker (commander in chief of the army). He gathered nearly all the available high-ranking generals in Istanbul under an extended war council (Meclis-i Umur-u Harbiye) and authorized this council as the supreme military authority. But he ignored the fact that all the talented generals, who were fit for service, were already assigned to active field command positions and, in reality, only elderly veterans and unreliable generals were available in Istanbul. Moreover, he created a privy military advisory council (Heyet-i Müşavere-i Harbiye), whose members were chosen not according to military merit but according to palace connections and loyalty.[28]

Consequently, three offices, independent of each other, were tasked to lead the war effort without any clear job descriptions or understanding of their roles in the command structure. Most of the members of these committees paid attention to their personal or group interests, and continuous infighting within and between offices adversely affected the decision-making process. To make things worse, none of these offices had the courage to withstand the wishes of Abdülhamid. So, in reality, Abdülhamid was the sole authority on everything. But, unfortunately, although he was wily he was not knowledgeable of fundamental military issues, let alone complex technical details. The problem was that he often and erratically chose the suggestion of one office without discussion or input from the other two offices. The ever-present intrigues of the palace were instrumental in the evolution of this erratic behavior. After a series of defeats suffered at the hands of the Russians, he lost his temper and began to sack and court-martial commanding generals. The threat of court-martial further disturbed the already timid commanders, most of whom owed their ranks to loyalty and absolute obedience.[29]

Abdülhamid's selection of high-ranking field commanders clearly showed his blurred understanding of the military. For example, he assigned one of the most talented (and the youngest) field marshals of the army, the 38-year-old Ahmed Muhtar Pasha, as the Serdar (literally commander in chief of a certain theater) of the Caucasus front. In contrast, he chose a veteran of the Crimean War, the 70-year-old Abdülkerim Nadir Pasha (the unlucky first commander of the Kars Army), as the Serdar of the Balkan front. This unintelligible mix of the old guard with young men was carried downward to all levels of the army.[30] In another example, Osman Nuri Pasha, another very young field marshal, was assigned as commander of the Vidin Army, but an elderly Alaylı, Eşref Mehmed Pasha, received command of the nearby Rusçuk Corps. Later, the administration replaced Eşref Pasha (due to his incapacity) with none other than the oldest admiral of the navy, the 81-year-old Kayserili Ahmed Pasha!

The Russian General Staff was more than ready to launch a new war against the Ottoman Empire as early as 1871. The series of Prussian victories against Denmark, Austria-Hungary, and France reinforced its position and increased its influence. Not surprisingly, the collapse of France against the Prussian war machine increased the activity of Russian staff planners to complete the perfect plan to destroy the Ottoman military. Following the trends of the time, the Russian plan was built on rapidly deploying cavalry-heavy mobile corps that would bypass fortified zones and reach the Turkish Straits in six weeks. The rapidity of the campaign would forestall the possible politico-military intervention of Britain and France. Rehearsals of the plan started one year before the start of the hostilities. To support these rehearsals with accurate maps and information, Russian spies, with the help of local Christian collaborators, conducted reconnaissance and collected as much information as possible about terrain and Ottoman military installations. When the war games and intelligence clearly pointed out the insufficiency of units allocated for this plan, the general staff requested at least one more year for the purpose of reorganization. But political pressures, as well as traditional misgivings about the validity of the army's staff planning, took precedence and war was declared on April 24, 1877, one day after the inspection of combat units by Tsar Alexander II in Kishinev.[31]

Interestingly, Russian planners sought decisive action and results in the Balkans instead of what was, traditionally, the weakest part of the empire; eastern Anatolia. The previous three wars showed that the Ottomans would deploy their best troops in the Balkans and would make use of their integrated fortress network there more effectively than in the remote and isolated fortresses of the east. Indeed, the Ottoman war council's decision to allocate 186,000 soldiers, excluding the units facing Serbia, Montenegro, and Greece, for the Balkans front and only 90,000 soldiers for the Caucasus front (a dispersion that curbed any chance of offensive action), proved the accuracy of the Russian intelligence estimates. But the proximity of the Straits and dreams of easy victory seduced the Russian decision-makers.[32]

The anarchic Ottoman high command could not agree upon a strategic plan and wasted valuable time until the very last moment. The experiences of the Crimean War clearly demonstrated the importance the northern bank of the Danube, where Ömer Pasha had famously fought the successful defense of the Ottoman Balkans. This was recognized publicly, as was the Russian intention to bypass the well-known quadrilateral fortresses (Kale-i Erbaa; Varna, Silistire, Rusçuk, and Vidin), and these were topics in contemporary European newspapers. Nevertheless, Abdülhamid and his advisors decided to follow the century's old defensive custom in which the main part of the army was distributed between the four fortresses, which established the first line of defense south of the Danube River.[33] A strong combat group, which was supposed to be mobile, was positioned in Şumnu, and a second final defensive line, with a reinforced elite division, was kept for the security of Istanbul. At the very last moment a corps-sized formation, the so-called Balkan Corps, was created to secure the Balkan passes and also cover a wide region between Sofia and İslimiye, in effect an intermediate line between the quadrilateral and Istanbul. The commander in chief of the Balkan front, Abdülkerim Nadir Pasha, planned to remain near Şumnu, and in the days before rapid communications thereby lost contact with most of the first- and second-line units.[34] All in all, the strategic importance of the northern bank, the defensive advantages of the Danube River, and the presence there of an important Ottoman river flotilla with ironclad monitors and gunboats were ignored.[35] The Ottoman strategic deployment and archaic defensive system thus presented Russian planners with excellent opportunities for success and created an ideal recipe for Ottomon disaster.

Russian forward units easily crossed the Danube in the delta region on June 22, 1877, and the weakly defended small fortifications of Kalas, İbrail, and İshakçı fell without a fight. The Ottoman screening force did not even try to establish contact or to apply skirmishing tactics but retreated, keeping a safe distance all the time. The main Russian army crossed the river in the vicinity of Rusçuk on June 27, an operation that the garrison watched helplessly. The Russians achieved similar easy victories all across the Danube front. Russian units crossed the river away from the guns of the fortresses and captured weakly defended towns, spreading fear throughout the area. For nearly one week, except for minor battalion or at most regimental counterattacks, Russian units were left alone to do whatever they wanted. Confusion and delay were the norms in the Ottoman headquarters at all levels. Abdülkerim Nadir Pasha, ever timid, reluctantly sent half of the units in Şumnu against the main Russian army around Rusçuk on July 3 but, before his units came into position to launch a counterattack, he recalled them on July 11.[36]

The Russians began to recruit local Bulgarians into irregular volunteer formations in the occupied regions, but in fact the first Bulgarian volunteer unit was raised well before the start of the hostilities, and it provoked the Bulgarians to rebel in the Ottoman-controlled regions. Bulgarian gangs created havoc behind the frontlines by attacking lightly defended logistics convoys, small units, and, most importantly, the Muslim civilian population. The success of the Bulgarian gangs was made possible by a fatal decision of the war council, which transformed local gendarmerie into combat units and sent them to the front, instead of reinforcing them and maintaining them in place. This decision left the local Muslim civilian population defenseless. The field commanders had limited means to protect Muslim civilians and under urgent orders coming from Istanbul they had to send all combat units to the frontline. The deliberate attacks against the undefended Muslim population frightened and uprooted the people. Thousands of civilians began to flee towards the south, creating further difficulties for the Ottoman units and logistics convoys marching north. To make things worse, local Redif soldiers began to desert their units in order to protect their families. For example, the Tırnova Müstahfız Battalion collapsed and became combat ineffective when most of its reserve soldiers deserted.[37]

After an easy advance, experiencing light casualties, receiving enthusiastic support from the Bulgarians, and the apparent passivity of the Ottoman main forces in Şumnu and Vidin, the Russian command decided to change its original plan. The Main Group, composed of the XII and XIII Corps, was allocated to blockade Rusçuk and to check the Şumnu Army. The Western Group, IX Corps, was tasked to capture the Niğbolu (Nicopolis) fortress and the city of Plevne, respectively, while the Southern Group was ordered to reach the Balkan passes as soon as possible. Niğbolu, the famous site of the battle of 1396, was an archaic fortress with a brigade-sized garrison. On June 23, after the Russians bypassed the fortress, leaving only a screening force to observe it, the commanding general, Hasan Hayri Pasha, sent repeated requests for reinforcements or permission to abandon it completely. But his requests and pleas fell on deaf ears. The Russian siege train reached Niğbolu on July 13, and the main assault was launched two days later. The garrison initially showed great resistance and courage against the massive frontal assault of a reinforced corps well supported by destructive artillery fire, but before nightfall all of the outer redoubts were turned into dust. Hasan Pasha lost heart and did not dare to attempt a breakthrough operation; however, a bold and independent-minded battalion commander succeeded in breaking out against orders with one and a half battalions. The fortress with its garrison of 7,000 capitulated the next morning.[38]

The speed of the Russian advance caught the Balkan Corps off-guard. Its units, which were supposed to be guarding the Balkan passes, were not yet in their assigned positions, leaving only weak forward elements in place. So, while the high command in Istanbul and Abdülkerim Nadir Pasha were trying to come up with a workable solution to stop the Russian advance, the Russian Southern Group, under the able command of General Gurko, easily captured the weakly defended and seemingly unimportant Hainboğazı defile on July 14. This allowed the group to advance immediately through the mountains towards the main pass at Şıpka (coming unexpectedly from the south). On the way, Gurko repulsed two uncoordinated and timid Ottoman counterattacks. Unfortunately, the Şıpka Pass defensive system was built against a northern assault, not against an assault coming from its rear. Thereupon a hopeless defense was crushed in a single day, and Şıpka Pass fell on July 19, opening the door to the Straits.[39]

Except for the defenders of Şıpka, the Ottoman army failed to provide serious resistance and, most of the time, its main units remained in their fortifications. Its available mobile units likewise displayed limited capabilities other than harassing the rapidly advancing Russian columns. But, interestingly, the immensity of success created huge problems for the Russian command and control system, and their logistics broke down under the strain. The Russian commander in chief of the Balkan front, Grand Duke Nicholas, decided to stop further advances to the south and, instead, concentrated his forces to capture Rusçuk and Plevne, in order to secure the Russian rear. The grand duke's check effectively ended any chance of reaching the Ottoman city of Edirne in six weeks, which was the key objective in the Russian plan.[40]

After much discussion, Abdülhamid sent Serasker Redif Pasha and veteran Namık Pasha to help Abdülkerim Nadir Pasha in reorganizing the defenses and stopping the Russian advance. As could be expected, neither the old and ignorant Redif Pasha nor the ailing and deeply mystic Namık Pasha provided any ideas, only creating confusion for the field command and Istanbul.[41] Abdülhamid then had to approve a series of measures that he had refused to approve before the start of the hostilities. The Vidin Army was ordered to move east and attack the Russian flank. Ongoing combat operations against Montenegro were suspended, and two divisions, under the command of Süleyman Hüsnü Pasha, were ordered to redeploy in order to fill the gaps in the Balkan passes. Units allocated for interior security duties were also ordered to reinforce the Balkan front. For the first time in decades, the conscription of the eligible male population of Istanbul was also brought into force. But, unfortunately, except for the redeployment of the Vidin Army and the divisions from the Montenegrin front, the other measures were not practical in terms of time. Even Süleyman

Pasha's divisions spent 20 days reaching the combat theater because of poor transportation and a lack of coal for steamships.[42]

The series of Russian successes came to an abrupt end in the city of Plevne. Surprisingly, the Russian vanguard captured undefended Plevne on June 8 but, blinded by easy victories, ignored its strategic importance and evacuated it. Abdülkerim Nadir Pasha suddenly realized the importance of this little city and hurriedly ordered a reinforced Ottoman infantry regiment to occupy Plevne immediately after the Russian evacuation. The commander of the Vidin Army, Osman Nuri Pasha, filled the vacuum by deploying most of his troops to a critical road junction, after marching to Plevne on June 18. Osman Pasha had a very strong and relatively well-trained army. He had waited impatiently for action in his isolated fortress for nearly one month, and his repeated urgings for action and his plans to attack the Russians in several alternative places had fallen on deaf ears. Finally, Abdülkerim Nadir Pasha and the high command had remembered this important asset and given him an open-ended order to counterattack the Russian flank. The order might have been an ideal excuse for inactivity for a typically selfish Ottoman general, but Osman Pasha was an aggressive professional and the ideal man for the job.[43] He was a graduate of the academy class of 1853 and was rapidly promoted because of his courage, valor, and merit. Even though he was a very conservative officer and deeply suspicious of European military advisors, he dedicated his life to learning and teaching modern European military ideas. Throughout his life and career, he remained a strange blend of conservatism and reformism, patriotic yet devoutly Muslim.[44]

Osman Pasha had to face the Russian vanguard immediately after his arrival, and the first main assault came two days later—before he had time to organize the defense. Luckily the Russians launched their assault carelessly without even the most basic preparations on July 20. The tired soldiers of the long, forced march, in their makeshift trenches, beat back waves of Russian attackers. Well-placed ambushes and continuous counterattacks took a toll, and the Russians suffered about 2,500 casualties.[45] The Ottoman victory not only surprised the Russian high command, but also attracted its full attention at the expense of other operational problems. Several brigade-sized units were diverted to Plevne, and another assault was launched on July 30. This time the attackers were more numerous and better organized, but the Russians were still excessively confident of their ability to shatter the Ottoman defenders. Unknown to the Russians, Osman Pasha had already improved the fortifications with the help of civilians, and reinforcements had poured into Plevne after the surprise victory reestablished communications with Sofia. So, the Russian's repeated assaults perished before the upgraded defense system. For the first time, the Ottoman military had an opportunity to make use of its new arsenal effectively—Peabody-Martini rifles and Krupp guns. The Russians paid a heavy price for underestimating the defenders of Plevne. Over one-third of the Russian soldiers were either wounded or killed, 7,000 casualties out of a combat strength of 20,000. An unorganized retreat by the attackers turned into a rout in a short time, but Osman Pasha was unable to pursue them due to a lack of cavalry (which turned out to be the main weakness of the Ottoman military in every action of the war).[46]

Interestingly, Osman Pasha used Plevne as a testing ground for the application of his ideas. Actually, his ideas were not novel. Earthen redoubts with wide ramparts, trenches, zigzag approaches, foxholes, and use of artillery, infantry, and cavalry together were not new concepts. The novelty was the massive use of defensive works based on the technical capabilities of modern weapons. Most probably, Osman Pasha was the first tactician to formulate and apply what would become the principles of modern trench warfare, four decades before World War I. Repeated Russian attacks, and long intervals between them, gave Osman Pasha golden opportunities to correct mistakes and further improve the integrity of the defense. The active defensive measures of Osman Pasha proved that, if properly led, the Ottoman infantry had offensive capacity in addition to its world-famous defensive capacity. Even though the foolhardy Russian assaults provided excellent opportunities for counterattacks, Osman's infantry battalions instead excelled in crushing the flanks of the enemy's assault columns and pushing them towards enfilading fire. His emphasis on active countermeasures and his methods of combat leadership, asking all officers to be in the firing line, gave a strong boost to his soldiers, albeit with a heavy cost of officer casualties.[47]

In the meantime, Abdülhamid sacked and court-martialed both the Serasker Redif Pasha and the commander of the Balkan front, Abdülkerim Nadir Pasha.[48] He assigned the young and talented Mehmed Ali Pasha (Karl Detroit) as the new Serdar of the Balkan front on July 21. Detroit was originally a German (descended from a French Huguenot family), who converted and enlisted in the Ottoman military at a young age and graduated from the Military Academy. He made effective use of his language ability and became one of the most sought-after staff officers in the army. His solid military background and his well-placed connections within the administration were instrumental in this assignment.[49]

Unfortunately for the Ottoman side, Mehmed Ali Pasha was promoted to field marshal rank and was unable to enforce his authority on his subordinates, who were more senior than him in terms of rank and service. To make things worse, Abdülhamid continued the age-old Ottoman practice of playing one commander against another in order to make them more loyal, which further weakened Mehmed Ali Pasha's position. The trusted aide of Abdülkerim Nadir Pasha, Ahmed Eyüp Pasha, was left as a corps commander, and Mehmed Ali Pasha's archenemy Süleyman Hüsnü Pasha, the hero of the Montenegrin Campaign, was assigned as the new Balkan Corps commander.[50] Süleyman Pasha was well trained, from the Military Academy class of 1860, and a very successful officer. He was also well versed in military science and served as a lecturer, dean of academics, and superintendent of the Military Academy. Due to his superior academic background and newly earned fame against the Montenegrins,[51] he was deeply resentful of being under the command of Mehmed Ali Pasha and did his best to undermine his authority (most probably being a pioneer Turkish nationalist, he also hated to be under a renegade). Not surprisingly, Abdülhamid kept Süleyman Pasha's archenemy Rauf Pasha as his immediate subordinate to control this ambitious general. In short, neither Mehmed Ali Pasha nor Süleyman Pasha was willing to work with the other at this critical junction in time. This caused the front to be divided ineffectively into three independent groupings facing three Russian concentrations: Osman Pasha in Plevne, Süleyman Pasha facing Şıpka Pass, and Mehmed Ali Pasha facing the Lom River. None of these commanders paid attention to the others and prioritized only their own interests, making coordination impossible. Abdülhamid exacerbated this dangerous situation by communicating with these three field army commanders directly and treating them as if they were equal.[52]

Mehmed Ali Pasha took over command of the Balkan front on July 21. He had the full support of the public and the sultan. But he failed to show inspired combat leadership by not establishing centralized command and control or aggressively attacking the Russians from all possible directions. Instead, he simply repeated the same mistakes of his predecessor, Abdülkerim Nadir Pasha. First of all, Mehmed Ali did not dare oppose Abdülhamid's habit of communicating directly with his subordinates, Osman Pasha and Süleyman Pasha, which served to undermine badly his authority. Similarly, instead of reacting to the requirements of the whole front, he paid attention only to his immediate vicinity. He then spent more than one month reorganizing the Şumnu Army into two mobile corps, thereby giving the Russians a free hand to concentrate against Plevne. He disregarded urgent calls of help from Osman Pasha as well as the sultan's orders to attack as soon as possible. Oddly, he paid more attention to the news coming from Europe than to the intelligence reports coming from his units, because, unlike Osman Pasha, he did not know enough about his immediate subordinates and his units. And, just as important, his subordinates and units were equally unacquainted with him. He had one of the empire's most courageous and trustworthy generals, Ahmed Eyüp Pasha, under his command, but he was unable to make use of him or any others for that matter. He was unable to see the larger strategic and operational picture, thereby forfeiting the urgency of offensive action against the Russian left flank. He wavered and invented a series of excuses for inaction. He deceived the high command, and most probably himself also, by launching limited attacks against weak Russian positions around the Lom River for a period of time and, at last, was relieved of command on October 2 (just before the initiation of a long-awaited major assault).[53]

Süleyman Pasha reached the Balkan ridges with his two veteran divisions of the Montenegrin Campaign on July 23 after a 20-day journey, slowed mainly by a shortage of coal. He spent another 20 days reorganizing his units and then beat back the Russian forward elements to the high ridgeline. He wasted an excellent opportunity at Eski Zağra because of discord with Rauf Pasha. His slow and overt preparations not only gave the Russians time to consolidate their gains and dig into a defense, but also allowed them to predict his avenue of approach, which was none other than via Şıpka Pass.

Süleyman Pasha launched his long-awaited assault on August 21, two days after conducting a reconnaissance. His elite and battle-hardened divisions launched repeated attacks through rugged mountainous terrain under terrible Russian artillery fire for four days and nights. It was an impossible mission under the conditions. Poor coordination at the brigade level and lack of effective fire support were instrumental in the waste of tactical opportunities. The Balkan Corps lost one-fourth of its combat strength, 1,700 dead and 5,000 wounded. Süleyman Pasha refused to accept the futility of a continuation of assaults against Şıpka. His immense self-esteem and hatred of Mehmed Ali Pasha blinded him, and he refused to join forces with Mehmed Ali Pasha in order to make use of the opportunities created by the defenders of Plevne, who had attracted an important percentage of the Russian army. The Balkan Corps remained stuck in front of Şıpka until the assignment of Süleyman Pasha as the new Serdar of the Balkan front on September 26.[54]

Osman Pasha's army continued to achieve fame through its heroic defense against all odds. This created such a drain on the Russian military that Tsar Alexander II tried every method possible, including threats, to convince the Romanians to take part actively in the war by providing a corps for the forthcoming assault on Plevne. For more than a month, Russian and Romanian reinforcements and additional siege trains arrived. The planners carefully calculated all factors, and engineers dug out approaches to protect the assault formations. Four army corps assembled around the circumference of the fortifications. In spite of meticulous preparations, all the Russian plans depended on the frontal attacks of massed waves of infantry. The ill-fated joint Russian-Romanian assault started on September 7, with a huge artillery preparation fire that inflicted damage on the outer earthen works but left the main redoubts intact. Some attacking units achieved tactical surprise, but generally the defenders waited patiently until the tightly packed enemy infantry columns were well inside their fields of fire. Hundreds of enemy infantry perished without having a chance to fire back. For the next four days, the Russian generals stubbornly forced their infantry to continue frontal assaults. The third battle of Plevne demonstrated clearly the futility of, and the dreadful effects from, frontal attacks against the combination of modern defensive engineering and firepower; there were 15,000 casualties out of 96,000 attackers, whereas the defenders suffered only 3,000 casualties.[55]

Their units were so disorganized and panic-stricken that, for several days, the Russian generals paid limited attention to the Ottoman defenders, trying their best to reorganize units, of which some had already withdrawn miles away. Unfortunately for the Ottomans, Osman Pasha once again could not make use of the excellent opportunity to pursue and annihilate at least some of the demoralized enemy units. Similarly, the nearby Ottoman units under competing commanders watched these developments from a safe distance without active intervention. Grand Duke Nicholas reluctantly accepted the suggestion of abandoning an offensive strategy, instead enforcing an effective blockade around Plevne and starving its defenders into capitulation. The successive defeats damaged Russian pride so much that the high command paid little attention to its original aim of bypassing strongly defended places to reach Edirne as quickly as possible.

At the same time, the Ottoman high command was trying to come up with a better front commander now that the Russians were providing the Ottomans with excellent opportunities and, more importantly, was taking time to reconfigure the command structure. As a result, the government's newest hope, Süleyman Pasha, handed over his old post to his archenemy Rauf Pasha and arrived at Şumnu to take over his new post from another archenemy, Mehmed Ali Pasha. But, surprisingly, he had to wait until November 10 for the official proclamation of his assignment. It was a deliberate delay. Abdülhamid never forgot the role of Süleyman Pasha in the dethronement of Sultan Abdülaziz, and he and many influential figures would have been more than happy to see the failure of Süleyman Pasha. Valuable time was thus wasted for these Byzantine intrigues, during which time the Russians, taking advantage of Ottoman inactivity, effectively sealed off Plevne on September 24. Süleyman Pasha understood the importance of relieving Plevne and destroying the main Russian army. But he also knew in his heart that only a well-coordinated concentric attack by the Şumnu army, the Balkan Corps, and the newly created Orhaniye Regional Command could achieve this objective. However, his two archenemies were the commanders of these two important forces, Rauf Pasha and Mehmed Ali Pasha, who had somehow been forgiven and had been assigned as the Orhaniye commander. He had no control over these forces, and Abdülhamid ignored the urgent requests coming from him. Out of frustration, Süleyman Pasha launched several limited attacks in the direction of Plevne. Some of them, like the battle of Elena on December 4, actually achieved their planned objectives, but such local successes failed to relieve Plevne because of a lack of support (which was compounded by a lack of knowledge about enemy vulnerabilities).[56]

Osman Pasha was hard-pressed after the enemy cut the last open road out of Plevne. The Russian strategy of starving the garrison of Plevne began to take effect in November. The winter and lack of provisions began to take its toll on the combat-tired soldiers, who had lost all hope of salvation. Osman Pasha had no other choice than to try to break through the siege ring. It was a hopeless operation. The Russians were fully aware of it, and with the arrival of imperial guards, their numbers swelled to exceed 200,000 men. Osman Pasha launched the operation on the night of December 9. He achieved surprise, and his attacking units, with a combat strength of 30,000, crushed the first siege ring. But, the timely arrival of Russian reserves enabled the Russian commanders to encircle most of the troops attempting the breakout. Osman Pasha surrendered in the morning with little more than 40,000 soldiers (including noncombatants).[57]

The fall of Plevne released the Russian army. There were two alternatives for future operations; one was to press on Rusçuk while waiting for the end of winter season and delay the southern move until spring, while the other was to bypass immediately Ottoman concentrations via the Orhaniye-Sofia axis and capture Edirne. After much discussion, the second alternative of launching a winter offensive was chosen. The Ottoman high command and field commanders were in disarray. The few available Ottoman units could neither build a defense line between Sofia and the Balkan ridge nor retreat back to Meriç River to protect Edirne and Istanbul. The entrance of Serbia, Montenegro, and Greece into the war on behalf of the Russians increased the Ottoman's insurmountable problems. Russian assault columns easily captured Sofia on January 3. The Balkan Corps was encircled and surrendered on February 8. The Ottoman army, on its own ground, launched desperate but uncoordinated attacks and was beaten back. Some units managed to retreat to the safety of the Black Sea coast.

Süleyman Pasha tried his best to conduct a fighting retreat with nearly seven brigades, but he managed only to delay the Russian onslaught for a few days. Most of his units were encircled or disintegrated at some stage of the withdrawal. Then he decided to regroup within the safety of the Rodop Mountains, which turned out to be a fatal decision, because it decreased the number of possible forces available for the defense of Edirne. One Russian column managed to bypass the retreating Ottoman force and captured Edirne on January 20, even as the Ottoman peace delegation was trying to come to terms with their Russian counterparts. Even the armistice of January 31 did not stop the Russian advance, and the vanguard reached Yeşilköy (San Stefano) on February 6. This effectively ended any hope of defending the capital, as Yeşilköy lay inside the famous defensive position of Çatalca and was, in fact, a suburb of Istanbul.[58]

In other theaters, the flow of combat actions followed a completely different pattern than on the Balkan front. In the Caucasus, hostilities started immediately after the declaration of war. The Russians, under the command of General Loris Melikov, crossed the border from two directions. The Ottoman commander in chief Ahmed Muhtar Pasha retreated to Kars without a fight and established his position on the dominant ground of the Soğanlı block. Due to his limited combat strength, he had no other choice but to canalize the Russians toward a relatively better prepared defensive line. The primary group under Melikov himself attacked and captured the Ardahan fortress in four days (May 16–20) with few casualties, thanks to the cowardice of the commanding general and the timidity of the garrison. This easy victory shook the already weak faith of the Ottoman soldiers. Fortunately, Ahmed Muhtar Pasha took effective actions to increase their confidence.[59]

The secondary assault group targeting Batum struck into trackless forests under constant attack by irregulars. The commander of the Batum fortress, Hüseyin Pasha, had effectively mobilized the warlike populations of Acars (or Acaras) and Lazs by providing them with brand new weapons and by promoting their hatred of the Russians. Instead of employing more than 6,000 irregulars with his regular troops, which was a common mistake most Ottoman generals made, he ordered them to conduct guerrilla warfare. He deployed them all around the two small roads leading to Batum and laid a series of ambushes. The Russian units moving on these roads then suffered heavy casualties while trying to improve the roads, build bridges, and move supplies. The elusive bands of irregulars so weakened the Russian assault columns that they could not penetrate into the Ottoman forward defense positions. The Russians renewed their assault toward Batum on June 23. In the meantime, the Ottoman Batum Army already received reinforcements and one of the best generals of the entire Ottoman military, Lofçalı Derviş Pasha, took command. Derviş Pasha was a unique officer who came up from the ranks, but his extensive combat experience qualified him to command large units better than most of his contemporary Mekteblis. He took advantage of the tactical initiative he had received from his predecessor and improved it further. The Russians were not only beaten back, but to their horror, saw well-coordinated actions by both Ottoman regulars and irregulars in their rear areas. Even though a subsequent Ottoman counterattack failed to achieve any result, the Russians hurriedly retreated back, suspending operations against Batum.[60]

At the same time, uncoordinated and limited Ottoman naval bombardments and amphibious operations against the Russian Caucasian coast caused panic within the local population and frightened the Russian commander in chief, Grand Duke Mikhail. He immediately sent reinforcements to the coastline, thereby crippling the main effort—the offensive of General Melikov. The evacuation of the Suhumkale (Sukhumi) region after an ineffective naval bombardment on May 14 clearly showed the potential of well-coordinated diversionary attacks on the Russian coasts. But unfortunately, the Ottoman high command failed to use its naval superiority or to employ the thousands of recently emigrated Circassians (who had fled from Russian oppression) effectively. Only 1,000 Abkhazian émigrés landed at Gudauta on May 12 and 1,500 Circassian émigrés at Adler on May 23. Even these small numbers of émigrés, having no support from regular units, created havoc, and disaffected local groups immediately joined them. Ottoman regular troops, four Redif battalions, and one artillery battery landed at Ochamchira three weeks after the initiation of this operation. The panic-stricken Russian Caucasus command allocated more troops, and by July 20 the number of men assigned to the cleansing operation exceeded 17,000 men. The Russian troops had to spend nearly two months, and hundreds of casualties, in order to suppress the Abkhazian rebellion and beat back the Ottoman battalions. In short, these diversionary attacks, with very little commitment, achieved remarkable results by pulling much-needed reserves away from the main theater of operations. Had they been planned and launched with more troops and better local coordination, the diversionary attacks had the potential to change the outcome of the entire Caucasus campaign.[61]

In the meantime, Ahmed Muhtar Pasha stopped the Russian advance in front of the Soğanlı block on June 25, thanks to his strategic foresight and the timidity of his adversary. This success turned the tide. Melikov had to order a general retreat in which the victorious Russian column in the Eleşkirt valley participated as well. Thousands of Ottoman Armenians, who were afraid of retributions for their active collaboration with the enemy, followed the retreating Russians. Again, none of the Ottoman field commanders could pursue the retreating enemy, a common problem for the entire military throughout the campaign.[62]

Ahmed Muhtar Pasha was the ideal large unit commander that the Ottoman military had longed for, but without an effective staff (his staff numbered only a bit more than 10) and lacking a single command and control hierarchy, he encountered difficulty translating his ideas into action. His immediate subordinates were often able to evade his orders by making use of their influential friends in Istanbul. Consequently, each group or division commander saw his unit as his personal fiefdom and paid attention only to his immediate area of operations. Not surprisingly, severe punishments for defeats and ever-present intrigues within the field army and in Istanbul reinforced the tendency to be passive and defensive, discouraging any risky undertaking or offensive operations. And in several cases, Ahmed Muhtar Pasha could not sack apparently incapable commanding generals due to the unavailability of any talented generals to replace them.[63]

Ahmed Muhtar Pasha was constrained by other factors also: the absence of Mektebli generals (the high command assigned most of them to the Balkan front), constant interventions by Istanbul, and the need to maintain the internal regional balance of power. Actually, the high command used the Caucasus front for dumping useless or problematic general officers. At least six generals assigned there, four of them lieutenant generals, were in this category. The last constraint generated the granting of general officer rank to some of the most influential tribal leaders, who played the role of mediator between state and tribes to recruit or actually hire tribal warriors. İsmail Hakkı Pasha was one of the most notorious of them. He was illiterate, selfish, corrupt, and lazy but, thanks to his tribal position, Ahmed Muhtar Pasha had no power over him. Out of necessity, the execution of a brilliant plan to conduct a diversionary attack on Russian positions around Mount Ağrı (Ararat) was given to none other than İsmail Hakkı Pasha. He initially achieved complete surprise by making use of his tribal allies' intimate knowledge of the terrain. However, he refrained from achieving decisive results over a weak enemy. Instead, he waited leisurely on dominant ground, forfeiting all initiative to the Russians. He even refused to send any reinforcements to the main front, violating the urgent orders of Ahmed Muhtar Pasha immediately prior to the Russian attack on Yahniler and Alagöz. As a result, İsmail Hakkı Pasha's passivity forfeited an excellent opportunity that might have affected the fate of the campaign, and valuable units remained dug in on the highlands of Ağrı.[64]

Against all odds, Ahmed Muhtar Pasha managed to organize a new defense line in the Alacadağ block by doing most of the work himself, even emplacing artillery pieces one by one. Despite the poor leadership of İsmail Hakkı Pasha, his diversionary attack on Ağrı did achieve some diversion of Russian reserves from the main front. He was hard-pressed and received no reinforcements. To make things worse, the tribal levies began to desert the army because of hardships and the oncoming winter. Under these adverse conditions, Ahmed Muhtar Pasha decided to act immediately instead of waiting for the Russians to attack. He launched daring, but limited, harassment attacks and lured the Russians against the strongest part of his defense line. He defeated the Russians in two battles—Kızıltepe on August 25 and Yahniler on October 2—albeit not decisively. Unfortunately for his army, his excessive self-reliance, his increasing tendency to ignore his subordinates, and his obvious reluctance to retreat to the safer defense position of Soğanlı created the conditions for a humiliating defeat on October 15 at Alacadağ. There, after Russian encircling maneuvers, he lost nearly half of his regular units, including 8,000 prisoners, and then nearly all of his irregulars during a disastrous retreat.[65]

The final phase of the campaign on the Caucasus front was marked by obstinate defense against superior Russian forces. The defeat not only shattered the morale of the Ottoman army and the nation, but also that of the northern Caucasus nations. Their rebellions came to a sudden end, thereby releasing more Russian units to be deployed against the Ottomans. Luckily, the impatient Abdülhamid did not sack Ahmed Muhtar Pasha, and the professional Ahmed Muhtar Pasha showed the wisdom of this decision in a short time. He decided to face the Russians in front of the Erzurum fortress, which was the key to the defense of all Anatolia. Thanks to the efforts of two able commanders, Hasan Pasha and Crimean War veteran Feyzi (Collman) Pasha, the fortification of the city was already well improved. However, his first confrontation with the Russians at the forward defense line in Deveboynu on November 4 was very disappointing. He was unable to control his forces in three defensive positions, and his ill-fated decision to launch a massive infantry counterattack gave Russian cavalrymen in covered positions excellent targets. The defenders withdrew to the city in panic, losing many cannons and their baggage trains.[66]

Ahmed Muhtar Pasha refused to surrender the city. His meager force was demoralized, and he had limited fire power to withstand the might of the Russian army. The Russians launched a daring night attack on November 8. The attackers gained some ground and, in fact, captured an important redoubt but, well-timed and well-led counterattacks of regulars reinforced with civilian volunteers (including women) beat back the enemy and recaptured the lost ground. The spirit of the defenders and the approach of winter discouraged the Russians, who did not renew their attacks or blockade the city. In complete contrast, the Ottoman garrison of Kars, with better guns and a more modern fortress network, did not show the same spirit and zeal against a Russian night attack on November 17. The legendary fortress of the Crimean War fell the next day, and 17,000 prisoners were taken, which was a serious blow for the Ottoman Army of the Caucasus.[67]

The fall of Kars and the series of victories in the Balkans gave impetus to the Russian command to continue military operations against the two remaining Caucasian fortresses, Erzurum and Batum. The imminence of an armistice also played an important role in this decision. Ahmed Muhtar Pasha made a difficult decision to take the very best of the Erzurum garrison troops and withdrew them to Bayburt because of the outbreak of an epidemic that ravaged the population. The Russians completely sealed the city after January 5, 1878, but the harsh winter and outbreak of epidemics eliminated any chances of storming the city. Finally, they managed to occupy the city on February 8, after the signing of the armistice.[68]

The continuation of operations against Batum turned out to be more damaging to the Russians than to Erzurum. Once again, Russian planners and commanders on the ground ignored the difficult terrain, winter conditions, and, more importantly, local guerrilla bands. They had a numerical advantage and a new assault formation coming from the south, near Ardahan, thereby giving them a pincer movement opportunity. The plan fell to pieces immediately after the start of its implementation. The Ardahan group spent one and a half months, only to reach Batum with little combat strength. The Russian commander, under heavy political pressure, then ordered a frontal assault on January 30. Derviş Pasha placed his regulars and artillery into excellent defensive positions, a small Ottoman fleet was ready to provide fire support, and guerrillas infested most of the combat area. He waited patiently for the attackers to cross a difficult stream, and the Russians were trapped in a firestorm from which there was no way out. The following combat action was, in reality, a slaughter. All the Russian frontline units were decimated, and thanks to guerrilla sharpshooters, most of their officers were killed, leaving units leaderless. Only a timely retreat order saved the rest of the Russian units.[69]

The Ottoman-Russian War of 1877–1878 was, without doubt, one of the most important wars of the nineteenth century. In terms of the extent of the combat area, the numbers of participants, the use of modern weapons, and the vast logistical requirements, it was the largest-ever conflict between the Ottomans and the Russians. It also caught the popular attention of the world, albeit temporarily, but few, including military professionals, paid much attention to the lessons learned from it. This is surprising, because it was the first war in which numbers of military observers from neutral nations freely roamed the battlefields monitoring the developments from both sides (but their reports failed to generate meaningful interest). Most probably, the highly prejudiced military circles of Europe saw it as an obscure war between two semi-civilized nations that had little to do with contemporary European military culture.[70] Surprisingly, even today, it fails to receive the attention it deserves in comparison to other similar wars. For example, only the Plevne battles are still remembered by Turkish scholars and the wider public; all other battles have been, more or less, forgotten. And for the nations of the Balkans, the war is only remembered as far as its relation to their respective national independence struggles.

Unfortunately for the Ottoman military, the mistake of spreading its forces too thinly around the Danube basin and northern Bulgaria (as an army notorious for its lack of mobility) not only turned out to be deadly and irreversible, but also overshadowed its performance during the war.[71] Not surprisingly, this still creates problems for current researchers of the war. The analysis of an army beaten in detail looms large in every aspect of its performance and our focus is on the war's affect on the levels of transformation, shortcomings, and new trends within the Ottoman military. Consequently, this work purposefully avoids further analysis of this strategic mistake and associated nationalist interpretations.

One of the most important lessons of the war was to reaffirm once again the importance of the officer corps in the combat performance of the Ottoman military.[72] For the first time in the history of the empire, Military Academy graduates—Mekteblis—occupied most of the high-ranking field commands, 45 out of 70 serving generals, and nearly all of the key staff positions. There were also several foreign academy graduates. In truth, Mekteblis participation remained confined to the top ranks of the army, while most of the field grade positions were left to Alaylıs. Moreover, the war showed clearly that this new generation of officers was far from perfect. Bit they were better in every aspect than the rankers or protégés of the grandees. Osman Pasha and Ahmed Muhtar Pasha were the most outstanding examples of Mekteblis. However, they were not above some of the traditional Ottoman military illnesses, chief among them jealousy and envy-related personal discord, which was mainly the result of an unjust promotion and assignment system that remained largely based on favoritism and patron-client relations.[73] The personal discord between Mehmed Ali Pasha and Süleyman Pasha was the most infamous example of this flaw. Each was very talented and successful, but their bitter private feud negated their professional qualities. Their personal issues took priority and not only destroyed the command and control structure, but also any chances of cooperation between two important field armies. Inflaming this situation, Abdülhamid and the palace cliques stirred the pot by playing one side against the other.[74]

As already mentioned, Abdülhamid, his two military councils, and his individual advisors destroyed not only the command and control hierarchy and authority of their field commanders, but also negated operational or tactical opportunities by their frequent interventions, which were based on limited intelligence. We can safely say that the army of Balkans fought without a commander in chief from the beginning till the end.[75] Istanbul was far from the combat theaters, and they only received glimpses of developments (that were always late or outdated). Unfortunately, neither their military ignorance nor inaccurate intelligence deterred them from meddling in combat affairs, which in the end was instrumental in the creation of chaos. Consequently, the only Ottoman strategic achievement, the extended defense of Plevne, was wasted. The army's commanding generals were relieved of duty and threatened with court-martial, thereby giving no chance for them to correct their mistakes or learn from experience and, understandably, increasing their reluctance to take calculated risks. Oddly, some of the sacked generals were reinstated to command positions after a short while due to the acute shortage of qualified generals. This ridiculous policy of punishment followed by parole not only took away the limited initiative of the generals, but also destroyed their reputations in the eyes of their subordinates, therefore further weakening their authority.[76]

In contrast to the Crimean War, the employment of numbers of foreign-born officers was limited, and their contributions were minor. The administration actively tried to enlist or hire only foreign doctors, but it did not refuse the applications of various foreign officers, who mostly sought adventure and fame. There were only a couple of foreign-born generals available, like the veteran of the Crimean War Hungarian émigré Feyzi Pasha and the British adventurer Valentine Baker Pasha. We know that about 100 foreign junior or middle-ranking officers enlisted and served in the Ottoman military, mostly at the field grade level. The number of Germans exceeded all other nationalities and, surprisingly, there were also several Russian-trained officers available, like the famous Ossetian tribal chief Musa Kundukov Pasha and the Russian Military Academy graduate Ömer Pasha. Some figures like William von Herbert achieved fame (after the publication of his memoirs), but the impact of most of the foreign-born participants still remains unknown.[77] In short, non-Ottoman commissioning sources did not fill the officer shortage as they had done during the Crimean War.

The general weakness of the officer corps exaggerated the "on paper only" character of large unit structures and staff positions. The lowly battalion remained the only functioning unit. Even regiments failed in their respective roles due to the lack of effective staffs and proficient logistical and administrative detachments.[78] The situation was far worse at higher echelons. Brigade and division commanders had only a couple of staff officers, no headquarters' units, and no effective means of communication (only corps and field army commands had telegraphs). In effect this left them with no other choice but to move with one of their subordinate units all the time, leaving their other subordinate commands with limited command and direction.

Most of the time, the commander himself had to prepare all the details of his plans and orders and then transmit them to his subordinates. Then, if any of his subordinates was an Alaylı, he had no other choice than to lend one of his own staff members to insure the proper execution of the plan. Moreover, none of the Ottoman officer corps had adequate experiences in commanding large units in the field or performing staff duties under combat conditions. Before the war, only the Second Army conducted division-level maneuvers, which were welcomed as the first large unit maneuvers since the abolishment of the Janissaries. So, Ottoman commanding generals had neither enough experience and staff to lead their respective units nor could their units function as a part of a larger formation, thanks to the small-unit (Müfreze) traditions of the army. The Serdar of the Caucasus, Ahmed Muhtar Pasha, had a staff of less than 20, including scribes, and some orderlies. Most of the time, he had to use his staff officers as heralds or umpires monitoring the conduct of his less reliable subordinates.[79]

The Ottoman soldiers showed their traditional valor, courage, obedience, and sturdiness, especially in defensive operations, but once again only when properly led. The inexperienced, but highly trained, Egyptian soldiers also showed their presence for the last time under Ottoman command. Obviously the army's general weakness in offensive capacity had much to do with the problem of leadership, not ignoring the importance (and absence of) training and maneuvers. It is important to note that the same stock of Ottoman soldiers performed differently under different officers. Osman Pasha, Ahmed Muhtar Pasha, and Derviş Pasha achieved fame by making use of the potential of their soldiers effectively, but Abdülkerim Nadir Pasha and Hasan Sabri Pasha ruined their careers and stained the reputation of the Ottoman military with the same soldiers. If we couple this with the high casualty rates of Ottoman officers, it becomes clear that the Ottoman military was becoming more and more of an officers' army that correlated closely with the increasing duties of the Mekteblis. Without finding a viable solution for the lack of an NCO corps or ways to commission and educate talented rankers, the Mekteblis had no other choice than to do everything by themselves and lead their units from the front ranks. The understandable result was that units frequently dispersed after their commanding officers were put out of action, which remained a serious problem throughout the war.[80]

Closely related with the uneven performance of Ottoman soldiers was the administration's failure, or neglect, to mobilize its entire pool of citizens for the war effort. The successive reform efforts had failed to enlarge the pool of recruits or to destroy the empire's traditional military-civilian separation. For the typical Ottoman citizen, military service was considered a duty and privilege for an elite group but not a compulsory duty for all.[81] Understandably, without widespread nationalism or the patriotism of the nation-in-arms concept, it was nearly impossible to destroy this traditional apathy toward military issues shown by the common people. The civil and military Ottoman leaders neither understood the modern nation-in-arms concept nor the severe limitations of an obsolete economy and social system on military reforms. However, even under these conditions and with this mentality, the administration had the means to mobilize Muslim groups within the combat zone by simply pointing out the dangers of defeat and enemy occupation. But, without any preparations including either intellectual or emotional appeals, it failed to organize these available resources. Few effective guerrilla-type operations were conducted in the Russian rear as they advanced and occupied Ottoman territory. There were minor exceptions to this when large groups of local Muslims helped the army, most famously in the defense of Plevne. This passive behavior becomes more apparent when compared with the military activities of the Bulgarians and Armenians, who launched guerrilla-type operations in the Ottoman rear or, more importantly, who provided provisions and intelligence to the enemy.[82]

The performance of the artillery and cavalry corps remained nearly the same as in the Crimean War. Apparently the full attention of the administration and the employment of French experts did improve the training and quality of the regular cavalry corps, but its numbers remained low so that its effect on the outcome of the war remained limited. Thousands of recently emigrated Caucasians, fleeing from Russian policies of forced expulsion and terror, provided a valuable source of Başıbozuk cavalry. In fact, these men provided the majority of Başıbozuks in both theaters of operations, but in neither theater were commanders able to make use of their potential. And, occasionally they created larger problems with their obsession with looting and their frequent breaches of the laws of war.[83]

The small number of regular infantry units achieved remarkable success, even in humiliating disasters. The veteran units of campaigns against Serbia and Montenegro (which were mostly employed in Plevne and Şıpka) especially surprised even the most pessimistic observers of the Ottoman military. Surprisingly, the famous fortifications of Plevne (and many other fortified positions as well) were built by the infantry corps and not by engineers, who were few in number in the Ottoman army. The performance of the Redifs, however, remained problematic as usual. Some of the Balkan Redif units reached the same standards as the regulars, thanks to their frequent mobilizations, but the Anatolian and Syrian Redifs disappointed everyone. Müstahfız units were so untrustworthy that they could do no more than guard fortified positions. The artillery corps remained the jewel of the Ottoman military, and with new Krupp cannons, was clearly superior to the Russian artillery. The main problem was the limited number of available field artillery batteries due to the initial heavy emphasis on fortress artillery.[84]

Thanks to the attention and efforts of the late Sultan Abdülaziz, the Ottoman military was better equipped and armed in this war than in previous wars. The Ottoman infantry used rapid-fire modern rifles such as the American Martini-Peabody (a close copy of the British Martini-Henry) and the British Snider, which were far superior to the Russian Krnk and Berdan rifles. Similarly, cavalry was armed with the Winchester Model 73 and Martini-Peabody carbines. However, not all units were able to make use of them effectively, especially reserve units that were called up at the very last minute. The imported Krupp steel cannons especially showed their worth in Plevne. Abdülaziz's decisions to improve the Tophane artillery foundry and other military industrial institutions by acquiring steam machinery, to hire

British and American engineers and foremen, and to introduce the British Woolwich system turned out to be very wise decisions. These improvements paid off during the war years when both Britain and France enforced a semi-official embargo of military-related merchandise to the Ottoman Empire. Additionally, the quality of gunpowder and cartridges produced by these factories was of superior quality. The Ottoman rifle factory converted thousands of old rifles to the Snider design, which were then distributed to newly recruited third-line Redif battalions. Finally, the baggy-looking Ottoman uniforms were more functional and sturdy than Russian ones, and winter clothing, backpacks, and blankets were of higher quality as well.[85]

Regrettably, the administration did not show the same interest and zeal for all critical equipment, especially the nonglamorous ones needed for staff work. In particular, there were no reliable maps available even for field army-level staffs due to the lack of surveying kit and military map-making equipment within the Ottoman military. Individual officers often bought copies of Austrian maps out of their own pockets.[86] These small-scale commercial maps could not compensate for the lack of detailed and scaled military maps necessary for proper staff work. So it is no great wonder that problems frequently occurred in coordinating assaults or that often even brigade-size units lost their way in the rugged terrain of the combat theaters.

Although Abdülaziz solved production and purchasing problems, the notoriously corrupt Ottoman logistics system remained the same, and every member of the field armies from the commanding generals down to private soldiers suffered from it. In contrast to historical Ottoman military strengths, no effective forward mounting bases were created. Transportation was a nightmare and traveling, even on the main roads, remained a huge challenge. Provisions spoiled and cartridges were rusted because of want of transportation and poor depot facilities, negatively affecting units that then could not perform their duties. The recently built railway system, as well as river and coastal steamboats, relieved some of the burden, but supplying coal became a large problem in a short time because of the lack of foresight and coordination. Well-trained and seasoned troops idled for weeks or months in distant provinces waiting for transportation, while teenagers and elderly men were forcefully recruited in and around the conflict zones.[87]

In conclusion, the end result of the war seemed to be a complete disaster in which both fronts collapsed. The Russians managed to reach the Istanbul suburbs for the first time. The final Peace Treaty of Berlin was humiliating in all respects; Romania and Serbia gained independence, an autonomous Greater Bulgaria was carved out, and the Armenian question was officially recognized. However, in relative terms, the defeated Ottoman army proved to be more capable than the victorious army of the Crimean War, clearly demonstrating that the Ottomans were on the right track with their reforms. The Russians paid dearly for their underestimation of the Ottoman military. Osman Pasha and Ahmed Muhtar Pasha showed the world that, if properly led, the Ottoman army had the potential to defeat its militarily stronger neighbor. Their successes became more important when taking into account the anarchic and disastrous strategic leadership of Abdülhamid and his favorites. More importantly, the Mekteblis made their presence felt for the first time, and the junior ones especially achieved remarkable success in comparison to either the Alaylıs or the protégés of the palace.[88]

The Hamidian Army: Attempts to Create an Apolitical and Loyal Army

The disastrous defeat and humiliating peace treaty shook the empire from top to bottom—especially the establishment of the Bulgarian Princedom, which created an independent enclave at the core of the empire and forced a flow of thousands of refugees, which not only created socioeconomic problems but emotional ones as well. Abdülhamid made use of this crisis effectively and came out of it stronger than before. Unfortunately, the Ottoman military, as the only institution with enough power to counter Abdülhamid, did not present any resistance to the sultan's increased autocracy due to its tarnished image and identity crisis. Some of its most powerful generals were court-martialed and sent into exile, while the victorious generals of the war, i.e., Osman Pasha, Derviş Pasha, and Ahmed Muhtar Pasha, were pacified by deliberate assignments to prestigious but ineffectual posts. Abdülhamid reinforced his position further by assigning loyal officers to key positions and by establishing a totally new imperial guard division and a secret police dedicated to monitoring and spying on everything within his administration and the public as a whole.

After securing his position and eliminating all real or imaginary opposition circles, Abdülhamid began to reorganize the Ottoman military according to his vision. However, several factors constrained his project from the very beginning. First, the Berlin Peace Treaty carved out the Ottoman Balkans in such a way that only a strip of territory ranging from the Adriatic Sea to the Aegean and Black Seas remained under direct Ottoman control. It was a territory bordered by hostile and irredentist Balkan nations and was impossibly difficult to defend against foreign aggression, let alone the internal problems. Two field armies (the Second and Third) were allocated entirely for the purpose of safeguarding this territory. Second, the already shaky Ottoman finance system, thanks to the costly armament projects of Abdülaziz and irresponsible government spending, collapsed after the costly war and the subsequent huge war indemnity. The creditor nations secured their investments by forcing the Ottoman administration to approve the founding of the Duyun-u Umumiye (Ottoman Public Debt Administration) on December 20, 1881, which would administer the tax revenues of the empire independent of the government for repayment of the credits and their interest. Consequently, the administration's ability to finance military reorganization and reforms was further crippled.

Under these constraints Abdülhamid tried to create an apolitical and absolutely loyal military that could safeguard the empire against foreign and internal aggression. As mentioned above, Abdülhamid shared the same passion as Abdülaziz for technical military reforms and military education. However, the huge burden of foreign debt and the costs of war hard-pressed the state budget so much that Abdülhamid had no other alternative than to sacrifice the navy. All available financial assets were allocated to the army, which undertook the almost impossible mission of defending the Ottoman Balkans. Abdülhamid was unable to follow the same generous military spending policy of the past, but he still pushed resources to the limits to acquire new weapons. Financial constraints played an important role in the renewed interest for military education, which was far cheaper than any armament projects. Without doubt, Abdülhamid achieved remarkable success in military education. He continued the policy of Abdülaziz to open military secondary and high schools not only in core regions but also in distant provinces. The dates and the places of the new military schools are instrumental in understanding Abdülhamid's zeal: Baghdad (first 1876 and the second 1886); Beirut and Damascus (1877); Edirne (1879); Bursa, Manastır, Erzurum, Trabzon, Erzincan, Elazığ, and Diyarbakır (1881); Aleppo (1882); Sivas (1883); Kastamonu and Salonika (1884); Tripoli (1886); Sana'a (1889); Van and Bitlis (1890); Süleymaniye-Iraq (1892); Benghazi (1892); Mosul, Üsküb, and Taiz-Yemen (1893); and Abha-Asir (1896). In effect he created a network of military schools all around the empire, encompassing every province and all Muslim groups.[89]

Unlike Abdülaziz, he did not see military education in military terms only, but also as a strategic instrument for his political vision and ideology. The total defeat at the hands of the Russians, increased political opposition, and subversive activities convinced him to reconsider the state ideology and formulate a new one; known as official Ottomanism. He actually borrowed the essentials from the opposition and redesigned them to be subservient to the state. Official Ottomanism was built around the personality cult of the sultan, a kind of patriotism and loyalty to the sultan in a multiethnic, multireligious, and multicultural empire. Unlike contemporary Ottoman intellectuals, Abdülhamid was pragmatic and a realist. He mainly targeted the Muslim population and tried to unite them under his political and spiritual leadership into a loosely unified Ottoman Muslim nation. So understandably, he saw the military schools as an important part of the effort to integrate distinct Muslim ethnic groups into the political, economic, and cultural fabric of the empire. He gave special emphasis to the predominantly Albanian and the much neglected Arab populated provinces, which had not been well represented previously in the Ottoman military. This policy became successful especially, in the larger provincial centers like Damascus and Baghdad, where poor and middle income families willingly sent their children to military schools. After commissioning, Arab and Albanian officers often served in their hometowns and became examples of success for the younger generations.[90] A special military school (*Aşiret Mekteb-i Hümayun*) was even opened for the nomadic tribal chieftains' children for a brief period of time (1892–1907).[91]

Abdülhamid's emphasis on enlarging the recruit pool of the military and encompassing less well-represented Muslim groups played an important role in experimenting with new ideas like the establishment of irregular tribal cavalry regiments. Abdülhamid, as a conservative, was very proud of the Ottoman past and tried to make use of old recipes in order to overcome new problems. He decided to revitalize the old tribal levies and irregular formations under his own name: Hamidiye Aşiret

Süvari Alayları (Hamidian tribal cavalry regiments). It is thought that the famous Russian Cossack irregulars also gave inspiration to this idea. The first experiments in this sense took place in the remote provinces of Libya and Yemen. In both provinces, young members of the ex-military social groups, the Kuloğlus, were conscripted and, after passing through intensive military training, were sent back to their provinces as a kind of local militia tasked with military and police duties.[92]

After these limited and encouraging experiences, Abdülhamid decided to apply the model on a massive scale in eastern Anatolia, where the Armenian question had already become an important internal threat and limited Iranian interventions required better border control. Obviously, a possible war against Russia was also taken into consideration. Abdülhamid invited notable Sunni Kurdish, Arab, Karapapak, and Turcoman tribal chiefs to Istanbul to renew with honor the old bonds of loyalty. However, he was careful to eliminate troublesome chiefs at the same time. Most of the tribal chiefs were well aware of the potential threat posed by the Armenian revolutionary committees and welcomed the idea of transforming their tribes into irregular regiments. Clearly, they increased their power by gaining legitimacy and receiving funds and weapons. According to the establishment decree, each cavalry regiment would consist of four to six troops with combat strengths ranging between 512 men to 1,052 men. Ideally, individual tribes would each man a respective regiment, but flexibility was provided for small tribes to man some regiments jointly. Thirty regiments were founded, for a total strength of 43,730 men, and organized into two brigades in less than four years. The reluctant tribes who had not joined initially eagerly asked to join the system after witnessing the benefits of it. So the number of regiments eventually reached 65 by 1908. For understandable reasons, most of the officers were commissioned from the respective tribe's notables; however, regular officers were assigned to man some posts and organize and help train these regiments.[93]

These regiments saw action immediately after their establishment. They showed their value during the Armenian Sason Rebellion in 1894, even though their heavy-handed tactics were highly criticized later on. Hamidiye regiments also managed to stop sporadic Iranian interventions. Sometimes, however, the tribes used their government-sponsored power against their rivals, thereby increasing tribal unrest for periods of time (like the feud between the Sunni Cibran and the Alawi Hormek tribes). Additionally, military experts remained skeptical about their conventional military capability against a power like Russia, even after their apparent success against internal dissidents and insurgents. From time to time, reform and reorganization teams were sent east, but none of them produced any meaningful results. The presence of regular officers, mostly retired Alaylıs and graduates of Aşiret Mektebi, helped to improve the overall bearing and manners of the regiments, but not their combat value. After the end of the Hamidian period, the Hamidiye regiments were reorganized and redesignated Aşiret Süvari Alayları (tribal cavalry regiments) in 1912 (dropping the name of the deposed sultan but preserving their tribal identity).[94]

The establishment of new imperial guard battalions composed solely of Albanians and Arabs was another novel attempt to integrate the empire's different Muslim nations. The Albanian Imperial Guard Battalion's (known as Fesli Zuhaf) soldiers were recruited from men from Prizren, who were well known for their sturdiness and loyalty. The Arab Imperial Guard Battalion's (known as Sarıklı Zuhaf) recruitment area was northern Syria. Even though a bloody clash between Arab and Albanian guards in 1905 abruptly ended this novel experience, it did achieve remarkable success in gaining the support of the sizable Albanian and Arab populations. Abdülhamid did not forget the Turks and also paid homage to the founders of Ottoman dynasty by establishing the Ertuğrul Cavalry Guard Regiment (named after the eponymous father of Osman Gazi, the first sultan) from the Turcomans of Bilecik (birthplace of the Ottoman Emirate).[95]

One instrumental outcome of Abdülhamid's fascination with the military technical and educational sides of reform, his autocratic way of governing, his suspicion of Ottoman generals, and the prevailing international atmosphere was that he chose the German military as a model and asked for help from Germany to carry out reforms. Actually, the official presence of German, or more correctly Prussian, military advisory teams was half a century old, starting with the Moltke Mission of 1835–1839. In contrast to the commonly accepted legend, the short-lived Moltke Mission, barely a dozen officers and other ranks, played a minor role in Ottoman military affairs. In truth, the effects of several other Prussian officers, who were enlisted to assist Ottoman military individually without official credentials, produced a more enduring legacy. For example, five Prussian artillery officers, Kotshkofski (Muhlis Pasha), Wendt (Nadir Pasha), Lohling (Mahir Bey), Schwenzfeier (Rami Pasha), and Wiesental, played important roles in the reorganization of the Ottoman artillery. These Prussian soldiers of fortune and the Moltke Mission started a tradition in which different Ottoman administrations looked to the Germans for various kinds of help and also purchased Prussian-manufactured weapons.[96]

As a very cautious and conservative man, Abdülhamid initially requested military advisors from a traditional ally, France, well before asking for German help. Most probably he planned to balance German influence with French. However, the French ignored repeated Ottoman requests, and by doing so France unknowingly destroyed any doubts or barriers regarding the acceptance of a solely German military mission. The official request for German military assistance was made in May 1880. After many discussions and a long negotiation process, only a small team of four officers under the leadership of Colonel Kaehler (and captains Kamphövener, von Hobe, and Ristow) was dispatched on April 29, 1882. After a brief investigation and analysis, Kaehler, now a newly commissioned Ottoman general, prepared a long reform and reorganization proposal. The proposal was discussed at the reform council that was headed by Ahmed Muhtar Pasha and approved by Abdülhamid on December 11, 1882. The plan dealt with three major shortcomings: a lack of an effective general staff system at all levels and anarchic command-control systems, the problematic Redif system, and the serious limitations of the military educational and training system. His findings were not novel and not unknown to the Ottoman administration. Grand Vizier Küçük Said Pasha was presented with similar findings and suggestions two years previously, and more or less every high-ranking general agreed with them.

However, neither Abdülhamid nor some of the influential figures like the hero of Plevne, Osman Pasha (who became an obstruction to increased German influence), were willing to start structural changes.[97]

Abdülhamid was deeply suspicious of his generals and was completely against the establishment of a clear and effective command-control architecture and hierarchy. Instead, he did the opposite and established numerous military commissions at various levels, reporting directly to him. Most importantly, he founded the Teftiş-i Askeri Dairesi (Department of Military Inspection) and Maiyet-i Seniye-i Erkân-ı Harbiye Dairesi (Department of Privy General Staff) within the palace structure as parallel organizations in order to control and check the Seraskeriye and Erkân-ı Harbiye-i Umumiye (The General Staff), respectively. Moreover, most of his military advisors were against the idea of a general staff department independent from the Seraskeriye, a legacy of old French models, and thus it remained part of Seraskeriye. Abdülhamid then curbed the power of the Seraskeriye more by establishing direct communications with his field army commanders. Most often, field army commanders would receive direct orders from the sultan without regard for or informing the Seraskeriye.[98]

To the astonishment of all contemporary observers, Abdülhamid's intrigue and distrust-based governance established stability and continuity for the first time in many centuries. He retained the same generals, who were selected for their loyalty and competence, in high posts for decades. For example, Rıza Pasha remained as Serasker for 18 years (1890–1908), Edhem Pasha served as chief of the general staff for 25 years (1880–1905), and Zeki Pasha as chief of artillery and engineer corps and superintendent of military schools for 17 years (1891–1908). Of course, keeping the same figures in the same positions had some negative effects, such as limiting the promotion opportunities for younger generations, encouraging patron-client relations at all levels, and increasing corruption. However, Hamidian stability and concord improved the general level of military efficiency up until the early 1900s.[99]

The Redif proposal of Kaehler was also ignored. Abdülhamid preferred quantity to quality and allocated barely enough financial assets for the survival of the Redif system. So even though the numbers of the Redif units increased drastically, without new officer cadres or effective and regular training programs, the system remained as it had been.[100] Not surprisingly, it was only Kaehler's last proposal regarding the military educational system that was taken seriously into consideration by the sultan. Because of Abdülhamid's support, a new German military advisor, namely Major Colmar von der Goltz, who would deal with military educational issues, was dispatched on June 18, 1883. Von der Goltz initially came to Istanbul for a short term of service but was destined to remain until 1895, and then returned several times afterwards. Had it not been for the presence of von der Goltz, the German military mission and its successors would certainly have failed to achieve the immense effect that they actually had on the Ottoman military.[101]

Von der Goltz was a highly talented general staff officer who had already established a reputation within German military circles, and he was a prolific military writer. However, his intellectual activities and his criticism of the German system (especially his book about Gambetta's army) effectively destroyed his chances of promotion, which was the reason for his new assignment to the Ottoman Empire.[102] After a brief inspection, von der Goltz came to the same conclusion as Kaehler. He was surprised by the high scientific level of the French style semi-engineering curriculum, but he found the Military Academy useless in terms of practical military matters. According to his observations, the cadets spent most of their time trying to learn the principles and theories of various sciences including civil and mechanical engineering, ballistics, and geography, but no time was allocated for the military application of these courses. The cadets were commissioned without any field experience, let alone any opportunity for small-unit leadership. He came to the conclusion that the current academic system was useless in its support of the military profession and should be discarded. Von der Goltz, importantly for the Ottoman army, recommended that the German officer training system, which was based upon military application and frequent regimental tours, should be introduced to replace it.[103]

In 1884, new military application lessons were added to the curriculum, and some engineering subjects were discarded. But the core lessons of the previous curriculum were retained.[104] Even though most of the young general staff officers and some influential figures like Küçük Said Pasha were very supportive of his suggestions, von der Goltz was unable to persuade Osman Pasha and the Military Academy officials to embrace his ideas. They refused to exclude advanced mathematics and physics from the curriculum. Obviously, they saw the officer training process not only in the military sense, but also as a part of the modernization of the Ottoman Empire. For them, it was essential to continue the semi-engineering curriculum in order to have officers who were capable enough to transfer to and handle civilian duties in the government.[105]

Von der Goltz's effect on general staff (Erkân-ı Harb) officer education turned out to be more important and more enduring. He not only drastically changed the education and training system itself, but also changed the overall status of the general staff officer corps within the army. First of all, according to his new evaluation system, only the best and brightest of the cadets were selected, 20 to 30 out of 1,000 cadets, for the General Staff College, which was three years long and academically very demanding. After graduation, the newly designated general staff officers would spend three to five years on probation, serving at the field level in all combat corps in the army. This shared experience made them a part of a special and privileged brotherhood within which every member knew and supported each other. They were protected against arbitrary assignment and promotion practices. Moreover, nearly all the influential command and staff positions were designated to be filled by general staff officers. Not surprisingly, many general staff officers became disillusioned with their unskilled superior officers in a relatively short time. Consequently, their work ethic, military-political culture and closely knit group structure were instrumental in the establishment and organization of secret opposition circles aimed at overthrowing the sultan.[106]

Understandably, the biggest impact of the German military mission was establishing the German army as the model for every aspect of the Ottoman military system and Germany itself as a political model. Contemporary German military manuals and other military literature replaced French and British versions. The German armaments industry also established a monopoly on nearly every weapon system and all equipment acquired by the empire. Von der Goltz played a crucial role in all aspects. Initially, several officers, growing by 1909 to hundreds of officers and other military specialists, were sent to Germany for training. These officers not only learned military subjects, but also German culture, lifestyles, and political systems. Even though the German advisors and other officials paid special attention to the political sensitivities of Abdülhamid and tried their best to stay away from Ottoman politics, in practice they played a crucial role by promoting the merits of their system, providing an institutional model, and demonstrating new training methods and work ethics.[107]

The Ottoman-Greek War of 1897 is instrumental in understanding the successes and shortcomings of the Hamidian military. Actually, the conflict was a limited war in every aspect. The combat actions lasted barely a month. Only 10 Ottoman divisions, reinforced with partial mobilization, took part, and overall casualty figures were low. But it was large enough for an evaluation of the extent of Hamidian reforms.

The Ottoman administration tried its best to stay away from war. However, the over-confident Greek leadership saw the situation for annexing Crete and even expanding on the mainland further north as ripe for exploitation. This was partly due to miscalculation of the Great Powers' policy and an exaggerated view of the internal problems of the Ottomans, especially regarding the recent Armenian rebellions. Two Greek regular battalions openly landed on Crete and joined with the local rebels on February 15, 1897 (the so-called Vassos Operation). Within two weeks, Greek semi-official gangs, called the Ethnike Hetairia, reinforced with regular officers and soldiers, began to launch guerrilla raids into Ottoman Thessaly. The Ottoman administration reluctantly increased the alert level and reinforced the border guards with regular infantry battalions. On April 9 a reinforced battalion-sized Greek gang with some Italian volunteers attacked Ottoman border towers and defeated a border company in Kranya (Krania). Even though they were repulsed and retreated back to Greece the next day, the incident forced the administration, which was already under intense public pressure, to declare war on Greece on April 17.[108]

The Ottoman-Greek War of 1897 was fought in two separate theaters of operations—Alasonya-Thessaly and Yanya (Janina)-Epirus—but in most of the contemporary works the Yanya theater is neglected due to the fact that combat operations near Yanya remained at divisional level (two Ottoman divisions against a Greek division) and did not affect the outcome of the war. We can divide the combat operations in the main theater (the Alasonya front) into three stages: first, border clashes and the occupation of mountain passes (April 16–22); second, the Mati-Deliler battle and the occupation of Tırnova (Tournavos) and Yenişehir (Larissa) (April 23–May 4); and finally, the battles of Velestin (Valestinos), Çatalca (Pharsalos), and Dömeke (Domokos) (May 5–17).

For the first time, the Ottoman high command put contingency plans into use. The plan against Greece was prepared by none other than von der Goltz in 1886. It was revised just before the start of the hostilities. The plan was simple—strategic defense by an army corps (two infantry divisions) in the Yanya region and strategic offensive by a field army (seven infantry divisions and one cavalry division) in the Alasonya region. The main idea was to force Greeks to overstretch their initial defensive lines, which were very near to the border. The main body of the Ottoman Alasonya Army would try to fall behind the Greeks before they were able to retreat back to the Yenişehir line. Von der Goltz supposed that the Great Powers would not let the Greeks be beaten and would intervene in the conflict in less than 15 days. So the Greek army had to be crushed in less than two weeks. Obviously, the revised plan demanded the rapid mobilization and transportation of combat units to the front, to fix the main body of the Greek army quickly along the border and enable the encirclement maneuver of cavalry-rich mobile divisions.[109]

The partial mobilization proceeded smoothly in less than two months. Thousands of reserve soldiers enthusiastically flooded the recruitment centers, and officials encountered difficulties forcing them to send home excess numbers of reserves. Similarly, hundreds of Albanian irregulars saw the conflict as a once-in-a-lifetime opportunity and joined the mobilized divisions as additional assets. Thanks to the availability of good railways, most of the units reached their destination on time (40,000 personnel and 8,000 pack animals were transported in 20 days). However, problems immediately started after debarkation from the troop trains. Transportation of baggage from the last train station to Alasonya, a distance of only 21 kilometers, took an inordinate amount of time and effort due to poor road conditions and lack of transportation assets. The high command was unable to find a satisfactory solution to this problem, and units had to wait days for resupply during the war.[110]

The initial stage of the campaign showed all the shortcomings of an inexperienced but excessively enthusiastic army. Officers and soldiers sometimes ran towards the enemy as if in a race without paying attention to combat tactics and techniques, and the first casualty figures of officers (52 casualties) jumped to abnormally high levels (10 percent for the first stage, 6 percent for the whole campaign) in comparison with the intensity of the combat. Two brigade and several regiment commanders were killed in action during the initial stage (four days long). Typically, regiment and higher-level unit commanders were unable to command and control effectively their battalions. Instead of conducting the encirclement maneuver as planned, most units simply tried to push the Greek defenders back by frontal assaults. Once again, the problematic Ottoman command-control hierarchy and logistics proved clearly deficient after the start of the Greek withdrawal. Confusion, delay, and lack of coordination and communication were the norms of the day. Ottoman forward units reached weakly defended Yenişehir two days after the Greeks withdrew from the town.[111]

Abdülhamid was extremely disillusioned with the performance of his commander in chief, Edhem Pasha, who preferred to spend more time with western journalists than with his subordinates. To make things worse, Edhem Pasha, after showing poor and wavering leadership, suddenly began to ask for reinforcements. The famous commander of the Plevne defense, Osman Pasha, was chosen to replace him, but then at the very last moment the fall of Yenişehir saved Edhem Pasha. The administration also decided to strengthen faltering staff positions by assigning all available general staff officers including military attachés and lecturers from the Military Academy.[112]

The second stage proceeded along the same lines as the first. Ottoman units pushed the Greek defenders back without attempting encirclement maneuvers, and the Greeks safely evacuated their defenses retreating to their last defensive line. Although confidence and firmer control under fire replaced the combat inexperience of the Ottoman rank and file, the first battle of Velestin was a disaster. In this encounter, a forced reconnaissance turned into a futile and bloody assault, which proved that the Ottoman officers, especially, were in need of more experience.[113]

The three pitched battles (Velestin, Çatalca, and Dömeke) in front of the last Greek defensive line turned out to be decisive. The Greek defenders were beaten in detail and lost any chance to safeguard the road to Athens.[114] However, thanks to the limited nature of Ottoman aims and the timely intervention of the Great Powers, Greece was saved from further humiliation. Against the expectations of the Ottoman public, the victory did not result in the return of the Thessaly region, which had been lost in 1882. In fact, the victorious Ottoman troops retreated as if defeated, and Abdülhamid spent several tense months trying to explain why the war had been won by the army but subsequently lost by the diplomats.

Obviously, the Ottoman military was better trained, led, and equipped than the overconfident Greeks. The Hamidian reforms were successful in most respects. For the first time, the Ottoman General Staff functioned like a real general staff rather than as a mere scribal bureau. The artillery corps (thanks to a high percentage of Mektebli officers) lived up to its own high standards and effectively crushed any Greek counterattacks. The newly reformed medical corps performed its medical treatment tasks by opening field hospitals at divisional-level and stationery hospitals in the rear. However, battlefield casualty evacuation, during which casualties spent hours—even entire days—without proper treatment, still lagged behind other armies. The costly investment in railways improved the performance of the ever-faulty transportation and logistics system. Even the enthusiasm of the common people overcame the shortages of the Redif system. And thanks to the frequent mobilization of the Anatolian Redifs, most Anatolian Redif battalions performed as well as their regular counterparts, and the Trabzon Redifs (the only mobilized unit from Fourth Army) became famous as the best of all.[115]

Abdülhamid and the Ottoman high command, blinded by the easy victories and by the apparent success of the improvements, paid little attention to the army's serious problems and shortcomings. First of all, they happily ignored the Ottoman defeat that had been suffered on the Yanya front in front of Loros (Louros). The unexpected Greek assault of April 18 dislocated the Yanya Corps and defeated the 2nd Division. Even though the Yanya Corps gained confidence and recaptured the lost ground in two weeks, the serious shortcomings of the Albanian Redifs and irregulars were exposed. Indeed, the friendly fire of the raw Redifs turned out to be more fatal to their comrades than that of the enemy. The failure to benefit from the lessons of this defeat would play an important role in the collapse of Ottoman regional defense units during the Balkan Wars of 1912–1913.[116]

Second, Abdülhamid still did not comprehend the cost of his paranoia—his banning of divisional and higher-unit maneuvers and all live firing exercises. He was suspicious of all combat training and any large-unit movement, due to his fear of military uprisings or coup d'états against his sultanate. Consequently, the Ottoman generals simply did not have the basic understandings of how to command their units under combat conditions. They were too slow in comprehending the rapidly unfolding modern battles, and they became a liability for their units, which were equally slow to react. The units were unable to perform complex maneuvers, failed to establish and maintain contact, and were notoriously unable to follow up victory. Abdülhamid was so paranoid that he categorically refused the distribution of modern long-range Mauser repeating rifles (fantastically, there were 480,000 7.5 mm and 220,000 9.5 mm rifles on hand) that had been purchased at the cost of increasing the foreign debt. Only one out of ten divisions that took part in the Greek War hurriedly armed themselves with these new rifles; all the others used the veteran Sniders and Martinis during the war.[117]

Third, keeping the same generals for the sake of stability and loyalty frozen in the higher posts effectively limited the opportunity for promotion for an ambitious new generation of officers. The poor leadership performance of these privileged old guards increased the fault line between old and new generations. This especially affected the young general staff officers, who were trained by Germans, and who admired the German model and were already critical of their generals.[118] In part due to their counterinsurgency experiences, they became so disillusioned that their military frustration, coupled with political aspirations, turned them into conspirators. They began to plot against the Hamidian regime and established relations with civilian opposition circles.

In conclusion, Abdülhamid achieved remarkable results with the military reforms and reorganization of the Ottoman military after the disastrous defeats at the hands of the Russians. However, his paranoia and lack of confidence in the officer corps that he himself had created limited the overall end results of the reforms. The Ottoman-Greek War not only showed the successes and shortcomings of the Hamidian military, but also acted as a catalyst in which disaffection and disillusionment of the highly trained young officers reached record levels. In a way, Abdülhamid created his own nemesis by providing a better military educational system, but not fulfilling the high expectations of the officers so educated.[119]

Counterinsurgency Experiences

One of the least-known aspects today of the Ottoman military experience is doubtless that of its counterinsurgency campaigns. The studies of the effects of counterinsurgency experiences on the officer corps and the Ottoman military as a whole are much neglected. On the political side, the effects are indirectly discussed in various scholarly works without establishing direct relationships, but the military effects are altogether neglected. Similar to the French and British colonial experiences with low-intensity conflicts or small wars, the Ottoman officers spent an important percentage of their careers fighting against various types of insurgents, social bandits, and tribal warriors. Their continuous occupation with counterinsurgency operations left its stamp on the identity and performance of these officers. It is nearly impossible to understand the political and military developments of the time without paying attention to this counterinsurgency heritage.

From the very beginning, the Ottoman military had been tasked to provide internal security and public order. The timariot cavalrymen's main duty, especially, was to act as local constabularies during peacetime. Even during mobilization a certain percent would remain behind to perform these duties. Consequently, even though, as time went on, the administration established various police and other constabulary organizations to deal specifically with law enforcement duties, the Ottoman military remained an important policing instrument.[120]

As already mentioned in the previous chapter, Mahmud II initially designed and founded the Mansure army to safeguard his regime and to perform law enforcement duties. Mansure soldiers acted as policemen first in Istanbul and later in the province centers and other towns. The Mansure army did not fulfill the expectations of its founder against foreign aggression but was successful in establishing the central administration's authority over the entire empire for the first time in centuries. The dual use of the Mansure army created a tradition in which law enforcement became permanent duty of the military.[121]

The establishment of the Zabtiye (literally law enforcement) organization, modeled after Prussian and French examples, in 1840 did lessen the burden on the military by taking over ordinary law enforcement duties. However, the administration kept its paramilitary character (except its civilian police branch, which was mainly based in Istanbul). The Zabtiye passed through a series of reforms (some as a part of general military reforms, others to please Great Powers) and transformed into the Jandarma (gendarmerie) organization during the 1870s. Interestingly, the Great Powers' persistent requests for the establishment of a centrally controlled hierarchic agency that would provide law enforcement services (chief among them protecting Christian minorities) all over the Ottoman territory further militarized the new Jandarma. The unit structures were close copies of the relevant military ones, and its personnel were either recruited directly from military ranks or passed through military training before assignment. Hundreds of military academy graduates were selected and assigned to new Jandarma units, which were manned with the best recruits available. The overall strength of Jandarma exceeded 26,000 personnel at the end of the nineteenth century. New on-the-job training centers were founded in provincial centers to train NCOs and soldiers. Weapons and equipment were purchased. The Ottoman Public Debt Administration, which was very reluctant about any military expenditure, eagerly financed the Jandarma's projects due to Great Power support. Not surprisingly, in a relatively short time, it lost its organizational independence and became officially subservient to the Seraskeriye.[122]

The breaking away of an independent Greece started a process that the Ottoman administration had little understanding of and little means to counter. Mahmud and his successors did not fully understand the level of threat posed by separatist nationalist movements. They saw the threat from a traditional perspective and employed traditional methods such as negotiation with traditional local leaders, trying to crush rebellions with military power only. Their negligent posture toward Great Power interventions as well as the political, social, economic, and cultural demands of newly born nationalism turned out to be fatal for the empire. Consequently, each nationalist movement, imitating its predecessor, launched its respective separatist campaign and carved a homeland from the empire by making use of Russian victories. In turn, Romanians, Serbians, Montenegrins, and Bulgarians followed the Greek path to independence.

After the success of the first wave of separatist nationalism, the empire had to face a second wave. The Berlin Peace Treaty recast the Ottoman Balkan possessions in such a way that it was not militarily feasible to defend them against either foreign aggression or internal insurrection. Except for Romania, all of the newly independent Balkan nations had significant national minorities left within the Ottoman provinces, and irredentist plans were quickly hatched to create larger Christian states by swallowing large portions of Ottoman territory. So it is not surprising that, immediately after the signing of the Berlin Treaty, a second wave of separatist nationalism began with many Christian minorities demanding union with their respective motherlands. The situation became more complicated and dangerous with the beginning of separatist Armenian nationalism. The Armenians living in eastern Anatolia were only able to secure the promise of reforms, which was far from satisfying their aims.

Abdülhamid and his advisors were unable to create an effective and viable strategy to deal with this second wave of separatism. In fact, the administration paid much attention to the effects of this wave of nationalism on its diplomatic relations with the Great Powers, in order to avoid interventions. However, the problem of how to deal with it internally was totally left in the hands of the military. The Seraskeriye neither refused the duty nor created a strategy. Instead, it handed over the duty to the respective field army commanders, who were in most of the cases governors as well. These generals (all of whom were still assigned according to loyalty and patron-client relations) usually did not bother themselves with the problem but passed it down to their subordinate commanders, who were actually in the field fighting against the insurgents. In short, the counterinsurgency campaigns against separatist nationalist movements were left entirely in the hands of regiment- and battalion-level junior officers, who were on their own without any clear orders and without the cooperation of other government agencies.[123]

The island of Crete is a good example that illustrates the chronic state of the nationalist rebellions even after successful military interventions and counterinsurgency operations. Beginning in 1841, turmoil began in Crete with the arrival of instigators from Greece. An Ottoman expeditionary force under the command of Mustafa Naili Pasha, a native Cretan, suppressed the rebellion easily and the administration assigned another native Cretan, Veli Pasha, to deal with the demands of the rebels and solve their grievances. But the tolerant administration of Veli Pasha did not solve much, and an outright rebellion started in 1861, which was suppressed by another talented general, İsmail Pasha, one year later. The negotiation process and further Ottoman reforms did not satisfy the Greek nationalists, and a well-organized rebellion broke out in 1866. This time the insurgents were well organized and able to mobilize 12,000 personnel. The veteran İsmail Pasha was assigned once again as the governor and the commander of an expeditionary force of 45,000 men. The insurgency continued on for nearly four years and terminated only after the successful application of counterinsurgency tactics and techniques, combined with what might be called today Mustafa Naili Pasha's "hearts and minds" campaign. However, low-level insurgency continued nonstop on the island with periodic large-scale rebellions in 1878, 1888, and 1896.[124]

The administration showed its structural limitations, especially, during these interim low-level conflict periods. Expeditionary forces, with their capable commanders, were repeatedly pulled out prematurely, leaving barely enough troops to patrol the conflict area. Junior officers, on their own, were left behind to fight against insurgents and to protect Muslim civilians who were prime targets of ethnic cleansing by nationalists. Moreover, in addition to their military responsibilities, these officers often had to perform civil governmental duties such as education, sanitation, reconstruction, and even tree planting. And in many locations, particularly in the Balkans, they had to deal with the representatives of the Great Powers, who were assigned to monitor conflicts and were empowered to sack officials.[125]

In comparison to Crete where there was only one insurgency group, which was relatively easy to isolate, the Ottoman Balkans, especially Macedonia, were most difficult to control and govern. First of all, there were four states and four major insurgent nationalist organizations[126] that were vying for portions of it. Additionally, the population was far more cosmopolitan, and settlements more mixed. Second, the irredentist desires of all four states overlapped each other so much that most often the insurgent organizations were fighting each other at the same time that they were fighting against the Ottoman military. Third, the introduction of Italian anarchism and Russian nihilism further radicalized the separatist nationalist groups. The Macedonian insurgent organization, especially, which carried the title of "Inner Macedonian Revolutionary Organization" (IMRO), managed to blend militant nationalist ideology with insurgency tactics and techniques so effectively that it could be called the first modern guerrilla organization.[127]

The Komitacıs (literally member of a secret political organization and the word most commonly used in the empire to describe such groups themselves) waged relentless terror campaigns (murder, robbery, extortion, kidnapping, and occasionally massacre) not only against the state and its functionaries, but also against Muslim and Christian populations (and sometimes even against their own supporters). For them, terrorism and employing all sorts of violence were proper tools to gain the support of the population and, most importantly, to capture European attention and encourage the intervention of the Great Powers. Komitacıs, as the first modern guerrillas, made effective use of the military potential of the civilian population. The population provided them with sanctuary, food, intelligence, funding, and recruits. The Komitacıs had support bases in neighboring Christian countries (in fact controlled by them) and most often had the direct support of the host country armed forces in terms of expertise, weapons, and sometimes personnel. Their organizational structures were a combination of the Italian Carbonari cell system and the Russian nihilist dual political front and armed wing structure. So most often, village notables, teachers, and clergy belonged to the political front, whereas the youngsters indoctrinated by them were guerrilla fighters. Of course, not all the Komitacı organizations were on equal footing. The IMRO was the most modern and complex organization, whereas the Greek ones were more traditional and less sophisticated.[128]

In comparison, the Ottoman officers had to learn by themselves under very adverse conditions how to conduct counterinsurgency operations against these guerrilla organizations. Most of the academy-graduated officers had to spend several rotations (sometimes whole careers) in Macedonia fighting on their own against these ideologically motivated, well-equipped, and well-led guerrilla organizations. Their main problem was the lack of government support as well as a lack of doctrinal tactics to combat these unconventional fighters. The administration was more than happy to leave everything to the officers on the scene, providing no substantial support unless the situation became completely unmanageable. This was also true for the wider Ottoman public in that ordinary citizens paid limited attention to the problem, even in neighboring provinces like Salonika (Selânik).[129]

The officers involved were quick to realize the evolution of traditional insurgents and social bandits, which were named interchangeably Asi (rebel) and Haydut (literally bandit, better known in Balkan languages as Hajduk or Hajdamak), into Komitacıs (ideologically motivated and highly disciplined guerrilla fighters). In a relatively short time, they understood the importance of gaining support from the population and made use of not only the potential of the Muslim population, but also of the different Christian groups, pitting them against each other. For example, Greeks were valuable allies in predominantly Macedonian or Bulgarian regions, whereas Bulgarians were Ottoman allies in Greek-dominated areas.[130]

Surprisingly, the Seraskeriye or Ministry of War remained aloof from the formulation and application of counterinsurgency doctrines and operations. And publication of any military manuals or texts on the subject was even forbidden. There was no curriculum regarding counterinsurgency in any military school, and even discussions about the subject were discouraged. Similarly, the administration tried its best not to inform the public about anything related to insurgencies, rebellions, or social unrest. Thanks to the administration's efforts to isolate conflict zones from the wider public, and because of its distancing itself from insurgency-related problems, the officer corps in a unique blend of initiative gained control of the conflict zones. Consequently, independent of the administration and the Seraskeriye, various tactics and techniques were invented, and more or less an unofficial but widely accepted uniform counterinsurgency doctrine was in use after the 1890s. By making use of their academy-acquired competencies in foreign languages, the Ottoman officer corps also followed developments in foreign militaries. For example, the British practice of constructing blockhouses in order to control and secure rugged terrain during the Boer War was immediately introduced under the same name (Blokhavz) and widely used. These unofficial counterinsurgency strategies, tactics, and techniques eventually paid off, and most of the Komitacı groups were crushed and lost ground after 1904.[131]

In effect, combat units became alternative military schools, and mess halls became clubs where one could discuss anything without fear of prosecution. As could be expected, this rare blend of freedom and conflict affected the political understanding and consciousness of the Mektebli officers. Their academic training, such as theoretical backgrounds and competency in foreign languages, gave them the necessary tools to follow and evaluate these developments. The effect of academic training becomes more obvious when the Alaylı officers are taken into consideration. The Alaylıs also lived through the same experiences, but they remained staunchly loyal to the sultan.[132]

The Mekteblis saw themselves as the new elite of the empire, and they felt responsible to act in its interest. As active combatants on the frontiers, they were visibly reminded of the empire's shrinking borders and loss of provinces. The constant fear of the imminent loss of the Ottoman Balkans especially shaped their perspective. They were also well aware of Great Power interventions and their activities within the empire. Resentment toward the presence of foreign diplomats, military observers, and missionaries was widespread. Ottoman officers increasingly became conscious of the insufficiency of the official state ideology and general lack of patriotism.[133]

Two other factors played an important role in shaping the political consciousness of the officers. The first factor was the effect of the ideologies of their guerrilla enemies. The constant conflicts created channels of information between combatants. The militant nationalism of the guerrillas—the continuous flow of political thoughts and their ways of propaganda and organization—greatly inspired the officers. And in the end, they applied what they had learned. The second factor was the solidarity between officers and the local Muslim (especially those who were Turkish) population. For obvious reasons, the Muslim population felt themselves deserted by the administration. The only agents of the government who were trying to protect the Muslims from the attacks of the various guerrilla groups (and trying to provide various civil services) were officers of the Ottoman army. The army and Muslims not only jointly fought against insurgents, but also built and repaired roads, bridges, schools, and mosques and performed other public tasks together. Understandably, a strong bond of solidarity was established between these groups.[134]

For most of the Mekteblis, neither the official nor the unofficial version of Ottomanism had any meaning. Similarly, Islamism began to lose ground, especially after Albanian unrest and the refusal of several Albanian units to fight against Albanian rebels and bandits. Turkish nationalism seemed for many the only viable solution. The appeal of Turkish nationalism becomes clearer when taking into account the unfair burden placed on reliable Anatolian units (composed of ethnic Turks) to conduct counterinsurgency operations in all parts of the empire. Officers who fought consistently alongside of the Anatolian soldiers began to identify themselves more with them. Officers, who were ethnically Turkish, hesitantly but continuously became nationalists, even if the majority was still reluctant to drop Ottomanism and Islamism altogether.[135]

Interestingly, even the most pragmatic officers believed in the merits of more democracy. They admired the German political system and, as military personnel, were well accustomed to its accompanying military discipline. However, due to the legacy of the short-lived first constitutional period, they naively interpreted political freedom as a magical potion that would cure all societal illness. For them, the autocratic regime of Abdülhamid was the root of all ills and problems. Obviously, these naive admirers of constitutional monarchy had limited backgrounds and did not understand the complexity of the problems of the empire, but they had the courage and will to act.[136]

The first political protests by military members were conducted (and secret organizations were founded) by cadets in Istanbul at the end of the 1880s such as the establishment of the Osmanlı İttihad Cemiyeti (Ottoman Union Committee) in 1889 by Imperial Medical School cadets.[137] The officer corps became organized after 1904, and several secret organizations, all of which carried the same phrase—Vatan (motherland)—within their names, were established and flourished at the field army headquarters (the Third Army headquarters in Salonika became the epicenter of the most powerful group). Not surprisingly, general staff officers (as a part of a privileged and educated elite brotherhood) took the lead. They made use of their positions and command and control channels in order to open new branches and to recruit new members. In a relatively short time, the İttihad ve Terakki Cemiyeti (Committee of Union and Progress or CUP) became the most prominent, and it absorbed the other groups into it.[138]

The officers involved in the CUP, in opposition to civilian intellectuals and some fellow conspirators, saw no other way than violent action to reinstate a constitutional regime. Some of them supported various types of military coup d'états while others, under the influence of their counterinsurgency experiences, advocated mutiny and guerrilla warfare. After the widely admired but failed Russian Revolution of 1905 and uprisings in Iran, the civilian conspirators unwillingly converted to the officers' way of thinking and accepted their leadership.[139]

Despite much preparation and secrecy, events unfolded without a master plan, with the failed attempt to assassinate the Chief of the Salonika Military Police on April 29, 1908. Abdülhamid immediately sent an investigation team with extraordinary powers to which the conspirators gave the alarm and reacted with disobedience and insubordination.[140] Even at this stage, things might have remained under control had the details of the Reval meeting of Russian Tsar Nicholas II and British King Edward VII on June 9–10 not been revealed (the so-called Isvolski-Harding project on Macedonia).[141] According to the information leaked to the press, Britain had given a free hand to Russia for the dismemberment of the Ottoman Empire. This news exploded on the scene and enraged the officers involved in the movement. Niyazi Bey, with his battalion and civilian volunteers, rebelled and took refuge in the mountains near Resne on July 3. Other junior officers soon followed his example and rebelled in other provinces. Government functionaries, including even reactionary generals, were assassinated by army officers. The civilian population joined the cause of the officers by holding public demonstrations and sending mass petitions to the sultan. Clearly, the officers were making use of their accumulated experience in counterinsurgency by following the blueprints of the Komitacıs.[142]

In the end, Abdülhamid gave up under intense pressure and restored the constitution that he had suspended in 1878. The Meşrutiyet (literally constitutional monarchy) was a remarkable victory won by the Mektebli junior officers. All of a sudden, they became the praetorian guards and kingmakers. Although at this stage they did not have the means to control the state, which the counterrebellions of April 1909 (31 Mart Vakası) would show, they did become the dominant political actors in the empire. Unfortunately for the empire, as the officers became part of active politics, and in a relatively short time, partisan politics destroyed the solidarity and unity of the Ottoman officer corps. Disappointed officers established their own parties opposing the CUP and began to conspire not only in the political arena but also within the military. Not surprisingly, several dissident officers rebelled with their units, and the Macedonian mountains once again became home for these military gangs. This infighting would be instrumental in the poor performance of the Ottoman military during the forthcoming wars.[143]

The military effects of the army's counterinsurgency experiences are more complicated than the political ones. More research is needed to unveil the real dimensions of this issue, but it is possible to point out some of the more obvious ones. First of all, most of the Ottoman officers preferred small-unit tactics and techniques to large-scale operations. During the Balkan Wars, company- and battalion-level units were able to beat enemy units soundly if they were employed independently, but when the same units were a part of a regiment or higher units, they were unable to reach the same level of efficiency. The wide-scale employment of snipers is also a good example of the army's counterinsurgency heritage.

The second effect was that of initiative. The Ottoman officers were well accustomed to act independently and to receive short, task-oriented operational orders. For example, during the Libyan War, the future founder of the Turkish Republic, Mustafa Kemal Atatürk, launched his famous assault on Tobruk against a much superior Italian force after receiving only half-a-page-long divisional order. In effect, this well-established sense of initiative sometimes was instrumental in officers disobeying orders.

The third effect was the most dangerous one. The officers schooled in counterinsurgency often suffered difficulty in adjusting themselves to the realities of conventional warfare and massive firepower. They became used to insurgents with limited firepower. So when faced with infantry supported by machine guns and quick firing artillery, they did not adapt well. Similarly, most of the regular soldiers were veterans of long counterinsurgency campaigns and encountered difficulties understanding the dynamics of conventional warfare. The infamous Bolayır frontal assaults at the last stage of the First Balkan War are good examples of this tendency. The Ottoman infantry literally decimated itself against Bulgarian firepower while trying to overcome troops well established in trenches protected with barbed wire and other engineering works.[144] The same mistakes were repeated again and again, especially during the Gallipoli Campaign of World War I.

Balkan Wars: Losing the Core Regions

The restoration of the constitution and the reopening of the parliament did not fulfill the high hopes and expectations of the younger modernizers. The French formula of liberty, equality, and fraternity managed to rally the citizens of the empire together for only a few months. The joyful mass demonstrations and public speeches of goodwill presented colorful stories for the western newspapers but, in the end, the so-called revolution of the Meşrutiyet did just the opposite—enlarging the fault lines and fractures between different ethnic and religious groups. Political radicalism and frustration took hold of many when developments did not meet expectations. In turn, the rank and file of the army became perennial actors in political protests and demonstrations. Once again, military cadets led the way.[145]

The serious limitations of the Ottoman version of liberty and democracy were instrumental in creating societal fault lines and fractures, which convinced most of the officer corps of the wisdom of an enlightened dictatorship of the military. Several other developments escalated the crisis in government and were seen as proof of the need for military rule. Among these were the proclamation of independence by Bulgaria on October 5, 1908 (actually the Bulgarian Princedom had been already enjoying de facto independence), the annexation of Bosnia and Herzegovina by the Austro-Hungarian Empire on October 6 (it had already been under Austro-Hungarian supervision for nearly 30 years), and the proclamation of union with Greece by the Cretan Assembly on October 12. So once again, aggressive foreign machinations increased regional instability and impaired the fragile peace and stability within the empire.[146]

The Meşrutiyet obviously did not establish an efficient and viable system in terms of politics, economics, and social life, but it did provide an unforeseen advantage for the military reformers. As already discussed above, the military reforms were led by sultans who were very willing but, at the same time, inexperienced and uninformed regarding military art and science. Even though they had native and foreign military advisors, they still encountered difficulty in differentiating important issues from the less important ones. For example, all of the last five sultans (starting with Selim III) spent months designing uniforms for their soldiers instead of allocating their valuable time to work on structural changes. Moreover, in most of the cases, the structural military reforms were perceived by the sultans as a direct threat to their authority. The command structure is a good example of this paradigm. Nearly all of the sultans of the period (chief among them Abdülhamid) created parallel or shadow organizations in order to curb the power of the military commanders and sometimes played one against another to maximize their power. In truth, unity of command and control, a single hierarchy, and communication and reports lines are key elements for the efficiency and success of any modern military. Therefore, the sultans sabotaged their own reforms by maintaining their self-interests as paramount.

The Meşrutiyet and the later dethronement of Abdülhamid reduced the power of the sultan in military affairs to a minimum. Additionally, the old and obsolete Seraskeriye, which became the last stronghold of the old guard after 1900, was formally disbanded, and its authority and duties were distributed to their rightful owners—the Harbiye Nezareti (Ministry of War, founded in 1900) and the General Staff. However, the Ministry of War was unable to fulfill its mission due to the political instability caused by a continual succession of 11 ministers of war in a six-year period. Consequently, thanks to the continuous leadership of Ahmed İzzet Pasha, who remained chief of the General Staff during the turbulent period between 1908 and 1914, the General Staff became the sole authority on military affairs by willingly assuming most of the duties of the ministry. In doing so, it also became independent of any political control. Ahmed İzzet Pasha further extended the control of the General Staff by improving its bureaucratic capacity and efficiency. The complex structure was simplified; the numbers of departments and bureaus were consolidated into five new functional departments (training, intelligence, mobilization, topography, and correspondence), and staff specialization was encouraged. In contrast, the ministry remained as it had been.[147]

Ahmed İzzet Pasha was a highly trained and talented general staff officer. He became the protégé of von der Goltz immediately after graduation and was one of the first five officers sent to Germany at the suggestion of General Kaehler. He spent four years as an exchange officer and served at different levels of staff positions with distinction. He not only understood the German military system thoroughly, but also was well versed in the German intellectual discussions and future plans. He also mastered the intricacies of von der Goltz's various treatises about the Ottoman military.[148]

The reorganization regulation of 1910 was the brainchild of Ahmed İzzet Pasha and his fellow German-trained general staff officers. First of all, the general unit architecture was reorganized drastically according to a new triangular division concept. Basically, the concept involved replacing the square division structure (two brigades each with two regiments) with a division composed of three regiments, each with three battalions, which eliminated both brigade headquarters and a regiment. Although the number of regiments was reduced in divisions, combat strength was preserved, because command and control was more effective. It was an innovative idea born out of German-Ottoman military intellectual discussions. World War I would show the advantages of this concept, but it was the Ottoman military that created initially this innovative organization. The introduction of triangular divisions started a chain reaction. Much-needed army corps headquarters were established (also triangular and each with three divisions and additional support units) at last on January 8, 1911. Previously, the term "army corps" was used for two or three divisional groups without a permanent standing corps staff. Understandably, there was little need for large field army headquarters, which were already obsolete and clumsy. Instead, field army inspectorates (Ordu Müfettişliği), which were leaner and focused only on operational issues, were created. Unfortunately, neither Ahmed İzzet Pasha, nor his fellow general staff officers, paid enough attention to the personnel, doctrinal, and technical issues related to these drastic reforms. Reorganizational problems such as how to man new staff positions and combat service support systems, how to write new operational and tactical doctrines, and how to create communication lines and assign responsibilities were all but ignored.[149]

Second, a wide-ranging and systematic purge of officers was initiated. The CUP and the General Staff decided to get rid of the unruly Alaylı officers and the protégés of the former regime. Certainly, political priorities and loyalties played an instrumental role in this decision but, in terms of its military aspects, it was the fulfillment of at least a two-decade-long discussion on how to create a homogeneous and capable officer corps (von der Goltz himself was the initiator of this discussion). Initially tens and later hundreds of Alaylıs were purged by making use of various excuses such as age limitations, poor performance, and disciplinary issues. None of the reformers paid any attention to the positive sides of the Alaylı system. As could be expected, the Alaylıs reacted to these purges and, in a relatively short time, their professional grievances took political and religious forms, which would in turn play an instrumental role in the counterrevolutionary military uprisings of April 1909 (better known as 31 Mart Vakası). In these uprisings, soldiers led by Alaylı officers and NCOs rebelled against the new regime in several field army centers (chief among them Istanbul and Erzurum). The uprisings were seen as additional proof of the wisdom of the purges, and most of the Alaylıs were dismissed immediately after the suppression of the uprisings.[150]

Third, after decades-long discussions and various failed attempts, the exemption of non-Muslim male citizens from conscription was totally abolished on August 7, 1909. The administration and the General Staff not only wished to enlarge the manpower pool, but also desired to use compulsory military service as an instrument of integration. Similarly, other exemptions such as geographic and professional exemptions were also abolished. Even though most of the non-Muslim parliamentarians supported the legislation process, their communities did not appreciate it. They were not pleased to lose what they understood as their traditional and inherent rights. At the same time (except for the Jews), it went against their nationalist convictions. Most Christian communities tried to prevent or resist the census and registration for military service. Hundreds fled to foreign countries, and passport applications reached record levels. Nevertheless, against all odds, after 1910, recruitment officials managed to conscript more than two-thirds of all eligible non-Muslim citizens into the army. This problematic start was not well received by the optimistic General Staff planners who had aimed to recruit 25 percent of the army's soldiers from non-Muslims without paying attention to the realities on the ground.[151]

Fourth, the General Staff initiated a revolution in military education and training. The forbidden subjects of the previous regime (like Ottoman military history, unconventional warfare, and political history) were added to the curriculum of military schools. Cadets had to spend more time in the application of theoretical lessons. For the first time, units higher than battalions began to conduct realistic field maneuvers and firing exercises using modern tactics. Indeed, the rank and file enjoyed using modern weapons and equipment that had been locked in the depots for years due to the paranoia of Abdülhamid. Command post exercises and staff rides became the most important duties of the divisional and corps staffs.[152]

Unfortunately for the Ottoman military, the timing of these drastic reforms was overcome by international events. Only two years after the initiation of the military reforms, the Italians launched a surprise assault against the Ottoman province of Trablusgarb (Libya or Tripolitania). This unprovoked foreign aggression was followed one year later by the Balkan League (Bulgaria, Serbia, Greece, and Montenegro), which decided to act before the Ottoman reforms produced results. The Ottoman military was caught in an interim stage of transformation in which the pillars of the old order were destroyed while the new ones were unready to carry the whole system.[153]

The province of Libya was always a backwater of the empire. It was conquered not by the regular army, but by Ottoman corsairs in 1551 and remained an autonomous province afterwards, including a period of literal independence between 1711 and 1835. But Mahmud II managed to curb the power of the local Karamanlıs dynasty and restored central authority in 1835 during the upheaval of Governor of Egypt Mehmed Ali Pasha's rebellion. However, the control of the central government remained minimal, not only over the local population but also over the provincial administration. The geographic remoteness and isolation of the province from the core regions, its minor economic and military importance, as well as corruption and the urgency of problems elsewhere, seriously hampered the administration's efforts to integrate it. Furthermore, Libya became an ideal place for exiling dissidents and problematic characters during the Hamidian period.[154]

The general weakness and vulnerability of Ottoman authority in Libya gave encouragement to an Italian governing elite longing to prove the might of the recently united nation and build a colonial empire. The Italians had already peacefully penetrated into Libya by economic means and were hoping to establish sovereignty without a fight. Not surprisingly, the drastic Meşrutiyet reform efforts and its meager results in Libya increased colonial competition between France and Germany, which frightened the Italian decision-makers. They hastily declared war on September 29, 1911, and hostilities began immediately. The Italian navy, which would face no naval resistance throughout the war, bombarded the Ottoman Adriatic and Libyan coastline. The few obsolete coastal fortifications were no match for the Italian onslaught. Tobruk was conquered on October 4, and the provincial center of Trablus (Tripoli) fell one day later, shortly followed by the fall of the remaining coastal cities.[155]

The 42nd Independent Division, one of the worst divisions of the whole empire, was equally helpless. It was under strength (less than half of its established combat strength of 10,000), ill-equipped, and poorly led.[156] But surprisingly, its poor conventional capacity turned out to be an enormous advantage. Instead of trying to resist the initial Italian amphibious landing, which would have been futile, Ottoman units moved out of the range of the naval guns at the cost of leaving heavy equipment. The majority of the local recruits (around 2,000), most of whom were of urban origin, deserted their units.[157] The acting commander Colonel Neşet had no other choice under these conditions than to initiate conventional warfare against the Italian invaders. The Italian military was completely unprepared for this type of war. Small bands of Ottoman soldiers easily infiltrated into Italian defense perimeters and inflicted small but humiliating defeats. The local population was encouraged by these easy victories and began to actively support the Ottoman troops. In turn, heavy-handed Italian tactics that targeted the civilian population more than the actual fighters were counterproductive and increased the hatred of the locals. Hundreds of volunteers and tribal warriors joined the Ottoman troops. But it was the support of the Sanusiyya religious order (or more correctly, fraternity) which dramatically changed the flow of the war.[158]

The Sanusiyya was not only a religious brotherhood, but also an economic and social alliance of the tribes. It was the only effective cement within the otherwise socially fragmented tribal society of Libya (especially the Cyrenaica region).[159] Moreover, the Sanusis were well-known fighters and had already fought against another colonial power; France, at the southern extremes of the Sahara desert. The Ottoman-Sanusiyya alliance achieved remarkable results in terms of a dramatic increase in manpower and logistical support for the fight. But it was the arrival of Ottoman officer-volunteers which tipped the balance. The apparent failure of the government to respond to Italian aggression created a moral crisis and outburst of patriotic and religious feelings in which many young officers volunteered to fight. The Ottoman General Staff and CUP military committee (without the authorization and support of the government) selected its best and brightest (including the hero of the Meşrutiyet revolution Enver Bey, future president of the Turkish Republic Mustafa Kemal [Atatürk] Bey, counterinsurgency mastermind Süleyman Askeri Bey, and Halil [Kut] Bey). Most of them were veterans of the Balkan counterinsurgency campaigns. In addition to these men, Libyan and other officers from predominantly Arab provinces (including ardent Arab nationalist Aziz al Masri, Muhittin [Kurtiş] Bey, and Ali Sami [Sabit] Bey) were also assigned.[160]

The first group of officers arrived in the conflict zone via Egypt and Tunis in the middle of October 1911, but groups and individuals continued to arrive through the summer of 1912. Their arrival changed the character and tempo of the war immediately. The theater of war was divided into four theaters of operations in which Tripoli and Bingazi (Benghazi) were the main ones. Regular soldiers, gendarmeries, volunteers, and tribal warriors were organized into flexible mission-oriented units under the command and control of regular officers. All operations were closely coordinated and integrated according to a *de facto* strategic plan, which simply sought to wage a campaign of long and attritional unconventional warfare. As veterans of counterinsurgency campaigns themselves, the Ottoman officers were well aware that such a war would be long and bloody and, in the end, moral factors would become paramount. They were hoping to frustrate the Italians by inflicting as many casualties as possible. In opposition to the geographic orientation of the Italians, the Ottomans were not targeting the recapture of coastal cities but choosing instead to annihilate the enemy.[161]

The asymmetric nature of the conflict frustrated the Italian command and staff planners. Even though they tried several novel methods successfully, such as the use of aviation for reconnaissance and artillery forward observation duties, for the first time,[162] they still stubbornly stuck to conventional tactics and techniques, even if the results were disastrous and costly. The infantry-rich Italian assault columns offered excellent targets for the ever-elusive Ottoman combat groups and bands. They would lure Italians deep into desert valleys and, after exhausting and disorganizing them with repeated hit-and-run skirmishes and small ambushes, the main group would suddenly attack and destroy the isolated groups (sometimes whole assault columns). Even the heavily fortified coastal towns were not safe and immune from the Ottoman guerrillas. Night raids, infiltration into defensive perimeters, and the hunting of isolated guards and patrols became a continuous activity.[163]

The Italian setbacks and blunders gave the Ottoman field commanders time to reorganize and train their mostly local troops. The assignment of regular officers as the superior authority for tribal forces created immense problems initially. The tribal warriors had a traditional way of war fighting, which was always anarchic and uncoordinated and which prevented performing even the simplest maneuvers. The Ottoman officers managed to overcome this serious problem by treating combat operations more or less as step-by-step training exercises and by accommodating their military priorities with the interests of the tribesmen. Interestingly, the tribal cavalry learned to evade aerial observation and attacks while the local infantry units learned to employ successfully antiaircraft fire techniques.[164]

The furious Italians, who were suffering casualties at an alarming rate and were unable to fix and destroy the elusive enemy, increasingly targeted the civilian population and its livelihood. The execution of real or imaginary supporters, collective punishments, and other elements of a scorched-earth policy became part of the daily routine. For understandable reasons, these heavy-handed and misguided actions helped the Ottomans greatly, not only increasing civilian support in terms of volunteers and logistics, but also providing them with a sense of moral and ethical superiority.[165]

After several bitter experiences, the Italian expeditionary forces decided to remain within range of naval gunnery and, instead of trying to expand their occupation deep into the hinterlands, they preferred to remain on the coastline. At the same time, they tightened the naval blockade and tried to close the Egyptian and Tunisian borders. Even though this strategic shift created enormous logistics problems for the Ottoman side, it also gave them a free hand to transform blockades of the Italian-occupied zones into sieges. The confident Ottoman troops and their local allies began to launch bolder and more concentrated night attacks and raids.[166] They also tried to solve logistics problems by using captured spoils of war. Specially organized detachments plundered the Italian depots and magazines during the night raids.[167]

At last, the Italian political leadership came to the understanding that their proud expeditionary force would not be able to defeat the Ottoman defenders and conquer the interior of Libya. Instead the leaders decided to move the war to the core regions of the empire in order to force the Ottoman political leadership to give up Libya. Understandably, they could not risk another land confrontation with the Ottoman military, so they decided to use solely their navy. In April 1912, the Italian navy tried various tactics including naval demonstrations and limited shelling of the Red Sea and Syrian and Aegean coastlines, blockading the Straits, and even supporting the Sheikh Idris rebellion in Asir on the Arabian Peninsula.[168] Out of frustration, the Italians occupied the weakly defended Dodecanese Islands between April 24 and May 20, 1912. The occupation of the main island of Rhodes is instrumental in understanding the aftereffects of Ottoman success and the Italians' exaggerated sense of caution. (A reinforced division was employed against the tiny Ottoman defensive force consisting of a single infantry battalion with four light artillery pieces, despite the fact that the Italians enjoyed the popular support of the predominantly Greek population.[169])

The Ottoman administration reluctantly came to terms with Italy due to the imminent threat coming from the Balkan states. The Ouchy Peace Treaty, which was signed on October 15, 1912, effectively ended Ottoman sovereignty in Libya. The field commanders received the order three days later. This was a serious blow to the Ottoman officers who were more than sure of their ability to win the war, and they encountered huge difficulties explaining why the empire had given up after so many successful engagements by their local soldiers and allies. However, the military members of the CUP decided to establish a sound base for keeping the insurgency alive in hopes of restarting the war after the end of Balkan crisis. Some officers and other ranks (overall 300 personnel) were selected to remain, and nearly all the heavy weapons and ammunition were left behind. Selected local NCOs and soldiers were passed through an intense military technical training in order to operate the heavy weapons and various devices during the three-month-long evacuation period. As a part of this scheme, more than 100 young Libyan students were transferred to military schools in Istanbul for the training of the next generation of leaders and officers, who would lead the next war. Unfortunately for the empire, this bold scheme fell victim to the Balkan defeats and was only partially realized during the First World War.[170]

In the fall of 1912, the Ottoman political and military leadership was caught completely by surprise and was unprepared for the aggression of the Balkan states.[171] The army's seasoned recruits had just demobilized (more than 70,000 soldiers) and, moreover, many talented officers were fighting against the Italians or were on their way to join the war. A reinforced divisional group under the command of Chief of the General Staff Ahmed İzzet Pasha (composed of 29 crack battalions from First, Second, and Third Armies) had just suppressed a rebellion in Yemen and were too far away to return to the war zone on time. The infant army corps and triangular divisions, which were still battling to finish the reorganization, did not have the means to overcome the efflux of trained and seasoned soldiers and the influx of untrained raw recruits. Furthermore, there was a serious political crisis in which different partisan officer cliques were doing everything possible to establish political control and exterminate their rivals.[172]

Additionally, several other factors seriously limited the combat power of the Ottoman military. As previously mentioned, the Berlin Treaty had shaped the borders of the Ottoman Balkans in such a way that it was nearly impossible to defend it against multiple enemies. Coupled with this, Ottoman political and military leadership obstinately determined to preserve every inch of the empire's territory, and they had great faith in the military capacity of territorial defense units. Moreover, overconfident general staff officers insisted on being on the offensive at the operational level while conducting defensive operations at strategic level, which was a key element in the newly introduced German doctrine. They naively hoped that the small militaries of the Balkan states would not have the means to launch coordinated assaults, thereby giving Ottoman units ample opportunities to defeat them one by one. Ottoman planners disregarded all the viable alternatives and tried in vain to design a war strategy that would fit these conflicting ideas. Unfortunately, they neglected to remember the main lesson of the Ottoman-Russian wars, namely, to not spread forces too thinly over the theaters of operation and to avoid the splitting of field armies into composite groups.[173]

The flawed outcome of all these priorities and factors was the grouping of available units into two geographically isolated field armies—the Garb Ordusu (Western Army) and the Şark Ordusu (Eastern Army). Once again, instead of making use of the established field army structure, the General Staff planners molded three numbered armies and some additional divisions from the Fourth Army into two new field army groups in order to meet the demands of defending all the Balkan provinces and safeguarding Istanbul. Both of the armies consisted of regular army corps (three each), Redif army corps (five and four, respectively), independent detachments, cavalry divisions, and various combat support and combat service support detachments. To make matters worse, army commanders had to allocate strong garrisons for the defense of several fortresses (Edirne, İşkodra [Scutari], and Yanya), Çanakkale (the Dardanelles) fortified zone, provincial centers, lines of transportation and communication, and, of course, strategic terrain. Two corps-sized divisional groups were tasked to perform the impossible mission of maintaining the connection between the two armies by securing the Istanbul-Salonika railway line. Further drains on resources were evident, as several regiments were still conducting counterinsurgency operations in Macedonia, while others guarded the Aegean Sea harbors and islands against possible Italian (and later on Greek) amphibious attacks.[174]

From every aspect, the revised contingency plan for war against four Balkan states was very problematic. Even though it looked smart and simple on paper, in reality, it was a very difficult plan to carry out. The planning assumptions were the weakest part of it. According to the plan, there would be enough time to complete mobilization (30 days) and concentration. All lines of transportation, including sea lines, would be open and logistics mobilization would finish well before the arrival of units from Anatolia. But in reality the mobilization went slowly. Half of the Anatolian units never reached their destinations. The single-track railway system collapsed under the sheer volume of traffic, while the Greek navy effectively blocked any use of the sea lanes. Above all, the rapidly mobilizing Balkan armies were ready to launch attacks from all directions first and were unwilling to give the Ottomans the time to complete their preparations.[175]

The public and rank and file of the military were unaware of these dangers, and mobilization was heartily welcomed. Military morale was high, and even well-informed circles were talking of taking back lost provinces and reestablishing Ottoman control over the Balkans once again. Amidst both hope and uncertainty, the Ottoman Empire was forced into war.[176]

The First Balkan War (October 1912–May 1913) was actually fought in two separate theaters of operation and was comprised of various separate battles and engagements. The main campaign was, without doubt, the Eastern Thracian Campaign between the Bulgarians and the Ottoman Eastern Army. One large campaign (Macedonia) and two smaller (Greece and Montenegro) campaigns were fought in the western theater of operations. Additionally, there were Greek amphibious operations against the eastern Aegean islands, which were actually small regimental-level engagements.

The Ottoman Eastern Army under the command of Abdullah Pasha did not defend the border region and immediately fell behind the Kırkkilise (Kırklareli) line, leaving a weak screening force against the Bulgarian main force, which had crossed the border. Interestingly, not only the Bulgarians were surprised by this, but also the Ottoman junior officers and soldiers because of the plan's extreme secrecy.[177] The Ottoman plan was to fix an important percentage of Bulgarian units in front of the Edirne fortress, pulling the remaining units towards Kırkkilise and thereby giving the Eastern Army an opportunity to envelop them from the north (III Corps) and south (IV Corps and Edirne garrison). The strategic objective behind this plan was the assumption that, once the Bulgarians were annihilated, the fragile Christian alliance would collapse. Therefore it was the most vital operation of the war.[178]

However, the Bulgarian command left a weak field army around Edirne and brought its full strength against the Ottoman Kırkkilise defense line. In doing so, they established numerical superiority, foiling the Ottoman plan from the very beginning. The III Corps commander, Mahmud Muhtar Pasha, began the encirclement maneuver late due to bad weather, poor visibility, and control and communication problems on October 22. The assaulting divisions achieved limited success and bogged down after a while when facing an enemy with more than twice their strength and better artillery support. The other Ottoman corps were less lucky. Their attacks died down immediately, neither achieving flanking maneuvers nor fixing the enemy units. The next day, it was the turn of the Bulgarians. Massive Bulgarian frontal assaults and well-coordinated artillery fire inflicted heavy casualties on the Ottoman units that were deployed on open ground. The Bulgarians quickly established superiority in small-unit infantry tactics and techniques. Their excellent use of cover and camouflage, well-coordinated fire and maneuver, and concentrated bayonet assaults pushed back the Ottoman defenders. Abdullah Pasha ordered a full retreat on October 24. It was a premature order, and the retreat turned into a rout (except for Mahmud Muhtar's III Corps) under Bulgarian artillery fire and battlefield confusion. Demoralized units abandoned most of their artillery, baggage, and other heavy equipment. Consequently, instead of annihilating the Bulgarians, the Eastern Army suffered a humiliating defeat because of flawed assumptions, poor intelligence, weak artillery support, and lack of communications.[179]

The next engagement, the five-day-long (October 29–November 2) battle around the Lüleburgaz-Pınarhisar line that became the largest and costliest battle of the war, was a repetition of the previous one. The Eastern Army (this time partially reorganized into two armies with the arrival of more Redif units) tried the same formula of strategic defensive and operational offensive without success. The Bulgarians were stronger, artillery-rich, and more mobile, and they clearly possessed better morale. The Ottoman troops were demoralized, lacked everything, and suffered under three independent-minded commanding generals (Nazım Pasha, Abdullah Pasha, and Mahmud Muhtar Pasha). Repetitive and costly Ottoman counterattacks achieved temporary successes only, and massive Bulgarian frontal assaults crushed all hopes. The Ottoman retreat once again turned into a rout, and much of the remaining artillery and baggage was lost along the way. The overstretched logistical system collapsed as well, casualties could not get treatment or evacuation, and soldiers were unable to find food and safe drinking water. Hundreds perished, and thousands were infected with cholera and dysentery.[180]

The exhausted Bulgarians could not follow up the victory, and the routed troops managed to reach the last defensive line at Çatalca (a mere 25 kilometers away from Istanbul). Çatalca was actually a fortified zone that had been fortified several times from as early as 1878. Even though the demoralized, disorganized, and disease-ridden units initially created immense problems,[181] the leisurely approach of the Bulgarians enabled acting commander in chief Nazım Pasha, who was French-trained and a very talented officer,[182] to occupy the line successfully. The Eastern Army successfully finished its reorganization, recovery, and reconstitution and was renamed the Çatalca Army. The over-confident Bulgarians launched several massive frontal assaults without paying serious attention to the defensive capabilities of the Çatalca Army in well-fortified positions, which had the support of a centralized fire support system (including naval gunfire support). The Bulgarian infantry was decimated during the two-day-long assault (November 17–18), which became known as the First Battle of Çatalca. The Bulgarian high command did not comprehend the impregnability of the Çatalca line or the strength of its determined defenders. And they stubbornly repeated the frontal assaults between March 24 and April 3, 1913, with the same disastrously high casualties.[183]

The Ottoman Western Army tried to employ the same blend of strategic defense with the operational offensive. But in contrast to its eastern sister, the Western Army divided its units into the Vardar Army, four corps-sized groups (Yanya, Ustruma, İşkodra, and Müretteb [provisional] VIII Corps) and four independent detachments in order to protect every inch of its area of responsibility against the concentric attacks of its four adversaries. Additionally, only a bit more than half of the assigned troops were mobilized due to a lack of transportation and slow mobilization, which further limited the army's chances of success.[184] The Ottoman planners identified the Serbian army (possibly reinforced with Bulgarian divisions) as the main threat and so tasked the Vardar Army to block and then annihilate it. Most of the Vardar Army divisions had to travel more than 100 kilometers in order to reach their concentration area near Kumonova. The commanding general, Halepli Zeki Pasha, employed aggressive covering force tactics while some of his divisions were still trying desperately to reach their tactical destinations between October 14 and 21. Zeki Pasha's tactics worked quite well and the First Serbian Army could not establish contact with the Second Serbian-Bulgarian Army. However, he did not wait for his remaining four divisions to arrive as he thought the time was ripe for attack, even though the Serbs had twice the number of men on hand as did the Ottomans. Three divisions fixed the Serbs, and three more launched flanking attacks from both sides on October 23. The ambitious assault achieved remarkable success initially, but at the end of the day, without effective artillery support and reserves, Zeki Pasha was unable to tip the balance in his favor. The ill-trained, ill-equipped, and poorly led Redif divisions began to waver, and massive Serbian artillery fire crushed and demoralized them the next day. Zeki Pasha somehow managed to keep his demoralized Redifs in their makeshift defensive positions against the all-day-long infantry assaults. However, panic seized them immediately after Zeki Pasha ordered a retreat, and all discipline and order was lost (similar to the Eastern Army experiences). Because of this, Zeki Pasha was accused of stupidity by later commentators.[185]

The ever-optimistic general staff officers then planned to concentrate the broken Vardar Army around the centrally located town of Manastır (Bitola) in order to face both the Serbians from the north and the Greeks from the south. The Vardar Army reached Manastır on November 7, but it lost most of its limited artillery and baggage on the way. Once again, Zeki Pasha tried to encircle the Serbs by launching a surprise attack with his demoralized units. It was a gamble and he lost it completely. This was the Vardar Army's second disastrous defeat, and only the iron will of its subordinate commanding officers saved the day. The Vardar Army retreated into Albania with half the original strength and without artillery and baggage. To make matters even worse, Albanian nationalists proclaimed independence, and the already reluctant Albanian soldiers began to desert their units in the hundreds.[186]

The other independent units of the Western Army (except the garrisons of Yanya and İşkodra) were unable to show the same determination and courage that the Vardar Army had shown. The Ustruma Corps, Kırcaali, and Nevrekop Detachments failed to perform their mission to protect the Salonika-Istanbul railway and preserve contact with the Eastern Army. They melted away after a series of inconclusive engagements.[187] Similarly, the Müretteb VIII Corps, which was tasked to protect the Greek border, tried in vain on its own to stop the much stronger Greek army advances. Its disorganized fighting withdrawal ended with the ignominious fall of Salonika on November 10.[188] The concept of employing territorial defense units composed of loose groupings of Redif regiments and a few regular battalions failed completely. The three independent detachments—İpek, Taşlıca, and Priştine, tasked to protect Kosova and Yeni Pazar provinces, dissolved in less than 15 days without showing any resistance against Serbian and Montenegrin forces. Most probably, the lack of regular officers and the uneasy relations between Albanians and the Ottoman state after the rebellions of 1910 played into the hands of the Serbs and Montenegrins.[189]

Although the territorial defense units failed, some independent-minded junior officers did achieve remarkable success by making use of their accumulated counterinsurgency experiences. The most famous example was the defense of Grebene (a small town at the Ottoman-Greek border). A certain provincial gendarmerie officer, Captain Bekir Fikri (a veteran of the Macedonian and Yemen Campaigns), united all the available border guards, Redifs, and gendarmeries (approximately 800 strong) under his command. He also effectively mobilized the civilian population. He waged a relentless guerrilla campaign against Greek regular units and irregular gangs, which started immediately after the defeat and withdrawal of the Müretteb VIII Corps. At the height of his power, Bekir Fikri covered a 100-kilometer-long strip of mountainous region between Kozana and Yanya and fixed 10–15 regular Greek battalions and various irregular gangs. His six-month-long guerrilla campaign showed clearly that, had the General Staff employed guerrilla warfare strategically and made use of the civilian population, the conclusion of the Greek and Montenegrin Campaigns might have been different.[190]

In contrast, Bulgaria actively employed former Komitacıs against the Ottoman military and civilian population. Bulgarian Komitacı gangs, reinforced with local volunteers and deserters from the Ottoman army, achieved remarkable success in blocking traffic and destroying logistics convoys by occupying strategic positions and passes. However, their biggest contribution to the war effort was, without doubt, their role in uprooting the Muslim population, achieving an ethnic cleansing that pushed thousands of people into Ottoman-held areas.[191]

As could be expected, the unexpected and humiliating defeats turned the politics of the empire upside down. The disillusioned officer members of CUP decided to overthrow the government, which was labeled by many as too lenient, unpatriotic, and conciliatory. A small group of officer conspirators under the leadership of Lieutenant Colonel Enver launched a raid into the offices of the prime ministry and forced the government to resign. It was a well-planned coup d'état and was executed smoothly by a small number of individuals, once again showing a high level of staff planning and courage. The so-called Raid on the Sublime Porte (Bab-ı Ali Baskını) changed drastically the political dynamics of the empire. The new Grand Vizier and Minister of War, Mahmud Şevket Pasha (who was a German-trained talented officer and a protégé of von der Goltz), drastically increased the efficiency and influence of the military by immediately assigning capable young officers to the nerve centers of the large army staffs.[192]

The armistice between December 3, 1912 and February 3, 1913, not only gave the Ottoman military much needed rest and recovery time, but also gave the regime time to consolidate its power. The Western Army was practically dissolved, and only the Yanya and İşkodra garrisons and some remnants of the Vardar Army defended the region between Yanya and İşkodra. The Çatalca (old Eastern) Army, which managed to preserve most of its main units, received reinforcements from Anatolia and Syria and defended the Edirne fortress, Istanbul City, and the Gallipoli Peninsula. Ahmed İzzet Pasha, who had just returned back from the counterinsurgency campaign in Yemen, led the reorganization, recovery, and reconstitution of the Çatalca Army by making use of his predecessor Nazım Pasha's achievements. All available resources were mobilized, and training became the main activity. The arrival of fresh troops, ever-increasing public support, and the reverses of the Bulgarians in front of the Çatalca line, as well as the heroic defenses of Edirne, Yanya, and İşkodra, increased morale and confidence. Even the enormous toll of the epidemics, including typhus and cholera, did not affect the positive atmosphere.[193]

The ever-resourceful General Staff once again took the initiative and displayed its offensive tendency by planning the Şarköy amphibious operation against the Fourth Bulgarian Army in an attempt to save Edirne by hitting the concentrated Bulgarian forces in front of Çatalca from behind. The plan was not only ambitious and innovative, but also demonstrated state-of-the-art staff work involving the technical details of a combined army and navy operation. Regrettably, a series of unfortunate incidents and developments like weather, technical failures, and communication and coordination problems handicapped the operation. The first leg of the operation, the frontal assault of the Müretteb Corps on the neck of the Gallipoli Peninsula died under the fire of well-entrenched Bulgarian infantry supported by massive coordinated artillery and machine gunfire on February 8. Nevertheless, the Şarköy amphibious landing succeeded in establishing beachheads against which recently reinforced Bulgarian divisions launched uncoordinated but effective assaults, forcing termination of the operation two days later on February 10. To the amazement of the Bulgarians, the Ottoman units managed to break off contact and embark on ships with light casualties, showing a rare combination of leadership, discipline, and courage.[194]

The increased vigilance and combat power of the Ottoman military demonstrated itself better during the Second Battle of Çatalca (March 24–April 3, 1913). Stubborn and massive Bulgarian frontal assaults were crushed repeatedly by the skillful use of fortifications and centralized fire support. Even so, the victorious defenders could not revel in their success because of the surrender of Edirne (March 26) and İşkodra (April 23). Moreover, the Yanya fortress had capitulated well before the others on March 6.[195] The fall of the fortresses instrumentally finished the actual hostilities and, with the intervention of the Great Powers, the final peace treaty was signed in London on May 30, 1913. The new European border of the empire was drawn in the middle of Eastern Thrace, leaving the important city of Edirne to Bulgaria.

The peace treaty was a serious blow to the prestige of the new CUP-led regime, which had legitimized its military coup by promising to retain Edirne at all costs. Nevertheless, the regime was saved at the last minute with the initiation of hostilities between Bulgaria (which was furious over the loss of Macedonia at the peace table to its allies) and Greece and Serbia on June 29. Young general staff officers immediately demanded action, while the civilian wing of the CUP and the generals (who together bore the full pressure of Great Power diplomacy) were still indecisive and wavering. Soon the real authors of the coup d'état, hawkish general staff officers led by Enver, forced the timid leaders to act. Amidst the fear of a new war, advancing Ottoman units liberated Edirne without a fight on July 21.[196]

The liberation of Edirne was a turning point for the empire and its military. The officer corps consolidated their position as saviors and as the new governing elite, whereas the old political cadres lost their remaining prestige as if all the disastrous defeats and humiliating treaties were authored by them. In less than one year, the last barriers between full control of the empire by the Young Turks were removed, sometimes violently. Not surprisingly, only a small group of intellectuals questioned the wisdom of military-led governance; for many it seemed the only alternative.[197]

The Ottoman military was clearly defeated in a series of mostly independent and unconnected battles. Seemingly, the only bright spots were the stubborn defenses of the three fortress cities (Edirne, Yanya, and İşkodra) and the Çatalca line. For many western observers of the war, it confirmed European prophecies of decadence and the inevitable collapse of the empire. In fact, most of them merely witnessed the flight of the southern wing of the Eastern Army after Kırkkilise and Lüleburgaz, or they witnessed the long convoys of refugees fleeing from the wrath of Balkan conquerors. They did not observe or understand how the Ottoman military functioned before and during combat. Consequently, they were unable to identify the real reasons behind the defeats. However, despite this serious limitation, their portrayals of the Ottoman military strengthened the already well-established European stereotype and biased view—that of a notoriously corrupt and degenerate army commanded by untrained, ignorant, and incapable officers. This view affected western political and military decision-makers before and during World War I and, surprisingly, still persists today.[198]

As mentioned above, some of the shortcomings or problem areas are easy to identify. The expeditionary forces were, once again, dispersed all over the theater in order to defend every inch of territory. Moreover, at the outbreak of hostilities the Ottoman units were still trying desperately to reach their respective concentration regions on time. The Balkan armies easily isolated each separate unit and defeated them in detail. The notoriously inefficient Redif reserve system once again disappointed even the most pessimistic officers. Except for some unusual battalions, Redif units failed in nearly every engagement and, by doing so, limited or destroyed the combat power of the regular units associated with them. There were two key issues that the General Staff was unable to find solutions for. The first one was an overall lack of individual and unit training. The second was the lack of trained officers. Only a few officers had been assigned to Redif regiments during peacetime and most of these were failed or incapable officers. During the mobilization, officers who had been working in military schools or administrative staff jobs and away from combat units for many years were assigned to fill key positions in the Redif structure. Understandably, these officers with problematic backgrounds were liabilities more than they were assets.[199] The decision to strengthen Redifs by lending them soldiers from regular units turned out to be a gross mistake and miscalculation. These lent regulars were unable to increase the combat efficiency of the Redifs, and their mother units were weakened substantially by this decision. The ever poor and corrupt logistical system failed completely. Without effective forward mounting bases and peacetime logistical arrangements, any unit located away from city centers suffered huge difficulties. Moreover, the small but effective Greek navy stopped the use of sea lines of communications, and the serious limitations of Ottoman railways (in terms of coverage, capacity, and wartime confusion) forced units to depend more on pack animals and roads. Taking into consideration the poor state of roads, weather conditions, and the total absence of motorized transportation, the problem becomes more obvious. The desperate measures of the administration, including commandeering all transportation means, did not lighten the burden and many of the commandeered animals perished due to the harsh weather and neglect.[200]

Intelligence about the enemy militaries remained a significant problem. The Ottoman General Staff did not have any system to gather information and to process it in order to develop intelligence. Due to the lack of strategic intelligence, the General Staff was not able to forecast enemy intentions, mobilization or concentration, nor was it able to assess the structure, composition, and overall combat power of enemy forces. Similarly, field units ignored the chief elements of gathering combat intelligence such as reconnaissance, observation, operating behind enemy lines, and the like. Above all, the underestimation of the Balkan states' capacity to launch coordinated and rapid offensive operations hampered intelligence gathering at all levels. Consequently, based upon poor and grossly flawed intelligence about their adversaries, the Ottomans made ambitious plans for offensive operations and put them into use. At Kırkkilise or Kumonova, Ottoman field armies were faced with stronger and more mobile enemy units than had been anticipated, and they still tried in vain to encircle them with catastrophic results.[201]

The army's planners and field unit commanders neglected the civilian population in the combat zones. Obviously the lessons of the Ottoman-Russian War of 1877–1878 were totally forgotten. There was no plan to employ civilians actively against enemy troops. Except at Grebene, Ottoman officers did not make use of their counterinsurgency experience. Similarly, the units on the ground did not have any understanding about how to protect civilians from the effects of combat, not even evacuation or how to handle refugees and transport them without using limited military corridors. The deliberate attacks against civilians by regular or irregular enemy combatants uprooted thousands immediately after the start of hostilities.[202] Thousands tried to get away and endless convoys with makeshift ox-carts or wagons flooded the roads. It was horrible and demoralizing for soldiers to see their families or fellow Muslim citizens suffering from cold, hunger, and epidemics. Also, the convoys placed a huge burden on the military corridors that were supposed to support expeditionary forces. The limited food sources on hand were quickly exhausted, and the already poorly maintained roads turned into quagmires. Epidemics followed the refugees wherever they went and thousands of civilians and soldiers perished. The ever-problematic medical services rapidly broke down under this strain.[203]

The erroneous strategic dispersion, the Redifs, logistics, and intelligence were well-known problem areas which the General Staff did little to improve and were badly neglected by planners. However, most of the army's other problems involved the outcomes of its unfinished transformation effort. The transformation and newly introduced German doctrine gave false confidence to generals in influential positions. They were more than sure that the Ottoman military would not repeat past humiliations and disasters. In their minds, even the Hamidian army had achieved success against Greece a decade previously, so there was no reason to worry about the new army with its better trained officers and without the corrupt elements of the Hamidian regime. They paid scant attention to the fact that transformation was still largely unfinished and that the officers were unfamiliar with the ambitious triangular division system. They were neither capable of establishing command and control and communication lines nor capable of adjusting combat support and combat service support units accordingly. Thus the famed Ottoman artillery corps faltered in nearly every combat action and only after the drastic centralization by the Çatalca Army did it regain its former efficiency. Similarly, other arms and branches encountered difficulty when supporting infantry regiments, such as the engineers, maintenance, and transportation units.[204] The newly established but weak aviation corps was also lost within the mire of transformation and was not employed effectively.

One of the other adverse side effects of the transformation was, without doubt, the purge of the Alaylı officers. The Alaylıs were of limited military use, but there were no extra Mektebli officers to replace them in vacant positions. The newly founded reserve officers' training center provided less than 100 officers, and the total absence of a trained NCO corps further worsened the problem. Therefore, Ottoman units went to war with very few officers (overall only 55% of the officer positions were manned). The regular infantry companies averaged only two officers per company at the beginning of the war. The problem in the Redif companies was even more acute in that a single officer was assigned to lead two companies. This was a significant problem for the Ottoman military, because it was essentially an officers' army in which officers performed all of the key tasks. The dimensions of the problem became clearer as the war progressed, when heavy officer casualties worsened the situation.[205]

The much-hoped-for reform of recruitment of non-Muslims embarrassed its avid supporters when an important percentage of them evaded the service. Instead, an important percentage of them volunteered for the armies or the militias of the Balkan states.[206] The unlucky non-Muslim recruits suffered huge problems in acclimating themselves to the totally foreign atmosphere of military service. They were ill-prepared and unaccustomed to the hardships of military life, which their Turkish counterparts endured indifferently. At the same time, except for Jewish citizens, very few of them were willing to fight and risk their lives for the sake of the empire. As could be expected, the desertion rates of non-Muslim recruits set record highs. They fled or surrendered at the first opportunity, which verified the suspicions that Muslim soldiers held toward them.[207]

Despite all these shortcomings and problem areas, the Ottoman military achieved some remarkable feats. First of all, the Ottoman General Staff and its planners clearly surpassed their Balkan counterparts in the preparation of staff products at high levels. Unfortunately, the tactical superiority of the Balkan armies effectively negated the otherwise superior Ottoman General Staff planning. There was no novelty in any of the Balkan armies' strategic plans or the application of them. Likewise, the Ottoman officers at the front achieved remarkable feats with ill-trained, ill-equipped, and often demoralized soldiers in the realization of the army's plans. This came at the cost of a huge number of officer casualties, a problem that would reoccur during World War I.[208]

Interestingly, the Ottoman field units easily reorganized into new provisional formations when needed, even under adverse conditions. For example, the Eastern Army passed through reorganization three times. Many mission-oriented provisional formations were established, and subordinate units easily merged with one another. Obviously, the unconventional counterinsurgency heritage helped greatly in this respect. Unfortunately, the combat service support units did not have the same flexibility. The most serious problem again was a lack of officers, which limited the army's flexibility but, nevertheless, units adjusted themselves as necessary to the frequent reorganizations, recovery, and reconstitution processes.[209]

Second, the officer corps displayed tactical and operational proficiency when employed properly. The successful defense of Edirne, İşkodra, and Yanya were, and are, seen by many contemporary and modern commentators as the embodiment of the Ottoman soldiers' inherent characteristic of staunch defense in fortified places. However, in reality these so-called fortress cities were nothing more than old, neglected, and isolated fortifications with limited value against modern siege trains. The main factor behind these successes was the General Staff's choice of assigning its best, brightest, and most innovative officers as the commanding officers (Mehmed Şükrü Pasha to Edirne, Hasan Rıza Pasha to İşkodra, and Esat Pasha and Vehib Bey to Yanya). These four officers achieved remarkable results against difficult odds, largely unsupported by the army as a whole.[210]

Last but not least, the Ottoman military showed a rare blend of determination and courage in recovering from a series of humiliating and disastrous defeats. This successful recovery was instrumental in the defense of Çatalca, the amphibious operation at Şarköy, and the liberation of Edirne. Clearly the unexpected defeats and loss of the Ottoman Balkans left physical and emotional scars on the Ottoman military. However, in little more than a year, it was rejuvenated like a phoenix from the ashes.

World War I: The Last Episode
Ante-bellum

The unexpected military defeats inflicted by the Balkan League nations were perceived by the Great Powers as a final sign of the collapse of the Ottoman Empire. The image of the sick man of Europe loomed large once again, and the powers separately decided to be proactive in its demise. The Russian decision-makers, especially, were determined to follow the Italian example of sudden invasion. To make things worse, internal centrifugal tendencies gained strength and ground. Not only did the well-established Armenian separatists, but also the Arab nationalist circles and even Kurdish tribal notables, began preparations to carve homelands for themselves at the right time.[211]

Surrounded by predatory states, amidst the intense competition of the Great Powers, and trying desperately to cope with the gravest political and socioeconomic crisis in the empire's history, the new governing elite drew the conclusion that the old diplomacy of domestic politics involving playing one faction against another was ill-suited to the times. At the same time, they were looking for a long-term solution that would provide security, integrity, and modernization for the empire. They understood that it needed a centralized and regular administration. The ideal solution for the tight-knit CUP leadership evolved as an enlightened dictatorship of the military. The self-made leaders of the officer corps, chief among them Enver Bey, determined not to remain in the background and refused to hand over power to the elder statesmen and retired generals.[212]

There were, however, doubts about the officer corps itself. Indeed, all parties, including the officers themselves, blamed the officer corps for the recent series of humiliating defeats. Additionally, they blamed partisan politics and infighting as the root causes for poor performance. Interestingly, many still wished to have a Hamidian-type of apolitical and absolutely loyal military institution.[213] Unfortunately for the empire, separatist nationalism began to show itself at this time within the officer corps. The administration became suspicious of nationalist movements within the officer corps after the fateful desertion of several Albanian officers during a counterinsurgency operation against Albanian rebels in 1910. This and other incidents created questions regarding the loyalty of non-Turkish officers in the minds of Ottoman military leaders.[214]

Contrary to common perceptions, Albanian and Arab nationalism did not create serious problems during the Ottoman-Italian War of 1911 or the Balkan Wars of 1912–1913, and soldiers of both groups fought loyally under the Ottoman flag. However, the infamous betrayal of Esat Toptani Pasha (an Albanian provincial grandee) during the defense of İşkodra, the subsequent resignation of several Albanian officers immediately after the fall of İşkodra province, and proto-nationalist declarations and meetings of several Arab officers in Gallipoli blurred relations and increased tensions.[215]

The actual effects of both wars manifested themselves after the end of the hostilities in 1913. The disastrous defeats, humiliating peace treaties, and the independence of Albania were perceived as the end of the Ottoman Empire by some Arab intellectuals and officers.[216] Semi-secret clubs and organizations were organized and became centers of disaffection under the watchful eyes of the new governing elite. The driving force behind these subversive activities was the empire's obvious incapacity to protect the vital region of Rumelia against small Balkan states, from which it was deduced that it could not retain its distant Arab provinces either. There were two Arab camps. The majority group was supportive of the Ottoman Empire but wanted an overall reorganization and creation of a union within which the Arabs would govern the empire jointly with the Turks, similar to the Austro-Hungarian model. The minority group saw the empire as already defunct and wanted total independence of the Arab provinces as a whole.[217]

Simultaneously, Turkish intellectuals and officers reacted to these developments, and they also founded clubs and organizations imitating the other ethnic-based organizations.[218] In line with their Arab counterparts, the majority of them wanted to maintain the empire as a whole but supported the unifying ideologies of Ottomanism and Pan-Islamism. The minority focused on the predominantly Turkish provinces and dreamt of a new country that would be created around the core of Turkish Anatolia and a new society. Several attempts were made to revitalize Pan-Islamist and Ottomanist ideology, which failed, thereby further increasing frustration. This vicious circle of opposing creeds reached a high point just before the outbreak of World War I.[219]

In the interim period, Grand Vizier and Minister of War Mahmud Şevket Pasha decided to overcome partisan politics and disaffection by using German military advisors in command positions. This idea was not new but the tendency towards Germany increased after the apparent failure of rapprochements with the other Great Powers. It was the increasing influence of young General Staff officers that encouraged Mahmud Şevket Pasha to act immediately when several German-trained officers including Ahmed İzzet Pasha brought this idea forward. Similarly, in Germany decision-makers were discussing how to drive the politics out of the Ottoman military. After much consultation with German diplomatic and military representatives, the Ottoman government officially asked for an enlarged military mission under the command of a prominent general on May 22, 1913.[220]

Despite the fact that the Balkan disaster adversely affected the German perception of Ottoman military capacity and its usefulness, still this was a welcome development for the German General Staff, which had wanted such an enlargement for several decades. Indeed, within the German governing elite, a school of thought had emerged advocating the military advantages of using Ottomans against Russians. Mahmud Şevket Pasha did not live to see the realization of his beloved project, as he was assassinated on June 11, 1913. In turn, the triumvirate of the CUP (Lieutenant Colonel Enver, Colonel Cemal, and Talat) became the undisputed leaders of the empire immediately thereafter. Surprisingly, it would be the most politicized officer of the Ottoman military, Enver Bey, who finally achieved the dreams of his predecessors by purging politicized officers and eliminating all the elements of partisan politics from within the military.[221]

The final contract between Germany and the Ottoman Empire (for the duration of five years and with the possibility of extension) was signed on October 27, 1913, which seemingly handed over not only all of the military reform packages but also the direct command and control of many key units to the German military mission. Moreover, the mission leader would become an essential part of all military decision-making processes including officer promotions and assignments. The German General Staff chose a senior division commander of the Prussian army, Major General

Otto Liman von Sanders, who arrived in Istanbul with a small group of mission members on December 14, 1913.[222]

Liman von Sanders was a successful field unit commander, but the traits that made him a good unit commander were not the ones needed to carry out the diplomatic duties of a military advisory mission leader. Immediately after his arrival, the obstinate and rude German general became involved in disputes or clashed with nearly all of his Ottoman counterparts. Neither the Ottoman high command nor the German diplomats and veteran military advisors in the embassy liked the man, who in turn found the old hands much too Turkified and degenerated. Similarly, he pessimistically exaggerated the condition of the postwar Ottoman military. According to von Sanders, the entire army was in a wretched condition without any élan or morale. He viewed Ottoman officers as unreliable, selfish, and corrupt and thought they paid attention only to their own interests at the cost of unfortunate soldiers who stoically accepted all misconducts and suffering. His high regard for Turkish soldiers but low regard for Ottoman officers remained the same throughout the war. His initial observations and deductions about military training and education were similarly negative. Even after von der Goltz's reforms, the military educational system was still reliant on excessive theory and showed a general lack of practical work, especially in field maneuvers and exercises.[223]

The German Military Mission consisted of 41 officers (the numbers rose to 70 during the summer of 1914 and 800 at the end of the war) and started work amidst a diplomatic crisis in which Russian diplomats effectively blocked the assignment of von Sanders as an army corps commander. Instead, he was promoted and assigned as the chief inspector general and the other German officers were assigned to critical positions as well; the command posts of a division, three regiments, eleven military educational institutions (including the prestigious superintendency of the Military Academy), and several other minor positions. The main idea behind these assignments was to train officers, NCOs, and units as a whole according to current German models.[224]

The most important posting turned out to be the assignment of Colonel Friedrich Bronsart von Schellendorf as the First Assistant Chief of General Staff (Erkân-ı Harbiye-i Umumiye Dairesi Erkân-ı Harbiye Reis-i Saniliği). This assignment was born out of necessity to coordinate staff activity at the top. It was offered to von Sanders first but he insisted on an assignment as a senior-level field commander. Although he was destined to play a crucial role in the Gallipoli Campaign, by refusing this post (combined with his inability to get along with Ottoman leaders, especially self-appointed generalissimo of the Ottoman military Enver Pasha) von Sanders was sidelined by von Schellendorf, who would become the most influential German military advisor in the empire until his recall in 1917.[225] In short and in opposition to commonly held opinions, von Sanders's affect on the Ottoman war effort was limited.

Bronsart von Schellendorf was, and still is, an obscure figure. He was the ideal staff officer not only because Enver Pasha personally liked him so much but also because he was a master of General Staff operations. He worked diligently and reorganized the Ottoman General Staff to become a mirror image of the German staff. Young and talented Ottoman General Staff officers, most of whom were also German-trained, were assigned as branch chiefs.[226] Under his close control, the staff amended the strategic mobilization and concentration plan and rewrote most of the future campaign plans. Nominally, Enver Pasha was the Chief of the General Staff in addition to his job as the Minister of War. However, Enver Pasha neither had the necessary experience and background to handle the highly technical and demanding General Staff duties nor did he like to be occupied with staff work. Instead, he preferred to deal with grant issues, but even so, only roughly. After the humiliating end of the Sarıkamış Campaign and other personal setbacks, he lost even his meager interest in the General Staff, and von Schellendorf became the *de facto* chief of the General Staff after January 1915.[227]

In the meantime, the German General Staff decided to become involved in Ottoman military affairs and decision-making processes more directly, due to the imminence of war and also because optimism about the military capacity of the Ottoman army was increasing. This was the result of a completely independent communications and reports-returns system designed and operated by the ever-increasing number of German staff officers assigned to the Ottoman General Staff. These documents were archived separately and at the end of the war were smuggled to Germany.[228] The Ottoman branch chiefs did not like the new arrangements and began to resist the ever-increasing control of the German General Staff in Ottoman affairs. In a relatively short time (between August and September 1914), von Schellendorf either replaced the Ottoman branch chiefs with German officers or sidelined them. He also increased the number of the staff branches, thereby reducing their respective powers. Bronsart von Schellendorf and his successor (after December 1917), General Hans von Seeckt, continued this policy of keeping Ottoman officers away from positions of influence and keeping them uninformed about developments. As a conclusion, it may be argued that after September 1914 the Ottoman General Staff became, more or less, a field army headquarters under the direct command and control of the German General Staff with little real Ottoman influence.[229]

Why did Enver Pasha and other Ottoman military leaders allow the degradation of the Ottoman General Staff into a *de facto* German field army headquarters? The answer seems complex, but very simply, Enver Pasha and the inner circle of the CUP believed in the superiority of German military thinking and in the imminence of victory. They were convinced that the Ottoman military could draw in enough Entente troops so as to enable the Germans to win decisive victories on the main fronts. This thinking was welcomed by the German General Staff, which saw the Ottoman military as a useful tool to divert attention and force the enemy to allocate more troops for "Oriental side shows." After the Sarıkamış defeat in January 1915, Enver's reliance on German staff officers increased dramatically in spite of the opposition of most of the high-ranking Ottoman officers.[230] Interestingly, von Sanders and several other German officers resented and criticized the subjugation of the Ottoman General Staff and removal of the Ottoman officers from important staff positions. According to them, the German General Staff and its agents at the Ottoman General Staff neither had the understanding and experience nor had the language skills to carry out the immense task of directing the Ottoman war effort.[231] This forecast would prove prophetic as the strategic direction of the Ottoman high command disintegrated over the course of the war.

Obviously, the German Military Mission contributed greatly to military reforms and the war effort, but contrary to widespread beliefs, it was not the main factor behind the Ottoman revival and combat success. First of all, von Sanders and most of his mission members were not officers of the high caliber one expects to see in such a delicate mission. Except for some unusual characters, most of them were mediocre officers without any background or talent to perform their highly demanding jobs. Moreover, they arrived in the empire at the end of December 1913 and had only nine months of work before the Ottoman entrance to the war. They were prohibited from starting work due to the diplomatic crisis created by their arrival and lost a valuable two months. Additionally, most of them were reassigned to new positions shortly after spending barely two or three months at their original posts. For example, Lieutenant Colonel Friedrich Freiherr Kress von Kressenstein spent less than three months as the director of the artillery branch school and training center. He was then reassigned as the operational branch chief of the Ottoman General Staff in order to plan the Suez Canal Campaign (and also as a part of von Schellendorf's ongoing elimination of Ottoman staff officers). Similarly, the prospective superintendent of the Military Academy, Lieutenant Colonel Back von Erlich, was reassigned as a division commander after spending less than six months at the academy. When taking into account the total lack of language skills and cultural awareness of local conditions, it is no surprise that most of the German officers were barely acclimated to the empire and were unable to affect the Ottoman military at the outbreak of the war.[232]

Secondly, the German Military Mission did not make any institutional or structural changes in the Ottoman army. The general unit architecture, the triangular division concept, which had been introduced just before the Balkan Wars, remained the same. The faulty Redif reserve system had been abolished after the Second Balkan War and the recruitment system was newly renovated as well. Moreover, before the arrival of the Germans, the Ottoman General Staff already started and was supervising the massive transformation and reorganization of the entire field army headquarters system (down to regimental level). This was a result of the disastrous defeats of 1912–1913, after which headquarters returned to their respective recruitment regions to rebuild their cadres. Due to the destruction of so many headquarters during the Balkan Wars, the administration reassigned one or two divisional headquarters from each relatively intact army corps to establish new army units around these divisional headquarters. Some divisional and regimental headquarters were also exchanged at the army corps level. As an example, the VI Army Corps, which escaped the Balkan Wars unharmed, was designated as the Second Army Inspectorate, gave its two veteran divisional headquarters (the 17th and 18th) to the Third Army (the former Western Army), and received two newly activated headquarters (the 24th and 26th which had been destroyed in the war). The 17th Division became the nucleus of the IX Army Corps whereas the 18th Division became the XI Army Corps' nucleus. The 18th Division also gave two of its regiments (the 52nd and 54th) for the establishment of the 33rd and 34th Divisions. The administration quickly created relative homogeneity at all levels but at the cost of weakening the veteran and established formations.[233]

Thirdly, the officer education and training system was already in the process of transformation. Furthermore, Enver Pasha deeply believed that the oncoming war would be a young man's war. For this reason, he purged the remaining members of the old guard and the incapable commanders of the Balkan Wars (some of them were punished as well). Overall, more than 800 high-ranking officers were sacked, including two field marshals, three lieutenant generals, 30 major generals, and 35 brigadier generals. Young and highly trained general staff officers were then assigned to positions of influence, and they soon turned to the hard task of completing the unfinished reforms of the pre-Balkan Wars period.[234] The order of battle of the III Army Corps, which would become the backbone of the defense of the Gallipoli Peninsula, provides a good example of the new system. The corps commander, Esat (Bülkat) Pasha, who was the hero of the defense of Yanya, was 53 years old. The 19th Division commander, Lieutenant Colonel Mustafa Kemal (Atatürk) Bey was 34 and his 57th Regiment commander, Lieutenant Colonel Hüseyin Avni Bey (who was a very successful officer but not a General Staff officer) was 43 years old. Mustafa Kemal Bey's classmate from the Military Academy and the Staff College, Major Mehmet Arif (Ayıcı) Bey (who was also a General Staff officer), was the chief of staff of the 5th Division.[235] This pattern of youthful commanders and staff officers was repeated throughout the corps.

Fourthly, the modern German military system was already well established within the closely-knit Ottoman General Staff officer corps. As already mentioned, hundreds of Ottoman officers passed through on-the-job training in Germany beginning in 1885. These officers had already played important roles by following German doctrines as closely as possible in order to transform the Ottoman military into a modern war machine well before the arrival of the von Sanders' mission. So, in reality, the German Military Mission merely gave additional fuel to the ongoing process by providing guidance and additional influence for these German-trained officers. These officers also played the crucial role of intermediary between German officers and Ottoman personnel by acting as interpreters and translators.[236]

The last but probably the most important factor was the Ottoman military renaissance.[237] Beginning with the restoration of the constitution in 1908, officers began to write and publish their thoughts and ideas about various aspects of the military, especially their combat experiences and criticisms of past campaigns. Various journals and newly opened literary clubs became the centers of discussion for the exchange of ideas. Furthermore, for the first time in the history of the empire, the military authorities encouraged these activities. Illustrating this, the official military science journal *Mecmua-i Askeri* (*Military Magazine*)[238] became the most important vehicle for the transmission of new ideas and critiques in the Ottoman military renaissance.

However, the real breakthroughs came after the humiliating defeats suffered at the hands of the small Balkan states. The defeats caused a very serious mental depression to take hold of the officer corps, which forced them to discuss openly their concerns about the fate of the empire and the possible scenarios facing it. Most of the career officers voiced their frustrations about the apparent weakness of the army and its obvious military incapacity.[239] Every publication (especially memoirs) immediately created new discussions and new publications. Even though most of them pointed out political issues, military problems and possible solutions were the essential components of these discussions. Some of the most favored topics were the performance of the Ottoman General Staff, outdated and cumbersome methods and procedures, the triangular divisional system, the mechanism and dynamics of attack and defense, new weapons (especially machine guns), combat support and service support, recruitment, and how to increase morale and élan.[240] Ottoman military history was often used (not always scientifically) to prove the validity of one's claims.

Interestingly, as the Turkish officers hesitantly but continuously became nationalistic, their publications also mirrored this development. They tried to reach a wider public by simplifying their ideas or making use of various literary prose forms and poems. Ottoman historical figures, famous conquests, and victories were widely used in earlier times to transmit nationalist messages. But this time the authors tried to blend military commentary with nationalism, religion, and other popular feelings.[241]

This military renaissance was the main force behind the vigorous reorganization of the Ottoman military. However, neither German officers, who were working within the Ottoman army, nor other foreign military officers in the empire, seemed to notice these intellectual developments. They continued to perceive and describe the Ottoman military as archaic and its officer corps as ill-trained, corrupt, and highly politicized. In short, western officers in the empire uniformly asserted that the Ottoman military was a hopeless case. Throughout the interim period and even during World War I, Turkish officers continued to communicate their ideas through official reports and personal letters to higher command echelons. Moreover, many of them maintained pocket diaries even during the most intense combat operations.[242]

In addition to the above stated factors, common problems that affect any kind of military advising mission, such as lack of communication, suspicion, ignorance, inherent conservatism, stiff resistance by established interest groups, or simply downright xenophobia, limited the relative effectiveness of the German Military Mission. Therefore, in view of these factors, it is a mistake to give credit for every victory to German leadership (or more correctly German mentors) while at the same time assigning blame to the so-called corrupt and incompetent Ottoman officers or military system for every failure.

An Uninspiring Start: The Sarıkamış Campaign

By the fall of 1914, for most Ottoman officers, neutrality was no longer an option, and there was a deep conviction that the survival of the empire depended on siding with Germany. However, most were equally adamant that war should be delayed for at least two more years, especially after witnessing the humiliating defeats the Habsburgs suffered against the Serbs and Russians. Nevertheless, after three months of wavering and diplomatic maneuvers the empire committed itself to the German side and entered the war following the *fait accompli* of a sudden Ottoman naval raid under the command of German Admiral Wilhelm Souchon on several Russian Black Sea ports on October 29, 1914.[243]

The Ottoman military entered the war with many shortcomings. The mobilization went on slowly due to the drastic changes within the recruitment system and an uncertainty regarding the recruitment districts. The General Staff was still trying desperately to move army corps and divisional headquarters that were massed around the Çatalca lines back to their respective regions. The confusion was so great that some of the headquarters and units moved forward and backward and passed through several transformations and reorganizations.[244] For example, the Second Army headquarters transformed into an inspectorship structure and moved to Damascus. However, less than a year later a totally new army headquarters (Fourth Army) was founded in Damascus on September 6, 1914, while the Second Army returned back to Istanbul (leaving behind half of its cadre) and retransformed into a regular army headquarters structure.[245]

In terms of weapons, equipment, and ammunition the situation was dire. More than half of the heavy equipment and weapons, which were recently purchased at a disastrous cost to the state treasury, were lost during the ignominious retreats and surrenders of the Balkan Wars. Understandably, the ammunition stocks (especially artillery shells) were exhausted. The logistics mobilization proceeded very slowly and was scandalously corrupted. To make matters worse, the state treasury did not have the means to cover new purchases, nor was the international atmosphere conducive for mass purchases based on loans. Against all expectations, the new alliance with Germany did not improve the situation because of the lack of direct railway connections. All transportation between Germany and the Ottoman Empire was at the mercy of Romania and Bulgaria, and only a fraction of the promised help arrived from Germany.[246]

Against all odds, the mobilization of personnel turned out to be the easiest part of the daunting problems. Thousands of men flooded the recruitment centers, and at least a quarter of them were sent home due to the serious limitations of feeding, clothing, and equipping them. The mobilized personnel strength of the military was imposing—more than a million men with a combat strength of 820,000. However the strength of regular officer corps was only 12,469, so for every 100 combatant soldiers the administration provided only 1.5 officers, literally a drop in an ocean of men.[247]

The administration tried several methods to man the empty officer posts and replace casualties; some of the discharged *Alaylıs* were called back, Military Academy cadets were immediately assigned to units as brevet lieutenants (*Zabit Vekili*), and senior cadets of the military secondary schools and civilian high school graduates or students were introduced into the military as officer candidates (*Zabit Namzeti*) after brief combat training. Several officer training courses (*Zabit Talimgâhları*) were opened to provide a continuous supply of junior officers to the units of the army.[248]

Cadets took basic officer training for six to eight months and were sent to the fronts with the rank of corporal. According to regulations, unit commanders would decide to commission them as officers or not after examining them for six months. In this way, the officer candidates, by acting as NCOs, for the first six months or more, fulfilled a very important duty for the army.[249] As mentioned previously, the Ottoman military did not have professional NCO corps, and often, experienced soldiers were left to perform the NCO tasks.[250] NCOs trained in military schools were a very small minority and often they were assigned to junior officer positions rather than to NCO positions.[251] Thus, the brevet officers filled a very important gap in the army's junior leadership. The empire's high schools had only enough graduates and students to fill the necessary quotas for one year. After 1915, the high command decided to enroll religious school (*medrese*) graduates and students and, later on, every available untapped source was used in order to overcome the ever-increasing casualty figures.[252]

The Sarıkamış Campaign is instrumental in understanding not only the problems of, but also the high caliber of planning and execution in, the Ottoman General Staff. Bronsart von Schellendorf and his German staff prepared a single mobilization and concentration plan (the so-called Plan Number One) in which most of the army corps and divisions (overall 26 divisions out of 37 regular divisions, excluding the newly established ones) would be concentrated around Istanbul and the Dardanelles Straits. According to their assessments, the most vulnerable part of the empire was its capital, Istanbul, and the Straits. Additionally, they planned to make use of two army corps against Russia (either at the Romanian border or around Odessa) in order to lighten the burden of the Habsburgs. Therefore, one army corps from the Third Army, two army corps headquarters and three divisions from the Iraq Regional Command (leaving only one division there), and nearly all the divisions of the Fourth Army were deployed to Thrace. However, due to conflicting messages coming from the German political and military leadership, they began to make drastic changes in these plans. In order to launch a surprise attack against the Suez Canal, two army corps, each with two divisions, were reallocated to the Fourth Army. X Army Corps was given back to its mother unit, the Third Army, due to the changing strategic concept against Russia. These sudden changes created havoc within the units, which had to march first forward and then back. For example, the X Army Corps spent four months moving to and from one concentration area to another and literally exhausted itself before firing a single bullet when it finally returned to Erzurum in order to participate in the Sarıkamış Campaign.[253]

The war plan had many pitfalls and flawed assumptions even after several amendments. First of all, the planners naively assumed that the British would not attack Basra province. Obviously, they paid no attention to the combat strength of British India and the nearly autonomous decision-making process of the colonial Government of India. Secondly, there was effectively no strategic reserve other than the oversized theater reserves around the Straits. Thirdly, the plan was unrealistic in terms of logistics and transportation. The logistics annexes lacked even the basic technical details or were totally irrational and unrealistic. Last, but not least, the planners totally ignored the problem of interior security. To create more mobile tactical units for the army, the planners reorganized the gendarmerie according to conventional military needs and established divisions and regiments, which were then deployed to the frontiers. Consequently, even the most volatile provinces were left without adequate interior security, while the governors attempted to maintain order with only old or unfit ex-servicemen and the always-problematic village guards.[254]

Thanks to the inconsistent planning and confused messages coming from the General Staff, the Third Army commander, Hasan İzzet Pasha (the heroic but unfortunate commander of the Vardar Army), and his staff encountered difficulty in the positioning of their units. Initially, he received orders to conduct a strategic defense against possible Russian incursions, but there was no strategic directive regarding where to establish the main defense line. Some orders advised the use of the archaic Erzurum fortress and surrounding high ground, whereas others advised different lines near to the border. Amidst the confusion, Hasan İzzet Pasha received a division from Iraq while lending his best army corps (X Army Corps) for possible operations in the European theater. Moreover, nearly all of his divisional and regimental headquarters had arrived from Thrace within the previous six months and were still trying desperately to finish transformation, reorganization, and the manning of their cadres.[255]

To make things even more complex for the Third Army, Enver Pasha decided to employ two new mobilization schemes to generate combat power. The first one was to raise four reserve cavalry divisions and one cavalry brigade from the tribesmen of southeastern and eastern Anatolia. In reality this was a reconstitution of the old Hamidian cavalry regiments that had been more or less defunct for a decade, which attempted to group them under the command of regular officers and headquarters.[256] The second one was to raise guerrilla bands from the warlike eastern Black Sea region locals (mainly Lazes and Acaras) under the command of mainly civilian high-ranking CUP members (but later on several regular officers were also charged to raise more bands). In contrast to the reserve cavalry units, these guerrilla bands were under the control of the Teşkilât-ı Mahsusa (literally the Special Organization) and independent of conventional military control. However, the army commanders were tasked to provide personnel, weapons, equipment, and sometimes whole units in emergencies, which created much tension and ill will between the military and the CUP.[257]

Fortunately for the Ottomans, the Russian General Staff (under the illusion that the Ottomans did not constitute credible threat) not only largely ignored its Caucasian region but also transferred most of the regular divisions from there to Poland, leaving a single regular army corps and a newly raised reserve army corps. Its Caucasus front plan was to remain on the defensive strategically but to occupy the high ground and passes on the Ottoman side of the border as soon as possible (which they did immediately after the declaration of war against the Ottomans on November 4, 1914). However, the aggressive Russian General Bergmann mistook the rapid withdrawal of the Ottoman border guards as a sign of strategic weakness and great opportunity, and disregarded the maxims of the plan by advancing deep into Ottoman territory. Hasan İzzet Pasha gropingly counterattacked the weak Russian assault formation, but only after the urgings of Enver Pasha, on the Köprüköy lines on November 6. He stopped and defeated the Russians but he missed a golden opportunity to annihilate them due to his cautious approach of sending divisions in piecemeal rather than *en masse*.[258]

The five-day-long Köprüköy battle was a costly victory that gave confidence to the troops and Enver Pasha but not to the commanding general Hasan İzzet Pasha. Once again Enver Pasha interfered and forced him to attack prematurely the shaky Russian defenses. Hasan İzzet Pasha's reluctance and anxiety hampered his staff work, and the Third Army launched an uncoordinated blind assault without much intelligence about the enemy positions on November 17. The ensuing two-day-long Azap battle turned out to be even costlier for both sides. Due to uncertain intelligence, the Ottoman divisions were unable to achieve flanking attacks as planned and executed frontal assaults. The high casualty figures frightened Hasan İzzet Pasha so much that he ordered a general retreat at the climax of a battle in which General Bergmann had already decided to withdraw his exhausted units. The ensuing disorderly withdrawal caused more harm to the Third Army than the bloody melee against the Russians.[259]

The Köprüköy and Azap battles clearly showed the shortcomings of the sweeping reforms of the post-Balkan War period. Obviously, most of the regular units fought bravely and obediently. In particular, the officers did their best to show their absolute willingness to support their superiors in order to cleanse the stigmas of the Balkan Wars. As a result, officer casualty figures were unnecessarily high.[260] Nevertheless the battles acted as a litmus test and showed the vast differences between the established army battalions and newly raised ones. The 18th Division's veteran regiments could not overcome the unwillingness and inexperience of the XI Army Corps' soldiers (from the Van recruitment region), who were conscripted from mostly unruly Kurdish tribesmen and Armenian villagers with shaky loyalty. On at least in one occasion these soldiers panicked and fled. Similarly, the soldiers of the unfortunate 37th Division, who had marched all the way from Baghdad, lost their confidence at the first clash of arms and literally dissolved in their second encounter.[261]

From higher staffs down to battalions, the Ottoman war machine faltered seriously at each level of command. Intelligence gathering and processing remained problematic, whereas logistics were catastrophic. The highly trained but naïve staff planners once again paid limited attention to serious institutional deficiencies and overestimated the army's tactical advantages.[262] The willingness of the officers and soldiers did solve some, but not all, of the command-control and communication problems, which were caused mainly by immature and unsettled unit structure. The reserve cavalry divisions were unable to perform even the simplest tasks and shattered all plans to cover and guard the flanks as well as conduct flanking attacks. Understandably, without military training, effective discipline, fire support, and above all willingness and patriotism, the tribesmen often deserted the first time they came under enemy fire. They were only capable of harassing the enemy rear and, at most, diverting the attention of enemy combat units albeit temporarily. Surprisingly, some units even changed sides and served with the Russians. Reluctantly, Enver dissolved the four reserve cavalry divisions. The best remaining men were reformed into two cavalry brigades and put under the direct command and control of the regular cavalry division on November 21.[263]

Surprisingly, the Ottoman General Staff and Enver Pasha ignored the sorry state of the Third Army and paid attention only to the poor performance of the Russians and to the opportunities that were lost. Moreover, the acclaim bestowed on the German battle of annihilation at Tannenberg infected the Ottoman decision-makers, who then became enamored with planning their own encirclement victory. Enver Pasha dismissed cautious commanders and assigned younger, dashing and less critical men. As far as he was concerned, even the Teşkilat-ı Mahsusa guerrilla bands, with limited manpower and fire support, which had achieved complete surprise and captured a long strip of the Eastern Black Sea coast, served to demonstrate the vulnerability of the exposed Russian salient. Enver Pasha, who had an immense ego and an exaggerated sense of self-confidence, personally took over the command of the Third Army on December 18, 1914.[264] He came to the front from Istanbul, bringing von Schellendorf with him as chief of staff.

The Sarıkamış Campaign plan, which was authored by the aggressive new commander of the X Army Corps, Colonel Hafız Hakkı Bey, was simple but daring. The XI Army Corps and the 2nd Regular Cavalry Division would fix the Russians by frontal assaults, thereby creating a window of opportunity for the IX and X Army Corps to encircle and assault to the right and the rear of the enemy, respectively. In addition, the Teşkilat-ı Mahsusa guerrilla bands working in concert with the infantry detachment of German Major Wilhelm Stange, and the Fethi Bey regimental group would launch diversionary raids deep into enemy territory from the north. The planning parameters depended on total surprise, swift action by highly mobile units, and fixing the enemy successfully. Unfortunately for the Ottomans, neither the chief planner Hafız Hakkı nor Enver Pasha paid attention to the lack of intelligence, incomplete logistical planning, the absence of heavy artillery, poor roads and, most importantly, winter weather conditions. The winter of 1914 turned out to be one of the harshest with record levels of snow and temperature drops. Making things worse and far more complex, Hafız Hakkı decided to alter the plan decisively after a brief reconnaissance. Instead of targeting the enemy, the altered plan targeted the enemy main supply bases in the town of Sarıkamış and in the vicinity of the Kars fortress so as to block any Russians from escaping the encirclement and so as to establish a secure launching pad for an invasion of Georgia.[265]

After many delays, the operation began on December 22. The IX and X Army Corps left all their heavy artillery and equipment behind and took only light mountain guns in order to move fast. In fact, total surprise was achieved and, by the end of the second day, the Russian high command caught only a glimpse of the Ottoman design.[266] However, the marching corps lost contact with each other and the soldiers (without proper winter clothing and equipment) encountered difficulty in adjusting themselves to the tempo of the operation and the harsh winter conditions (in which the dirt roads and tracks were nearly impassable due to the heavy snowfall). Moreover, unforeseeable problems such as the stiff defense of the weak Russian screening force and small border guard posts, encountering strong Russian covering forces at critical junctions, incidents of friendly fire (92nd and 94th Regiments inflicted heavy casualties on each other in front of the Russian position at Oltu during a half-day-long amicicide), and troops becoming lost on the mountainous tracks hampered the tempo even more.[267] The forward elements of the IX Army Corps reached the vicinity of Sarıkamış on the third day, but the main group could not make it on time and the Ottomans missed a golden opportunity to capture the weakly defended city. Russian reinforcements then began to arrive in numbers because of the ineffective fixing assaults of the XI Army Corps.[268]

The Ottoman army still had a chance to achieve its aim, thanks to the paralysis of the Russian command, which in confusion and panic repeatedly issued orders and counterorders for a general withdrawal until December 30. But by that date the Ottoman units were exhausted, and the IX Army Corps had barely one third of its combat strength and was outgunned by the Russian defenders. Consequently, it was unable to capture Sarıkamış on its own and Enver Pasha ordered the X Army Corps to retreat. Hafız Hakkı gave the fateful order to cross over the Allahüekber Mountain instead of detouring around it. The X Army Corps made the crossing but at a disastrous cost of losing two thirds of its personnel on the trackless mountain. The desperate attacks of both army corps did not achieve any meaningful result against ever-increasing numbers of Russians, who enjoyed effective fire support. The costly frontal assaults, exhaustion, frostbite, and malnutrition took their toll, and the total numbers of the combatants dropped below 1,000 for the IX Army Corps and to less than 2,000 for the X Army Corps.[269]

On January 1, 1915, nearly all of the high-ranking Ottoman officers understood the futility of continuing the operation. Nevertheless, Enver Pasha stubbornly refused any suggestion of retreat. Encouraged by the apparent failure of the Ottoman offensive maneuver and achieving total superiority in every respect with the arrival of more troops, the Russians decided to launch their own version of an encirclement attack, which began on January 2. A desperate defense by the IX Army Corps enabled its sister X Army Corps to retreat but at the cost of encirclement and eventual surrender of the corps and three divisional headquarters (over 200 Ottoman officers, including the IX Army Corps commander, were captured). The victorious Russian troops were unable to pursue and outflank the remnants of the Third Army thanks to the heroic sacrifices of the rear guards.[270]

Whatever the potential was for an Ottoman victory, it became a self-inflicted disaster. Out of 118,174 combat effectives of December 22, 1914, only 8,900 personnel remained available. Some authors suggest the Sarıkamış Campaign effectively ended any chance of Ottoman offensive action against Russia for at least two more years.[271] It was also instrumental in the cancellation of joint German-Ottoman designs of conquering Iranian Azerbaijan and inciting rebellion within the subject nations of Afghanistan, Central Asia, and India. Two divisional groups (1st and 5th Expeditionary Forces) that were moving toward fantastic objectives deep inside Iran and Dagestan were immediately diverted to reinforce the shattered Third Army.[272] From the perspective of our study, the Sarıkamış Campaign as a whole was not something unusual or extraordinary but an understandable undertaking within the institutional development of the Ottoman military.

First of all, the general idea and outline of the plan can be easily linked to the Ottoman's operational encirclement doctrine and planning as shown in the Balkan Wars. And it is also true the army repeated the same type of planning errors (lack of effective fire support, inadequate logistics, poor coordination, overly optimistic time tables, and ignoring the effects of weather) and flawed assumptions (expectations of a weak enemy without fire support and a deteriorating Russian command and control; high expectations of Mahsusa bands and tribal cavalry). In spite of this, the officers and regular units performed to a very high standard and against all odds and, for a period of time, they were within reach of victory.

Secondly, Enver Pasha and Hafız Hakkı, both of whom were seeking combat glory, displayed the same dangerous habit of assuming all command functions within their immediate area and interfering with the spheres of their subordinates (as had happened to the commanders of the Eastern and Western armies of the Balkan Wars). Coupled with the obsession to exhibit absolute obedience borne out of the Balkan syndrome, the Ottoman commanders and staff officers had no choice but to carry out orders in which they had little confidence. From the very beginning until the very end, dozens of officers were sacked, court-martialed and even put to death. This was the reason why the entire command group and staff of the IX Army Corps were captured while fighting hopelessly as riflemen.[273]

Thirdly, the idea of the creation of Mahsusa guerrilla bands was not unique, but rather was the clear outcome of a decades-long counterinsurgency experience and can be traced back to Sultan Abdülhamid's dreadful spy agency.[274] Party leaders and politically motivated officers (including the hitmen of the CUP who were useless for regular military purposes) were enlisted in the creation of guerrilla bands from warlike local populations (these were the Lazes and Acaras on the Caucasus front) and from troublesome characters like bandits and ex-convicts. These bands were reinforced sometimes with regular officers, small fire support elements (artillery and machine gun teams) and, in several cases, entire regular units (most often border guard and gendarmerie units). The allocation of valuable assets for these bands, as well as their independence from military authorities, was an obvious source of tension for the regular command structure. For this reason, several control mechanisms were created such as assigning a regular officer as overall commander for special missions like the assignment of Major Stange during the Sarıkamış Campaign, or giving clear command authority to the highest military officer present.[275] Against the expectations of the CUP leadership (especially Enver Pasha and the civilian boss of the party Talat Bey) and despite an inspiring start, the Mahsusa bands achieved meager results due to their failure to mobilize effectively the local populations. However, they managed to frighten the Russian high command and caused the diversion of a sizable number of troops. The Mahsusa bands continued to operate at the Caucasus front until the very end. Some continued to be used in direct conventional operations while others were used in guerrilla-type hit and run operations deep into enemy rear and in combating the increasing numbers of Armenian gangs. The apparent failure of the Mahsusa bands just increased the disdain of conventional units towards them. Not surprisingly, they became the ideal scapegoat for any operation that went wrong.[276]

The second offensive enterprise, the Suez Canal Campaign, fell short of its planners' expectations. Only two reinforced divisions of a newly organized expeditionary force (of two army corps each with two divisions) were assigned as the first echelon of the campaign. They managed to pass through the inhospitable Sinai desert undetected by British surveillance teams and patrols. The logistics preparation and planning turned out to be unprecedented in terms of sophistication and foresight. The Ottoman logistics convoys advanced two days in front of the main group and provided adequate water, food, and fodder, not only during the advance, but also during the retreat. Nevertheless, the operational part of the campaign failed in every respect. Once again, Ottoman intelligence grossly underestimated the total combat strength of the enemy (instead of 20,000 British and colonial soldiers they faced 100,000). Weak firepower and lack of bridging and water-crossing equipment further weakened the chances of success. The vanguard 25th (Damascus) Division, which was totally untrained in water-crossing operations did actually establish a small bridgehead on the west bank of the canal but could not hold it until the arrival of the second echelon. The theater commander, Büyük Cemal Pasha, understood the futility of continuing the offensive and managed to break contact skillfully and withdraw the Ottoman units professionally. The secrecy and boldness of the undertaking increased the concerns of the British colonial administration and effectively pinned down the large British garrison of Egypt for more than a year. So in opposition to conventional wisdom, we can easily label the Suez Canal Campaign a long-term success when taking into account the light casualties and paucity of resources committed to the enterprise compared against the much larger British commitment.[277]

Unconventional Warfare against Conventional and Unconventional Enemies

Simultaneously with operations on the Caucasus front, the Teşkilat-ı Mahsusa organized and employed guerrilla bands in Iraq, Palestine, Hejaz, Libya, and even in the Balkans. But this time, the size of the formations (except in the Balkans) exceeded regimental levels, with the enlistment of entire Bedouin and other nomadic tribes. Moreover, unlike the Caucasus bands, their tasks were far greater in scope than simply supporting conventional military operations. The Mahsusa Balkan operations were actually a continuation of prewar operations in Western Thrace. The Mahsusa operatives, who operated from bases on the Bulgarian side of the border, sent small guerrilla bands to achieve specific missions in Serbia and Greece, which consisted mostly of sabotaging critical infrastructure like the destruction of the Valedova Bridge or annihilating isolated units. Due to their heavy reliance on local collaborators, their areas of operations were of a confined nature. Even though Bulgarian bands were also involved in these operations from time to time, suspicion, envy, and outward xenophobia poisoned relations and hampered the operations greatly which, in the end, caused the suspension of all operations in September 1917.[278]

In Libya, the Mahsusa already had operatives and a well-functioning alliance with the Sanusis and other local forces, thanks to the foresight of keeping a core cadre of officers and technicians, as well as continuing military aid to the insurgents after the Ouchy Peace Treaty of 1912. Moreover, the Libyans heartily welcomed the declaration of Jihad on November 14, 1914. Oddly, they paid no attention to the fact that the Jihad was aimed at only the enemies of the Ottoman Empire, which did not include Italy at that time. The major problem for the Mahsusa operatives was the sociopolitical nature of the locals, who were perpetually divided and factionalist and reluctant to fight against British troops. The Libyans merely wanted to continue their struggle for independence against the Italians, which Mahsusa operatives were unable to target openly due to the precarious neutrality of Italy. They were not willing to commit forces for inciting rebellion within the Egyptian population, and they had no designs for an invasion of Western Egypt. In effect, aggressive actions such as these put Ottoman military advice and aid at great risk.[279]

Groups of Ottoman officers and other volunteers began to arrive in Libya after September 1914. With their arrival, the spirit of resistance gained new ground. The Sanusis and other groups managed to reconquer the interior of the country, and the Italians once again took refuge in their coastal fortified bases.[280] After a series of victories against the Italians and the arrival of Nuri (Killigil) Pasha (younger brother of Enver Pasha) and Major Cafer Askeri (Jafar al Askari, who would change sides after his capture by British troops and thereafter become the commander of Sheikh Faisal's regular troops) with a command group, technicians, and an infantry battalion, the Sanusis were forced to bow to the continuous requests coming from Istanbul and reluctantly and slowly initiated attacks against British targets. Interestingly, the actual hostilities between Sanusis and the British garrison of Sollum began after a provocative raid that was orchestrated by Ottoman officers on a British outpost in Sidi Barani on November 22, 1915. The uncontrolled events unfolded and a crisis escalated quickly in which the British garrison evacuated Sollum and retreated to Mersa Matruh the following day.[281]

Nuri Pasha had to transform tribal warriors into conventional units in order to occupy and keep at least a portion of Western Egypt so as to incite rebellion. It was an impossible mission under the conditions, with the limited numbers of Ottoman officers, a problematic supply of weapons and ammunition (the only source other than spoils of war were infrequent German submarine shipments), and the questionable loyalty of the Sanusi and tribal leaders. The Sanusi leader Sidi Ahmad al-Sharif (also known as the Grand Sanusi) was so reluctant that most often he personally sabotaged Nuri's offensive plans. The tribal warriors were unwilling to face danger and hardship away from their tribal areas. Moreover, the only reliable forces, the Ottoman-trained Sanusi regular troops, were no match for their adversaries (with the chief exception of the Numune [model] Battalion) and encountered difficulties when fighting against a conventional enemy using conventional tactics and techniques. British firepower, airplanes, and especially armored cars were instrumental in terrifying the Libyan soldiers and tribal levies.[282]

The British theater command easily concentrated two reinforced brigades and some other auxiliary units with armored cars and planes. After minor setbacks, the British troops stopped the Ottoman-Sanusi attackers at Bir-i Ebu Tunus (Halazin) on January 24, 1916 and recaptured Sollum on March 15. The reversal broke up the fragile alliance between Sanusis and Mahsusa operatives for a period of time. Nuri Pasha managed to regain the confidence of the Sanusi leaders with the help of ardent patriots like Sulayman al-Baruni and Ottoman-trained Libyan officers. This time Nuri convinced Sidi Ahmad to attack from the south where the British military presence was ephemeral. The Sanusis easily captured the Western Oases between April 24 and June 15, 1916. Actually this was their second offensive operation against the oases, but they now had the support of the local population. A much anticipated British expedition marched in September 1916 and ended with success in February 1917.[283] The Mahsusa continued its operations in Libya, this time aimed exclusively against the Italians even after the new Sanusi leader Muhammad Idris al-Mahdi reached agreement both with Italians and British. Thanks to the transfer of the majority of the Italian troops to the European theater, the Mahsusa and its allies achieved control on an important percentage of the country in which officially assigned Ottoman governors and provincial administration functioned properly up until the end of World War I.[284]

The Libya operation did not fulfill the overly exaggerated expectations of Enver Pasha and the Mahsusa chiefs who dreamt of wide-scale and far-reaching rebellions in Egypt and North Africa. Militarily, the Ottoman-led Sanusi attacks did not achieve anything meaningful. But psychologically these attacks, in combination with the repeated Ottoman Suez Canal Campaigns, were seen by the British authorities as the fulfillment of their worst fears for a period of time. The desertion of several Egyptian officers and even whole companies immediately after the fall of Sollum increased their fears. When taking into account the resources committed for this operation by the Ottoman Empire, it becomes apparent that it was inexpensive (less than 100 operatives, limited amounts of war material, largely financed by Germans) and cost effective, forcing both the British and Italians to allocate much needed forces away from major theaters and to spend large amounts of money to keep the local grandees loyal. Furthermore, Mahsusa propagandists made use of the Libyan resistance against "infidels" to gain the support of other Muslim groups and to increase the prestige of the empire.[285]

In Hejaz and Palestine, the Mahsusa was initially charged with conducting raids against British targets and raising a tribal army to support the first Suez Canal Campaign. The project totally failed.[286] Later its mission changed to fight against the rebellion of Sharif Hussein of Hejaz. So instead of fighting a conventional enemy, the Mahsusa operatives suddenly found themselves engaged in a fight against an unconventional enemy that had the material and financial support of Britain.

Although the timing of the rebellion caught the Ottoman administration unprepared, the rebellious and separatist desires of the Arab traditional leadership and intellectuals were not unknown. And even for a period of time the Mahsusa leadership (foremost among them Major Mümtaz Bey and Captain Kuşçubaşızade Eşref Bey) thought to handle the rebellion solely with Mahsusa units.

Mümtaz and Eşref had extensive experiences with the Arabian Peninsula tribes and were well-known figures within the region. They hoped to enlist most of the important tribes by making use of their traditional feuds and power struggles. They and other operatives did succeed in enlisting one of the major sheikhs, Rashid of Shammar, who remained more or less loyal throughout the war and pacified Abd al-Aziz ibn Saud of Najd. Nevertheless, they were unable to cope with the British intelligence service, which had more funds to buy the services or loyalty of most of the tribes.[287] Fortuitously the new commander of the Hejaz region, Fahreddin Pasha, understood the serious limitations of the Mahsusa and built his strategy instead around his regular units. Against all odds, he managed to defend one of the two holy cities of Islam, Medina, for two and a half years until January 9, 1919 (outlasting the end of World War I).

In Ottoman military history, the defense of Medina clearly ranks with the defense of Plevne. Fahreddin Pasha not only had to defend Medina but also the single-track narrow gauge Hejaz Railway on which his entire logistics depended. Even though sabotaging the railway tracks and attacking the trains were generally attributed to the larger than life figure, Captain T. E. Lawrence, in fact the Bedouin tribes had been experimenting with these ideas from the onset of construction of the Hejaz Railway in the early 1900s. Understandably, regular Ottoman infantry and cavalry had to learn how to secure the railway while finding ways to cope with the increasing professionalism of the tribesmen, even before the Arab Revolt.[288] Thanks to this decade-long experience and the novel tactics of Fahreddin Pasha, such as emplacing rapid reaction forces not along the tracks but deep in the desert and sending long-range desert patrols for harassment raids, the effects of interdiction were minimal. Surprisingly, Ottoman garrisons of isolated small train stations not only withstood the continuous night attacks to their bunker-like buildings (a clear legacy of Ottoman blockhouses of the Balkans) stoically, but also secured the tracks against ever-increasing numbers of sabotages (around 130 major attacks in 1917 and hundreds in 1918, including exploding more than 300 bombs in a single day on April 30, 1918).

It was in Iraq that the power and the influence of the Teşkilat-ı Mahsusa reached its apex. As mentioned above, thanks to the flawed assumption of the German-led General Staff that there would be no immediate danger to Basra province and Iraq as a whole, both army corps headquarters and three out of four regular divisions that were manned by Iraqi recruits were transferred elsewhere. The gendarmerie and border guard battalions (which were notoriously ill-trained, poorly led, and scattered all over the province) and tribal warriors were the only forces available other than the understrength 38th Division (three regiments each with two battalions).[289] The General Staff planners equally ignored the sorry state of interior security and the chronic rebellions and lawlessness, which infected the area.[290]

The Iraq Regional Command made the fatal mistake of establishing several independent defensive positions by spreading its thin and already weak garrisons. Provisional units were created for each position by mixing regular companies and battalions with gendarmerie and border guards and reinforcing them with tribal warriors, which instrumentally aggravated the vulnerability of the garrison. Most probably, Enver Pasha's order to make use of tribes as the fulcrum of the defense and the positive Libyan experience of employing the mixed regular and tribal forces influenced these decisions.[291]

Contrary to the Ottoman General Staff's planning assumptions, the Indian Government rapidly concentrated a reinforced divisional group (so-called Indian Expeditionary Force "D") in Bahrain. Force D set sail immediately after the formal declaration of war and captured easily the crucial beachhead of Fav (Fao) after a day-long bombardment on November 6, 1914. The tribal warriors and other militias were in full flight after experiencing the bombardment. The remaining regular component of the Fav Composite Force showed ephemeral resistance and melted away. Neither the divisional headquarters nor the Iraq Regional Command learned any lessons from this ignominious flight and continued to repeat the same flawed defensive concept again and again.[292]

Force D crushed the defensive positions of Seyhan (Saihan) and Kütüzzeyn (Zain) in two days and captured Basra on November 20. The enemy riverine flotilla played an especially crucial role by shelling the Ottoman positions and flanking them. In each confrontation, the tribal warriors immediately fled and local soldiers soon followed their lead, whereas Turkish regular soldiers tried to defend their positions in vain. The unabated British advance came to a stop at Kurna (Qurna) on November 25. The first British assault failed thanks to the successful application of a series of small ambushes in the marshland. The British did not repeat their frontal assault and instead flanked the Ottoman positions by employing their tribal allies. The hard-pressed defenders surrendered two days later on December 9. The fall of Kurna was a serious blow for the Ottoman side. Not only was the most strategic position that could threaten Basra lost, but also the headquarters of the 38th Division surrendered, thereby leaving its remaining scattered divisional troops leaderless.[293]

After urgent requests were received from Iraq, Enver Pasha decided to assign his loyal friend, Lieutenant Colonel Süleyman Askeri Bey, as the Iraq regional commander. As the *de facto* director of the Teşkilat-ı Mahsusa, Süleyman Askeri had all the qualifications needed to direct unconventional warfare on a grand scale. He was a highly talented officer and a veteran of the decade-long counterinsurgency operations against the Komitacıs. After the end of the Balkan Wars, he organized and led several unconventional campaigns against Serbia, Albania, and Greece. He orchestrated Mahsusa bands and operatives, which tried to manipulate the regime crisis in Albania to establish Ottoman control once again. In Serbia, they sabotaged critical bridges and conducted raids by using the hospitality and cooperation of Bulgarian authorities. In Western Thrace, they proclaimed independence (between August 31 and October 25, 1913) of the Turkish enclave, the so-called Garbi Trakya Hükümeti Müstakilesi (The Independent Government of Western Thrace), by making use of the power vacuum caused by the Greek-Bulgarian conflict.[294] These experiences gave him confidence to launch larger scale operations with the support of Enver Pasha, who was also an ardent believer in unconventional warfare. Iraq provided an excellent opportunity for Süleyman Askeri, who already knew the region intimately, to experiment with his concepts of unconventional warfare against a conventional enemy.[295]

Süleyman Askeri arrived in Baghdad with his special staff and the elite Mahsusa unit, the Osmancık (named after the founder of the dynasty Osman Gazi) Volunteer Battalion (composed of six companies) on December 20, 1914.[296] He immediately introduced his concept of operations and made drastic changes. He reorganized the scattered defense forces into a composite division and several regimental size composite detachments. He tried to concentrate all his available forces near Kurna. In his view, success could be achieved by fixing the British troops with regular units and then hitting them from every direction at every opportunity by using tribes. He was well aware of the Indian government's plan to reinforce Force D. In order to divert and fix as many enemy units as he could from the main theater, he decided to send a detachment (Kerha Müfrezesi), reinforced with tribal warriors, to Southern Iran. The Kerha Detachment (a regimental group) was tasked with destroying the Abadan oil pipeline and attacking British outposts.[297]

Unlike his predecessor, he did not remain in Baghdad away from the combat zone. He also did not delegate his authority, and personally took over the entire operation. In less than a month, his new approaches achieved small but encouraging successes. The Kerha Detachment succeeded in making the British theater command anxious and forced it to divert an infantry brigade to protect the vital oil facilities. He launched a guerrilla campaign to harass and to tire the British. Unfortunately, the weather suddenly turned to heavy showers and catastrophic levels of flooding seriously limited his campaign. However, contrary to his ideas, it was the regular units that managed unexpectedly to repel the overconfident British advance on the Rota (Ruta) canals on January 20, 1915. But unfortunately for the Ottoman side, Süleyman Askeri was seriously wounded in this battle.[298]

Süleyman Askeri, ever confident and optimistic, refused to hand over his duties even temporarily. His confidence and faith in the martial potential of the local tribes was so great that he even declined Enver's offer of a special task force. The General Staff did not share the optimism of Süleyman Askeri and sent the 35th Division (two regiments each with two battalions), which was an original Iraqi unit, and the elite Istanbul Fire Brigade Regiment (two battalions). Süleyman Askeri distributed the new battalions to provisional formations. Most probably, he simply tried to strengthen his weak formations in the well-established Müfreze tradition.[299]

Süleyman Askeri decided to attack the British positions at Şuayyibe (Shaiba) at once before the British buildup could reach an insurmountable scale. His timing was correct, but he paid no attention to the fact that he had organized his units to wage an unconventional war rather than to attack conventional infantry in entrenched positions with superior firepower. His plan was flawed by an exaggerated force assessment of the tribal contribution (he would get only half of his estimate of

20,000 tribal warriors and only a bit more than 1,000 actually joined the battle) and poor reconnaissance and combat intelligence. The main idea was to breach the British line of defense using regulars (9,000 strong) and then employ tribal cavalry to annihilate the enemy.[300]

The Ottoman regular units launched four massive frontal attacks beginning on the morning of April 12, 1915, which continued until midnight. Their heroism did not help much against superior British firepower and their simple but effective entrenchments. The tribal warriors patiently waited for the breakthrough and most of them stayed out of the battle. A similarly planned diversionary attack by the Dicle (Tigris) and Kerha Müfrezes did not make any significant contribution. A British counterattack efficaciously ended any chances of success, but Süleyman Askeri, who was still hoping to make one last effort, stubbornly refused any suggestion for general withdrawal. This fatal decision gave the British defenders an excellent opportunity to crush the disorganized and exhausted Ottoman troops, which they did on April 14. After a hopeless stand, the Ottoman troops were routed (losing more than half of their numbers). The hapless, but excessively proud, Süleyman Askeri committed suicide, thereby leaving his force leaderless (Askeri's wound had never healed and had left him bedridden). Even though the British did not pursue, most of the heavy weapons and equipment were left behind, and isolated soldiers and small units fell prey to their former tribal allies, who plundered everyone and everything during the ignominious flight.[301]

The Şuayyibe battle definitely ended Süleyman Askeri's concept of unconventional warfare, which was actually an imitation of the successful Libyan campaign. In truth, the British and Indian army did not resemble the Italians nor did the Iraqi tribes have the motivation of the Libyans. The local population either watched the unfolding events passively or tried to benefit from the power vacuum by various means, including sporadic rebellions and attacking friend and foe alike. Enver Pasha and the Mahsusa leadership learned the hard way that it was impossible to wage unconventional war against a highly trained and disciplined modern conventional army without popular and active support.[302]

The new Ottoman strategy for Iraq was a conventional attritional war in which the available forces would try to do their best to lure, tire, and delay the British advance, which would be canalized along the riverbeds and annihilated deep inside Iraq. The tribal warriors would be employed only as auxiliary troops for screening tasks and harassing the enemy. The Ottoman General Staff's assessment and arrangements turned out to be more than correct. The victory of Şuayyibe and the fall of Amara (June 3) and Nasıriyye (July 24) at comparatively small loss of life not only instrumentally increased the confidence of the Indian government and its field commanders, but also blinded them to the hard facts of an insufficiency of logistics and lines of transportation and communication that were already stretched dangerously thin.[303]

The British expeditionary force (the reinforced 6th Poona Division) pulled the Ottoman defenders out of their Kut al-Amara defensive position after a successful flanking maneuver on September 28. It was an embarrassing failure, but the

Ottoman troops made excellent use of the leisurely approach of their adversary and fortified a new defensive position further north at Selman-ı Pak (Ctesiphon). The battle of Selman-ı Pak was a terrible ordeal and lasted four days. Both sides unbeknownst to each other began to withdraw nearly at the same time. The Ottoman side realized the development a bit sooner and immediately pursued the enemy, albeit without much success. The British commander, Major General Charles Townshend, retreated to avoid encirclement but decided to make a stand in Kut al-Amara in order to keep his territorial gains and to protect Basra. Townshend received approval from his superiors to entrench at Kut because another Indian army corps of two combat-experienced divisions was coming into Iraq, which could relieve his force.[304]

Even though the Ottoman side was lacking a modern siege train, the commander, Colonel Nurettin (Sakallı) Bey (who was replaced by Halil [Kut] Pasha on January 10), still managed to carry out the siege professionally. First, he isolated the Kut garrison and then emplaced the majority of his units downstream against the British relieving force. Obviously, he paid dearly for his underestimation of the will and capacity of the Kut defenders during the initial month of the siege. But his assessment of the relieving force and its operational methods was correct. The British relieving force failed to break in the Ottoman lines of contravallation after a series of bloody assaults between January 6 and April 22, 1916. The British offer of a huge sum of bribery also failed to affect the Ottoman field commanders. Townshend had no choice other than unconditional surrender, which he duly carried out on April 29. The surrender of 13,309 British military personnel (including the noncombatants) was a terrible blow for the prestige of Britain, especially after the Gallipoli blunder. It was the largest surrender of a British army between Yorktown in 1781 and Singapore in 1942. In addition to this loss of prestige, the British had to commit valuable assets away from the main theater of operations and, moreover, suffered around 25,000 casualties during nearly a five-month-long standoff.[305]

Interestingly, both Halil Pasha and Nurettin were veterans of counterinsurgency campaigns, and Halil Pasha was also a high-ranking Mahsusa member. They realized partially the dream of Süleyman Askeri. But the victory was gained by regular units using conventional methods and neither ever tried to revert to unconventional warfare in their subsequent commands. The obvious failure of the Mahsusa's operations in Iraq brought to an end all Mahsusa-led combat operations against conventional enemies. However, for understandable reasons (chief among them the immensity and scale of the theater), the Mahsusa could not handle the interior security duties either. In a bit more than one year, its operations against rebels and other unconventional enemies were more or less suspended and handed over to military authorities, thereby leaving the Mahsusa organization with only intelligence gathering and propaganda campaigns that mostly targeted native and foreign Muslim groups.

Overall, the Teşkilat-ı Mahsusa achieved meager results in contrast to the extravagant expectations of its grand master, Enver Pasha. And clearly its achievements were more psychological than military. The idea to make use of the military potential of tribal and other conventionally useless groups, as a concept, was novel. But the

Mahsusa operatives did not fully understand the selfish, pragmatic, and ever-fluid loyalties of the tribes, which were mostly trying their best to gain as much as they could from the ongoing conflict.[306] They received varying degrees of cooperation from the locals, depending upon the operational and tactical situation on the ground. The Mahsusa's mixed and, in a way, conflicting character of being Islamist and Turkish at the same time did not help its mission to keep the different ethnic Muslim groups loyal. Not surprisingly, the Mahsusa's attempts to incite rebellion within the subject nations of Egypt, Tunis, Iran, Afghanistan, and Central Asia (by making use of several native nationalists or notables like Abd al-Aziz Shawish, Muhammad Farid and Dr. Ahmad Fuad of Egypt, Ali Baş Hamba and Salih al-Tunisi of Tunis) failed to achieve anything meaningful. Similarly, joint Mahsusa-German operations in Iran and Afghanistan went wrong and only increased the paranoia of British and Russian provincial officials. As a conclusion, while there were some isolated tactical successes, Mahsusa operations might be categorized as merely a serious nuisance for the allies.

Realization of the Long-Cherished Dream: The Gallipoli Victory

The Gallipoli Campaign was and still is seen as a "narrowly missed victory" by many western military historians and enthusiasts. They have a tendency to blame everything ranging from command and coordination problems and poor planning to geography and climate. Speculation is rife with many might-have-beens, which are still popular.[307] From the Turkish official and popular perspective, it was not only a magnificent victory but also signified the birth of the new Turkish nation from the wreck of the Ottoman Empire. It is beyond the scope of this study to examine or to question the relative validity of these commonly held beliefs. Instead, this section will focus on the military maxims behind the fulfillment of a long-cherished dream; defeating the allied forces of the Great Powers.

Many researchers tend to forget that the Straits and Gallipoli Peninsula had been a fortress command from very early times. Many fortresses and other fortifications were built, enlarged, and rebuilt during the reign of several Ottoman sultans. Up until the activation and assignment of the Fifth Army on March 24, 1915, the main responsibility of the defenses remained under the command of the Ottoman artillery corps. In fact, nearly every artillery officer, especially the heavy artillery branch, served at least one term in Dardanelles Fortified Zone Command (Çanakkale Müstahkem Mevki Kumandanlığı) before 1914. They knew the area thoroughly. And during the Balkan Wars the entire peninsula was fortified against possible amphibious operations.[308] Although the peninsula defense system was immature, it gave an opportunity for staff and artillery officers to analyze and practice the concepts of defense against amphibious operations.[309] Whatever the merits of the German artillery and naval experts under the leadership of Admiral Guido von Usedom, it was the Fortified Zone Command which played the crucial role in the achievement of the naval victory of March 18, 1915.

Likewise, the leadership of von Sanders as the commanding general of the theater of operations has been deemed as the major factor behind the land victory against the British and French troops.[310] In reality it was von Sanders and some of his fellow German officers who created the impasse of the early operations.[311] Von Sanders and his small staff arrived and took command of the Dardanelles fortified zone on March 26. After a brief inspection, von Sanders disregarded the experience and advice of the Fortified Zone Area Command and disbanded the old defense system.[312] According to the old plan, all units placed their main bodies near the possible landing sites and kept small reserves in the interior. The Fortified Area Command expected the main attacks to come at the southern tip of the peninsula (Seddülbahir-Cape Helles region) and Kabatepe (Gaba Tepe) region, because according to their estimate, only these two areas offered a favorable opportunity to overcome the straits' defenses.[313]

Von Sanders categorically rejected the Ottoman plan and its assumptions as unsuitable for defense against modern amphibious warfare. According to his own ideas and plan, units would be placed in an observation and screening force watching over the beaches while maintaining main bodies as mobile reserves. Moreover, he identified the Bolayır (Bulair)-Saros region and Beşika bays as the probable main landing sites.[314] It is now well known that von Sanders's concept of defense was ineffective in preventing landings. Allied units did land at the southern tip of the peninsula and at Arıburnu (Anzac Cove, one mile north of Kabatepe) and not at von Sanders' probable landing sites.[315] The small screening forces were not able to oppose the landings of April 25, 1915 effectively. Additionally, the large reserves encountered great difficulty in reaching the landing sites due to the poor roads, shortage of transportation, and the effects of the allied naval bombardment.[316] Von Sanders also failed to understand the unfolding events and ineffectively managed the crisis. Had all the Turkish unit commanders followed his orders exactly, the Anzac landing at Arıburnu would have been successful, and the 9th Division would have been unable to offer the kind of resistance that stopped the further enlargement of the beach head at Cape Helles. The 19th Division Commander, Mustafa Kemal (Atatürk) Bey, managed to stop the Anzacs only after openly disregarding von Sanders's orders.[317]

The statistical data concerning the high-ranking officers who actually fought at Gallipoli clearly show that the German officers in command and critical staff positions actually constituted a minority. According to the August 1915 order of battle of the Gallipoli front, there were two field armies, five army corps, 17 divisions, and 57 infantry regiments (not counting the supporting arms). So, altogether, there were 80 commanding officers and 23 chiefs of staff. Only eight of them were Germans.[318] This means that there were 95 Ottoman officers assigned to important combat posts (or 92% of the total available command and chief of staff posts). As a conclusion, Ottoman officers, rather than German ones, provided the majority of the important leadership roles on the peninsula in August 1915.[319]

The performance of the Ottoman troops during the amphibious landing phase exceeded all estimates and expectations, surprising not only the Allied planners but also the Ottoman General Staff. Company and platoon size units kept the amphibious landings at bay for hours and, in some cases, more than a day. For example, a sole infantry company (10th Coy, 3–26 Infantry) stopped the multibrigade British advance in Ertuğrul Koyu (V Beach), and another company (7th Coy, 2–26 Infantry) blocked a similar advance of British troops in İkiz Koyu (X Beach), which was undefended and which created the gravest danger to the whole front.[320] When taking into account the primitive nature of the field fortifications (except for a small strip of Seddülbahir there were only defensive works composed of minimally wired trenches and light bunkers) and artillery support, the achievements of these isolated screening forces becomes more clear.

Unfortunately for the Ottoman defenders, von Sanders and later on Enver Pasha did not comprehend the deadly effect of the combination of modern fire power and entrenched infantry. Equally, they were unable to calculate the destructive power of naval bombardment on the infantry units attacking in dense formations.[321] Their flawed counterattack concept of destroying the landing parties was unsuccessful and ended with heavy Ottoman casualties during the fateful month of May 1915, and after a brief pause during the first half of June. As an example, the 15th and 2nd Divisions, which were first line formations, were annihilated as effective fighting forces after the costly failures of the night attack of May 3–4 and the day attack of May 19, respectively. The most critical damage to the divisions came from the loss of officers (more than 60 percent), and the divisions were never able to recover.[322]

Why did the Ottoman commanding officers not challenge their orders? The first reason was related to the Balkan Wars. Many of the officers were psychologically affected by the disasters and the desertion of whole units during the Balkan Wars. Accordingly, they saw the Gallipoli Campaign as an opportunity to cleanse the Ottoman army's reputation.[323] The second reason was the inexperience of some of the unit commanders in trench warfare. Their counterinsurgency experiences affected their conduct of conventional combat operations. In effect, they learned about modern trench warfare the hard way.[324] The third reason was the exaggeration and misleading statements that crept into the combat reports going up the chain of command. Consequently, the Ottoman General Staff saw the situation completely differently from the commanders who knew the realities at the front.[325] As a result, commanders were reluctant to disobey the orders of von Sanders or Enver Pasha. Any commander who dared to oppose the orders was immediately sacked. This policy succeeded in some cases but, generally, it was counterproductive among the officer corps.[326]

After the apparent failure of amphibious operations on April 25 and the following costly stalemate, the Allied theater command decided to try their chances by landing troops around Suvla Bay in order to conquer the dominating ground behind the already fixed Ottoman units surrounding Anzac Cove. The idea was not novel but the combined operations of landings at Suvla and diversionary attacks at Arıburnu and Helles on August 6 and 7 achieved initial surprise and, for two days, the Ottoman theater command encountered difficulty understanding and reacting to the situation. Von Sanders's belated decision to assign Mustafa Kemal (Atatürk) Bey as the Northern Group commander changed the situation dramatically. Mustafa Kemal committed all available forces against the enemy, and waves of massive infantry attacks destroyed any chances of success for the Allied troops. Likewise, the second Allied offensive between August 21 and 27 also failed to achieve its objective.[327]

Even though the August offensive (or better known as the Suvla disaster) was nothing more than a tactical opportunity, it was widely seen as the very last chance for conquering the Straits. Its failure, which coincided with the growing importance of the western front, convinced British decision-makers of the futility of the continuation of the campaign. The new Allied theater commander immediately proposed evacuation, which was duly carried out during December 1915 and early January 1916. The Ottoman field commanders ignored the early signs of evacuation and did little to hamper the operation, which turned out to be the sole success for the Allied forces during the whole campaign.[328]

An important percentage of the Ottoman army (17 out of 40 numbered divisions) and its officers (a bit less than half of the regular officers) served in the Gallipoli Campaign. The casualty figures were astonishing; overall 166,507 in which 1,658 of them were officers.[329] Units were decimated and battlefields were covered with deteriorating bodies. The Ottoman military was never able to overcome these losses (especially the officer losses). The availability of trained rank and file within Ottoman units was never again as high as it was prior to Gallipoli. "The flower of the Turkish army" was lost there.[330] This great sacrifice adversely affected the army in materialistic sense. But the pride of victory was so great that, psychologically, it improved the combat effectiveness of the entire military. The prestige and cohesion of the military was greatly improved. The units, which took part in the campaign, created a special identity and managed to protect it until the very end of the war.[331] The example of the 25th Regiment was very interesting in this sense. The 25th Regiment, which took part in nearly all of the major battles, was one of the most heroic units of the Gallipoli Campaign.[332] The regiment was sent to the Caucasus front afterwards. It took over the responsibility of some parts of the defense line, ranging near the city of Bayburt. The Russians attacked on the very same day of the takeover (July 3, 1916), but the 25th Regiment easily stopped the main Russian assault and chased the withdrawing attackers. All of the veteran units of the Caucasus front watched this performance with awe, and their admiration for the veterans of Gallipoli greatly increased.[333]

The Gallipoli victory also provided many benefits to the military in terms of military proficiency. A large number of officers served in the campaign and learned their trade in a modern trench warfare environment. They already had a good educational and theoretical background, but their practical combat experiences made them real leaders. They learned the tactics and techniques of modern warfare and were able to defeat or at least stand firm against the modern and powerful militaries of Britain and France.[334] But the most important benefit of the campaign was the creation of new bonds within the rank and file. Facing danger and hardship every day, their shared experiences in the trenches created a special brotherhood. Being a veteran of Gallipoli became a clear distinction and endowed prestige. It was not a chain of coincidences that the future commanders of the Turkish Independence War (27 out of 91 commanding officers higher than regimental level) and the new Turkish Republican Army were veterans of the Gallipoli Campaign.[335]

The Gallipoli victory was the clear result of the efforts of Ottoman officers, and without their contributions, the outcome would have been very different. But the Gallipoli Campaign itself also greatly affected the entire Ottoman officer corps. Before the campaign, Ottoman officers served under the psychological burden of complete defeat at the hands of the Balkan nations. Although several drastic measures and a dramatic reorganization of the army helped to overcome this stigma, psychological pressures continued to affect the officer corps. The Gallipoli victory cleansed the stains of defeats and improved the morale and cohesion of the officer corps.[336] It became a symbol of Ottoman determination and courage against the invaders. It also helped to improve the position and prestige of officers among the public. They began to see themselves proudly as the saviors and protectors of the nation once again.

The Last Episode

The year 1916 started with the glory of Gallipoli and the imminence of another victory at Kut al-Amara. For the first time after the Sarıkamış blunder, the future seemed bright as the Ottoman General Staff at last had both a strategic reserve (the divisions massed around Gallipoli Peninsula) and the strategic initiative. Nevertheless, Enver Pasha and his German advisors once again lost touch with the realities on the ground and decided to realize their vision of becoming a full participant in the European theaters of operations. They rightfully predicted that the British would not dare to advance until the end of year at the Sinai-Palestine front, and they were very sure of their strength on the Mesopotamian front. However, their estimates of Russian intentions and plans could not have been more erroneous. The victor of the Sarıkamış Campaign, General Yudenich, launched a massive assault on January 10, 1916 by making good use of winter conditions and vulnerabilities against the hapless Third Army. The Russian cavalry penetrated eight to ten kilometers deep into the Ottoman rear. Overloaded with assaults coming from a multitude of different directions, and unable to respond to the high Russian tempo, Third Army units had no other choice than to retreat nearly fifty kilometers in six days.[337]

Against the high expectations of the General Staff, which hoped to see a repetition of the glories of the Balkan Wars' city defenses, the key fortress city of Erzurum fell in three days on February 16. After dislodging and dislocating the Third Army, Yudenich skillfully captured the main port city of Trabzon (April 16) and the key transport junction and logistics base of Erzincan (July 25) by massing superior strength at the exact time and place. The understrength Third Army experienced more than 30,000 casualties, and an equal number of soldiers fell prisoner (most were the inexperienced products of a series of call-ups). Thus, all the preparation and fruits of a year-long effort were ruined.[338]

Worse still, the ongoing Armenian insurgency and rebellion reached its apex with the severe reverses suffered by the Ottoman military. As already mentioned, a significant percentage of Ottoman Armenians saw the war as a once-in-a-lifetime opportunity to carve out an independent state for themselves. From the very beginning,

Armenian conscripts deserted their units at the first opportunity. The Russian military raised four regiments of Armenian volunteers and sent agent-provocateurs into Ottoman territory well before the start of the hostilities. Instigated and armed by the Russian government and organized by revolutionary groups (foremost among them were the Dashnaks), Armenian rebels captured the city of Van on April 14, 1915. The Third Army hurriedly deployed a mobile gendarmerie division, a few regulars and reserve cavalry regiments, to besiege the city. The rebels withstood the assaults for more than a month, and a Russian relief force reached the city at the end of May.[339]

The Ottoman political and military leaders were aware of the Armenian designs before the war and even tried to reach a deal with the revolutionary groups.[340] For whatever reason, they totally ignored the possibility of a well-coordinated rebellion and paid little attention to the increasingly urgent intelligence reports. Therefore, the rebellion of Van and its timing petrified the leaders, who were already encountering difficulty coming up with a workable plan against possible Russian onslaughts and protecting lines of communication while committing most of the assets to the Gallipoli Campaign. The controversial relocation decree of May 31, which aimed to remove the Armenian population of eastern and southern Anatolia, was the outcome of these fears and urgency.[341]

The relocation of the Armenians did lighten the interior security and counterinsurgency duties of the regular units on the Caucasus front. But the Fourth Army continued to be plagued by Armenian rebels and in fact, in order to conduct counterinsurgency and secure the coastline, raised three new divisions (41st, 43rd, and 44th Divisions) from depot battalions and gendarmerie during the spring of 1915. These operations were difficult and costly. As an example, the 41st Division spent four months (between August and November 1915) trying to subdue rebels on and near the Musa Dağı mountain complex in Antakya (Antioch).[342]

In the meantime, the Second Army (nine divisions strong), which was just released when the Gallipoli front was reorganized, refurbished (with the help of Austro-Hungarians and Germans) and reinforced with the best recruits available for its new mission to help Austria-Hungary. Although the Ottoman General Staff reluctantly had to deploy most of the Second Army to the Caucasus front, its best divisions were stripped off to help their allies in Europe. To make things worse, one division was rerouted to Iraq and another one to Syria. Second Army units began their long journey to the Caucasus front late and, thanks to the severe limitations of the transportation system (under ideal conditions it would take more than 50 days for a single division to reach the Caucasus), they were unable to reach their respective concentration points before the end of the summer.[343]

Interestingly, the Third Army Commander, Vehib Pasha (who was just a major when Ahmed İzzet Pasha was the Chief of the General Staff in 1908) refused to serve under the operational command of the Second Army Commander, Ahmed İzzet Pasha. Equally, Ahmed İzzet Pasha refused to help his sister Third Army, even though some of his divisions had already arrived in theater on the grounds of conserving strength. So their personal animosity and discord blurred their perceptions and decision-making processes. The Second Army divisions leisurely acclimated while the Third Army continued its desperate struggle. Not surprisingly, in return, the Third Army sat idle when Ahmed İzzet Pasha launched his long-awaited assault on August 2. The real culprit for this lack of unity of command was the Ottoman General Staff, which neglected to assign a theater-level commander empowered to coordinate and direct the overall effort.[344]

The August offensive of the Second Army achieved meager results (only one army corps was able to reach its initial target) largely because the Russians were able to concentrate their troops against it, thanks to the inactivity of the Third Army. The Second Army paid a terrible price for its separate and ill-planned assault. Overall, 30,000 well-trained and combat-hardened Gallipoli veterans were lost, thereby further crippling the Ottoman military. In short, the feud of Ahmed İzzet Pasha and Vehib Pasha effectively drained available troop strength and put the whole region under threat and at the mercy of the Russians.[345]

Undeterred by the fate of the Second and Third Armies and amidst intense criticism coming from both Ottoman officers and the German Advisory Mission, Enver Pasha insisted on sending Ottoman troops to the European theater. This was a welcome decision for Germany and Austro-Hungary, which were trying hard to compensate for the huge casualties inflicted by the Brusilov Offensive of June 1916. The best divisions of the empire, the heroic 19th and 20th Divisions, reinforced with picked officers and soldiers, were sent to Galicia in August 1916 and remained there until September 1917.[346] After another urgent request from the German General Staff, the VI Army Corps (the elite 15th and 25th Divisions) was assigned to help joint operations against Romania between September 1916 and May 1918.[347] Similarly, the XX Army Corps (46th and 50th Divisions) was sent to relieve the hard-pressed Bulgarians on the Salonika front in October 1916 and remained there until March 1917.[348]

The overall performance and contribution of the Ottoman troops in these operations was significant in relation to the forces committed. Ottoman officers and soldiers fought willingly and in many cases heroically even though they were far away from their country and fighting for causes alien to them. Their conduct becomes more apparent when the conduct of Austro-Hungarians and Bulgarians, who were supposed to be fighting for their national aims, are taken into account. There were no cases of insubordination, desertion, or mass surrender, which badly affected their fellow allies, the Austro-Hungarians. They withstood the hardship of trench warfare and privation on the European fronts stoically.[349]

From the Ottoman perspective the units sent to Europe gained much experience and learned modern tactics and techniques of trench warfare. Many Ottoman officers and NCOs were sent to training centers to learn various new weapons, equipment, tactics, and techniques.[350] For example, the assault troop concept (stosstruppen or storm troops) which came to dominate German tactical thinking in the final year of the war was passed on to the Ottoman infantry corps. "Hücum Kıtaatı" or assault detachments[351] were formed and experimented within the 19th Division and, later on, were introduced into the Ottoman military in Palestine.

Similarly, light machine guns and infantry trench-guns were employed by Ottoman infantry companies for the first time in Galicia. They also experienced the administrative and logistical functioning of a modern military. Not surprisingly, both the officers and soldiers perceived the German logistical support as luxurious in comparison to the Ottoman system. For the first time, they received uniforms and equipment when they asked for it and enjoyed it greatly. Unfortunately for the Ottoman military, these valuable experiences and lessons learned were imported too late to be disseminated for the benefit of the entire system. However, the later Turkish nationalist army made good use of these accumulated experiences during the Turkish Independence War.[352]

Another strategic misstep occurred when the Ottoman General Staff appeared to underestimate the importance of the Sinai-Palestine front and the risk of a constantly growing British military presence, which was forming into an expeditionary force while the last strategic reserve was expended irresponsibly on the Caucasus front and in Europe. Most probably, in addition to its inborn myopia to see the strategic picture, the early Ottoman victories at very low cost in the Sinai and the slow British buildup deceived the General Staff. The Sinai-Palestine front was seen as nothing more than a sideshow to draw away the largest possible number of British troops from the European fronts. Thanks to the pipe dream of renewing another Suez Canal assault, the VIII Army Corps remained in the theater and carried out small raids, which maintained high levels of British angst. After the success of a much smaller raid against an outpost at Katya (Katia) on April 23, 1916, the commanding officer Kress von Kressenstein decided to launch a major assault against the British positions around Romani in order to push the enemy back to its original position on the canal. Unfortunately for the Ottomans, the Katya raid alerted the British command which in turn strengthened its positions. Thus, the British easily dealt with the two-day-long Ottoman assault (August 4 and 5) but did not follow up their victory efficaciously.[353]

The British command paid little attention to Ottoman tactical weakness and instead focused on constructing a railway, water pipeline, and other supply facilities that could support a large campaign. The Fourth Army Commander, Cemal Pasha, and von Kress evacuated all of the indefensible forward positions and began to entrench a defensive line between Gazze (Gaza) and Birüs-Sebi (Beersheba). The Ottoman entrenchments and defense works had little depth but were of modern design. However, due to the shortage of barbed wire and entrenchment tools, priority was given to the Gaza fortifications, whereas the large expanse between Gaza and Beersheba was superficially prepared. In March 1917, General Archibald Murray, commander in chief of Egyptian Expeditionary Forces (EEF), at last satisfied with the level of logistics preparation and force buildup, launched his long-awaited offensive targeting Gaza on March 26. Initially, surprise was complete as the Ottoman side, which had grown weary of waiting, saw its forward defense troops easily taken prisoner by British cavalry. But poorly coordinated piecemeal, slow British assaults died down in front of secondary Ottoman positions. An equally uncoordinated Ottoman counterattack the next day failed, but Ottoman flanking movements in the desert forced the British troops to withdraw in safety.[354]

Von Kress improved the fortified positions around Gaza and tried in vain to strengthen his defense line linking Beersheba. Undeterred by his old plan's failure, Murray launched a similar assault (once again paying limited attention to the weak Ottoman defenses between Gaza and Beersheba) on April 14. This time he made use of heavy artillery fires, naval gunfire, aerial bombardment and, for the first time in the Middle East, poisonous gases (against the deep reservations of most of his officers), and even a small tank unit. The Ottoman troops had absolutely no protection against gases but, due to weather conditions or poor delivery, the gas shells (around 2,500 chlorine shells) did no harm to the defenders. Similarly, small numbers of tanks did not alter the situation and fell prey to deadly Ottoman artillery fire. In short, the staunch Ottoman area defense effectively stopped the British assault waves and inflicted heavy casualties.[355]

The disastrous end of the Second Battle of Gaza disappointed the British High Command, and General Murray and other high-ranking officers were replaced immediately. The new commander, General Edmund Allenby, was a notable cavalry officer but was also known to be cautious. So another half a year was spent waiting for the arrival of reinforcements and improving lines of communication and logistics. While the British expeditionary forces in Palestine were undergoing a major transformation and expansion, the Ottoman General Staff turned its attention to another front; Iraq and its imminent collapse.[356]

As already discussed above, the successful end of the Kut al-Amara siege dazzled the Ottoman General Staff, and a spirit of adventurous offensive thinking against Iran and Azerbaijan was revived. The XIII Army Corps (three and a half divisions) was redeployed from the Iraq front to advance into Iran. The order was open-ended; to safeguard the rear of the Sixth Army against possible Russian advance, to clear foreign elements from Iran and conquer as much territory as possible. Enver Pasha and his advisors were convinced that the Iranians would immediately rebel against the Russians and support the Ottoman advance. The forward elements of the expeditionary force crossed into Iran on June 8, 1917. After an inspiring start, the Ottoman advance stopped with the capture of Hamadan on August 9. Despite Enver's assurances, there was no local support (except, oddly, from the Swedish-trained Iranian gendarmerie units) and no rebellion at all. Desultory fighting with the Russians went on while Ottoman soldiers fell easy prey to epidemics (dysentery, cholera, and spotted typhus) caused by malnutrition and lack of efficient medical support. Against these unfavorable conditions and without any meaningful aim, the XIII Army Corps continued to remain in Iran until the collapse of the Iraq front (at which time they were duly called back). The withdrawal was started on February 22, 1917, which was too late.[357]

The Iraqi theater of operations passed through a massive transformation after the humiliation at Kut al-Amara. The new British commander, General Stanley Maude, was a capable officer and received additional divisions (boosting his army to more than 160,000 men) and assets (especially additional riverine flotillas). However, he cautiously waited and nurtured the troop buildup and construction of supply facilities until December 1916 (in a very similar fashion to the logistics buildups on the Sinai-Palestine front). In the meantime, the Ottoman Sixth Army lost half of its combat strength to the Iranian campaign and epidemics, desertion, and various interior security duties further depleted its available cadres. Worse still, there were two strategic avenues of approaches to Baghdad following the riverbeds of the Dicle (Tigris) and Fırat (Euphrates) Rivers. So the remaining elements of the Sixth Army divided into two defense groups in order to cover both approaches, which were a wide distance apart and which offered no chances of mutual support. Luckily Halil Pasha invested more troops in covering the Tigris approach, which Maude would choose to follow. However, Halil emplaced most of the XVIII Army Corps strength on the northern bank (between Falahiya and Rashid) and left only a weak guard force on the southern bank. It was an ideal recipe for disaster. The Ottomans had limited means of water crossing, whereas the British had strong riverine flotillas and bridging equipment, which gave them greater operational mobility. Maude launched a series of relentless attacks between December 14, 1916 and February 20, 1917 against the Ottoman positions in order to develop the situation and weaken the defenders.[358]

After inflicting heavy casualties and fixing the XVIII Army Corps on the north bank, Maude exploited the Ottoman situational weakness by flanking the defense positions in two days from the south bank. The Ottoman units managed to escape from encirclement on February 23, 1917 (in the nick of time), albeit leaving most of their baggage and artillery behind. The XVIII Army Corps had to be reorganized after severe losses in which two division headquarters (including the heroic 45th Division of the Kut siege) and five regiments were disbanded. For a period of time, Halil Pasha toyed with the idea of defending Baghdad at all costs. However, the sheer power of the British was too much for the outnumbered, outgunned, and demoralized Sixth Army units. The city was abandoned and the surviving Ottoman troops took refuge at Cebeli Hamrin after a 15-day-long fighting withdrawal. The British troops entered Baghdad on March 11. In short, Maude turned a tactical breakthrough into a major victory by making full use of his great numerical superiority and enormous resources.[359]

At this point in time, the German General Staff unveiled a surprising project to establish a German-led army group (the so-called Heeres Gruppen Kommando F) in the Middle East. Actually, the idea evolved well before the fall of Baghdad as a reaction to the impasse in the Sinai and the Arab Revolt. According to the German General Staff, Ottoman soldiers (especially the ethnic Turks) were of superior quality but needed equipment and leadership. Moreover, the Germans believed the Ottoman officer corps and military system as a whole was ill-trained and ill-equipped to command and make use of this superior human material. Germany had more than enough trained officers and technical branches to command and control any given Ottoman unit.

Additionally, the Arab Revolt clearly demonstrated ethnic fractures within the fabric of the empire. Germany as a neutral player could easily bridge the fractures and mobilize both sides for the common cause of defeating the entente powers. For these reasons, the German military offered to provide an army group headquarters (composed overall of 65 German staff officers—with the last-minute addition of 9 Ottoman officers) to command and control more than two Ottoman field armies. Additionally, the Germans promised to send a combat support and service support group nicknamed Pasha II[360] (comprised of a light infantry division [reduced to a brigade later on], artillery battalions, signal companies, field hospitals, flak guns, aviation, automobile, railway, and some other detachments). Moreover, the army group would have an independent budget financed mainly by Germany in order to overcome the supply problems that plagued the Ottoman military. Surprisingly, the German General Staff did not bother to consult the Ottoman General Staff (except for some private communications with Enver Pasha), nor the German Military Mission and, instead, relied on the individual input of several German officers, chief among them former Military Attaché to Istanbul, Colonel Otto von Lossow.[361]

Almost all of the Ottoman officers welcomed the German combat support and service support elements but rightly saw the whole project as an insult to themselves and the Ottoman military. Amidst intense criticism and ill feelings, the Army Group F staff, which was christened in Turkish as the Yıldırım (thunderbolt) Army Group, started working under its commanding general, Field Marshal Erich von Falkenhayn. Von Falkenhayn was one of the highest-ranking German generals and a former Prussian Minister of War and a former Chief of General Staff, who reached Istanbul in July 1917. Originally, the Yıldırım Army Group was tasked to reconquer Baghdad, Iraq, and Iran by taking the Sixth and newly formed Seventh Army under its command. However, the situation drastically changed after the enemy concentration against Gaza and Beersheba became much stronger. Instead, the Yıldırım Army Group was rerouted to the Palestine front before finishing its deployment to Aleppo in September 1917 (just before the initiation of Allenby's assault on Gaza).[362]

Von Falkenhayn and the Yıldırım staff encountered immense difficulty and intense opposition (indeed, the overconfidence and arrogance of von Falkenhayn added fuel to Ottoman uneasiness and xenophobia) during the takeover of command responsibility for the Palestine front (the Fourth, Seventh, and Eighth Armies). The previous generalissimo of the region, Büyük Cemal Pasha, was more than obstructive in showing his opposition and blocking each step but, more importantly, the Seventh Army Commander, Mustafa Kemal Pasha, who was highly influential within the Ottoman officer corps, resigned from his post after voicing his criticism and frustration with von Falkenhayn. Unfortunately for the Ottoman military, the Third Battle of Gaza and Beersheba began during this period of slow deployment and infighting among the Ottoman commanders.[363]

Kress von Kressenstein, now the commander of the newly established Eighth Army, adamantly expected the main British assault to come against well-entrenched Gaza (very similar to the previous engagements) and ignored the urgent calls coming from the III Army Corps commander, Colonel İsmet (İnönü) Bey, who was tasked with defending the main water supply center in the town of Beersheba with only a reinforced infantry division and a cavalry screening force. Although there were intelligence reports about a possible massive cavalry-rich flanking attack on the town, von Kress was deceived by a British intelligence ruse into believing that an attack on Gaza was more likely. Allenby, slowly but surely, massed two infantry and two cavalry divisions while conducting a deception operation to convince the Turks that a frontal assault against Gaza was imminent. After a massive bombardment, the well-synchronized attack on Beersheba began on October 31, 1917. The cavalry and other mounted units successfully flanked the Ottoman positions and captured Beersheba's wells intact, while the infantry fixed the defenders. Some elements of the corps headquarters and half of the units managed to escape the closing jaws of the British cavalry (around 1,500 soldiers were taken prisoners). Allenby then turned his attention on Gaza, employing his remaining troops and arsena,l including a large number of heavy artillery groups. The relentless tempo, orchestration, and simultaneity of the British assault effectively dislocated the Ottoman defenders, but they staunchly defended their positions for seven more days. Abandoning Gaza, strong Ottoman rearguards sacrificed themselves in a series of bloody engagements that saved the main group from annihilation. This enabled the Turks to reorganize their forces in a series of temporary defense positions by occupying the Jaffa-Lud-Jerusalem line.[364]

Von Falkenhayn and the Yıldırım staff took over the responsibility of the front during the chaos after the collapse. As a veteran of the European fronts, von Falkenhayn had little faith in the capacity of his field armies to construct a solid area defense without entrenchment materials, engineers, and heavy artillery support. Instead, he decided to delay and wear the enemy down by making use of a series of temporary defensive positions and limited counterattacks. However, his plan to trade space for time while strengthening the Jerusalem defensive perimeter did not work very well. The Ottoman infantry regiments had limited mobility, whereas the British had aerial superiority, strong cavalry, and mechanized units. To make things even worse, locally recruited soldiers began to desert their units at every opportunity, and Arab tribes harassed lines of communication, thereby forcing field commanders to allocate more troops to provide rear area security. The battle for Jerusalem and Jaffa lasted nearly one month (November 16–December 8, 1917). The XX Army Corps bore the full brunt of the enemy attacks and losses reached record levels. Against the opposition of von Falkenhayn, the corps commander, Ali Fuat (Cebesoy) Pasha, evacuated Jerusalem in order to save his corps (then numbering less than 8,000 infantry) and the holy city from total annihilation during the night of December 7–8. The battered Yıldırım Army Group managed to withdraw in a more or less orderly fashion to the Tabsur-Sinya-Cebeli Ektef line at the end of December.[365]

During the winter and spring of 1918, both sides preferred to economize their efforts. Allenby lost most of his experienced infantry battalions, which had to be sent to the western front after the German spring offensive. He once again turned his attention on supply and lines of communication and satisfied himself with several reconnaissance-in-force operations and limited attacks to capture key terrain features. On the Ottoman side, von Falkenhayn was replaced by von Sanders at the end of February. The departure of von Falkenhayn (most of the original German staff also went home with him) validated the bankruptcy of the German General

Staff's project of taking full control of the Ottoman Middle East. Instead of improving the command and control system, the establishment of the Yıldırım Army Group did the opposite and became a heavy burden. Valuable time and assets were lost in the transfer, takeover, settling in, and acclimation process of the German command group. The Pasha II units and detachments arrived too late to have an effect on the outcome of the Gaza and Jerusalem battles. Von Falkenhayn and his staff spent more time bickering with the Turks than leading the combat effort during their brief service of four months (excluding the out-of-theater period).[366]

Von Sanders received definitive orders to defend the remaining portion of Lebanon and Syria at all costs and to keep the lines of communication with Hejaz secure. Under the conditions, it was an impossible mission. He did bring with him the experienced Turkish-German Fifth Army staff from Istanbul, which restored some of the harmony between the allies. The strategic posture of his new command was dismal. The number of combat effectives in his army group was around 40,000, so it was actually the size of a standard army corps (although on paper von Sanders commanded five army corps, two corps equivalent groups, 14 infantry divisions, and a cavalry division, excluding various small formations and militia). After the loss of the large storage facilities near Jerusalem and Gaza and the utter mismanagement of logistics, there were shortages of everything including ammunition, food, fodder, water, and supplies. The overburdened transportation network, which also had to support other fronts (Iraq and Hejaz), simply collapsed from the sheer volume of traffic and as well from the transfer of administrative personnel and civilians.[367]

Von Sanders obediently tried his best. He knew the intricacies of defensive and offensive operations, but his predecessor had recklessly drained the available forces by committing them too early and in piecemeal fashion. This left him with no operational reserve and not enough men to properly man the lines. Moreover, he had little sense of contemporary combat tactics (as they had evolved by 1918) due to the fact that his only combat experience was in the early phases of trench warfare in the confined spaces of the Gallipoli Peninsula. Even though he was a former cavalry officer, he ignored the massive British superiority in cavalry, the use of which was instrumental in breaking the deadlock on the Gaza-Beersheba line. In any case, he had extremely limited means to counter it. Consequently, he ordered his units to defend every centimeter of the line and committed his cavalry not as an operational reserve but to defend the passes in the army's rear area.[368]

Allenby, in contrast to von Sanders, built his strategy around mobility based on cavalry and combined infantry-artillery operations. He conducted a sophisticated deception operation to convince his adversary that the main assault would come, once again, from the Şeria (Jordan) Valley. Instead, Allenby massed five infantry divisions and the Desert Mounted Corps on the western sector near the coastline (establishing a 14 to 1 local superiority). On September 19, 1918, Allenby launched his long-awaited assault, which was destined to become famous as the last great cavalry operation in history. The Ottomans called it the Battle of Nablus, but it is better known today as the Battle of Megiddo (taking the name of the biblical town of Armageddon). Under the protection of massive artillery fire (more than 1,000 shells per minute), highly mobile British colonial infantry easily breached the Ottoman main defense line, which the cavalry then tore through and raced to block the Ottoman lines of retreat. In a single day, the XXII Army Corps ceased to exist as a fighting force. During the following days, Ottoman field commanders, independent of each other, tried in vain to save their respective units under the relentless British cavalry pursuit and pressure. Only half of the units of the Seventh and Eighth Armies made it to the safety of the far bank of the Şeria River, albeit without their baggage and losing most of their artillery.[369]

Even though it became more than obvious that there was no chance of stopping the British advance short of the Aleppo-Taurus Mountains line, von Sanders still decided to defend Damascus with the remnants of the Yıldırım Army Group. It was a fatal decision, and most of the surviving Ottoman units were surrounded and taken prisoner (around 20,000 soldiers) on the way. The ones that made it to Damascus were betrayed by Ali Rıza Pasha (an ethnic Arab better known as Ali Rida al-Rikabi), who was the commander of the central sector of the city defenses. The city surrendered on October 1. The remnants of the Fourth and Seventh Army under the able command of Mustafa Kemal Pasha, who was operating despite the confusion and disorder, fought with determination to retain as much territory as possible until the armistice. He lost Aleppo on October 25 but managed to stop further advances into the Anatolian plains.[370]

Obviously, von Falkenhayn and von Sanders and some other field commanders made serious operational mistakes, but the real culprits behind the collapse of the Palestine-Syria front were Enver Pasha and the German-dominated Ottoman General Staff. Beginning with the Second Battle of Gaza, every field commander on the Palestine front repeatedly asked for reinforcements and for the evacuation of the Medina garrison (which amounted to the strategic abandonment of Arabia). The urgency of the situation became so apparent after the Third Battle of Gaza that even von Falkenhayn (who was an early advocate of the Baghdad project) changed his mind and supported the field commanders. Unfortunately for the empire, Enver Pasha (ever the dreamer) decided to commit the surplus troops made available by the collapse of Russia to reopening the Caucasus front.

The Third Army, which was reinforced with the personnel and weapons of the inactivated Second Army, had more than enough forces to recapture the occupied provinces of eastern Anatolia.[371] The last regular Russian troops either self-disbanded or retreated into Russia very soon after the signing of the Erzurum Armistice Protocol by the opposing army commanders on December 18, 1917. The Armenian National Army and some other self-raised militia groups, which replaced the Russians, were no match for the Ottoman regulars. After much discussion about the wisdom of another offensive operation during the winter, anarchy and atrocities committed in the Armenian-occupied zone against Muslims persuaded the military leaders to act at once. The Third Army launched a two-prong attack from the north and south, liberating Erzincan on February 12, Trabzon on February 25, and Erzurum on March 12, 1918. Vanguard units crossed the frontier of 1914 on March 25. The infamous target of the ill-fated Sarıkamış Campaign fell easily on

April 5. The Third Army crossed the frontier of 1877 at the end of April, whereas a reinforced army corps had already penetrated into Iran. Ever enthusiastic, Enver Pasha then decided to relaunch his Pan-Turkish dream of conquering large tracts of the Caucasus, Iran, and Central Asia at this critical moment instead of stopping and consolidating the territorial gains and sending the surplus troops to reinforce the Palestine front.[372]

Enver's newly raised Army of Islam (in reality only a corps-sized formation including Caucasian volunteer units) marched into Transcaucasia as the Ninth Army was activated on June 7, 1918, to conquer as much Iranian territory as it could from the Russians. Surprisingly, selected Ottoman officers from the Yıldırım Army Group were assigned to these new armies and the German General Staff, alarmed by Enver's Pan-Turkish designs, pulled a reinforced battalion from the German Asia Corps and redeployed it to Georgia (in order to protect German interests in the Caucasus) immediately before the start of Allenby's massive assault. The elite 15th Division (its combat effectives were more numerous than any of the corps at the Syrian front) was also assigned and transported from Romania to the Caucasus theater of operation. The Ninth Army conquered Tabriz on August 23, and the Caucasian Islam Army captured Baku after a series of small but bloody engagements on September 15. Derbent fell on October 7 while the Ottoman political leadership was requesting an armisticem and Petrovsk was conquered on November 8—a full week after the signing of an armistice with the victorious Entente Powers.[373]

The collapse of the Palestine-Syria front and Bulgaria effectively ended any chance for the Ottoman Empire to continue the war. The ruling triumvirate of the CUP unwillingly handed over leadership to a neutral government council, and the Mudros Armistice Agreement was hurriedly signed on October 30, 1918. In opposition to its Austrian and Bulgarian allies and its ardent enemy Russia, the Ottoman army, although seriously beaten, was still in the field. Its units were passing through a massive reorganization while some of them were still fighting in Azerbaijan, Dagestan, and Iran. Even the harsh clauses of the armistice and disarmament did not destroy its organization and solidarity. The Ottoman military lived on to fight a new war. In less than a year, it was reborn as a nationalist army of liberation. A new multifront war broke out, this time against invaders bent on seizing the Ottoman Empire's core Anatolian regions. After an exhausting war climaxed by the liberation of İzmir on September 9, 1922, the army victoriously ended the Turkish Independence War. The former Ottoman military under its new name, the Turkish Nationalist Army, recovered its honor by making use of its centuries-old institutional knowledge, seasoned combat commanders, and its veteran rank and file.

An overall evaluation of the Ottoman military in World War I is very difficult and complex because of a general lack of unbiased academic studies about it. The collapse of the empire and the birth of new nations blurred an accurate understanding of its performance. For years, the nationalist historians of the former Ottoman subject nations distorted historical facts to accommodate the demands of their newly created nationalist histories. Similarly, the Turkish Republic paid more attention to its victorious Independence War and to the famously successful Gallipoli Campaign at the expense of all other campaigns. Many of the veterans of the war preferred to keep silent about their achievements and failures. This was especially true of most of the officers of the new armies of Syria, Iraq, and Jordan, where it was not politically wise to talk, let alone, to write about their experiences. For the others, either they preferred not to remember their traumatic experiences (especially if they had spent some time in prisoner of war camps), or they found few avid readers or listeners as an audience.

Ten years of sustained intensive combat left a population unwilling to come to grips with the memory of war. Only one person—the Chief of the General Staff of the Turkish Republican Armed Forces, Field Marshal Fevzi Çakmak, actively supported and actually wrote down his experiences. By the mid-1930s, renewed interest in these events emerged and a brief period of publishing and lessons-learned discussions erupted. Unfortunately, World War II cooled down this brief period of intellectual activity, and the Cold War effectively ended almost all interest in military history and affairs in Turkey.

The Ottoman army as the military arm of a preindustrial multiethnic peasant-based empire encountered huge difficulties accommodating itself to the demands of a multifront global war, which was at the same time long and attritional. When the disastrous effects of the Balkan Wars are taken into account, the immense problems that the Ottoman military had to face become more apparent. In truth, officers and the rank and file fought a bit more than 10 years with little interruption, beginning with the Ottoman-Italian War of 1911 and ending with the Turkish Independence War of 1919–1922.

We can easily identify the insurmountable problems facing the Ottomans. The Ottoman Empire was less prepared than any of the belligerents to face the economic consequences and logistical demands of a global war which was not realized by its leaders. Poor lines of communication effectively negated the geographic advantages of interior lines. Worse still, the British and Russian blockade ended the coastal shipping trade on which the empire's trade depended. This caused nearly two times more personnel and ten times more pack animals to be allocated in sustaining the notoriously deficient lines of communication. The blockade was also instrumental in starving millions of Ottoman citizens (although the empire was rated as an agricultural country, it was unable to feed its citizens in normal years). The theater commanders had to compete with each other to get priority for the use of the empire's single-track railway and operational trains (usually less than 100 available at any time). Moreover, even this single-track railway was not fully operable. The line was interrupted in two places (small but crucial interruptions) and after the Rayak Station another gauge was used. Consequently, all sorts of supplies and passengers had to be loaded and unloaded three times between Istanbul and its final destination. The Second Army lost nearly half of its combat effectives during its deployment from Thrace to the Caucasus front. Similarly, poor and corrupt logistics continued to plague the military. More food and fodder were lost during transportation and storage and at the black markets than were actually consumed by troops and military animals. A notoriously bad medical system was instrumental in the loss of 10 to

11 times more soldiers than were lost in actual combat. For example, the Third Army suffered around 14,000 killed in action and deaths due to wounds between 1915 and 1918, but more than 110,000 of its military personnel fell prey to epidemics (spotted typhus, dysentery, cholera, and the like), simple diseases, and unhealed combat wounds.[374]

The Ottoman administration proved unable to deal with other well-known structural problems in addition to logistics and transportation. Once again, the internal security of the empire was largely neglected. Instead of taking extra security measures to deal with the impending Armenian and Arab rebellions, the administration decided to transform gendarmerie and other law enforcement agencies into line infantry or irregular combat units, due to the urgent requests coming from the General Staff. So not surprisingly, ever-present banditry and tribal unrest reached record levels, thanks to the security vacuum and increasing numbers of deserters. The field commanders had to allocate a sizable percentage of their combat effectives in order to fight against rebels and bandits during most of the campaigns (especially on the Eastern, Syrian, and Iraqi fronts). The internal security problems became so threatening that the General Staff had to mobilize new divisions to deal with them. But even employing these new divisions turned out to be another type of stop-gap measure. The law and order was broken everywhere except in a few big cities, and all sorts of illegal bands continued to roam behind the lines, attacking military and civilian targets at every opportunity until the end of the war.[375]

Of the major branches, the cavalry corps remained weakest in quality and quantity. Overall, only three regular cavalry divisions and very small numbers of independent regular cavalry detachments could be raised throughout the war. The short-lived tribal cavalry and other volunteer regiments were unable to perform the simplest tasks and proved to be anything but military assets. Reconnaissance, screening, vanguard, and rearguard duties, in short, the standard cavalry missions, remained an enormous problem for Ottoman commanders throughout the war. And regrettably, the grandsons of the legendary Ottoman timariot cavalry found themselves powerless against the last large cavalry action at Megiddo in 1918.

The ever-problematic recruitment and mobilization of the empire's citizens improved significantly in comparison with previous war periods. Even though the burden of military service continued to fall almost entirely on the ethnic Turkish peasant population, the Ottoman military of 1914 was far more representative of the empire's population than in any other period. Clearly, the shocking impact of world war exposed the ethnic, religious, and regional fractures of an archaic and pre-industrial sociocultural system of empire and expanded the limits of integration. But amazingly, the military forces of the Ottoman Empire turned out to be sturdier and more enduring than the Austro-Hungarian Empire and the Russian Empire. Of the empire's minorities, only the Armenians tried to evade conscription and to desert at the very first opportunity (especially after the relocation decree).

A review of the Arab officers and rank and file is important in understanding the relative effectiveness of the Ottoman conscription system and the issue of loyalty throughout the war. As indicated earlier, the Arab population of the empire vehemently opposed conscription for decades, a trend which was carried forward into the World War I period. From the very beginning of the war, British authorities orchestrated a propaganda campaign to win hearts and minds of the Arab rank and file. Indeed, British intelligence even established relations with the secret Arab nationalist organizations well before the war. Famously, it recruited many Orientalist scholars or adventurers, who happened to know bits and pieces about the Middle East, into a newly created intelligence establishment better known as the Arab Bureau in Cairo. Like many European diplomats and travelers, the bureau was too quick to look for sources of local uneasiness as a clear sign of Arab nationalism. Moreover, these eager but novice intelligence experts immediately came under the influence of Arab nationalist circles in Egypt and forecast that the Arab rank and file would not shed blood for the Ottoman cause. They predicted the Arabs would rebel at the first instance. In fact, one of the most important reasons behind the British negotiations with Sharif Hussein of Hejaz was to incite the Arab rank and file within the Ottoman military to rebel or at least refuse to obey orders.[376] Interestingly, their cleverly designed propaganda convinced the British authorities themselves more than the originally targeted Arab population. Except for a few thousand tribesmen, most Arabs remained loyal to the empire during the traumatic events of the times.

The long-awaited Arab crisis started at the beginning of 1917 when all combatant nations were beginning to develop war weariness. To the surprise of most observers, Ottoman soldiers as a whole, and Arabs particularly, instead of openly resisting the Ottoman high command, simply chose desertion. For understandable reasons, the number of deserters increased if the respective unit was near to its home garrison. Most deserters took refuge in their hometowns and only a minority escaped to the enemy side. There were no collective outbreaks of indiscipline like the Russian Revolution-type outbursts of rebellions or the Italian- and French-type mutinies.[377]

The British authorities decided to make use of Ottoman prisoners of war to man Sharif Hussein's rebel army and to perform intelligence missions. This policy gained importance after hopes for a collapse of the Ottoman military and large numbers of deserters did not materialize. Prisoners were immediately grouped not according to rank, as the law of war clauses provided, but according to their nationality. The Arab officers were a prime target and were isolated from Turkish officers. The officers and soldiers, who showed a willingness to collaborate, gained material advantages, whereas the others were punished. When taking into account the high mortality rate of Ottoman prisoners (7.1 %) in comparison with Austro-Hungarian or German POWs (2.9% and 2.6%, respectively), the choice of collaboration was actually a choice between life and death. According to British statistics, a total of 10,742 Ottoman POWs out of 150,041 died for various reasons—chief among them was pellagra disease, which was caused by a niacin deficiency.[378] Nearly all of Sharif Hussein's prominent commanders were ex-prisoners like Jafar al Askari, Mavlud Mukhlis, İbrahim al Husseini, and Cemil al Madfai. The Arab legion of Sharif Hussein was also manned by ex-prisoners and Bedouin fighters.[379]

The S. S. Pandua and S. S. Kara Deniz affair is a good example, showing the efforts of British authorities to enlist Arab prisoners as well as showing its failure. Beginning in

June 1916, British intelligence officers desperately asked the Viceroy of India to find volunteers for Sharif Hussein's army from the ranks of Arab prisoners. They especially asked for officers and artillery experts. After much delay and hesitation, 300 prisoners were selected from different camps in India and sent to the Hejaz on board the S. S. Pandua and S. S. Kara Deniz. Interestingly, except for a handful of individuals, none of these so-called volunteers was willing to fight for Sharif Hussein against his Turkish comrades, and the British authorities tried to keep this fact a secret. A small rebellion took place when the secret was leaked just before the start of the voyage. The ships arrived off the Hejaz coast at the end of November 1916, and negotiations with prisoners started immediately thereafter. Only four prisoners (a police officer, a journalist, and two medical doctors) volunteered for the Sharif's cause after a week-long effort to enlist them. Almost to a man, they preferred to remain prisoners rather than be part of Sharif's army, which was also lavishly provisioned and supplied in comparison to the Ottoman army.[380]

Reciprocally, the Ottoman military tried to enlist Muslim prisoners of war. Unfortunately, there is not enough data available at the present time to draw a concrete picture. But we do know that the Ottomans and Germans tried their best to encourage the defection of Muslim prisoners and use them for propaganda purposes against their countrymen. It is known that a number of ex-POWs—officers and soldiers from the French and British armies who were of Algerian, Tunisian, Egyptian, and Indian origins—were purposefully assigned by the Ottomans to problematic Ottoman units and the Palestine-Syria front. These ex-prisoners whose homelands had been occupied by European colonial powers influenced the Arab rank and file greatly.[381]

The situation of the Arab officers is far more interesting. Using a sample of statistical data, a better understanding emerges regarding the fallacy of commonly held opinions about Arab officers. In order to highlight generational differences, data from two typical Military Academy graduating classes, the class of 1903 (1319) and the class of 1914.C (1330.C), are presented.[382] From the class of 1903, 740 officers were commissioned, of which 109 came from Arab provinces. Fourteen Arab officers had left the military by 1914 for a variety of reasons (chief among them was being killed in action), so 16 percent of officers from the class of 1903 were Arab officers. From the class of 1914.C, 295 officers were commissioned, of which 75 came from Arab provinces. The density of Arab officers raised to 25 percent, a remarkable increase in 10 years.[383] Of the 95 serving Arab officers of the class of 1903, only 2 deserted, 75 of them were either killed during the war or resigned at the end of the war, 18 of them took part in the Turkish Independence War, and 14 of them continued to serve in the Republican Turkish military. Of the 75 serving Arab officers of the class of 1914.C, only 1 deserted, 42 were either killed during the war or resigned at the end of the war, and 32 took part in the Turkish Independence War, to later serve in the Republican Turkish military.

The statistics tell a completely different story than the ones most commonly told today; the Ottoman Arab officers did not desert *en masse*; instead most of them fought until the very end. If we pay attention to the positions of the sample classes, the reality becomes more obvious. The class of 1903 officers were middle ranking officers from battalion level to brigade level in the war. The class of 1914.C officers were junior officers and most of them ended up as company commanders during the war. These two classes, therefore, experienced the full horror of the war by remaining in frontline assignments. However, except for a few individuals, none deserted the Ottoman military, and they loyally fought until the very end. Most surprisingly, a remarkable percentage of them took part in the Turkish Independence War, which was in many ways a nationalist war for the survival of the Turkish nation. Most of these veterans of the Independence War continued their careers in the newly established Republican military.

Several individual cases help us to understand the success or failure of the Ottoman methods to manage the crisis of disloyalty. The most famous incident in this sense was the desertion of a prominent figure of the Arab rebellion, Lieutenant Mehmed Şerif el Faruki (better known as Muhammad Sharif al Faruqi). He was a member of the secret Arab organization *al-Ahd* before the war. He and some of his friends planned to rebel or to escape to join Sharif Hüssein of Mecca. But Faruki was arrested and sent to the First Army in İstanbul. He was then assigned to the Gallipoli (Çanakkale) front as a platoon leader, but he deserted to the British on August 20, 1915, after spending 10 days in his unit.[384]

Obviously, sending a well-known Arab nationalist to the frontline might seem more than naïve, but it worked with most of the implicated Arab nationalists like Lieutenant Colonel Yasin al Hashimi (Yasin Hilmi in Ottoman documents) from Baghdad. Yasin was the real leader of the Arab nationalist officers in Syria. He was widely known as the chief plotter behind the scheme, that Faruki was part of, to support an Allied landing in İskenderun (Alexanderatta) Bay, by inciting the rebellion of whole Syrian units. The administration decided to send him and his division to the European front rather than to punish him and his fellow conspirators.[385] He was promoted to major general rank due to his valiant and meritorious service at the Galicia front. In the final stages of the war, he was the commander of VIII Army Corps and was seriously wounded by the Arab volunteers of Sherif Faisal's army during the final retreat to Damascus. After a brief recovery, he served as the Chief of General Staff of the short-lived Faisal's Syria government. Interestingly, he applied for a job in the Turkish army in late 1921, but his application was declined. Yasin enrolled in the new Iraqi army in 1922 and served in various capacities, including prime minister.[386]

Even though the majority of Ottoman soldiers did not defect, desertion remained a significant problem throughout the war, especially after the year 1916. Poor supply and medical services, coupled with fighting long years on far away fronts, took their toll. Harsh military punishments did little to deter desertion, and hundreds of deserters were executed after brief court-martials, often in front of their units or the civilian public, as an example. However, when numbers reached the 300,000 level during 1917, the administration had no other choice than to lighten the punishments (by the summer of 1918 the figure amounted to 500,000). Most often soldiers deserted their units when passing near their respective hometowns. For example, the elite 19th Division lost around 4,800 of its soldiers (from an initial strength of some 13,000 men) to desertion during its long journey from Galicia to Aleppo.

To make things worse, many deserters who could not return back to their hometowns joined criminal gangs and waged terror within the country. As the war progressed, these gangs became one of the most important problems in eastern Anatolia and Syria. Surprisingly, many officers began to show sympathy for the deserters, especially after 1917, when the chances of victory faded to nil and the futility of fighting far from Anatolia became more apparent.[387]

From our perspective, the most important question of the war deals with the overall performance of the Ottoman officer corps. The Ottoman military reforms specifically tried to raise highly trained officers, who would be equal to their European counterparts in every respect. Their performance then also reflects the importance and the relative success of the centuries-long reforms.

Even though the strategic leadership of the Ottoman generals seems to have failed the test of war, in reality, none really had any chance of affecting the strategic decision-making process. All of the Ottoman generals were sidelined by Enver Pasha and the German-led Ottoman General Staff. Any opposition to their plans and orders was taken seriously and punished harshly. Many talented and experienced generals lost their jobs or were reassigned to prestigious but passive posts. By silencing all high-ranking Ottoman generals, Enver Pasha and his German advisors then encountered difficulty grasping the strategic situation from their luxurious offices in Istanbul, far away from any theaters of war. The German General Staff easily influenced them to prioritize the immediate interests of Germany. Many strategic mistakes and flawed assumptions came out of this sheltered existence and absolute deference to the German General Staff. For example, the Ottoman General Staff did not foresee a multifront war and committed a critical mistake by concentrating most of its available divisions around Istanbul and the Straits, which played an important role in the collapse of the Iraq front and the disastrous ending of the Sarıkamış Campaign. Moreover, they were proved equally incapable of dealing with the social and economic consequences of the war.

The performance of the officer corps at the operational level is more complex. Enver Pasha created enormous opportunities for young General Staff officers by purging a large number of the older officers and rankers. These staff officers were highly trained, good in military doctrine and staff work but, in terms of career development, they sadly lacked professional experience and expertise in commanding units larger than regiments.[388] Worse still, they gained field experience mostly during counterinsurgency operations and had only brief conventional experiences during the disastrous Balkan Wars. They learned their trade the hard way by learning from their mistakes. They suffered difficulty in commanding and controlling large formations, and their ignorance of defensive-offensive relationships and templates was more than apparent, especially during the complex maneuvers of the Sarıkamış Campaign. After 1915, a new generation of successful battlefield commanders emerged from the cauldron of war, chief among them were Mustafa Kemal (Atatürk) Pasha, Fevzi (Çakmak) Pasha, Kazım (Karabekir) Pasha, Fahrettin (Türkkan) Pasha, İsmet (İnönü) Pasha, Ali Fuat (Cebesoy) Pasha, Yakup Şevki (Subaşı) Pasha, Ali İhsan (Sabis) Pasha, and Refet (Bele). Regrettably, the Ottoman military was unable to make full use of the talents of these successful commanders because of the general decline in the quality and quantity of the troops available after 1916 and the preferential assignment of German officers to important positions.

At the tactical level, Ottoman officers showed a rare blend of enormous motivation, high morale, and physical endurance, even through the worst possible moments. The Ottoman military was an officers' army. Even though Ottoman peasant soldiers (especially Turks) were sturdy, stoic to all kinds of hardship, and highly regarded by foreign observers, they needed constant leadership, orientation, and role models to imitate.[389] This created a "lead from the front" mentality, which often resulted in more officer casualties than necessary. Most of the Ottoman officers preferred small-unit tactics and techniques rather than large-scale operations because of their counterinsurgency experiences. Their contributions to the war effort became even more important during the difficult days of 1918, when the empire's dispirited soldiers only did their duties under the sheer discipline and close control of their officers. Unfortunately, the real contributions of Ottoman officers in battle remain largely forgotten. The available Turkish sources have been generally silent about the individual unit commanders. Even in the very detailed Turkish official military history series, it is nearly impossible to find the names of junior unit commanders, let alone understand their contributions. Western sources are also instrumental in continuing this error. Most of the western observers had high regard for Turkish soldiers but had a very low regard for the Turkish officer corps. And thanks to their psychological, racist, or colonial mentalities, they highlighted the role of individual German officers at the expense of Ottoman officers. Unfortunately, the resulting constructed myth that categorizes Ottoman officers as incompetent and corrupt is still in existence today.

Conclusion

Without doubt, the Ottoman military remained the backbone of the empire throughout its lifespan. It is very difficult to envisage the empire without taking into consideration its military. However, as a state it neither "lived for war" nor for "a near perfect military society" as some have suggested. The Ottoman Empire was one of the greatest and longest-lasting empires of the world and, more precisely, it was the last Mediterranean empire. At its zenith in the seventeenth century, the empire occupied an area that stretched from the southern and eastern shores of the Mediterranean to the Caspian Sea, and from Poland in the north to the Indian Ocean in the south. Even though certain provinces like Hungary, the Danubean Principalities, and the Caucasian and Iranian frontier regions experienced almost continuous warfare, most of the other provinces enjoyed long periods of peace and prosperity, thanks to the efficiency of the Ottoman bureaucracy. In fact, it is entirely proper to label the empire as more bureaucratic than military. However, the military is credited with being the first to introduce modern bureaucratic methods and techniques (such as tax and census registers, detailed bookkeeping, and archives), regular and fair taxation, well-designed law codes, and complex networks of transportation and communication (not only in the Middle East but in Europe as well).

Against the overly simplistic and negative views, the Ottoman military played decisive roles in the formation and evolution of both European and Middle Eastern military art and science. Arguably, the Ottomans initiated the revival of an infantry-based standing army (the first since the fall of Rome) well before any in Europe. The elite Janissary regiments, which were the first modern light infantry units of the world, introduced for the first time standard uniforms with rank and branch tabs, state-owned weapons and arsenals, military bands, and social security benefits for the deceased and elderly. Likewise, land-based seasonally mobilized timariot cavalry, which provided their own horses, weapons, and equipment, were the first modern light cavalry troops. Musters and reviews, which ensured minimum standards of dress, equipment, and detailed inspection, were Ottoman standard operating procedure decades before their employment in Europe. In terms of logistics, the Ottoman soldiers had better rations, better medical and sanitation arrangements, and qualitatively and quantitatively better supply. In order to provide high levels of logistics superiority, the empire employed thousands of men and organized them into self-sufficient corps. The system worked well most of the time, thanks to the efficient financial bureaucracy, which managed to extract taxes and resources from the population without provoking opposition and destroying the local economy.

Because of these pioneering initiatives and many victorious campaigns, European generals, politicians, and even philosophers like Machiavelli and Montesquieu developed a grudging admiration for the Ottoman military.

The greatest achievement of the Ottoman Empire was building an efficient bureaucracy and military, based on the principles of conservatism, pragmatism, elasticity, and tolerance. Instead of imposing a clean break with the past, the empire had a tendency to preserve or transform the existing systems into systems of its own. The empire was tolerant in accommodating, to a certain extent, the assimilation of various cultures and ethnic groups into its patrimonial realm. The Christian military classes of the Balkan countries are very good examples in this sense. By using various methods of coercion, offering incentives, and preserving the privileges of these classes, the empire easily conquered and kept the Balkans for centuries. Local notables were bonded closely to the empire and its military through an elaborate system of entitlements (as well as by the allocation and redistribution of resources). While the empire's military elite included a disproportional number of ethnic Turks, the Ottoman military emerged as the engine in the creation of a multiethnic, multireligious, and multicultural empire.

Similarly, its inherent pragmatism and adaptability were instrumental in enabling the free borrowing and learning of useful technology and methods from its enemies. Of course, methods of pragmatism, coexistence, and cohabitation were not always successful, which was why the empire had to send strong expeditionary forces time and again to reassert its power as well as maintain strong garrisons on distant frontiers. In addition to well-trained, well-armed and well-led troops, this unique synthesis was the key to the success of the Ottoman military against enemies (real or potential) on all sides.

Even the catastrophic Treaty of Karlowitz did not hamper the military might of the empire. Although it lost important provinces and border defense systems, it survived for another two centuries (outliving, in fact, most of its ardent enemies) by transforming its military to adapt to developments in the west. Obviously, the transformation, adaptation, and reform processes were laden with inconsistencies, contradictions, corruption, and half-hearted efforts, but these attempts eventually led to the creation of a professional officer corps and a sturdy standing army. Most contemporary observers and modern scholars tend to exaggerate the impact of the contending Great Powers and balance of power system for the longevity of the empire, whereas ignoring or underestimating the contributions of the Ottoman military, which fought not only against foreign adversaries on two fronts most of the time, but also against ever-present internal security threats.

The profound dilemma for the Ottoman military was that the reforms required to resist western expansion and insure the integrity of the empire turned out to be a double-edged sword, requiring enormous financial resources and provoking intense domestic and foreign hostility, thereby weakening further the entire state. Moreover, and unfortunately for the empire, most of the reformers were ill equipped to understand the relationship between the failures of military reforms and the overall inadequacy of the politico-administrative structure, agrarian economy, and social fabric.

At the start of the twentieth century, the Ottoman military was in the midst of a dramatic transformation in which its frustrated officers (who had learned their trade from decades' long counterinsurgency operations against nationalist Balkan guerrillas) dethroned the sultan and tried to transform completely the empire along modern European lines. This eleventh-hour attempt fell victim to a series of disastrous wars. Although its endurance in the face of World War I deserves praise, in the end, the Ottoman military failed the acid test of total warfare.

In November 1918, the Ottoman military did not quit the war, as Lenin remarked about the Russian army, by 'voting with its feet'. Unlike Austro-Hungary which literally disintegrated, or Germany which had to surrender immediately its war fleet and heavy weapons and suffered huge difficulties to contain its now rebellious army and navy, the Ottoman military managed to reserve its discipline, cohesion, and surviving divisions (most of which were composed of ethnic Turks from the Anatolian heartland).

Even though the armistice obligated the Ottoman military to demobilize its combat units quickly, the actual demobilization proceeded slowly and came to a full stop with the start of a new war—this time to save what was remained of the empire in 1919–1921—against Greek, French, Italian, and Armenian forces. A new generation of combat-tested battlefield commanders, under the supreme leadership of Mustafa Kemal Pasha, found a willing audience within the ranks of the postwar Ottoman military. Most of the surviving Ottoman officers (including reserves and retirees), as well as the conscripts, were drawn to the nationalist cause. Almost overnight, regiment after regiment abandoned the Istanbul-based government and joined the forces of liberation. By changing its loyalty from the sultan to the Turkish nationalist cause, the Ottoman military also transformed itself from the Sultan's army to the new Turkish Nationalist Army well before the successful end of the Independence War.

Notes

Preface

1. Charles Messenger, *Reader's Guide to Military History* (London: Fitzroy Dearborn Publishers, 2001), xv–xx.

Chapter 1

1. Halil İnalcık, "The Rise of Ottoman Historiography," in *From Empire to Republic: Essays on Ottoman and Turkish Social History* (İstanbul: The Isis Press, 1995), 13–14, 17, 21, 23, 25; Colin Imber, *The Ottoman Empire 1300–1481* (İstanbul: The Isis Press, 1990), 1–13; William L. Langer and Robert P. Blake, "The Rise of the Ottoman Turks and Its Historical Background," *The American Historical Review* vol. 37, no. 3, April 1932, 468–475; Caroline Finkel, *Osman's Dream: The Story of the Ottoman Empire 1300–1923* (London: John Murray, 2005), 5; Daniel Goffman, *The Ottoman Empire and Early Modern Europe* (Cambridge: Cambridge University Press, 2002), 27.

2. Uzi Baram and Lynda Carroll, "The Future of the Ottoman Past," in (ed.) Uzi Baram and Lynda Carroll, *A Historical Archaeology of the Ottoman Empire: Breaking New Ground*, (New York: Kluwer Academic Publishers, 2002), 3–13, 20–21; Jacques Lefort, "Tableau de la Bithynie au XIIIe Si'ecle," in (ed.) Elizabeth A. Zachariadou, *Ottoman Emirate 1300–1389*, (Heraklion: Crete University Press, 1993), 101–117; İlber Ortaylı, "Menkıbe," in *Osmanlı Devleti'nin Kuruluşu: Efsaneler ve Gerçekler*, (Ankara: İmge Kitabevi, 2004), 18; For a modest but an inspiring attempt *see* Great Arab Revolt Project, February 14, 2008, http://www.jordan1914-18archaeology.org.

3. Goffman, *Ottoman Empire and Early Modern Europe*, 11–12.

4. Friar Giovanni DiPlano Carpini, *The Story of the Mongols Whom We Call the Tartars*, (ed.) Erik Hildinger, (Boston: Branden Publishing, 1996), 72–74; Laszlo Torday, *Mounted Archers: The Beginnings of Central Asian History*, (Durham: The Durham Academic Press, 1997), 11; John Masson Smith Jr., "Mongol Society and Military in the Middle East: Antecedents and Adaptations," in (ed.) Yaacov Lev, *War and Society in the Eastern Mediterranean 7th–15th Centuries*, (Leiden: E.J. Brill, 1997), 250–251.

5. Torday, *Mounted Archers*, 80, 187; Carpini (Hildinger), *Story of the Mongols*, 74.

6. Carpini (Hildinger), *Story of the Mongols*, 74–76; Smith, "Mongol Society and Military in the Middle East," 249, 251–253; May noted that the encirclement tactics of nomadic armies originated in mass hunting practices. *See* Timothy May, "The Training of an Inner Asian Nomad Army in the Pre-Modern Period" *The Journal of Military History*, vol. 70, no. 3, July 2006, 620.

7. Torday, *Mounted Archers*, 88–89, 191; Carpini (Hildinger), *Story of the Mongols*, 71–72; Boris Y. Vladimirtsov, *Moğolların İçtimai Teşkilatı: Moğol Göçebe Feodalizmi*, (trans.) Abdülkadir İnan, (Ankara: Türk Tarih Kurumu, 1995), 155–166.

8. Ünal Yücel, *Türk Okçuluğu*, (Ankara: Atatürk Kültür Merkezi Yayınları, 1998), 5, 21; Alaaddin Ata Melik Cüveyni, *Tarih-i Cihan Güşa*, (trans.) Mürsel Öztürk, (Ankara: Kültür Bakanlığı Yayınları, 1998), 88–89; May, "Training of an Inner Asian Nomad Army," 618–623, 630–632; Vladimirtsov, *Moğolların İçtimai Teşkilatı*, 169.

9. Denis Sinor, "Introduction: The Concept of Inner Asia," in (ed.) Denis Sinor, *The Cambridge History of Early Inner Asia*, (Cambridge: Cambridge University Press, 1990), 10, 13.

10. Smith, "Mongol Society and Military in the Middle East," 254–259, 262–266.

11. The Seljukid or Seljuks were a Turcoman dynasty that arose in the early 1030s. By 1055, Tuğrul Bey forced the Abbasid Caliph in Baghdad to recognize his rule.

12. Walter Emil Kaegi Jr., "The Contribution of Archery to the Turkish Conquest of Anatolia," *Speculum*, vol. 39, no. 1, January 1964, 96–108.

13. Feridun Dirimtekin, *Malazgirt Meydan Muharebesi: 26 Ağustos 1017*, (İstanbul: Askeri Matbaa, 1936), 30–48; Speros Vryonis Jr., *The Decline of Medieval Hellenism in Asia Minor and the Process of Islamization from the Eleventh through the Fifteenth Century*, (Berkeley: University of California Press, 1971), 96–103; Speros Vryonis Jr., "The Greek and Arabic Sources on the Battle of Mantzikert, 1071 A.D.," in (ed.) Speros Vryonis Jr., *Byzantine Studies: Essays on the Slavic World and the Eleventh Century*, (New Rochelle: Aristide D. Caratzas, 1992), 125–136; Erdoğan Merçil, "Türkçe Selçukname'ye Göre Malazgirt Savaşı,"*İstanbul Üniversitesi Tarih Enstitüsü Dergisi*, no. 2, October 1971, 19–49.

14. Hugh Kennedy, *The Armies of the Caliphs: Military and Society in the Early Islamic State*, (London: Routledge, 2001), 1–9, 13–14; Fred McGraw Donner, *The Early Islamic Conquests*, (Princeton: Princeton University Press, 1981), 221–250; Patricia Crone, "The Pay of Client Soldiers in the Umayyad Period," *Der Islam*, vol. 80, no. 2, 2003, 285–292; Clifford Edmond Bosworth, "Recruitment, Muster and Review in Medieval Islamic Armies" in (ed.) V. J. Parry and M. E. Yapp, *War, Technology and Society in the Middle East*, (London: Oxford University Press, 1975), 59–61.

15. David Ayalon, "Preliminary Remarks on the Mamluk Military Institution in Islam," in (ed.) V. J. Parry and M. E. Yapp, *War, Technology and Society in the Middle East*, (London: Oxford University Press, 1975), 44–48.

16. Osman Turan, "İkta," *İslam Ansiklopedisi*, vol. 5/2, (İstanbul: Milli Eğitim Bakanlığı Yayınları, 1993), 949–952.

17. Kennedy, *Armies of the Caliphs*, 26–34, 45–47, 96; Crone, "Pay of Client Soldiers in the Umayyad Period," 293–300; David Ayalon, "The Military Reforms of Caliph Al Mutasim: Their Background and Consequences," in David Ayalon, *Islam and the Abode of War*, (Aldershot: Variorum, 1994), 2–4; Yaacov Lev, "Regime, Army and Society in Medieval Egypt, 9th–12th Centuries," in (ed.) Yaacov Lev, *War and Society in the Eastern Mediterranean 7th–15th Centuries*, (Leiden: E.J. Brill, 1997), 129.

18. Kennedy, *Armies of the Caliphs*, 104–105; Ayalon, "Preliminary Remarks on the Mamluk Military Institution in Islam," 49–50, 56–57; Jere L. Bacharach, "African Military Slaves in the Medieval Middle East: The Cases of Iraq (869–955) and Egypt (868–1171)," *International Journal of Middle East Studies*, vol. 13, no. 4, November 1981, 471–472, 489–491.

19. Kennedy, *Armies of the Caliphs*, 36–37.

20. Matthew S. Gordon, *The Breaking of a Thousand Swords: A History of the Turkish Military of Samarra (A.H. 200–275/ 815–889 C.E.)*, (New York: State University of New York Press, 2001), 1, 24–27, 55; Clifford Edmond Bosworth, *The Ghaznavids: Their Empire in Afghanistan and Eastern Iran 994–1040*, (New Delhi: Munshiram Monoharhal Publishers, 1992), 99–100; Ayalon, "Military Reforms of Caliph Al Mutasim," 4–39; Bacharach, "African Military Slaves in the Medieval Middle East," 476–477.

21. Peter B. Golden, "The Karakhanids and Early Islam," in (ed.) Denis Sinor, *The Cambridge History of Early Inner Asia*, (Cambridge: Cambridge University Press, 1990), 347; Kennedy, *Armies of the Caliphs*, 118– 122; Gordon, *Breaking of a Thousand Swords*, 12, 50.

22. Gordon, *Breaking of a Thousand Swords*, 62; Lev, "Regime, Army and Society in Medieval Egypt," 134, 146.

23. Kennedy, *Armies of the Caliphs*, 100.

24. Bosworth, *The Ghaznavids*, 100; Bacharach, "African Military Slaves in the Medieval Middle East," 477–482.

25. Hassanein Rabie, "The Training of the Mamluk Faris," in (ed.) V. J. Parry and M. E. Yapp, *War, Technology and Society in the Middle East*, (London: Oxford University Press, 1975), 153–162; May, "Training of an Inner Asian Nomad Army," 624–626.

26. Gordon, *Breaking of a Thousand Swords*, 80–104; Kennedy, *Armies of the Caliphs*, 141; Lev, "Regime, Army and Society in Medieval Egypt," 150–151; David Ayalon, "Mamluk: Military Slavery in Egypt and Syria," in David Ayalon, *Islam and the Abode of War*, (Aldershot: Variorum, 1994), 1–19; Rabie, "Training of the Mamluk Faris," 162–163.

27. M. Fuad Köprülü, *Bizans Müesseselerinin Osmanlı Müesseselerine Tesiri*, (İstanbul: Ötüken Neşriyat, 1981), passim.; Herbert Adams Gibbons, *Foundation of the Ottoman Empire*, (London: Frank Cass, 1968), passim.

28. Some Byzantinists belittle the impact of Manzikert battle. See Jean-Claude Cheynet, "Manzikert: Un Désastre Militaire?," *Byzantion*, vol. 50, 1980, 410–438.

29. John Haldon, *Warfare, State and Society in the Byzantine World, 565–1204*, (London: UCL Press, 1999), passim.; Ralph-Johannes Lilie, "Twelfth-Century Byzantine and Turkish States," in (ed.) Anthony Bryer and Michael Ursinus, *Manzikert to Lepanto: The Byzantine World and the Turks 1071–1571*, (Amsterdam: Adolf M. Hakkert, 1991), 35–52.

30. Istvan Vasary, *Cumans and Tatars: Oriental Military in the Pre-Ottoman Balkans, 1185–1365*, (Cambridge: Cambridge University Press, 2005), 4–11, 32–33, 67–68, 114–117; Rudi Paul Lindner, *Nomads and Ottomans in Medieval Anatolia*, (Bloomington: Indiana University Press, 1983), 12; Paul Wittek, *Menteşe Beyliği: 13–15nci Asırda Garbi Küçük Asya Tarihine Ait Tetkik*, [Turkish translation of German original *Das Fürstentum Mentesche*], (trans.) Orhan Şaik Gökyay, (Ankara: Türk Tarih Kurumu Basımevi, 1986), 9–10, 12–13.

31. Donald M. Nicol, *Bizans'ın Son Yüzyılları (1261–1453)*, [Turkish translation of English original *The Last Centuries of Byzantium 1261–1453*], (İstanbul: Tarih Vakfı Yurt Yayınları, 1999), 27–28.

32. Nicol, *Bizans'ın Son Yüzyılları (1261–1453)*, 87–91, 116, 133–134; Vryonis, *Decline of Medieval Hellenism in Asia Minor*, 4, 234; Halil İnalcık, "The Rise of Turcoman Maritime Principalities in Anatolia, Byzantium and Crusades" in *The Middle East and the Balkans under the Ottoman Empire: Essays on Economy and Society*, (Bloomington: Indiana University Turkish Studies, 1993), 311–312; Keith R. Hopwood, "The Byzantine-Turkish Frontier c1250–1300," in (ed.) M. Kohbach, G. Prochaska-Eisl and C. Romer, *Acta Viennensia Ottomanica*, (Vienna: Im Selbrstverlag des Instıtuts fur Orientalistik, 1999), 158–159.

33. Aşıkpaşazade Derviş Ahmed, *Aşıkpaşaoğlu Tarihi*, (ed.) Nihal Atsız, (İstanbul: Milli Eğitim Bakanlığı Yayınları, 1992), 39; Oruç, *Oruç Beğ Tarihi*, (ed.) Nihal Atsız, (İstanbul: Kervan Kitapçılık, 1972), 23.

34. Aşıkpaşazade (Atsız), *Aşıkpaşaoğlu Tarihi*, 29; Mehmet Neşri, *Neşri Tarihi*, vol. 1, (ed.) M. Altay Köymen, (Ankara: Kültür Bakanlığı Yayınları, 1983), 62.

35. Nicol, *Bizans'ın Son Yüzyılları (1261–1453)*, 134–135; Vryonis, "Decline of Medieval Hellenism in Asia Minor," 441; Charles M. Brand, "The Turkish Element in Byzantium, Eleventh-Twelfth Centuries," *Dumbarton Oaks Papers*, vol. 43, 1989, 2; M. Tayyib

Gökbilgin, *Rumeli'de Yürükler, Tatarlar ve Evlad-ı Fatihan*, (İstanbul: Osman Yalçın Matbaası, 1957), 9–12.

36. Claude Cahen, *Pre-Ottoman Turkey: A General Survey of the Material and Spiritual Culture and History 1071–1330*, (London: Sidgwick & Jackson, 1968), 230–232; Vryonis, "Decline of Medieval Hellenism in Asia Minor," 234; Hopwood, "Byzantine-Turkish Frontier c1250–1300," 153–154.

37. Cahen, *Pre-Ottoman Turkey*, 231; Haldon, *Warfare, State and Society in the Byzantine World, 565–1204*, 183–189.

38. Brand, "Turkish Element in Byzantium, Eleventh-Twelfth Centuries," 1–25.

39. Köprülü, *Bizans Müesseselerinin Osmanlı Müesseselerine Tesiri*, 145, 226.

40. Cemal Kafadar, *Between Two Worlds: The Construction of the Ottoman State*, (Berkeley: University of California Press, 1995), 119, 134; Donald Quataert, *The Ottoman Empire 1700–1922*, 2nd Edition, (Cambridge: Cambridge University Press, 2005), 13, 17.

41. Kafadar, *Between Two Worlds*, 2.

42. Mükrimin Halil Yinanç, "Ertuğrul Gazi," *İslam Ansiklopedisi*, vol. 4, (İstanbul: Milli Eğitim Bakanlığı Yayınları, 1993), 328–337.

43. Yaşar Yücel, *XIII. ve XV. Yüzyıllar Kuzey-Batı Anadolu Tarihi: Çobanoğulları ve Candaroğulları Beylikleri*, (Ankara: Türk Tarih Kurumu Basımevi, 1980), 43; M. Fuad Köprülü, *Osmanlı İmparatorluğu'nun Kuruluşu*, (Ankara: Başnur Matbaası, 1972), 86, 132.

44. Goffman, *Ottoman Empire and Early Modern Europe*, 34; Quataert, *Ottoman Empire 1700–1922*, 13–15.

45. Osman Turan, "Anatolia in the Period of the Seljuks and the Beyliks," in (ed.) P. M. Holt, Ann K. S. Lambton and Bernard Lewis, *The Cambridge History of Islam*, vol. 1, (Cambridge: Cambridge University Press, 1970), 233, 248–253; Halil İnalcık, "Osman Ghazi's Siege of Nicaea and the Battle of Bapheus," in Halil İnalcık, *Essays in Ottoman History*, (İstanbul: Eren Yayıncılık, 1998), 59–60; Lindner, *Nomads and Ottomans in Medieval Anatolia*, 10; Kafadar, *Between Two Worlds*, 5–6.

46. Lindner, *Nomads and Ottomans in Medieval Anatolia*, 13–16; Langer and Blake, "Rise of the Ottoman Turks and Its Historical Background," 493–494; Speros Vryonis Jr., "Nomadization and Islamization in Asia Minor," *Dumbarton Oaks Papers*, vol. 29, 1975, 46–47; Vryonis *Decline of Medieval Hellenism in Asia Minor*, 76–77.

47. Yücel, *XIII. ve XV. Yüzyıllar Kuzey-Batı Anadolu Tarihi*, 48–49.

48. Himmet Akın, *Aydın Oğulları Tarihi Hakkında Bir Araştırma*, (Ankara: Ankara Üniversitesi Yayınları, 1968), 45–48; İnalcık, "Rise of Turcoman Maritime Principalities," 313–320; Nicol, *Bizans'ın Son Yüzyılları (1261–1453)*, 185–186.

49. Lindner, *Nomads and Ottomans in Medieval Anatolia*, 26–27; Nicol, *Bizans'ın Son Yüzyılları (1261–1453)*, 137–142; Mustafa Çetin Varlık, *Germiyanoğulları Tarihi (1300–1429)*, (Ankara: Ankara Üniversitesi Yayınları, 1974), 39.

50. Colin Imber, "Othman I." in (ed.) P. Bearman, Th. Bianquis, C. E. Bosworth, E. van Donzel and W. P. Heinrichs, *Encyclopaedia of Islam*, 2nd Edition, vol. 8; (Leiden: E.J. Brill, 2008), online edition.

51. Lindner, *Nomads and Ottomans in Medieval Anatolia*, 21–23; Peter F. Sugar, *Southeastern Europe under Ottoman Rule, 1354–1804*, (Seattle: University of Washington Press, 1977), 15.

52. Aşıkpaşazade (Atsız), *Aşıkpaşaoğlu Tarihi*, 15, 18, 20; Neşri (Köymen), *Neşri Tarihi*, 39–40, 63–64; Kafadar, *Between Two Worlds*, 123–124, 127–128.

53. Vryonis, "Nomadization and Islamization in Asia Minor," 47.

54. İnalcık, "Osman Ghazi's Siege of Nicaea and the Battle of Bapheus,", 67–78; Lindner, *Nomads and Ottomans in Medieval Anatolia*, 25–26; Nicol, *Bizans'ın Son Yüzyılları (1261–1453)*, 135–136; Neşri (Köymen), *Neşri Tarihi*, 56.
55. Imber, *Ottoman Empire 1300–1481*, 19.
56. Neşri (Köymen), *Neşri Tarihi*, 57–58; Köprülü, *Osmanlı İmparatorluğu'nun Kuruluşu*, 45, 93, 109–110; Kafadar, *Between Two Worlds*, 61, 125; Feridun M. Emecen, "Tavaif-i Mülukdan Osmanlılaşmaya," *İlk Osmanlılar ve Batı Anadolu Beylikler Dünyası*, (İstanbul: Kitabevi Yatınları, 2003), 18; Halil İnalcık, "The Ottoman State: Economy and Society, 1300–1600" in (ed.) Halil İnalcık and Donald Quataert, *An Economic and Social History of the Ottoman Empire, 1300–1914*, (Cambridge: Cambridge University Press, 1994), 31.
57. Lindner, *Nomads and Ottomans in Medieval Anatolia*, 15, 18.
58. Köprülü, *Osmanlı İmparatorluğu'nun Kuruluşu*, 118, 153–158; G. G. Arnakis, "Futuwwa Traditions in the Ottoman Empire Akhis, Bektashi Dervishes and Craftsmen," *Journal of Near Eastern Studies*, vol. 12, no. 4, October 1953, 232–247; Franz Taeschner, "İslam Ortaçağında Fütüvvet Teşkilatı," *İstanbul Üniversitesi İktisat Fakültesi Mecmuası*, vol. 15, no. 1–4, 1953–1954, 3–22; Langer and Blake, "Rise of the Ottoman Turks and Its Historical Background," 500–503.
59. Lindner, *Nomads and Ottomans in Medieval Anatolia*, 6–7, 10, 29–31.
60. Goffman, *Ottoman Empire and Early Modern Europe*, 228; Linda T. Darling, "Contested Territory: Ottoman Holy War in Comparative Context," *Studia Islamica*, no. 91, 2000, 137, 157–158.
61. Wittek and Köprülü saw the whole conflict from the perspectives of holy war *see* Paul Wittek, *The Rise of the Ottoman Empire: Studies on the History of Turkey, 13th–15th Centuries*, (London: Routledge, 2002), passim.; M. Fuad Köprülü, *Osmanlı İmparatorluğu'nun Kuruluşu*, (Ankara: Başnur Matbaası, 1972), passim. For the English translation see *The Origins of the Ottoman Empire*, (ed.) Garry Leiser, (Albany: State University of New York Press, 1992); Lindner ignored the importance of religion on the conflict *see* Lindner, *Nomads and Ottomans in Medieval Anatolia*, 2, 35; For general evaluation of Gazi thesis *see* Ronald C. Jennings, "Some Thoughts on the Gazi Thesis," in Ronald C. Jennings, *Studies on Ottoman Social History in the Sixteenth and Seventeenth Centuries*, (İstanbul: Isis Press, 1999), 719–726.
62. Darling, "Contested Territory," 133–137; Kafadar, *Between Two Worlds*, 79–80; Feridun M. Emecen, "Gazaya Dair: XIV. Yüzyıl Kaynakları Arasında Bir Gezinti," *İlk Osmanlılar ve Batı Anadolu Beylikler Dünyası*, (İstanbul: Kitabevi Yayınları, 2003), 75–85.
63. Kafadar, *Between Two Worlds*, 56, 62, 65, 144; Haldon, *Warfare, State and Society in the Byzantine World, 565–1204*, 31–33; Darling, "Contested Territory," 139–154; Köprülü, *Osmanlı İmparatorluğu'nun Kuruluşu*, 146–151; Anthony Bryer, "Han Turali Rides Again," *Byzantine and Modern Greek Studies*, vol. 11, 1987, 193–206.
64. Ahmet Yaşar Ocak, "Osmanlı Devleti'nin Kuruluşunda Dervişlerin Rolü," in *Osmanlı Devleti'nin Kuruluşu: Efsaneler ve Gerçekler*, (Ankara: İmge Kitabevi, 2004), 75–89; Iréne Mélikoff, "L'origine Sociale des Premiers Ottomans," in (ed.) Elizabeth A. Zachariadou, *Ottoman Emirate 1300–1389*, (Heraklion: Crete University Press, 1993); Kafadar, *Between Two Worlds*, 74, 128–129, 133.
65. Varlık, *Germiyanoğulları Tarihi (1300–1429)*, 32–33, 40; Akın, *Aydın Oğulları Tarihi Hakkında Bir Araştırma*, 6, 16; Emecen, "Tavaif-i Mülukdan Osmanlılaşmaya," 19.
66. Kafadar, *Between Two Worlds*, 9, 15–16, 89; Lindner, *Nomads and Ottomans in Medieval Anatolia*, 9, 33; İsenbike Togan, "İç Asya'dan, Orta Asya'dan Türkiye'ye Bir Bağlantı ve Uzanış," in *Osmanlı Devleti'nin Kuruluşu: Efsaneler ve Gerçekler*, (Ankara: İmge Kitabevi, 2004), 70.

67. Aşıkpaşazade (Atsız), *Aşıkpaşaoğlu Tarihi*, 35, 50; Imber, *Ottoman Empire 1300–1481*, 20; it is nearly impossible to get some details about early Ottoman siege operations. Wittek's examination of the Ottoman chronicles about a certain siege operation against a castle is showing clearly the inherent problems. See Paul Wittek, "The Taking of Aydos Castle: A Ghazi Legend and Its Transformation," in (ed.) George Makdisi, *Arabic and Islamic Studies in Honor of A. R. Gibb*, (Leiden: E.J. Brill, 1965), 662–672.

68. Aşıkpaşazade (Atsız), *Aşıkpaşaoğlu Tarihi*, 26–28, 33–34, 41–42; Imber, *Ottoman Empire 1300–1481*, 21.

69. Aşıkpaşazade (Atsız), *Aşıkpaşaoğlu Tarihi*, 15.

70. Altay Köymen, *Alp Arslan ve Zamanı*, vol. 2, (Ankara: Ankara Üniversitesi DTCF Basımevi, 1967), 251–252, 255; Köprülü, *Osmanlı İmparatorluğu'nun Kuruluşu*, 100–101, 139–140.

71. Feridun M. Emecen, "Osmanlılar ve Türkmen Beylikleri (1350–1450)," *İlk Osmanlılar ve Batı Anadolu Beylikler Dünyası*, (İstanbul: Kitabevi Yayınları, 2003), 58–59.

72. Aşıkpaşazade (Atsız), *Aşıkpaşaoğlu Tarihi*, 40–41; Oruç (Atsız), *Oruç Beğ Tarihi*, 34; Halime Doğru, *Osmanlı İmparatorluğunda Yaya-Müsellem-Taycı Teşkilatı: XV. ve XVI. Yüzyılda Sultanönü Sancağı*, (İstanbul: Eren Yayıncılık, 1990), 2–7; İsmail Hakkı Uzunçarşılı, *Osmanlı Tarihi*, vol. 1, (Ankara: Türk Tarih Kurumu, 1995), 127–128; Nazlı Esim Mergen, *The Yaya and Müsellem Corps in the Ottoman Empire*, (Ankara: Bilkent University Unpublished M.A. Thesis, 2001), 1–29; Köprülü, *Osmanlı İmparatorluğu'nun Kuruluşu*, 49; According some documents and legends Ottomans borrowed the distinctive white bonnet from Aydınıds. See Akın, *Aydın Oğulları Tarihi Hakkında Bir Araştırma*, 49.

73. Doğru, *Osmanlı İmparatorluğunda Yaya-Müsellem-Taycı Teşkilatı*, 8.

74. Mergen, *Yaya and Müsellem Corps*, 31–37, 50–56; Doğru, *Osmanlı İmparatorluğunda Yaya-Müsellem-Taycı Teşkilatı*, 40–41.

75. Doğru, *Osmanlı İmparatorluğunda Yaya-Müsellem-Taycı Teşkilatı*, 11–13, 145–146.

76. Köprülü, *Bizans Müesseselerinin Osmanlı Müesseselerine Tesiri*, 102–106, 111, 113, 126; İsmail Hakkı Uzunçarşılı, *Anadolu Beylikleri ve Akkoyunlu, Karakoyunlu Devleti*, (Ankara: Türk Tarih Kurumu Basımevi, 1937), 72–73; Varlık, *Germiyanoğulları Tarihi (1300–1429)*, 101–105.

77. Neşri (Köymen), *Neşri Tarihi*, 59, 76.

78. Oruç (Atsız), *Oruç Beğ Tarihi*, 32–33.

79. Ömer Lütfi Barkan, "Timar," *İslam Ansiklopedisi*, vol. 5/2, (İstanbul: Milli Eğitim Bakanlığı Yayınları, 1993), 287, 293–296.

80. Köprülü, *Osmanlı İmparatorluğu'nun Kuruluşu*, 181–182, 122–123.

81. Emecen, "Osmanlılar ve Türkmen Beylikleri (1350–1450)," 60.

82. J. A. B. Palmer, "The Origins of the Janissaries," *Bulletin of the John Rylands Library*, vol. 35, no. 2, March 1953, 454–455; A similar institution Bahadır was also known by the Turks but early Ottomans preferred to use Nöker term. Carl Max Kortepeter, "The Origins and Nature of Turkish Power," in Carl Max Kortepeter, *The Ottoman Turks: Nomad Kingdom to World Empire*, (İstanbul: Isis Press, 1991), 22.

83. Vladimirtsov, *Moğolların İçtimai Teşkilatı*, 133–146.

84. David Ayalon, "From Ayyubids to Mamluks," in David Ayalon, *Islam and the Abode of War*, (Aldershot: Variorum, 1994), 44.

85. Aşıkpaşazade (Atsız), *Aşıkpaşaoğlu Tarihi*, 51–52; Oruç (Atsız), *Oruç Beğ Tarihi*, 41–42; Palmer, "Origins of the Janissaries," 458–464, 468–475; Elizabeth Zachariadou, "The Conquest of Adrianople by he Turks," in *Romania and the Turks (c.1300–c.1500)*, (London: Variorum Reprints, 1985), XII/211–217.

86. Palmer, "Origins of the Janissaries," 449–452; V. L. Ménage, "Some Notes on the Devshirme," *Bulletin of the School of Oriental and African Studies*, vol. 29, part 1, 1966, 72–78.

87. İsmail Hakkı Uzunçarşılı, *Osmanlı Devleti Teşkilatından Kapukulu Ocakları*, vol. 1, (Ankara: Türk Tarih Kurumu Basımevi, 1988), 5–12.

88. Glabas's sermon is clearly showing that Devşirme was common at least in the year 1395. *See* Speros Vryonis Jr., "Isidore Glabas and the Turkish Devshirme," *Speculum*, vol. 31, no. 3, July 1956, 435–438.

89. Vryonis, *Decline of Medieval Hellenism in Asia Minor*, 175.

90. Vassilis Demetriades, "Some Thoughts on the Origins of the Devsirme," in (ed.) Elizabeth A. Zachariadou, *Ottoman Emirate 1300–1389*, (Heraklion: Crete University Press, 1993), 23–33; Uzunçarşılı, *Osmanlı Devleti Teşkilatından Kapukulu Ocakları*, vol. 1, 13–17; Palmer, "Origins of the Janissaries," 464–468.

91. Ménage, "Some Notes on the Devshirme," 64–72; V. L. Ménage, "Sidelights on the Devshirme from Idris and Saduddin," *Bulletin of the School of Oriental and African Studies*, vol. 18, part 1, 1956, 181–183.

92. Palmer, "Origins of the Janissaries," 455–457.

93. İnalcık, "Ottoman State," 13–14; Goffman, *Ottoman Empire and Early Modern Europe*, 39; Rossitsa Gradeva, "Administrative System and Provincial Government in the Central Balkan Territories of the Ottoman Empire," in Rossitsa Gradeva, *Rumeli Under the Ottomans, 15th–18th Centuries: Institutions and Communities*, (İstanbul: The Isis Press, 2004), 25–28; G. Leiser, "Malkoč-oghulları," in (ed.) P. Bearman, Th. Bianquis, C. E. Bosworth, E. van Donzel and W. P. Heinrichs, *Encyclopaedia of Islam*, 2nd Edition, vol. 7; (Leiden: E.J. Brill, 2008), online edition.

94. Emecen, "Osmanlılar ve Türkmen Beylikleri (1350–1450)," 57.

95. İnalcık, "Rise of Turcoman Maritime Principalities," 310, 325.

96. Konstantin Mihailović, *Memoirs of a Janissary*, (trans.) Benjamin Stolz, (Ann Arbor: The University of Michigan, 1975), 165–167; Agostino Pertusi, *İstanbul'un Fethi: Çağdaşların Tanıklığı*, vol. 1, (Turkish translation of the Italian original *La Caduta di Constantinopoli: Le Testimonianze dei Contemporanei)*, (trans.) Mahmut H. Şakiroğlu, (İstanbul: İstanbul Fetih Cemiyeti, 2004), 105–106.

97. İsmail Hakkı Uzunçarşılı, "Azab," *İslam Ansiklopedisi*, vol. 2/1, (İstanbul: Milli Eğitim Bakanlığı Yayınları, 1993), 82–83; Rahmi Egemen and Hayri Aytepe, *Türk Silahlı Kuvvetleri Tarihi*, vol. 3, section 1, (Ankara: Genelkurmay Basımevi, 1964), 228–230.

98. Aşıkpaşazade (Atsız), *Aşıkpaşaoğlu Tarihi*, 43–44; Neşri (Köymen), *Neşri Tarihi*, 82, 86–87; Elizabeth A. Zachariadou, "The Emirate of Karasi and That of the Ottomans: Two Rival States" in (ed.) Elizabeth A. Zachariadou, *Ottoman Emirate 1300–1389*, (Heraklion: Crete University Press, 1993), 225–236; Kate Fleet, "Early Turkish Naval Activities," *Oriento Moderno*, vol. 20, no. 1, 2001, 129–138; Emecen, "Tavaif-i Mülukdan Osmanlılaşmaya," 22; Feridun M. Emecen, "Siyasi ve Jeopolitik Dinamikler Hakkında Bazı Mülahazalar (1300–1389)," *İlk Osmanlılar ve Batı Anadolu Beylikler Dünyası*, (İstanbul: Kitabevi Yatınları, 2003), 31; Kafadar, *Between Two Worlds*, 138; Uzunçarşılı, *Osmanlı Tarihi*, , vol. 1, 123–124.

99. Nicol, *Bizans'ın Son Yüzyılları (1261–1453)*, 183–187, 212–214, 217, 234, 253, 255, 258; Nicolae Jorga, *Osmanlı İmparatorluğu Tarihi*, [Turkish translation of German original *Geschichte des Osmanischen Reiches*], vol. 1, (trans.) Nilüfer Epçeli, (İstanbul: Yeditepe Yayınevi, 2005), 166, 168, 172–176, 178–183, 186–189; Emecen, "Siyasi ve Jeopolitik Dinamikler Hakkında Bazı Mülahazalar (1300–1389)," 32; Halil İnalcık, "The Emergence of the Ottomans," in (ed.) P. M. Holt, Ann K. S. Lambton and Bernard Lewis, *The Cambridge History of Islam*, vol. 1, (Cambridge: Cambridge University Press, 1970), 274

100. Nicolas Oikonomides, "The Turks in Europe (1305–13) and the Serbs in Asia Minor," in (ed.) Elizabeth A. Zachariadou, *Ottoman Emirate 1300–1389*, (Heraklion: Crete University Press, 1993), 160–165; Nicol, *Bizans'ın Son Yüzyılları (1261–1453)*, 145–149.

101. Nicolas Oikonomides, "From Soldiers of Fortune to Gazi Warriors: The Tzympe Affair," in (ed.) Colin Heywood and Colin Imber, *Studies in Ottoman History in Honour to Professor V. L. Ménage*, (İstanbul: Isis Press, 1994), 239–247; Nicol, *Bizans'ın Son Yüzyılları (1261–1453)*, 258–259, 284–285, 300–301; İnalcık, "Emergence of the Ottomans," 274; John V. A. Fine, *The Late Medieval Balkans: A Critical Survey from the Late Twelfth Century to the Ottoman Conquest*, (Ann Arbor: The University of Michigan Press, 1994), 325–326.

102. Aşıkpaşazade (Atsız), *Aşıkpaşaoğlu Tarihi*, 48–50, 56–57, 65–66; Neşri (Köymen), *Neşri Tarihi*, 87–90, 104; Gökbilgin, *Rumeli'de Yürükler, Tatarlar ve Evlad-ı Fatihan*, 12–29; Uzunçarşılı, *Osmanlı Tarihi*, vol. 1, 157–166; Gradeva, "Administrative System and Provincial Government," 23–24, 28–39.

103. Sugar, *Southeastern Europe under Ottoman Rule, 1354–1804*, 3.

104. Solakzade Mehmed Hemdeni Çelebi, *Solakzade Tarihi*, vol. 1, (ed.) Vahid Çabuk, (Ankara: Kültür Bakanlığı Yayınları, 1989), 43–44; Fine, *Late Medieval Balkans*, 379–380; Jorga, *Osmanlı İmparatorluğu Tarihi*, vol. 1, 226–227; Imber, *Ottoman Empire 1300–1481*, 29; Nicol, *Bizans'ın Son Yüzyılları (1261–1453)*, 294–295; Ottoman chronicles' accounts are very confusing. They are mentioning not one battle but two different battles in the same location in 1364 and 1371 respectively. See Aşıkpaşazade (Atsız), *Aşıkpaşaoğlu Tarihi*, 53; Oruç (Atsız), *Oruç Beğ Tarihi*, 43–44; Neşri (Köymen), *Neşri Tarihi*, 99–100; Uzunçarşılı, *Osmanlı Tarihi*, vol. 1, 167–172.

105. Aşıkpaşazade (Atsız), *Aşıkpaşaoğlu Tarihi*, 65–66; Neşri (Köymen), *Neşri Tarihi*, 104; These strategic routes are Serrae-Monastir-Ohrid, Salonika-Tesselia-Morae, Marica-Sofia-Niš-Belgrade and Tunja-Karnobud-Dobruca.

106. İnalcık, "Emergence of the Ottomans," 275–276.

107. Kate Fleet, "The Treaty of 1387 Between Murad I and the Genoese," *Bulletin of the School of Oriental and African Studies*, vol. 56, no. 1, 1993, 16–32.

108. Goffman, *Ottoman Empire and Early Modern Europe*, 91.

109. Sugar, *Southeastern Europe under Ottoman Rule, 1354–1804*, 16–17; Halil İnalcık, "On the Social Structure of the Ottoman Empire: Paradigms and Research,"*From Empire to Republic: Essays on Ottoman and Turkish Social History*, (İstanbul: The Isis Press, 1995), 43.

110. Kafadar, *Between Two Worlds*, 142.

111. İnalcık, "Social Structure of the Ottoman Empire," 41; Halil İnalcık, "The Çifthane System and Peasant Taxation,"*From Empire to Republic: Essays on Ottoman and Turkish Social History*, (İstanbul: The Isis Press, 1995), 74–75, 82.

112. Aşıkpaşazade (Atsız), *Aşıkpaşaoğlu Tarihi*, 43–44, 53, 55; Neşri (Köymen), *Neşri Tarihi*, 82, 102.

113. Emecen, "Siyasi ve Jeopolitik Dinamikler Hakkında Bazı Mülahazalar (1300–1389)," 33–34; İnalcık, "Emergence of the Ottomans," 276–277; Stanford J. Shaw, *History of the Ottoman Empire and Modern Turkey*, vol. 1, (Cambridge: Cambridge University Press, 1976), 20–21; Sugar, *Southeastern Europe under Ottoman Rule, 1354–1804*, 15.

114. Emecen, "Osmanlılar ve Türkmen Beylikleri (1350–1450)," 54–55, 58.

115. Neşri (Köymen), *Neşri Tarihi*, 141.

116. Presentation of the statistics in Egemen-İşgüven is very problematic but due to the lack of sources I based my calculations on these statistics. Rahmi Egemen and Hazım İşgüven, *Türk

Silahlı Kuvvetleri Tarihi Osmanlı Devri: Birinci Kosova Meydan Muharebesi, vol. 3, section 1 annex, (Ankara: Genelkurmay Basımevi, 1987),, 51–58; Neşri (Köymen), *Neşri Tarihi*, 131–134.

117. Egemen and İşgüven, *Türk Silahlı Kuvvetleri Tarihi Osmanlı Devri*, 46–48, 73–76; Ahmet Muhtar Paşa, *Muharebat-ı Meşhure-i Osmaniye Albümü*, (ed.) Kemal Yılmaz, (İstanbul: Harp Akademileri Basımevi, 1971), 46–51; Mükerrem, *Türk Ordusunun Eski Seferlerinden Bir İmha Muharebesi Kosova 1389*, (İstanbul: Askeri Matbaa, 1931), 16–18; Necati Tacan, *Batı Türklerinin (Osmanlılar) Teessüs ve İstila Devirlerinde Harb Güdemi Usulleri*, (İstanbul: Askeri Matbaa, 1936), 5, 12, 19.

118. Neşri (Köymen), *Neşri Tarihi*, 141–144; Oruç (Atsız), *Oruç Beğ Tarihi*, 46–47; Solakzade (Çabuk), *Solakzade Tarihi*, vol. 1, 59–69; Egemen and İşgüven, *Türk Silahlı Kuvvetleri Tarihi Osmanlı Devri*, 60–69; Mükerrem, *Türk Ordusunun Eski Seferlerinden Bir İmha Muharebesi Kosova 1389*, 22–28 Kafadar, *Between Two Worlds*, 56, 62, 65, 144; Haldon, *Warfare, State and Society in the Byzantine World, 565–1204*, 31–33; Darling, "Contested Territory," 139–154; Köprülü, *Osmanlı İmparatorluğu'nun Kuruluşu*, 146–151; Anthony Bryer, "Han Turali Rides Again," *Byzantine and Modern Greek Studies*, vol. 11, 1987, 193–206.

119. Stephen W. Reinert, "A Byzantine Source on the Battle of Bileća (?) and Kosovo Polje: Kydones' Letters 396 and 398 Reconsidered," in (ed.) Colin Heywood and Colin Imber, *Studies in Ottoman History in Honour to Professor V. L. Ménage*, (İstanbul: Isis Press, 1994), 253–254; Fine, *Late Medieval Balkans*, 410–411.

120. Imber, *Ottoman Empire 1300–1481*, 37–45; Reinert, "Byzantine Source on the Battle of Bileća (?) and Kosovo Polje," 269–272; Fine, *Late Medieval Balkans*, 412–424.

121. Even though outdated Atiya's book is still the most complete account of Nicopolis *see* Aziz Suryal Atiya, *The Crusade of Nicopolis*, (London: Methuen & Co., 1934), passim.; Uzunçarşılı, *Osmanlı Tarihi*, vol. 1, 279–288.

122. Lindner, *Nomads and Ottomans in Medieval Anatolia*, 51, 111–113.

123. Ahmet Muhtar, *Muharebat-ı Meşhure-i Osmaniye Albümü*, 9–12; Aşıkpaşazade (Atsız), *Aşıkpaşaoğlu Tarihi*, 69; Neşri (Köymen), *Neşri Tarihi*, 167; Solakzade (Çabuk), *Solakzade Tarihi*, vol. 1, 94–104; Ömer Halis, *Timurun Anadolu Seferi ve Ankara Savaşı*, (İstanbul: Askeri Matbaa, 1934), passim.; Uzunçarşılı, *Osmanlı Tarihi*, vol. 1, 301–315.

124. Dimitris J. Kastritsis, "Religious Affiliations and Political Alliances in the Ottoman Succession Wars of 1402–1413," *Medieval Encounters*, vol. 13, no. 2, June 2007, 223–242; Jorga, *Osmanlı İmparatorluğu Tarihi*, vol. 1, 293–319; Imber, *Ottoman Empire 1300–1481*, 55–73; Fine, *Late Medieval Balkans*, 499–509; Uzunçarşılı, *Osmanlı Tarihi*, vol. 1, 325–345; Elizabeth Zachariadou, "The Ottoman World," in (ed.) Christopher Allmand, *The New Cambridge Medieval History*, vol. 7, (Cambridge: Cambridge University Press, 1998), 812–86; Janos Bak, "Hungary: Crown and Estates," in (ed.) Christopher Allmand, *The New Cambridge Medieval History*, vol. 7, (Cambridge: Cambridge University Press, 1998), 708–709; İnalcık, "Emergence of the Ottomans," 285–286.

125. Imber, *Ottoman Empire 1300–1481*, 75–90; Uzunçarşılı, *Osmanlı Tarihi*, vol. 1, 347–374; Zachariadou, "Ottoman World," 817–819; Halil İnalcık, "Mehemmed I" in (ed.) P. Bearman, Th. Bianquis, C. E. Bosworth, E. van Donzel and W. P. Heinrichs, *Encyclopaedia of Islam*, 2nd Edition, vol. 7; (Leiden: E.J. Brill, 2008), online edition

126. Imber, *Ottoman Empire 1300–1481*, 91–132; Uzunçarşılı, *Osmanlı Tarihi*, vol. 1, 375–433; Zachariadou, "Ottoman World," 819–820, 822–824.

127. Solakzade (Çabuk), *Solakzade Tarihi*, vol. 1, 237–240; Imber, *Ottoman Empire 1300–1481*, 133–134; Tacan, *Batı Türklerinin (Osmanlılar) Teessüs ve İstila Devirlerinde Harb Güdemi Usulleri*, 36.

128. Emanuel Constantin Antoche, "Du Tabor de Jan Žižka et de Jean Hunyadi au Tabur Çengi des Armées Ottomanes: L'art Militaire Hussite en Europe Orientale, au Proche et au Moyen Orient (XV-XVII siécles)," *Turcica*, vol. 36, 2004, 104–106, 110–116. [The authors express their appreciation to Lt. Col. Cyrille Frayer for the translation of the article.]; Stephen Turnbull, *The Hussites Wars*, (Oxford: Osprey Publishing, 2004), 9, 19, 23–34; Halil İnalcık, "The Socio-Political Effects of the Diffusion of Fire-arms in the Middle East," in (ed.) V. J. Parry and M. E. Yapp, *War, Technology and Society in the Middle East*, (London: Oxford University Press, 1975), 204; Bert S. Hall, *Weapons and Warfare in Renaissance Europe*. (Baltimore: Johns Hopkins University Press, 1997), 107–114.

129. Solakzade (Çabuk), *Solakzade Tarihi*, vol. 1, 245–250; Tacan, *Batı Türklerinin (Osmanlılar) Teessüs ve İstila Devirlerinde Harb Güdemi Usulleri*, 36–38; Imber, *Ottoman Empire 1300–1481*, 140–141.

130. Tacan, *Batı Türklerinin (Osmanlılar) Teessüs ve İstila Devirlerinde Harb Güdemi Usulleri*, 39.

Chapter 2

1. Oruç, *Oruç Beğ Tarihi*, (ed.) Nihal Atsız, (İstanbul: Kervan Kitapçılık, 1972), 97–98; Solakzade Mehmed Hemdemi, *Solakzade Tarihi*, (ed.) Vahid Çabuk, (Ankara: Kültür Bakanlığı Yayınları, 1989), 241–243; Halil İnalcık, "İstanbul'un Fethinden Önce Fatih Sultan Mehmed" in *Fatih Devri Üzerinde Tetkikler ve Vesikalar*, vol. 1, 3rd Edition, (Ankara: Türk Tarih Kurumu Basımevi, 1995), 92–07; Colin Imber, *The Ottoman Empire 1300–1481*, (İstanbul: The Isis Press, 1990), 136–138; İsmail Hakkı Uzunçarşılı, *Osmanlı Tarihi*, vol. 1, (Ankara: Türk Tarih Kurumu Basımevi, 1995), 439–441.

2. İnalcık, "İstanbul'un Fethinden Önce Fatih Sultan Mehmed," 113–114, 118; Kritovoulos, *History of Mehmed the Conqueror*, (trans.) Charles T. Riggs, (Princeton: Princeton University Press, 1954), 15; Solakzade (Çabuk), *Solakzade Tarihi*, 260; Nicolae Jorga, *Osmanlı İmparatorluğu Tarihi*, vol. 2, (trans.) Nilüfer Epçeli, (İstanbul: Yeditepe Yayınevi, 2005), 24–25; Uzunçarşılı, *Osmanlı Tarihi*, vol. 1, 454.

3. Gábor Ágoston, Guns for the Sultan, *Military Power and the Weapons Industry in the Ottoman Empire* (Cambridge: Cambridge University Press, 2005), 20.

4. Jorga, *Osmanlı İmparatorluğu Tarihi*, vol. 2, 33; Pertusi, *İstanbul'un Fethi: Çağdaşların Tanıklığı*, 60.

5. The biggest bombard had the bore diameter of 62.8 cm and could fire 600 kg shots up to one mile. Ahmed Muhtar Paşa, *Feth-i Celil-i Konstantıniyye*, (ed.) Mehmet Ş. Eygi, (İstanbul: Bedir Yayınevi, 1994), 31–32; Selahattin Tansel, *Osmanlı Kaynaklarına Göre Fatih Sultan Mehmet'in Siyasi ve Askeri Faaliyeti*, (İstanbul: Milli Eğitim Basımevi, 1971), 51–52.

6. Rahmi Egemen and Naci Çakın, *Türk Silahlı Kuvvetleri Tarihi: İstanbul'un Fethi 1453*, vol. 3, annex to section 3, (Ankara: Genelkurmay Basımevi, 1979), 97; Pertusi, *İstanbul'un Fethi: Çağdaşların Tanıklığı*, 70–72.

7. Mehmet Neşri, *Neşri Tarihi*, vol. 2, (ed.) M. Altay Köymen, (Ankara: Kültür Bakanlığı Yayınları, 1983), 133; Ahmed Muhtar, *Feth-i Celil-i Konstantıniyye*, 35; Egemen and Çakın, *Türk Silahlı Kuvvetleri Tarihi*, 66–67, 84.

8. Steven Runciman, *The Fall of Constantinople 1453*, (Cambridge University Press, 1965), 60–62, 64; Jorga, *Osmanlı İmparatorluğu Tarihi*, vol. 2, 25–26, 28; Imber, *Ottoman Empire 1300–1481*, 145–146; Uzunçarşılı, *Osmanlı Tarihi*, vol. 1, 453; Tansel, *Osmanlı Kaynaklarına Göre Fatih Sultan Mehmet'in Siyasi ve Askeri Faaliyeti*, 33–39, 53.

9. *See* Halil İnalcık, "The Rise of Turcoman Maritime Principalities in Anatolia, Byzantium and Crusades" in *The Middle East and the Balkans under the Ottoman Empire: Essays on Economy and Society*, (Bloomington: Indiana University Turkish Studies, 1993), 309–329.

10. Egemen and Çakın, *Türk Silahlı Kuvvetleri Tarihi*, 52–55, 67–68; Runciman, *Fall of Constantinople 1453*, 75–76; Tansel, *Osmanlı Kaynaklarına Göre Fatih Sultan Mehmet'in Siyasi ve Askeri Faaliyeti*, 50–51.

11. Hüseyin Dağtekin, "Rumeli Hisarı'nın Askeri Ehemmiyeti," *Fatih ve İstanbul Dergisi*, vol. 1, no. 1–2, May–July 1953, 117–137, 177–186; Kritovoulos (Riggs), *History of Mehmed the Conqueror*, 15–16, 18–21; Tursun Bey, *Fatih'in Tarihi: Tarih-i Ebul Feth*, (ed.) Ahmet Tezbaşar, (İstanbul: Kervan Kitapçılık, not dated), 41–45; Egemen and Çakın, *Türk Silahlı Kuvvetleri Tarihi*, 55–63; Zorzo Dolfin, "1453 Yılında İstanbul'un Muhasara ve Zaptı" (Turkish translation of the Italian original *Cronaca Delle Famiglie Nobili Di Venezia e Della Stessa Citta Dalla Sua Origine Sino L'anno 1478*), *Fatih ve Istanbul Dergisi*, vol. 1, no. 1, May 1953, 23–24.

12. For a short summary of the walls of Constantinople *see* Runciman, *Fall of Constantinople 1453*, 87–92; For details *see* Stephen Turnbull, *The Walls of Constantinople AD 324–1453*, (Oxford: Osprey Publishing, 2004), passim.; *See also* Ahmed Muhtar, *Feth-i Celil-i Konstantıniyye*, 38–108.

13. Ahmed Muhtar, *Feth-i Celil-i Konstantıniyye*, 161–177; Egemen and Çakın, *Türk Silahlı Kuvvetleri Tarihi*, 91–92, 94–95.

14. Neşri (Köymen), *Neşri Tarihi*, 132; Dolfin, "1453 Yılında İstanbul'un Muhasara ve Zaptı," 27; Jorga, *Osmanlı İmparatorluğu Tarihi*, vol. 2, 34; Imber, *Ottoman Empire 1300–1481*, 148–149; Egemen and Çakın, *Türk Silahlı Kuvvetleri Tarihi*, 91–92.

15. Kelly De Vries, "Gunpowder Weapons at the Siege of Constantinople, 1453," in (ed.) Yaacov Lev, *War and Society in the Eastern Mediterranean 7th–15th Centuries*, (Leiden: E.J. Brill, 1997), 348–349.

16. Kritovoulos (Riggs), *History of Mehmed the Conqueror*, 39–40, 48; Egemen and Çakın, *Türk Silahlı Kuvvetleri Tarihi*, 104–105; Runciman, *Fall of Constantinople 1453*, 96–98; Pertusi, *İstanbul'un Fethi: Çağdaşların Tanıklığı*, 105.

17. Ahmed Muhtar, *Feth-i Celil-i Konstantıniyye*, 217–222; Dolfin, "1453 Yılında İstanbul'un Muhasara ve Zaptı," 27–29; Jorga, *Osmanlı İmparatorluğu Tarihi*, vol. 2, 42; Imber, *Ottoman Empire 1300–1481*, 154–155; Egemen and Çakın, *Türk Silahlı Kuvvetleri Tarihi*, 108–109, 128–134; Runciman, *Fall of Constantinople 1453*, 99, 116–120; Pertusi, *İstanbul'un Fethi: Çağdaşların Tanıklığı*, 81, 110, 139–141; Tansel, *Osmanlı Kaynaklarına Göre Fatih Sultan Mehmet'in Siyasi ve Askeri Faaliyeti*, 57–60.

18. Ahmed Muhtar, *Feth-i Celil-i Konstantıniyye*, 228–243; Dolfin, "1453 Yılında İstanbul'un Muhasara ve Zaptı," 32; Egemen and Çakın, *Türk Silahlı Kuvvetleri Tarihi*, 107–108, 110–115; Kritovoulos (Riggs), *History of Mehmed the Conqueror*, 50–55; Runciman, *Fall of Constantinople 1453*, 98, 100–103; Tansel, *Osmanlı Kaynaklarına Göre Fatih Sultan Mehmet'in Siyasi ve Askeri Faaliyeti*, 68–70.

19. Ahmed Muhtar, *Feth-i Celil-i Konstantıniyye*, 243–260; Kritovoulos (Riggs), *History of Mehmed the Conqueror*, 51–52, 55–57; Dolfin, "1453 Yılında İstanbul'un Muhasara ve Zaptı," 31, 33; Egemen and Çakın, *Türk Silahlı Kuvvetleri Tarihi*, 115–127; Runciman, *Fall of Constantinople 1453*, 98, 104–111; Pertusi, *İstanbul'un Fethi: Çağdaşların Tanıklığı*, 106, 108, 110–111, 139; Tansel, *Osmanlı Kaynaklarına Göre Fatih Sultan Mehmet'in Siyasi ve Askeri Faaliyeti*, 72–79.

20. Ahmed Muhtar, *Feth-i Celil-i Konstantıniyye*, 283–286; Kritovoulos (Riggs), *History of Mehmed the Conqueror*, 33; Runciman, *Fall of Constantinople 1453*, 58–59, 61, 104, 123;

Imber, *Ottoman Empire 1300–1481*, 152–153; Egemen and Çakın, *Türk Silahlı Kuvvetleri Tarihi*, 138–141; Tansel, *Osmanlı Kaynaklarına Göre Fatih Sultan Mehmet'in Siyasi ve Askeri Faaliyeti*, 70–72, 84–85.

21. Ahmed Muhtar, *Feth-i Celil-i Konstantıniyye*, 287–291, 295–390, 405, 409–411; Kritovoulos (Riggs), *History of Mehmed the Conqueror*, 64–75; Dolfin, "1453 Yılında İstanbul'un Muhasara ve Zaptı," 41–42, 45–49; Tursun (Tezbaşar), *Fatih'in Tarihi*, 51–55; Egemen and Çakın, *Türk Silahlı Kuvvetleri Tarihi*, 141–153; Jorga, *Osmanlı İmparatorluğu Tarihi*, vol. 2, 42–46; Imber, *Ottoman Empire 1300–1481*, 156–158; Runciman, *Fall of Constantinople 1453*, 124–144; Pertusi, *İstanbul'un Fethi: Çağdaşların Tanıklığı*, 112–119; Tansel, *Osmanlı Kaynaklarına Göre Fatih Sultan Mehmet'in Siyasi ve Askeri Faaliyeti*, 85–103.

22. İsmail Hakkı Uzunçarşılı, *Osmanlı Tarihi*, vol. 2, 7th Printing, (Ankara: Türk Tarih Kurumu Basımevi, 1995), 8–11; Tansel, *Osmanlı Kaynaklarına Göre Fatih Sultan Mehmet'in Siyasi ve Askeri Faaliyeti*, 110–111.

23. Cemal Kafadar, *Between Two Worlds: The Construction of the Ottoman State*, (Berkeley: University of California Press, 1995), 147, 149.

24. De Vries, "Gunpowder Weapons at the Siege of Constantinople, 1453," 345–346, 362; Kritovoulos (Riggs), *History of Mehmed the Conqueror*, 43, 45, 48–49; Uzunçarşılı, *Osmanlı Tarihi*, vol. 1, 464–465.

25. İsmail Hakkı Uzunçarşılı, *Osmanlı Devleti Teşkilatından Kapukulu Ocakları*, vol. 1, 3rd Printing, (Ankara: Türk Tarih Kurumu Basımevi, 1988), 173, 384–389.

26. Ibid., vol. 1, 35–37, 61–65, 79; Reşad Ekrem Koçu, *Yeniçeriler*, 2nd Printing, (İstanbul: Doğan Kitapçılık, 2004), 47–48.

27. Uzunçarşılı, *Osmanlı Devleti Teşkilatından Kapukulu Ocakları*, vol. 1, 40–42, 57–60; Koçu, *Yeniçeriler*, 48–50.

28. Kritovoulos (Riggs), *History of Mehmed the Conqueror*, 175; Imber, *Ottoman Empire 1300–1481*, 164–165, 226.

29. Uzunçarşılı, *Osmanlı Devleti Teşkilatından Kapukulu Ocakları*, vol. 1, 14–18, 21–29, 623; Koçu, *Yeniçeriler*, 34–43.

30. Uzunçarşılı, *Osmanlı Devleti Teşkilatından Kapukulu Ocakları*, vol. 1, 14, 17–21, 108–109, 122–123; Koçu, *Yeniçeriler*, 44.

31. Uzunçarşılı, *Osmanlı Devleti Teşkilatından Kapukulu Ocakları*, vol. 1, 31–34, 306–307.

32. Some sources are giving the credit to Selim I. *See* Uzunçarşılı, *Osmanlı Devleti Teşkilatından Kapukulu Ocakları*, vol. 1, 168–169; Emin Aysan and Muzaffer Kan, *TSK Tarihi Osmanlı Devri Yavuz Sultan Selim'in Mısır Seferi Mercidabık (1516) ve Ridaniye (1517)*, vol. 3, annex to section 2, (Ankara: Genelkurmay Basımevi, 1990), 76–77.

33. Uzunçarşılı, *Osmanlı Devleti Teşkilatından Kapukulu Ocakları*, vol. 1, 64, 165, 169, 178–179.

34. Ibid., 155–156, 159, 163–164, 167–168, 170; Koçu, *Yeniçeriler*, 78–79.

35. Uzunçarşılı, *Osmanlı Devleti Teşkilatından Kapukulu Ocakları*, vol. 1, 612–614; Koçu, *Yeniçeriler*, 82–83.

36. Frank Tallett, *War and Society in Early-Modern Europe, 1495–1715*, (London: Routledge, 1992), 7.

37. Uzunçarşılı, *Osmanlı Devleti Teşkilatından Kapukulu Ocakları*, vol. 1, 158–159, 230–232.

38. For the standard, flags and symbols of the Janissaries *see* Mahmud Şevket, *Osmanlı Askeri Teşkilatı ve Kıyafeti: Osmanlı Ordusunun Kuruluşundan 1908 Yılına Kadar*, (ed.) N. Türsan and S. Türsan, (Ankara: Kara Kuvvetleri Komutanlığı Basımevi, 1983), 25–32;

Uzunçarşılı, *Osmanlı Devleti Teşkilatından Kapukulu Ocakları*, vol. 1, 258–259, 290–305; Koçu, *Yeniçeriler*, 84–87, 110–111.

39. Ogier Ghiselin de Busbecq, *The Turkish Letters of Ogier Ghiselin de Busbecq*, (trans.) Edward S. Forster, (Oxford: The Clarendon Press, 1968), 5, 8; Geoffrey Parker, *The Military Revolution: Military Innovation and the Rise of the West, 1500–1800*, 2nd Edition, (Cambridge: Cambridge University Press, 1996), 72; Mahmud Şevket, *Osmanlı Askeri Teşkilatı ve Kıyafeti*, 16.

40. Busbecq (Forster), *Turkish Letters of Ogier Ghiselin de Busbecq*, 61, 146–147; For the uniforms of Janissary and other Kapıkulu corps *see* Mahmud Şevket, *Osmanlı Askeri Teşkilatı ve Kıyafeti*, 22, 38–65; Also *see* Uzunçarşılı, *Osmanlı Devleti Teşkilatından Kapukulu Ocakları*, vol. 1, 263–284, 376; Koçu, *Yeniçeriler*, 123–126.

41. Uzunçarşılı, *Osmanlı Devleti Teşkilatından Kapukulu Ocakları*, vol. 1, 147–150, 159–160; Koçu, *Yeniçeriler*, 116–118.

42. Uzunçarşılı, *Osmanlı Devleti Teşkilatından Kapukulu Ocakları*, vol. 1, 288–289, 356–358; Koçu, *Yeniçeriler*, 85–86; Busbecq (Forster), *Turkish Letters of Ogier Ghiselin de Busbecq*, 155, 158–159.

43. Uzunçarşılı, *Osmanlı Devleti Teşkilatından Kapukulu Ocakları*, vol. 1, 214–218, 234–237, 285–287; Koçu, *Yeniçeriler*, 89–90, 92; Mahmud Şevket, *Osmanlı Askeri Teşkilatı ve Kıyafeti*, 43–44, 61; Arthur Leon Horniker, "The Corps of Janizaries,"*Military Affairs*, vol. 8, Autumn 1944, 188.

44. Uzunçarşılı, *Osmanlı Devleti Teşkilatından Kapukulu Ocakları*, vol. 1, 174, 192–213; Koçu, *Yeniçeriler*, 92–93.

45. Uzunçarşılı, *Osmanlı Devleti Teşkilatından Kapukulu Ocakları*, vol. 1, 175–176, 195, 349–354.

46. Andre Corvisier, *Armies and Societies in Europe, 1494–1789*, (trans.) A. T. Siddall, (Bloomington: Indiana University Press, 1979), 151–152; Tallett, *War and Society in Early-Modern Europe, 1495–1715*, 100.

47. Uzunçarşılı, *Osmanlı Devleti Teşkilatından Kapukulu Ocakları*, vol. 1, 152, 397–400; Mahmud Şevket, *Osmanlı Askeri Teşkilatı ve Kıyafeti*, 43–44.

48. Uzunçarşılı, *Osmanlı Devleti Teşkilatından Kapukulu Ocakları*, vol. 1, 254–256, 337–344, 411–463; Koçu, *Yeniçeriler*, 126–138; Mahmud Şevket, *Osmanlı Askeri Teşkilatı ve Kıyafeti*, 58–59; Caroline Finkel, *The Government of Warfare: The Ottoman Military Campaigns in Hungary, 1593–1606*, (Wien: VWGÖ, 1988), 71–77, 79–80, 82–83.

49. Uzunçarşılı, *Osmanlı Devleti Teşkilatından Kapukulu Ocakları*, vol. 1, 287, 289, 311–320, 349–354, 381–383, 378; Finkel, *Government of Warfare*, 69–70; Mahmud Şevket, *Osmanlı Askeri Teşkilatı ve Kıyafeti*, 2.

50. Uzunçarşılı, *Osmanlı Devleti Teşkilatından Kapukulu Ocakları*, vol. 1, 165, 199, 377.

51. Ibid., 377; Mahmud Şevket, *Osmanlı Askeri Teşkilatı ve Kıyafeti*, 22–23; Busbecq (Forster), *Turkish Letters of Ogier Ghiselin de Busbecq*, 146; Gabor Agoston, *Guns for the Sultan: Military Power and the Weapons Industry in the Ottoman Empire*, (Cambridge: Cambridge University Press, 2005), 23–24.

52. Ünsal Yücel, *Türk Okçuluğu*, (Ankara: Atatürk Kültür Merkezi Yayınları, 1998), 22–25, 43–48; Adam Karpowicz, "Ottoman Bows—An Assesment of Draw Weight, Performance and Tactical Use," *Antiquity*, vol. 81, no. 313, September 2007, 680–683; Halim Baki Kunter, "Atıcılar Kanunnamesi," *Tarih Vesikaları*, vol. 2, no. 10, İlkkanun 1942, 254; Alan Williams, "Ottoman Military Technology: The Metallurgy of Turkish Armour," in (ed.) Yaacov Lev, *War and Society in the Eastern Mediterranean 7th–15th Centuries*, (Leiden: E.J. Brill, 1997), 374; Kenneth Chase, *Firearms: A Global History to 1700*, (Cambridge: Cambridge University Press, 2003), 24, 73–74; Parker, *Military Revolution*, 17.

53. Uzunçarşılı, *Osmanlı Devleti Teşkilatından Kapukulu Ocakları*, vol. 1, 226–232, 332–333; Mahmud Şevket, *Osmanlı Askeri Teşkilatı ve Kıyafeti*, 23; Koçu, *Yeniçeriler*, 139–142.

54. Paul E. Klopsteg, *Turkish Archery and the Composite Bow*, (Lyn: Derrydale Press, 1992), 14, 79; Yücel, *Türk Okçuluğu*, op.cit., 35–36, 163–165, 193–197, 233–235; Busbecq (Forster), *Turkish Letters of Ogier Ghiselin de Busbecq*, 133–135.

55. Uzunçarşılı, *Osmanlı Devleti Teşkilatından Kapukulu Ocakları*, vol. 1, 374–376; Ahmet Muhtar, *Muharebat-ı Meşhure-i Osmaniye Albümü*, 53.

56. Solakzade (Çabuk), *Solakzade Tarihi*, 346.

57. Ahmed Muhtar, *Feth-i Celil-i Konstantıniyye*, 58–59.

58. Koçu, *Yeniçeriler*, 163–164.

59. Imber, *Ottoman Empire 1300–1481*, 174.

60. For various examples *see* Jorga, *Osmanlı İmparatorluğu Tarihi*, vol. 2, 90, 100, 111, 116, 127, 232.

61. Uzunçarşılı, *Osmanlı Devleti Teşkilatından Kapukulu Ocakları*, vol. 1, 82–83, 196–197, 321–330; Koçu, *Yeniçeriler*, 50–51, 78–79, 150–151; Busbecq (Forster), *Turkish Letters of Ogier Ghiselin de Busbecq*, 8, 89, 138–139; Mustafa Akdağ, *Türk Halkının Dirlik ve Düzenlik Kavgası: Celali İsyanları*, (Ankara: Barış Yayınları, 1999), 19, 89.

62. İsmail Hakkı Uzunçarşılı, *Osmanlı Devleti Teşkilatından Kapukulu Ocakları*, vol. 2, 3rd Printing, (Ankara: Türk Tarih Kurumu Basımevi, 1988), 137, 146; Mahmud Şevket, *Osmanlı Askeri Teşkilatı ve Kıyafeti*, 4.

63. Busbecq (Forster), *Turkish Letters of Ogier Ghiselin de Busbecq*, 114.

64. Uzunçarşılı, *Osmanlı Devleti Teşkilatından Kapukulu Ocakları*, vol. 2, 138–139, 162–163.

65. Ibid., 172–173, 175.

66. Ibid., 213–216; Rhoads Murphey, *Ottoman Warfare, 1500–1700*, (New Brunswick: Rutgers University Press, 1999), 45.

67. Busbecq (Forster), *Turkish Letters of Ogier Ghiselin de Busbecq*, 145–146.

68. Ibid., 123–124; Emin Aysan, *TSK Tarihi Osmanlı Devri Kıbrıs Seferi (1570–1571)*, vol. 3, annex to section 3, (Ankara: Genelkurmay Basımevi, 1971), 66.

69. Uzunçarşılı, *Osmanlı Devleti Teşkilatından Kapukulu Ocakları*, vol. 2, 147–153, 182; Mahmud Şevket, *Osmanlı Askeri Teşkilatı ve Kıyafeti*, 5.

70. Rahmi Egemen, Lütfü Güvenç and Rıza Bozkurt, *Türk Silahlı Kuvvetleri Tarihi Osmanlı Devri (1451–1566)*, vol. 3, section 2, (Ankara: Genelkurmay Basımevi, 1977), 525.

71. Uzunçarşılı, *Osmanlı Devleti Teşkilatından Kapukulu Ocakları*, vol. 2, 156–161, 175–177, 182–183; Mahmud Şevket, *Osmanlı Askeri Teşkilatı ve Kıyafeti*, 4–5; Finkel, *Government of Warfare*, 81–82.

72. Akdağ, *Türk Halkının Dirlik ve Düzenlik Kavgası*, 19–20, 89.

73. Uzunçarşılı, *Osmanlı Devleti Teşkilatından Kapukulu Ocakları*, vol. 2, 137; Koçu, *Yeniçeriler*, 205–208.

74. Mücteba İlgürel "Osmanlı Topçuluğunun İlk Devirleri," *Hakkı Dursun Yıldız Armağanı*, (İstanbul: Marmara Üniversitesi Yayınları, 1995), 285–293; Salim Aydüz, "Osmanlı Askeri Teknoloji Tarihi: Ateşli Silahlar, *Türkiye Araştırmaları Literatür Dergisi*, vol. 2, no. 4, 2004, 267–269; Some authors like de Vries claimed that Ottomans began to use cannons after the first quarter of 15th century. See De Vries, "Gunpowder Weapons at the Siege of Constantinople, 1453," 354; Also *see* V. J. Parry, "Barud-iv. The Ottoman Empire," in (ed.) P. Bearman, Th. Bianquis, C. E. Bosworth, E. van Donzel and W. P. Heinrichs, *Encyclopaedia of Islam*, 2nd Edition, vol. 1; (Leiden: E.J. Brill, 2008), online edition.

75. Uzunçarşılı, *Osmanlı Devleti Teşkilatından Kapukulu Ocakları*, vol. 2, 35–37; Agoston, *Guns for the Sultan*, 16–18, 20, 28; Djurdjica Petrović, "Fire-arms in the Balkans on the Eve of and After the Ottoman Conquests of Fourteenth and Fifteenth Centuries," in (ed.) V. J. Parry and M. E. Yapp, *War, Technology and Society in the Middle East*, (London: Oxford University Press, 1975), 193–194.

76. John E. Woods, *The Aqquyunlu: Clan, Confederation, Empire*, (Salt Lake City: The University of Utah Press, 1999), 118–120; Hazım İşgüven, *TSK Tarihi Osmanlı Devri Otlukbeli Meydan Muharebesi (11 Ağustos 1473)*, vol. 3, annex to section 2, (Ankara: Genelkurmay Basımevi, 1986), 124, 136.

77. For details about this institution *see* Salim Aydüz, *Osmanlı Devleti'nde Tophâne–i Âmire'nin Faaliyetleri ve Top Döküm Teknolojisi (XIV–XVI. Yüzyıl)*, (İstanbul: İstanbul Üniversitesi Unpublished Ph.D. Dissertation, 1998), passim.

78. Agoston, *Guns for the Sultan*, 66, 178–181; Uzunçarşılı, *Osmanlı Devleti Teşkilatından Kapukulu Ocakları*, vol. 2, 39–41, 45–46.

79. Solakzade (Çabuk), *Solakzade Tarihi*, 349.

80. Uzunçarşılı, *Osmanlı Devleti Teşkilatından Kapukulu Ocakları*, vol. 2, 56.

81. Parker, *Military Revolution*, 126–128; Williams, "Ottoman Military Technology," 375.

82. Agoston, *Guns for the Sultan*, 35, 186–187.

83. Parry, "Barud-iv. The Ottoman Empire"; For details about these foundries and gunpowder works *see* Agoston, *Guns for the Sultan*, 96–189.

84. Agoston, *Guns for the Sultan*, 38, 42–48, 192–195; Petrović, "Fire-arms in the Balkans," 190–191.

85. R. M. Savory, "Barud-iv. The Safawids," in (ed.) P. Bearman, Th. Bianquis, C. E. Bosworth, E. van Donzel and W. P. Heinrichs, *Encyclopaedia of Islam*, 2nd Edition, vol. 1; (Leiden: E.J. Brill, 2008), online edition.

86. Uzunçarşılı, *Osmanlı Devleti Teşkilatından Kapukulu Ocakları*, vol. 2, 37.

87. Ibid., 53–54, 61–62; Agoston, *Guns for the Sultan*, 30, 33.

88. Uzunçarşılı, *Osmanlı Devleti Teşkilatından Kapukulu Ocakları*, vol. 2, 52–53.

89. Agoston, *Guns for the Sultan*, 30–31, 135–138, 180, 182; Klara Hegyi, "The Ottoman Military Force in Hungary," in (ed.) Geza David and Pal Fodor, *Hungarian–Ottoman Military and Diplomatic Relations in the Age of Süleyman the Magnificent*, (Budapest: Lorand Eötvös University, 1994), 134–138; Parry, "Barud-iv. The Ottoman Empire."

90. Uzunçarşılı, *Osmanlı Devleti Teşkilatından Kapukulu Ocakları*, vol. 2, 57, 261–263; Eyup Sabri, "Devri İstilamızda Osmanlı Ordusununda Geri Hidematı," in *Türk Ordusunu Eski Seferlerinde İki İmha Muharebesi*, (İstanbul: Askeri Matbaa, 1930), 33.

91. Uzunçarşılı, *Osmanlı Devleti Teşkilatından Kapukulu Ocakları*, vol. 2, 3–5.

92. Ibid., 3, 23, 26; Eyup Sabri, "Devri İstilamızda Osmanlı Ordusununda Geri Hidematı," 33.

93. Uzunçarşılı, *Osmanlı Devleti Teşkilatından Kapukulu Ocakları*, vol. 2, 8, 21–22; Agoston, *Guns for the Sultan*, 30.

94. Mahmud Şevket, *Osmanlı Askeri Teşkilatı ve Kıyafeti*, 50.

95. Uzunçarşılı, *Osmanlı Devleti Teşkilatından Kapukulu Ocakları*, vol. 2, 11–14, 27, 29–30.

96. Ibid., 12, 15, 29.

97. Ibid., 247, 366.

98. Chase, *Firearms*, 86.

99. Uzunçarşılı, *Osmanlı Devleti Teşkilatından Kapukulu Ocakları*, vol. 2, 97; Hayati, "Bin Senei Hicriyesine Kadar Osmanlı Ordusunun Teşkilatı, Bu Teşkilatın Kuvvetli ve Zayıf

Nukuatı" in *Türk Ordusunu Eski Seferlerinde İki İmha Muharebesi*, (İstanbul: Askeri Matbaa, 1930), 9.

100. Chase, *Firearms*, 97; Emanuel Constantin Antoche, "Du Tabor de Jan Žižka et de Jean Hunyadi au Tabur Çengi des Armées Ottomanes: L'art Militaire Hussite en Europe Orientale, au Proche et au Moyen Orient (XV–XVII siécles)," *Turcica*, vol. 36, 2004, 104–106, 110–116.

101. Tacan, *Batı Türklerinin (Osmanlılar) Teessüs ve İstila Devirlerinde Harb Güdemi Usulleri*, 36, 50–51; Egemen and Çakın, *Türk Silahlı Kuvvetleri Tarihi*, 241.

102. Vernon J. Parry, "La Maniére de Combattre," in in (ed.) V. J. Parry and M. E. Yapp, *War, Technology and Society in the Middle East*, (London: Oxford University Press, 1975), 221–233.

103. Chase, *Firearms*, 123, 132.

104. Uzunçarşılı, *Osmanlı Devleti Teşkilatından Kapukulu Ocakları*, vol. 2, 97–100.

105. Ibid., 102, 105; Agoston, *Guns for the Sultan*, 30–31.

106. Uzunçarşılı, *Osmanlı Devleti Teşkilatından Kapukulu Ocakları*, vol. 2, 117–118; Mahmud Şevket, *Osmanlı Askeri Teşkilatı ve Kıyafeti*, 4, 51; Colin Imber, "The Navy of Süleyman the Magnificent," in Colin Imber, *Studies in Ottoman History and Law*, (İstanbul: The Isis Press, 1996), 25, 29, 47; Aysan, *TSK Tarihi Osmanlı Devri Kıbrıs Seferi (1570–1571)*, 69.

107. Aysan, *TSK Tarihi Osmanlı Devri Kıbrıs Seferi (1570–1571)*, 69–70.

108. Uzunçarşılı, *Osmanlı Devleti Teşkilatından Kapukulu Ocakları*, vol. 2, 131–132; Egemen, Güvenç and Bozkurt, *Türk Silahlı Kuvvetleri Tarihi Osmanlı Devri (1451–1566)*, 248–249.

109. Uzunçarşılı, *Osmanlı Devleti Teşkilatından Kapukulu Ocakları*, vol. 2, 131; Agoston, *Guns for the Sultan*, 40–42.

110. Aysan, *TSK Tarihi Osmanlı Devri Kıbrıs Seferi (1570–1571)*, 41–45, 95–100.

111. Ibid., 117–131.

112. Uzunçarşılı, *Osmanlı Devleti Teşkilatından Kapukulu Ocakları*, vol. 2, 131–132; Egemen, Güvenç and Bozkurt, *Türk Silahlı Kuvvetleri Tarihi Osmanlı Devri (1451–1566)*, 194.

113. Barkan, "Timar," 298, 301; Gyula Kaldy-Nagy, "The First Centuries of the Ottoman Military Organization," A *cta Orientalia Academiae Scientiarum Hungaricae*, vol. 31, no. 2, 1977, 151–152, 154–157; Halil İnalcık, *Osmanlı İmparatorluğu: Klasik Çağ (1300–1600)*, (trans.) R. Sezer, (İstanbul: Yapı Kredi Yayınları, 2003), 35; Some scholars question the validity of the scope and radical nature of the Mehmed's land reforms. See Oktay Özel, "Limits of the Almighty: Mehmed II's Land Reform Revisited," *Journal of the Economic and Social History of the Orient*, vol. 42, no. 2, 1999, 227–244.

114. Geza David, "Assigning a Zeamet in the 16th Century: Revenue-Limits and Office-Holding," in Geza David, *Studies in Demographic and Administrative History of Ottoman Hungary*, (İstanbul: The Isis Press, 1997), 216–222.

115. Mahmud Şevket, *Osmanlı Askeri Teşkilatı ve Kıyafeti*, 5; Cengiz Orhonlu and Nejat Göyünç, "Has," *Türkiye Diyanet Vakfı İslam Ansiklopedisi*, vol. 16, (İstanbul: Türkiye Diyanet Vakfı Yayınları, 1997), 268–269.

116. Mahmud Şevket, *Osmanlı Askeri Teşkilatı ve Kıyafeti*, 5; Barkan, "Timar," 288–290; Kaldy-Nagy, "First Centuries of the Ottoman Military Organization," 150; David, "Assigning a Zeamet in the 16th Century," 222.

117. For several examples of Timar grants and financial arrangements *see* Geza David, "The Sancakbegis of Arad and Gyula," in Geza David, *Studies in Demographic and Administrative History of Ottoman Hungary*, (İstanbul: The Isis Press, 1997), 143–163.

118. Barkan, "Timar," 313–316; Kaldy-Nagy, "First Centuries of the Ottoman Military Organization," 153–154, 157–159; Julius Kaldy-Nagy, "The Strangers (Ecnebiler) in the

16th Century Military Organization," in (ed.) György Kara, *Between the Danube and the Caucasus*, (Budapest: Akademiai Kiado, 1987), 167–169.

119. For various examples of this policy *see* Halil İnalcık, "Stefan Duşan'dan Osmanlı İmparatorluğuna" in *Fatih Devri Üzerinde Tetkikler ve Vesikalar*, vol. 1, 3rd Edition, (Ankara: Türk Tarih Kurumu Basımevi, 1995), 137–184.

120. Barkan, "Timar," 323–324; Halil İnalcık, "The Ottoman State: Economy and Society, 1300–1600," in (ed.) Halil İnalcık and Donald Quataert, *An Economic and Social History of the Ottoman Empire, 1300–1914*, (Cambridge: Cambridge University Press, 1994), 90.

121. Mahmud Şevket, *Osmanlı Askeri Teşkilatı ve Kıyafeti*, 49.

122. Ibid., 5, 49; Kaldy-Nagy, "First Centuries of the Ottoman Military Organization," 152.

123. Barkan, "Timar," 317–318, 325–326; Kaldy-Nagy, "First Centuries of the Ottoman Military Organization," 160–161; Finkel, *Government of Warfare*, 28–29, 49–56; İşgüven, *TSK Tarihi Osmanlı Devri Otlukbeli Meydan Muharebesi (11 Ağustos 1473)*, 67; Aysan and Kan, *TSK Tarihi Osmanlı Devri Yavuz Sultan Selim'in Mısır Seferi Mercidabık (1516) ve Ridaniye (1517)*, 67.

124. Barkan, "Timar," 287–291; Murphey, *Ottoman Warfare, 1500–1700*, 37–41.

125. İşgüven, *TSK Tarihi Osmanlı Devri Otlukbeli Meydan Muharebesi (11 Ağustos 1473)*, 60–61, 112–113; Busbecq (Forster), *Turkish Letters of Ogier Ghiselin de Busbecq*, 137; Parry, "La Maniére de Combattre," 218–219.

126. Aysan and Kan, *TSK Tarihi Osmanlı Devri Yavuz Sultan Selim'in Mısır Seferi Mercidabık (1516) ve Ridaniye (1517)*, 55, 98–99.

127. Imber, "Navy of Süleyman the Magnificent," 46–51.

128. Nenad Moačanin, "Hacı Mehmed Ağa of Požega, God's Special Protégé (CA. 1490–CA. 1580)," in (ed.) Geza David and Pal Fodor, *Hungarian-Ottoman Military and Diplomatic Relations in the Age of Süleyman the Magnificent*, (Budapest: Lorand Eötvös University, 1994), 171–181; Pal Fodor, "Making a Living on the Frontiers: Volunteers in the Sixteenth-Century Ottoman Army," in (ed.) Geza David and Pal Fodor, *Ottomans, Hungarians, and Habsburgs in Central Europe: The Military Confines in the Era of Ottoman Conquest*, (Leiden: E.J. Brill, 2000), 234–247.

129. Barkan, "Timar," 313–317; Kaldy-Nagy, "First Centuries of the Ottoman Military Organization," 155–156, 160; Kaldy-Nagy, "Strangers (Ecnebiler) in the 16th Century Military Organization," 168.

130. Barkan, "Timar," 310–312.

131. Parry, "La Maniére de Combattre," 223; Chase, *Firearms*, 93.

132. İsmail Hakkı Uzunçarşılı, "Akıncı," *İslam Ansiklopedisi*, vol. 1, (İstanbul: Milli Eğitim Bakanlığı Yayınları, 1993), 239–240; Jorga, *Osmanlı İmparatorluğu Tarihi*, vol. 2, 181–182.

133. Uzunçarşılı, "Akıncı," 239.

134. Mihailović, *Memoirs of a Janissary*, 177.

135. Jorga, *Osmanlı İmparatorluğu Tarihi*, vol. 2, 165–166, 194–196, 228, 334–335; Maria Pia Pedani, "Turkish Raids in Friuli at the End of the Fifteenth Century," in (ed.) M. Kohbach, G. Prochaska-Eisl and C.Romer, *Acta Viennensia Ottomanica*, (Vienna: Im Selbrstverlag des Instıtuts fur Orientalistik, 1999), 287–289.

136. Neşri (Köymen), *Neşri Tarihi*, 129, 131–132; Uzunçarşılı, "Akıncı," 239; Eyup Sabri, "Devri İstilamızda Osmanlı Ordusununda Geri Hidematı," 31.

137. Neşri (Köymen), *Neşri Tarihi*, vol. 2, 73–75.

138. Carl Max Kortepeter, "Gazi Giray II, Khan of the Crimea and Ottoman Policy in Eastern Europe and the Caucasus, 1588–94," in Carl Max Kortepeter, *The Ottoman Turks:*

Nomad Kingdom to World Empire, (İstanbul: The Isis Press, 1991), 127–128, 148–150; Finkel, *Government of Warfare*, 97–106.

139. Jorga, *Osmanlı İmparatorluğu Tarihi*, vol. 2, 163, 226; Mihailović (Stolz), *Memoirs of a Janissary*, 179–181.

140. Enes Pelidija and Feridun Emecen, "İsa Bey," *Türkiye Diyanet Vakfı İslam Ansiklopedisi*, vol. 22, (İstanbul: Türkiye Diyanet Vakfı Yayınları, 2000), 475–476; Jorga, *Osmanlı İmparatorluğu Tarihi*, vol. 2, 140–142.

141. Uzunçarşılı, *Osmanlı Devleti Teşkilatından Kapukulu Ocakları*, vol. 2, 573–574; Jorga, *Osmanlı İmparatorluğu Tarihi*, vol. 2, 297; Egemen, Güvenç and Bozkurt, *Türk Silahlı Kuvvetleri Tarihi Osmanlı Devri (1451–1566)*, 188.

142. Finkel, *Government of Warfare*, 47–48.

143. Murphey, *Ottoman Warfare, 1500–1700*, 32–33.

144. Hegyi, "Ottoman Military Force in Hungary," 136–143; Strashimir Dimitrov, "Introduction," in Asparuch Velkov and Evgeniy Radushev, *Ottoman Garrisons on the Middle Danube*, (Budapest: Akademiai Kiado, 1996), 13–27.

145. Uzunçarşılı, *Osmanlı Devleti Teşkilatından Kapukulu Ocakları*, vol. 2, 574–575.

146. Fodor, "Making a Living on the Frontiers," 230–237, 240–241, 247–255; Dimitrov, "Introduction," 24–27; Finkel, *Government of Warfare*, 83–84.

147. Uzunçarşılı, *Osmanlı Devleti Teşkilatından Kapukulu Ocakları*, vol. 2, 574.

148. Nazlı Esim Mergen, *The Yaya and Müsellem Corps in the Ottoman Empire*, (Ankara: Bilkent University Unpublished M.A. Thesis, 2001), 73–79; İnalcık, "Ottoman State," 92–93.

149. Cengiz Orhonlu, *Osmanlı İmparatorluğunda Derbend Teşkilatı*, 2nd Printing, (İstanbul: Eren Yayınları, 1990), 9–16.

150. Orhonlu, *Osmanlı İmparatorluğunda Derbend Teşkilatı*, 23–24, 40, 45–46, 68–69.

151. Aşıkpaşazade Derviş Ahmed, *Aşıkpaşaoğlu Tarihi*, 48, 65–66; Neşri (Köymen), *Neşri Tarihi*, vol. 1, 117; Gökbilgin, *Rumeli'de Yürükler, Tatarlar ve Evlad-ı Fatihan*, 12–18.

152. Busbecq (Forster), *Turkish Letters of Ogier Ghiselin de Busbecq*, 108–109; İnalcık, "Ottoman State," 35–37; Gökbilgin, *Rumeli'de Yürükler, Tatarlar ve Evlad-ı Fatihan*, 19–100; Uzunçarşılı, *Osmanlı Devleti Teşkilatından Kapukulu Ocakları*, vol. 2, 570–572; Suraiya Faroqhi, "Camels, Wagons, and the Ottoman State in the Sixteenth and Seventeenth Centuries," *International Journal of Middle East Studies*, vol. 14, no. 4, November 1982, 524–536.

153. David Ayalon, "The End of the Mamluk Sultanate: Why did the Ottomans Spare the Mamluks of Egypt and Wipe out the Mamluks of Syria," in David Ayalon, *Islam and the Abode of War: Military Slaves and Islamic Adversaries*, (Aldershot: Variorum, 1994), 127–148; Egemen, Güvenç and Bozkurt, *Türk Silahlı Kuvvetleri Tarihi Osmanlı Devri (1451–1566)*, 625–626.

154. Neşri (Köymen), *Neşri Tarihi*, 45, 90; Tursun (Tezbaşar), *Fatih'in Tarihi*, 80–81, 114–116; Mihailović (Stolz), *Memoirs of a Janissary*, 183.

155. Hegyi, "Ottoman Military Force in Hungary," 137.

156. Robert Anhegger, "Martolos," *İslam Ansiklopedisi*, vol. 7, (İstanbul: Milli Eğitim Bakanlığı Yayınları, 1993), 341–344; Abdülkadir Özcan, "Martolos," *Türkiye Diyanet Vakfı İslam Ansiklopedisi*, vol. 28, (İstanbul: Türkiye Diyanet Vakfı Yayınları, 2003), 64–66; Orhonlu, *Osmanlı İmparatorluğunda Derbend Teşkilatı*, 85–93.

157. Yavuz Ercan, *Osmanlı İmparatorluğunda Bulgarlar ve Voynuklar*, (Ankara: Türk Tarih Kurumu Basımevi, 1989), 1, 11, 25–29; Rhoads Murphey, "Woynuk," in (ed.) P. Bearman, Th. Bianquis, C. E. Bosworth, E. van Donzel and W. P. Heinrichs, *Encyclopaedia of Islam*, 2nd Edition, vol. 9; (Leiden: E.J. Brill, 2008), online edition.

158. İnalcık, "Stefan Duşan'dan Osmanlı İmparatorluğuna," 153–156; Istvan Vasary, *Cumans and Tatars: Oriental Military in the Pre-Ottoman Balkans, 1185–1365*, (Cambridge: Cambridge University Press, 2005), 19–20.

159. Orhonlu, *Osmanlı İmparatorluğunda Derbend Teşkilatı*, 96–99; "Panduri," *Vojna Enciklopedija*, vol. 6, (Beograd: Izdanje Redakcije Vojne Enciklopedije, 1973), 522–523.

160. Pal Fodor, "The Way of a Seljuq Institution to Hungary: The Cerehor" in Pal Fodor, *In Quest of the Golden Apple: Imperial Ideology, Politics and Military Government in the Ottoman Empire*, (İstanbul: The Isis Press, 2000), 244–273; Mihailović (Stolz), *Memoirs of a Janissary*, 183; Uzunçarşılı, *Osmanlı Devleti Teşkilatından Kapukulu Ocakları*, vol. 2, 571; Jorga, *Osmanlı İmparatorluğu Tarihi*, vol. 2, 194.

161. Neşri (Köymen), *Neşri Tarihi*, 128.

162. Petrović, "Fire-arms in the Balkans," 193.

163. Rossitsa Gradeva, "War and Peace Along the Danube: Vidin at the End of the Seventeenth Century," in Rossitsa Gradeva, *Rumeli Under the Ottomans, 15th–18th Centuries: Institutions and Communities*, (İstanbul: The Isis Press, 2004), 110–111.

164. Ercan, *Osmanlı İmparatorluğunda Bulgarlar ve Voynuklar*, 20–24, 67–73; İnalcık, "Ottoman State," 91.

165. Ercan, *Osmanlı İmparatorluğunda Bulgarlar ve Voynuklar*, 34–37, 93.

166. Geza David, "Government in Ottoman Europe," in Geza David, *Studies in Demographic and Administrative History of Ottoman Hungary*, (İstanbul: The Isis Press, 1997), 199–200.

167. Ercan, *Osmanlı İmparatorluğunda Bulgarlar ve Voynuklar*, 46.

168. David, "Government in Ottoman Europe," 193–194.

169. Jorga, *Osmanlı İmparatorluğu Tarihi*, vol. 2, 128.

170. R. Nisbet Bain, "The Siege of Belgrade by Muhammad II, July 1–23, 1456," *The English Historical Review*, vol. 7, no. 26, April 1892, 242–252; Imber, *Ottoman Empire 1300–1481*, 166–169; Egemen, Güvenç and Bozkurt, *Türk Silahlı Kuvvetleri Tarihi Osmanlı Devri (1451–1566)*, 419–426; Tansel, *Osmanlı Kaynaklarına Göre Fatih Sultan Mehmet'in Siyasi ve Askeri Faaliyeti*, 119–127.

171. Kritovoulos (Riggs), *History of Mehmed the Conqueror*, 198–204; Jorga, *Osmanlı İmparatorluğu Tarihi*, vol. 2, 116–117; Egemen, Güvenç and Bozkurt, *Türk Silahlı Kuvvetleri Tarihi Osmanlı Devri (1451–1566)*, 475–480.

172. Fine, *Late Medieval Balkans*, 596–600; Jorga, *Osmanlı İmparatorluğu Tarihi*, vol. 2, 83–84, 127–128, 167; Egemen, Güvenç and Bozkurt, *Türk Silahlı Kuvvetleri Tarihi Osmanlı Devri (1451–1566)*, 480–483, 485–487, 519, 536–543; Tansel, *Osmanlı Kaynaklarına Göre Fatih Sultan Mehmet'in Siyasi ve Askeri Faaliyeti*, 133–146.

173. Imber, *Ottoman Empire 1300–1481*, 248–251; Jorga, *Osmanlı İmparatorluğu Tarihi*, vol. 2, 169–170; Egemen, Güvenç and Bozkurt, *Türk Silahlı Kuvvetleri Tarihi Osmanlı Devri (1451–1566)*, 552–555; Tansel, *Osmanlı Kaynaklarına Göre Fatih Sultan Mehmet'in Siyasi ve Askeri Faaliyeti*, 240–247.

174. Giovan-Maria Angiolello, *Angiolello on the Fall of Negroponte*, November 9, 2006, http://angiolello.net; Imber, *Ottoman Empire 1300–1481*, 200–203, 250–251; Jorga, *Osmanlı İmparatorluğu Tarihi*, vol. 2, 134–136, 170; Egemen, Güvenç and Bozkurt, *Türk Silahlı Kuvvetleri Tarihi Osmanlı Devri (1451–1566)*, 491–497, 555–556; Tansel, *Osmanlı Kaynaklarına Göre Fatih Sultan Mehmet'in Siyasi ve Askeri Faaliyeti*, 202–207.

175. Solakzade (Çabuk), *Solakzade Tarihi*, 365, 367; Sydney Nettleton Fisher, "Civil Strife in the Ottoman Empire, 1481–1503," *The Journal of Modern History*, vol. 13, no. 4, December 1941, 449–465.

176. Randal H. Munsen, "Stephen the Great: Leadership and Patronage on the Fifteenth-Century Ottoman Frontier," *East European Quarterly*, vol. 39, no. 3, September 2005, 281–283; Jorga, *Osmanlı İmparatorluğu Tarihi*, vol. 2, 155, 160–161; Imber, *Ottoman Empire 1300–1481*, 224, 230–232; Egemen, Güvenç and Bozkurt, *Türk Silahlı Kuvvetleri Tarihi Osmanlı Devri (1451–1566)*, 521–523, 526–530.

177. Jorga, *Osmanlı İmparatorluğu Tarihi*, vol. 2, 231–233; Uzunçarşılı, *Osmanlı Devleti Teşkilatından Kapukulu Ocakları*, vol. 2, 182–183; Egemen, Güvenç and Bozkurt, *Türk Silahlı Kuvvetleri Tarihi Osmanlı Devri (1451–1566)*, 560–563.

178. Shai Har-El, *Struggle for Domination in the Middle East: The Ottoman–Mamluk War 1485–94*, (Leiden: E.J. Brill, 1995), 54–59, 115–130, 134–141; Egemen, Güvenç and Bozkurt, *Türk Silahlı Kuvvetleri Tarihi Osmanlı Devri (1451–1566)*, 563–565.

179. Har-El, *Struggle for Domination in the Middle East*, 163–191; Egemen, Güvenç and Bozkurt, *Türk Silahlı Kuvvetleri Tarihi Osmanlı Devri (1451–1566)*, 566–568E.

180. Har-El, *Struggle for Domination in the Middle East*, 138, 142, 188.

181. İşgüven, *TSK Tarihi Osmanlı Devri Otlukbeli Meydan Muharebesi (11 Ağustos 1473)*, 97–100, 126, 128–130; Tansel, *Osmanlı Kaynaklarına Göre Fatih Sultan Mehmet'in Siyasi ve Askeri Faaliyeti*, 313–324; Mihailović (Stolz), *Memoirs of a Janissary*, 171–172.

182. Emin Aysan and Nafiz Orhun, *TSK Tarihi Osmanlı-İran Savaşı: Çaldıran Meydan Muharebesi 1514*, (Ankara: Genelkurmay Basımevi, 1979), 31–32, 90, 149–161; Egemen, Güvenç and Bozkurt, *Türk Silahlı Kuvvetleri Tarihi Osmanlı Devri (1451–1566)*, 585–592.

183. Aysan and Orhun, *TSK Tarihi Osmanlı-İran Savaşı*, 132–143; Kazım, "Osmanlı-İran Muharebelerinde 1514 Tarihinde Vukua Gelen Çaldıran Seferi," in *Türk Ordusunu Eski Seferlerinde İki İmha Muharebesi*, (İstanbul: Askeri Matbaa, 1930), 40–42.

184. Aysan and Orhun, *TSK Tarihi Osmanlı-İran Savaşı*, 90–97, 101–102, 108–109; Kazım, "Osmanlı-İran Muharebelerinde 1514 Tarihinde Vukua Gelen Çaldıran Seferi," 43–46.

185. R. M. Savory, "Safavid Persia," in (ed.) P. M. Holt, Ann K. S. Lambton and Bernard Lewis, *The Cambridge History of Islam*, vol. 1, (Cambridge: Cambridge University Press, 1970), 400.

186. Aysan and Orhun, *TSK Tarihi Osmanlı-İran Savaşı*, 110–117; Kazım, "Osmanlı-İran Muharebelerinde 1514 Tarihinde Vukua Gelen Çaldıran Seferi," 46–53, 55.

187. Chase, *Firearms*, 120–122, 125–126; Busbecq (Forster), *Turkish Letters of Ogier Ghiselin de Busbecq*, 110; Savory, "Safavid Persia," 404–405; Murphey, "Woynuk," 4–5, 22.

188. Aysan and Orhun, *TSK Tarihi Osmanlı-İran Savaşı*, 22–28, 90; Uzunçarşılı, *Osmanlı Devleti Teşkilatından Kapukulu Ocakları*, vol. 2, 230–231, 346–347; Egemen, Güvenç and Bozkurt, *Türk Silahlı Kuvvetleri Tarihi Osmanlı Devri (1451–1566)*, 588–589, 644–647.

189. Chase, *Firearms*, 19–27.

190. Aysan and Kan, *TSK Tarihi Osmanlı Devri Yavuz Sultan Selim'in Mısır Seferi Mercidabık (1516) ve Ridaniye (1517)*, 87–90, 98–99; Hüsnü, "Yavuz Sultan Selim'in Mısır Seferi 1516–1517," in *Türk Ordusunu Eski Seferlerinde İki İmha Muharebesi*, (İstanbul: Askeri Matbaa, 1930), 61–84.

191. Aysan and Kan, *TSK Tarihi Osmanlı Devri Yavuz Sultan Selim'in Mısır Seferi Mercidabık (1516) ve Ridaniye (1517)*, 114–121; Hüsnü, "Yavuz Sultan Selim'in Mısır Seferi 1516–1517," 95–105.

192. Aysan and Kan, *TSK Tarihi Osmanlı Devri Yavuz Sultan Selim'in Mısır Seferi Mercidabık (1516) ve Ridaniye (1517)*, 122–123; Hüsnü, "Yavuz Sultan Selim'in Mısır Seferi 1516–1517," 105–106; Egemen, Güvenç and Bozkurt, *Türk Silahlı Kuvvetleri Tarihi Osmanlı Devri (1451–1566)*, 614–616.

193. Jorga, *Osmanlı İmparatorluğu Tarihi*, vol. 2, 83–84, 127–129; Fine, *Late Medieval Balkans*, 596–601; Egemen, Güvenç and Bozkurt, *Türk Silahlı Kuvvetleri Tarihi Osmanlı Devri (1451–1566)*, 480–483, 485–487, 519, 536–543; Tansel, *Osmanlı Kaynaklarına Göre Fatih Sultan Mehmet'in Siyasi ve Askeri Faaliyeti*, 133–146.

194. Ferenc Szakaly, "Nandorfehervar, 1521: The Beginning of the End of the Medieval Hungarian Kingdom," in (ed.) Geza David and Pal Fodor, *Hungarian–Ottoman Military and Diplomatic Relations in the Age of Süleyman the Magnificent*, (Budapest: Lorand Eötvös University, 1994), 47, 50–51, 57–62; Uzunçarşılı, *Osmanlı Devleti Teşkilatından Kapukulu Ocakları*, vol. 2, 311–312.

195. Szakaly, "Nandorfehervar, 1521," 53, 56, 58–68; Janos Bak, "Hungary: Crown and Estates," in (ed.) Christopher Allmand, *The New Cambridge Medieval History*, vol. 7, (Cambridge: Cambridge University Press, 1998), 724–726; Jorga, *Osmanlı İmparatorluğu Tarihi*, vol. 2, 327–328; Egemen, Güvenç and Bozkurt, *Türk Silahlı Kuvvetleri Tarihi Osmanlı Devri (1451–1566)*, 626–631.

196. Uzunçarşılı, *Osmanlı Devleti Teşkilatından Kapukulu Ocakları*, vol. 2, 313–316; Jorga, *Osmanlı İmparatorluğu Tarihi*, vol. 2, 312–315; Egemen, Güvenç and Bozkurt, *Türk Silahlı Kuvvetleri Tarihi Osmanlı Devri (1451–1566)*, 631–635.

197. Gabor Basta, "A Forgotten Theatre of War 1526–1528: Historical Events Preceding the Ottoman-Hungarian Alliance of 1528," in (ed.) Geza David and Pal Fodor, *Hungarian–Ottoman Military and Diplomatic Relations in the Age of Süleyman the Magnificent*, (Budapest: Lorand Eötvös University, 1994), 93–114; Geza Palffy, "The Origins and Development of the Border Defence System Against the Ottoman Empire in Hungary (up to the Early Eighteenth Century)," in (ed.) Geza David and Pal Fodor, *Ottomans, Hungarians, and Habsburgs in Central Europe: The Military Confines in the Era of Ottoman Conquest*, (Leiden: E.J. Brill, 2000), 13–14; Szakaly, "Nandorfehervar, 1521," 71–72.

198. Şeref, *Muhaç Meydan Muharebesi: 1526 (Türk–Macar) Seferi*, (İstanbul: Askeri Matbaa, 1930), 8–22; Jorga, *Osmanlı İmparatorluğu Tarihi*, vol. 2, 336–338.

199. Egemen, Güvenç and Bozkurt, *Türk Silahlı Kuvvetleri Tarihi Osmanlı Devri (1451–1566)*, 647–656, 682–690, 700–705, 725–730; Busbecq (Forster), *Turkish Letters of Ogier Ghiselin de Busbecq*, 240–241.

200. M. N. Pearson, *The New Cambridge History of India: The Portuguese in India*, vol. 1.1, (Cambridge: Cambridge University Press, 1987), 5–31.

201. Palmira Brummett, *Ottoman Seapower and Levantine Diplomacy in the Age of Discovery*, (Albany: State University of New York Press, 1994), 22–23, 48, 112–114; Kamal Salibi, *A History of Arabia*, (New York: Caravan Books, 1980), 132–137.

202. Brummett, *Ottoman Seapower and Levantine Diplomacy*, 32–36, 114–121; S. Soucek, "Selman Reis," in (ed.) P. Bearman, Th. Bianquis, C. E. Bosworth, E. van Donzel and W. P. Heinrichs, *Encyclopaedia of Islam*, 2nd Edition, vol. 9; (Leiden: E.J. Brill, 2008), online edition.

203. Brummett, *Ottoman Seapower and Levantine Diplomacy*, 172–174; Salibi, *History of Arabia*, 137–141; Soucek, "Selman Reis."

204. İsmail Hakkı Uzunçarşılı, *Osmanlı Tarihi*, vol. 3, section 1, (Ankara: Türk Tarih Kurumu Basımevi, 1995), 32–33; G. Venstein, "Sokollu Mehmed Pasha," in (ed.) P. Bearman, Th. Bianquis, C. E. Bosworth, E. van Donzel and W. P. Heinrichs, *Encyclopaedia of Islam*, 2nd Edition, vol. 9; (Leiden: E.J. Brill, 2008), online edition.

205. C. R. Boxer, "A Note on Portuguese Reactions to the Revival of the Red Sea Spice Trade and the Rise of Atjeh 1540–1600," *Journal of Southeast Asian Studies*, vol. 10, no. 3, 418–427; Leonard Y. Andaya, "Interactions with the Outside World and Adaptation in

Southeast Asian Society, 1500–1800," in (ed.) Nicholas Tarling, *The Cambridge History of Southeast Asia*, vol. 1, (Cambridge: Cambridge University Press, 1992), 383–387.

206. Richard Blackburn, "The Collapse of Ottoman Authority in Yemen, 968/1560-976/1568," *Die Welt des Islams*, vol. 19, no. 1–4, 1979, 119–176.

207. Pearson, *New Cambridge History of India*, 34, 44–46; Jon E. Mandaville, "The Ottoman Province of Al-Hasa in the Sixteenth and Seventeenth Centuries," *Journal of the American Oriental Society*, vol. 90, no. 3, July–September 1970, 488–491.

208. Giancarlo Casale, "Global Politics in the 1580s: One Canal, Twenty Thousand Cannibals, and an Ottoman Plot to Rule the World," *Journal of World History*, vol. 18, no. 3, 2007, 273–277.

209. Brummett, *Ottoman Seapower and Levantine Diplomacy*, 24–26; Boxer, "Note on Portuguese Reactions," 416–422; Salibi, *History of Arabia*, 139–140, 144–152.

210. Finkel, *Government of Warfare*, 8–10; Murphey, "Woynuk," 2–3, 6–7; Palffy, "Origins and Development of the Border Defence System," 40.

211. Finkel, *Government of Warfare*, 11–14.

212. Peçevi İbrahim, *Peçevi Tarihi*, vol. 2, (ed.) Bekir Sıtkı Baykal, (Ankara: Kültür Bakanlığı Yayınları, 1999), 194–195.

213. Peçevi (Baykal), *Peçevi Tarihi*, 196–203; Hayri Aytepe and Lütfü Güvenç, *Türk Silahlı Kuvvetleri Tarihi Osmanlı Devri (1566–1683)*, vol. 3, section 3, (Ankara: Genelkurmay Basımevi, 1981), 226–229.

214. Finkel, *Government of Warfare*, 15–20.

215. Palffy, "Origins and Development of the Border Defence System," 54–56; Finkel, *Government of Warfare*, 20.

216. Jozsef Kelenik, "The Military Revolution in Hungary," in (ed.) Geza David and Pal Fodor, *Ottomans, Hungarians, and Habsburgs in Central Europe: The Military Confines in the Era of Ottoman Conquest*, (Leiden: E.J. Brill, 2000), 130–137.

217. Caroline Finkel, "French Mercenaries in the Habsburg–Ottoman War of 1593–1606: The Desertion of the Papa Garrison to the Ottomans in 1600," *Bulletin of the School of Oriental and African Studies*, vol. 55, no. 3, 1992, 451–470.

218. Finkel, *Government of Warfare*, 34–38.

Chapter 3

1. For some classical examples *see* İsmail Hakkı Uzunçarşılı, *Osmanı Tarihi*, vol. 3, section 2, (Ankara: Türk Tarih Kurumu Basmevi, 1983), vol. 3, 270–288; Halil İnalcık, "The Ottoman State: Economy and Society, 1300–1600," in (ed.) Halil İnalcık and Donald Quataert, *An Economic and Social History of the Ottoman Empire, 1300–1914*, (Cambridge: Cambridge University Press, 1994), 22; Ömer Lütfi Barkan and Justin McCarthy, "The Price Revolution of the Sixteenth Century: A Turning Point in the Economic History of the Near East," *International Journal of Middle East Studies*, vol. 6, no. 1, January 1975, 3–28; Sugar, *Southeastern Europe under Ottoman Rule, 1354–1804*, 65.

2. Chase, *Firearms*, 98.

3. For some important examples of revisionist literature *see* Virginia Aksan, *Ottoman Wars 1700–1870: An Empire Besieged*, (Harlow: Pearson, Longman, 2007), 1–8, 34; Metin Kunt, *The Sultan's Servants: The Transformation of Ottoman Provincial Government, 1550–1650*, (New York: Columbia University Press, 1983), 98–99; Rifaat Ali Abou El-Haj, *Formation of the Modern State: The Ottoman Empire Sixteenth to Eighteenth Centuries*, (New York: State University

of New York Press, 1991), 2–11, 22–23, 25–26; Karen Barkey, *Bandits and Bureaucrats: The Ottoman Route to State Centralization*, (Ithaca: Cornell University Press, 1994), ix, 45; Rhoads Murphey, "Continuity and Discontinuity in Ottoman Administrative Theory and Practice during the Late Seventeenth Century," *Poetics Today*, vol. 14, no. 2, Summer 1993, 420–425; Şevket Pamuk, "Institutional Change and the Longevity of the Ottoman Empire, 1500–1800," *Journal of Interdisciplinary History*, vol. 35, no. 2, Autumn 2004, 225–247.

4. Finkel, *Osman's Dream*, 160, 164.
5. Parker, *Military Revolution*, 43; El-Haj, *Formation of the Modern State*, 6, 9, 11, 18.
6. Busbecq (Forster), *Turkish Letters of Ogier Ghiselin de Busbecq*, 111–112.
7. Parker, *Military Revolution*, 61; Tallett, *War and Society in Early-Modern Europe, 1495–1715*, 172.
8. Finkel, *Government of Warfare*, 151.
9. Murphey, *Ottoman Warfare, 1500–1700*, 21–22, 68–69.
10. These were Rumeli Sağ Kol (İstanbul-Vize-Aydos-İsmail), Rumeli Orta Kol (which was also known as Via Militaria; İstanbul-Edirne-Filibe-Sofya-Belgrat), Rumeli Sol Kol (which was also known as Via Egnatia; İstanbul-Selanik), Anadolu Sağ Kol (İstanbul-Yalova-Bursa-İzmir), Anadolu Orta Kol (İstanbul-Eskişehir-Konya-Adana) and Anadolu Sol Kol (İstanbul-İzmid-Bolu-Tosya-Merzifon-Sivas-Malatya-Diyarbakır). Rıza Bozkurt, *Osmanlı İmparatorluğunda Kollar, Ulak ve İaşe Menzilleri*, (Ankara: Genelkurmay Basımevi, 1966), 1–4; Konstantin Josif Ireček, *Belgrad-İstanbul-Roma Askeri Yolu*, (Turkish Translation of the Bulgarian original *Via Militaris Singidunum-Constantinopolis*), (trans.) Ali Kemal Balkanlı, (Ankara: Kültür Bakanlığı Yayınları, 1990), 108–130; Rhoads Murphey, *The Functioning of the Ottoman Army under Murad IV (1623–1639/1032–1049): Key to the Understanding of the Relations Between Center and Periphery in Seventeenth Century Turkey*, Chicago: University of Chicago Unpublished Ph.D. Dissertation, 1979), 91–107; Mehmet İnbaşı, *Ukrayna'da Osmanlılar: Kamaniçe Seferi ve Organizasyonu (1672)*, (İstanbul: Yeditepe Yayınevi, 2004), 55–57.
11. Bozkurt, *Osmanlı İmparatorluğunda Kollar, Ulak ve İaşe Menzilleri*, 21–24; For the transportation and billeting phases of Kamanets (Kamaniçe) campaign of 1672 *see* İnbaşı, *Ukrayna'da Osmanlılar*, 60–114; Also *see* the transportation and billeting phases of Morae campaign of 1714. Mehmet Yaşar Ertaş, *Sultanın Ordusu: Mora Fethi Örneği 1714–1716*, (İstanbul: Yeditepe Yayınevi, 2007), 31–79.
12. Finkel, *Government of Warfare*, 151–154, 198–203.
13. Bozkurt, *Osmanlı İmparatorluğunda Kollar, Ulak ve İaşe Menzilleri*, 21–29, 37–40; İnbaşı, *Ukrayna'da Osmanlılar*, 212–289; Ertaş, *Sultanın Ordusu*, 85–106, 119–145; Busbecq (Forster), *Turkish Letters of Ogier Ghiselin de Busbecq*, 109–110.
14. Martin van Creveld, *Supplying the War: Logistics from Wallenstein to Patton*, (Cambridge: Cambridge University Press, 2004), 18–21.
15. Busbecq (Forster), *Turkish Letters of Ogier Ghiselin de Busbecq*, 12–13; Gradeva, "War and Peace Along the Danube," 120–127; İnbaşı, *Ukrayna'da Osmanlılar*, 109–114.
16. Finkel, *Government of Warfare*, 154–155.
17. Bülent Çelik, *Osmanlı Sefer Organizasyonlarından Kentli Esnafın Getirdiği Çözümler: Orducu Esnafı*, (Ankara: University of Ankara Unpublished Ph.D. Dissertation, 2002), supra. 57.
18. Çelik, *Osmanlı Sefer Organizasyonlarından Kentli Esnafın Getirdiği Çözümler*, 59–68.
19. M. Münir Aktepe, "Ahmed III. Devrinde Şark Seferine İştirak Edecek Ordu Esnafı Hakkında Vesikalar," *İstanbul Üniversitesi Edebiyat Fakültesi Tarih Dergisi*, vol. 7, no. 10, September 1954, 16–19; Robert W. Olson, "The Esnaf and the Patrona Halil Rebellion of 1730: A Realignment in Ottoman Politics?," *Journal of the Economic and Social History of the Orient*, vol. 17, no. 3, September 1974, 335–344.

20. Finkel, *Government of Warfare*, 160–161.
21. Agoston, *Guns for the Sultan*, 135–138.
22. Murphey, *Functioning of the Ottoman Army under Murad IV (1623–1639/1032–1049)*, xviii, 26; İnbaşı, *Ukrayna'da Osmanlılar*, 78–109, 222–242.
23. Tallett, *War and Society in Early-Modern Europe, 1495–1715*, 62.
24. As an example a bit more than 80,000 personnel (excluding labor units and camp followers) took part in Kamanets campaign in 1672. These were; 34,825 Kapıkulu soldiers (52 % of them Janissaries), 21,500 provincial soldiers (Sipahis and all sorts of provincial infantry), 10,000 Crimean Tatars, 9,000 Wallachians and Moldavians and 5,000 Cossacks. İnbaşı, *Ukrayna'da Osmanlılar*, 119–121.
25. Tallett, *War and Society in Early-Modern Europe, 1495–1715*, 56, 150–151; Creveld, *Supplying the War*, 25; Corvisier, *Armies and Societies in Europe, 1494–1789*, 5; Aşir Arkayın, *TSK Tarihi Osmanlı Devri İkinci Viyana Kuşatması 1683*, vol. 3, annex to section 4, (Ankara: Genelkurmay Basımevi, 1983), 113.
26. Gabor Agoston, "The Costs of the Ottoman Fortress System in Hungary in the Sixteenth and Seventeenth Centuries," (ed.) Geza David and Pal Fodor, *Ottomans, Hungarians, and Habsburgs in Central Europe: The Military Confines in the Era of Ottoman Conquest*, (Leiden: E.J. Brill, 2000), 222–228; Tallett, *War and Society in Early-Modern Europe, 1495–1715*, 149–150.
27. Busbecq (Forster), *Turkish Letters of Ogier Ghiselin de Busbecq*, 52–53, 110–111; Tallett, *War and Society in Early-Modern Europe, 1495–1715*, 54; Finkel, *Government of Warfare*, 173, 191.
28. Pamuk, "Institutional Change and the Longevity," 246–247; J. L. Price, "A State Dedicated to War? The Dutch Republic in the Seventeenth Century," in (ed.) Andrew Ayton and J. L. Price, *The Medieval Military Revolution*, (New York: Barnes & Noble Books, 1998), 184–186.
29. Stanford J. Shaw, "Some Aspects of the Aims and Achievements of the Nineteenth-Century Ottoman Reformers," in (ed.) William R. Polk and Richard L. Chambers, *Beginnings of Modernization in the Middle East: The Nineteenth Century*, (Chicago: The University of Chicago Press, 1968), 30.
30. Murphey, *Functioning of the Ottoman Army under Murad IV (1623–1639/1032–1049)*, 17.
31. Finkel, *Government of Warfare*, 130–137, 260–265; İnalcık, "Ottoman State," 74.
32. Murphey, "Continuity and Discontinuity in Ottoman Administrative Theory," 431–433.
33. Finkel, *Government of Warfare*, 130–137, 141–143; Çelik, *Osmanlı Sefer Organizasyonlarından Kentli Esnafın Getirdiği Çözümler*, 11–12, 30–31, 64–70; İnbaşı, *Ukrayna'da Osmanlılar*, 223–228; Ertaş, *Sultanın Ordusu*, 266–270.
34. Pamuk, "Institutional Change and the Longevity," 239–240; Tallett, *War and Society in Early-Modern Europe, 1495–1715*, 174, 187.
35. Finkel, *Government of Warfare*, 255–257; Kunt, *Sultan's Servants*, 88; Aksan, *Ottoman Wars 1700–1870*, 54–55; Ertaş, *Sultanın Ordusu*, 230–232, 319–320.
36. El-Haj, *Formation of the Modern State*, 15.
37. Murphey, *Ottoman Warfare, 1500–1700*, 51–52.
38. Orhonlu, *Osmanlı İmparatorluğunda Derbend Teşkilatı*, 34–37; Finkel, *Government of Warfare*, 257–260.
39. Murphey, *Functioning of the Ottoman Army under Murad IV (1623–1639/1032–1049)*, 17–19; Ziya and Rahmi, *Girit Seferi*, (İstanbul: Askeri Matbaa, 1933), 23–26.

40. Murphey, *Functioning of the Ottoman Army under Murad IV (1623–1639/1032–1049)*, 19.
41. Ibid., 63.
42. Creveld, *Supplying the War*, 8.
43. Corvisier, *Armies and Societies in Europe, 1494–1789*, 11, 73–77; Tallett, *War and Society in Early-Modern Europe, 1495–1715*, 118–119, 188, 198, 202, 204.
44. Murphey, "Continuity and Discontinuity in Ottoman Administrative Theory," 425–430, 436–440; Cornell H. Fleischer, *Bureaucrat and Intellectual in the Ottoman Empire: The Historian Mustafa Ali (1541–1600)*, (Princeton: Princeton University Press, 1986), 35, 214–221.
45. The combat strength of the Janissaries fluctuated between 20,000 and 35,000 during the first half of the 17th century. Murphey, *Functioning of the Ottoman Army under Murad IV (1623–1639/1032–1049)*, 42–47.
46. İsmail Hakkı Uzunçarşılı, *Osmanlı Devleti Teşkilatından Kapukulu Ocakları*, vol. 1, 3rd Printing, (Ankara: Türk Tarih Kurumu Basımevi, 1988), 329–330.
47. Amon Cohen, "The Army in Palestine in the Eighteenth Century: Sources of Its Weakness and Strength," *Bulletin of the School of Oriental and African Studies*, vol. 34, no. 1, 1971, 41–43; Jane Hathaway, "The Military Household in Ottoman Egypt," *International Journal of Middle East Studies*, vol. 27, no. 1, February 1995, 40–44; Daniel Goffman, *The Ottoman Empire and Early Modern Europe*, (Cambridge: Cambridge University Press, 2004), 120–121; Gradeva, "War and Peace Along the Danube," 112–116; Murphey, *Functioning of the Ottoman Army under Murad IV (1623–1639/1032–1049)*, 12–14.
48. Uzunçarşılı, *Osmanlı Devleti Teşkilatından Kapukulu Ocakları*, vol. 1, 24–26, 31–34, 172; Murphey, *Functioning of the Ottoman Army under Murad IV (1623–1639/1032–1049)*, 9–11.
49. Uzunçarşılı, *Osmanlı Devleti Teşkilatından Kapukulu Ocakları*, vol. 1, 64–69.
50. Ibid., 169, 183; Kunt, *Sultan's Servants*, 32–33.
51. Uzunçarşılı, *Osmanlı Devleti Teşkilatından Kapukulu Ocakları*, vol. 1, 466–471.
52. Tallett, *War and Society in Early-Modern Europe, 1495–1715*, 141–142.
53. Uzunçarşılı, *Osmanlı Devleti Teşkilatından Kapukulu Ocakları*, vol. 1, 464–478, 488; Kunt, *Sultan's Servants*, 83; Cohen, "Army in Palestine in the Eighteenth Century," 42–43.
54. Cemal Kafadar, "On the Purity and Corruption of the Janissaries," *The Turkish Studies Association Bulletin*, vol. 15, no. 2, September 1991, 273–278.
55. İsmail Hakkı Uzunçarşılı, "Levend," *İslam Ansiklopedisi*, vol. 6, (İstanbul: Milli Eğitim Bakanlığı Yayınları, 1993), 46–47; M. Tayyib Gökbilgin, "Sekban," *İslam Ansiklopedisi*, vol. 8, (İstanbul: Milli Eğitim Bakanlığı Yayınları, 1993), 326–327.
56. Akdağ, *Türk Halkının Dirlik ve Düzenlik Kavgası*, 16–17; Kunt, *Sultan's Servants*, 24.
57. Karen Barkey, "In Different Times: Scheduling and Social Control in the Ottoman Empire, 1550 to 1650," *Comparative Studies in Society and History*, vol. 38, no. 3, July 1996, 460, 463–472; Kunt, *Sultan's Servants*, 73–76.
58. Barkey, "In Different Times," 76–84, 164–165; Kunt, *Sultan's Servants*, 77; Cohen, "Army in Palestine in the Eighteenth Century," 45–47.
59. M. Çağatay Uluçay, *XVII. Asırda Saruhan'da Eşkiyalık ve Halk Hareketleri*, (İstanbul: Resimli Ay Matbaası, 1944), 78–89; Barkey, "In Different Times," 165–166, 172–173; Ertaş, *Sultanın Ordusu*, 232–237.
60. Akdağ, *Türk Halkının Dirlik ve Düzenlik Kavgası*, 70–71.
61. Uzunçarşılı, "Levend," vol. 6, 47–48; Goffman, *Ottoman Empire and Early Modern Europe*, 113.

62. Hayri Aytepe and Lütfü Güvenç, *TSK Tarihi Osmanlı Devri (1566–1683)*, vol. 3, section 3, (Ankara: Genelkurmay Basımevi, 1981), 203–221; Uzunçarşılı, *Osmanlı Tarihi*, vol. 3, 482.
63. Avni Savaşkurt, *Kanije Müdafaası*, (İstanbul: Askeri Matbaa, 1945), 10–21.
64. Aytepe and Güvenç, *TSK Tarihi Osmanlı Devri (1566–1683)*, 246–247.
65. Uzunçarşılı, *Osmanlı Devleti Teşkilatından Kapukulu Ocakları*, vol. 1, 478, 486–488; Barkey, "In Different Times," 68–70.
66. Akdağ, *Türk Halkının Dirlik ve Düzenlik Kavgası*, 70, 99–100; Gökbilgin, "Sekban," 326; Virginia H. Aksan, "Locating the Ottomans Among Early Modern Empires," in *Ottomans and Europeans: Contacts and Conflicts*, (İstanbul: The Isis Press, 2004), 96–97, 106.
67. R. M. Savory, "Barud-iv. The Safawids," in (ed.) P. Bearman, Th. Bianquis, C. E. Bosworth, E. van Donzel and W. P. Heinrichs, *Encyclopaedia of Islam*, 2nd Edition, vol. 1; (Leiden: E.J. Brill, 2008), online edition.
68. Akdağ, *Türk Halkının Dirlik ve Düzenlik Kavgası*, 98.
69. Halil İnalcık, "The Socio-Political Affects of Diffusion Fire-arms in the Middle East," in (ed.) V. J. Parry and M. E. Yapp, *War, Technology and Society in the Middle East*, (London: Oxford University Press, 1975), 204; Giancarlo Casale, "The Ethnic Composition of Ottoman Ship Crews and the Rumi Challenge to Portuguese Identity," *Medieval Encounters*, vol. 13, no. 2, June 2007, 132, 137; Chase, *Firearms*, 131–132.
70. Nicholas C. J. Pappas, "Stradioti: Balkan Mercenaries in Fifteenth and Sixteenth Century Italy," http://www.shsu.edu/%7Ehis_ncp/Stradioti.html; Philippe Contamine, *War in the Middle Ages*, (trans.) Michael Jones, (Oxford: Blackwell Publications, 1984), 128–129; Corvisier, *Armies and Societies in Europe, 1494–1789*, 136.
71. İnalcık, "Socio-Political Affects of Diffusion Fire-arms in the Middle East," 24; Suraiya Faroqhi, "Crisis and Change, 1590–1699," in (ed.) Halil İnalcık and Donald Quataert, *An Economic and Social History of the Ottoman Empire, 1300–1914*, (Cambridge: Cambridge University Press, 1994), 434–435.
72. Barkey, "In Different Times," 24; Parker, *Military Revolution*, 59.
73. Aytepe and Güvenç, *TSK Tarihi Osmanlı Devri (1566–1683)*, 178.
74. Tallett, *War and Society in Early-Modern Europe, 1495–1715*, 79.
75. Fleischer, *Bureaucrat and Intellectual in the Ottoman Empire*, 19; El-Haj, *Formation of the Modern State*, 45–46; Kunt, *Sultan's Servants*, 34, 43, 67–68.
76. Barkey, "In Different Times," 48–50; Akdağ, *Türk Halkının Dirlik ve Düzenlik Kavgası*, 45.
77. Sydney Nettleton Fisher, "Civil Strife in the Ottoman Empire, 1481–1503," *The Journal of Modern History*, vol. 13, no. 4, December 1941, 449–465; Solakzade, *Solakzade Tarihi*, 365–367; Finkel, *Government of Warfare*, 77, 82; Faroqhi, "Crisis and Change, 1590–1699," 414–415.
78. Faroqhi, "Crisis and Change, 1590–1699," 419, 435–436; Finkel, *Government of Warfare*, 251, 295–304; Barkey, "In Different Times," 36; H. G. Majer, "Othman Pasha, Yegen," in (ed.) P. Bearman, Th. Bianquis, C. E. Bosworth, E. van Donzel and W. P. Heinrichs, *Encyclopaedia of Islam*, 2nd Edition, vol. 8; (Leiden: E.J. Brill, 2008), online edition.
79. Koçi Bey, *Koçi Bey Risalesi*, (ed.) Zuhuri Danışman, 3rd printing, (İstanbul: MEB Yayınları, 1997), 35–36.
80. Akdağ, *Türk Halkının Dirlik ve Düzenlik Kavgası*, 69–72, 85; Barkey, "In Different Times," 141, 147; Uluçay, *XVII. Asırda Saruhan'da Eşkiyalık ve Halk Hareketleri*, 23–30, 90–96.
81. Akdağ, *Türk Halkının Dirlik ve Düzenlik Kavgası*, 14, 19; Barkey, "In Different Times," 144; Faroqhi, "Crisis and Change, 1590–1699," 418.

82. İnalcık, "Socio-Political Affects of Diffusion Fire-arms in the Middle East," 195–198, 200–201; Mücteba İlgürel, "Osmanlı İmparatorluğunda Ateşli Silahların Yayılışı," *İstanbul Üniversitesi Edebiyat Fakültesi Tarih Dergisi*, no. 32, March 1979, 302–304.

83. İlgürel, "Osmanlı İmparatorluğunda Ateşli Silahların Yayılışı," 305–315; Ronald C. Jennings, "Firearms, Bandits, and Gun-Control: Some Evidence on Ottoman Policy towards Firearms in the Possession of Reaya, from Judicial Records of Kayseri, 1600–1627," in *Studies on Ottoman Social History in the Sixteenth and Seventeenth Centuries*, (İstanbul: The Isis Press, 1999), 330–344.

84. Barkey, "In Different Times," x, 22, 55–56, 85–102; Murphey, "Continuity and Discontinuity in Ottoman Administrative Theory," 424–425.

85. Mücteba İlgürel, "İl Erleri," *Türkiye Diyanet Vakfı İslam Ansiklopedisi*, vol. 22, (Ankara: Türkiye Diyanet Vakfı Yayınları, 2002), 59–60; Akdağ, *Türk Halkının Dirlik ve Düzenlik Kavgası*, 89–90; Barkey, "In Different Times," 160, 167–169.

86. Uluçay, *XVII. Asırda Saruhan'da Eşkiyalık ve Halk Hareketleri*, 13–19; Akdağ, *Türk Halkının Dirlik ve Düzenlik Kavgası*, 25.

87. Bernard Lewis, "Some Reflections on the Decline of the Ottoman Empire," *Studia Islamica*, vol. 9, 1958, 115.

88. John Stoye, *The Siege of Vienna*, (London: Collins, 1964), 30–34.

89. Ahmet Ağa, *Devlet-i Aliyye Teşrifatçıbaşısı Ahmet Ağa'nın Viyana Kuşatması Günlüğü*, (ed.) Richard F. Kreutel, (trans.) Esat N. Erendor, (İstanbul: Aksoy Yayıncılık, 1998), 115; Stoye, *Siege of Vienna*, 42–45.

90. Arkayın, *TSK Tarihi Osmanlı Devri İkinci Viyana Kuşatması 1683*, 32–34.

91. Stoye, *Siege of Vienna*, 20–22, 52; Arkayın, *TSK Tarihi Osmanlı Devri İkinci Viyana Kuşatması 1683*, 42–46; Ivan Parvev, *Habsburgs and Ottomans: Between Vienna and Belgrade (1683–1739)*, (Boulder: East European Monographs, 1995), 31–32.

92. Stoye, *Siege of Vienna*, 51–52; Arkayın, *TSK Tarihi Osmanlı Devri İkinci Viyana Kuşatması 1683*, 48–50; Palffy, "Origins and Development of the Border Defence System," 13–56.

93. Stoye, *Siege of Vienna*, 52, 67–71.

94. Ibid., 123–131.

95. Ibid., 132–144; Arkayın, *TSK Tarihi Osmanlı Devri İkinci Viyana Kuşatması 1683*, 52–54, 58–65.

96. Stoye, *Siege of Vienna*, 150.

97. Ziya and Rahmi, *Girit Seferi*, 7–21, 26–32.

98. Ahmet Ağa (Kreutel), *Devlet-i Aliyye Teşrifatçıbaşısı Ahmet Ağa'nın Viyana Kuşatması Günlüğü*, 26–30, 114; Stoye, *Siege of Vienna*, 48, 151–159; Arkayın, *TSK Tarihi Osmanlı Devri İkinci Viyana Kuşatması 1683*, 71–79.

99. Stoye, *Siege of Vienna*, 161–166, 171.

100. Ahmet Ağa (Kreutel), *Devlet-i Aliyye Teşrifatçıbaşısı Ahmet Ağa'nın Viyana Kuşatması Günlüğü*, 44–45, 49, 51, 55, 63–64, 88; Stoye, *Siege of Vienna*, 168–173; Arkayın, *TSK Tarihi Osmanlı Devri İkinci Viyana Kuşatması 1683*, 76–80.

101. Ahmet Ağa (Kreutel), *Devlet-i Aliyye Teşrifatçıbaşısı Ahmet Ağa'nın Viyana Kuşatması Günlüğü*, 58–59, 76–80, 83; Stoye, *Siege of Vienna*, 174–177, 203–217, 244–246; Arkayın, *TSK Tarihi Osmanlı Devri İkinci Viyana Kuşatması 1683*, 66–71.

102. Ahmet Ağa (Kreutel), *Devlet-i Aliyye Teşrifatçıbaşısı Ahmet Ağa'nın Viyana Kuşatması Günlüğü*, 81; Stoye, *Siege of Vienna*, 238–242, 244–256; Arkayın, *TSK Tarihi Osmanlı Devri İkinci Viyana Kuşatması 1683*, 81–83.

103. Ahmet Ağa (Kreutel), *Devlet-i Aliyye Teşrifatçıbaşısı Ahmet Ağa'nın Viyana Kuşatması Günlüğü*, 97–106, 112; Stoye, *Siege of Vienna*, 257–264; Arkayın, *TSK Tarihi Osmanlı Devri İkinci Viyana Kuşatması 1683*, 84–85.

104. Stoye, *Siege of Vienna*, 273–277; Arkayın, *TSK Tarihi Osmanlı Devri İkinci Viyana Kuşatması 1683*, 98–99; Parvev, *Habsburgs and Ottomans*, 41–42.

105. Gürsoy Şahin, "Osmanlı Devleti'nin 1684 Avusturya-Macaristan Seferi Hazırlıkları ve Bunların Afyonkarahisar Kazasında Halka Yansımaları," *Uludağ Üniversitesi Sosyal Bilimler Dergisi*, vol. 4, no. 4, 2003, 113–116.

106. Nicolae Jorga, *Osmanlı İmparatorluğu Tarihi*, vol. 4, (trans.) Nilüfer Epçeli, (İstanbul: Yeditepe Yayınevi, 2005), 177–230; Aşir Arkayın and A. Rıza Bozkurt, *TSK Tarihi Osmanlı Devri İkinci Viyana Kuşatmasından Nizam-ı Cedidin Teşkiline Kadar Olan Devre (1683–1793)*, vol. 3, section 4, (Ankara: Genelkurmay Basımevi, 1982), 186–212; Parvev, *Habsburgs and Ottomans*, 43–127.

107. Murphey, *Ottoman Warfare, 1500–1700*, 10.

108. Murphey, "Continuity and Discontinuity in Ottoman Administrative Theory," 426–428.

109. Finkel, *Government of Warfare*, 293–300.

110. Gradeva, "War and Peace Along the Danube," 112–119.

111. Parvev, *Habsburgs and Ottomans*, 76–98; Jorga, *Osmanlı İmparatorluğu Tarihi*, vol. 4, 208–209; Gradeva, "War and Peace Along the Danube," 112; Finkel, *Government of Warfare*, 306; Murphey, "Continuity and Discontinuity in Ottoman Administrative Theory," 439; Aksan, "Locating the Ottomans," 99.

112. Aksan, *Ottoman Wars 1700–1870*, 19–22; *See also* Joseph S. Roucek, "The Geopolitics of Danubia," *American Journal of Economics and Sociology*, vol. 5, no. 2, January 1946, 217–226.

113. İsmail Hakkı Uzunçarşılı, *Osmanlı Tarihi*, vol. 4, section 1, (Ankara: Türk Tarih Kurumu, 1978), 7–9; Gradeva, "War and Peace Along the Danube," 111–119; Ertaş, *Sultanın Ordusu*, 217–218.

114. Michael Robert Hickok, *Ottoman Military Government in Eighteenth-Century Bosnia*, (Leiden: E.J. Brill, 1997), 20–22, 41–52, 57–65, 78–98; Kunt, *Sultan's Servants*, 84–87; Gradeva, "War and Peace Along the Danube," 115–117.

115. Habsburg military border defense system, which depended basically on Orthodox and Catholic refugees from Ottoman provinces and locals was actually founded much earlier during 1530s by making use of the remains of the old Hungarian one. However, the system gained its unique character during 17th century especially after Treaty of Karlowitz (following more or less the rivers of Una, Sava, and Danube). *See* Gunther Rothenberg, *The Austrian Military Border in Croatia, 1522–1747*, (Urbana: University of Illinois, 1960), passim.

116. Hickok, *Ottoman Military Government in Eighteenth-Century Bosnia*, 1–2, 40–42, 54–55; Aksan, "Locating the Ottomans," 110–116.

117. Hickok, *Ottoman Military Government in Eighteenth-Century Bosnia*, 26–36; Uzunçarşılı, *Osmanlı Tarihi*, vol. 4, 274–277.

118. S. Soucek, "Özi," in (ed.) P. Bearman, Th. Bianquis, C. E. Bosworth, E. van Donzel and W. P. Heinrichs, *Encyclopaedia of Islam*, 2nd Edition, vol. 8; (Leiden: E.J. Brill, 2008), online edition.

119. Virginia H. Aksan, "Manning a Black Sea Garrison in the Eighteenth Century: Ochakov and Concepts of Mutiny and Rebellion in the Ottoman Context," in *Ottomans and Europeans: Contacts and Conflicts*, (İstanbul: The Isis Press, 2004), 251–261; Orhan Şaik Gökyay, "Kamaniçe Muhafızlarının Çektiği," *İstanbul Üniversitesi Edebiyat Fakültesi Tarih Dergisi*, no. 32, March 1979, 294–299.

120. Necati Salim, *Prut (1711)*, (İstanbul: Askeri Matbaa, 1931), 14–42; Aksan, *Ottoman Wars 1700–1870*, 90–97; Uzunçarşılı, *Osmanlı Tarihi*, vol. 4, 76–85.

121. Hopefully some bold and innovative international and interdisciplinary projects that would bring together various specialists and would employ field investigation and archive research like Akkerman Fortress Project would surely enrich our understanding of Ottoman defensive system and fill the vacuum. See. *Akkerman Fortress Project*, http://www.akkermanfortress.org.ua/akkerman_face/external/main/go/aqk_home.

122. Karl K. Barbir, *Ottoman Rule in Damascus 1708–1758*, (Princeton: Princeton University Press, 1980), 13; Abdul-Karim Rafeq, *The Province of Damascus 1723–1783*, (Beirut: Khayats, 1966), 58–59; Uzunçarşılı, *Osmanlı Tarihi*, vol. 4, 3, 5.

123. Barbir, *Ottoman Rule in Damascus 1708–1758*, 33–35, 37–38; Rafeq, *Province of Damascus 1723–1783*, 65–72.

124. Barbir, *Ottoman Rule in Damascus 1708–1758*, 89–96; Rafeq, *Province of Damascus 1723–1783*, 24–42; Shimon Shamir, "Asad Pahsa al-Azm and Ottoman Rule in Damascus (1743–58)," *Bulletin of the School of Oriental and African Studies*, vol. 26, no. 1, 1963, 6–8.

125. Rafeq, *Province of Damascus 1723–1783*, 82–83, 98–101, 133–141, 165–175, 209–212, 222–226; Barbir, *Ottoman Rule in Damascus 1708–1758*, 33–34, 44–45, 85; Shamir, "Asad Pahsa al-Azm and Ottoman Rule," 11–16, 27–28.

126. Barbir, *Ottoman Rule in Damascus 1708–1758*, 39, 61–64, 72; Aksan, *Ottoman Wars 1700–1870*, 117–118.

127. El-Haj, *Formation of the Modern State*, 12–13, 44; Kunt, *Sultan's Servants*, 93; Dennis N. Skiotis, "From Bandit to Pasha: First Steps in the Rise to Power of Ali Of Tepelen, 1750–1784," *International Journal of Middle East Studies*, vol. 2, no. 3, July 1971, 219–220.

128. Pal Fodor, "State and Society, Crisis and Reform Century: Ottoman Mirror for Princes," in *In Quest of the Golden Apple: Imperial Ideology, Politics and Military Government in the Ottoman Empire*, (İstanbul: The Isis Press, 2000), 23–28; Virginia H. Aksan, "Ottoman Political Writing, 1768–1808," in *Ottomans and Europeans: Contacts and Conflicts*, (İstanbul: The Isis Press, 2004), 25–27; Fleischer, *Bureaucrat and Intellectual in the Ottoman Empire*, 99, 101–102.

129. Koçi Bey (Danışman), *Koçi Bey Risalesi*, xiii–ix, xv–xvi; Ömer Faruk Akgün, "Koçi Bey," *Türkiye Diyanet Vakfı İslam Ansiklopedisi*, vol. 26 (Ankara: Türkiye Diyanet Vakfı Yayınları, 2002), 143–148.

130. Koçi Bey (Danışman), *Koçi Bey Risalesi*, 48–49; Fleischer, *Bureaucrat and Intellectual in the Ottoman Empire*, 101.

131. Koçi Bey (Danışman), *Koçi Bey Risalesi*, 6, 13–15, 27–29, 30–32; Kaldy-Nagy, "Strangers (Ecnebiler) in the 16th Century Military Organization," 167–169; El-Haj, *Formation of the Modern State*, 10, 33.

132. Koçi Bey (Danışman), *Koçi Bey Risalesi*, 9–12, 17–18, 24–26; Fodor, "State and Society, Crisis and Reform Century," 28–37; Barkan, "Timar," 319–322; El-Haj, *Formation of the Modern State*, 30–31, 36, 84–89.

133. Koçi Bey (Danışman), *Koçi Bey Risalesi*, 5–8, 16–18, 37, 39–43, 55–58, 46–47, 60–62; Barkan, "Timar," 320–322; El-Haj, *Formation of the Modern State*, 34–40; Fleischer, *Bureaucrat and Intellectual in the Ottoman Empire*, 139, 192, 226–227.

134. Kunt, *Sultan's Servants*, 79; Fodor, "State and Society, Crisis and Reform Century," 31–32.

135. Barkey, "In Different Times," 47–48; Barkan, "Timar," 322–325; Fleischer, *Bureaucrat and Intellectual in the Ottoman Empire*, 182, 231.

136. El-Haj, *Formation of the Modern State*, 21–28; Fleischer, *Bureaucrat and Intellectual in the Ottoman Empire*, 71, 129, 282.

137. İsmail Hakkı Uzunçarşılı, *Osmanlı Tarihi*, vol. 3, section 1, (Ankara: Türk Tarih Kurumu, 1983), 186–204, 306–308, 367–372, 402–407, 430–432; Ibid., sec. 2, 414–420, 586–588.

138. Aytepe and Güvenç, *TSK Tarihi Osmanlı Devri (1566–1683)*, 265–274, 297–300, 304–311; Murphey, *Ottoman Warfare, 1500–1700*, 9; Murphey, *Functioning of the Ottoman Army under Murad IV (1623–1639/1032–1049)*, 139–159; İnbaşı, *Ukrayna'da Osmanlılar*, 135–163.

139. El-Haj, *Formation of the Modern State*, 5, 45–46, 55–56.

140. El-Haj, *Formation of the Modern State*, 14, 37–38, 44; Corvisier, *Armies and Societies in Europe, 1494–1789*, 10–13.

141. Murphey, *Ottoman Warfare, 1500–1700*, 8–11; Hickok, *Ottoman Military Government in Eighteenth-Century Bosnia*, 8–38.

142. Koçi Bey (Danışman), *Koçi Bey Risalesi*, 37.

143. Niyazi Berkes, *Türkiye'de Çağdaşlaşma*, (İstanbul: Doğu-Batı Yayınları, 1978), 42–44.

144. Virginia, H., *An Ottoman Statesman in War and Peace: Ahmed Resmi Efendi 1700–1783*, (Leiden: E.J. Brill, 1995), 35–37; El-Haj, *Formation of the Modern State*, 68.

145. Faik Reşit Unat, *Osmanlı Sefirleri ve Sefaretnameleri*, 3rd Printing, (Ankara: Türk Tarih Kurumu, 1992), s. 53–58; Enver Ziya Karal, *Osmanlı Tarihi*, vol. 5, (Ankara: Türk Tarih Kurumu Basımevi, 1947) 57–59; Berkes, *Türkiye'de Çağdaşlaşma*, 44–45.

146. Joseph von Hammer Purgstall, *Osmanlı Devleti Tarihi*, (Turkish translation of the German original *Geschichte des Osmanischen Reichs*) vol. 15, (trans.) V. Bürün, (İstanbul: Üçdal Neşriyat, n.d.), 233–235; Berkes, *Türkiye'de Çağdaşlaşma*, 46–50; Abdülhak Adnan Adıvar, *Osmanlı Türklerinde İlim*, 4th Printing, (İstanbul: Remzi Kitabevi, 1982), 181.

147. Peçevi (Baykal), *Peçevi Tarihi*, 111–112; Busbecq, *Turkish Letters of Ogier Ghiselin de Busbecq*, 135.

148. Franz Babinger, "18.Yüzyılda İstanbul'da Kitabiyet," (ed.) Nedret Kuran-Burçoğlu, *Müteferrika ve Osmanlı Matbaası*, (İstanbul: Tarih Vakfı Yurt Yayınları, 2004), 7–11; Berkes, *Türkiye'de Çağdaşlaşma*, 57–62.

149. Actually the Ottoman Ulema's (who were divided into two camps; privileged Ulema leadership and highly dissatisfied lower Ulema and Softas) reception and reaction to the various reform efforts based on their immediate group interests. Seemingly progressive Ulema leadership sided with sultans and high ranking reformers whereas lower Ulema and Softas objected (sometimes violently) reforms which they perceived as a threat to their economic prospects and religious beliefs. See Uriel Heyd, "The Ottoman Ulema and Westernization in the time of Selim III and Mahmud II," in (ed.) Albert Hourani, Philip Khoury and Mary C. Wilson, *The Modern Middle East*, 2nd edition, (London: I.B. Tauris, 2004), 29–39.

150. Babinger, "18.Yüzyılda İstanbul'da Kitabiyet," 11–34; Adıvar, *Osmanlı Türklerinde İlim*, 167; Berkes, *Türkiye'de Çağdaşlaşma*, 57–65.

151. İbrahim Müteferrika, *Milletlerin Düzeninde İlmi Usüller* (Usul-ül Hikem fi Nizami'l Ümem), (ed.) Ömer Okutan, (İstanbul: Milli Eğitim Bakanlığı Yayınları, 1990), 29–31, 59, 63–112; Berkes, *Türkiye'de Çağdaşlaşma*, 50–57.

152. Olson, "Esnaf and the Patrona Halil Rebellion of 1730," 335–344.

153. Joseph von Hammer Purgstall, *Osmanlı Devleti Tarihi*, vol. 14, (trans.) V. Bürün, (İstanbul: Üçdal Neşriyat, n.d.), 129–134; İsmail Hakkı Uzunçarşılı, *Osmanlı Tarihi*, vol. 4, section 1, (Ankara: Türk Tarih Kurumu, 1978), 204–218.

154. Necdet Sakaoğlu, "Ahmed Paşa (Humbaracı)," *İstanbul Ansiklopedisi*, vol. 1, (İstanbul: Toplumsal Tarih Vakfı Yayınları, 1993), 129–130; Uzunçarşılı, *Osmanlı Tarihi*, vol. 4, 322–323; Berkes, *Türkiye'de Çağdaşlaşma*, 66.

155. Hammer, *Osmanlı Devleti Tarihi*, vol. 14, 118; Hammer, *Osmanlı Devleti Tarihi*, vol. 15, 8, 45–46, 81–83, 202–231, 246–260; Uzunçarşılı, *Osmanlı Tarihi*, vol. 4, 322–325; Berkes, *Türkiye'de Çağdaşlaşma*, 6–68.

156. Joseph von Hammer Purgstall, *Osmanlı Devleti Tarihi*, vol. 16, (trans.) V. Bürün, (İstanbul: Üçdal Neşriyat, n.d.), 41–42, 65–69; Hüseyin Yorulmaz, "Şair Devlet Adamı Koca Ragıb Paşa," *Tarih ve Toplum*, vol. 13, no. 76, April 1990, 34–42.

157. Aksan, "An Ottoman Statesman in War and Peace," 1–33, 185.

158. Ibid., 92–94.

159. Ibid., 91–92, 94–97; Virginia H. Aksan, "An Ottoman Portrait of Frederick the Great," in *Ottomans and Europeans: Contacts and Conflicts*, (İstanbul: The Isis Press, 2004), 67–80.

160. Aksan, "An Ottoman Statesman in War and Peace," 117–122, 126–127; Aksan, *Ottoman Wars 1700–1870*, 46; Uzunçarşılı, *Osmanlı Tarihi*, vol. 4, 365–375.

161. Aksan, "An Ottoman Statesman in War and Peace," 129–141, 144–153; Uzunçarşılı, *Osmanlı Tarihi*, vol. 4, 375–389, 395–401.

162. Aksan, "An Ottoman Statesman in War and Peace," 130–134, 153–164; Uzunçarşılı, *Osmanlı Tarihi*, vol. 4, 410–419.

163. İsmail Hakkı Uzunçarşılı, "Sadrazam Halil Hamid Paşa," *Türkiyat Mecmuası*, vol. 5, 1935, 22; Berkes, *Türkiye'de Çağdaşlaşma*, 78–79.

164. Aksan, "An Ottoman Statesman in War and Peace," 165–167; Uzunçarşılı, *Osmanlı Tarihi*, vol. 4, 419–425.

165. Aksan, "An Ottoman Statesman in War and Peace," 117–143, 198–200.

166. Ibid., 188–194; Jacob M.Landau, "Saint-Priest and His Mémoire sur les Turcs," in *Exploring Ottoman and Turkish History*, (London: Hurst & Co., 2004), 85–87.

167. Aksan, "An Ottoman Statesman in War and Peace," x–xviii, 188–200.

168. Virginia H. Aksan, "Breaking the Spell of the Baron de Tott: Reframing the Question of Military Reform in the Ottoman Empire, 1760–1830," in *Ottomans and Europeans: Contacts and Conflicts*, (İstanbul: The Isis Press, 2004), 113–126.

169. Uzunçarşılı, *Osmanlı Tarihi*, vol. 4, 226; Çağatay Uluçay and Enver Kartekin, *Yüksek Mühendis Okulu*, (İstanbul: Berksoy Matbaası, 1958), 20–22.

170. Uzunçarşılı, *Osmanlı Tarihi*, vol. 4, 226–227, 233–234; Uluçay and Kartekin, *Yüksek Mühendis Okulu*, 21–26; For the details about Naval Engineering School *see* Fevzi Kurtoğlu, *Deniz Mektepleri Tarihçesi*, (İstanbul: Deniz Matbaası, 1931), passim.

171. Virginia H. Aksan, "Choiseul Gouffier at the Sublime Porte 1784–1792," in *Ottomans and Europeans: Contacts and Conflicts*, (İstanbul: The Isis Press, 2004), 60–65; Berkes, *Türkiye'de Çağdaşlaşma*, 79–81; Uzunçarşılı, *Osmanlı Tarihi*, vol. 4, 226, 235–257.

172. Stanford J. Shaw, *Between Old and New: The Ottoman Empire Under Sultan Selim III 1789–1807*, (Cambridge: Harvard University Press, 1971), 86–93, 98–110; Besim Özcan, "Tatarcık Abdullah Efendi ve Islahatlarla İlgili Layihası," *Türk Kültürü Araştırmaları*, vol. 25, no. 1, 1987, 55–64; Enver Ziya Karal, *Selim III'ün Hattı Hümayunları: Nizam-ı Cedit*, (Ankara: Türk Tarih Kurumu, 1988), 34–41; Sipahi Çataltepe, *19. Yüzyıl Başlarında Avrupa Dengesi ve Nizam-ı Cedit Ordusu*, (İstanbul: Göçebe Yayınları, 1997), 73–81.

173. Fatih Yeşil, *III. Selim Döneminde Bir Osmanlı Bürokratı: Ebubekir Ratib Efendi*, (Ankara: University of Hacettepe Unpublished M.A. Thesis, 2002), 276–277; İsmail Hakkı Uzunçarşılı, "Tosyalı Ebubekir Ratib Efendi," *Belleten*, vol. 39, no. 153, January 1975, 49–76; J. M. Stein, "An Eighteen-Century Ottoman Ambassador Observes the West: Ebu Bekir Ratib Efendi Reports on the Habsburg System of Roads and Posts," *Archivum Ottomanicum*,

vol. 10, 1985, 225–232; Abdullah Uçman (ed.), *Ebubekir Ratib Efendi'nin Sefaretnamesi*, (İstanbul: Kitabevi Yayınları, 1999), passim.

174. Yeşil, *III. Selim Döneminde Bir Osmanlı Bürokratı*, 62, 87, 101–110, 147; Enver Ziya Karal, "Ebu Bekir Ratib Efendi'nin Nizam-ı Cedit Islahatında Rolü," *V. Türk tarih Kongresi: Kongreye Sunulan Tebliğler*, (Ankara: Türk Tarih Kurumu, 1960).

175. Karal, "Ebu Bekir Ratib Efendi'nin Nizam-ı Cedit Islahatında Rolü," 347–348.

176. Stanford J. Shaw, "The Established Ottoman Army Corps Under Sultan Selim III (1789–1807)," *Der Islam*, vol. 40, February 1965, 144–148, 151–152; Karal, *Osmanlı Tarihi*, vol. 5, 66–74.

177. Shaw, "Established Ottoman Army Corps," 153.

178. Ibid., 149–151, 153.

179. Ibid., 153–172; Turgud Işıksal, "III. Selim'in Türk Topçuluğuna Dair Bir Hattı Hümayunu," *İ.Ü.Ed.Fak. Tarih Dergisi*, vol. 8, no. 11–12, September 1955, 179–182.

180. Stanford J. Shaw, "The Origins of Ottoman Military Reform: The Nizam-ı Cedid Army of Sultan Selim III," *The Journal of Modern History*, vol. 37, no. 3, September 1965, 292–293; Çataltepe, *19. Yüzyıl Başlarında Avrupa Dengesi ve Nizam-ı Cedit Ordusu*, 97.

181. Shaw, "Origins of Ottoman Military Reform," 293–297; Yavuz Cezar, *Osmanlı Maliyesinde Bunalım ve Değişim Dönemi: XVIII. Yüzyıldan Tanzimat'a Mali Tarih*, (İstanbul: Alan Yayıncılık, 1986), 55–234.

182. Shaw, "Origins of Ottoman Military Reform," 297–309; Yücel Özkaya, "Orta Anadolu'da Nizam-ı Cedid'in Kuruluşu ve Kaldırılışı," *A.Ü. Dil Tarih Coğrafya Fakültesi Dergisi*, 1982, 514–529; Musa Çadırcı, "Ankara Sancağında Nizam-ı Cedid Ortasının Teşkili ve Nizam-ı Cedid Askeri Kanunnamesi," *Belleten*, vol. 36, no. 141, January 1972, 7–13; Çataltepe, *19. Yüzyıl Başlarında Avrupa Dengesi ve Nizam-ı Cedit Ordusu*, 98–104, 120–210.

183. Çataltepe, *19. Yüzyıl Başlarında Avrupa Dengesi ve Nizam-ı Cedit Ordusu*, 85–90.

184. Kemal Beydilli, İlhan Şahin, *Mahmud Raif Efendi ve Nizam-ı Cedid'e Dair Eseri*, (Ankara: Türk Tarih Kurumu, 2001), passim.; Kemal Beydilli, "İlk Mühendislerimizden Seyyid Mustafa ve Nizam-ı Cedid'e Dair Risalesi," *Tarih Enstitüsü Dergisi*, no. 13, 1987, 387–479.

185. Kemal Beydilli, *Türk Bilim ve Matbaacılık Tarihinde Mühendishane, Mühendishane Matbaası ve Kütüphanesi (1776–1826)*, (İstanbul: Eren Yayıncılık, 1995), 23–32; Uluçay and Kartekin, *Yüksek Mühendis Okulu*, 17–29; Kemal Beydilli, "Ignatius D'Ohsson Mouradgea (Muradcan Tosunyan)," *İ.Ü. Edebiyat Fakültesi Tarih Dergisi*, no. 34, 1984, 247–314.

186. Beydilli, *Türk Bilim ve Matbaacılık Tarihinde Mühendishane, Mühendishane Matbaası ve Kütüphanesi (1776–1826)*, 32–92; Uluçay and Kartekin, *Yüksek Mühendis Okulu*, 39–41; Mustafa Kaçar, "Osmanlı İmparatorluğu'nda İlk Mühendishane'nin Kuruluşu," *Toplumsal Tarih*, vol., 9, no. 54, June 1998, 7–9; Çataltepe, *19. Yüzyıl Başlarında Avrupa Dengesi ve Nizam-ı Cedit Ordusu*, 108–110, 117–119.

187. Naci Çakın and Nafiz Orhon, *TSK Tarihi Osmanlı Devri (1793–1908)*, vol. 3, section 5, (Ankara: Genelkurmay Basımevi, 1978), 397–407; İsmail Hakkı Uzunçarşılı, "Nizam-ı Cedid Ricalinden Kadı Abdurrahman Paşa I," *Belleten*, vol. 35, no. 138, April 1971, 271–272; For the character and composition of Cezzar's mercenary army *see* Cohen, "Army in Palestine in the Eighteenth Century," 47–53.

188. William Wittman, *Travels in Turkey, Asia-Minor, Syria and Across the Desert into Egypt during the Years 1799, 1800 and 1801*, (London: Richard Phillips, 1803), 147–149, 251–252; John Philip Morier, *Memoir of a Campaign with the Ottoman Army in Egypt from February to July 1800*, (London: Debrett, 1801), 7–17.

189. Wittman, *Travels in Turkey, Asia-Minor, Syria and Across the Desert into Egypt*, 121–123, 137–140, 186–188, 191, 194–196, 198–199, 201–206, 232–233, 252–255, 275, 316; Morier, *Memoir of a Campaign with the Ottoman Army*, 21–33.

190. Wittman, *Travels in Turkey, Asia-Minor, Syria and Across the Desert into Egypt*, 237–245; Morier, *Memoir of a Campaign with the Ottoman Army*, 17–21, 47.

191. Morier, *Memoir of a Campaign with the Ottoman Army*, 71–77, 89–92; Çakın and Orhon, *TSK Tarihi Osmanlı Devri (1793–1908)*, 407–413; Shaw, "Origins of Ottoman Military Reform," 302–303.

192. İsmail Hakkı Uzunçarşılı, *Meşhur Rumeli Ayanlarından Tirsinikli İsmail, Yılık Oğlu Süleyman Ağalar ve Alemdar Mustafa Paşa*, (İstanbul: Maarif Matbaası, 1942), 5–39; Çakın and Orhon, *TSK Tarihi Osmanlı Devri (1793–1908)*, 413–430, 504–511; Aksan, *Ottoman Wars 1700–1870*, 215–224.

193. Uzunçarşılı, *Osmanlı Tarihi*, vol. 4, 254–261, 272–296; Shaw, "Origins of Ottoman Military Reform," 301–302, 304–305; Özkaya, "Orta Anadolu'da Nizam-ı Cedid'in Kuruluşu ve Kaldırılışı," 529–532.

194. Yavuz Senemoğlu (ed.), *Vaka-ı Cedid: Yayla İmamı Tarihi ve Yeni Olaylar*, (İstanbul: Kervan Kitapçılık, n.d.), 67–89; Shaw, "Origins of Ottoman Military Reform," 304; Çakın and Orhon, *TSK Tarihi Osmanlı Devri (1793–1908)*, 514–519; Özkaya, "Orta Anadolu'da Nizam-ı Cedid'in Kuruluşu ve Kaldırılışı," 533–535.

195. Çakın and Orhon, *TSK Tarihi Osmanlı Devri (1793–1908)*, 520–523; Uzunçarşılı, *Osmanlı Tarihi*, vol. 4, 82–123.

196. Senemoğlu, *Vaka-ı Cedid*, 103–108; İsmail Hakkı Uzunçarşılı, "Nizam-ı Cedid Ricalinden Kadı Abdurrahman Paşa II," *Belleten*, vol. 35, no. 139, July 1971, 417–444.

197. For the details of the operations from the Russian perspective *see* Alexander Mikhailovsky-Danilevsky, *Russo-Turkish War of 1806–1812*, 2 vols., (ed.) Alexander Mikaberidze, (West Chester: The Nafzinger Collection, 2002), passim.

198. Çakın and Orhon, *TSK Tarihi Osmanlı Devri (1793–1908)*, 421–430, 511–514; Aksan, *Ottoman Wars 1700–1870*, 270–285.

199. Ali Pasha's rebellion and his eventual demise caught the imagination of the contemporary European writers (including Lord Byron and Alexandre Dumas) thereby several popular but largely inaccurate accounts of the event were published. For a representative example *see* R. A. Davenport, *The Life of Ali Pasha of Tepeleni: Surnamed Aslan, or the Lion*, (London: Thomas Tegg and Son, 1807), 215–418.

200. The best account of the sufferings of the Ottoman soldiers and the way how the war had been fought is the diary of an Ottoman mercenary. *See* Jan Schmidt, "The Adventures of an Ottoman Horseman: The Autobiography of Kabudlı Vasfi Efendi," in Jan Schmidt, *The Joys of Philology, Studies in Ottoman Literature, History and Orientalism (1500–1923)*, (İstanbul: The Isis Press, 2002), 214–241.

201. Çakın and Orhon, *TSK Tarihi Osmanlı Devri (1793–1908)*, 534–541.

202. Khaled Fahmy, *All the Pasha's Men: Mehmed Ali, His Army and the Making of Modern Egypt*, (Cambridge: Cambridge University Press, 1997), 9–12, 79–82, 89–93, 170–171, 175–180; Alain Silvera, "The First Egyptian Student Mission to France Under Muhammad Ali," *Middle Eastern Studies*, vol. 16, no. 2, May 1980, 6–7.

203. Thomas Gordon, *History of the Greek Revolution and of the Wars and Campaigns*, 2nd Edition, (London: T. Cadell, 1844), 193–267.

204. Fahmy, *All the Pasha's Men*, 55–60, 268–275; Howard A. Reed, *The Destruction of the Janissaries by Sultan Mahmud II in June 1826*, (Princeton: Princeton University Unpublished Ph.D. Dissertation, 1951), 16–19.

205. Reed, *Destruction of the Janissaries*, 45–46, 52–69, 99–102; Avigdor Levy, "The Ottoman Ulema and the Military Reforms of Sultan Mahmud II," *Asian and African Studies*, vol. 7, 1971, 13–16.

206. *Başbakanlık Osmanlı Arşivi (Turkish Prime Ministry Ottoman Archive)* (Hereafter *BOA*), Hatt-ı Hümayun (Imperial Rescript) Catalog no. 17479, year 1241; Avigdor Levy, "The Eşkenci Project: An Ottoman Attempt at Gradual Reform (1826)," Offprint Paper Read to *28th International Congress of Orientalists-Canberra*, 1971, 6–13; Çuhadar İlyas Ağa, *Tarih-i Enderun (Letaif-i Enderun)*, (ed.) Cahit Kayra, (İstanbul: Güneş Yayınları, 1981), 273; Reed, *Destruction of the Janissaries*, s. 107–189.

207. Reed, *Destruction of the Janissaries*, 190–287; Ahmet Cevat Eren, *Mahmud II Zamanında Bosna-Hersek*, (İstanbul: Nurgök Matbaası, 1969), 71–83.

Chapter 4

1. Helmuth von Moltke, *The Russians in Bulgaria and Rumelia in 1828 and 1829*, (trans.) Lucie D. Gordon, (London: John Murray, 1854), 12; Avigdor Levy, *The Military Policy of Sultan Mahmud II, 1808–1839*, (Cambridge: Harvard University Unpublished Ph.D. Dissertation, 1968), 195–196; Edward Engelhardt, *Tanzimat ve Türkiye*, (Turkish translation of the French original *La Turquie et le Tanzimat*), (trans.) Ali Reşad, (İstanbul: Kaknüs Yayınları, 1999), 23–24, 31–32, 41.

2. Engelhardt, *Tanzimat ve Türkiye*, 23; Charles Mac Farlane, *Kismet; or the Doom of Turkey*, (London: Thomas Bosworth, 1853), 6.

3. Levy, *Military Policy of Sultan Mahmud II, 1808–1839*, 161–165, 169–171.

4. Eren, *Mahmud II Zamanında Bosna-Hersek*, 48–97; Moltke, *Russians in Bulgaria and Rumelia*, 14–15, 269–270.

5. Khaled Fahmy, *All the Pasha's Men*, 53–54.

6. R. Walsh, *Narrative of a Journey from Constantinople to England*, (Philadelphia: Carey, Lea & Carey, 1828), 42; Engelhardt, *Tanzimat ve Türkiye*, 20.

7. İlyas Ağa, *Tarih-i Enderun (Letaif-i Enderun)*, 281–282, 292–293; Levy, *Military Policy of Sultan Mahmud II, 1808–1839*, 176–177, 388–390.

8. Levy, *Military Policy of Sultan Mahmud II, 1808–1839*, 268–270.

9. Ahmet Yaramış and Mehmet Güneş (eds.), *Askeri Kanunnameler (1826–1827)*, (Transliteration of Ottoman original *Kanunname-i Asakir-i Mansure-i Muhammediye*, (Ankara: Asil Yayın, 2007), 100–114.

10. İlyas Ağa (Kayra), *Tarih-i Enderun (Letaif-i Enderun)*, 285; Levy, *Military Policy of Sultan Mahmud II, 1808–1839*, 242–247, 544–545.

11. Levy, *Military Policy of Sultan Mahmud II, 1808–1839*, 177–179, 182, 360–361, 390; Yaramış and Güneş, *Askeri Kanunnameler (1826–1827)*, 45–58.

12. Levy, *Military Policy of Sultan Mahmud II, 1808–1839*, 366–371; Yaramış and Güneş, *Askeri Kanunnameler (1826–1827)*, 61–62.

13. Levy, *Military Policy of Sultan Mahmud II, 1808–1839*, 250–267; Yaramış and Güneş, *Askeri Kanunnameler (1826–1827)*, 67–79.

14. Levy, *Military Policy of Sultan Mahmud II, 1808–1839*, 323–345, 545–554; Yaramış and Güneş, *Askeri Kanunnameler (1826–1827)*, 88–100.

15. Levy, *Military Policy of Sultan Mahmud II, 1808–1839*, 179–181, 187–189, 399–401.

16. Ibid., 226–230; Charles Napier, *The War in Syria*, (London: John W. Parker, 1842), 4–7; Helmuth von Moltke, *Türkiye Mektupları*, (Turkish translation of the German original

Briefe über Zuftände und Begebenheiten in der Türkei, (trans.) Hayrullah Örs, (İstanbul: Remzi Kitabevi, 1969), 32–34; İlber Ortaylı, *İmparatorluğun En Uzun Yüzyılı*, (İstanbul: İletişim Yayınları, 2005), 41.

17. İlyas Ağa (Kayra), *Tarih-i Enderun (Letaif-i Enderun)*, 292, 294; Levy, *Military Policy of Sultan Mahmud II, 1808–1839*, 230–232, 235.

18. Levy, *Military Policy of Sultan Mahmud II, 1808–1839*, 232–238.

19. İlyas Ağa (Kayra), *Tarih-i Enderun (Letaif-i Enderun)*, 62–261; Levy, *Military Policy of Sultan Mahmud II, 1808–1839*, 377–378.

20. İlyas Ağa (Kayra), *Tarih-i Enderun (Letaif-i Enderun)*, 227–228, 281, 288–289.

21. Ibid., 305–306, 309, 311–313, 321–322, 349; Levy, *Military Policy of Sultan Mahmud II, 1808–1839*, 380–381.

22. İlyas Ağa (Kayra), *Tarih-i Enderun (Letaif-i Enderun)*, 307, 320–321, 328, 346; Levy, *Military Policy of Sultan Mahmud II, 1808–1839*, 380–382.

23. F. R. Chesney, *The Russo-Turkish Campaigns of 1828 and 1829 with a View of the Present State of Affairs in the East*, 3rd Edition, (London: Smith, Elder & Co., 1854), 16–24.

24. Eren, *Mahmud II Zamanında Bosna-Hersek*, 98–101; Moltke, *Russians in Bulgaria and Rumelia*, 13–15; Walsh, *Narrative of a Journey*, 50.

25. Çakın and Orhon, *TSK Tarihi Osmanlı Devri (1793–1908)*, 436–437; Moltke, *Russians in Bulgaria and Rumelia*, 14, 16, 19–20.

26. Humphry Sandwith, *A Narrative of the Siege of Kars*, (London: John Murray, 1856), 149–161; Edward Money, *Twelve Months with the Bashi-Bozouks*, (London: Chapman and Hall, 1857), 7–10, 26–29; George Dodd, *Pictorial History of the Russian War*, (London: W & R Chambers, 1856), 31–33.

27. "Widin," in (ed.) P. Bearman, Th. Bianquis, C. E. Bosworth, E. van Donzel and W. P. Heinrichs, *Encyclopaedia of Islam*, 2nd Edition, vol. 9; (Leiden: E.J. Brill, 2008), online edition; Svetlana Ivanova, "Warna," in (ed.) P. Bearman, Th. Bianquis, C. E. Bosworth, E. van Donzel and W. P. Heinrichs, *Encyclopaedia of Islam*, 2nd Edition, vol. 9; (Leiden: E.J. Brill, 2008), online edition.

28. Chesney, *Russo-Turkish Campaigns of 1828 and 1829*, 32–46, 64–68, 93; Moltke, *Russians in Bulgaria and Rumelia*, 40–46, 56.

29. Chesney, *Russo-Turkish Campaigns of 1828 and 1829*, 69–84; Moltke, *Russians in Bulgaria and Rumelia*, 57–58, 68–104.

30. Chesney, *Russo-Turkish Campaigns of 1828 and 1829*, 85–92, 101–113; Moltke, *Russians in Bulgaria and Rumelia*, 108–137; Çakın and Orhon, *TSK Tarihi Osmanlı Devri (1793–1908)*, 438–439.

31. Chesney, *Russo-Turkish Campaigns of 1828 and 1829*, 113–139; Moltke, *Russians in Bulgaria and Rumelia*, 138–190, 216–218; Çakın and Orhon, *TSK Tarihi Osmanlı Devri (1793–1908)*, 439–441.

32. Chesney, *Russo-Turkish Campaigns of 1828 and 1829*, 150–158; Moltke, *Russians in Bulgaria and Rumelia*, 220–232.

33. Chesney, *Russo-Turkish Campaigns of 1828 and 1829*, 163–165; Moltke, *Russians in Bulgaria and Rumelia*, 261–263.

34. W. Monteith, *Kars and Erzeroum; with the Campaigns of Prince Paskiewitch in 1828 and 1829*, (London: Longman, Brown, Green and Longmans, 1854), 122–157; Chesney, *Russo-Turkish Campaigns of 1828 and 1829*, 167–171.

35. Monteith, *Kars and Erzeroum*, 158; Chesney, *Russo-Turkish Campaigns of 1828 and 1829*, 172–179.

36. Monteith, *Kars and Erzeroum*, 158–214; Chesney, *Russo-Turkish Campaigns of 1828 and 1829*, 179–196; Çakın and Orhon, *TSK Tarihi Osmanlı Devri (1793–1908)*, 441–442.

37. Monteith, *Kars and Erzeroum*, 217–219, 221–223; Chesney, *Russo-Turkish Campaigns of 1828 and 1829*, 197–199.

38. Monteith, *Kars and Erzeroum*, 231–240; Chesney, *Russo-Turkish Campaigns of 1828 and 1829*, 257–266.

39. Monteith, *Kars and Erzeroum*, 242–274; Chesney, *Russo-Turkish Campaigns of 1828 and 1829*, 266–286; Çakın and Orhon, *TSK Tarihi Osmanlı Devri (1793–1908)*, 443.

40. Chesney, *Russo-Turkish Campaigns of 1828 and 1829*, 201–203; Moltke, *Russians in Bulgaria and Rumelia*, 269–274.

41. Chesney, *Russo-Turkish Campaigns of 1828 and 1829*, 204–206; Moltke, *Russians in Bulgaria and Rumelia*, 277–283.

42. Chesney, *Russo-Turkish Campaigns of 1828 and 1829*, 208–227; Moltke, *Russians in Bulgaria and Rumelia*, 326–357; Çakın and Orhon, *TSK Tarihi Osmanlı Devri (1793–1908)*, 444–445.

43. Chesney, *Russo-Turkish Campaigns of 1828 and 1829*, 232–240; Moltke, *Russians in Bulgaria and Rumelia*, 284–323.

44. Chesney, *Russo-Turkish Campaigns of 1828 and 1829*, 240–250; Moltke, *Russians in Bulgaria and Rumelia*, 370–418; Çakın and Orhon, *TSK Tarihi Osmanlı Devri (1793–1908)*, 445–448.

45. Chesney, *Russo-Turkish Campaigns of 1828 and 1829*, 293–296.

46. Moltke, *Russians in Bulgaria and Rumelia*, 256–257; Chesney, *Russo-Turkish Campaigns of 1828 and 1829*, 389, 398.

47. Moltke, *Russians in Bulgaria and Rumelia*, 19–20, 68–77, 255–256; Chesney, *Russo-Turkish Campaigns of 1828 and 1829*, 375–376.

48. Adolphus Slade, *Records of Travels in Turkey, Greece &c. and of a Cruise in the Black Sea with the Capitan Pasha in the Years 1829, 1830 and 1831*, vol. 2, (Philadelphia: E. L.Carey & A. Hart, 1833), 70–71; Monteith, *Kars and Erzeroum*, 301; Ufuk Gülsoy, *1828–1829 Osmanlı-Rus Savaşında Rumeli'den Rusya'ya*, (İstanbul: TKAE Yayınları, 1993), 27–39, 41–64; Aksan, *Ottoman Wars 1700–1870*, 400–401.

49. Moltke, *Russians in Bulgaria and Rumelia*, 410–411; Chesney, *Russo-Turkish Campaigns of 1828 and 1829*, 375.

50. Moltke, *Russians in Bulgaria and Rumelia*, 13, 17–19, 319; Walsh, *Narrative of a Journey*, 118–119.

51. Chesney, *Russo-Turkish Campaigns of 1828 and 1829*, 257–260.

52. Moltke, *Russians in Bulgaria and Rumelia*, 218–219, 233–235, 262, 279–281; Chesney, *Russo-Turkish Campaigns of 1828 and 1829*, 144–147, 204–206.

53. Mustafa Zarif, "Zarif Paşanın Hatıratı" (ed.) E. Ziya Karal, *Belleten*, vol. 4, no. 16, 1. Teşrin 1940, 456–457; Moltke, *Russians in Bulgaria and Rumelia*, 12–13, 17; Slade, *Records of Travels in Turkey, Greece &c.*, vol. 2, 145; Chesney, *Russo-Turkish Campaigns of 1828 and 1829*, 65–66; Mac Farlane, *Kismet; or the Doom of Turkey*, 10, 14; Engelhardt, *Tanzimat ve Türkiye*, 25–26; Bernard Lewis, *The Emergence of Modern Turkey*, (London: Oxford University Press, 1966), 98–100.

54. Chesney, *Russo-Turkish Campaigns of 1828 and 1829*, 288–289.

55. Dukakinzade Feridun, *Türk Ordusunun Eski Seferlerinden Nezip 1831–1840 Seferi*, (İstanbul: Askeri Matbaa, 1931), 1.

56. Fahmy, *All the Pasha's Men*, 41–51; Dukakinzade, *Türk Ordusunun Eski Seferlerinden Nezip 1831–1840 Seferi*, 3–5.

57. Dukakinzade, *Türk Ordusunun Eski Seferlerinden Nezip 1831–1840 Seferi*, 11–15; Fahmy, *All the Pasha's Men*, 61–63.

58. Dukakinzade, *Türk Ordusunun Eski Seferlerinden Nezip 1831–1840 Seferi*, 14–17; Fahmy, *All the Pasha's Men*, 63–66.

59. Dukakinzade, *Türk Ordusunun Eski Seferlerinden Nezip 1831–1840 Seferi*, 17–21; Fahmy, *All the Pasha's Men*, 66–67; Zarif, "Zarif Paşanın Hatıratı," 452–454.

60. Dukakinzade, *Türk Ordusunun Eski Seferlerinden Nezip 1831–1840 Seferi*, 21–23; Fahmy, *All the Pasha's Men*, 67–71.

61. Levy, *Military Policy of Sultan Mahmud II, 1808–1839*, 454–455.

62. Ibid., 197–200, 460–462.

63. Ibid., 462–464.

64. *Turkish Military Academy Archives* (here after *TMAA*), Künye Defteri (Registry Logbook) no. 1; Levy, *Military Policy of Sultan Mahmud II, 1808–1839*, 200–205, 465–469.

65. Mahmud Şevket, *Osmanlı Askeri Teşkilatı ve Kıyafeti*, 85–86; Levy, *Military Policy of Sultan Mahmud II, 1808–1839*, 480–489; Sandwith, *Narrative of the Siege of Kars*, 121–122.

66. *Harpokulu Tarihçesi*, (Ankara: Harpokulu Matbaası, 1945), 10; Fahmy, *All the Pasha's Men*, 90–91, 174–179, 243–251.

67. The government of Egypt sent the first group of students to Italy in 1813 and to Britain in 1818. However the bulk of the following groups were sent to France after 1826.

68. Mahmut Kemal İnal, *Son Sadrazamlar*, vol. 2, 3rd Edition, (İstanbul: Dergah Yayınları, 1982), 601–602.

69. Most probably the presence of an Egyptian school (Mekteb-i Mısri) in Paris had important effect on this decision.

70. Adnan Şişman, "Mekteb-i Osmani (1857–1864)," *Osmanlı Araştırmaları*, vol. 5, 1986, 84–100; Richard L. Chambers, "Notes on the Mekteb-i Osmani in Paris 1857–1874," in (ed.) William R. Polk and Richard L. Chambers, *Beginnings of Modernization in the Middle East: The Nineteenth Century*, (Chicago: The University of Chicago Press, 1968), 314–316.

71. Şişman, "Mekteb-i Osmani (1857–1864)," 106–118; Chambers, "Notes on the Mekteb-i Osmani," 317–329.

72. Levy, *Military Policy of Sultan Mahmud II, 1808–1839*, 382–384.

73. Zarif, "Zarif Paşanın Hatıratı," 454, 458.

74. Fahmy, *All the Pasha's Men*, 12, 80–82, 90, 170; Choosing short-term vocational training or long-term academic training remains an important dilemma in every underdeveloped nation.

75. Ahmet Nuri Sinaplı, *Şeyhülvüzera, Serasker Mehmed Namık Paşa*, (İstanbul: Yenilik Basımevi, 1987), 66–69.

76. The elitist character of the French educational system would have profound effects on the Ottoman military schools.

77. *BOA*, Hatt-ı Hümayun Catalog no. 17474, year 1242; *BOA*, Hatt-ı Hümayun Catalog no. 17474A, year 1242; *BOA*, Hatt-ı Hümayun Catalog no. 17700, year 1242; Ahmed Lütfi, *Vakanüvis Ahmed Lütfi Efendi Tarihi*, vol. 4–5, (İstanbul: Yapı Kredi Bankası Yayınları, 1999), 826; For contemporary eye-witness description of the Academy, see Julia Pardoe, *The City of the Sultan and Domestic Manners of the Turks in 1836*, vol. 1, (London: Henry Colburn, 1837), 194–204; Also see Mac Farlane, *Kismet; or the Doom of Turkey*, 47–49.

78. *TMAA*, Künye Defteri (Registry Logbook) no. 1; Mac Farlane, *Kismet; or the Doom of Turkey*, 95; Ortaylı, *İmparatorluğun En Uzun Yüzyılı*, 46, 187.

79. *TMAA*, Numara Defteri (Cadet Grade Logbook) no. 1; *BOA*, Hatt-ı Hümayun Catalog no. 46425, year 1253; *BOA*, Hatt-ı Hümayun Catalog no. 46425A, year 1253.

80. For the vivid description of the forceful recruitment in southeastern Anatolia *see* Moltke, *Türkiye Mektupları*, 180–198.

81. Dukakinzade, *Türk Ordusunun Eski Seferlerinden Nezip 1831–1840 Seferi*, 24–34, 37–38; Moltke, *Russians in Bulgaria and Rumelia*, 152–157, 252–263.

82. Dukakinzade, *Türk Ordusunun Eski Seferlerinden Nezip 1831–1840 Seferi*, 34–40; Moltke, *Russians in Bulgaria and Rumelia*, 263–274.

83. Fahmy, *All the Pasha's Men*, 199–209, 252–263.

84. *BOA*, Hatt-ı Hümayun Catalog no. 59153, year 1255; *BOA*, Hatt-ı Hümayun Catalog no. 59154, year 1255; *BOA*, Hatt-ı Hümayun Catalog no. 59168A, year 1255; *BOA*, Hatt-ı Hümayun Catalog no. 59171, year 1255; *BOA*, Hatt-ı Hümayun Catalog no. 59181, year 1256; *BOA*, Hatt-ı Hümayun Catalog no. 59187B, year 1256; *BOA*, Hatt-ı Hümayun Catalog no. 59197C, year 1256.

85. *Harpokulu Tarihçesi*, 10–13; Osman Ergin, *Türkiye Maarif Tarihi*, vol. 1–2, (İstanbul: Eser Matbaası, 1977), 357; Ahmed Lütfi, *Vakanüvis Ahmed Lütfi Efendi Tarihi*, 927; Fahmy, *All the Pasha's Men*, 161.

86. Dukakinzade, *Türk Ordusunun Eski Seferlerinden Nezip 1831–1840 Seferi*, 41–50.

87. Avigdor Levy, "The Officer Corps in Sultan Mahmud II's New Ottoman Army 1826–1839," *International Journal of Middle East Studies*, vol. 2, 1971, 32–36.

88. Except for the two officers who had died at an early age all of them served in the Academy as lecturers (one them remained in the permanent academic staff). Five of them served in several civilian posts like governor of province and diplomatic assignments. The most successful one (Hüseyin Avni Pasha) managed to become grand vizier. *TMAA*, Künye Defteri no. 1.

89. Atwell Lake, *Narrative of the Defence of Kars, Historical and Military*, (London: Richard Bentley, 1857), 61–62.

90. *TMAA*, Numara Defteri no. 1; Mehmed Esad, *Mirat-ı Mekteb-i Harbiye*, (İstanbul: Artin Asaduryan Matbaası, 1310 [1894]), 57–84.

91. *BOA*, Cevdet Askeri no. 3041, no date; *BOA*, Cevdet Askeri no. 8843, year 24 S 1253; *TMAA*, Künye Defteri no. 1 and 2; Mehmed Esad, *Mirat-ı Mekteb-i Harbiye*, 43–87.

92. For a list of Military Academy graduate artists *see* İlkay Karatepe, *Asker Ressamlar Kataloğu*, (İstanbul: Askeri Müze Yay., 2001); For a list of Military academy graduate poets and writers *see* İlhan Çiloğlu, *Asker Yazarlar ve Şairler*, (İstanbul: Elif Kitabevi, 2002).

93. Mac Farlane, *Kismet; or the Doom of Turkey*, 19, 36–37, 40.

94. Kemal Karpat, "Kossuth in Turkey: The Impact of Hungarian Refugees in the Ottoman Empire, 1849–1851," in (ed.) J. L. Bacque-Grammont, İ. Ortaylı, E. van Donzel, *CIEPO VII Sempozyumu Bildirileri*, (Ankara: Türk Tarih Kurumu, 1994), 109–116; Adolphus Slade, *Turkey and the Crimean War: A Narrative of Historical Events*, (London: Smith, Elder, 1867), 61–62; İlber Ortaylı, "Osmanlı İmparatorluğu'nda Askeri Reformlar ve Polonyalı Mülteci Subaylar," *Askeri Tarih Bülteni*, year: 14, no. 27, August 1989, 19–20; György Csorba, "Hungarian Emigrants of 1848–49 in the Ottoman Empire," in (ed.) H. C. Güzel, C. C. Oğuz and O. Karatay, *The Turks*, vol. 4, (Ankara: Yeni Türkiye Pub., 2002), 224–226.

95. Karpat, "Kossuth in Turkey," 117; Csorba, "Hungarian Emigrants of 1848–49," 226–229; Jerzy S. Lakta, *Lehistan'dan Gelen Şehit Mustafa Celaleddin Paşa-Konstanty Borzecki*, (İstanbul: Boyut Yayıncılık, 1987), 17–19; Sandwith, *Narrative of the Siege of Kars*, 115–116; Charles Duncan, *A Campaign with the Turks in Asia*, vol. 1, (London: Smith, Elder and Co., 1855), 154–167, 174–178.

96. Karpat, "Kossuth in Turkey," 119–121; Ortaylı, "Osmanlı İmparatorluğu'nda Askeri Reformlar ve Polonyalı Mülteci Subaylar," 20–21; Csorba, "Hungarian Emigrants of 1848–49," 230–231; Duncan, *Campaign with the Turks in Asia*, 171–176.

97. Karpat, "Kossuth in Turkey," 121; Lakta, *Lehistan'dan Gelen Şehit Mustafa Celaleddin Paşa-Konstanty Borzecki*, 27–31.

98. Levy, *Military Policy of Sultan Mahmud II, 1808–1839*, 374–375, 590–594, 632.

99. For official justification *see*. Musa Çadırcı, "Redif Askeri Teşkilatı," in *Yedinci Askeri Tarih Semineri*, vol. 1, (Ankara: Genelkurmay Basımevi, 2000), 58–60; Mübahat S. Kütükoğlu, "Sultan II. Mahmud Devri Yedek Ordusu, Redif-i Asakir-i Mansure," *İ.Ü. Edebiyat Fakültesi Tarih Enstitüsü Dergisi*, no. 12, 1981, 127.

100. Mahmud Şevket, *Osmanlı Askeri Teşkilatı ve Kıyafeti*, 87; Nihat Atakan, *Ordu Bilgisi*, (Ankara: Harp Okulu Matbaası, 1943), 22–23.

101. Kütükoğlu, "Sultan II. Mahmud Devri Yedek Ordusu, Redif-i Asakir-i Mansure," 128.

102. Çadırcı, "Redif Askeri Teşkilatı," 59–61; Kütükoğlu, "Sultan II. Mahmud Devri Yedek Ordusu, Redif-i Asakir-i Mansure," 129–131; Cahide Bolat, *Redif Askeri Teşkilatı (1834–1876)*, (Ankara: University of Ankara Unpublished Ph.D. Dissertation, 2000), 24–26.

103. Kütükoğlu, "Sultan II. Mahmud Devri Yedek Ordusu, Redif-i Asakir-i Mansure," 131–135; Bolat, *Redif Askeri Teşkilatı (1834–1876)*, 30–31; Fahrettin Tızlak, "Harput'tan Asker Alma ve Firariler Hakkında Bazı Tedbirler (1834–1838)," *Askeri Tarih Bülteni*, year 14, no. 1989.

104. Moltke, *Russians in Bulgaria and Rumelia*, 29.

105. Kütükoğlu, "Sultan II. Mahmud Devri Yedek Ordusu, Redif-i Asakir-i Mansure," 139–143; Bolat, *Redif Askeri Teşkilatı (1834–1876)*, 29–32.

106. Kütükoğlu, "Sultan II. Mahmud Devri Yedek Ordusu, Redif-i Asakir-i Mansure," 143–145, 149–157; Bolat, *Redif Askeri Teşkilatı (1834–1876)*, 27–28, 32–33, 38–46; Tızlak, "Harput'tan Asker Alma ve Firariler Hakkında Bazı Tedbirler (1834–1838)," 61–63; Adolphus Slade, *Records of Travels in Turkey, Greece &c. and of a Cruise in the Black Sea with the Capitan Pasha in the Years 1829, 1830 and 1831*, vol. 1, (Philadelphia: E. L. Carey & A. Hart, 1833), 411–412, 494; For a summary of Ottoman conscription system, *see* Erik Jan Zürcher, "The Ottoman Conscription System in Theory and Practice, 1844–1918," *International Review of Social History*, vol. 43, no. 3, 1998, 437–449.

107. Mac Farlane, *Kismet; or the Doom of Turkey*, 59–63, 67–68; Levy, *Military Policy of Sultan Mahmud II, 1808–1839*, 595–599; Aksan, *Ottoman Wars 1700–1870*, 357–359.

108. James Henry Skene, *The Three Eras of Ottoman History; A political Essay on the Late Reforms of Turkey*, (London: Chapman and Hall, 1851), 52–61; Lewis, *Emergence of Modern Turkey*, 104–109; Aksan, *Ottoman Wars 1700–1870*, 402–403; Engelhardt, *Tanzimat ve Türkiye*, 43–50.

109. Alexander W. Kinglake, *The Invasion of the Crimea: Its Origin and an Account of Its Progress*, vol. 1, 3rd Edition, (London: William Blackwood, 1863), infra. 181; Dodd, *Pictorial History of the Russian War*, 3–19; Chesney, *Russo-Turkish Campaigns of 1828 and 1829*, 297–334.

110. Mac Farlane, *Kismet; or the Doom of Turkey*, 5–6, 10–17, 26–37; John Reid, *Turkey and the Turks being the Present State of the Otoman Empire*, (London: Robert Tyas, 1840), 66–68; Sandwith, *Narrative of the Siege of Kars*, 117–119.

111. Chesney, *Russo-Turkish Campaigns of 1828 and 1829*, 353–354.

112. A. Tevfik Gürel, *1853–1855 Türk-Rus ve Müttefiklerin Kırım Savaşı*, (İstanbul: Askeri Matbaa, 1935), 20–27; Hikmet Süer, *TSK Tarihi Osmanlı Devri Osmanlı-Rus Kırım Harbi Kafkas Cephesi Harekatı (1853–1856)*, (Ankara: Genelkurmay Basımevi, 1986), 52–58.

113. Kinglake, *Invasion of the Crimea*, vol. 1, 182–197; Dodd, *Pictorial History of the Russian War*, 19–26; Slade, *Turkey and the Crimean War*, 105–115, 126–127; Gürel, *1853–1855 Türk-Rus ve Müttefiklerin Kırım Savaşı*, 26–32; Süer, *TSK Tarihi Osmanlı Devri Osmanlı-Rus Kırım Harbi Kafkas Cephesi Harekatı (1853–1856)*, 68–69.

114. Mahmud Şevket, *Osmanlı Askeri Teşkilatı ve Kıyafeti*, 83–84; Skene, *Three Eras of Ottoman History*, 77–81; Süer, *TSK Tarihi Osmanlı Devri Osmanlı-Rus Kırım Harbi Kafkas Cephesi Harekatı (1853–1856)*, 34–35; Dodd, *Pictorial History of the Russian War*, 26; Engelhardt, *Tanzimat ve Türkiye*, 71–76, 93–94; Atakan, *Ordu Bilgisi*, 24–25.

115. W. E. D. Allen and Paul Muratoff, *Caucasian Battlefields: A History of the Wars on the Turco-Caucasian Border*, (Cambridge: Cambridge University Press, 1953), 58–59; Skene, *Three Eras of Ottoman History*, 62–73; Chesney, *Russo-Turkish Campaigns of 1828 and 1829*, 389–390; Engelhardt, *Tanzimat ve Türkiye*, 120–124.

116. Sandwith, *Narrative of the Siege of Kars*, 119–120; Skene, *Three Eras of Ottoman History*, 61–63; Dodd, *Pictorial History of the Russian War*, 28; Süer, *TSK Tarihi Osmanlı Devri Osmanlı-Rus Kırım Harbi Kafkas Cephesi Harekatı (1853–1856)*, 33; Gürel, *1853–1855 Türk-Rus ve Müttefiklerin Kırım Savaşı*, 7; Duncan, *Campaign with the Turks in Asia*, 93–95.

117. Gürel, *1853–1855 Türk-Rus ve Müttefiklerin Kırım Savaşı*, 28–29, 105–106; Süer, *TSK Tarihi Osmanlı Devri Osmanlı-Rus Kırım Harbi Kafkas Cephesi Harekatı (1853–1856)*, 51; Slade, *Turkey and the Crimean War*, 58–64, 70–71; Sandwith, *Narrative of the Siege of Kars*, 96, 107.

118. Slade, *Turkey and the Crimean War*, 116–120; William H. Russell, *The British Expedition to the Crimea*, (London: G. Routledge, 1858), 69–70.

119. Süer, *TSK Tarihi Osmanlı Devri Osmanlı-Rus Kırım Harbi Kafkas Cephesi Harekatı (1853–1856)*, 34, 37–39, 59, 63–66, 71–72; Zarif, "Zarif Paşanın Hatıratı," 473–476; Dodd, *Pictorial History of the Russian War*, 31–36.

120. Gürel, *1853–1855 Türk-Rus ve Müttefiklerin Kırım Savaşı*, 108–109; Süer, *TSK Tarihi Osmanlı Devri Osmanlı-Rus Kırım Harbi Kafkas Cephesi Harekatı (1853–1856)*, 72–73; Allen and Muratoff, *Caucasian Battlefields*, 59–61.

121. Süer, *TSK Tarihi Osmanlı Devri Osmanlı-Rus Kırım Harbi Kafkas Cephesi Harekatı (1853–1856)*, 74–77; Allen and Muratoff, *Caucasian Battlefields*, 61–62; Zarif, "Zarif Paşanın Hatıratı," 476–479.

122. Kinglake, *Invasion of the Crimea*, vol. 1, 373–387; Süer, *TSK Tarihi Osmanlı Devri Osmanlı-Rus Kırım Harbi Kafkas Cephesi Harekatı (1853–1856)*, 77–82; Zarif, "Zarif Paşanın Hatıratı," 480–483; Sandwith, *Narrative of the Siege of Kars*, 92–94; Allen and Muratoff, *Caucasian Battlefields*, 62–64; Gürel, *1853–1855 Türk-Rus ve Müttefiklerin Kırım Savaşı*, 108–109.

123. Slade, *Turkey and the Crimean War*, 139–151; Dodd, *Pictorial History of the Russian War*, 56–74; Süer, *TSK Tarihi Osmanlı Devri Osmanlı-Rus Kırım Harbi Kafkas Cephesi Harekatı (1853–1856)*, 83–87.

124. Dodd, *Pictorial History of the Russian War*, 36–44; Gürel, *1853–1855 Türk-Rus ve Müttefiklerin Kırım Savaşı*, 38–44.

125. Gürel, *1853–1855 Türk-Rus ve Müttefiklerin Kırım Savaşı*, 46–47, 52–55; Dodd, *Pictorial History of the Russian War*, 44–47.

126. Dodd, *Pictorial History of the Russian War*, 47–51; Gürel, *1853–1855 Türk-Rus ve Müttefiklerin Kırım Savaşı*, 57–69, 77–78; Winfried Baumgart, *The Crimean War 1853–1856*, (London: Arnold Pub., 1999), 98–102.

127. Gürel, *1853–1855 Türk-Rus ve Müttefiklerin Kırım Savaşı*, 79–80; Dodd, *Pictorial History of the Russian War*, 51–55; Allen and Muratoff, *Caucasian Battlefields*, 69–71.

128. Moshe Gammer, *Muslim Resistance to the Tsar, Shamil and the Conquest of Chechnia and Daghestan*, (London: Frank Cass, 1994), 267–272; Dodd, *Pictorial History of the Russian War*, 120, 126–127, 130; Gürel, *1853–1855 Türk-Rus ve Müttefiklerin Kırım Savaşı*, 113–114; Süer, *TSK Tarihi Osmanlı Devri Osmanlı-Rus Kırım Harbi Kafkas Cephesi Harekatı (1853–1856)*, 74, 88–89, 91, 111–119.

129. Sandwith, *Narrative of the Siege of Kars*, 94–95, 235–238.

130. Süer, *TSK Tarihi Osmanlı Devri Osmanlı-Rus Kırım Harbi Kafkas Cephesi Harekatı (1853–1856)*, 94–95, 98–100; Allen and Muratoff, *Caucasian Battlefields*, 71–74; Sandwith, *Narrative of the Siege of Kars*, 99–100; Gürel, *1853–1855 Türk-Rus ve Müttefiklerin Kırım Savaşı*, 11–112.

131. Süer, *TSK Tarihi Osmanlı Devri Osmanlı-Rus Kırım Harbi Kafkas Cephesi Harekatı (1853–1856)*, 100–102.

132. Zarif, "Zarif Paşanın Hatıratı," 443–448; Duncan, *Campaign with the Turks in Asia*, 116–121.

133. Zarif, "Zarif Paşanın Hatıratı," 484–494; Duncan, *Campaign with the Turks in Asia*, 159–168; Sandwith, *Narrative of the Siege of Kars*, 97–109; Lake, *Narrative of the Defence of Kars*, 8–11; Süer, *TSK Tarihi Osmanlı Devri Osmanlı-Rus Kırım Harbi Kafkas Cephesi Harekatı (1853–1856)*, 102–106; Allen and Muratoff, *Caucasian Battlefields*, 74–79; Gürel, *1853–1855 Türk-Rus ve Müttefiklerin Kırım Savaşı*, 112–113.

134. Lake, *Narrative of the Defence of Kars*, 2–7; Sandwith, *Narrative of the Siege of Kars*, 113, 124–125; Süer, *TSK Tarihi Osmanlı Devri Osmanlı-Rus Kırım Harbi Kafkas Cephesi Harekatı (1853–1856)*, 123–125.

135. Lake, *Narrative of the Defence of Kars*, 18–43, 69–70, 72–82, 86, 105–106; Allen and Muratoff, *Caucasian Battlefields*, 81–82; Sandwith, *Narrative of the Siege of Kars*, 125–126, 130–132, 229–235, 246–247.

136. For military discussions *see* Alexander W. Kinglake, *The Invasion of the Crimea: Its Origin and an Account of Its Progress*, vol. 2, 3rd Edition, (London: William Blackwood, 1863), 66–130.

137. Gürel, *1853–1855 Türk-Rus ve Müttefiklerin Kırım Savaşı*, 84–87; Slade, *Turkey and the Crimean War*, 272–294; Kinglake, *Invasion of the Crimea*, vol. 2, 141–211; Dodd, *Pictorial History of the Russian War*, 202–210; John Adye, *A Review of the Crimean War to the Winter of 1854-5*, (London: Hurst and Blackett, 1860), 29–40; Albert Seaton, *The Crimean War: A Russian Chronicle*, (London: B. T. Batsford Ltd., 1977), 56–76.

138. Gürel, *1853–1855 Türk-Rus ve Müttefiklerin Kırım Savaşı*, 87–88; Slade, *Turkey and the Crimean War*, 295–299; Kinglake, *Invasion of the Crimea*, vol. 2, 226–512; Adye, *Review of the Crimean War*, 41–64; Dodd, *Pictorial History of the Russian War*, 210–216; Russell, *British Expedition to the Crimea*, 123–158; Seaton, *Crimean War*, 77–103.

139. Alexander W. Kinglake, *The Invasion of the Crimea: Its Origin and an Account of Its Progress*, vol. 3, 3rd Edition, (London: William Blackwood, 1863), 13–33; Slade, *Turkey and the Crimean War*, 299–324; Dodd, *Pictorial History of the Russian War*, 220–240, 250–253; Seaton, *Crimean War*, 107–137.

140. Adye, *Review of the Crimean War*, 98–100; Slade, *Turkey and the Crimean War*, 327; Kinglake, *Invasion of the Crimea*, vol. 3, 292–294; Russell, *British Expedition to the Crimea*, 183.

141. Somerset John Gough Calthorpe, *Letters from the Head-quarters; or, the Realities of the War in Crimea*, vol. 1, (London: John Murray, 1856), 105–106; James Henry Skene, *With Lord Stratford in the Crimean War*, (London: R. Bentley, 1883), 105–106; Christopher Hibbert, *The Destruction of Lord Raglan, A Tragedy of the Crimean War 1854–55*, (Ware: Wordsworth, 1999), 135, 166; Adye, *Review of the Crimean War*, 100–103; Dodd, *Pictorial History of the Russian War*, 254–258; Russell, *British Expedition to the Crimea*, 184–188; Baumgart, *Crimean War 1853–1856*, 127–128; Russian accounts are also conflicting. *See* Seaton, *Crimean War*, 139–146.

142. For the current discussion *see* Michael H. Mawson, "Television, Talking Heads, and Turks," *The War Correspondent*, vol. 21, no. 4, January 2004, 16–19; Colin Robins, "Ship,

Johnny Ship? Battlefield Detectives, UK Channel 5, August 2003," *The War Correspondent*, vol. 21, no. 3, October 2003, 11–12; For official Turkish version *see* Gürel, *1853–1855 Türk-Rus ve Müttefiklerin Kırım Savaşı*, 91–92.

143. Dodd, *Pictorial History of the Russian War*, 215–216.

144. Ibid., 287; Slade, *Turkey and the Crimean War*, 330–335; Russell, *British Expedition to the Crimea*, 232, 261–263, 266–267, 270, 286–287.

145. Dodd, *Pictorial History of the Russian War*, 330–335; Russell, *British Expedition to the Crimea*, 239, 266, 291, 315–321, 336; Gürel, *1853–1855 Türk-Rus ve Müttefiklerin Kırım Savaşı*, 92–95; Baumgart, *Crimean War 1853–1856*, 145–146.

146. Gürel, *1853–1855 Türk-Rus ve Müttefiklerin Kırım Savaşı*, 93–101; Dodd, *Pictorial History of the Russian War*, 434–436, 443–448, 450–456; Adye, *Review of the Crimean War*, 165; Slade, *Turkey and the Crimean War*, 375–378.

147. Süer, *TSK Tarihi Osmanlı Devri Osmanlı-Rus Kırım Harbi Kafkas Cephesi Harekatı (1853–1856)*, 128–129, 131–134; Slade, *Turkey and the Crimean War*, 378–384, 425–428; Russell, *British Expedition to the Crimea*, 197.

148. Allen and Muratoff, *Caucasian Battlefields*, 82–86, 89–91.

149. Lake, *Narrative of the Defence of Kars*, 64–66; Süer, *TSK Tarihi Osmanlı Devri Osmanlı-Rus Kırım Harbi Kafkas Cephesi Harekatı (1853–1856)*, 129–131; Allen and Muratoff, *Caucasian Battlefields*, 87–89; Gürel, *1853–1855 Türk-Rus ve Müttefiklerin Kırım Savaşı*, 115.

150. Lake, *Narrative of the Defence of Kars*, 86–94, 96–115, 260–275; Duncan, *Campaign with the Turks in Asia*, 121–122; Gürel, *1853–1855 Türk-Rus ve Müttefiklerin Kırım Savaşı*, 116; Sandwith, *Narrative of the Siege of Kars*, 252–254, 261.

151. Lake, *Narrative of the Defence of Kars*, 129–159, 189–194; Sandwith, *Narrative of the Siege of Kars*, 277–278; Slade, *Turkey and the Crimean War*, 429.

152. Lake, *Narrative of the Defence of Kars*, 195–233; Sandwith, *Narrative of the Siege of Kars*, 278–285; Süer, *TSK Tarihi Osmanlı Devri Osmanlı-Rus Kırım Harbi Kafkas Cephesi Harekatı (1853–1856)*, 138–139; Slade, *Turkey and the Crimean War*, 429–431; Allen and Muratoff, *Caucasian Battlefields*, 91–94.

153. Allen and Muratoff, *Caucasian Battlefields*, 95–99; Süer, *TSK Tarihi Osmanlı Devri Osmanlı-Rus Kırım Harbi Kafkas Cephesi Harekatı (1853–1856)*, 138, 140, 142–148; Gürel, *1853–1855 Türk-Rus ve Müttefiklerin Kırım Savaşı*, 116–118; Slade, *Turkey and the Crimean War*, 433–440; Lake, *Narrative of the Defence of Kars*, 236, 284–285, 290–304, 327–335.

154. Süer, *TSK Tarihi Osmanlı Devri Osmanlı-Rus Kırım Harbi Kafkas Cephesi Harekatı (1853–1856)*, 148–150; Gürel, *1853–1855 Türk-Rus ve Müttefiklerin Kırım Savaşı*, 121–123; Allen and Muratoff, *Caucasian Battlefields*, 100–102.

155. Dodd, *Pictorial History of the Russian War*, 298–311.

156. Süer, *TSK Tarihi Osmanlı Devri Osmanlı-Rus Kırım Harbi Kafkas Cephesi Harekatı (1853–1856)*, 155–164; Sandwith, *Narrative of the Siege of Kars*, 96, 203, 206–208; Duncan, *Campaign with the Turks in Asia*, 140–149.

157. Lake, *Narrative of the Defence of Kars*, 66–67; Sandwith, *Narrative of the Siege of Kars*, 25, 237.

158. Sandwith, *Narrative of the Siege of Kars*, 127–128; Lake, *Narrative of the Defence of Kars*, 143–145; Duncan, *Campaign with the Turks in Asia*, 102–106.

159. Lake, *Narrative of the Defence of Kars*, 13, 17, 61–62; Sandwith, *Narrative of the Siege of Kars*, 122; Duncan, *Campaign with the Turks in Asia*, 96.

160. Reid, *Turkey and the Turks*, 69–70.

161. Zarif, "Zarif Paşanın Hatıratı," 472, 486–488, 492–493; Lake, *Narrative of the Defence of Kars*, 29–31, 165–168, 275–284; Sandwith, *Narrative of the Siege of Kars*, 111–113, 122–123; Slade, *Turkey and the Crimean War*, 407–408, 413–414; Duncan, *Campaign with the Turks in Asia*, 167–170, 180.

162. Lake, *Narrative of the Defence of Kars*, 60–63, 114; Sandwith, *Narrative of the Siege of Kars*, 99–100, 107–108, 132, 208–209; Russell, *British Expedition to the Crimea*, 70; Duncan, *Campaign with the Turks in Asia*, 179–187; Slade, *Turkey and the Crimean War*, 173–176.

163. Money, *Twelve Months with the Bashi-Bozouks*, 7–10, 14–22, 30–32, 40–42, 119; Dodd, *Pictorial History of the Russian War*, 384; Sandwith, *Narrative of the Siege of Kars*, 154–155.

164. Money, *Twelve Months with the Bashi-Bozouks*, 23, 30–32, 35–37, 47–48, 49–55, 63–67, 76–79; Dodd, *Pictorial History of the Russian War*, 97–98; Russell, *British Expedition to the Crimea*, 73–74, 92.

165. Money, *Twelve Months with the Bashi-Bozouks*, 100–119, 199–219.

166. Cemil Karasu, "Kırım Savaşı'nda Kontenjan Askeri," in *Yedinci Askeri Tarih Semineri*, vol. 1, (Ankara: Genelkurmay Basımevi, 2000), 16–19; Dodd, *Pictorial History of the Russian War*, 384.

167. Karasu, "Kırım Savaşı'nda Kontenjan Askeri," 19–24.

Chapter 5

1. Nicolae Jorga, *Osmanlı İmparatorluğu Tarihi*, vol. 5, (trans.) Nilüfer Epçeli, (İstanbul: Yeditepe Yayınevi, 2005), 442–443; Bernard Lewis, *Emergence of Modern Turkey*, 118.

2. Ahmed Mithat, *Üss-i İnkılap*, vol. 1, (ed.) T. G. Seratlı, (İstanbul: Selis Kitaplar, 2004), 71–72, 79.

3. Jorga, *Osmanlı İmparatorluğu Tarihi*, vol. 5, 449, 451–453; Atakan, *Ordu Bilgisi*, 26.

4. J. Lewis Farley, *Modern Turkey*, (London: Hurst and Blackett, 1872), 134–136, 144–149; İ. Halil Sedes, *1877–1878 Osmanlı-Rus ve Romen Savaşı*, vol. 1, (İstanbul: Askeri Matbaa, 1935), 129–130.

5. Ahmet Nuri Sinaplı, *Şeyhülvüzera, Serasker Mehmed Namık Paşa*, (İstanbul: Yenilik Basımevi, 1987), 281; Ahmed Mithat, *Üss-i İnkılap*, 107–110.

6. The first military high school was founded in İstanbul in 1845 as a part of Military Academy.

7. Mahmud Şevket, *Osmanlı Askeri Teşkilatı ve Kıyafeti*, 88; Ahmed Mithat, *Üss-i İnkılap*, 75–76, 112–113.

8. Ahmed Muhtar, *Anılar: Sergüzeşt-i Hayatımın Cildi Sanisi*, (ed.) Nuri Akbayar, (İstanbul: Tarih Vakfı Yurt Yayınları, 1996), 50; Keçecizade İzzet Fuad, *Kaçırılan Fırsatlar: 1877 Osmanlı-Rus Savaşı Hakkında Eleştiriler ve Askeri Düşünceler*, (ed.) Rasim Süerdem, (Ankara: Genelkurmay Basımevi, 1997), 23.

9. Ahmed Muhtar, *Anılar*, 95; William von Herbert, *The Defence of Plevna, 1877*, (London: Longmans, Green and Co., 1895), 10, 44–45, 184; For an example of a high-ranking Alaylı officer's career *see* Ethem Erkoç, *Beşiktaş Muhafızı Yedi Sekiz Hasan Paşa ve Bir Devrin Hikayesi*, (Çorum: Pegasus, 2004), 24–39, 51–54.

10. Sedes, *1877–1878 Osmanlı-Rus ve Romen Savaşı*, vol. 1, 117–120; Hikmet Süer, *1877–1878 Osmanlı-Rus Harbi Rumeli Cephesi*, (Ankara: Genelkurmay Basımevi, 1993), 36; Jorga, *Osmanlı İmparatorluğu Tarihi*, vol. 5, 477.

11. Herbert, *Defence of Plevna, 1877*, 47–48; Jorga, *Osmanlı İmparatorluğu Tarihi*, vol. 5, 477.

12. Ahmed Muhtar, *Anılar*, 51, 87, 94, 127, 167, 186, 208, 214, 217, 228.
13. Charles Ryan and John Sanders, *Under the Red Crescent*, (New York: Charles Scribner's Sons, 1897), 6–13.
14. Ahmed Muhtar, *Anılar*, 271–272.
15. Mahmud Şevket, *Osmanlı Askeri Teşkilatı ve Kıyafeti*, 87; Jorga, *Osmanlı İmparatorluğu Tarihi*, vol. 5, 477.
16. Mahmud Şevket, *Osmanlı Askeri Teşkilatı ve Kıyafeti*, 87–88; Çakın and Orhon, *TSK Tarihi Osmanlı Devri (1793–1908)*, 206–207.
17. Mahmud Şevket, *Osmanlı Askeri Teşkilatı ve Kıyafeti*, 88–89; Çakın and Orhon, *TSK Tarihi Osmanlı Devri (1793–1908)*, 207–208; Atakan, *Ordu Bilgisi*, 27; Ahmed Mithat, *Üss-i İnkılap*, 87.
18. Çakın and Orhon, *TSK Tarihi Osmanlı Devri (1793–1908)*, 207–208; James Baker, *Turkey*, (New York: Henry Holt and Co., 1879), 259; Ahmed Muhtar, *Anılar*, 230.
19. Ahmed Cevdet, *Maruzat*, (ed.) Yusuf Hallaçoğlu, (İstanbul: Çağrı Yayınları, 1980), 116–120; Skene, *With Lord Stratford in the Crimean War*, 43–45.
20. Ahmed Muhtar, *Anılar*, 80.
21. Enver Behnan Şapolyo, *Gazi Osman Paşa ve Plevne Müdafaası*, (İstanbul: Türkiye Yayınevi, 1959), infra. 53.
22. Ahmed Muhtar, *Anılar*, 27.
23. Berkes, *Türkiye'de Çağdaşlaşma*, 269–297; Şerif Mardin, "Yeni Osmanlı Düşüncesi," in (ed.) Mehmet Ö. Alkan and Modern *Türkiye'de Siyasi Düşünce*, vol. 1, (İstanbul: İletişim Yayınları, 2001), 42–50; Selçuk Akşin Somel, "Osmanlı Reform Çağında Osmanlıcılık Düşüncesi (1839–1913)," in (ed.) Mehmet Ö. Alkan and Modern *Türkiye'de Siyasi Düşünce*, vol. 1, (İstanbul: İletişim Yayınları, 2001), 88–107.
24. Ahmed Mithat, *Üss-i İnkılap*, 171–184, 201–206; Lewis, *Emergence of Modern Turkey*, 147–164.
25. Lewis, *Emergence of Modern Turkey*, 158–165; Berkes, *Türkiye'de Çağdaşlaşma*, 301–329.
26. A. J. Schem, *An Illustrated History of the Conflict between Russia and Turkey with a Review of the Eastern Question*, (New York: H. S. Goodspeed & Co., 1878), 181–186; Ellis A. Bartlett, *The Battlefields of Thessaly: With Personal Experiences in Turkey and Greece*, (London: John Murray, 1897), 47–50; For the level of propaganda against Ottoman Empire *see* Gladstone's eighty pages long popular booklet. W. E. Gladstone, *Lessons in Massacre: An Exposition of the Conduct of the Porte in and About Bulgaria*, (London: John Murray, 1877); For a contemporary book supporting Ottoman thesis *see* G. Giacometti, *Russia's Work in Turkey*, (trans.) Edgar Whitaker, (London: Effingham Wilson, 1877); Also *see* Ahmed Mithat, *Üss-i İnkılap*, vol. 2, (ed.) T. G. Seratlı, (İstanbul: Selis Kitaplar, 2004), 55–57, 210–213.
27. Ahmed Mithat, *Üss-i İnkılap*, 77–102; Sedes, *1877–1878 Osmanlı-Rus ve Romen Savaşı*, vol. 1, 13–55; Schem, *Illustrated History of the Conflict between Russia and Turkey*, 186–189, 199–207.
28. Sedes, *1877–1878 Osmanlı-Rus ve Romen Savaşı*, vol. 1, 121–125; Şapolyo, *Gazi Osman Paşa ve Plevne Müdafaası*, 64; Ahmed Muhtar, *Anılar*, 38–39.
29. Ahmed Muhtar, *Anılar*, 4–7; Sedes, *1877–1878 Osmanlı-Rus ve Romen Savaşı*, vol. 1, 125–126.
30. İzzet Fuad, *Kaçırılan Fırsatlar*, 33, 35.
31. David A. Rich, "Building Foundations for Effective Intelligence: Military Geography and Statistics in Russian Perspective 1845–1905," in (ed.) D. S. van der Oye and B. W. Mennig, *Reforming the Tsar's Army: Military Innovation in Imperial Russia from Peter the Great to the Revolution*, (Cambridge: Cambridge University Press, 2004), 179–181; Schem, *Illustrated History*

of the Conflict between Russia and Turkey, 211–213; Süer, *1877–1878 Osmanlı-Rus Harbi Rumeli Cephesi*, 54–56.

32. Süer, *1877–1878 Osmanlı-Rus Harbi Rumeli Cephesi*, 38; Ahmed Muhtar, *Anılar*, 13.

33. İzzet Fuad, *Kaçırılan Fırsatlar*, 16, 19, 21; Sedes, *1877–1878 Osmanlı-Rus ve Romen Savaşı*, vol. 1, 67–75; Schem, *Illustrated History of the Conflict between Russia and Turkey*, 225–227.

34. İ. Halil Sedes, *1877–1878 Osmanlı-Rus ve Romen Savaşı*, vol. 2, (İstanbul: Askeri Matbaa, 1936), 10–17, 22–34; Süer, *1877–1878 Osmanlı-Rus Harbi Rumeli Cephesi*, 35, 72–76.

35. Sedes, *1877–1878 Osmanlı-Rus ve Romen Savaşı*, vol. 2, 17–21, 34–36; Süer, *1877–1878 Osmanlı-Rus Harbi Rumeli Cephesi*, 71, 76, 85; Herbert, *Defence of Plevna, 1877*, 52–53; Schem, *Illustrated History of the Conflict between Russia and Turkey*, 225–226.

36. İzzet Fuad, *Kaçırılan Fırsatlar*, 7, 16, 20, 24–30, 39–41; İ. Halil Sedes, *1877–1878 Osmanlı-Rus ve Romen Savaşı*, vol. 3, (İstanbul: Askeri Matbaa, 1937), 18–72; Süer, *1877–1878 Osmanlı-Rus Harbi Rumeli Cephesi*, 79–88, 99–114; Schem, *Illustrated History of the Conflict between Russia and Turkey*, 231–247.

37. Süer, *1877–1878 Osmanlı-Rus Harbi Rumeli Cephesi*, 104, 106–109, 137; İzzet Fuad, *Kaçırılan Fırsatlar*, 18; Herbert, *Defence of Plevna, 1877*, 32; Bartlett, *Battlefields of Thessaly*, 51–53, 368–384; Francis Stanley, *St. Petersburg to Plevna*, (London: Richard Bentley and Son, 1878), 99–103; For an eye-witness account of attacks against civilian population and Ottoman military's failure to protect them *see* Hüseyin Raci, *Tarihçe-i Vaka-i Zağra*, (ed.) E. Düzdağ, (İstanbul: Kervan Kitapçılık, not dated), passim.; İ. Halil Sedes, *1877–1878 Osmanlı-Rus ve Romen Savaşı*, vol. 5, (İstanbul: Askeri Matbaa, 1938), 27, 36–37, 39.

38. Süer, *1877–1878 Osmanlı-Rus Harbi Rumeli Cephesi*, 116–132; İ. Halil Sedes, *1877–1878 Osmanlı-Rus ve Romen Savaşı*, vol. 4, (İstanbul: Askeri Matbaa, 1937), 13–34; Schem, *Illustrated History of the Conflict between Russia and Turkey*, 252–254.

39. Sedes, *1877–1878 Osmanlı-Rus ve Romen Savaşı*, vol. 3, 101–136; Süer, *1877–1878 Osmanlı-Rus Harbi Rumeli Cephesi*, 138–154; Schem, *Illustrated History of the Conflict between Russia and Turkey*, 247–251.

40. Süer, *1877–1878 Osmanlı-Rus Harbi Rumeli Cephesi*, 175–176, 207.

41. İzzet Fuad, *Kaçırılan Fırsatlar*, 42.

42. Sedes, *1877–1878 Osmanlı-Rus ve Romen Savaşı*, vol. 5, 29–34; Süer, *1877–1878 Osmanlı-Rus Harbi Rumeli Cephesi*, 134–136, 177–184.

43. Sedes, *1877–1878 Osmanlı-Rus ve Romen Savaşı*, vol. 4, 35–58; Süer, *1877–1878 Osmanlı-Rus Harbi Rumeli Cephesi*, 154–157; Herbert, *Defence of Plevna, 1877*, 52–53, 78–80; İbrahim Edhem, *Plevne Hatıraları: Sebat ve Gayret Kıyametten Bir Alamet*, (ed.) Seyfullah Esin, (İstanbul: Kervan Kitapçılık, 1979), 37–42; Ryan and Sanders, *Under the Red Crescent*, 99–117.

44. Herbert, *Defence of Plevna, 1877*, 49–51, 224; Ryan and Sanders, *Under the Red Crescent*, 34.

45. Sedes, *1877–1878 Osmanlı-Rus ve Romen Savaşı*, vol. 4, 59–75; Süer, *1877–1878 Osmanlı-Rus Harbi Rumeli Cephesi*, 157–170; İbrahim Edhem, *Plevne Hatıraları*, 42–43; Ryan and Sanders, *Under the Red Crescent*, 121–137; Stanley, *St. Petersburg to Plevna*, 79–85.

46. İ. Halil Sedes, *1877–1878 Osmanlı-Rus ve Romen Savaşı*, vol. 6, (İstanbul: Askeri Matbaa, 1938), 1–58; Süer, *1877–1878 Osmanlı-Rus Harbi Rumeli Cephesi*, 218–246; İbrahim Edhem, *Plevne Hatıraları*, 43–46; Ryan and Sanders, *Under the Red Crescent*, 51–52, 166–177; Schem, *Illustrated History of the Conflict between Russia and Turkey*, 287–296; Stanley, *St. Petersburg to Plevna*, 152–153.

47. Ryan and Sanders, *Under the Red Crescent*, 219–224; Herbert, *Defence of Plevna, 1877*, 341; Süer, *1877–1878 Osmanlı-Rus Harbi Rumeli Cephesi*, 361; Sedes, *1877–1878 Osmanlı-Rus ve Romen Savaşı*, vol. 6, 9–16.

48. Sedes, *1877–1878 Osmanlı-Rus ve Romen Savaşı*, vol. 4, 81–86, 126–141.

49. Sedes, *1877–1878 Osmanlı-Rus ve Romen Savaşı*, vol. 5, 17–19; Süer, *1877–1878 Osmanlı-Rus Harbi Rumeli Cephesi*, 172–173; Herbert, *Defence of Plevna, 1877*, 56.

50. İzzet Fuad, *Kaçırılan Fırsatlar*, 43, 73; Sedes, *1877–1878 Osmanlı-Rus ve Romen Savaşı*, vol. 5, 18–22, 34.

51. Fethi Tevetoğlu, "Büyük Türkçü Süleyman Paşa," *Türk Kültürü*, year. VI, no. 70, August 1968, 707–730.

52. Sedes, *1877–1878 Osmanlı-Rus ve Romen Savaşı*, vol. 5, 23–25, 34, 43–52; Süer, *1877–1878 Osmanlı-Rus Harbi Rumeli Cephesi*, 174, 180–181, 185; İzzet Fuad, *Kaçırılan Fırsatlar*, 69; Herbert, *Defence of Plevna, 1877*, 51.

53. İzzet Fuad, *Kaçırılan Fırsatlar*, 44–49, 52, 70, 73, 77–80, 87, 91; Sedes, *1877–1878 Osmanlı-Rus ve Romen Savaşı*, vol. 5, 23–25, 57–61, 111–145; İ. Halil Sedes, *1877–1878 Osmanlı-Rus ve Romen Savaşı*, vol. 9, (İstanbul: Askeri Matbaa, 1950), 75–220; Süer, *1877–1878 Osmanlı-Rus Harbi Rumeli Cephesi*, 204–207, 307–344.

54. Sedes, *1877–1878 Osmanlı-Rus ve Romen Savaşı*, vol. 5, 57–102; İ. Halil Sedes, *1877–1878 Osmanlı-Rus ve Romen Savaşı*, vol. 8, (İstanbul: Askeri Matbaa, 1940), 1–180; Sedes, *1877–1878 Osmanlı-Rus ve Romen Savaşı*, vol. 9, 1–36, 44–74; Süer, *1877–1878 Osmanlı-Rus Harbi Rumeli Cephesi*, 177–203, 252–298; İzzet Fuad, *Kaçırılan Fırsatlar*, 45, 55, 78–79, 92; Schem, *Illustrated History of the Conflict between Russia and Turkey*, 298–303, 314–318; Stanley, *St. Petersburg to Plevna*, 30–40, 73.

55. Süer, *1877–1878 Osmanlı-Rus Harbi Rumeli Cephesi*, 344–358; İbrahim Edhem, *Plevne Hatıraları*, 46–66; Ryan and Sanders, *Under the Red Crescent*, 224–239; Stanley, *St. Petersburg to Plevna*, 139–203; Schem, *Illustrated History of the Conflict between Russia and Turkey*, 307–314.

56. İzzet Fuad, *Kaçırılan Fırsatlar*, 49, 52, 93; Süer, *1877–1878 Osmanlı-Rus Harbi Rumeli Cephesi*, 413–452; İbrahim Edhem, *Plevne Hatıraları*, 66–67; Richard Graf von Pfeil, *Experiences of a Prussian Officer in the Russian Service*, (trans.) C. W. Bowdler, (London: Edward Stanford, 1893), 127, 133.

57. Süer, *1877–1878 Osmanlı-Rus Harbi Rumeli Cephesi*, 452–486; İbrahim Edhem, *Plevne Hatıraları*, 67–78; Ryan and Sanders, *Under the Red Crescent*, 254–295; Schem, *Illustrated History of the Conflict between Russia and Turkey*, 324–326, 328–335; Stanley, *St. Petersburg to Plevna*, 224–241.

58. Süer, *1877–1878 Osmanlı-Rus Harbi Rumeli Cephesi*, 487–507; İzzet Fuad, *Kaçırılan Fırsatlar*, 111–114; Schem, *Illustrated History of the Conflict between Russia and Turkey*, 369–385.

59. Ahmed Muhtar, *Anılar*, 13, 44–56, 65; Schem, *Illustrated History of the Conflict between Russia and Turkey*, 263–271; Şadi Sükan, *TSK Tarihi Osmanlı Devri 1877–1878 Osmanlı-Rus Harbi Kafkas Cephesi Harekatı*, (Ankara: Genelkurmay Basımevi, 1985), 63, 72–80.

60. Allen and Muratoff, *Caucasian Battlefields*, 123–126, 152–154; Sükan, *TSK Tarihi Osmanlı Devri 1877–1878 Osmanlı-Rus Harbi Kafkas Cephesi Harekatı*, 85–89, 93–98.

61. Allen and Muratoff, *Caucasian Battlefields*, 126–131, 154–157; Sükan, *TSK Tarihi Osmanlı Devri 1877–1878 Osmanlı-Rus Harbi Kafkas Cephesi Harekatı*, 89–93, 98–99.

62. Ahmed Muhtar, *Anılar*, 56–61; Schem, *Illustrated History of the Conflict between Russia and Turkey*, 272–281; Sükan, *TSK Tarihi Osmanlı Devri 1877–1878 Osmanlı-Rus Harbi Kafkas Cephesi Harekatı*, 99–121.

63. Ahmed Muhtar, *Anılar*, 83, 122–123, 136, 149, 226–227.

64. Ibid., 8, 55, 72, 125; Allen and Muratoff, *Caucasian Battlefields*, 120–139, 160–164, 168–169; Sükan, *TSK Tarihi Osmanlı Devri 1877–1878 Osmanlı-Rus Harbi Kafkas Cephesi Harekatı*, 121–126; Vehbi Kocagüney, *Erzurum Kalesi ve Savaşları*, (İstanbul: Askeri Matbaa, 1942), 69, 87.

65. Ahmed Muhtar, *Anılar*, 148–217; Allen and Muratoff, *Caucasian Battlefields*, 158–160, 164–168, 170–188; Schem, *Illustrated History of the Conflict between Russia and Turkey*, 339–349; Sükan, *TSK Tarihi Osmanlı Devri 1877–1878 Osmanlı-Rus Harbi Kafkas Cephesi Harekatı*, 126–133, 138–156.

66. Kocagüney, *Erzurum Kalesi ve Savaşları*, 62, 71–72; Sükan, *TSK Tarihi Osmanlı Devri 1877–1878 Osmanlı-Rus Harbi Kafkas Cephesi Harekatı*, 159–163.

67. Allen and Muratoff, *Caucasian Battlefields*, 189–210; Ahmed Muhtar, *Anılar*, 218–245, 281–307; Sükan, *TSK Tarihi Osmanlı Devri 1877–1878 Osmanlı-Rus Harbi Kafkas Cephesi Harekatı*, 164–171; Kocagüney, *Erzurum Kalesi ve Savaşları*, 93, 99.

68. Ryan and Sanders, *Under the Red Crescent*, 330–340; Sükan, *TSK Tarihi Osmanlı Devri 1877–1878 Osmanlı-Rus Harbi Kafkas Cephesi Harekatı*, 171–181, 189–196; Allen and Muratoff, *Caucasian Battlefields*, 211–212.

69. Allen and Muratoff, *Caucasian Battlefields*, 212–215; Sükan, *TSK Tarihi Osmanlı Devri 1877–1878 Osmanlı-Rus Harbi Kafkas Cephesi Harekatı*, 157–158, 184–189.

70. O'Connor believed just the opposite that the war was "the object of serious contemporary scrutiny" of European militaries. See Maureen P. O'Connor, "The Vision of Soldiers: Britain, France, Germany, and the United States Observe the Russo-Turkish War," *War in History*, vol. 4, no. 3, 1997, 264–266.

71. İzzet Fuad, *Kaçırılan Fırsatlar*, 15.

72. Ahmed Muhtar, *Anılar*, 84.

73. İzzet Fuad, *Kaçırılan Fırsatlar*, 30; Ahmed Muhtar, *Anılar*, 96–97, 117–118, 121–122, 146; Baker, *Turkey*, 261.

74. Sedes, *1877–1878 Osmanlı-Rus ve Romen Savaşı*, vol. 9, 125–126.

75. Necati Tacan, "1877–78 Osmanlı-Rus Seferinde Türk Sevk ve İdaresinde Sevkulceyşi Hataları," *Askeri Mecmua*, vol. 8, no. 107, December 1937, 756–759.

76. İzzet Fuad, *Kaçırılan Fırsatlar*, 8, 54; Hüseyin Raci, *Tarihçe-i Vaka-i Zağra*, 192.

77. Herbert, *Defence of Plevna, 1877*, 13–15, 22, 37, 43, 63; Ahmed Muhtar, *Anılar*, 8, 72; Ryan and Sanders, *Under the Red Crescent*, 32–34, 50, 308.

78. Herbert, *Defence of Plevna, 1877*, 8; İzzet Fuad, *Kaçırılan Fırsatlar*, 39.

79. Ahmed Muhtar, *Anılar*, 27, 94, 275; İzzet Fuad, *Kaçırılan Fırsatlar*, 15, 90; Süer, *1877–1878 Osmanlı-Rus Harbi Rumeli Cephesi*, 37.

80. Herbert, *Defence of Plevna, 1877*, 48, 233–234; Ahmed Muhtar, *Anılar*, 83–84, 126–127, 208, 214, 217; Baker, *Turkey*, 273; Ryan and Sanders, *Under the Red Crescent*, 31, 67, 240–241, 296; Allen and Muratoff, *Caucasian Battlefields*, 217; İzzet Fuad, *Kaçırılan Fırsatlar*, 82–83.

81. İzzet Fuad, *Kaçırılan Fırsatlar*, x, 6, 13.

82. Ibid., 89; Ahmed Muhtar, *Anılar*, 63, 107.

83. Sedes, *1877–1878 Osmanlı-Rus ve Romen Savaşı*, vol. 9, 127–128.

84. Ibid., vol. 9, 113–117.

85. Farley, *Modern Turkey*, 136–144; Ahmed Mithat, *Üss-i İnkılap*, 80–87; Sedes, *1877–1878 Osmanlı-Rus ve Romen Savaşı*, vol. 9, 107–109, 147–149; Herbert, *Defence of Plevna, 1877*, 10; Stanley, *St. Petersburg to Plevna*, 35–36; Baker, *Turkey*, 261.

86. İzzet Fuad, *Kaçırılan Fırsatlar*, 91; Herbert, *Defence of Plevna, 1877*, 30.

87. Sedes, *1877–1878 Osmanlı-Rus ve Romen Savaşı*, vol. 9, 110–113.
88. İzzet Fuad, *Kaçırılan Fırsatlar*, 82; Jorga, *Osmanlı İmparatorluğu Tarihi*, vol. 5, 476–477, 487.
89. *Osmanlı Döneminde Askeri Okullarda Eğitim*, (Ankara: Milli Savunma Bakanlığı, 2000), 14–169.
90. *TMAA Numara Defteri (Cadet Grade Logbook) no. 2, 4, 5, 6, 9, 11, 12, 13, 14, 16, 18, 20, 22*.
91. Alişan Akpınar, *Osmanlı Devleti'nde Aşiret Mektebi*, (İstanbul: Göçebe Yayınları, 1997), passim.; Eugene L. Rogan, "Aşiret Mektebi: Abdülhamid II's School for Tribes (1892–1907)," *International Journal of Middle East Studies*, vol. 28, no. 1, 1996, 83–107.
92. Cevdet Ergül, *II.Abdülhamid'in Doğu Politikası ve Hamidiye Alayları*, (İzmir: Çağlayan Yayınları, 1997), 35–37, 45–46; Merwin A. Griffiths, *The Reorganization of the Ottoman Army under Abdülhamid II, 1880–1897*, (Los Angeles: University of California Unpublished Ph.D. Dissertation, 1965), 119.
93. Ergül, *II.Abdülhamid'in Doğu Politikası ve Hamidiye Alayları*, 43–66, 74–77; Çakın and Orhon, *TSK Tarihi Osmanlı Devri (1793–1908)*, 224–226; Griffiths, *Reorganization of the Ottoman Army*, 119–125.
94. Ergül, *II.Abdülhamid'in Doğu Politikası ve Hamidiye Alayları*, 65–82, 93–96; Griffiths, *Reorganization of the Ottoman Army*, 125–127; Çakın and Orhon, *TSK Tarihi Osmanlı Devri (1793–1908)*, 226; Edwin M. Bliss, *Turkey and the Armenian Atrocities*, (New York: M. J. Coghlan, 1896), 97–98, 121, 369–371.
95. Abbas Erdoğan Noyan, *Prizren-Dersaadet: II.Abdülhamid'in Yıldız Sarayı Muhafızlığına Getirilen Arnavut Taburunun Öyküsü*, (İstanbul: Kitap Matbaası, 1999), 21–88.
96. Jehuda L. Wallach, *Bir Askeri Yardımın Anatomisi*, (Turkish translation of the German original *Anatomie einer Miltaerhilfe*), (trans.) Fahri Çeliker, (Ankara: Genelkurmay Basımevi, 1977), 9–23; Tahsin Esencan, *Türk Topçuluğu ve Kaynakları*, (Ankara: Askeri Fabrika Basımevi, 1946), 9–11; Sedes, *1877–1878 Osmanlı-Rus ve Romen Savaşı*, vol. 9, 127; Griffiths, *Reorganization of the Ottoman Army*, 40–43, 151.
97. Wallach, *Bir Askeri Yardımın Anatomisi*, 25–42; Griffiths, *Reorganization of the Ottoman Army*, 40–43, 45–52, 56.
98. Çakın and Orhon, *TSK Tarihi Osmanlı Devri (1793–1908)*, 301–304; Griffiths, *Reorganization of the Ottoman Army*, 43–45, 71–72.
99. Griffiths, *Reorganization of the Ottoman Army*, 109–110.
100. Çakın and Orhon, *TSK Tarihi Osmanlı Devri (1793–1908)*, 212–217.
101. Wallach, *Bir Askeri Yardımın Anatomisi*, 42–47; Griffiths, *Reorganization of the Ottoman Army*, 54–57.
102. Actually the German General Staff previously proposed von der Goltz to the Japanese military delegation for the instructor post at the newly founded Japanese Military Academy. Japanese delegates found von der Goltz unsuited for the job due to his fame as a military theoretician. They preferred Major Clemens Meckel, a well-known practitioner. See Stewart Lone, *Army, Empire, and Politics in Meiji Japan: The Three Careers of General Katsura Taro*, (London: Macmillan Press, 2000), 19.
103. Wallach, *Bir Askeri Yardımın Anatomisi*, 47–49, 55–57; Griffiths, *Reorganization of the Ottoman Army*, 58–61, 65, 98.
104. *TMAA Numara Defteri (Cadet Grade Logbook) no. 5, 6, 9, 11, 12, 13, 14, 16, 18, 20, 22*.
105. İzzet Fuad, *Kaçırılan Fırsatlar*, 23; Wallach, *Bir Askeri Yardımın Anatomisi*, 49, 57.

106. Enver, *Enver Paşa'nın Anıları*, (ed.) H.Erdoğan Cengiz, (İstanbul: İletişim Yayınları, 1991), 36–39, 43–51; Wallach, *Bir Askeri Yardımın Anatomisi*, 49; Griffiths, *Reorganization of the Ottoman Army*, 99–101.

107. Wallach, *Bir Askeri Yardımın Anatomisi*, 23, 51–52, 57, 64, 82–83; Griffiths, *Reorganization of the Ottoman Army*, 67–72, 88–89, 102.

108. Bartlett, *Battlefields of Thessaly*, 11–44, 131–137, 147–148; Colmar von der Goltz, *Osmanlı-Yunan Harbi*, (Turkish translation of the German original *Der Thessalische Krieg und die Türkische Armee*), (trans.) Yakub Şevki, (İzmir: Akademi Kitabevi, 2001), 9–12; Clive Bigham, *With the Turkish Army in Thessaly*, (London: Macmillan and Co., 1897), 1–7, 36–41; Selim Sun, *1897 Osmanlı-Yunan Harbi*, (Ankara: Genelkurmay Basımevi, 1965), 22–28, 83–86.

109. Goltz, *Osmanlı-Yunan Harbi*, 35–64; Sun, *1897 Osmanlı-Yunan Harbi*, 57–63, 76–80; For a criticism of the von der Goltz plan and its revised version *see* Fahri, "1897 Türk-Yunan Harbine Ait Bir Tetkik," *Askeri Mecmua*, no. 95, December 1934, 927–933.

110. Bartlett, *Battlefields of Thessaly*, 75–82; Goltz, *Osmanlı-Yunan Harbi*, 12–16, 22–29; Bigham, *With the Turkish Army in Thessaly*, 11–12, 42–54; Sun, *1897 Osmanlı-Yunan Harbi*, 71–73, 83.

111. Bartlett, *Battlefields of Thessaly*, 127–158; Goltz, *Osmanlı-Yunan Harbi*, 91–108, 115–127; Sun, *1897 Osmanlı-Yunan Harbi*, 88–116.

112. Ahmed İzzet, *Feryadım*, vol. 1, (İstanbul: Nehir Yayınları, 1992), 11; Bartlett, *Battlefields of Thessaly*, 91–96, 112, 182; Bigham, *With the Turkish Army in Thessaly*, 124; Sun, *1897 Osmanlı-Yunan Harbi*, 119–121; Fahri, *Askeri Mecmua*, 934–936.

113. Bartlett, *Battlefields of Thessaly*, 159–173, 186–187, 189–193; Goltz, *Osmanlı-Yunan Harbi*, 108–115, 128–143; Ahmed İzzet, *Feryadım*, 12–15; Bigham, *With the Turkish Army in Thessaly*, 55–75; Sun, *1897 Osmanlı-Yunan Harbi*, 118–136.

114. Bartlett, *Battlefields of Thessaly*, 216–247; Goltz, *Osmanlı-Yunan Harbi*, 144–222; Ahmed İzzet, *Feryadım*, 15–24; Bigham, *With the Turkish Army in Thessaly*, 76–102; Sun, *1897 Osmanlı-Yunan Harbi*, 137–206.

115. Bartlett, *Battlefields of Thessaly*, 100, 107, 109, 146–147; Goltz, *Osmanlı-Yunan Harbi*, 21–23, 269, 272; Bigham, *With the Turkish Army in Thessaly*, 9–11; Sun, *1897 Osmanlı-Yunan Harbi*, 68–69, 247–252.

116. Bartlett, *Battlefields of Thessaly*, 248–260; Goltz, *Osmanlı-Yunan Harbi*, 228–260; Sun, *1897 Osmanlı-Yunan Harbi*, 218–243; Mahmud Muhtar, *3.Kolordu ve Doğu Ordusu'nun Muharebeleri: Balkan Savaşı*, (İstanbul: Güncel Yayıncılık, 2003), 166–167.

117. Bartlett, *Battlefields of Thessaly*, 92–93, 110–112; Goltz, *Osmanlı-Yunan Harbi*, 18–19, 263–265; Sun, *1897 Osmanlı-Yunan Harbi*, 66–68, 165–168, 267.

118. Bartlett, *Battlefields of Thessaly*, 92–93, 143; Goltz, *Osmanlı-Yunan Harbi*, 25, 70–78, 261–263, 265–267; Kazım Karabekir, *Hayatım*, (ed.) Faruk Özerengin, (İstanbul: Emre Yayınları, 1995), 356–357, 360–361; Bigham, *With the Turkish Army in Thessaly*, 28–33; Sun, *1897 Osmanlı-Yunan Harbi*, 266–267.

119. Enver, *Enver Paşa'nın Anıları*, 35; Resneli Niyazi, *Hürriyet Kahramanı Resneli Niyazi Hatıratı*, (ed.) Nurer Uğurlu, (İstanbul: Örgün Yayınevi, 2003), 144–147; Metin Ayışığı, *Mareşal Ahmet İzzet Paşa: Askeri ve Siyasi Hayatı*, (Ankara: Türk Tarih Kurumu Basımevi, 1997), 14–16, 19–21.

120. Glen W. Swanson, "The Ottoman Police," *Journal of Contemporary History*, vol. 7, no. 1/2, January–April 1972, 243–252.

121. Levy, *Military Policy of Sultan Mahmud II, 1808–1839*, 175–179.

122. Çakın and Orhon, *TSK Tarihi Osmanlı Devri (1793–1908)*, 248–253; Swanson, *Journal of Contemporary History*, 253–255; Nadir Özbek, "Policing the Countryside: Gendarmes of the Late 19th Century Ottoman Empire (1876–1908), *International Journal of Middle East Studies*, vol. 40, no. 1, 2008, 51–56, 62–63; Selahattin Günay, *Bizi Kimlere Bırakıp Gidiyorsun Türk? Suriye ve Filistin Anıları*, (İstanbul: Türkiye İş Bankası Yayınları, 2006), 13.

123. Enver, *Enver Paşa'nın Anıları*, 48–51; Karabekir, *Hayatım*, 496.

124. Çakın and Orhon, *TSK Tarihi Osmanlı Devri (1793–1908)*, 590–596.

125. Niyazi, *Hürriyet Kahramanı Resneli Niyazi Hatıratı*, 148–149, 159–161; Halil Kut, *İttihat ve Terakki'den Cumhuriyete Bitmeyen Savaş: Kutülamare Kahramanı Halil Paşanın Anıları*, (İstanbul: 7 Gün Yayınları, 1972), 29; Karabekir, *Hayatım*, 364.

126. These were St. Sava (supported and controlled by Serbia), Ethnike Hetairia (Greece), Supreme Committee of Macedonia (Bulgaria) and IMRO (more or less independent until 1903).

127. Duncan McVicar Perry, *The Macedonian Cause: A Critical History of the Macedonian Revolutionary Organization, 1893–1903*, (Ann Arbor: The University of Michigan Unpublished Ph.D. Dissertation, 1981), 4–12, 26–36, 49–67, 71–83; Fikret Adanır, *Makedonya Sorunu Oluşumu ve 1908'e Kadar Gelişimi*, (Turkish translation of the German original *Die Makedonische Frage*), (trans.) İhsan Catay, (İstanbul: Tarih Vakfı Yurt Yayınları, 1996), 108–121; Karabekir, *Hayatım*, 409, 427, 447; Mahmut Beliğ, *Bulgar Komitalarının Tarihi ve Balkan Harbinde Yaptıkları*, (İstanbul: Askeri Matbaa, 1936), 21–35; Kut, *İttihat ve Terakki'den Cumhuriyete Bitmeyen Savaş*, 28.

128. Perry, *Macedonian Cause*, 71–106, 151–190, 252–266, 272–298; Adanır, *Makedonya Sorunu Oluşumu ve 1908'e Kadar Gelişimi*, 125–171; Beliğ, *Bulgar Komitalarının Tarihi ve Balkan Harbinde Yaptıkları*, 37–39; Karabekir, *Hayatım*, 468–469; For the statute of the IMRO see Voin Bozhinov and L. Panayotov, *Macedonia: Documents and Material*, (Sofia: Bulgarska Akademiya na Naukite, 1979), 419–422.

129. Kut, *İttihat ve Terakki'den Cumhuriyete Bitmeyen Savaş*, 24–27; Karabekir, *Hayatım*, 443; Perry, *Macedonian Cause*, 17–19, 129, 155–156, 182–184.

130. Niyazi, *Hürriyet Kahramanı Resneli Niyazi Hatıratı*, 148–152; Karabekir, *Hayatım*, 353–354, 490; Kut, *İttihat ve Terakki'den Cumhuriyete Bitmeyen Savaş*, 37–42; Adanır, *Makedonya Sorunu Oluşumu ve 1908'e Kadar Gelişimi*, 221–223, 233–235, 243; Perry, *Macedonian Cause*, 38–41, 266–271.

131. Enver, *Enver Paşa'nın Anıları*, 52–57; Niyazi, *Hürriyet Kahramanı Resneli Niyazi Hatıratı*, 175–183; Kut, *İttihat ve Terakki'den Cumhuriyete Bitmeyen Savaş*, 30–50; Karabekir, *Hayatım*, 379–383, 407–411, 468–475, 503–518; Rahmi Apak, *Yetmişlik Bir Subayın Anıları*, (Ankara: Türk Tarih Kurumu Basımevi, 1988), 16–23; Adanır, *Makedonya Sorunu Oluşumu ve 1908'e Kadar Gelişimi*, 202–203, 212–213, 263–264; Perry, *Macedonian Cause*, 311–319, 332–333.

132. Kut, *İttihat ve Terakki'den Cumhuriyete Bitmeyen Savaş*, 24–27; Karabekir, *Hayatım*, 360, 373–375, 378, 384, 388–389; Yavuz Abadan, *Mustafa Kemal ve Çetecilik*, 2nd Edition, (İstanbul: Varlık Yayınevi, 1972), 24–29.

133. Apak, *Yetmişlik Bir Subayın Anıları*, 16, 27–28; Enver, *Enver Paşa'nın Anıları*, 45–51; Niyazi, *Hürriyet Kahramanı Resneli Niyazi Hatıratı*, 149–155; Karabekir, *Hayatım*, 365, 377–379, 396, 471–472, 487–488, 529–535; Adanır, *Makedonya Sorunu Oluşumu ve 1908'e Kadar Gelişimi*, 255–259, 262–266; Yusuf Hikmet Bayur, *Türk İnkılâbı Tarihi*, vol. 1, section 1, (Ankara: Türk Tarih Kurumu Basımevi, 1983), 355–367, 407–422.

134. Kut, *İttihat ve Terakki'den Cumhuriyete Bitmeyen Savaş*, 51–53; Enver, *Enver Paşa'nın Anıları*, 69–71; Niyazi, *Hürriyet Kahramanı Resneli Niyazi Hatıratı*, 157; Bekir Fikri,

Balkanlarda Tedhiş ve Gerilla: Grebene, (İstanbul: Belge Yayınları, 1978), 31–34; Adanır, *Makedonya Sorunu Oluşumu ve 1908'e Kadar Gelişimi*, 200–201.

135. Enver, *Enver Paşa'nın Anıları*, 57; Karabekir, *Hayatım*, 392–397; Kerem Ünüvar, "İttihatçılıktan Kemalizm'e İhya'dan İnşa'ya," in (ed.) Mehmet Ö. Alkan and Modern *Türkiye'de Siyasi Düşünce*, vol. 1, (İstanbul: İletişim Yayınları, 2001), 132–133; Bayur, *Türk İnkılâbı Tarihi*, 345–351; Ercümend Kuran, "The Impact of Nationalism on the Turkish Elite in the Nineteen Century," in (ed.) W. R. Polk and R. L. Chambers, *Beginnings of Modernization in the Middle East: The Nineteenth Century*, (Chicago: University of Chicago Press, 1968), 117.

136. Ahmed İzzet, *Feryadım*, 7–8; Niyazi, *Hürriyet Kahramanı Resneli Niyazi Hatıratı*, 155–156; Karabekir, *Hayatım*, 494; Bayur, *Türk İnkılâbı Tarihi*, 244–252, 385–396.

137. Military schools (especially the Military Academy) were the real cauldrons of dissidence and dissemination of ideologies and thoughts. See Niyazi, *Hürriyet Kahramanı Resneli Niyazi Hatıratı*, 133–138; Kut, *İttihat ve Terakki'den Cumhuriyete Bitmeyen Savaş*, 9–17; Karabekir, *Hayatım*, 247–349.

138. Enver, *Enver Paşa'nın Anıları*, 57–69, 75–76; Niyazi, *Hürriyet Kahramanı Resneli Niyazi Hatıratı*, 162–163; H Cemal, *Arnavutluk'tan Sakarya'ya Komitacılık: Yüzbaşı Cemal'in Anıları*, (ed.) Kudret Emiroğlu, (Ankara: Kebikeç Yayınları, 1996), 9–13; Karabekir, *Hayatım*, 406; Bayur, *Türk İnkılâbı Tarihi*, 64, 196–197, 207, 315–320; Şapolyo, *Gazi Osman Paşa ve Plevne Müdafaası*, 61; Tarık Zafer Tunaya, *Türkiye'de Siyasal Partiler*, vol. 3, (İstanbul: Hürriyet Vakfı Yayınları, 1989), 13–34, 249.

139. Bayur, *Türk İnkılâbı Tarihi*, 266–267, 297–301, 339–341.

140. Enver, *Enver Paşa'nın Anıları*, 79–90; Niyazi, *Hürriyet Kahramanı Resneli Niyazi Hatıratı*, 165–171; Bayur, *Türk İnkılâbı Tarihi*, 432–441.

141. Michael A. Reynolds, *The Ottoman-Russian Struggle for Eastern Anatolia and the Caucasus, 1908–1918: Identity, Ideology and the Geopolitics of World Order*, (Princeton: Princeton University Unpublished Ph.D. Dissertation, 2003), 44–45.

142. Enver, *Enver Paşa'nın Anıları*, 77, 90–121; Niyazi, *Hürriyet Kahramanı Resneli Niyazi Hatıratı*, 186–374; Bekir Fikri, *Balkanlarda Tedhiş ve Gerilla*, 17–28; Bayur, *Türk İnkılâbı Tarihi*, 441–475; Adanır, *Makedonya Sorunu Oluşumu ve 1908'e Kadar Gelişimi*, 183–187.

143. Cemal, *Arnavutluk'tan Sakarya'ya Komitacılık*, 21–24.

144. Hafız Hakkı, *Bozgun*, (İstanbul: Kervan Kitapçılık, not dated), 96–99; Karabekir, *Hayatım*, 413, 420; Ahmed İzzet, *Feryadım*, 176.

145. Adanır, *Makedonya Sorunu Oluşumu ve 1908'e Kadar Gelişimi*, 266–271; M. Naim Turfan, *Rise of the Young Turks: Politics, the Military and Ottoman Collapse*, (London: I.B.Tauris, 2000), 143–148; Eliezer Tauber, *The Emergence of the Arab Movements*, (London: Frank Cass, 1993), 54–58; Yücel Aktar, *İkinci Meşrutiyet Dönemi Öğrenci Olayları (1908–1918)*, (İstanbul: İletişim Yayınları, 1990), 68–78, 82–96; Enver, *Enver Paşa'nın Anıları*, 121–129.

146. Yusuf Hikmet Bayur, *Türk İnkılâbı Tarihi*, vol. 1, section 2, (Ankara: Türk Tarih Kurumu Basımevi, 1983), 113–124; Turfan, *Rise of the Young Turks*, 148–156.

147. Ahmed İzzet, *Feryadım*, 44, 49; Ayışığı, *Mareşal Ahmet İzzet Paşa*, 18–22; Selahattin Karatamu, *Türk Silahlı Kuvvetleri Tarihi*, vol. 3, section 6, book 1, (Ankara: Genelkurmay Basımevi, 1971), 241–254, 261,; Edward J. Erickson, *Defeat in Detail: The Ottoman Army in the Balkans, 1912–1913*, (Westport: Praeger, 2003), 33.

148. Ahmed İzzet, *Feryadım*, 2–3, 9–10; Ayışığı, *Mareşal Ahmet İzzet Paşa*, 8, 22–25.

149. Reşat Hallı, *Balkan Harbi (1912–1913)*, vol. 1, 2nd printing, (Ankara: Genelkurmay Basımevi, 1993), 93–100; Ahmed İzzet, *Feryadım*, 57–62; Erickson, *Defeat in Detail*, 26–28, 30–33; Ayışığı, *Mareşal Ahmet İzzet Paşa*, 23–25.

150. The figures of officer corps reduced from 26,310 to 16,121 after the purges of the Alaylıs. Karatamu, *Türk Silahlı Kuvvetleri Tarihi*, 187–189; Ahmed İzzet, *Feryadım*, 45–46, 62–73; Apak, *Yetmişlik Bir Subayın Anıları*, 31–41; Turfan, *Rise of the Young Turks*, 155–161; Bartlett, *Battlefields of Thessaly*, 52, 55–56; Griffiths, *Reorganization of the Ottoman Army*, 111.

151. Ufuk Gülsoy, *Osmanlı Gayri Müslimlerinin Askerlik Serüvenleri*, (İstanbul: Simurg, 2000), 127–162; Hallı, *Balkan Harbi (1912–1913)*, 120–121.

152. Hafız Hakkı, *Bozgun*, 100–104; Karabekir, *Hayatım*, 365–366; Ellis A. Bartlett, *With the Turks in Thrace*, (London: William Heinemann, 1913), 50; Erickson, *Defeat in Detail*, 29–30; Karatamu, *Türk Silahlı Kuvvetleri Tarihi*, 142–143.

153. Hallı, *Balkan Harbi (1912–1913)*, 119, 130–131; Bartlett, *With the Turks in Thrace*, 53–55; Richard C. Hall, *The Balkan Wars 1912–1913: Prelude to the First World War*, (London: Routledge, 2000), 9–15.

154. Rachel Simon, *Between Ottomanism and Nationalism: The Ottoman Involvement in Libya during the War with Italy (1911–1919)*, (Berlin: Klaus Schwarz Verlag, 1987), 1–10, 22–30; Hamdi Ertuna, *TSK Tarihi Osmanlı Devri, Osmanlı-İtalyan Harbi (1911–1912)*, (Ankara: Genelkurmay Basımevi, 1981), 17–27, 63, 463–464.

155. Yusuf Hikmet Bayur, *Türk İnkılâbı Tarihi*, vol. 2, section 1, (Ankara: Türk Tarih Kurumu Basımevi, 1983), 68–98; Ertuna, *TSK Tarihi Osmanlı Devri, Osmanlı-İtalyan Harbi (1911–1912)*, 117–128, 141–145, 153; Simon, *Between Ottomanism and Nationalism*, 47–65; J. Revol, *1911–1912 Türk-İtalyan Harbi*, (Turkish translation of the French original *La Guerre Italo-Turque, 1911–1912*), (trans.) Kadri Demirkaya, (İstanbul: Askeri Matbaa, 1940), 3–27, 36–48; Contemporary western sources give largely inflated numbers. See W. H. Beehlar, *The History of the Italian-Turkish War, September 29, 1911 to October 18, 1912*, (Annapolis: The Advertiser-Republican, 1913), 12–15.

156. Ertuna, *TSK Tarihi Osmanlı Devri, Osmanlı-İtalyan Harbi (1911–1912)*, 49–57; Revol, *1911–1912 Türk-İtalyan Harbi*, 59–64.

157. Ertuna, *TSK Tarihi Osmanlı Devri, Osmanlı-İtalyan Harbi (1911–1912)*, 129–135, 141–153, 217; Revol, *1911–1912 Türk-İtalyan Harbi*, 65–72, 86–98; Beehlar, *History of the Italian-Turkish War*, 19–21.

158. Ertuna, *TSK Tarihi Osmanlı Devri, Osmanlı-İtalyan Harbi (1911–1912)*, 159–160, 165–167, 169, 181, 183; Revol, *1911–1912 Türk-İtalyan Harbi*, 73–83, 98–99, 104–127.

159. For detailed information about Sanusiyya fraternity *see* E. Evans-Pritchard, *The Sanusi of Cyrenaica*, (Oxford: Oxford University Press, 1949), 11–28, 62–89.

160. Cemal Kutay, *Trablus-Garb'de Bir Avuç Kahraman*, (İstanbul: Tarih Yayınları, 1963), 14–54, 86–111; Simon, *Between Ottomanism and Nationalism*, 10–21, 76; Ertuna, *TSK Tarihi Osmanlı Devri, Osmanlı-İtalyan Harbi (1911–1912)*, 152, 158; Tauber, *Emergence of the Arab Movements*, 217–218.

161. Kut, *İttihat ve Terakki'den Cumhuriyete Bitmeyen Savaş*, 83–114; Ertuna, *TSK Tarihi Osmanlı Devri, Osmanlı-İtalyan Harbi (1911–1912)*, 171–177, 184–185, 188–213.

162. Ertuna, *TSK Tarihi Osmanlı Devri, Osmanlı-İtalyan Harbi (1911–1912)*, 187, 192, 199, 273; Bülent Yılmazer, "Balkan Harbi'nde Hava Gücü, Askeri Havacılıkta Perdenin Açılışı," in *Dokuzuncu Askeri Tarih Semineri Bildirileri*, vol. 2, (Ankara: Genelkurmay Basımevi, 2006), 232–233; Beehlar, *History of the Italian-Turkish War*, 31–34, 54.

163. Ertuna, *TSK Tarihi Osmanlı Devri, Osmanlı-İtalyan Harbi (1911–1912)*, 219–251; Beehlar, *History of the Italian-Turkish War*, 34–36, 48–50; Kutay, *Trablus-Garb'de Bir Avuç Kahraman*, 112–123.

164. Ertuna, *TSK Tarihi Osmanlı Devri, Osmanlı-İtalyan Harbi (1911–1912)*, 289, 331–333; Kutay, *Trablus-Garb'de Bir Avuç Kahraman*, 154–201; Yılmazer, *Dokuzuncu Askeri Tarih Semineri Bildirileri*, 233.

165. Ertuna, *TSK Tarihi Osmanlı Devri, Osmanlı-İtalyan Harbi (1911–1912)*, 181, 183.

166. Ibid., 282–288, 290–349, 404–410; Simon, *Between Ottomanism and Nationalism*, 112–118; Beehlar, *History of the Italian-Turkish War*, 64–66, 70–71, 78, 83–86.

167. Ertuna, *TSK Tarihi Osmanlı Devri, Osmanlı-İtalyan Harbi (1911–1912)*, 220, 310, 324–327, 432–434, 446–447; Revol, *1911–1912 Türk-İtalyan Harbi*, 128–144.

168. Ertuna, *TSK Tarihi Osmanlı Devri, Osmanlı-İtalyan Harbi (1911–1912)*, 278–280, 353–368, 372–383; Ahmed İzzet, *Feryadım*, 105–106; Beehlar, *History of the Italian-Turkish War*, 50–52, 56–60, 68–70, 87–90.

169. Ertuna, *TSK Tarihi Osmanlı Devri, Osmanlı-İtalyan Harbi (1911–1912)*, 383–393; Bayur, *Türk İnkılâbı Tarihi*, 127–129; Beehlar, *History of the Italian-Turkish War*, 73–76.

170. Ertuna, *TSK Tarihi Osmanlı Devri, Osmanlı-İtalyan Harbi (1911–1912)*, 411–421; Simon, *Between Ottomanism and Nationalism*, 98–101; Kut, *İttihat ve Terakki'den Cumhuriyete Bitmeyen Savaş*, 116; Tauber, *Emergence of the Arab Movements*, 218–219.

171. Ahmed İzzet, *Feryadım*, 117–119.

172. Mahmud Muhtar, *3ncü Kolordu ve Doğu Ordusu'nun Muharebeleri*, 156–158; Ahmed İzzet, *Feryadım*, 109; Abdurrahman Nafiz and Kiramettin, *1912–1913 Balkan Harbinde İşkodra Müdafaası*, (İstanbul: Askeri Matbaa, 1933), 80; Hamdi Baştepe, *26. P. Alayı Tarihçesi*, (Ankara: no publisher name, 1937), 3–4; Hallı, *Balkan Harbi (1912–1913)*, 101.

173. Mahmud Muhtar, *3ncü Kolordu ve Doğu Ordusu'nun Muharebeleri*, 7, 165–166; Ahmed İzzet, *Feryadım*, 120–129, 134; Hallı, *Balkan Harbi (1912–1913)*, 185–219E.

174. Hallı, *Balkan Harbi (1912–1913)*, 112–118.

175. Hafız Hakkı, *Bozgun*, 137–139, 149; Mahmud Muhtar, *3ncü Kolordu ve Doğu Ordusu'nun Muharebeleri*, 8, 10, 13; Hallı, *Balkan Harbi (1912–1913)*, 223–230; Ayışığı, *Mareşal Ahmet İzzet Paşa*, 25–33.

176. Philip Gibbs and Bernard Grant, *Adventures of War with Cross and Crescent*, (London: Methnen & Co., 1912), 141–143, 147–148, 152–153; Aram Andoyan, *Balkan Savaşı*, (Turkish translation of the Armenian original *Badgerazart Intartzag Badmutyun Balkanyan Baderazmin*), (trans.) Zaven Biberyan, (İstanbul: Aras Yayıncılık, 1999), 197–213, 28; Bartlett, *With the Turks in Thrace*, 10–11, 15–17; Hallı, *Balkan Harbi (1912–1913)*, 77–79.

177. H. Cemal, *Tekrar Başımıza Gelenler*, (ed.) Murat Çulcu, (İstanbul: Kastaş Yayınları, 1991), 23–39; Raif Necdet Kestelli, *Osmanlı İmparatorluğu'nun Batışı: Ufûl*, (ed.) Veliye Özdemir, (İstanbul: Arma Yayınları, 2001), 17; Şadi Sükan, *TSK Tarihi Balkan Harbi (1912–1913): Edirne Kalesi Etrafındaki Muharebeler*, vol. 2, section 3, 2nd printing, (Ankara: Genelkurmay Basımevi, 1993), 88–104.

178. Mahmud Muhtar, *3ncü Kolordu ve Doğu Ordusu'nun Muharebeleri*, 7–9; Sükan, *TSK Tarihi Balkan Harbi (1912–1913)*, 120–124.

179. Mahmud Muhtar, *3ncü Kolordu ve Doğu Ordusu'nun Muharebeleri*, 11–39; Sükan, *TSK Tarihi Balkan Harbi (1912–1913)*, 124–156; Erickson, *Defeat in Detail*, 86–100; Cemal, *Arnavutluk'tan Sakarya'ya Komitacılık*, 70–73; Gibbs and Grant, *Adventures of War with Cross and Crescent*, 63–66, 87–92; Hall, *Balkan Wars 1912–1913*, 23–28; Andonyan, *Balkan Savaşı*, 445–467; Herbert F. Baldwin, *A War Photographer in Thrace: An Account of Personal Experiences during the Turco-Balkan War*, (London: T. Fisher Unwin, 1913), 152–156.

180. Mahmud Muhtar, *3ncü Kolordu ve Doğu Ordusu'nun Muharebeleri*, 39–129; For the Bulgarian perspective see Murat Tunca (trans.), *1912–1913 Balkan Harbinde Türk-Bulgar*

Harbi: Lüleburgaz-Pınarhisar Muharebesi, vol. 3, (Turkish translation of Bulgarian official history), (İstanbul: Askeri Basımevi, 1945), passim.; Bartlett, *With the Turks in Thrace*, 139–166, 171–181, 204–226; Erickson, *Defeat in Detail*, 102–122; Hall, *Balkan Wars 1912–1913*, 28–31; Gibbs and Grant, *Adventures of War with Cross and Crescent*, 66–73, 172–175; Andonyan, *Balkan Savaşı*, 469–481.

181. Mahmud Muhtar, *3ncü Kolordu ve Doğu Ordusu'nun Muharebeleri*, 128–138; Mahmut Beliğ, Balkan *Harbinde Mürettep 1.Kolordunun Harekâtı*, (İstanbul: Askeri Matbaa, 1929), 3–24; Baldwin, *War Photographer in Thrace*, 178–182; Tunca, *1912–1913 Balkan Harbinde Türk-Bulgar Harbi*, 380–386.

182. Beliğ, *Bulgar Komitalarının Tarihi ve Balkan Harbinde Yaptıkları*, 61–88; Andonyan, *Balkan Savaşı*, 219–223.

183. Mahmud Muhtar, *3ncü Kolordu ve Doğu Ordusu'nun Muharebeleri*, 143–152; Beliğ, *Bulgar Komitalarının Tarihi ve Balkan Harbinde Yaptıkları*, 25–233; M. Kadri Alasya, *TSK Tarihi Balkan Harbi (1912–1913): Şark Ordusu Birinci Çatalca Muharebesi*, vol. 2, book 1, 2nd printing, (Ankara: Genelkurmay Basımevi, 1993), 20–245; Hikmet Süer, *TSK Tarihi Balkan Harbi (1912–1913): Şark Ordusu İkinci Çatalca Muharebesi ve Şarköy Çıkarması*, vol. 2, section 2, book 2, 2nd printing, (Ankara: Genelkurmay Basımevi, 1993), 273–374; Erickson, *Defeat in Detail*, 122–137, 285–290; Hall, *Balkan Wars 1912–1913*, 32–37; Gibbs and Grant, *Adventures of War with Cross and Crescent*, 175–211; Bartlett, *With the Turks in Thrace*, 266–291; Andonyan, *Balkan Savaşı*, 483–491; For the Ottoman way of defense in fortified zones *see* Karatamu, *Türk Silahlı Kuvvetleri Tarihi*, 322–323.

184. Reşat Hallı, *Balkan Harbi (1912–1913), Garp Ordusu, Vardar Ordusu ve Ustruma Kolordusu*, vol. 3, section 1, 2nd printing, (Ankara: Genelkurmay Basımevi, 1993), 36–41; Nafiz and Kiramettin, *1912–1913 Balkan Harbinde İşkodra Müdafaası*, 99–108, 111.

185. Hallı, *Balkan Harbi (1912–1913)*, 64–81, 105–110, 122–130, 154–211; K. Kocaman, "Kumanova Muharebesinde Sırp Ordusu," *Askeri Mecmua*, vol. 10, no. 114, September 1939, 674–678; Erickson, *Defeat in Detail*, 171–181; Andonyan, *Balkan Savaşı*, 323–333; Gibbs and Grant, *Adventures of War with Cross and Crescent*, 59–61.

186. Hallı, *Balkan Harbi (1912–1913)*, 211–314, 344–367; Erickson, *Defeat in Detail*, 182–197; Andonyan, *Balkan Savaşı*, 335–352; Cemal, *Arnavutluk'tan Sakarya'ya Komitacılık*, 24–25; Apak, *Yetmişlik Bir Subayın Anıları*, 69–72.

187. For the operations of Ustruma Corps and Nevrekop Detachment *see* Hallı, *Balkan Harbi (1912–1913)*, 314–343; For the operations of Kırcaali Detachment *see* Mehmet Murat, *1912–1913 Balkan Harbinde Kırcaali Kolordusunun Hareketleri*, (İstanbul: Askeri Matbaa, 1933), passim.; Also *see* Sükan, *TSK Tarihi Balkan Harbi (1912–1913)*, 347–452.

188. Raif Yaşar and Hüseyin Kabasakal, *Balkan Harbi (1912–1913), Garp Ordusu Yunan Cephessi Harekatı*, vol. 3, section 2, 2nd printing, (Ankara: Genelkurmay Basımevi, 1993), 157–323; Hellenic Army General Staff, *A Concise History of the Balkan Wars, 1912–1913*, (Athens: Army History Directorate Publication, 1998), 23–109, 117–122.

189. Fehmi Özatalay, *TSK Tarihi Balkan Harbi (1912–1913): Garb Ordusu Karadağ Cephesi*, vol. 3, section 3, 2nd printing, (Ankara: Genelkurmay Basımevi, 1993), 26–30, 38, 70–73, 116–136; Nafiz and Kiramettin, *1912–1913 Balkan Harbinde İşkodra Müdafaası*, 111, 17–168; Hallı, *Balkan Harbi (1912–1913)*, 150–151; Erickson, *Defeat in Detail*, 201–204, 214–225; Ahmed İzzet, *Feryadım*, 117; Andonyan, *Balkan Savaşı*, 272–273, 363–391; Apak, *Yetmişlik Bir Subayın Anıları*, 51–60.

190. Bekir Fikri, *Balkanlarda Tedhiş ve Gerilla*, supra 42; Yaşar and Kabasakal, *Balkan Harbi (1912–1913)*, 330–358; Fuat Balkan, *İlk Türk Komitacısı Fuat Balkan'ın Hatıraları*, (ed.) Metin Martı, (İstanbul: Arma Yayınları, 1998), 8–9.

191. Beliğ, *Bulgar Komitalarının Tarihi ve Balkan Harbinde Yaptıkları*, 50–61; Baştepe, *26. P. Alayı Tarihçesi*, 4; Selahattin Yurtoğlu, *Yüzbaşı Selahattin'in Romanı*, vol. 1, (ed.) İlhan Selçuk, (İstanbul: Cumhuriyet Kitapları, 2004), 67–68.

192. Turfan, *Rise of the Young Turks*, 208–213; Glen W. Swanson, "War, Technology, and Society in the Ottoman Empire from the Reign of Abdülhamid II to 1913; Mahmud Şevket and the German Military Mission," in in (ed.) V. J. Parry and M. E. Yapp, *War, Technology and Society in the Middle East*, (London: Oxford University Press, 1975), 368–373.

193. Hallı, *Balkan Harbi (1912–1913)*, 367–401; Erickson, *Defeat in Detail*, 226–235, 248–249, 274–282, 293–304, 306–313; Andonyan, *Balkan Savaşı*, 277–311; Baldwin, *War Photographer in Thrace*, 255–256; For the defense of Edirne see Remzi Yiğitgüden, *1912–1913 Balkan Harbinde Edirne Kale Muharebeleri*, vol. 1 and 2, (İstanbul: Askeri Matbaa, 1938 and 1939), passim.; Also see Sükan, *TSK Tarihi Balkan Harbi (1912–1913)*, 157–334; For the defense of Yanya see Yaşar and Kabasakal, *Balkan Harbi (1912–1913)*, 523–674; Also see Hellenic Army General Staff, *Concise History of the Balkan Wars*, 179–199; For the defense of İşkodra see Nafiz and Kiramettin, *1912–1913 Balkan Harbinde İşkodra Müdafaası*, 113–152, 206–592; Also see Özatalay, *TSK Tarihi Balkan Harbi (1912–1913)*, 8–116, 150–210.

194. Hüsnü Ersü, *1912–1913 Balkan Harbinde Şarköy Çıkarması ve Bulayır Muharebeleri*, (İstanbul: Askeri Matbaa, 1938), 53–228; Süer, *TSK Tarihi Balkan Harbi (1912–1913)*, 123–273; Erickson, *Defeat in Detail*, 253–272; For a criticism of this ambitious operation see Hüsnü Ersü, "1912–1913 Balkan Harbinin İkinci Devresinde Türk ve Bulgarların Hareket Planlarına Ait Bir Tetkik," *Askeri Mecmua*, vol. 8, no. 107, December 1937, 746–749.

195. Süer, *TSK Tarihi Balkan Harbi (1912–1913)*, 273–374; Erickson, *Defeat in Detail*, 285–290; Gibbs and Grant, *Adventures of War with Cross and Crescent*, 97–111.

196. Cemal Paşa, *Hatıralar*, (ed.) Alpay Kabacalı, (İstanbul: Türkiye İş bankası Yayınları, 2006), 57–61; Ahmed İzzet, *Feryadım*, 151–154; Süer, *TSK Tarihi Balkan Harbi (1912–1913)*, 375–457; Bartlett, *With the Turks in Thrace*, 313–326.

197. Turfan, *Rise of the Young Turks*, 331–346.

198. Gibbs and Grant, *Adventures of War with Cross and Crescent*, 72–73, 175–211; Bartlett, *With the Turks in Thrace*, 56–58, 179–180.

199. Kestelli, *Osmanlı İmparatorluğu'nun Batışı*, 10, 15–16, 18–19; Mahmud Muhtar, *3ncü Kolordu ve Doğu Ordusu'nun Muharebeleri*, 155–156, 163; Hallı, *Balkan Harbi (1912–1913)*, 122–123; Nafiz and Kiramettin, *1912–1913 Balkan Harbinde İşkodra Müdafaası*, 79–80, 89, 95–96; Mehmet Murat, *1912–1913 Balkan Harbinde Kırcaali Kolordusunun Hareketleri*, 24–25; Apak, *Yetmişlik Bir Subayın Anıları*, 47, 91.

200. Mahmud Muhtar, *3ncü Kolordu ve Doğu Ordusu'nun Muharebeleri*, 10–11, 164; Ahmed İzzet, *Feryadım*, 178–179; Beliğ, *Bulgar Komitalarının Tarihi ve Balkan Harbinde Yaptıkları*, 231–233; Baldwin, *War Photographer in Thrace*, 124–128; Gibbs and Grant, *Adventures of War with Cross and Crescent*, 179.

201. Bartlett, *With the Turks in Thrace*, 17–18; Baldwin, *War Photographer in Thrace*, 152.

202. Gibbs and Grant, *Adventures of War with Cross and Crescent*, 74–81, 84–85; Kestelli, *Osmanlı İmparatorluğu'nun Batışı*, 16; Mehmet Murat, *1912–1913 Balkan Harbinde Kırcaali Kolordusunun Hareketleri*, 198.

203. Gibbs and Grant, *Adventures of War with Cross and Crescent*, 78–79, 82–85, 154–156, 159–162, 212–219; Bartlett, *With the Turks in Thrace*, 134, 141, 217–222; Hallı, *Balkan Harbi (1912–1913)*, 143–149; Baldwin, *War Photographer in Thrace*, 35–36.

204. Mahmud Muhtar, *3ncü Kolordu ve Doğu Ordusu'nun Muharebeleri*, 160–162; Bartlett, *With the Turks in Thrace*, 143–145, 154, 156, 164; Hallı, *Balkan Harbi (1912–1913)*, 126–127, 139–140.

205. Hallı, *Balkan Harbi (1912–1913)*, 134, 149–150; H. Cemal, *Tekrar Başımıza Gelenler*, 73–74.

206. As an example more than 45,000 Ottoman Macedonians volunteered for the Bulgarian army and militia. Bozhilov and Panayatov, *Macedonia*, 625–627, 631–633.

207. Gülsoy, *Osmanlı Gayri Müslimlerinin Askerlik Serüvenleri*, 163–167; H. Cemal, *Tekrar Başımıza Gelenler*, 19, 122–123; Mahmud Muhtar, *3ncü Kolordu ve Doğu Ordusu'nun Muharebeleri*, 155; Andonyan, *Balkan Savaşı*, 215.

208. Hallı, *Balkan Harbi (1912–1913)*, 230–249; Bartlett, *With the Turks in Thrace*, 174.

209. Yiğitgüden, *1912–1913 Balkan Harbinde Edirne Kale Muharebeleri*, vol. 1, 74; Erickson, *Defeat in Detail*, 337.

210. Yiğitgüden, *1912–1913 Balkan Harbinde Edirne Kale Muharebeleri*, vol. 2, 99.

211. Reynolds, *Ottoman-Russian Struggle for Eastern Anatolia*, 59–65, 91–94; Tauber, *Emergence of the Arab Movements*, 76, 93, 106, 115, 121; Yusuf Hikmet Bayur, *Türk İnkılâbı Tarihi*, vol. 2, section 3, (Ankara: Türk Tarih Kurumu Basımevi, 1983), 18–230; Justin McCarthy, et al., *The Armenian Rebellion at Van*, (Salt Lake City: The University of Utah Press, 2006), 155–169.

212. Mustafa Aksakal, *Defending the Nation: The German-Ottoman Alliance of 1914 and the Ottoman Decision for War*, (Princeton: Princeton University Unpublished Ph.D. Dissertation, 2003), 6–7, 9–12.

213. Mahmud Muhtar, *3ncü Kolordu ve Doğu Ordusu'nun Muharebeleri*, 156–160; Nafiz and Kiramettin, *1912–1913 Balkan Harbinde İşkodra Müdafaası*, 576–577, 586–587, 590.

214. Adem Sarıgöl (ed.), *Harbiye Nazırı Sadrazam Mahmut Şevket Paşa'nın Günlüğü*, (İstanbul: IQ Kültürsanat, 2001), 223–224; Tarık Zafer Tunaya, *Türkiye'de Siyasal Partiler*, vol. 1, (İstanbul: Hürriyet Vakfı Yayınları, 1988), 535, 537; Cemal Kutay, *Türkiye İstiklâl ve Hürriyet Mücadeleleri Tarihi*, vol. 17, (İstanbul: Tarih Yayınları, 1961), 9837–9844; İsmet İnönü, *Hatıralar*, vol. 1, (ed.) Sebahattin Selek, (Ankara:Bilgi Yayınevi; 1985), 59; Nilüfer Hatemi (ed.), *Mareşal Fevzi Çakmak ve Günlükleri*, vol. 1, (İstanbul: Yapı Kredi Yayınları, 2002), 174–228; Ahmed İzzet, *Feryadım*, 77–81.

215. Nafiz and Kiramettin, *1912–1913 Balkan Harbinde İşkodra Müdafaası*, 352–359, 372, 569–575; Ahmed İzzet, *Feryadım*, 132–133; Apak, *Yetmişlik Bir Subayın Anıları*, 71, 78–82; Tauber, *Emergence of the Arab Movements*, 213–214; Friedrich Freiherr Kress von Kressenstein, *Son Haçlı Seferi Kuma Gömülen İmparatorluk*, (Turkish translation of the German original *Mit den Türken zum Suezkanal*), (İstanbul: Yeditepe Yayınevi, 2007), 27.

216. Ali İhsan Sabis, *Harp Hatıralarım: Birinci Dünya Harbi*, vol. 1, (İstanbul: Nehir Yayınları, 1990), 43; Sarıgöl, *Harbiye Nazırı Sadrazam Mahmut Şevket Paşa'nın Günlüğü*, 159.

217. Cemal Paşa, *Hatıralar*, 70–73; Apak, *Yetmişlik Bir Subayın Anıları*, 45–46; Yurtoğlu, *Yüzbaşı Selahattin'in Romanı*, 91.

218. İ. Hakkı Sunata, *Gelibolu'dan Kafkaslara: Birinci Dünya Savaşı Anılarım*, (İstanbul: Türkiye İş Bankası Yayınlaı, 2003), 12; Yurtoğlu, *Yüzbaşı Selahattin'in Romanı*, 90–91.

219. Ercümend Kuran, "The Impact of Nationalism on the Turkish Elite in the Nineteen Century," in (ed.) W. R. Polk and R. L. Chambers, *Beginnings of Modernization in the Middle East: The Nineteenth Century*, (Chicago: University of Chicago Press, 1968), 117; Kerem Ünüvar, "İttihatçılıktan Kemalizm'e İhya'dan İnşa'ya," in (ed.) Mehmet Ö. Alkan, *Modern Türkiye'de Siyasi Düşünce*, vol. 1, (İstanbul: İletişim Yayınları, 2001), 132–133; Aksakal *Defending the Nation*, 20–26.

220. Cemal Paşa, *Hatıralar*, 80–83; Ahmed İzzet, *Feryadım*, 157–158; Bayur, *Türk İnkılâbı Tarihi*, 55–58, 280–286; Wallach, *Bir Askeri Yardımın Anatomisi*, 118–122; Liman von Sanders, *Five Years in Turkey*, (trans.) Carl Reichmann, (Baltimore: The Williams & Wilkins Co., 1928),

1–3; Naim Turfan, "Reporting Him and His Cause Aright: Mahmud Şevket Paşa and the Liman von Sanders Mission," *Cahiers d'etudes sur la Méditerranée Orientale et la Monde Turco-Iranien*, no. 12, July–December 1991, 2–14, 28; Swanson, *Journal of Contemporary History*, 381–384; Karatamu, *Türk Silahlı Kuvvetleri Tarihi*, 192–193.

221. Turfan, *Rise of the Young Turks*, 16–18; Aksakal, *Defending the Nation*, 65–69, 90; Kressenstein, *Son Haçlı Seferi Kuma Gömülen İmparatorluk*, 1–2.

222. Sanders, *Five Years in Turkey*, 1–4; Bayur, *Türk İnkılâbı Tarihi*, 286–287; Wallach, *Bir Askeri Yardımın Anatomisi*, 122–123; Sabis, *Harp Hatıralarım*, 76–82; Karatamu, *Türk Silahlı Kuvvetleri Tarihi*, 193–194; Cemal Akbay, *Birinci Dünya Harbinde Türk Harbi*, vol. 1, (Ankara: Genelkurmay Basımevi, 1970), 271–278.

223. Sanders, *Five Years in Turkey*, 5–11; Wallach, *Bir Askeri Yardımın Anatomisi*, 128–139; Kressenstein, *Son Haçlı Seferi Kuma Gömülen İmparatorluk*, 14–15, 37; İnönü, *Hatıralar*, 88.

224. Bayur, *Türk İnkılâbı Tarihi*, 288–305; Sanders, *Five Years in Turkey*, 20–21; Wallach, *Bir Askeri Yardımın Anatomisi*, 148–149; Karatamu, *Türk Silahlı Kuvvetleri Tarihi*, 193–194, 197.

225. "Türkiye' de Alman Askerî Misyonu Subaylar-Generaller-Heyetler," *Belgelerle Türk Tarihi Dergisi*, no. 24, February 1987, 60; Kressenstein, *Son Haçlı Seferi Kuma Gömülen İmparatorluk*, 15–17; Karatamu, *Türk Silahlı Kuvvetleri Tarihi*, 197.

226. These talented general staff officers would destined to become the leaders of the Turkish Independence War (1919–1922) such as; Major İsmet (İnönü), Major Kazım (Karabekir), Major Ali İhsan (Sabis), Captain Kazım (Orbay). Akbay, *Birinci Dünya Harbinde Türk Harbi*, 169–170; İnönü, *Hatıralar*, 87.

227. Akdes Nimet Kurat, *Birinci Dünya Savaşı Sırasında Türkiye'de Buluna Alman Generallerinin Raporları*, (Ankara: TKAE Yayınları, 1966), 26–27; Kressenstein, *Son Haçlı Seferi Kuma Gömülen İmparatorluk*, 11–13; İnönü, *Hatıralar*, 146–148; Sabis, *Harp Hatıralarım*, 168–170, 256–257; Karatamu, *Türk Silahlı Kuvvetleri Tarihi*, 257, 287–288, 293.

228. For the smuggling of the Ottoman General Staff Archive *see* Mesut Uyar and Hayrullah Gök, "Birinci Dünya Savaşındaki Alman Askeri Yardım Heyetinin Bilinmeyen Bir Yönü: Bir Arşiv Yağmasının Hikayesi," *Toplumsal Tarih Dergisi*, vol. 14, no. 84, November 2000, 4–11.

229. Kâzım Karabekir, *Birinci Cihan Harbine Nasıl Girdik?*, vol. 2, (İstanbul: Emre Yayınları, 1994), 154–159; İnönü, *Hatıralar*, 148; Ahmed İzzet, *Feryadım*, 182–183, 193, 216; Sabis, *Harp Hatıralarım*, 143; Aydemir, *Makedonya'dan Orta Asya'ya Enver Paşa*, 380, 382, 412–423; Karatamu, *Türk Silahlı Kuvvetleri Tarihi*, 257–258.

230. Şerif İlden, *Birinci Dünya Savaşı Başlangıcında 3.Ordu: Sarıkamış Kuşatma Manevrası ve Meydan Savaşı*, (ed.) Sami Önal, (İstanbul: İş Bankası Kültür Yayınları, 1998), 257–258; Ahmed İzzet, *Feryadım*, 215; Sabis, *Harp Hatıralarım*, 180; İnönü, *Hatıralar*, 99, 147; Arif Baytın, *İlk Dünya Harbinde Kafkas Cephesi: Sessiz Ölüm Sarıkamış Günlüğü*, (ed.) İsmail Dervişoğlu, (İstanbul: Yeditepe Yayınevi, 2007), 170; Şevket Süreyya Aydemir, *Makedonya'dan Orta Asya'ya Enver Paşa*, vol. 3, (İstanbul: Remzi Kitabevi, 1985), 68; Kressenstein, *Son Haçlı Seferi Kuma Gömülen İmparatorluk*, 12–13, 16; Kurat, *Birinci Dünya Savaşı Sırasında Türkiye'de Buluna Alman Generallerinin Raporları*, 28, 32–34.

231. Sanders, *Five Years in Turkey*, 16–20; Kurat, *Birinci Dünya Savaşı Sırasında Türkiye'de Buluna Alman Generallerinin Raporları*, 77.

232. Kressenstein, *Son Haçlı Seferi Kuma Gömülen İmparatorluk*, xv, 24, 31–34; *Harpokulu Tarihçesi*, (Ankara: Harpokulu Matbaası, 1945), 37–38; Swanson, *Journal of Contemporary History*, 379.

233. İlden, *Birinci Dünya Savaşı Başlangıcında 3.Ordu*, 27–28; Hakkı Altınbilek and Naci Kır, *Birinci Dünya Harbinde Türk Harbi: Kafkas Cephesi 3ncü Ordu Harekatı*, vol. 2, section 1, book 1, (Ankara: Genelkurmay Basımevi, 1993), 35–40, 51; Cairo Intelligence Section, *Handbook of the Turkish Army*, 8th Edition, (Nashville: The Battery Press reprint, 1996), 21–28, 44–50.

234. İlden, *Birinci Dünya Savaşı Başlangıcında 3.Ordu*, 23–26; Sanders, *Five Years in Turkey*, 8–9; Ali Fuad Erden, *Birinci Dünya Harbinde Suriye Hatıraları*, (ed.) Alpay Kabacalı, (İstanbul: Türkiye İş Bankası Yayınları, 2003), 20–23; Carl Mühlmann, *Çanakkale Savaşı: Bir Alman Subayının Notları*, (Turkish translation of the German original *Der Kampf um die Dardanellen 1915*), (trans.) Sedat Umran, (İstanbul: Timaş Yayınları, 2004), 16.

235. İsmet Görgülü, *On Yıllık Harbin Kadrosu (1912–1922)*, (Ankara: Türk Tarih Kurumu Basımevi, 1993), 64–95.

236. Kressenstein, *Son Haçlı Seferi Kuma Gömülen İmparatorluk*, 23–24, 31–32.

237. Unfortunately, the Ottoman military renaissance has escaped the notice of scholars. No academic study is available covering these intellectual developments. Moreover, a good catalog of books and articles printed during this period is not available.

238. Sait Gürbüz, *Silahlı Kuvvetler Cephesinden Bir Tanıklık: Askeri Mecmua 1929–1950*, (İstanbul: University of İstanbul Unpublished M.A. Thesis, 2005), 6.

239. Following is a short list/sample of the kinds of publications that grew out of these discussions:; Mehmed Nuri, *Zabit ve Kumandan*, (İstanbul: Tanin Matbaası, 1330); Hafız İsmail Hakkı, *Bozgun*, (İstanbul: Matbaa-i Hayriye ve Şürekası, 1330); Mehmet Ali Nüzhet, *Balkan Harbi*, (İstanbul: Nefaset Matbaası, 1328); Safvet, *Balkan Harbinde Askeri Mağlubiyetlerimizin Esbabı*, (İstanbul: Artin Asaduryan Matbaası, 1329); Safvet, *Balkan Harbinde Neden Mültezim Olduk*, (İstanbul: Artin Asaduryan Matbaası, 1329); İbrahim Hilmi, *Balkan Harbinde Askeri Mağlubiyetlerimizin Esbabı*, (İstanbul: Artin Asaduryan, 1329); Bahri, *Balkan Harbinde Sırb Ordusu: Esbâb-ı Felâketimizin Orduya İsabet Eden Hisse-i Mesuliyetinden*, (İstanbul: Tanin Matbaası, 1329); Hamid Osman, *Balkan Harbi Hatıratı*, (İstanbul: Kader Matbaası, 1330).

240. Pertev, *Balkan Harbinde Büyük Karargah-ı Umumi*, (İstanbul: Tevsi-i Tıbaat Matbaası, 1329); Ahmed Suad, *Balkan Darül-harbine Dair Tedkikat-ı Coğrafiye ve Mütalaat-ı Sevkül-ceysiye*, (İstanbul: Mühendishane-i Berri Hümayun Matbaası, 1330); Mehmed Arif, *Balkan Harbinde Makineli Tüfekler*, (İstanbul: no publisher's name, 1329); Ragıb Rıfkı, *Balkan Hükümetlerinin Teşkilat-ı Askeriyesi*, (İstanbul: Şems Matbaası, 1328).

241. Ömer Seyfeddin, *Maneviyat-ı Askeriye Makaleleri*, (İstanbul: Türk Yurdu Kütübhanesi, 1330); Ömer Seyfeddin, *Yarınki Turan Devleti*, (İstanbul: Kader Matbaası, 1330); İsmail Hakkı, *Şanlı Asker Ali Çavuş*, (İstanbul: Tanin Matbaası, 1330); M.S., *Balkan'da Karagöz Neler Görmüş?*, (İstanbul: Yeni Osmanlı Matbaası, 1330).

242. Unfortunately, the Ottoman military renaissance has escaped the notice of scholars. No academic study is available covering these intellectual developments. Moreover, a good catalog of books and articles printed during this period does not exist. For a general catalog of military books and articles *see* Ekmeleddin İhsanoğlu et al., *Osmanlı Askerlik Literatürü Tarihi*, vol. 1, 2, (İstanbul: IRCICA, 2004).

243. Aksakal, *Defending the Nation*, 112–150, 156–175, 186–189; Cemal Paşa, *Hatıralar*, 130–163; Kressenstein, *Son Haçlı Seferi Kuma Gömülen İmparatorluk*, 4–9; Ahmed İzzet, *Feryadım*, 184–186.

244. İlden, *Birinci Dünya Savaşı Başlangıcında 3.Ordu*, 33–34; Baytın, *İlk Dünya Harbinde Kafkas Cephesi*, 13–14; Altınbilek and Kır, *Birinci Dünya Harbinde Türk Harbi*, 51; Mühlmann, *Çanakkale Savaşı*, 21–24.

245. Yahya Okçu, *Birinci Dünya Harbinde Türk Harbi, Sina-Filistin Cephesi*, vol. 4, section 1, (Ankara: Genelkurmay Basımevi, 1979), 71–74; Ahmed İzzet, *Feryadım*, 190–194.

246. Ulrich Trumpener, "German Military Aid to Turkey in 1914: A Historical Reevaluation," *The Journal of Modern History*, vol. 32, no. 2, June 1960, 145–149; Selahattin Selışık, *Kafkas Cephesinde 10ncu Kolordunun Birinci Dünya Savaşının Başlangıcından Sarıkamış Muharebelerinin Sonuna Kadar Olan Harekatı*, 2nd Edition, (Ankara: Genelkurmay Basımevi, 2006), 6–7, 11–16; Mühlmann, *Çanakkale Savaşı*, 29–34.

247. İlden, *Birinci Dünya Savaşı Başlangıcında 3.Ordu*, 39–40; Selışık, *Kafkas Cephesinde 10ncu Kolordunun Birinci Dünya Savaşının Başlangıcından Sarıkamış Muharebelerinin Sonuna Kadar Olan Harekatı*, 3–5; Sabis, *Harp Hatıralarım*, 159–164, 285.

248. Cairo Intelligence, *Handbook of the Turkish Army*, 12–14, 116–117.

249. Alaeddin Ören, "İlk Yedek Subay Yuvası: İhtiyat Zabitan Mektebi," *Piyade Yedek Subay Talimgâhı 35. Dönem Hatırası*, (Ankara: Güzel Sanatlar Matbaası, 1952); İhsan Ali Alpar, *Anı: Kahraman Türk Silahlı Kuvvetlerimizde 55 Yıl 11 Ay*, (İstanbul: Nilüfer Matbaası, 1974), 21–35; Faik Tonguç, *Birinci Dünya Savaşında Bir Yedek Subayın Anıları*, (İstanbul: T. İş Bankası Yayınları, 1999), 16–17, 63, 67.

250. The fist NCO school (Gedikli Küçük Zabit Okulu) was founded by Mahmud Şevket Paşa under the supervision of a German officer Ditfurt Pasha in İstanbul in 1909. Some more schools were opened in important regional centers like Konya and Beirut. These schools which were three years long, managed to graduate three classes before the war. Tahsin Yahyaoğlu, "Astsubay Okullarının Tarihçesi," *Türk Kültürü*, year: 3, no. 32, June 1965, 36; İsmail Hakkı Süerdem, *Anılarım: Osmanlı'dan Cumhuriyet'e*, (ed.) Orhan Avcı, (Ankara: Bilge Yayınevi, 2004), 23–24; Wallach, *Bir Askeri Yardımın Anatomisi*, 80.

251. The most successful NCO cadets from each class were commissioned as officers. So in reality the NCO schools turned out to be supplementary military academies. Süerdem, *Anılarım*, 39.

252. Başkatipzade Ragıp Bey, *Tarih-i Hayatım: Tahsil-Harp-Esaret-Kurtuluş Anıları*, (ed.) Ahmet Emin Güven, (Ankara: Kebikeç Yayınları, 1996), 49–52.

253. Fevzi Çakmak, *Birinci Dünya Savaşı'nda Doğu Cephesi*, 2nd Edition, (Ankara: Genelkurmay Basımevi, 2005), 5–12, 18–19; Selışık, *Kafkas Cephesinde 10ncu Kolordunun Birinci Dünya Savaşının Başlangıcından Sarıkamış Muharebelerinin Sonuna Kadar Olan Harekatı*, 17–25, 28–34; Sabis, *Harp Hatıralarım*, 170–174.

254. McCarthy, *Armenian Rebellion at Van*, 177.

255. Baki, *Büyük Harpte Kafkas Cephesi*, vol. 2, (İstanbul: Askeri Matbaa, 1933), 3–29; Baytın, *İlk Dünya Harbinde Kafkas Cephesi*, 14–23; İlden, *Birinci Dünya Savaşı Başlangıcında 3.Ordu*, 56–58, 62–66, 79–81; Altınbilek and Kır, *Birinci Dünya Harbinde Türk Harbi*, 69–71, 87–94; Selışık, *Kafkas Cephesinde 10ncu Kolordunun Birinci Dünya Savaşının Başlangıcından Sarıkamış Muharebelerinin Sonuna Kadar Olan Harekatı*, 35–37, 42–44; Çakmak, *Birinci Dünya Savaşı'nda Doğu Cephesi*, 12–13, 26–28.

256. Altınbilek and Kır, *Birinci Dünya Harbinde Türk Harbi*, 39, 50–61, 81; Aziz Samih İlter, *Birinci Dünya Savaşında Kafkas Cephesi Hatıraları*, (Ankara: Genelkurmay Basımevi, 2007), 1–2; Cairo Intelligence, *Handbook of the Turkish Army*, 64–65.

257. British intelligence called Mahsusa organization and its operatives as "Fedai" throughout the war. See Cairo Intelligence, *Handbook of the Turkish Army* 105, 207; Arif Cemil Denker, *Birinci Dünya Savaşında Teşkilat-ı Mahsusa*, (ed.) Metin Martı, (İstanbul: Arma Yayınları, 2006), 13–41; Hüsameddin Ertürk, *İki Devrin Perde Arkası*, (ed.) Samih Nafiz Tansu, (İstanbul: Hilmi Kitabevi, 1957), 111–112; Ali İhsan Sabis, *Harp Hatıralarım: Birinci Dünya Harbi*, vol. 2, (İstanbul: Nehir Yayınları, 1990), 34, 168; İlden, *Birinci Dünya*

Savaşı Başlangıcında 3.Ordu, 61, 68, 158–159; Selışık, *Kafkas Cephesinde 10ncu Kolordunun Birinci Dünya Savaşının Başlangıcından Sarıkamış Muharebelerinin Sonuna Kadar Olan Harekatı*, 78.

258. Nikolski, *Sarıkamış Harekatı*, (Turkish translation of the Russian original), (trans.) Nazmi, (Ankara: Genelkurmay Basımevi, 1990), 3–5; Baki, *Büyük Harpte Kafkas Cephesi*, 11–202; Baytın, *İlk Dünya Harbinde Kafkas Cephesi*, 45–48; İlden, *Birinci Dünya Savaşı Başlangıcında 3.Ordu*, 72–78, 82–84, 91–92, 97–111, 127–128, 137–138; Altınbilek and Kır, *Birinci Dünya Harbinde Türk Harbi*, 110–219; Çakmak, *Birinci Dünya Savaşı'nda Doğu Cephesi*, 30–36; Allen and Muratoff, *Caucasian Battlefields*, 240–246; İlter, *Birinci Dünya Savaşında Kafkas Cephesi Hatıraları*, 3–7; Reynolds, *Ottoman-Russian Struggle for Eastern Anatolia*, 190.

259. Baytın, *İlk Dünya Harbinde Kafkas Cephesi*, 55–75; Selışık, *Kafkas Cephesinde 10ncu Kolordunun Birinci Dünya Savaşının Başlangıcından Sarıkamış Muharebelerinin Sonuna Kadar Olan Harekatı*, 59–72; İlden, *Birinci Dünya Savaşı Başlangıcında 3.Ordu*, 138–147; Baki, *Büyük Harpte Kafkas Cephesi*, 203–363; Çakmak, *Birinci Dünya Savaşı'nda Doğu Cephesi*, 36–39; Altınbilek and Kır, *Birinci Dünya Harbinde Türk Harbi*, 219–221, 229–321.

260. Baytın, *İlk Dünya Harbinde Kafkas Cephesi*, 45, 163–164, 175; Altınbilek and Kır, *Birinci Dünya Harbinde Türk Harbi*, 232, 322–323.

261. İlden, *Birinci Dünya Savaşı Başlangıcında 3.Ordu*, 101, 106–109, 127, 130–135; Altınbilek and Kır, *Birinci Dünya Harbinde Türk Harbi*, 77–83, 90–91, 185, 329; Baytın, *İlk Dünya Harbinde Kafkas Cephesi*, 46.

262. İlden, *Birinci Dünya Savaşı Başlangıcında 3.Ordu*, 92–95, 141–143; Baytın, *İlk Dünya Harbinde Kafkas Cephesi*, 165–169.

263. Altınbilek and Kır, *Birinci Dünya Harbinde Türk Harbi*, 111, 119, 129, 149–150, 189, 203, 222, 276–278, 289–292, 304, 317–318, 328; Baki, *Büyük Harpte Kafkas Cephesi*, 34–37, 47–51, 61–68, 78–82, 107–109, 126–130, 194–197, 291–294, 356–359; İlden, *Birinci Dünya Savaşı Başlangıcında 3.Ordu*, 67–68, 113–116; Çakmak, *Birinci Dünya Savaşı'nda Doğu Cephesi*, 39, 41–42; İlter, *Birinci Dünya Savaşında Kafkas Cephesi Hatıraları*, 3–9.

264. İlden, *Birinci Dünya Savaşı Başlangıcında 3.Ordu*, 145–154, 165; Denker, *Birinci Dünya Savaşında Teşkilat-ı Mahsusa*, 107–144, 195; Çakmak, *Birinci Dünya Savaşı'nda Doğu Cephesi*, 14, 40–41, 44–48; Sabis, *Harp Hatıralarım*, 163–197, 224–225, 231–247, 262–263.

265. Baytın, *İlk Dünya Harbinde Kafkas Cephesi*, 85–95, 102, 174; Selışık, *Kafkas Cephesinde 10ncu Kolordunun Birinci Dünya Savaşının Başlangıcından Sarıkamış Muharebelerinin Sonuna Kadar Olan Harekatı*, 82–87, 91–94, 108, 111, 191–193; İlden, *Birinci Dünya Savaşı Başlangıcında 3.Ordu*, 161–165, 167–177, 190–191; Altınbilek and Kır, *Birinci Dünya Harbinde Türk Harbi*, 354–356, 368–369, 371–374, 378–381; Kressenstein, *Son Haçlı Seferi Kuma Gömülen İmparatorluk*, 19–20.

266. Altınbilek and Kır, *Birinci Dünya Harbinde Türk Harbi*, 382–383; Nikolski, *Sarıkamış Harekatı*, 7–13.

267. Baytın, *İlk Dünya Harbinde Kafkas Cephesi*, 91–118; Selışık, *Kafkas Cephesinde 10ncu Kolordunun Birinci Dünya Savaşının Başlangıcından Sarıkamış Muharebelerinin Sonuna Kadar Olan Harekatı*, 94–115; İlden, *Birinci Dünya Savaşı Başlangıcında 3.Ordu*, 179–188, 190–219; Çakmak, *Birinci Dünya Savaşı'nda Doğu Cephesi*, 49–52; Altınbilek and Kır, *Birinci Dünya Harbinde Türk Harbi*, 385–409.

268. Baytın, *İlk Dünya Harbinde Kafkas Cephesi*, 118–123; İlden, *Birinci Dünya Savaşı Başlangıcında 3.Ordu*, 189–190, 219–227; Çakmak, *Birinci Dünya Savaşı'nda Doğu Cephesi*, 52–60; Altınbilek and Kır, *Birinci Dünya Harbinde Türk Harbi*, 414–417, 429–437, 442–444.

269. Baytın, *İlk Dünya Harbinde Kafkas Cephesi*, 123–151; Selışık, *Kafkas Cephesinde 10ncu Kolordunun Birinci Dünya Savaşının Başlangıcından Sarıkamış Muharebelerinin Sonuna Kadar Olan Harekatı*, 114–159; İlden, *Birinci Dünya Savaşı Başlangıcında 3.Ordu*, 229–241; Nikolski, *Sarıkamış Harekatı*, 13–40; Çakmak, *Birinci Dünya Savaşı'nda Doğu Cephesi*, 60–61; Altınbilek and Kır, *Birinci Dünya Harbinde Türk Harbi*, 411–413, 426–427, 439–485.

270. Baytın, *İlk Dünya Harbinde Kafkas Cephesi*, 151–162; Selışık, *Kafkas Cephesinde 10ncu Kolordunun Birinci Dünya Savaşının Başlangıcından Sarıkamış Muharebelerinin Sonuna Kadar Olan Harekatı*, 159–188; İlden, *Birinci Dünya Savaşı Başlangıcında 3.Ordu*, 244–252; Nikolski, *Sarıkamış Harekatı*, 41–62; Çakmak, *Birinci Dünya Savaşı'nda Doğu Cephesi*, 61–63; Altınbilek and Kır, *Birinci Dünya Harbinde Türk Harbi*, 493–525.

271. Selışık, *Kafkas Cephesinde 10ncu Kolordunun Birinci Dünya Savaşının Başlangıcından Sarıkamış Muharebelerinin Sonuna Kadar Olan Harekatı*, 188–194; Çakmak, *Birinci Dünya Savaşı'nda Doğu Cephesi*, 71–75; İlter, *Birinci Dünya Savaşında Kafkas Cephesi Hatıraları*, 13–14.

272. Hulusi Baykoç, *Birinci Dünya Savaşı'nda Kafkas ve Irak Cephesi'nde 5nci Seferi Kuvvetler (52nci Tümen)*, (Ankara: Genelkurmay Basımevi, 2006), 1–4, 6–12; Kut, *İttihat ve Terakki'den Cumhuriyete Bitmeyen Savaş*, 136–142; Apak, *Yetmişlik Bir Subayın Anıları*, 95–98; Yurtoğlu, *Yüzbaşı Selahattin'in Romanı*, 93–99, 110–111; Çakmak, *Birinci Dünya Savaşı'nda Doğu Cephesi*, 44–46; İlter, *Birinci Dünya Savaşında Kafkas Cephesi Hatıraları*, 30, 38.

273. Baytın, *İlk Dünya Harbinde Kafkas Cephesi*, 120, 126–127, 137, 163–164, 172, 175–182; Ahmed İzzet, *Feryadım*, 196–198; Selışık, *Kafkas Cephesinde 10ncu Kolordunun Birinci Dünya Savaşının Başlangıcından Sarıkamış Muharebelerinin Sonuna Kadar Olan Harekatı*, 45, 129; Altınbilek and Kır, *Birinci Dünya Harbinde Türk Harbi*, 447; İlter, *Birinci Dünya Savaşında Kafkas Cephesi Hatıraları*, 8–9, 11, 15.

274. Philip H. Stoddard, *Teşkilat-ı Mahsusa*, (Turkish translation of the English original *The Ottoman Government and the Arabs, 1911 to 1918: A Study of the Teşkilat-ı Mahsusa*), (trans.) Tansel Demirel, (İstanbul: Arba Yayınları, 1994), 7–12, 43–47.

275. Denker, *Birinci Dünya Savaşında Teşkilat-ı Mahsusa*, 140–161; Selışık, *Kafkas Cephesinde 10ncu Kolordunun Birinci Dünya Savaşının Başlangıcından Sarıkamış Muharebelerinin Sonuna Kadar Olan Harekatı*, 78, 81–82; İlden, *Birinci Dünya Savaşı Başlangıcında 3.Ordu*, 158–159; İlter, *Birinci Dünya Savaşında Kafkas Cephesi Hatıraları*, 23–27, 63; Altınbilek and Kır, *Birinci Dünya Harbinde Türk Harbi*, 368–369, 375; Süleyman Gürcan, *Binbaşı Süleyman Bey'in Manzum Anıları*, (ed.) Ömer Türkoğlu, (Ankara: Kebikeç Yayınları, 1997), 130–133.

276. Denker, *Birinci Dünya Savaşında Teşkilat-ı Mahsusa*, 167–268; Çakmak, *Birinci Dünya Savaşı'nda Doğu Cephesi*, 81–82; Erden, *Birinci Dünya Harbinde Suriye Hatıraları*, 266–269; İlter, *Birinci Dünya Savaşında Kafkas Cephesi Hatıraları*, 26–27, 30, 33–34, 54–55; Gürcan, *Binbaşı Süleyman Bey'in Manzum Anıları*, 131–167.

277. Erden, *Birinci Dünya Harbinde Suriye Hatıraları*, 11–19, 30–76; Cemal Paşa, *Hatıralar*, 174–188; Kressenstein, *Son Haçlı Seferi Kuma Gömülen İmparatorluk*, 65–114; Okçu, *Birinci Dünya Harbinde Türk Harbi, Sina-Filistin Cephesi*, 177–262; Behçet, *Büyük Harpte Mısır Seferi*, (İstanbul: Askeri Matbaa, 1930), 4–34; Yigal Sheffy, *British Military Intelligence in the Palestine Campaign 1914–1918*, (London: Frank Cass, 1998), 2–20, 33–34, 48–49, 52–59.

278. Balkan, *İlk Türk Komitacısı Fuat Balkan'ın Hatıraları*, 13–46.

279. Şükrü Erkal, *Birinci Dünya Harbinde Türk Harbi: Hicaz, Asir, Yemen Cepheleri ve Libya Harekatı*, vol. 6, (Ankara: Genkur Basımevi, 1978), 32–38, 627–629; Jafar al-Askari, *A Soldier's Story: From Ottoman Rule to Independent Iraq*, (trans.) Tariq al-Askari, (London:

Arabian Publishing, 2003), 57–58, 65, 70; Simon, *Between Ottomanism and Nationalism*, 104–109.

280. Erkal, *Birinci Dünya Harbinde Türk Harbi*, 629–640; Simon, *Between Ottomanism and Nationalism*, 107–109.

281. al-Askari, *Soldier's Story*, 54–75; Erkal, *Birinci Dünya Harbinde Türk Harbi*, 641–648.

282. Erkal, *Birinci Dünya Harbinde Türk Harbi*, 642–654, 808–821; al-Askari, *Soldier's Story*, 58–60, 76–77; Simon, *Between Ottomanism and Nationalism*, 129–131; Ertürk, *İki Devrin Perde Arkası*, 162–164.

283. Erkal, *Birinci Dünya Harbinde Türk Harbi*, 655–680; al-Askari, *Soldier's Story*, 76–92.

284. Erkal, *Birinci Dünya Harbinde Türk Harbi*, 672–673, 684–725.

285. Ibid., 648–649, 680–681, 684, 735; Simon, *Between Ottomanism and Nationalism*, 109, 126, 132; al-Askari, *Soldier's Story*, 76.

286. Okçu, *Birinci Dünya Harbinde Türk Harbi, Sina-Filistin Cephesi*, 74, 77–78; Erkal, *Birinci Dünya Harbinde Türk Harbi*, 153–159; Kressenstein, *Son Haçlı Seferi Kuma Gömülen İmparatorluk*, 54–56; Sheffy, *British Military Intelligence in the Palestine Campaign 1914–1918*, 41; Sabis, *Harp Hatıralarım*, 217–218.

287. Cemal Paşa, *Hatıralar*, 174–175, 192.

288. Mustafa Tevfik, *Gelibolu Müfrezesi: Yüzbaşı Mustafa Tevfik'in Ölüm Kalım Mücadelesi*, (ed.) Zafer Güler, (İstanbul: Truva Yayınları, 2007), 33–98.

289. Nezihi Fırat and Behzat Balkış, *Birinci Dünya Harbinde Türk Harbi, İran-Irak Cephesi*, vol. 3, section 1, (Ankara: Genelkurmay Basımevi, 1979), 39–46.

290. Fırat and Balkış, *Birinci Dünya Harbinde Türk Harbi, İran-Irak Cephesi*, 20, 33–34.

291. Ibid., 42, 61–63; Sabis, *Harp Hatıralarım*, 35.

292. Fırat and Balkış, *Birinci Dünya Harbinde Türk Harbi, İran-Irak Cephesi*, 65–71.

293. Ibid., 72–107.

294. For details about Western Thrace enclave *see* Nevzat Gündağ, *Garbi Trakya Hükümet-i Müstakilesi*, (Ankara: Kültür ve Turizm Bakanlığı Yayınları, 1987); Also *see* Cemal Kutay, *1913'de Garbi Trakya'da İlk Türk Cumhuriyeti*, (İstanbul: Tarih Yayınları, 1962).

295. Denker, *Birinci Dünya Savaşında Teşkilat-ı Mahsusa*, 269–361; Cemal Paşa, *Hatıralar*, 61–64; Cemal, *Arnavutluk'tan Sakarya'ya Komitacılık*, 28–37; Balkan, *İlk Türk Komitacısı Fuat Balkan'ın Hatıraları*, 9–13; Stoddard, *Teşkilat-ı Mahsusa*, 48–50, 108; Sabis, *Harp Hatıralarım*, 212–214, 391–395.

296. Fırat and Balkış, *Birinci Dünya Harbinde Türk Harbi, İran-Irak Cephesi*, 120–121; Stoddard, *Teşkilat-ı Mahsusa*, 47; Sabis, *Harp Hatıralarım*, 392–393.

297. Fırat and Balkış, *Birinci Dünya Harbinde Türk Harbi, İran-Irak Cephesi*, 121–123, 131–132; Sabis, *Harp Hatıralarım*, 395–397.

298. Fırat and Balkış, *Birinci Dünya Harbinde Türk Harbi, İran-Irak Cephesi*, 123–131, 142–158; Orhan Avcı, *Irak'ta Türk Ordusu*, (Ankara: Vadi Yayınları, 2004), 33–37.

299. Fırat and Balkış, *Birinci Dünya Harbinde Türk Harbi, İran-Irak Cephesi*, 158–161.

300. Ibid., 172–179; Sabis, *Harp Hatıralarım*, 397–398.

301. Fırat and Balkış, *Birinci Dünya Harbinde Türk Harbi, İran-Irak Cephesi*, 179–204, 207–210.

302. Ibid., 204–207, 268–283, 284–287, 350–352; Sabis, *Harp Hatıralarım*, 397–398.

303. Fırat and Balkış, *Birinci Dünya Harbinde Türk Harbi, İran-Irak Cephesi*, 227–257, 261–265, 287–333.

304. Ibid., 352–421; Edward J. Erickson, *Ottoman Army Effectiveness in World War I: A Comparative Study*, (New York: Routledge, 2007), 74–79; Kut, *İttihat ve Terakki'den Cumhuriyete Bitmeyen Savaş*, 153–158.

305. Fahri Belen, *Birinci Cihan Harbinde Türk Harbi: 1916 Yılı Hareketleri*, vol. 3, (Ankara: Genelkurmay Basımevi, 1965), 111–150; Fırat and Balkış, *Birinci Dünya Harbinde Türk Harbi, İran-Irak Cephesi*, 421–782; Kut, *İttihat ve Terakki'den Cumhuriyete Bitmeyen Savaş*, 159–190; Erickson, *Ottoman Army Effectiveness in World War I*, 79–89, 92; Baykoç, *Birinci Dünya Savaşı'nda Kafkas ve Irak Cephesi'nde 5nci Seferi Kuvvetler (52nci Tümen)*, 36–59; Yurtoğlu, *Yüzbaşı Selahattin'in Romanı*, 177–224; Apak, *Yetmişlik Bir Subayın Anıları*, 134–148.

306. İlter, *Birinci Dünya Savaşında Kafkas Cephesi Hatıraları*, 53–54.

307. C. F. Aspinall-Oglander, *History of the Great War, Military Operations Gallipoli*, vol. 1, (Nashville: The Battery Press reprint, 1992), vii–ix, 70–71, 87–89; Basil H. Liddell-Hart, *History of the First World War*, (London: Book Club, 1977), 214–215, 223, 227, 239–242; Nigel Steel and Peter Hart, *Defeat at Gallipoli*, (London: Papermac, 1995), 46, 419–420; Robert Rhodes-James, "Gallipoli Campaign," in (ed.) Richard Holmes, *The Oxford Companion to Military History*, (Oxford: Oxford University Press, 2003), 345.

308. Süer, *TSK Tarihi Balkan Harbi (1912–1913)*, 47–50; Ersü, *1912–1913 Balkan Harbinde Şarköy Çıkarması ve Bulayır Muharebeleri*, 14–26; Muhterem Saral et al., *Birinci Dünya Harbinde Türk Harbi: Çanakkale Cephesi Harekâtı*, vol. 5, book 1, (Ankara: Genkur Basımevi, 1993), 33–39, 44–47.

309. Mustafa Kemal Atatürk, *Arıburnu Muharebeleri Raporu*, (ed.) Uluğ İğdemir, (Ankara: Türk Tarih Kurumu Basımevi, 1986), 6–7.

310. Aspinall-Oglander, *History of the Great War*, 18–19; Steel and Hart, *History of the First World War*, 45–47; Michael Hickey, *Gallipoli*, (London: John Murray, 1995), 23–24, 117, 125, 145–146.

311. Ahmed İzzet, *Feryadım*, 240; Şerif Güralp, *1918 Yılında Türk Ordusunun Filistin ve Suriye'den Çekilişinde 3. Sv. Tümeninin Harekatı*, 2nd edition, (Ankara: Genelkurmay Basımevi, 2006), 43.

312. Sanders, *Five Years in Turkey*, 57–59; Saral, *Birinci Dünya Harbinde Türk Harbi*, 217–230; Mühlmann, *Çanakkale Savaşı*, 71–72.

313. Saral, *Birinci Dünya Harbinde Türk Harbi*, 109–110; Selahattin Adil, *Hayat Mücadeleleri*, (İstanbul: Zafer Matbaası, 1982), 235–237; Atatürk, *Arıburnu Muharebeleri Raporu*, 6, 9–11.

314. Sanders, *Five Years in Turkey*, 59–61; Saral, *Birinci Dünya Harbinde Türk Harbi*, 225–230; İnönü, *Hatıralar*, 145–146; Adil, *Hayat Mücadeleleri*, 208–209, 257; Mühlmann, *Çanakkale Savaşı*, 73–78; Remzi Yiğitgüden et al., *Birinci Dünya Harbinde Türk Harbi: Çanakkale Cephesi Harekâtı*, vol. 5, book 2, (Ankara: Genkur Basımevi, 1978), 8–10; Fahrettin Altay, *10 Yıl Savaş ve Sonrası (1912–1922)*, (İstanbul: İnsel Yayınları, 1970), 80, 84–85.

315. Altay, *10 Yıl Savaş ve Sonrası (1912–1922)*, 85–86; Sanders, *Five Years in Turkey*, 63–67.

316. Aspinall-Oglander, *History of the Great War*, 292–293.

317. Atatürk, *Arıburnu Muharebeleri Raporu*, 19–26; Altay, *10 Yıl Savaş ve Sonrası (1912–1922)*, 87–89; Yiğitgüden, *1912–1913 Balkan Harbinde Edirne Kale Muharebeleri*, 12–37; Mühlmann, *Çanakkale Savaşı*, 83–90.

318. These German officers were 5th Army Commander Liman von Sanders Pasha, XIV Corps CO Trommer Pasha, 3rd ID CO Col. Nicolai, 9th ID. CO Lt. Col. Bötrich, Anafartalar Area Commander Lt. Col. Willmer, 13th ID CO Col. Heuck, V Corps Chief of Staff Lt. Col. Albrecht and 28th IR CO Maj. Hunker. Several other German officers served before August 1915; Weber Pasha, Col. von Sodenstern, Col. Kannengiesser, Col. Hovik, Lt. Col. Thauvenay, Maj. Mühlmann and Maj. Eggert. The German artillery, engineers and

naval officers who served at Fortified Area Zone Command and did not take part in land operations are not taken into account.

319. Necati Ökse et al., *Türk İstiklâl Harbi'ne Katılan Tümen ve Daha Üst Kademelerdeki Komutanların Biyografileri*, (Ankara: Genkur Basımevi, 1989), passim.; Görgülü, *On Yıllık Harbin Kadrosu (1912–1922)*, passim.; İsmet Görgülü, *Türk Harp Tarihi Derslerinde Adı Geçen Komutanlar*, (İstanbul: Harp Akademileri Basımevi, 1983), passim.

320. Baştepe, *26. P. Alayı Tarihçesi*, 8–44; Yiğitgüden, *1912–1913 Balkan Harbinde Edirne Kale Muharebeleri*, 239–240, 243–244; Hickey, *Gallipoli*, 221–222.

321. Cemil Conk, *Canlı Tarihler: Cemil Conk Hatıraları*, (İstanbul: Türkiye Yayınevi, 1947), 140; Yiğitgüden, *1912–1913 Balkan Harbinde Edirne Kale Muharebeleri*, 327–357; Altay, *10 Yıl Savaş ve Sonrası (1912–1922)*, 93–94; Sanders, *Five Years in Turkey*, 71, 73, 76; Mustafa Tevfik, *Gelibolu Müfrezesi*, 111, 146–147; Steel and Hart, *History of the First World War*, 127–128.

322. Yiğitgüden, *1912–1913 Balkan Harbinde Edirne Kale Muharebeleri*, 175–182, 191–211, 365–393; Altay, *10 Yıl Savaş ve Sonrası (1912–1922)*, 97–98; Adil, *Hayat Mücadeleleri*, 245, 248; Mühlmann, *Çanakkale Savaşı*, 95–114, 122–123.

323. Atatürk, *Arıburnu Muharebeleri Raporu*, 70; Yiğitgüden, *1912–1913 Balkan Harbinde Edirne Kale Muharebeleri*, 137–138; Adil, *Hayat Mücadeleleri*, 246, 270.

324. Adil, *Hayat Mücadeleleri*, 253; Conk, *Canlı Tarihler*, 140; Mustafa Tevfik, *Gelibolu Müfrezesi*, 115–117.

325. Yiğitgüden, *1912–1913 Balkan Harbinde Edirne Kale Muharebeleri*, 179–180.

326. Izzettin Çalışlar, *On Yıllık Savaşın Günlüğü: Balkan, Birinci Dünya ve İstiklal Savaları*, (ed.) İ. Gorgülü, İ. Çalışlar, (İstanbul: Yapı Kredi Yayınları, 1997), 116–117; Adil, *Hayat Mücadeleleri*, 259–260; Altay, *10 Yıl Savaş ve Sonrası (1912–1922)*, 108–110.

327. Adil, *Hayat Mücadeleleri*, 259–260; Altay, *10 Yıl Savaş ve Sonrası (1912–1922)*, 108–110; Mühlmann, *Çanakkale Savaşı*, 131–143.

328. Steel and Hart, *History of the First World War*, 285–286, 298.

329. İrfan Tekşüt and Necati Ökse, *Birinci Dünya Harbinde Türk Harbi: Çanakkale Cephesi Harekatı*, vol. 5, book 3, (Ankara: Genkur. Basımevi, 1980), table no. 4; Saral, *Birinci Dünya Harbinde Türk Harbi*, 276; Most of the Turkish sources persistently give 250,000 figures as the overall numbers of the casualties.

330. Altay, *10 Yıl Savaş ve Sonrası (1912–1922)*, 113; İnönü, *Hatıralar*, 149; Aspinall-Oglander, *History of the Great War*, ix; Hikmet Özdemir, *The Ottoman Army 1914–1918: Disease & Death on the Battlefield*, (Salt Lake City: The University of Utah Press, 2008), 68–76.

331. Güliz B. Erginsoy (ed.), *Dedem Hüseyin Atıf Beşe: Bir Cemiyet-i Osmaniye Askerinin Savaş Hatıratı*, (İstanbul: Varlık Yayınları, 2004), 173–175.

332. Adil, *Hayat Mücadeleleri*, 240–241.

333. Faik Tonguç, *Birinci Dünya Savaşı'nda Bir Yedek Subayın Anıları*, (İstanbul: Türkiye İş Bankası Yayınları, 1999), 161–164.

334. İnönü, *Hatıralar*, 146–147.

335. Tekşüt and Ökse, *Birinci Dünya Harbinde Türk Harbi*, passim.

336. Avni Çoker, *Çanakkale Şehitlerini Ziyaret Münasebetiyle*, (Ankara: Akın Matbaacılık, 1952), 14, 20–21.

337. Rasim Bayraktaroğlu, "Kafkas Cephesinde Köse Yarması," *Askeri Mecmua*, vol. 52, no. 92, March 1934, 52–64; Allen and Muratoff, *Caucasian Battlefields*, 331–347.

338. İlter, *Birinci Dünya Savaşında Kafkas Cephesi Hatıraları*, 67–95, 99–101; Allen and Muratoff, *Caucasian Battlefields*, 348–372, 375–383; Ragıp, *Tarih-i Hayatım*, 75–83.

339. A. P. Hacobian, *Armenia and the War: An Armenian's Point of View with an Appeal to Britain and the Coming Peace Conference*, (London: Hodder and Stoughton, 1917), 70–80; Garegin Pasdermadjian, *Why Armenia Should be Free: Armenia's Role in the Present War*, (Boston: Hairenik Publishing, 1918), 17–23; McCarthy, *Armenian Rebellion at Van*, 180–221; Sabis, *Harp Hatıralarım*, 30, 41, 183–184, 202, 425–442; Reynolds, *Ottoman-Russian Struggle for Eastern Anatolia*, 201–209, 259–266; Altınbilek and Kır, *Birinci Dünya Harbinde Türk Harbi*, 676–686; Allen and Muratoff, *Caucasian Battlefields*, 297–301; İlter, *Birinci Dünya Savaşında Kafkas Cephesi Hatıraları*, 38, 41; Apak, *Yetmişlik Bir Subayın Anıları*, 114, 150; Baykoç, *Birinci Dünya Savaşı'nda Kafkas ve Irak Cephesi'nde 5nci Seferi Kuvvetler (52nci Tümen)*, 14–20.

340. Cemal Paşa, *Hatıralar*, 407; Pasdermadjian, *Why Armenia Should be Free*, 15–17; Hacobian, *Armenia and the War*, 69–70; Bayur, *Türk İnkılâbı Tarihi*, 71–72; McCarthy, *Armenian Rebellion at Van*, 132–140.

341. Edward J. Erickson, "The Armenians and Ottoman Military Policy, 1915," *War in History*, vol. 15, no. 2, 2008, 150–167; Yusuf Hikmet Bayur, *Türk İnkılâbı Tarihi*, vol. 3, section 3, (Ankara: Türk Tarih Kurumu Basımevi, 1983), 35–49; McCarthy, *Armenian Rebellion at Van*, 180–186; Reynolds, *Ottoman-Russian Struggle for Eastern Anatolia*, 267–274; For the official documents about this decree and its application see *Osmanlı Belgelerinde Ermeniler (1915–1920)*, (Ankara: Başbakanlık Devlet Arşivleri Genel Müdürlüğü, 1995), 5–11, 18–178.

342. Edward J. Erickson, "Bayonets on Musa Dagh: Ottoman Counterinsurgency Operations 1915," *The Journal of Strategic Studies*, vol. 28, no. 3, June 2005, 536–544; Erden, *Birinci Dünya Harbinde Suriye Hatıraları*, 92, 141–155; Okçu, *Birinci Dünya Harbinde Türk Harbi, Sina-Filistin Cephesi*, 698–703.

343. Ahmed İzzet, *Feryadım*, 246–253; Fikri Güleç, *Birinci Dünya Harbinde Türk Harbi, Kafkas Cephesi, 2nci Ordu Harekatı 1916–1918*, vol. 2, section 2, (Ankara: Genelkurmay Basımevi, 1978), 37–69; Özdemir, *Ottoman Army 1914–1918*, 87.

344. Ahmed İzzet, *Feryadım*, 253–260; Güleç, *Birinci Dünya Harbinde Türk Harbi, Kafkas Cephesi, 2nci Ordu Harekatı 1916–1918*, 91–151; Hakkı Altınbilek and Naci Kır, *Birinci Dünya Harbinde Türk Harbi*, vol. 2, section 1, book 2, (Ankara: Genelkurmay Basımevi, 1993), 148–150, 160–162, 269–272; Çakmak, *Birinci Dünya Savaşı'nda Doğu Cephesi*, 146–153; Allen and Muratoff, *Caucasian Battlefields*, 390–418; Belen, *Birinci Cihan Harbinde Türk Harbi*, 74–75; İnönü, *Hatıralar*, 108; İlter, *Birinci Dünya Savaşında Kafkas Cephesi Hatıraları*, 98.

345. Ahmed İzzet, *Feryadım*, 261–270; Allen and Muratoff, *Caucasian Battlefields*, 419–428; İnönü, *Hatıralar*, 108–109; Güleç, *Birinci Dünya Harbinde Türk Harbi, Kafkas Cephesi, 2nci Ordu Harekatı 1916–1918*, 148–235; Çakmak, *Birinci Dünya Savaşı'nda Doğu Cephesi*, 153–162; Belen, *Birinci Cihan Harbinde Türk Harbi*, 75–98.

346. Ali Fuat Cebesoy, *Birüssebi-Gazze Meydan Muharebesi ve Yirminci Kolordu*, (İstanbul: Askeri Matbaa, 1938), 15–18; For the operations of XV Army Corps at Galicia see Ahmet Suat, *Büyük Harpte Galiçya Cephesinde 15. Türk Kolordusu*, (İstanbul: Askeri Matbaa, 1930), passim.; Also see Cihat Akçakayalıoğlu, *Birinci Dünya Harbi Avrupa Cepheleri: Galiçya Cephesi*, vol. 7, section 1, (Ankara: Genelkurmay Basımevi, 1967), passim.

347. For the operations of VI Army Corps at Galicia see M. Neşet, *Büyük Harpte Romanya Cephesinde 6. Türk Kolordusu*, (İstanbul: Askeri Matbaa, 1930), passim.; Also see Fikri Güleç, *Birinci Dünya Harbi Avrupa Cepheleri: Romanya Cephesi*, vol. 7, section 2, (Ankara: Genelkurmay Basımevi, 1967), passim.

348. For the operations of VI Army Corps at Galicia *see* Fazıl Karlıdağ, Kani Ciner, *Birinci Dünya Harbi Avrupa Cepheleri: Makedonya Cephesi*, vol. 7, section 3, (Ankara: Genelkurmay Basımevi, 1967), passim; Also *see* Mustafa Erem, and Büyük *Harpte Osmanlı Rumeli Müfrezesi (Takviyeli 177. Piyade Alayı)*, (İstanbul: Askeri Matbaa, 1940), passim.

349. İbrahim Arıkan, *Harp Hatıralarım: Bir Mehmetçiğin Çanakkale-Galiçya-Filistin Cephesi Hatıraları*, (İstanbul: Timaş Yayınları, 2007), 87–113, 132–176; M. Şevki Yazman, *Mehmetçik Avrupa'da*, (İstanbul: Ahmet Halit Yaşaroğlu Kitapçılık, 1953), 36–83, 150–160.

350. Yazman, *Mehmetçik Avrupa'da*, 87–92, 97, 118, 126, 131.

351. The Ottoman Hücum Kıtaatı was a mixture of the German assault detachment concept and a century old Nişancı and Avcı formations' traditions. Ahmed İzzet, *Feryadım*, 160.

352. Sedad, *Hücum Kıtaatının Talim ve Terbiyesi*, (İstanbul: Erkan-ı Harbiye Mektebi Matbaası, 1336), passim.; Rıfat, "Hücum Taburlarının Teşkilatıyla Talim ve Terbiyesi," *Mecmua-i Askeri*, no. 5, August 1335; Sedad, *Gaz Muharebesi*, (İstanbul: Askeri Matbaa, 1337), passim.

353. Erden, *Birinci Dünya Harbinde Suriye Hatıraları*, 93–127, 178–205, 210–214, 227–230, 286–298; Kressenstein, *Son Haçlı Seferi Kuma Gömülen İmparatorluk*, 115–131, 139–140, 165–225; Okçu, *Birinci Dünya Harbinde Türk Harbi, Sina-Filistin Cephesi*, 299–394; Cebesoy, *Birüssebi-Gazze Meydan Muharebesi ve Yirminci Kolordu*, 35–43.

354. Okçu, *Birinci Dünya Harbinde Türk Harbi, Sina-Filistin Cephesi*, 413–564; Erden, *Birinci Dünya Harbinde Suriye Hatıraları*, 317–323; Kressenstein, *Son Haçlı Seferi Kuma Gömülen İmparatorluk*, 227–229, 233, 245–276; Recep Balkan, "Harp Tarihi Tetkiklerine Göre Süvaride Atlı Muharebe mi, Yaya Muharebe mi Asıldır?," *Askeri Mecmua*, vol. 57, no. 114, September 1939, 705–706.

355. Okçu, *Birinci Dünya Harbinde Türk Harbi, Sina-Filistin Cephesi*, 564–651; Kressenstein, *Son Haçlı Seferi Kuma Gömülen İmparatorluk*, 277–294; Yigal Sheffy, "The Chemical Dimension of the Gallipoli Campaign: Introducing Chemical Warfare to the Middle East," *War in History*, vol. 12, no. 3, July 2005, 316.

356. Kressenstein, *Son Haçlı Seferi Kuma Gömülen İmparatorluk*, 297–308; Kamil Onalp and Hilmi Üstünsoy, *Birinci Dünya Harbinde Türk Harbi, Sina-Filistin Cephesi*, vol. 4, section 2, (Ankara: Genelkurmay Basımevi, 1986), 28–74.

357. Ali İhsan Sabis, *Harp Hatıralarım: Birinci Dünya Harbi*, vol. 3, (İstanbul: Nehir Yayınları, 1991), 178–349; Ibid., vol. 4, (İstanbul: Nehir Yayınları, 1991), 21–90; Necati Ökse and Özden Çalhan, *Birinci Dünya Harbinde Türk Harbi, İran-Irak Cephesi*, vol. 3, section 2, (Ankara: Genelkurmay Basımevi, 2002), 52–57, 183–241, 357–370; Kut, *İttihat ve Terakki'den Cumhuriyete Bitmeyen Savaş*, 193–197; Allen and Muratoff, *Caucasian Battlefields*, 430–447.

358. Ökse and Çalhan, *Birinci Dünya Harbinde Türk Harbi, İran-Irak Cephesi*, 76–138, 289–357; Şükrü Kanatlı, *Irak Muharebelerinde 3ncü Piyade Alayı Hatıraları*, 2nd Edition, (Ankara: Genelkurmay Basımevi, 2006), 11–57; Baykoç, *Birinci Dünya Savaşı'nda Kafkas ve Irak Cephesi'nde 5nci Seferi Kuvvetler (52nci Tümen)*, 59–74.

359. Ökse and Çalhan, *Birinci Dünya Harbinde Türk Harbi, İran-Irak Cephesi*, 138–175,; Baykoç, *Birinci Dünya Savaşı'nda Kafkas ve Irak Cephesi'nde 5nci Seferi Kuvvetler (52nci Tümen)*, 75–105; Kut, *İttihat ve Terakki'den Cumhuriyete Bitmeyen Savaş*, 198–202.

360. It was named sequentially after Pasha I; the composite German detachments of artillery, aviation, medical and transport that had deployed to the Middle East during 1916.

361. Werner Steuber, *Yıldırım*, (Turkish translation of the German original *Jildirim Deutsche Streiter auf Heiligem Boden*), (trans.) Nihat, (İstanbul: Askeri Matbaa, 1932), 5–19; Sanders, *Five Years in Turkey*, 173–177; Hüseyin Hüsnü Emir (Erkilet), *Yıldırım*, (Ankara:

Genelkurmay Basımevi, 2002), 4–5, 11–13, 15–17, 19; Kressenstein, *Son Haçlı Seferi Kuma Gömülen İmparatorluk*, 301; Cebesoy, *Birüssebi-Gazze Meydan Muharebesi ve Yirminci Kolordu*, 23–26.

362. Erkilet, *Yıldırım*, 15–26, 36–83; Cemal Paşa, *Hatıralar*, 210–221; Kressenstein, *Son Haçlı Seferi Kuma Gömülen İmparatorluk*, 301, 309–311; Onalp and Üstünsoy, *Birinci Dünya Harbinde Türk Harbi, Sina-Filistin Cephesi*, 88–99; Wallach, *Bir Askeri Yardımın Anatomisi*, 210–211, 215–216.

363. Erkilet, *Yıldırım*, 48–83; Kressenstein, *Son Haçlı Seferi Kuma Gömülen İmparatorluk*, 302, 313–318; Cemal Paşa, *Hatıralar*, 210–214, 224–226; Cebesoy, *Birüssebi-Gazze Meydan Muharebesi ve Yirminci Kolordu*, 26–35; Onalp and Üstünsoy, *Birinci Dünya Harbinde Türk Harbi, Sina-Filistin Cephesi*, 105–115; Sanders, *Five Years in Turkey*, 76–77.

364. Onalp and Üstünsoy, *Birinci Dünya Harbinde Türk Harbi, Sina-Filistin Cephesi*, 15–18, 128–315; Cebesoy, *Birüssebi-Gazze Meydan Muharebesi ve Yirminci Kolordu*, 54–80; İnönü, *Hatıralar*, 120–123; Kressenstein, *Son Haçlı Seferi Kuma Gömülen İmparatorluk*, 319–362; Erickson, *Ottoman Army Effectiveness in World War I*, 111–124; Sheffy, *British Military Intelligence in the Palestine Campaign 1914–1918*, 316; Altay, *10 Yıl Savaş ve Sonrası (1912–1922)*, 128–137.

365. Kressenstein, *Son Haçlı Seferi Kuma Gömülen İmparatorluk*, 354–364; Altay, *10 Yıl Savaş ve Sonrası (1912–1922)*, 139–147.

366. Erkilet, *Yıldırım*, 258–312; Sanders, *Five Years in Turkey*, 196–204; Wallach, *Bir Askeri Yardımın Anatomisi*, 212–213, 217–218; İnönü, *Hatıralar*, 124–125; M. Neşet, *Büyük Harpte Suriye Cephesinde 48. Piyade Fırkası*, (İstanbul: Askeri Matbaa, 1930), 23–52; Onalp, Üstünsoy, *Birinci Dünya Harbinde Türk Harbi, Sina-Filistin Cephesi*, 536–539.

367. Onalp and Üstünsoy, *Birinci Dünya Harbinde Türk Harbi, Sina-Filistin Cephesi*, 614–619.

368. Sanders, *Five Years in Turkey*, 204–262; Onalp and Üstünsoy, *Birinci Dünya Harbinde Türk Harbi, Sina-Filistin Cephesi*, 540–541.

369. Onalp and Üstünsoy, *Birinci Dünya Harbinde Türk Harbi, Sina-Filistin Cephesi*, 619–676; Güralp, *1918 Yılında Türk Ordusunun Filistin ve Suriye'den Çekilişinde 3. Sv. Tümeninin Harekatı*, 7–18; Sanders, *Five Years in Turkey*, 269–285; İnönü, *Hatıralar*, 128–132; Erickson, *Ottoman Army Effectiveness in World War I*, 140–151; Balkan, *İlk Türk Komitacısı Fuat Balkan'ın Hatıraları*, 708–711; Neşet, *Büyük Harpte Romanya Cephesinde 6. Türk Kolordusu*, 52–90.

370. Onalp and Üstünsoy, *Birinci Dünya Harbinde Türk Harbi, Sina-Filistin Cephesi*, 677–742; Güralp, *1918 Yılında Türk Ordusunun Filistin ve Suriye'den Çekilişinde 3. Sv. Tümeninin Harekatı*, 19–30, 40–41; Sanders, *Five Years in Turkey*, 285–319; Ahmed İzzet, *Feryadım*, 236; İnönü, *Hatıralar*, 132–135; Neşet, *Büyük Harpte Romanya Cephesinde 6. Türk Kolordusu*, 90–101; The cavalry corps of the nationalist Turkish army successfully employed the lessons learned from the battle of Megiddo against Greeks during Turkish Independence War. Altay, *10 Yıl Savaş ve Sonrası (1912–1922)*, 136; Also see Güralp, *1918 Yılında Türk Ordusunun Filistin ve Suriye'den Çekilişinde 3. Sv. Tümeninin Harekatı*, 38.

371. Güleç, *Birinci Dünya Harbinde Türk Harbi, Kafkas Cephesi, 2nci Ordu Harekatı 1916–1918*, 309–318.

372. Altınbilek and Kır, *Birinci Dünya Harbinde Türk Harbi*, 413–506; Sabis, *Harp Hatıralarım*, 165–282; Allen and Muratoff, *Caucasian Battlefields*, 457–467; Reynolds, *Ottoman-Russian Struggle for Eastern Anatolia*, 276–285, 376–396; Nasır Yüceer, *Birinci Dünya Savaşı'nda Osmanlı Ordusu'nun Azerbaycan ve Dağıstan Harekatı*, (Ankara: Genelkurmay Basımevi, 1996), 14–28.

373. Yüceer, *Birinci Dünya Savaşı'nda Osmanlı Ordusu'nun Azerbaycan ve Dağıstan Harekatı*, 72–157; Altınbilek and Kır, *Birinci Dünya Harbinde Türk Harbi*, 507–618; Rüştü Türker, *Birinci Dünya Harbinde Bakü Yollarında 5nci Kafkas Tümeni*, 2nd Edition, (Ankara: Genelkurmay Basımevi, 2006), 20–210; Süleyman İzzet Yeğin, *Birinci Dünya Harbinde Azerbaycan ve Dağıstan Muharebelerinde 15nci Piyade Tümeni*, 2nd Edition, (Ankara: Genelkurmay Basımevi, 2006), 4–15, 65–228; Kut, *İttihat ve Terakki'den Cumhuriyete Bitmeyen Savaş*, 219–246; Allen and Muratoff, *Caucasian Battlefields*, 467–507; Reynolds, *Ottoman-Russian Struggle for Eastern Anatolia*, 436–490; Wallach, *Bir Askeri Yardımın Anatomisi*, 236–238.

374. Ahmed Emin, *Turkey in the World War*, (New Haven: Yale University Press, 1930), 84–91, 107–109, 119–122, 128–130; Özdemir, *Ottoman Army 1914–1918*, 28–133; Altınbilek and Kır, *Birinci Dünya Harbinde Türk Harbi*, 775–778; Baykoç, *Birinci Dünya Savaşı'nda Kafkas ve Irak Cephesi'nde 5nci Seferi Kuvvetler (52nci Tümen)*, 4–12; For the general evaluation of the logistics dimension of war *see* Necmi Koral et al., *Birinci Dünya Harbi İdari Faaliyetler ve Lojistik*, vol. 10, (Ankara: Genelkurmay Basımevi, 1985), passim.

375. İlter, *Birinci Dünya Savaşında Kafkas Cephesi Hatıraları*, 22; McCarthy, *Armenian Rebellion at Van*, 177, 187–191, 195–197.

376. Ann Scoville, *British Logistical Support to Hashemites of Hejaz: Taif to Maan 1916–1918*, (Los Angeles: University of California Unpublished Ph.D. Dissertation, 1982), 22, 38–42, 47.

377. Naci Kaşif Kıcıman, *Medine Müdafaası: Yahud Hicaz Bizden Nasıl Ayrıldı*, (İstanbul: Sebil Yayınevi, 1994), 168–169, 340.

378. Yücel Yanıkdağ, *Ill-fated Sons of the Nation: Ottoman Prisoners of War in Russia and Egypt, 1914–1922*, (Ohio State University Unpublished Ph.D. Dissertation, 2002), 149–150.

379. Eliezer Tauber, *The Arab Movements in World War I*, (London: Frank Cass, 1993), 114–127.

380. H. V. F. Winstone, *The Diaries of Parker Pasha*, (London: Quartet Books, 1983), 181–184; Scoville, *British Logistical Support to Hashemites of Hejaz*, 73–74, 79, 81, 120–122, 126–127.

381. Fırat and Balkış,, *Birinci Dünya Harbinde Türk Harbi, İran-Irak Cephesi*, 356; Erden, *Birinci Dünya Harbinde Suriye Hatıraları*, 315–316.

382. These statistics are derived from Military Academy cadet logbooks, Ministry of Defense Archive (Milli Savunma Bakanlığı Arşiv Müdürlüğü) officer logbooks and several graduation anniversary publications.

383. Unfortunately due to the complex nature of Ottoman military record keeping and archive system, it is very demanding and time consuming to research the files of an entire class.

384. Eliezer Tauber, "The Role of Lieutenant Muhammad Sharif al-Faruqi: New Light on Anglo-Arab Relations during the First World War," *Asian and African Studies*, vol. 24, no. 1, March 1990, 19–20.

385. *The Arab Bulletin: Bulletin of the Arab Bureau in Cairo, 1916–1919*, vol. 2, (Oxford: Archive Editions, 1986), 80; T. E. Lawrence, *Seven Pillars of Wisdom: A Triumph*, (Harmondsworth: Penguin Books, 1969), 49–50; Erden, *Birinci Dünya Harbinde Suriye Hatıraları*, 87–91.

386. Tauber, *Emergence of the Arab Movements*, 60–61; Mohammad Tarbush, *The Role of the Military in Politics: A Case Study of Iraq to 1941*, (London: KPI Ltd., 1985), 116–117; Neşet, *Büyük Harpte Romanya Cephesinde 6. Türk Kolordusu*, 98.

387. Erik Jan Zürcher, "Between Death and Desertion: The Experieces of the Ottoman Soldier in World War I," *Turcica*, vol. 28, 1996, 242–257; İnönü, *Hatıralar*, 126–127; Ahmed

Emin, *Turkey in the World War*, 261–262, 265; Altay, *10 Yıl Savaş ve Sonrası (1912–1922)*, 122; Cebesoy, *Birüssebi-Gazze Meydan Muharebesi ve Yirminci Kolordu*, 18; Ahmet Rifat Çalıka, *Kurtuluş Savaşında Adalet Bakanı Ahmet Rifat Çalıka'nın Anıları*, (ed.) Hurşit Çalıka, (İstanbul: no publisher name, 1992), 20–22.

388. Kressenstein, *Son Haçlı Seferi Kuma Gömülen İmparatorluk*, 30–31; Mühlmann, *Çanakkale Savaşı*, 15–16.

389. Kressenstein, *Son Haçlı Seferi Kuma Gömülen İmparatorluk*, 36–37; Mühlmann, *Çanakkale Savaşı*, 14–15.

Selected Bibliography

Abdurrahman Nafız, and Kiramettin. *1912–1913 Balkan Harbinde İşkodra Müdafaası*. İstanbul: Askeri Matbaa, 1933.

Abou El-Haj, Rifa'at Ali. *Formation of the Modern State: The Ottoman Empire Sixteenth to Eighteenth Centuries*. New York: State University of New York Press, 1991.

Adanır, Fikret. *Makedonya Sorunu Oluşumu ve 1908'e Kadar Gelişimi* (Turkish Translation of the German Original, *Die Makedonische Frage*). (trans.) İhsan Catay. İstanbul: Tarih Vakfı Yurt Yayınları, 1996.

Ágoston, Gábor. *Guns for the Sultan, Military Power and the Weapons Industry in the Ottoman Empire*. Cambridge: Cambridge University Press, 2005.

Ahmet Ağa. *Devlet-i Aliyye Teşrifatçıbaşısı Ahmet Ağa'nın Viyana Kuşatması Günlüğü*. (ed.) Richard F. Kreutel. (trans.) Esat N. Erendor. İstanbul: Aksoy Yayıncılık, 1998.

Ahmed İzzet. *Feryadım*. 2 vols. İstanbul: Nehir Yayınları, 1992.

Ahmed Mithat. *Üss-i İnkılap*. 2 vols. (ed.) T. G. Seratlı. İstanbul: Selis Kitaplar, 2004.

Ahmed Muhtar Paşa [Katırcızade]. *Anılar: Sergüzeşt-i Hayatımın Cildi Evveli*. (ed.) Nuri Akbayar. İstanbul: Tarih Vakfı Yurt Yayınları, 1996.

———. *Anılar: Sergüzeşt-i Hayatımın Cildi Sanisi*. (ed.) Nuri Akbayar. İstanbul: Tarih Vakfı Yurt Yayınları, 1996.

Ahmed Muhtar Paşa. *Feth-i Celil-i Konstantıniyye*. (ed.) Mehmet Ş. Eygi. İstanbul: Bedir Yayınevi, 1994.

———. *Muharebat-ı Meşhure-i Osmaniye Albumu*. (ed.) Kemal Yılmaz. İstanbul: Harp Akademileri Basımevi, 1971.

Akbay, Cemal. *Birinci Dünya Harbinde Türk Harbi*. Vol. 1. Ankara: Genelkurmay Basımevi, 1970.

Akdağ, Mustafa. *Türk Halkının Dirlik ve Düzenlik Kavgası: Celali İsyanları*. Ankara: Barış Yayınları, 1999.

Aksakal, Mustafa. *Defending the Nation: The German-Ottoman Alliance of 1914 and the Ottoman Decision for War*. Princeton: Princeton University Unpublished Ph.D. Dissertation, 2003.

Aksan, Virginia H. *Ottomans and Europeans: Contacts and Conflicts*. İstanbul: The Isis Press, 2004.

———. *An Ottoman Statesman in War and Peace: Ahmed Resmi Efendi 1700–1783*. Leiden: E.J. Brill, 1995.

———. *Ottoman Wars 1700–1870: An Empire Besieged*. Harlow: Pearson, Longman, 2007.

Allen, W. E. D., and Paul Muratoff. *Caucasian Battlefields: A History of the Wars on the Turco-Caucasian Border*. Cambridge: Cambridge University Press, 1953.

Altay, Fahrettin. *10 Yıl Savaş ve Sonrası (1912–1922)*. İstanbul: İnsel Yayınları, 1970.

Altınbilek, Hakkı, and Naci Kır. *Birinci Dünya Harbinde Türk Harbi: Kafkas Cephesi 3ncü Ordu Harekâtı*. Vol. 2, section 1, book 1. Ankara: Genelkurmay Basımevi, 1993.

Andoyan, Aram. *Balkan Savaşı* (Turkish Translation of the Armenian Original, *Badgerazart Intartzag Badmutyun Balkanyan Baderazmin*). (trans.) Zaven Biberyan. İstanbul: Aras Yayıncılık, 1999.

Antoche, Emanuel Constantin. "Du Tabor de Jan Žižka et de Jean Hunyadi au Tabur Çengi des Armées Ottomanes: L'art Militaire Hussite en Europe Orientale, au Proche et au Moyen Orient (XV-XVII siécles)." *Turcica*. vol. 36, 2004.

Apak, Rahmi. *Yetmişlik Bir Subayın Anıları*. Ankara: Türk Tarih Kurumu Basımevi, 1988.

Arkayın, Aşir. *TSK Tarihi Osmanlı Devri İkinci Viyana Kuşatması 1683*. Vol. 3, annex to section 4. Ankara: Genelkurmay Basımevi, 1983.

Arkayın, Aşir, and A. Rıza Bozkurt. *TSK Tarihi Osmanlı Devri İkinci Viyana Kuşatmasından Nizam-ı Cedidin Teşkiline Kadar Olan Devre (1683–1793)*. Vol. 3, section 4. Ankara: Genelkurmay Basımevi, 1982.

Aşıkpaşazade Derviş Ahmed. *Aşıkpaşaoğlu Tarihi*. (ed.) Nihal Atsız. İstanbul: Milli Eğitim Bakanlığı Yayınları, 1992.

al-Askari, Jafar. *A Soldier's Story: From Ottoman Rule to Independent Iraq*. (trans.) Tariq al-Askari. London: Arabian Publishing, 2003.

Atatürk, Mustafa Kemal. *Arıburnu Muharebeleri Raporu*. (ed.) Uluğ İğdemir. Ankara: Türk Tarih Kurumu Basımevi, 1986.

Ayalon, David. *Islam and the Abode of War: Military Slaves and Islamic Adversaries*. Aldershot: Variorum, 1994.

Aydemir, Şevket Süreyya. *Makedonya'dan Orta Asya'ya Enver Paşa*. 3 vols. İstanbul: Remzi Kitabevi, 1985.

Aysan, Emin. *TSK Tarihi Osmanlı Devri Kıbrıs Seferi (1570–1571)*. Vol. 3, annex to section 3. Ankara: Genelkurmay Basımevi, 1971.

Aysan, Emin, and Muzaffer Kan. *TSK Tarihi Osmanlı Devri Yavuz Sultan Selim'in Mısır Seferi Mercidabık (1516) ve Ridaniye (1517)*. Vol. 3, annex to section 2. Ankara: Genelkurmay Basımevi, 1990.

Aysan, Emin, and Nafiz Orhun. *TSK Tarihi Osmanlı-İran Savaşı: Çaldıran Meydan Muharebesi 1514*. Ankara: Genelkurmay Basımevi, 1979.

Aytepe, Hayri, and Lütfü Güvenç. *Türk Silahlı Kuvvetleri Tarihi Osmanlı Devri (1566–1683)*. Vol. 3, section 3. Ankara: Genelkurmay Basımevi, 1981.

Barbir, Karl K. *Ottoman Rule in Damascus 1708–1758*. Princeton: Princeton University Press, 1980.

Barkey, Karen. *Bandits and Bureaucrats: The Ottoman Route to State Centralization*. Ithaca: Cornell University Press, 1994.

Bartlett, Ellis A. *The Battlefields of Thessaly: With Personal Experience in Turkey and Greece*. London: John Murray, 1897.

Bayur, Yusuf Hikmet. *Türk İnkılâbı Tarihi*. 10 vols. Ankara: Türk Tarih Kurumu Basımevi, 1983.

Berkes, Niyazi. *Türkiye'de Çağdaşlaşma*. İstanbul: Doğu-Batı Yayınları, 1978.

Beydilli, Kemal. *Türk Bilim ve Matbaacılık Tarihinde Mühendishane, Mühendishane Matbaası ve Kütüphanesi (1776–1826)*. İstanbul: Eren Yayıncılık, 1995.

Bigham, Clive. *With the Turkish Army in Thessaly*. London: Macmillan and Co., 1897.

Bozkurt, Rıza. *Osmanlı İmparatorluğunda Kollar, Ulak ve İaşe Menzilleri*. Ankara: Genelkurmay Basımevi, 1966.

Brummett, Palmira. *Ottoman Seapower and Levantine Diplomacy in the Age of Discovery*. Albany: State University of New York Press, 1994.

Bryer, Anthony, and Michael Ursinus, eds. *Manzikert to Lepanto: The Byzantine World and the Turks 1071–1571*. Amsterdam: Adolf M. Hakkert, 1991.
de Busbecq, Ogier Ghiselin. *The Turkish Letters of Ogier Ghiselin de Busbecq*. (trans.) Edward S. Forster. Oxford: The Clarendon Press, 1968.
Çakın, Naci, and Nafiz Orhon. *TSK Tarihi Osmanlı Devri (1793–1908)*. Vol. 3, section 5. Ankara: Genelkurmay Basımevi, 1978.
Çakmak, Fevzi. *Birinci Dünya Savaşı'nda Doğu Cephesi*. 2nd edition. Ankara: Genelkurmay Basımevi, 2005.
Carpini, Friar Giovanni DiPlano. *The Story of the Mongols Whom We Call the Tartars*. (ed.) Erik Hildinger. Boston: Branden Publishing, 1996.
Çelik, Bülent. *Osmanlı Sefer Organizasyonlarından Kentli Esnafın Getirdiği Çözümler: Orducu Esnafı*. Ankara: University of Ankara Unpublished Ph.D. Dissertation, 2002.
Cemal Paşa. *Hatıralar*. (ed.) Alpay Kabacalı. İstanbul: Türkiye İş bankası Yayınları, 2006.
Chase, Kenneth. *Firearms: A Global History to 1700*. Cambridge: Cambridge University Press, 2003.
Corvisier, Andre. *Armies and Societies in Europe, 1494–1789*. (trans.) A. T. Siddall. Bloomington: Indiana University Press, 1979.
Çuhadar İlyas Ağa. *Tarih-i Enderun (Letaif-i Enderun)*. (ed.) Cahit Kayra. İstanbul: Güneş Yayınları, 1981.
Cüveyni, Alaaddin Ata Melik. *Tarih-i Cihan Güşa*. (trans.) Mürsel Öztürk. Ankara: Kültür Bakanlığı Yayınları, 1998.
David, Geza. *Studies in Demographic and Administrative History of Ottoman Hungary*. İstanbul: The Isis Press, 1997.
David, Geza, and Pal Fodor, eds. *Hungarian-Ottoman Military and Diplomatic Relations in the Age of Süleyman the Magnificent*. Budapest: Lorand Eötvös University, 1994.
———. *Ottomans, Hungarians, and Habsburgs in Central Europe: The Military Confines in the Era of Ottoman Conquest*. Leiden: E.J. Brill, 2000.
Dirimtekin, Feridun. *Malazgirt Meydan Muharebesi: 26 Ağustos 1017*. İstanbul: Askeri Matbaa, 1936.
Dodd, George. *Pictorial History of the Russian War*. London: W&R Chambers, 1856.
Doğru, Halime. *Osmanlı İmparatorluğunda Yaya-Müsellem-Taycı Teşkilatı: XV. Ve XVI. Yüzyılda Sultanönü Sancağı*. İstanbul: Eren Yayıncılık, 1990.
Dukakinzade Feridun. *Türk Ordusunun Eski Seferlerinden Nezip 1831–1840 Seferi*. İstanbul: Askeri Matbaa, 1931.
Egemen, Rahmi, and Hayri Aytepe. *Türk Silahlı Kuvvetleri Tarihi Osmanlı Devri (1299–1451)*. Vol. 3, section 1. Ankara: Genelkurmay Basımevi, 1964.
Egemen, Rahmi, and Hazım İşgüven. *Türk Silahlı Kuvvetleri Tarihi Osmanlı Devri: Birinci Kosova Meydan Muharebesi*. Vol. 3, section 1 annex. Ankara: Genelkurmay Basımevi, 1987.
Egemen, Rahmi, and Naci Çakın. *Türk Silahlı Kuvvetleri Tarihi: İstanbul'un Fethi 1453*. Vol. 3, annex to section 3. Ankara: Genelkurmay Basımevi, 1979.
Egemen, Rahmi, Lütfü Güvenç, and Rıza Bozkurt. *Türk Silahlı Kuvvetleri Tarihi Osmanlı Devri (1451–1566)*. Vol. 3, section 2. Ankara: Genelkurmay Basımevi, 1977.
Ercan, Yavuz. *Osmanlı İmparatorluğunda Bulgarlar ve Voynuklar*. Ankara: Türk Tarih Kurumu Basımevi, 1989.
Erden, Ali Fuad. *Birinci Dünya Harbinde Suriye Hatıraları*. (ed.) Alpay Kabacalı. İstanbul: Türkiye İş Bankası Yayınları, 2003.

Erickson, Edward J. *Defeat in Detail: The Ottoman Army in the Balkans, 1912–1913*. Westport: Praeger, 2003.

———. *Ottoman Army Effectiveness in World War I: A Comparative Study*. New York: Routledge, 2007.

Erkal, Şükrü. *Birinci Dünya Harbinde Türk Harbi: Hicaz, Asir, Yemen Cepheleri ve Libya Harekâtı*. Vol. 6. Ankara: Genkur Basımevi, 1978.

Erkilet, Hüseyin Hüsnü Emir. *Yıldırım*. 2nd Printing. Ankara: Genelkurmay Basımevi, 2002.

Ertaş, Mehmet Yaşar. *Sultanın Ordusu: Mora Fethi Örneği 1714–1716*. İstanbul: Yeditepe Yayınevi, 2007.

Ertuna, Hamdi. *TSK Tarihi Osmanlı Devri, Osmanlı-İtalyan Harbi (1911–1912)*. Ankara: Genelkurmay Basımevi, 1981.

Fahmy, Khaled. *All the Pasha's Men: Mehmed Ali, His Army and the Making of Modern Egypt*. Cambridge: Cambridge University Press, 1997.

Fine, John V. A. *The Late Medieval Balkans: A Critical Survey from the Late Twelfth Century to the Ottoman Conquest*. Ann Arbor: The University of Michigan Press, 1994.

Finkel, Caroline. *The Government of Warfare: the Ottoman Military Campaigns in Hungary, 1593–1606*. Wien: VWGÖ, 1988.

———. *Osman's Dream: The Story of the Ottoman Empire 1300–1923*. London: John Murray, 2005.

Fırat, Nezihi, and Behzat Balkış. *Birinci Dünya Harbinde Türk Harbi, İran-Irak Cephesi*. Vol. 3, section 1. Ankara: Genelkurmay Basımevi, 1979.

Fodor, Pal. *In Quest of the Golden Apple: Imperial Ideology, Politics and Military Government in the Ottoman Empire*. İstanbul: The Isis Press, 2000.

Goffman, Daniel. *The Ottoman Empire and Early Modern Europe*. Cambridge: Cambridge University Press, 2002.

Gökbilgin, M. Tayyib. *Rumeli'de Yürükler, Tatarlar ve Evlad-ı Fatihan*. İstanbul: Osman Yalçın Matbaası, 1957.

von der Goltz, Colmar. *Osmanlı-Yunan Harbi*. (trans.) Yakub Şevki. İzmir: Akademi Kitabevi, 2001.

Gordon, Matthew S. *The Breaking of a Thousand Swords: A History of the Turkish Military of Samarra (A.H. 200–275/ 815–889 C.E.)*. New York: State University of New York Press, 2001.

Gradeva, Rossitsa. *Rumeli Under the Ottomans, 15th–18th Centuries: Institutions and Communities*. İstanbul: The Isis Press, 2004.

Griffiths, Merwin A. *The Reorganization of the Ottoman Army under Abdülhamid II, 1880–1897*. Los Angeles: University of California Unpublished Ph.D. Dissertation, 1965.

Güleç, Fikri. *Birinci Dünya Harbinde Türk Harbi, Kafkas Cephesi, 2nci Ordu Harekatı 1916–1918*. Vol. 2, section 2. Ankara: Genelkurmay Basımevi, 1978.

Gürel, A. Tevfik. *1853–1855 Türk-Rus ve Müttefiklerin Kırım Savaşı*. İstanbul: Askeri Matbaa, 1935.

Hallı, Reşat. *Balkan Harbi (1912–1913)*. Vol. 1, 2nd printing. Ankara: Genelkurmay Basımevi, 1993.

Hall, Richard C. *The Balkan Wars 1912–1913: Prelude to the First World War*. London: Routledge, 2000.

von Hammer Purgstall, Joseph. *Osmanlı Devleti Tarihi*. Vols. 14–16 (Turkish Translation of the German Original, *Geschichte des Osmanischen Reichs*). (trans.) V. Bürün. İstanbul: Üçdal Neşriyat, not dated.

Har-El, Shai. *Struggle for Domination in the Middle East: The Ottoman-Mamluk War 1485–94*. Leiden: E.J. Brill, 1995.

von Herbert, William. *The Defence of Plevna, 1877*. London: Longmans, Green and Co., 1895.

Hickok, Michael Robert. *Ottoman Military Government in Eighteenth-Century Bosnia*. Leiden: E.J. Brill, 1997.

İbrahim Edhem. *Plevne Hatıraları: Sebat ve Gayret Kıyametten Bir Alamet*. (ed.) Seyfullah Esin. İstanbul: Kervan Kitapçılık, 1979.

İlden, Şerif. *Birinci Dünya Savaşı Başlangıcında 3.Ordu: Sarıkamış Kuşatma Manevrası ve Meydan Savaşı*. (ed.) Sami Önal. İstanbul: İş Bankası Kültür Yayınları,1998.

İlter, Aziz Samih. *Birinci Dünya Savaşında Kafkas Cephesi Hatıraları*. 2nd edition. Ankara: Genelkurmay Basımevi, 2007.

Imber, Colin. *The Ottoman Empire 1300–1481*. İstanbul: The Isis Press, 1990.

İnalcık, Halil. *Essays in Ottoman History*. İstanbul: Eren Yayıncılık, 1998.

———. *Fatih Devri Üzerinde Tetkikler ve Vesikalar*. Vol. 1, 3rd ed. Ankara: Türk Tarih Kurumu Basımevi, 1995.

———. *The Middle East and the Balkans under the Ottoman Empire: Essays on Economy and Society*. Bloomington: Indiana University Turkish Studies, 1993.

İnalcık, Halil, and Donald Quataert, eds. *An Economic and Social History of the Ottoman Empire, 1300–1914*. Cambridge: Cambridge University Press, 1994.

İnbaşı, Mehmet. *Ukrayna'da Osmanlılar: Kamaniçe Seferi ve Organizasyonu (1672)*. İstanbul: Yeditepe Yayınevi, 2004.

İnönü, İsmet. *Hatıralar*. Vol. 1. (ed.) Sebahattin Selek. Ankara: Bilgi Yayınevi, 1985.

İşgüven, Hazım. *TSK Tarihi Osmanlı Devri Otlukbeli Meydan Muharebesi (11 Ağustos 1473)*. Vol. 3, annex to section 2. Ankara: Genelkurmay Basımevi, 1986.

Jennings, Ronald C. *Studies on Ottoman Social History in the Sixteenth and Seventeenth Centuries*. İstanbul: The Isis Press, 1999.

Jorga, Nicolae. *Osmanlı İmparatorluğu Tarihi*. 5 vols (Turkish Translation of German Original, *Geschichte des Osmanischen Reiches*). (trans.) Nilüfer Epçeli. İstanbul: Yeditepe Yayınevi, 2005.

Kaegi Jr., Walter Emil. "The Contribution of Archery to the Turkish Conquest of Anatolia." *Speculum* vol. 39, no. 1, January 1964.

Kafadar, Cemal. *Between Two Worlds: The Construction of the Ottoman State*. Berkeley: University of California Press, 1995.

Karabekir, Kazım. *Hayatım*. (ed.) Faruk Özerengin. İstanbul: Emre Yayınları, 1995.

Karatamu, Selahattin. *Türk Silahlı Kuvvetleri Tarihi (1908–1920)*. Vol. 3, section 6, book 1. Ankara: Genelkurmay Basımevi, 1971.

Keçecizade İzzet Fuat. *Kaçırılan Fırsatlar: 1877 Osmanlı-Rus Savaşı Hakkında Eleştiriler ve Askeri Düşünceler*. (ed.) Rasim Süerdem. Ankara: Genelkurmay Basımevi, 1997.

Kennedy, Hugh. *The Armies of the Caliphs: Military and Society in the Early Islamic State*. London: Routledge, 2001.

Kinglake, Alexander W. *The Invasion of the Crimea: Its Origin and an Account of Its Progress*. 3 vols, 3rd edition. London: William Blackwood, 1863.

Kocagüney, Vehbi. *Erzurum Kalesi ve Savaşları*. İstanbul: Askeri Matbaa, 1942.

Koçi Bey. *Koçi Bey Risalesi*. (ed.) Zuhuri Danışman, 3rd printing. İstanbul: MEB Yayınları, 1997.

Koçu, Reşad Ekrem. *Yeniçeriler*. 2nd Printing. İstanbul: Doğan Kitapçılık, 2004.

Köprülü, M. Fuad. *Bizans Müesseselerinin Osmanlı Müesseselerine Tesiri*. İstanbul: Ötüken Neşriyat, 1981.

———. *The Origins of the Ottoman Empire*. (ed.) Garry Leiser. Albany: State University of New York Press, 1992.

Kortepeter, Carl Max. *The Ottoman Turks: Nomad Kingdom to World Empire*. İstanbul: The Isis Press, 1991.

von Kressenstein, Friedrich Freiherr Kress. *Son Haçlı Seferi Kuma Gömülen İmparatorluk* (Turkish Translation of the German Original, *Mit den Türken zum Suezkanal*). (trans.) Tahir Balaban. İstanbul: Yeditepe Yayınevi, 2007.

Kritovoulos. *History of Mehmed the Conqueror*. (trans.) Charles T. Riggs. Princeton: Princeton University Press, 1954.

Kunt, Metin. *The Sultan's Servants: The Transformation of Ottoman Provincial Government, 1550–1650*. New York: Columbia University Press, 1983.

Kut, Halil. *İttihat ve Terakki'den Cumhuriyete Bitmeyen Savaş: Kutülamare Kahramanı Halil Paşanın Anıları*. İstanbul: 7 Gün Yayınları, 1972.

Lake, Atwell. *Narrative of the Defence of Kars, Historical and Military*. London: Richard Bentley, 1857.

Lev, Yaacov, ed. *War and Society in the Eastern Mediterranean 7th–15th Centuries*. Leiden: E.J. Brill, 1997.

Levy, Avigdor. *The Military Policy of Sultan Mahmud II, 1808–1839*. Cambridge: Harvard University Unpublished Ph.D. Dissertation, 1968.

Lindner, Rudi Paul. *Nomads and Ottomans in Medieval Anatolia*. Bloomington: Indiana University Press, 1983.

Mahmud Muhtar. *Balkan Savaşı: 3. Kolordu ve 2. Doğu Ordusu'nun Muharebeleri*. İstanbul: Güncel Yayıncılık, 2003.

Mahmud Şevket. *Osmanlı Askeri Teşkilatı ve Kıyafeti: Osmanlı Ordusunun Kuruluşundan 1908 Yılına Kadar*. (ed.) N.Türsan, S.Türsan. Ankara: Kara Kuvvetleri Komutanlığı Basımevi, 1983.

May, Timothy. "The Training of an Inner Asian Nomad Army in the Pre-Modern Period." *The Journal of Military History* vol. 70, no. 3, July 2006.

Mehmed Esad. *Mirat-ı Mekteb-i Harbiye*. İstanbul: Artin Asaduryan Matbaası, 1310 [1894].

Mehmed Neşet. *Büyük Harpte Suriye Cephesinde 48. Piyade Fırkası*. İstanbul: Askeri Matbaa, 1930.

Mihailović, Konstantin. *Memoirs of a Janissary*. (trans.) Benjamin Stolz. Ann Arbor: The University of Michigan, 1975.

von Moltke, Helmuth. *The Russians in Bulgaria and Rumelia in 1828 and 1829*. (trans.) Lucie D. Gordon. London: John Murray, 1854.

Monteith, W. *Kars and Erzeroum; with the Campaigns of Prince Paskiewitch in 1828 and 1829*. London: Longman, Brown, Green and Longmans, 1854.

Morier, John Philip. *Memoir of a Campaign with the Ottoman Army in Egypt from February to July 1800*. London: Debrett, 1801.

Mühlmann, Carl. *Çanakkale Savaşı: Bir Alman Subayının Notları* (Turkish Translation of the German Original, *Der Kampf um die Dardanellen 1915*). (trans.) Sedat Umran. İstanbul: Timaş Yayınları, 2004.

Mükerrem. *Türk Ordusunun Eski Seferlerinden Bir İmha Muharebesi Kosova 1389*. İstanbul: Askeri Matbaa, 1931.

Murphey, Rhoads. *The Functioning of the Ottoman Army under Murad IV (1623–1639/ 1032–1049): Key to the Understanding of the Relations between Center and Periphery in

Seventeenth Century Turkey. Chicago: University of Chicago Unpublished Ph.D. Dissertation, 1979.
———. *Ottoman Warfare, 1500–1700*. New Brunswick: Rutgers University Press, 1999.
Mustafa Zarif. "Zarif Paşanın Hatıratı". (ed.) E. Ziya Karal. *Belleten* vol. 4, no. 16, 1.Teşrin 1940.
Necati Salim. *Prut (1711)*. İstanbul: Askeri Matbaa, 1931.
Neşri, Mehmet. *Neşri Tarihi*. 2 vols, (ed.) M. Altay Köymen. Ankara: Kültür Bakanlığı Yayınları, 1983.
Okçu, Yahya. *Birinci Dünya Harbinde Türk Harbi, Sina-Filistin Cephesi*. Vol. 4, section 1. Ankara: Genelkurmay Basımevi, 1979.
Ökse, Necati, and Özden Çalhan. *Birinci Dünya Harbinde Türk Harbi, İran-Irak Cephesi*. Vol. 3, section 2. Ankara: Genelkurmay Basımevi, 2002.
Ömer Halis. *Timur'un Anadolu Seferi ve Ankara Savaşı*. İstanbul: Askeri Matbaa, 1934.
Onalp, Kamil, and Hilmi Üstünsoy. *Birinci Dünya Harbinde Türk Harbi, Sina-Filistin Cephesi*. Vol. 4, section 2. Ankara: Genelkurmay Basımevi, 1986.
Orhonlu, Cengiz. *Osmanlı İmparatorluğunda Derbend Teşkilatı*. 2nd printing. İstanbul: Eren Yayınları, 1990.
Oruç. *Oruç Beğ Tarihi*. (ed.) Nihal Atsız. İstanbul: Kervan Kitapçılık, 1972.
Palmer, J. A. B. "The Origins of the Janissaries." *Bulletin of the John Rylands Library* vol. 35, no. 2, March 1953.
Parker, Geoffrey. *The Military Revolution: Military Innovation and the Rise of the West, 1500–1800*. 2nd Edition. Cambridge: Cambridge University Press, 1996.
Parry, V. J., and M. E. Yapp. *War, Technology and Society in the Middle East*. London: Oxford University Press, 1975.
Parvev, Ivan. *Habsburgs and Ottomans: Between Vienna and Belgrade (1683–1739)*. Boulder: East European Monographs, 1995.
Peçevi İbrahim. *Peçevi Tarihi*. 2 vols, (ed.) Bekir Sıtkı Baykal. Ankara: Kültür Bakanlığı Yayınları, 1999.
Perry, Duncan McVicar. *The Macedonian Cause: A Critical History of the Macedonian Revolutionary Organization, 1893–1903*. Ann Arbor: The University of Michigan Unpublished Ph.D. Dissertation, 1981.
Quataert, Donald. *The Ottoman Empire 1700–1922*. 2nd edition. Cambridge: Cambridge University Press, 2005.
Rafeq, Abdul-Karim. *The Province of Damascus 1723–1783*. Beirut: Khayats, 1966.
Reed, Howard A. *The Destruction of the Janissaries by Sultan Mahmud II in June 1826*. Princeton: Princeton University Unpublished Ph.D. Dissertation, 1951.
Reynolds, Michael A. *The Ottoman-Russian Struggle for Eastern Anatolia and the Caucasus, 1908–1918: Identity, Ideology and the Geopolitics of World Order*. Princeton: Princeton University Unpublished Ph.D. Dissertation, 2003.
Runciman, Steven. *The Fall of Constantinople 1453*. Cambridge University Press, 1965.
Ryan, Charles, and John Sanders. *Under the Red Crescent*. New York: Charles Scribner's Sons, 1897.
Sabis, Ali İhsan. *Harp Hatıralarım: Birinci Dünya Harbi*. 4 vols. İstanbul: Nehir Yayınları, 1990–1991.
von Sanders, Liman. *Five Years in Turkey*. (trans.) Carl Reichmann. Baltimore: The Williams & Wilkins Co., 1928.
Sandwith, Humphry. *A Narrative of the Siege of Kars*. London: John Murray, 1856.

Saral, Muhterem et al. *Birinci Dünya Harbinde Türk Harbi: Çanakkale Cephesi Harekâtı.* Vol. 5, book 1. Ankara: Genkur Basımevi, 1993.

Savaşkurt, Avni. *Kanije Müdafaası.* İstanbul: Askeri Matbaa, 1945.

Schem, A. J. *An Illustrated History of the Conflict between Russia and Turkey with a Review of the Eastern Question.* New York: H. S. Goodspeed & Co., 1878.

Sedes, İ.Halil. *1877–1878 Osmanlı-Rus ve Romen Savaşı.* 11 vols. İstanbul: Askeri Matbaa, 1935–1952.

Selışık, Selahattin. *Kafkas Cephesinde 10 ncu Kolordunun Birinci Dünya Savaşının Başlangıcından Sarıkamış Muharebelerinin Sonuna Kadar Olan Harekâtı.* 2nd edition. Ankara: Genelkurmay Basımevi, 2006.

Şeref. *Muhaç Meydan Muharebesi: 1526 (Türk-Macar) Seferi.* İstanbul: Askeri Matbaa, 1930.

Shaw, Stanford J. *Between Old and New: The Ottoman Empire Under Sultan Selim III 1789–1807.* Cambridge: Harvard University Press, 1971.

Shaw, Stanford J., and Ezel K. Shaw. *History of the Ottoman Empire and Modern Turkey.* 2 vols. Cambridge: Cambridge University Press, 1976–1978.

Simon, Rachel. *Between Ottomanism and Nationalism: The Ottoman Involvement in Libya during the War with Italy (1911–1919).* Berlin: Klaus Schwarz Verlag, 1987.

Sinor, Denis, ed. *The Cambridge History of Early Inner Asia.* Cambridge: Cambridge University Press, 1990.

Slade, Adolphus. *Turkey and the Crimean War: A Narrative of Historical Events.* London: Smith, Elder, 1867.

Solakzade Mehmed Hemdeni Çelebi. *Solakzade Tarihi.* 2 vols, (ed.) Vahid Çabuk. Ankara: Kültür Bakanlığı Yayınları, 1989.

Stoye, John. *The Siege of Vienna.* London: Collins, 1964.

Süer, Hikmet. *1877–1878 Osmanlı-Rus Harbi Rumeli Cephesi.* Ankara: Genelkurmay Basımevi, 1993.

———. *TSK Tarihi Osmanlı Devri Osmanlı-Rus Kırım Harbi Kafkas Cephesi Harekatı (1853–1856).* Ankara: Genelkurmay Basımevi, 1986.

Sugar, Peter F. *Southeastern Europe under Ottoman Rule, 1354–1804.* Seattle: University of Washington Press, 1977.

Sun, Selim. *1897 Osmanlı-Yunan Harbi.* Ankara: Genelkurmay Basımevi, 1965.

Sükan, Şadi. *TSK Tarihi Osmanlı Devri 1877–1878 Osmanlı-Rus Harbi Kafkas Cephesi Harekâtı.* Ankara: Genelkurmay Basımevi, 1985.

Tacan, Necati. *Batı Türklerinin (Osmanlılar) Teessüs ve İstila Devirlerinde Harb Güdemi Usulleri.* İstanbul: Askeri Matbaa, 1936.

Tallett, Frank. *War and Society in Early-Modern Europe, 1495–1715.* London: Routledge, 1992.

Torday, Laszlo. *Mounted Archers: The Beginnings of Central Asian History.* Durham: The Durham Academic Press, 1997.

Turfan, M. Naim. *Rise of the Young Turks: Politics, the Military and Ottoman Collapse.* London: I. B. Tauris, 2000.

Türk Ordusunu Eski Seferlerinde İki İmha Muharebesi. İstanbul: Askeri Matbaa, 1930.

Tursun Bey. *Fatih'in Tarihi: Tarih-i Ebul Feth.* (ed.) Ahmet Tezbaşar. İstanbul: Kervan Kitapçılık, not dated.

Uluçay, M. Çağatay. *XVII. Asırda Saruhan'da Eşkiyalık ve Halk Hareketleri.* İstanbul: Resimli Ay Matbaası, 1944.

Uluçay, Çağatay, and Enver Kartekin. *Yüksek Mühendis Okulu.* İstanbul: Berksoy Matbaası, 1958.

Uzunçarşılı, İsmail Hakkı. *Osmanlı Devleti Teşkilatından Kapukulu Ocakları*. 2 vols. Ankara: Türk Tarih Kurumu Basımevi, 1988.

———. *Osmanlı Tarihi*. 6 vols. Ankara: Türk Tarih Kurumu, 1995.

Vryonis Jr., Speros. *The Decline of Medieval Hellenism in Asia Minor and the Process of Islamization from the Eleventh through the Fifteenth Century*. Berkeley: University of California Press, 1971.

Wallach, Jehuda L. *Bir Askeri Yardımın Anatomisi* (Turkish Translation of the German Original, *Anatomie einer Miltaerhilfe*). (trans.) Fahri Çeliker. Ankara: Genelkurmay Basımevi, 1977.

Wittek, Paul. *The Rise of the Ottoman Empire: Studies on the History of Turkey 13th–15th Centuries*. London: Routledge, 2002.

Wittman, William. *Travels in Turkey, Asia-Minor, Syria and Across the Desert into Egypt during the Years 1799, 1800 and 1801*. London: Richard Phillips, 1803.

Woods, John E. *The Aqquyunlu: Clan, Confederation, Empire*. Salt Lake City: The University of Utah Press, 1999.

Yaramış, Ahmet, and Mehmet Güneş, eds. *Askeri Kanunnameler (1826–1827)*. Ankara: Asil Yayın, 2007.

Yiğitgüden, Remzi et al. *Birinci Dünya Harbinde Türk Harbi: Çanakkale Cephesi Harekâtı*. Vol. 5, book 2. Ankara: Genkur Basımevi, 1978.

Yüceer, Nasır. *Birinci Dünya Savaşı'nda Osmanlı Ordusu'nun Azerbaycan ve Dağıstan Harekâtı*. Ankara: Genelkurmay Basımevi, 1996.

Yücel, Ünal. *Türk Okçuluğu*. Ankara: Atatürk Kültür Merkezi Yayınları, 1998.

Zachariadou, Elizabeth A., ed. *Ottoman Emirate 1300–1389*. Heraklion: Crete University Press, 1993.

Ziya, Rahmi. *Girit Seferi*. İstanbul: Askeri Matbaa, 1933.

Index

Abbasid caliphs, 6, 7–8
Abdülhamid I, Sultan, 119, 176
Abdülhamid II, Sultan, 177, 213, 217, 249; command and control by, 183–84, 198, 206, 219–20; constitution and, 183, 218; Hamidian army and, 202–5; military reorganized by, 202–6, 211; war with Greece and, 209–11; war with Russia and, 185, 187, 189–90, 192, 195, 201
Abdülhaziz, Sultan, 200, 201, 202; coup d'état and, 182–83, 192; military schools and, 176–77, 203
Abdullah Efendi, Tartarcik, 120
Abdullah Pasha, 227, 228
Abdülmecid, Sultan, 160, 161, 168, 172
Abkazian rebellion, 194
Acemi Ocaği training, 18, 37, 41, 47, 51, 91
Adana, battle of (1486), 68–69
Administration, 23, 133, 215, 216, 240; law enforcement, 212; Sipahi, 57. See also Bureaucracy
Adrianople. See Edirne
Ahis (artisan guilds), 13, 15
Ahiska fortress, siege of, 138
Ahmed I, Sultan, 31
Ahmed Pasha, 162, 163
Ahmed Pasha, Cezzar, 123
Ahmed Pasha, Humbaraci, 115
Ahmed Pasha, Kayserli, 184
Akhirman, siege of (1484), 68
Akinci raiders, 20, 28, 36, 45, 74, 87; in battle of Kosovo, 25, 26; Delis compared to, 60; as frontier units, 57–60
Akkoyunlu, 46, 69
Akritai (border guards), 9, 11

Alaeddin Paşa, 15
Alan mercenaries, 10, 12
Alayli (commissioned officers), 147, 177, 178, 197, 199, 202, 216; purge of, 221, 234; recalled, for World War I, 243
Albania (Albanians), 126, 181, 203, 216, 254; conquest of (1456–1478), 72; in imperial guard, 204–5; mercenaries from, 93, 94, 124, 136, 141; nationalism in, 229, 230, 236
Al-Baruni, Sulayman, 252
Alexander II, Tsar of Russia, 185, 191
Alexious Philanthropens, 13
Al Hashimi, Yasin, 277
Ali Pasha, Mehmed, 189–90, 191, 192, 197–98
Ali Pasha, Tepedelenli, 143
Allenby, Edmund, 266, 269, 270
Al-Mutasim, Caliph, 7
Alp Arslan, Sultan, 1, 5
Al-Sharif, Sidi Ahmad, 251
Amcazade Hüseyin Pasha, 105
Amphibious landing, 150, 158, 170, 231; at Gallipoli, 258, 259–60
Anatolia, 120, 172, 245, 272; counterinsurgency in, 217; expansion into, 24; Ibrahim Pasha in, 160–61; mercenaries from, 136; nomadic rebellions in, 71; rebellions in, 94; Redifs (reserves) from, 200, 210
Andronikov (Russian general), 165
Ankara, battle of (1402), 27–28, 69
Arabaci (wagoner) corps, 90
Arab nationalism, 236–37, 275, 277
Arab provinces, 203. See also Egypt; Iraq; Syria
Arab revolt, 253, 267, 274–77
Arab tribes, 6, 204–5

Archery, 4, 24, 25, 42. *See also* Composite bows
Arif (Ayici) Bey, Mehmet, 241
Aristocrats, 36, 63; estates (Timars) of, 53–54
Armenia, 139, 141, 194, 201, 246, 250; nationalism in, 213, 236; rebellion in (1894), 204, 208; rebellion in (1915), 262–63, 274
Armorers (Cebecis), 49–50, 90
Army corps headquarters, 220–21
Army of Islam, 272
Artillery corps, 25, 42, 50, 90, 258; Krupp cannon and, 200; in Mansure army, 141, 144; officers for, 177–78, 210; Prussian advisors in, 205; Russian, 138, 139, 190, 191; in siege of Constantinople, 32, 33, 34, 36; Topçu Ocağı, 46–48
Artisan guilds, 13, 15, 85, 91
Asakir-i Mansure-i Muhammediya. *See* Mansure army
Askeri, Cafer, 251
Askeri Bey, Süleyman, 223, 254, 255–56, 257
Askeri class, 6, 55, 63, 79
Atatürk, Mustafa Kemal, 223, 241, 268, 271, 283; at Gallipoli, 259, 260; at Tobruk, 218
Austro-Hungarian Empire, 219, 237, 263, 264, 274, 283. *See also* Hapsburgs
Aviation, 224, 234
Avni Bey, Hüseyin, 241
Aydinid emirate, 11, 15
Azabs (semi–mercenaries), 20–21, 25, 37, 61–62; combat formations and, 42, 48, 50, 55, 70
Azerbaijan, 71, 138, 248, 266, 272

Babur Khan, 51
Baghdad, 203, 255, 267; fall of, 75, 82
Bahrain, 254
Baker Pasha, Valentine, 198
Balaclava, battle of, 167–68
Balkan Corps, 185, 187, 189, 191, 192, 198
Balkan League, 222
Balkan states, 26, 28, 203, 242, 262; aristocrats of, 63; castles in, 22; Christian military of, 282; nationalism in, 141, 180–81; Ottoman conquest, 22–23, 54, 73; Redifs (reserves) from, 200; Turkoman mercenaries in, 21–22; vassal policy in, 24; in war with Russians (1877–1878), 185, 187, 190, 197
Balkan Wars (1912–1913), 175, 211, 219–35, 236, 243, 258, 273; counterinsurgency in, 226, 233, 260, 278; Libyan invasion and, 218, 222–25; mobilization for, 226–27
Baltic fleet, 117
Banditry (Harami), 57–58, 212; rebellion and, 96–98, 181, 274
Bapheus, battle of (1301), 12
Başıbozuk cavalry, 136, 142, 144, 160, 161; British recruitment of, 172–73; lawlessness of, 200
Basra, 76, 254
Battles. *See* Combat/battle formation; specific battles
Bayezid I, Sultan, 2, 26, 27, 38, 46; Akinci power base and, 58
Bayezid II, Sultan, 53, 67–69, 70
Beatson (British general), 173
Bebutov (Russian commander), 162, 166
Bedouins, 108, 250, 253
Bekir Fikri, 230
Bektaşi religious order, 39
Belgrade, 106; siege of (1456), 66–67; siege of (1521), 73
Bem, Jozef (Murad Pasha), 152
Bergmann (Russian general), 245–46
Berlin Peace Treaty, 201, 202, 213, 226
Bismarck, Otto von, 183
Bithynia, 13
Black Sea region, 107, 118, 245, 247; Crimean War in, 162, 164; naval raids in, 243
Boer War, 216
Bombardiers, 51–52, 115, 121
Bombards, 32, 34, 47
Bonneval, Claude Alexandre Comte de, 115
Bosnia, 52, 59, 65, 135, 141; in Austro-Hungarian Empire, 219; border defense units in, 106; Janissaries in, 128;

mercenaries from, 93, 94; recruitment from, 115, 121; resistance in, 130
Bosquet (French general), 167
British (Great Britain), 150, 217, 265–66, 270, 271; in Crimean War, 157–58, 162–63, 164, 166–67; at Gallipoli, 260, 261; intelligence, 275; in Iraq, 253–57; Mahsusas and, 251–52; military advisors, 160, 171, 201; military embargo and, 201; navy of, 123, 176, 254; Ottoman rigidity and, 183; Suez Canal and, 250, 252
British India, 244, 254, 255–57
Bucharest Treaty (1812), 126
Bulgaria, 141, 243, 251, 254, 264, 272; autonomy of, 201, 202; in Balkan Wars, 227–28, 230, 231; Greece and, 255; counterinsurgency in, 183; independence of, 213, 219; volunteers from, 186
Bureaucracy, 27, 37, 281, 282; financial, 47, 89, 281; Murad I and, 23, 24; reformist, 109, 111, 116
Burg bastion, siege of, 101
Byzantines, 21–22, 34–35; military system of, 8–10; Seljukid defeat of, 1–2, 5; wars with Ottomans, 12, 13–14. *See also* Constantinople

Cairo, 72, 123, 275
Çaldiran, battle of (1514), 51
Camels and camel drivers, 63, 85
Canbulatoğlu of Syria, 97
Candia (Kandiya) siege of, 101
Canning, Stratford, 161, 172, 173
Cannon, 33, 36, 46–47, 141, 144; bombards, 32, 34, 47; foundries for, 32, 46, 48, 117, 122; Krupp, 200; logistics and, 86; transport of, 51. *See also* Artillery corps
Cannoneers (Topçus), 89, 105
Caprara (Habsburg envoy), 99
Catalan Company, 22
Çatalca, battles of, 193, 228, 231, 235
Caucasus region, 161, 245, 249–50; in Crimean War, 159, 160, 161, 164–65, 168; mercenaries from, 10, 12, 93, 124; in wars with Russia, 136, 137–39, 141, 142, 185, 193–96; in World War I, 272
Cavalry (horsemen), 69, 129, 245, 274; Başibozuk, 136, 142, 144, 160, 161, 172–73, 200; Cossack, 153, 173, 180, 204; in Crimean War, 162; Deli, 59–60, 74, 126; European system, 158; in Sarikamis campaign, 246–47; steppe-nomadic tradition, 3; Süvaris, 44–46, 88, 90, 121; Timariot, 53–57, 115, 212, 274, 281; Turcoman, 17, 132. *See also* Sipahis
Cebecis (armorers), 49–50, 90, 128
Cebeli (armed retinue), 17, 92
Celaeddin Pasha, Mustafa (Konstanty Borzecki), 153
Celali rebellions, 96–98, 112
Çelebi Mehmed Efendi, Yirmisekiz, 112–13
Cemal Pasha, Büyük, 250, 265
Central Asian traditions. *See* Steppe-nomadic tradition
Cerehor/Serehor mercenaries, 64
Černomen, battle of (1371), 23
Çeşme, 117
Charles of Lorraine, 100–101
Child tribute system.*See* Devşirme
Chilia, siege of (1484), 68
Christians, 24, 28, 63–66, 147; Balkan, 141, 227; in battle of Kosovo, 29; as collaborators, 185; conversion to Islam, 13, 54; Cossacks, 132, 133; Devşirme, 19; disloyalty of, 105; Martoloses, 58, 63–64, 65, 83; as mercenaries, 61, 62, 63, 94, 141; nationalism and, 130, 180; Orthodox, 157, 183; Reaya, 64–65; recruitment of, 221
Circassians, 165, 194
Civil war, 28
Çobanid beys, 11, 117
Çolok, battle of (1854), 165
Combat/battle formation, 45; Janissary, 42–43, 51; Sipahi cavalry, 55–56; steppe-nomadic tradition, 3–4, 12; Tabur Cengi, 42, 48, 50–51, 56, 70, 90
Command-and-control structure, 8, 118, 217, 237, 246; Abdlhamid II and, 183–84, 198, 206, 219–20; Crimean War,

160, 161; Janissary, 40–41; Mahmud's reforms of, 144–46; in Ottoman-Russian War (1877–1878), 183–84, 198–99; reform of, 179; Russian, 187; Sipahi cavalry, 55; steppe-nomadic tradition, 4; in war with Greece (1897), 209

Committee of Union and Progress. *See* CUP

Composite bow, 3, 21, 62; Janissary, 19, 41, 42

Conscription system, 129, 154, 155–56, 174, 180; Arab opposition to, 274–75; Crimean War, 159; Hamidian army, 204; provincial nature of, 160; Prussian, 178–79; in war with Russians (1877–1878), 187

Constantinople, 9, 11; conquest of (1453), 31, 32–36, 37, 46. *See also* Istanbul

Constitution, 156–57, 183; restored, 218, 219

Corruption, 91, 110, 140, 156, 166, 201

Cossacks, 106, 132, 133, 141; cavalry, 153, 173, 180, 204

Counterinsurgency campaigns, 181, 183, 211–19, 223; in Armenia, 263; in Balkan Wars, 226, 233, 260, 278; guerrilla warfare and, 214–17, 249; Komitaci groups in, 130, 154, 214–15, 216; officer corps and, 212, 214, 215–18, 279, 283; Turkish nationalism and, 216–17

Coup d'état, 182–83, 211, 217, 230, 231–32

Crete, 208, 219; campaigns in (1645–1669), 82, 88, 101; insurgency in, 213–14

Crimea, 116; Tatars of, 59, 60, 63, 68, 84, 118

Crimean War, 130, 151, 157–74, 176, 185; Britain and France in, 157–58, 162–63, 164, 166–67; Gökdere disaster in, 148, 166, 172; modernization in, 170, 171; refugee officers in, 152–53, 160, 171, 198; Russia in, 152, 157–58, 161–70, 171; and war with Russia (1878–1888) compared, 198, 200, 201

Crusaders, 9, 11; at battle of Nicopolis, 26–27

CUP (Committee of Union and Progress), 223, 225, 237, 239, 272; in Balkans Wars, 230; coupe d'état and, 231–32; and officer corps purge, 221; in Sarikamiş campaign, 245, 249

Currency, debasement of, 87, 91

Cyprus, conquest of, 52

Czajkowski, Michal, 153

Damascus, 107–8, 203, 243, 271

Danube border, 27, 77, 105; in Crimean War, 158–59, 160, 163; in wars with Russians, 136, 137, 141, 185, 186

Danube flotilla, 66, 67, 73, 84

Dardanelles, 244, 259

Davud Ağa, 131

Deli (daredevil) cavalry, 59–60, 74, 126

Derbendcis, 62–63, 64, 83

Dervishes, 13, 14

Derviş Pasha, Lofçali, 181, 193, 196, 199, 202

Desertion, in World War I, 277–78

De Tott, François Baron, 117, 118–19

Devşirme, 19, 37–38, 90, 93

Diebitsch (Russian commander), 139, 164

Dobruca, 136–37

Dutch Republic, 87

Edhem Pasha, 206, 209–10

Edirne (Adrianople), 32, 164, 187, 193; in Balkan Wars, 227, 231–32; battle of (1352), 22; Treaty of (1829), 158

Edward VII, King of England, 217

Eflak (Vlach) groups, 64, 83

Eger, siege of (1596), 77

Egypt, 8, 63, 72, 75, 251; Arab nationalism in, 275; French conquest of, 123–24; under Mehmed Ali Pasha, 126–27, 130–31, 146, 222; provincial army of, 149–50, 199; Suez Canal campaign in, 244, 250, 252, 265

Elite. *See* Governing elite

Enderun (palace school), 134–35

Engineers, 47, 52–53

Entente powers (France, England, Russia), 175, 239, 272

Enver Bey, 223, 230, 232, 236, 237
Enver Pasha, 238–39, 252, 254, 257, 264, 266; at Gallipoli, 260, 262; Iraq and, 255, 256; officer purge by, 241, 278; Pan-Turkish dream of, 272; Sarikamis campaign and, 245, 246, 247, 248, 249
Erlich, Back von, 240
Ertuğrul Bey, 11
Erzurum fortress, 169, 195–96, 262
Erzurum Armistice Protocol (1917), 271
Esat (Bülkat) Pasha, 241
Eşkinci (campaigner) project, 127–28
Eşref Bey, Kuşçubaşizade, 253
Estergon fortress, 77, 78
European militaries, 81, 82, 113, 114, 129; Mansure officers and, 132; Nizam–i Cedid reforms and, 121, 122; officer training in, 150; rebellion in, 94–95; Spanish Army of Flanders, 94–95; technology from, 47; transformation of, 111. *See also* specific country
Eyalet Askerleri. *See* Provincial army
Eyüp Pasha, Ahmed, 189, 190

Fahreddin Pasha, 253
Faisal, Sherif, 277
Famagusta, siege of, 52–53
Family farm system (Çiftlik), 23–24
Fethi Bey, 247
Fevzi Çakmak, 273
Feyzi (Collman) Pasha, 196, 198
Finance, 87–89, 107, 202–3, 281, 282; currency debasement, 87, 91; salaries, 41, 87, 88, 91
Firearms, 49, 63, 90; arquebus, 50, 62; introduction of, 5, 29, 82; of Janissaries, 38, 42, 74, 90, 99; logistics and, 86; machine guns, 218, 242, 265; muskets, 50, 62, 74, 79, 90, 91, 92, 96, 108; rebellions and, 97, 98; rifles, 171, 188, 200, 201, 211
Firka-i Islahiyye, 181
First (Dersaadet) Army, 179
Foreign debt/loans, 171, 202, 211, 243
Fortress garrisons, 61, 90, 107, 179, 258; Hungarian, 54, 83, 100; Janissaries in, 89; in war with Russia, 136–37, 185

Foundations, of Ottoman military, 10–30; crossing into Europe, 21–30; Gazi warriors, 10–15, 18, 21; Janissaries, 17, 18–21, 26–27; Kosovo battles, 23, 24–26, 29–30
France, 26, 78, 223, 261; Çelebi Mehmed in, 112–13; conquest of Egypt by, 123–24; in Crimean War, 157–58, 162–63, 164, 166–67; military embargo and, 201; under Napoleon, 123, 126, 132, 134; Ottoman rigidity and, 183.
Frederick the Great, king of Prussia, 116
French advisors, 122, 127, 134, 172; de Tott, 117, 118–19
French military model, 81; in academy curriculum, 151, 207; for officer training, 146–47, 148
Frontier units (Serhat), 57–61
Fuat (Cebesoy) Pasha, Ali, 269

Gallipoli, 175, 219, 231, 236; assault on (1311), 21, 22; dockyards in, 33; Janissary training center in, 18, 37; in World War I, 238, 241, 258–62, 263, 270, 272–73
Gaza and Beersheba, battle of (1916), 265–66, 268, 270
Gazi warriors, 10–15, 18, 21, 57
Gedikler, battle of (1854), 162, 163, 172
Gendarmerie, 211–12, 230, 253, 263
General Staff, 206, 220, 223, 242, 254, 255; in Balkan Wars, 226, 231, 233, 234, 235; at Gallipoli, 259, 260, 262; German military and, 237, 238–40, 241, 253, 264, 278; Mansure army, 145–46; Sarikamiş campaign and, 243, 245, 247; at Sinai-Palestine, 265; in war with Greece, 210, 211
General Staff College, 207
Georgia, 126, 247, 272
German doctrine, 217, 226, 234
German military advisors, 175, 205, 206–8, 267–68, 279; General Staff, 237, 238–40, 241, 253, 264, 278; officer corps and, 198; prior to World War I, 237–40, 241, 242; in war with Greece, 209, 211
Germany, in World War I, 243, 283

Germiyanid emirate, 14
Ghulams (military slaves), 6–8
Gladstone, William, 183
Gökdere disaster, 148, 166, 172
Gönder, 65
Gönüllü (volunteers), 61
Gouffier, Choiseul, 119
Governing elite, 81, 98, 104, 153; CUP leadership and, 236; death of Mehmed II and, 96; finance and, 87, 89; foreign policy and, 118; German, 237; infighting among, 116–17; modernization and, 129; officer training and, 151; personal retinue of, 92; printing and, 113; reforms and, 111, 119. *See also* Bureaucracy;
Great Britain. *See* British
Great Powers, 208, 212–13, 235, 258, 282; competition of, 236; intervention by, 215, 216, 231
Greece, 143, 219, 255; in Balkan Wars, 227, 229, 230, 233, 234; nationalism in, 213, 214; rebellion in, 117, 126, 127, 131, 132, 148; war with Ottomans, 208–11
Guerrilla warfare, 208, 224, 245, 247, 249, 255; in Balkans Wars, 230; in Caucasus front, 165, 249–50; counterinsurgency and, 214–17; Mahsusa bands (Teskilat-i Mahsusa), 247, 249–50, 251, 252–55, 256–58; in war with Russia (1877–1878), 193, 196, 200
Guilds, 13, 15, 85, 91
Gunpowder mills, 47, 48, 122
Gurebas, 44, 45
Guyon, Richard Debaufre, 152

Habsburgs, 57, 77–78, 82, 85, 111; alliance with Poland, 81, 99, 102, 103; campaign against, 94; defensive strategy against, 105; fortress renovation by, 74; siege of Vienna and, 100–102; war with (1737–1739), 106; World War I and, 243, 244. *See also* Austro-Hungarian Empire; Long War
Haci Ilbeyi, 23
Haci Mehmed, 56
Hafiz Pasha, 148

Haj (pilgrimage), 107, 108
Hakki Bey, Hafiz, 247, 248, 249
Hakki Pasha, Ismail, 195
Halil Ece, 22
Halil Kut Bey, 223
Halil Pasha, 257, 267
Halil Pasha, Çandarh, 32
Hamidian army, 202–11, 222, 234, 236; German advisors and, 205, 206–8, 209; in war with Greece, 208–11
Hamidid archers, 24, 25
Hamid Pasha, Halil, 119
Hand grenades (elkumbarasi), 42, 50
Harami. *See* Banditry
Hasan Kafi, 110
Hasan Pasha, Cezayirli Gazi, 119, 164
Hasan Pasha, Sabri, 196, 199
Has estates, 53
Hassa (imperial guard), 131, 149, 179
Hayri Pasha, Hasan, 186–87
Hejaz, 143, 252–53; Sharifian emirate of, 75, 252, 275
Hekimoğlu Ali Pasha, 106
Heliopolis, battle of (1800), 124
Hendesehane military school, 115, 119, 127
Herbert, William von, 198
Herzegovina, 219
Hildburghausen, Prince, 106
Holy Alliance, War of (1684–1690), 86, 95, 103–4
Horsemen. *See* Cavalry (horsemen)
Huguenot project, 113
Hulâsatü'l Itibar (Resmi), 118
Humbaraci (bombardiers), 51–52, 115, 121
Hungary, 28–29, 65, 78; Akinci raids on, 26; cannon foundry and mills in, 48; fortress building in, 59, 83, 100; Ottoman interests in, 86, 99, 103; refugee officers from, 152, 160, 171; siege victories in, 47. *See also* Austro-Hungarian Empire
Hunting parties, 4, 38
Hunyadi, John, 28–29, 66
Hursid Pasha (Richard Debaufre Guyon), 166

Hüseyin Pasha, Avni, 178, 179, 182, 183, 193
Husrevbegova, 59
Hüsrev Pasha, Mehmed, 133–34, 135, 139, 145; officer training and, 146–47, 148–49; Redif (reserve) training and, 155

Ibn Khaldun, 110
Ibn Saud of Najd, Abd al-Aziz, 253
Ibrahim Pasha, 112, 113, 127, 143–44, 150
Idris al-Mahdi, Muhammad, 252
Imperial guard, 204–5; Hassa, 131, 149, 179
Imperial Medical School, 153
Imperial Naval Engineering School, 176
India. See British India
Infantry. See Janissaries; Yaya corps
Inner Macedonian Revolutionary Organization (IMRO), 214, 215
Insurgency, campaigns against. See Counterinsurgency campaigns
Intellectuals, 182
Intelligence gathering, 246, 250, 269; British, 275; reconnaissance and, 185, 233, 256
Internal security, 180, 274
Iqta system, 6, 8, 17
Iran, 255, 266–67; Azerbaijan and, 71, 138, 248, 266; campaigns against, 84, 85, 93, 94; neutrality of, 165; Shiite propaganda, 69, 70. See also Persian Safavids
Iraq, World War I in, 253–57, 266
Isa Bey (Isakoğlu), 59
Islam: conversion to; 13, 54, 60, 113, 115, 152; Devşirme and, 38, 93
Islamic law (Sharia), 19, 24
Islamic military system, 6–8
Ismail, shah of Persia, 70–71
Ismail Pasha, 214
İsmet (İnönü) Bey, 278
Istanbul, 36, 44, 120, 124, 185; cannon foundry in, 46; cavalry units in, 45; rebellion in, 114; Sarikamis campaign and, 243, 244; training center in, 37. See also Constantinople

Italy, 214, 215, 236; invasion of Libya by, 218, 222–25, 251, 252, 256
İzzet Pasha, Ahmed, 220, 225, 237, 263–64
İzzet Pasha, Hasan, 245, 246

Jam, battle of (1527), 51
Jandarma, 212–13. See also Gendarmerie
Janissaries, 1, 17, 18–20, 36–44, 124; at Angora, 27; Azabs and, 20–21, 42; in battle against Mamluks, 72; cavalry (Süvaris) and, 45–46; combat formations, 42–43, 48, 51, 56, 70; command-control structure of, 40–41; criminal element within, 121; Devşirme, 19, 37–38, 90, 93; disbanding of, 81, 128, 129, 130, 133; élan and cohesion in, 39, 41; in fortress garrisons, 89; loyalty of, 32, 41; military identity and, 31; at Nicopolis (1396), 26–27; nomad rebellion and, 71; officer corps of, 39–41, 43; Orta regiment, 38; pensions for, 41; rebellions by, 108, 126, 128; reform of, 127–28; reorganization of, 37; sons of (Kulogus), 90, 91, 204; standardization in, 37, 281; training of (Acemi Ocağı), 18, 37, 41, 47, 51, 91; urban middle class and, 91; in war with Russia, 107; weaponry of, 38, 41–42, 49, 50, 74, 99
Jerusalem, battle of, 269, 270
Jewish refugees, 113–14
Jihad, 14, 251

Kadi Abdurrahman Pasha, 125
Kaehler (German officer), 205, 206, 220
Kahlenberg, battle of, 102
Kalafat, 163
Kaletülmeydan, battle of (1840), 150
Kampel Mustafa Aga (Ramsay Campbell), 119, 124
Kanitzsa, seige of (1601), 93
Kapikulu corps, 17, 27, 28, 36–53, 61; commercial activities of, 91; demise of, 109, 110–11; in Istanbul, 124; Janissaries and, 20, 36–44; in Kosovo battles, 25, 26, 29; mercenaries compared to, 93, 94; new regulations

for, 121; renewal of, 126; salaries paid to, 91; in seige of Constantinople, 33, 36; Sipahis and, 96; Süvaris (cavalry), 44–46, 88, 90, 121; technical corps of, 127, 128, 131; Timars awarded to, 54; war wagons of, 29
Kara Halil, Çandarli, 13, 15, 18
Karamanids of Anatolia, 24, 33, 94
Karamanlis dynasty of Lybia, 222
Kara Rüstem of Karaman, 18
Karesi emirate, 21, 22
Karlowitz, Treaty of (1699), 103, 105, 282
Kars fortress, 166, 168, 196; siege of, 138, 169, 171
Kartal, battle of (1770), 117
Kazanci Doğan, 32
Kemal, Mustafa. *See* Atatürk, Mustafa Kemal
Khorasan army, 6
Knez Lazar, 25, 26
Knights of St. John, 73
Koca Sekbanbasi Risalesi, 122
Koçi Bey, 109
Komitaci groups, 214–15, 216, 230, 254
Köprüköy, battle of (1914), 246
Köprülü viziers, 110, 112, 246
Kosovo: battle of (1389), 23, 24–26, 46; battle of (1448), 29–30, 50
Kossuth, Lajos, 152
Kressenstein, Friedrich Freiherr Kress von, 240, 265, 266, 268–69
Küçük Kaynarca, Treaty of (1774), 118
Kuloğlus, 90, 91, 204
Kundukov Pasha, Musa, 198
Kurdish tribes, 60–61, 108, 126, 165, 236; loyalty of, 246; in war with Russia, 136, 138, 139
Kütahya, Treaty of (1833), 144
Kut al-Amara, battle of (1916), 256–57, 262, 266

Lağimci (miner) corps, 34, 52–53, 90
Landownership, 27, 92, 121. *See also* Timar system
Lascarids of Nicaea, 9
Latas, Michael, 145
Law enforcement, 182, 212. *See also* Gendarmerie

Lawrence, T. E., 253
Lebanon, rebellion in, 181
Leopold I, Emperor of Austria, 100–101
Lepanto, battle of (1571), 82
Levend mercenaries, 91–94, 96, 108
Libyan War, 218, 222–25, 251, 254, 256
Logistics (Orducu), 25, 34, 83–87, 117, 226, 281; in Balkans Wars, 228, 233; corruption in, 201; in Crimean War, 161, 166; in Independence War (1919–1922), 273, 274; in Sarikamis campaign, 243, 245, 246; in Suez Canal campaign, 250
Longo di Giustinianni, Giovanni, 34
Long War (1593–1606), 40, 55, 59, 76–79, 82; Hungarian frontier and, 86; Sipahi rebellion in, 97
Lossow, Otto von, 268
Louis (Lajos), king of Hungary, 74
Lüftü Pasha, Ömer, 145, 159, 161
Lüleburgaz-Pinarhisat, battle of, 228

Macedonia, 214, 215, 226, 227
MacFarlane, Charles, 158
Machine guns, 218, 242, 265
Mahan, Sylvanus Thayer, 149
Mahmud II, Sultan, 125, 130–35, 144–49, 170, 176; death of, 150; Egypt and, 130–31; Janissary reform and, 127–28, 130; Lybia and, 222; Mansure army and, 131–35, 145, 153, 212; officer training and, 144–49, 146–49; palace school cadets and, 134–35; recruitment problem and, 153–54; Redif (reserve) system and, 154–55, 156; reforms of, 142, 158; war with Russia, 135, 137, 139, 140, 142
Mahmud Pasha, 43
Mahsusa bands, 247, 249–50, 251, 252–56, 257–58
Malta campaign (1565), 56
Mamluks, 5, 8, 19, 63; Bayezid's campaigns against, 67, 68–69; conquest of, 72, 75
Mansure army, 131–35, 141, 212; command structure of, 145; officer corps and, 153
Manzikert, battle of (1071), 1–2, 5, 8
Marriage, 38

Martoloses, 58, 63–64, 65, 83
Maude, Stanley, 266–67
Mawali (freedmen), 6–7
Mecca, pilgrimage to, 107, 108
Medical services, 170, 178, 180, 233, 273–74
Medina, 107, 253
Megiddo, battle of, 270–71
Mehmed Ali Pasha (Egypt), 126–27, 130–31, 149, 150, 156; conscription success of, 154; officer corps of, 146, 148; rebellion of, 143–44, 148, 153, 222
Mehmed Efendi, Said, 113
Mehmed I, Sultan, 2; appeasement policy of, 28, 33
Mehmed II, Sultan, 43, 44, 52, 73, 77; and conquest of Constantinople, 31, 32–36, 37, 46; death of, 96; reforms of, 53; and seige of Belgrade (1456), 66–67
Mehmed IV, Sultan, 100, 103
Mehmed Pasha, Abaza, 97
Mehmed Pasha, Eşref, 184
Mehmed Pasha, Kalenderoğlu, 98
Mehmed Pasha, Muhsinzade, 117
Mehmed Pasha, Piri, 73
Mehmed Pasha, Reşid, 127, 139
Mehmed Pasha, Silahdar, 117
Mehmed Pasha, Sokullu, 75
Mektebli (academy-trained) officers, 174, 234; in artillery corps, 177–78, 210; counterinsurgency and, 216, 218; coup d'etat and, 182–83; in war with Russia (1877–1878), 193, 195, 197, 199, 201–2
Melikov, Loris, 193, 194
Menshikov, A. S., 166, 168
Mercenaries, 64, 89, 95, 97; Albanian, 93, 94, 124, 141; Caucasian (Alan), 10, 12, 93, 124; Christian, 61, 62, 63, 93, 94, 141; Levend, 91–94, 96, 108; musket-bearing, 91, 92, 96, 108; new weapons and tactics of, 78; Prussian, 205. See also Azabs
Mercidabik, battle of (1516), 56, 72
Mesih Pasha, army of, 67
Mesrutiyet, 218, 219–20, 222, 223. See also Constitution
Michael, Voivode, 60

Middle class, 91
Mikhail (Russian commander), 194
Military Academy, 129, 130, 146, 147–49, 175, 207; Arabs in, 276; cadets from, 243; graduates of, 150–52, 189 (See also Mektebli); limitations of, 177; Polish and Hungarian refugees in, 152–53
Military corridors (Kol), 83, 84, 86, 233
Military councils, 146
Military coup. See Coup d'état
Military renaissance, 241–42
Military schools, 115, 119, 123, 127; officer training in, 244; provincial, 203; reform of, 177, 221–22. See also Military Academy; Training systems
Military slaves, 6–8. See also Janissaries
Miner (Lağimci) corps, 34, 52–53, 90
Ministry of War (Harbiye Nezareti), 220
Mir Ali Bey, 76
Mithat Pasha, 183
Mobilizations, 83, 199, 209, 239; for Balkan Wars, 226–27; for Sarikamiş campaign, 243, 244, 245. See also Logistics
Modernization, 222. See also Reforms
Mohacs, battle of (1526), 51, 74
Mohammad Ali. See Mehmed Ali Pasha
Moldavia, 77. 107, 136; campaign in (1484), 59, 67–68; in Crimean War, 158; Russian invasion of, 124
Moltke, Helmut von, 142, 149, 155, 205
Mongols, 5, 11
Montecuccoli, 100
Montenegro, 227, 230; campaign in (1863–1864), 181, 189, 190; independence of, 213
Morea, rebellion in, 117, 126
Mouradgea d'Ohsson (Muradcan Tosunyan), 123
Mouzolon (Byzantine commander), 12
Müfreze (small unit) traditions, 181, 199, 255–56
Mughals of India, 76
Mühendishane-i Berri Hümayun, 123
Muhtar Pasha, Ahmed, 184, 193, 194–96, 197, 199, 201, 202; on reform council, 205
Muhtar Pasha, Mahmud, 227

Mümtaz Bey, 253
Murad I, Sultan, 2, 26, 44; campaigns of, 16; reorganization of, 23, 24–25
Murad II, Sultan, 2, 29, 32
Murad IV, Sultan, 109, 110, 112
Murad Pasha, Kuyucu, 98, 112
Murad Pasha (Jozef Bem), 152
Muravyev (Russian commander), 168–69, 170
Murray, Archibald, 265–66
Musa Pasha, 164
Müsellem corps, 16, 62
Muskets, 50, 62, 74, 79, 90; of mercenaries, 91, 92, 96, 108
Muslims, 105, 156, 171. *See also* Islam
Mustafa Ali, Gelibolulu, 110
Mustafa IV, Sultan, 125
Mustafa Pasha, Lala, 52–53, 125–26
Mustapha Pasha, Merzifonlu Kara, 99–103
Müteferrika, Ibrahim, 113, 114

Nadir Pasha, Abdülkerim, 161, 162, 163; court marshal of, 189, 199; in war with Russians, 185, 186, 187–88, 190
Naili Pasha, Mustafa, 214
Namik Pasha, Mehmed, 148–49, 177, 187
Napoleon, 123, 126, 132, 134
Nationalism, 130, 141, 153, 213, 214; Albanian, 229, 230, 236; Arab, 236–37, 275, 277; Balkan, 141, 180–81; Turkish, 216–17, 242, 258, 265, 283 (*See also* Ottomanism)
Nation-in-arms concept, 199
Navy (warships), 56, 68, 74, 88, 119, 194, 203; British, 123, 176, 254; Danube flotilla, 66, 67, 73, 84; Dutch, 76; in Gallipoli campaign, 258, 259, 260; Greek, 227, 233; Italian, 222, 224, 225; logistical work of, 70; modernization of, 176; Portuguese, 75; raids by, in Black Sea, 243; Russian, 117, 162, 164, 166; in siege of Constantinople, 33, 34–35
Nazim Pasha, 228, 231
NCOs (non-commisioned officers), 131, 178, 199, 221, 225; training of, 234, 244, 264. *See also* Officer corps
Negroponte campaign (1470), 67
Nevers, Comte de, 26

Nicholas, Tsar of Russia, 158
Nicholas II, Tsar of Russia, 217
Nicholas (Russian commander), 187, 191
Nicopolis, battle of (1396), 26–27
Nicosia, siege of (1570), 52
Nigbolu, siege of (1877), 186–87
Nightingale, Florence, 178
Niyazi Bey, 218
Nizam–i Cedid reforms, 120–23, 124, 125, 127, 131; end of, 134
Nizamiye (regular) troops, 159, 160, 165, 169
Nökers (royal guards), 18
Nomads: Anatolia rebellion, 71; as combat support group, 63, 69. *See also* Mamluks; Steppe-nomadic tradition; specific nomadic group
North African mercenaries, 108
Nurettin (Sakalli) Bey, 257
Nuri (Killigil) Pasha, 251, 252

Officer corps, 118, 278–79; academy-trained, 130; Alayli (commissioned), 177, 178, 197, 199, 202, 243; Arab, 275–76; artillery units, 48; Balkan Wars and, 175, 232, 235; career patterns of, 181–82; casualties, 189, 234, 246, 261; counterinsurgency and, 212, 214, 215–18, 279, 283; in Crimean War, 160–71; at Gallipoli, 259, 260, 261, 262; general staff, 207; Hungarian and Polish refugees in, 152–53, 160, 171, 198; insurgency problems and, 214, 215–18; Janissary (Ağasi), 39–41; in Libyan war, 223; non-commissioned (NCO), 131, 178, 199, 221, 225, 234, 244, 264; purge of, 221, 237, 241, 249; Quwwad, 7–8; in war with Russia (1877–1878), 197, 198–99. CUP (Committee of Union and Progress); General Staff; Mektebli
Officer training, 95, 120, 134, 146–49, 150–51, 241, 244; German system for, 207–8, 209. *See also* Military Academy
Ömer Pasha, 163–64, 168, 169, 170, 185
On-the-job training, 111, 112
Operational encirclement doctrine, 249
Oral tradition, 111, 112

Orducus. *See* Logistics
Orhan, Sultan, 2
Orthodox Christians, 157, 183
Osman Gazi, Sultan, 11–12, 13
Osman II Genç, Sultan, 110
Osmanli dynasty, 2
Osman Pasha, Nuri, 181, 197, 199, 201, 202, 207; Plevne defense and, 188–89, 190, 191, 192, 206, 210; in war with Greece, 210
Osman Pasha, Özdemiroğlu, 93
Osman Pasha, Topal, 115
Otlukbeli, battle of (1473), 46, 69
Otranto, siege of (1481), 67
Ottoman-French War (1798–1802), 123–24
Ottoman-Greek War (1897), 208–11
Ottoman-Habsburg-Russian War (1787–1791), 120
Ottoman-Habsburg War (1737–1739), 106
Ottomanism, 157, 182, 203, 216–17, 237
Ottoman-Italian War (1911), 218, 222–25, 236, 273
Ottoman-Russian War (1877–1878), 174, 178, 183–202, 233; Balkan Corps in, 185, 187, 189, 191, 192, 198; Caucasian front in, 185, 193–96; command-control hierarchy in, 183–84, 198; guerrilla tactics in, 193, 196, 200; mobilization in, 180, 199–200; Plevni battles, 188–89, 191–92, 197, 198, 200
Ottoman-Russian wars, 157, 226; (1768–1774), 116–18; (1806–1812), 124, 126; (1828–1829), 132, 134, 135–42, 153
Ottoman Union Committee, 217. *See also* CUP
Ouchy Peace Treaty (1912), 225, 251

Palestine front, World War I, 252, 262, 264–66, 268, 271, 272
Pandor groups, 64, 93
Pan-Islamism, 237
Pan-Turkish dream, of Enver Pasha, 272
Papacy, 103
Paris, military academy in, 147
Parkany, battle of (1683), 98

Paskievitch, Ivan Fedorovich, 138, 139, 164
Passarowitz, Treaty of (1718), 112
Patrona Halil rebellion, 114
Patron-client relations, 95, 121, 171, 178, 197; military school and, 148, 149
Pençik tax, 18
Persian Gulf, 76
Persian Safavids, 51, 57, 61, 67, 76, 78; campaign against, 70–71 scorched-earth tactics of, 84;
Persian Sasanids, Islamic conquest of, 6
Peter I, Tsar of Russia, 107, 121
Plevne, battle of, 191–92, 197, 198, 200; Osman Pasha and, 188–89, 192, 206, 210
Poison gas, 266
Poland, 245; alliance with Habsburgs, 81, 99, 102, 103; campaign in (1620), 93; refugee officers from, 152–53, 171; Russian excursions against, 116
Polish-Lithuanian Commonwealth, 103
Portugal, campaign against, 74–76
Printing house, 113–14
Provincial army (Eyalet Askerleri), 53–66, 85, 92, 98; auxiliary corps and units, 61–66; Egyptian, 149–50; frontier units (Serhat Kulu), 57–61; governors and, 99, 105–9; rise of, 105–9; Timariot cavalry, 53–57
Prussian military, 116, 149, 184; advisors, 205 (*See also* Moltke, Helmut von); conscription system, 178–79; reserve system, 154; 155
Publications, 241, 242

Quwwad (qaid), 7–8, 9

Raab (Yanik) fortress, 100
Ragib Pasha, Koca, 115
Raglan, Lord, 166, 167
Raiding parties. *See* Akinci raiders
Raif Efendi, Mahmud, 122–23
Railways, 210, 243, 253, 273; in Balkan Wars, 226, 227, 229, 233
Rashid of Shammar, 253
Ratib Efendi, Ebubekir, 120–21, 123, 125

Rauf Pasha, 189, 190, 191, 192
Reaya (civilians), 6, 36, 64–65
Rebellions, 124–25, 225; in Anatolia, 94; Arab, 253, 267, 274–77; in Armenia (1894), 204; banditry and, 96–98, 181, 274; Celali, 96–98; in Egypt, under Mehmed Ali Pasha, 143–44, 148, 153, 222; Greek, 126, 127; Janissary, 108, 126, 128; military, 95; Patrona Halil, 114; separatist, 213–14
Reconnaissance, 65, 163, 164, 224; intelligence and, 185, 233, 256
Recruitment, 90–91, 121, 124, 132, 153–54; of Basibozuks, 172–73; Devşirme, 19, 37–38, 90, 93; Jandarma units, 212; non-Muslim, 221, 234; prior to World War I, 243; for Redif battalions, 180; renovation of, 240
Redif Pasha, Serasker, 184, 187, 189
Redif (reserve) troops, 154–56, 159, 178; abolition of, 240; Anatolian, 200, 210; in Balkan Wars, 226, 229, 232–33, 234; in Crimean War, 171, 173, 179; German proposal for, 206; old guard (Müstafhiz) category, 179–80; in war with Greece (1897), 210–11; in war with Russians (1877–1878), 186, 194, 200, 201
Red Sea, 75, 76, 179
Reforms, 81–82, 109–12; advice literature, 109–10, 111; bureaucracy and, 109, 111; Janissary, 127–28; in military education, 177; Nizam-i Cedid, 120–23, 127; of Selim III, 53, 120–23, 125, 127; Tanzimat, 129; Tulip Period (1718–1730), 112–14
Reorganization regulation (1910), 220–21
Reserve system. *See* Redif (reserve) troops
Reşid Pasha, Mehmed, 118, 144, 148
Resmi Efendi, Ahmed, 116, 118
Reval meeting (1908), 217
Rhodes, 225; siege of (1522), 73
Rifles, 188, 200, 201, 211
Riza Pasha, Ali, 161–62, 206
Riza Pasha Reforms (1843), 159
Romania, 243, 264, 272; allied with Russia, 183, 191; independence of, 201, 213

Romanus IV Diogenes, Byzantine emperor, 5
Rumelia, 22, 120, 161, 236; army units from, 27, 33–34; Russian invasion of, 126, 156
Rumeli Hisari fortress, 33
Rumiantsev, Peter, 117
Russia, 81, 105, 130, 236; Armenian rebels and, 263; in Crimean War, 152, 157–58, 161–70, 171; nihilism in, 214, 215; in Sarikamiş campaign, 244, 245–46, 248; in World War I, 243, 261
Russia, wars with Ottomans: (1768–1774), 116–18; (1806–1812), 124, 126, 129; (1828–1829), 132, 134; (1877–1878), 174, 178
Russian Cossacks. *See* Cossacks
Russo-Turkish War of 1711, 107
Rüştü Pasha, Mehmed, 182

Sacred cauldron, 39, 40
Safavids. *See* Persian Safavids
Şahin Paşa, Lala, 22–23
Said Pasha, Küçük, 205, 207
St. Arnaud, Marshal, 166–67
St. Priest, reports of, 117, 118
Şakirds (artillery novices), 47
Salary payments, 41, 87, 88, 91
Sanusis of Libya, 223, 251–52
Sardunyah Hurşid, 134
Sarikamiş campaign, 175, 239, 242–50, 262, 278; winter conditions in, 247–48
Şarköy amphibious landing, 231
Sason rebellion (Armenia), 204, 208
Satih Pasha, Selim, 146, 150
Schwendi, Lazarus von, 57
Scorched-earth tactics, 84, 170, 224
Scouting. *See* Reconnaissance
Seeckt, Hans von, 239
Sekban Cedid reforms, 125–26
Sekban (hound keepers), 32, 38, 91
Selim III, reforms of, 53, 120–23, 125, 127, 131, 146
Selim I Yavuz (the Grim), 69, 73
Selim Pasha, Ahmed, 165
Seljukids, 1–2, 5, 14, 18; Iqta system of, 6, 8, 17; military legacy of, 10–11
Selman-i Pak, battle of, 257

Şemseddin Yama Candar, 11
Separatist movements, 213
Seraskeriye, 146, 206, 213, 215, 220
Serbian army, 229; in battle of Kosovo, 23, 25–26; Voynuks, 64, 83
Serbia (Serbs), 126, 230, 243, 254; independence of, 201, 213; rebellion by, 132
Serhat Kulu (frontier units), 57–61
Sevastopol, siege of, 166–67, 169
Seven Years' War (1756–1763), 116
Şevket Pasha, Mahmud, 230, 237
Seyyid Mustafa Efendi, Küçük, 123
Shamil, Sheikh, 165
Sharia (Islamic law), 19, 24
Sharif al Faruqi, Muhammad, 277
Sharif Hussein of Hejaz, 75, 252, 275–76
Shiite propaganda, 69, 70
Sidi Ahmad, 252
Siege operations, 34, 52–53, 60
Sigismund of Hungary, 26
Silahdar cavalry, 44–45
Silistire fortress, 137, 164; cavalry of, 132, 141
Sinai-Palestine front, 262, 265
Sinan Pasha, Koca, 60, 77
Sipahis (cavalry), 44–45, 79, 81, 90; combat formation, 55–56, 74; funding of, 84; loyalty of, 69; nomadic tactics of, 71; provincial officials and, 92; rebellions by, 94, 96–98; Timarli, 17, 20, 25, 26, 53–57, 88, 110; weaponry of, 54; winter quarters and, 85
Sipka Pass, defense of, 187
Skanderberg (George Kastrioti), 72
Slade, Adolphus, 172
Slave-based army, 6–7. *See also* Janissaries
Social upheaval, 94. *See also* Rebellions
Soldiers of fortune. *See* Mercenaries
Souchon, William, 243
Spanish Army of Flanders, 94–95
S. S. Kara Deniz affair, 275–76
S. S. Pandua affair, 275–76
Standardization, 37, 281; Murad I and, 23, 24
Stange, Wilhelm, 247, 249
Steppe-nomadic tradition, 2, 3–5, 12
Suayyibe, battle of (1915), 255–56
Suez Canal campaign, 244, 250, 252
Sülemiş, 11
Süleyman Bey, Baltaoğlu, 33
Süleyman II, Sultan, 56
Süleyman I (the Magnificent), Sultan, 31, 45, 53, 54, 64; campaign delays, 83; golden age of, 109; Hungarian campaign of (1521), 73–74; Janissaries and, 40, 44
Süleyman Pasha, 22, 166
Süleyman Pasha, Baltaci, 107
Süleyman Pasha, Hadim, 75
Süleyman Pasha, Hüsnü, 189–192, 182, 187–88, 193, 197–98
Şumnu army, 137, 186, 192
Süvaris (cavalry), 44–46, 88, 90, 121
Swahili coast, 76
Syria, 123, 143, 156, 263, 272; Arab nationalism in, 277; Canbulatoğlu of, 97; Mamluks in, 63; Redifs (reserves) from, 200

Tabur Cengi (battle formation), 42, 48, 50–51, 56, 70, 74
Tanzimat edict (1839), 129, 147, 156–57, 159, 160, 180
Tatars, 78, 100, 132; Crimean, 59, 60, 63, 68, 84, 116
Taxation, 157, 182, 202, 281; exemption from, 16, 21, 65; wartime (Avariz), 87–88
Tekfur, 9
Telli Hasan Pasha, 76–77
Terrorism, 214–15
Teşkilat-i Mahsusa. *See* Mahsusa bands
Thirty Years War, 86
Thököly, Imre, 99, 100, 102
Thrace, 245, 254; Ottoman conquest of, 22, 23
Timariot cavalry, 53–57, 108, 115, 212, 274, 281
Timarli Sipahis, 17, 20, 25, 26. *See also* Sipahis
Timar system, 17, 40, 53, 61, 62, 95, 108; Balkan aristocrats and, 63; bombadiers in, 51–52; family farms and, 23–24; of Sipahis, 17, 53–57, 88, 110; weakening of, 109–10
Timur (Tamerlane), 27–28

Tiryaki Hasan Pasha, 93
Tobruk assault, 218, 222
Topçu Ocağı. *See* Artillery corps
Tophane artillery foundry, 200–201
Toptani Pasha, Esat, 236
Townshend, Charles, 257
Training systems, 49, 95–96, 113, 116, 129, 174; Jandarma, 212; Mansure reforms and, 132, 134–35; on-the-job, 111, 112. *See also* Acemi Ocağı; Military schools; Officer training
Transportation services, 63, 83, 209, 245; challenges in, 201; war wagons, 28, 29, 50–51. *See also* Railways
Transylvania, 77, 78, 84, 99; printing center in, 114
Trench warfare, 189, 219, 260, 261, 270
Triangular division concept, 240
Tribal chiefs, 204
Tribal warriors, 212, 223, 224, 251, 254–56. *See also* specific tribal groups
Tulip Period (1718–1730), 112–14
Turcoman tribes, 1–2, 10–11, 13; Azabs and, 61–62; cavalry, 17, 132; emirates, 14, 17, 27; nomadic tactics of, 70; rebels, 57; warriors, 21, 36, 61–62, 69, 126
Turkish Independence War (1919–1922), 261, 265, 272, 273, 283; Arab officers in, 276, 277
Turkish military, 7; cavalry, 10
Turkish nationalism, 216–17, 242, 258, 265, 283
Turkish Republic, 272
Türkmençay, Treaty of (1826), 138

Ulema (judiciary) class, 120, 127, 128
Ulufecis, 44, 45
Umayyadid caliphs, 6
Uniforms, 142; headgear, 15, 20, 39
Usedom, Guido von, 258
Uzbek army, 51

Vaka-i Hayriyye, 128
Vardar Army, 228–29, 231
Varna: battle of (1444), 50; siege of (1828), 137
Vasfi Pasha, Ahmed, 166, 169

Vehib Pasha, 263, 264
Veli Pasha, 214
Venice, 28, 81, 103
Vienna, siege of (1683), 98–103, 106; Mustafa Pasha and, 99–103
Vivian (British officer), 173
Vladislav, king of Hungary, 29
Volunteers, 198, 223, 234; Gönüllü, 61; Kul Karindaşi, 90; Serdengeçti, 102
Von der Goltz, Colmar, 206–8, 209, 220, 221, 230; reforms of, 238
Von Falkenhayn, Erich, 268, 269–70, 271
Von Sanders, Otto Liman, 239, 240, 241, 269–70, 271; at Gallipoli, 238, 259, 260
Von Schellendorf, Friedrich Bronsart, 238–39, 244, 247
Voronzov, Mikhail, 161
Voynuk groups, 64, 83

Wahhabi rebellion (Hejaz), 143
Wallachia, 81, 84, 99, 107, 136; campaign in (1595), 77; Russian invasion of, 124, 142, 158
War of the Holy Alliance (1684–1690), 86, 95, 103–4
War wagons, 28, 29, 50–51
Weaponry, 78; Ahi guilds, 13; Azab, 21; cavalry, 54; Janissary, 38, 41–42, 49, 50, 74, 99; manufacture of, 49–50; modern, 222; nomadic tradition, 3; Prussian, 205. *See also* Cannon; Firearms
Williams, Fenwick, 151, 166, 172
Winter periods, 85, 94, 247–48
World War I, 175–76, 235–79, 283; build up to, 235–42; demobilization following, 283; desertion in, 277–78; Gallipoli campaign, 175, 219, 258–62, 270, 272–73; Iraq in, 253–57, 266; Palestine front in, 252, 262, 264–66, 268, 271; Sarikamiş campaign, 242–50

Yamak (apprentice), 90
Yaya corps, 15–16, 62, 65, 87; in battle of Kosovo, 25, 26
Yeğen Osman, 96
Yemen, 75, 76, 225
Yeniçeriler. *See* Janissaries

Yeni Osmanlilar (New Ottomans), 182
Yergögü, defeat of (1595), 60
Yildirim Army, 268
Yörük (auxiliary) corps, 22, 63, 83
Young Turks, 182, 232
Yudenich (Russian general), 262
Yusuf Pasha, Koca, 122

Zabtiye. *See* Law enforcement
Zamoyski, Wladyslaw, 153
Zarif Pasha, Mustafa, 148, 166
Zeamat estates, 53, 54
Zeki Pasha, Halepli, 206, 229
Ziya Pasha, Yusuf, 124
Zsitvatorok peace agreement (1606), 78, 79

About the Authors

MESUT UYAR, Ph.D., graduate of Turkish Military Academy, is a career military officer. He teaches international relations and security studies at the Turkish Military Academy. A specialist in war studies and military history, he has published articles on Ottoman military and operations other than war. As a career officer, he served at platoon, company, and battalion commander positions in various infantry units and in several tours of peace support operations in Afghanistan, Georgia, and Bosnia.

EDWARD J. ERICKSON, Lieutenant Colonel, U.S. Army (retired), is a combat veteran of the first and second Gulf Wars. He is currently an Associate Professor of Military History at the United States Marine Corps University in Quantico, Virginia, and he has a Ph.D. from the University of Leeds in the United Kingdom. Colonel Erickson is the author of numerous books and articles on the Ottoman army during the early twentieth century.